ORIGINS & DESTINATIONS

41 ESSAYS ON CHINESE AMERICA

A Joint Project of

CHINESE HISTORICAL SOCIETY OF SOUTHERN CALIFORNIA
and
UCLA ASIAN AMERICAN STUDIES CENTER

Library of Congress Catalog Card Number: 94-067955
ISBN No. 0-930377-03-6

Published by
Chinese Historical Society of Southern California, Inc. and
UCLA Asian American Studies Center
Los Angeles, California, U.S.A.

Printed in the United States of America.

10 9 8 7 6 5 4 3 2 1

Cover photograph courtesy
of El Pueblo de Los Angeles
Historical Monument: a gift of
Dorothy Siu

Consultant: RUSSELL C. LEONG
Production/ Book Editor: DENNIS NG
Cover Design by: PETER NGUYEN

Acknowledgments

This book is made possible in part by funds donated to the Chinese Historical Society of Southern California for this project, and in part by funds from a publications fund jointly administered by CHSSC and the UCLA Asian American Studies Center.

The editorial committee was headed by co-editors Munson A. Kwok and Ella Yee Quan. Committee members Suellen Cheng, Margaret D. Lew, Susie Ling, Donald Loo, Franklin Mah, and Pauline R. Wong provided support for typing and proofreading. The Editorial Assistant (intern) was Philip Cheng.

The compilation of essay presentations was assembled by the 1992 Conference Program Committee, chaired by Lucie Cheng, with members: Suellen Cheng, Eugene Cooper, Lloyd Inui, Munson Kwok, Him Mark Lai, Marjorie Lee, Russell Leong, Philip Leong, San-Pao Li, Susie Ling, John Liu, Emma Woo Louie, Thomas McDannold, Stanley Mu, Gay Wong, Ruth Wu, and Judy Yung. Other session chairs who managed conference panels included Roberta Greenwood, Alice Hom, Enid Lim, Patricia Lin, Paul Louie, Eugene Wong Moy, Jean Bruce Poole, and Jo Yang. Staff assistant to the Program Committee was Scott Gruber of the UCLA Center for Pacific Rim Studies.

During the project period, Chinese Historical Society of Southern California presidents were Kipham Kan, Thomas McDannold, Sue Yee, and, most recently, Irvin R. Lai. The UCLA Asian American Studies Center is headed by Don Nakanishi, professor of education. At the time of the conference, Lucie Cheng, UCLA professor of sociology, and Ruth Wu, dean of the School of Health and Human Services, represented the UCLA Center for Pacific Rim Studies and the California State University, Los Angeles, respectively.

Special thanks is given to Scott Gruber for supporting the 1992 conference.

Foreword

Origins and Destinations: A Conference on Chinese Americans was held on the campus of California State University, Los Angeles (CSLA), August 28–30, 1992. This conference was hosted by the Institute for Asian American and Pacific Asian Studies at CSLA, the Center for Pacific Rim Studies and the Asian American Studies Center of University of California at Los Angeles (UCLA), and the Chinese Historical Society of Southern California (CHSSC).

This conference provided a forum for the presentation of research papers, oral history papers, and theses. I hope that the information from the conference, as well as the face to face exchanges developed there, will enhance relationships between Chinese Americans and their communities by increasing the understanding of the roles that Chinese Americans played in the history of the United States. I also hope that this conference and future such conferences will help to minimize stereotyping of Chinese Americans and help authors to portray accurate accounts of Chinese Americans in United States history.

We all hope that this conference initiated a new series of Chinese American studies symposia that will become a biennial event hosted in turn by different historical societies, cultural societies, or Asian American studies programs at universities throughout the country. In addition, with adequate interest, the conference can be expanded to include other areas of the Pacific Rim and its immigrants who have made an impact on the United States.

As director, I am grateful to all the presenters and volunteers who worked hard to make the conference a great success. There are too many to mention by name, so to all of you, please accept my heartfelt thanks.

This volume contains 41 essays submitted by author/presenters at the conference. The essence and representations of the conference are fairly complete and preserved. Little alteration of length and content of each essay has been made; editing has principally focused in arranging the manuscripts into a readable format and common style. We hope you will enjoy this book.

> Stanley Mu
> Los Angeles, California
> August 1994

Contents

Challenges for Chinese Americans

JUDY CHU
City Council, Monterey Park, California

Let me tell you about Monterey Park.

For many years, Monterey Park was a sleepy farming town, populated mainly by whites until the 1950s, when housing tracts were built. Latino, Chinese, and Japanese families moved in; Monterey Park was seen as a step out of East L.A., Chinatown, and Little Tokyo.

It wasn't, however, until the late 1970s and early 1980s that a dramatic change occurred. Asian immigrants, mostly Chinese, came in big numbers. The face of the city started to change. The eggs and bacon coffee shop was replaced by the Chinese noodle shop. The big Alpha Beta supermarket was gone and replaced by Ai Hoa Supermarket, a name the older residents could not pronounce.

In 1980, the Asian population was 30%. By 1990, it was 56%. We are perhaps the only city on the U.S. mainland with an Asian majority. Inevitably, conflicts started to arise between the old residents and the new. Monterey Park had a new-immigrant population, many of whom were not familiar with the language, rules, and customs here. Many, of course, felt more comfortable hanging out with members of their own groups. While PTAs declined in membership, the Chinese PTA grew. While the original Lions Club members got older and older, a new Little Taipei Lions Club blossomed with younger, Chinese members. Early morning Chinese exercise groups proliferated all over the city in the parks, and it would not be surprising to hear the strains of music from Chinese opera groups when walking through city buildings.

The old time residents had mixed reactions. The vast majority were somewhat bewildered, and they hoped they would not become strangers in their own city. Many tried their best to adjust to the change. But unfortunately, there were a small, but loud, minority who blamed the new immigrants for everything from bad driving to over development. We even heard complaints from them about those Chinese seniors who wore pajamas on the streets!

These attitudes were most exemplified by a man who was elected to the City Council in 1986. This man was a proponent of English Only. He wanted English Only on signs and English only in libraries. He was against bilingual education, and he felt that children in bilingual classrooms were subcultured. He wanted a moratorium on all immigration to the U.S.; he frequently said that immigrants were destroying the nation, and that if they didn't like it, they could go back to where they came from. He felt that most problems of the city could be blamed on immigrants. When he talked about the problems with garbage landfills reaching their capacity, he launched into a tirade about immigrants coming over the border bringing their garbage with them.

You can imagine what it was like with someone like this on the council spouting his rhetoric. The media came flocking to interview him and to profile Monterey Park as a city torn by racism. As a result, we gained national attention; we were covered by everyone from "20/20" to the *New York Times, Atlantic Monthly, Washington Post, California Journal*; and we had a full-time *L.A. Times* reporter covering us. Now, you know you're in trouble when you go to the office and see "20/20" on your doorsteps!

After two years of this, I ran for election to the city council to present a contrast to these views; but more importantly, I ran for council to be an impetus for bridging the gaps that existed in our community between the different groups. Rather than polarizing people, there needed to be leadership that could bring the concerns of the people together.

As you can see, I won; in fact, I won with the highest number of votes. And it's a good thing I did, too, because if I had not, we would have had an all-white city council in a town that is 56% Asian, 31% Latino, and 12% white. The town is 87% comprised of people of color, and yet would have had an all-white city council. As it was, I was the only person of color out of the five city council members for my first two years.

There is a good ending to this part of the story. In the last election, the English Only advocate was trounced in the election, coming in last out of six. We gained two Latinos and another Asian on the city council, and so we are much more representative. I became the Mayor of the city in 1990, and will be the mayor again in 1994. I have played a part in setting a different tone for the city.

I tell you our story because I feel that Monterey Park is just a microcosm of the rapid change occurring in California. By the year 2000, we will be a majority minority state where Latinos, Asians, and blacks will comprise the majority. Already, the 1990 census has shown the dramatic change in the growth of the Asian population, which has now become the second largest minority group in California. There is no doubt that Asians are certainly making their stamp on California. And yet, where is our power? Where is our clout? Where are we represented in the decision making process that affects our lives?

Certainly, Asians have serious issues to face. In 1989, an *L.A. Times* poll found that 57% of the residents polled felt that there were too many immigrants here. No wonder anti-Asian hate crimes are up.

A decade ago, we were shocked to find that Vincent Chin was murdered by two unemployed autoworkers in Detroit because they thought he was Japanese; and we were shocked that his killers were given only probation and a fine. But only three years ago, Patrick Purdy gunned down five Asian school children in a Stockton, California, school yard because of his hatred of Asians. And only three years ago, Chinese immigrant Jim Loo was killed by two whites outside a Raleigh, North Carolina, pool hall because they thought he was Vietnamese and blamed him for their brothers' deaths during the war. Only two weeks ago, a Vietnamese pre-med student at the University of Miami was killed by a mob yelling racial epithets.

As much as we are shocked by this violence, it is the light punishment that is even more disturbing because it shows that for many, anti-Asian hate crimes are still not taken seriously.

In the U.C. system and other universities around the country, Asians are still not sure whether they are being denied admission because they are considered to be over represented in the student body. UC Berkeley was forced to conclude that there were irregularities that resulted in lower admissions for Asian applicants. At UCLA, the Department of Justice confirmed anti-Asian bias in the admissions policy of one of the graduate schools.

In employment, Asians are blocked from reaching their potential because they face the glass ceiling. Asians are well represented in the professional technical fields, but underrepresented in management, even in the aerospace industry, where the number of Asian American professionals exceed those of African American or Latino. According to complaints filed at the Equal Employment Opportunity Commission, there is a perception by management that Asians are good researchers, but are too studious, quiet, and clannish.

And in the area of politics, there are clear problems. How many Asians are in Congress? Since Asians are 2.7% of the population, we would theoretically have 12 in the House of Representatives. Instead, we have three: one from Hawaii and two from Northern California. None are from Southern California and none are Chinese American.

How many Asians are in the California State Legislature? In the state with the greatest Asian population, where we comprise 10% of the state? Out of the 40 Senate seats? We have none. Out of the 80 Assembly seats? Again, we have none.

Education is supposed to be such an important area to Asians. Yet, out of the 7,000 school board seats in the state, less than 1% are occupied by Asians.

While the obstacles that Chinese Americans face are many, we should never fall into a victim mentality. Victims stay in the past; Chinese Americans need to look to the future. As a group, we are relatively new, with many of us being first or second generation. We have many new immigrants who are still learning about American norms. So we need to educate and empower Chinese Americans so that they have the tools they need.

We need to help Chinese Americans acquire the skills that help them to advance, whether it be public speaking or knowing how to network. We need to urge Chinese Americans to participate in the American democratic system, by registering to vote and getting involved in campaigns. We have to teach that it doesn't always work to take the safe route. Sometimes we have to risk and speak up in order to change the perceptions that society has of us. Chinese Americans have to be educated about the issues that we face as a community. With education comes awareness, and with awareness will come the advocacy and the public pressure to change things.

Education and awareness is one reason Chinese American studies plays an important role in our communities.

On a personal level, Chinese American studies, and, in fact, Asian American studies, have played a large and critical role in my life. Many people think that I must have always wanted to get into politics since I was a kid. But the opposite was true.

My mother is an immigrant from China. I grew up in South-Central L.A. in a black neighborhood. But even though my neighborhood was black, the media was all white, and believe me, inside the house, it was all China.

What I remember about growing up were the traditional Chinese messages. All that mattered was going to Chinese school, studying hard, working hard, and marrying a nice Chinese boy. Strangely enough, I did all these things. I was quiet and I studied hard and I was not very involved in extracurricular activities. And when I went to college, I decided to major in math. I really thought that I could do okay in life by mainly studying hard.

It wasn't until college when I took my first Asian American studies class, in my first year during that stormy period when ethnic studies was established a little over 20 years ago. A light went on in my head and I woke up. I discovered that I had swallowed many stereotypes about Asians, and that I knew virtually nothing about my history and the barriers that Asians before me had faced. I discovered that we had many goals that still had to be met.

I was so inspired that I got involved in community organizations and changed my major to psychology. I taught classes in Asian American studies and watched over and over again as new students in my class went through the same process of discovery and insight. Now, I see them out in the community, joining groups, leading organizations, and advocating on issues. They are making an impact on their community.

Like many Chinese Americans, when I grew up, I was not encouraged to learn public skills. It took many years of involvement to learn how to organize, how to conduct meetings, and how to interact with the powers that be. Ultimately, it led to my getting involved in the political arena, so that I could make changes right in the heart of the institutions that so profoundly affect all our lives.

Through Asian American studies, we learn about our history, so that we can make sure abuses will not repeat themselves. We find role models and learn that there were models of survival. We learn about the range of experiences across the country. Asian American studies give us the larger vision and it is that larger vision that tells us what we need to do next to better our communities for the next generation.

Our history shows that the first Chinese Americans came to America in the 1850s and named America the gold mountain. They hoped to find prosperity and great wealth. Instead, there were great difficulties.

In 1882, the Chinese were the subject of the first anti-immigration law ever to be passed, the Chinese Exclusion Act. Up until the turn of the century, Chinese were not allowed to work in the public sector, nor were they allowed to testify against whites in court. Asian children were not allowed in the same classrooms as white children, and Asian children were not allowed to speak their own languages. In 1913, immigrant Asians were not allowed to purchase land.

In 1992, this treatment does not have to happen anymore.

Today is a time of significant change, and California is in the forefront of this change. But the future of California depends on whether it can become a truly pluralistic society, a society where all kinds of people exist side by side—not the melting pot where cultural identities are submerged into one uniform whole, but the salad bowl where cultures co-exist and benefit from one another.

This is the challenge I have in Monterey Park, creating a moral authority for cultural diversity. To that end, I am pushing culturally appropriate social and city services, neighborhood watch programs, sister cities, and a harmony month. These were a series of citywide activities to have neighbors interact with one another, which included a multicultural film series, a community roundtable on local issues, and a citywide essay contest on living in a multicultural society.

There has been a turnaround in Monterey Park, but it happened because the community demanded a change, and that caused the leadership to change. And I believe that if California is going to seriously tackle the problems that it is facing in the coming decade, it will need the community to advocate just as strong for change.

If anything, the L.A. Riots showed us how critical these issues are. I have just been appointed on the board of Rebuild L.A., where it has become clear to me that racial tension and economic disparity are still our number one priority, and that Chinese Americans need to be in the forefront of the effort. As Chinese Americans, we have dual challenges. We need to make sure our needs are heard. Many people are unaware, for instance, that Chinese Americans lost over $200 million and shared in 30% of the damage during the riots. At the same time, we need to work with other ethnic groups. We cannot let L.A. deteriorate further into a society where ethnic group is pitted against ethnic group, where economic fears automatically result in racial scapegoating. We need to work to resolve these issues together, not only between Asian groups, but within the larger community.

I am optimistic. Today, Chinese Americans have the strength and the tools we didn't have 140 years ago. We have the education and the financial base. We have the economic strength of the Pacific Rim, where trade with the U.S. is already twice that of Europe. We have the entrepreneurial spirit of immigrants, whose burst of energy is leading Los Angeles to replace New York as a financial center of the United States. With our growing numbers, political sophistication, and knowledge, I think it will be an exciting time for Asian Americans in the coming decade.

It is no coincidence that we have made many breakthroughs only within the last five years. Due to public pressure, last year was the first time Asians were successful in getting a federal conviction for the murderers of an Asian victim, Jim Loo. Public pressure caused investigations into admissions practices for Asian applicants at UC Berkeley, Brown, and Harvard universities. This last year, we had the first state-wide coalition to advocate for Asian Americans for fair reapportionment in California. At UC Berkeley, the first Chinese American was appointed as chancellor. L.A. City Council, L.A. School Board, and the L.A. Community College Board had never had an Asian elected to a seat before. But in the last few years, Mike Woo, Warren Furutani, and Julia Wu were elected. And now, Mike Woo may be L.A.'s next mayor.

It is my hope that we are visible and that we help each other, and if we become effective participants in our communities, we can look forward to the day when we can finally climb the peak of that lost gold mountain to claim a truly equal and democratic America.

A New Agenda for Chinese Americans

JOHN KUO WEI TCHEN
Queens College, New York

Twelve years ago, I attended the last Chinese American studies conference in San Francisco, and at that time, I was the young kid on the block. I had just finished researching the Genthe book (it had not come out yet) and, with my colleagues in New York, I was just getting the Chinatown History Project underway. Now, over a decade later, my students at Queens College are reminding me that, although I still think of myself as young, I'm not so young anymore. The great thing about being older is that I get to see, and be stimulated by, a new generation of scholars and activists.

While thinking about what to say for tonight, I was reminded of a phrase that New York Chinatown "old-timers" have taught me. Many of you know the phrase. In my fractured Cantonese, it is "lok yip gwai gun." In Mandarin, it is "luo yeh gwei gun." In English, it is "Falling leaves return to their roots." At first glance, this phrase appears to be a sojourner's statement about their heart-felt desire to return to his or her home village in China. After all, even if earlier generations of Chinese wanted to stay and sink their roots here, few could do so. The racism, the Exclusion laws, the anti-marriage laws, and the isolation from their families clearly signaled that they were not welcome.

But like any really good aphorism, the phrase has other interpretations. In a more metaphorical and modern sense, falling leaves are subject to the unpredictable currents of blowing winds, implying a sense of alienation. Returning to the roots can be understood as a search for origins, or home. The phrase can also be interpreted in the sense that we are all subject to cycles of birth, growth, death, and rebirth; perhaps this is closer to the original naturalistic meaning. A rebellious contemporary twist on this saying, used by recent immigrants intent on settling in the United States, is "Let falling leaves root wherever they land."

No matter which interpretation one subscribes to, this metaphor serves as an important example of how we Chinese of the global diaspora try to link our present situations with our individual and collective pasts for one of life's most important instinctual tasks: our finding meaning for the future. More broadly stated, we as human beings create and recreate the past from the vantage of the ever-shifting present. And as our experiences change to the ever-changing social and political realities of our time, we constantly reach back into the past to gain some sense of wisdom and guidance to improve the present for the future.

With this perspective of the interrelationship of present, past, and future in mind, I would like to discuss two aspects of our present-day situation in Chinese American studies, and offer you two historical interpretations that challenge us on how to proceed for the remaining years of the 20th century (or at least until our next conference). Whichever comes first.

Over the past 12 years, we have witnessed an unprecedented efflorescence of Chinese American studies and an explosion of Chinese American communities all over the United States. In terms of the field that until recently was made up of a handful of people, and in terms of a people that were severely limited by racist immigration policies, we are finally gaining enough of a mass to make a difference. A field which was nurtured by a few devoted, self-trained historians is now finally on the verge of sprouting into tenured-tracked positions and programs all across this nation. University and commercial presses are at long last searching and competing for Chinese and Asian American titles. And, miracles of miracles, the emerging generation of nationally-acclaimed Chinese American writers, film makers, artists, and cultural creators are using and contributing to the historical research and interpretation we have pioneered. Most important of all, non-Chinese and non-Asian Americans are beginning to believe that they are not informed Americans unless they also know something about the Chinese American experience. We still have a long way to go, no doubt, but who would have imagined this happening so rapidly and so pervasively?

I need not remind this group that these developments have not come out of thin air. They have been driven by the breaking down of racial barriers because we have actively joined with others, especially African Americans and Latinos, in various civil rights and equality movements. They have been driven by the striking down of racist immigration quotas and policies which has made it possible for Chinese and other Asians to immigrate. And they have been driven by Chinese, among other Asian Americans, working and sacrificing like crazy to do well and to make their mark in this society. We have never been so many, nor have we ever risen higher. We seem to be on the verge of acceptance, legitimacy, and—dare I say it?—equality. Indeed, we have done well enough in this recent past to be described by the powers-that-be to be members of a "model minority:" a successful, self-reliant racial minority group that most Republicans, Democrats, or Independents love.

But, as our Chinese American ancestors before us have known, there are deceptions in those dazzling golden mountains; there are mirages in how close we are to what Puritan leader John Winthrop described as "the city on a hill."

What separates us from gaining inclusion? Is it just a matter of climbing up a few more thousand yards? Or are we actually perched on a cliff, separated from that vision by a deep and dangerous chasm?

We have to answer these questions for ourselves and from within the groups to which we belong. I would like to offer my understanding of the field of Chinese American studies and my interpretation of Chinese American history, especially as it relates to my recent New York research.

Chinese American Studies. It is my view that our recent success is positive and should not be dismissed. Yet it is also full of hazards and pitfalls that can divorce our work from its moorings. In terms of Chinese American studies, I want to offer some personal stories about my 17 years of work as a historian and as an activist.

I have been keenly aware of how my work on Arnold Genthe and his San Francisco photographs, the Chinese American laundry experience, and New York Chinatown had been based on the insights and work of prior generations of thinkers and doers.

My work has been guided by individuals long gone and long forgotten, such as Wong Ching Foo, the satiric, Chinese activist journalist who stood up in New York City's Cooper Unions Great Hall in 1884 and attempted to shout down none other than Denis Kearney, the leader of the 1870s anti-Chinese movement which culminated in the Chinese Exclusion Law of 1882. Wong toured the East, lecturing in tongue-in-cheek fashion the virtues of Buddhism mocking American missionaries in Chinatowns and China. He also offered a $5,000 reward (money he didn't have) to anyone who could find a Chinese eating rats in New York, but more importantly, he actively wrote in American mainstream journals and newspapers, trying to debunk misinformation and replace it with real insight.

My work has also been immeasurably aided by those I consider my mentors, two of them being Paul C.P. Siu and Him Mark Lai. I first learned of Dr. Siu's work when we were researching the New York Chinatown History Projects series of projects on Chinese laundry life. I found his 1952 University of Chicago Ph.D. dissertation, "The Chinese Laundryman: A Study of Social Isolation," on microfilm. I was stunned and dazzled by his participant observation work and I could not figure out why we did not know more about this man. Was he still alive? What other work had he done? I called the American Sociological Association and found out that he was an active member. Out of the blue, I called the number given to me and found myself talking to a soft-spoken man with sharp insight. Years later, when he retired to New Jersey, we became friends and I learned of his story.

Paul Siu was the son of a laundry operator. He did his participant observation fieldwork in the later 1930s and 1940s, but he interrupted his writing to work in a social service agency serving Boston Chinese and to pay the bills for his family. His professors at Chicago liked his work a great deal, but they did not believe it should be published. He went from job to job at a series of smaller midwestern colleges in the 1950s, where he and his family had a hard time finding landlords who would rent to Chinese, and where European American students resisted learning about sociology from a Chinese professor. He finally found a job at the Detroit Institute of Technology, where he thrived in a multi-cultural environment. There he eventually became a full professor and chair of the department. We were finally able to get his dissertation published in 1987. He died just a few months before his book came out, some 35 years after it was completed as a dissertation and 50 years after the original research.

Just about everyone here knows Him Mark Lai. At a time when scholars jealously guard their own research, Mark unfailingly shares his work. Before his recent retirement, he was a full-time engineer by day and a prodigious (more than full-time) historian at all other times. I went to him when I was researching the Genthe book and he spent many hours with me, giving me leads and his measured assessments. Many individuals have published their own work with his help. Yet, as less committed scholars have published, made their names, and gained tenure in the larger academic world, he has been steadfast in researching and writing in a community context. Those of us who follow Mark's whereabouts know he is always traveling, but not for vacation. He is always in a local library to do field research. He is a scholar in the purest sense of the term. He does it for the belief of the importance of history and for his commitment of the Chinese American community.

Indeed, all three of these individuals did their work against all odds, if only because of their love for their community and the political belief that it was important. Chinese American studies have truly been a labor of love, and not remunerative or career-building. It has been a collective endeavor in which we have had no choice but to rely on each other. Generations of community-based scholars have stood on each other's shoulders. This is how we have gotten anywhere!

While we have been able to build on these pioneers' works, and individuals have been able to gain tenure, recognition, and some money, our field now risks a new set of challenges.

American academia, which was founded on the German model, has clear-cut rules of tenure, peer review, and publish or perish. Although in recent years, much has been said about the importance of giving recognition to teaching or even community service, security and advancement are still overwhelmingly doled out by publishing in journals and with presses deemed professionally acceptable. How valuable this knowledge is for a community or how committed that individual has been to inspire others in pursuing history are simply not calculated in these decisions.

So someone like me, who has worked as a community-based historian and is now in academia, is torn. Now that I have a two-and-a-half-year-old child to think about, voices are always whispering in my head, "You're not getting any younger! Think about tenure." Or, "Maybe you shouldn't publish in a local Chinese American newspaper or *Chinese America History and Perspectives* or *Amerasia* because it won't help with tenure or a salary increase."

Ideally, we can do both. But I do not want to underestimate the difficulty of doing both and how all the material and career incentives are skewed toward professional scholarship. Those who are unproblematically seduced by that siren call of professionalism are easily isolated from the people their work is about. Sure, the community is proud of its success stories, but does the scholarship (even when it is written with the community in mind) truly speak in a voice, rigor, and content which is engaged and helpful for real, everyday people—and not simply elitist work that may even be in the rhetoric of being community-minded but primarily advances an individual's career or ego? The rising generations of professional historians have to understand the long and important tradition of community-based scholarship that precedes them. They cannot try to advance by disdaining community-based work as "unsophisticated," and their own individual work as the ultimate flying machine. Within our still-tiny field, we risk engaging in turf wars and hoarding our research, which runs counter to the larger spirit and purpose of what we should be about.

My point here is that, while we have made huge strides as a field, we cannot unproblematically enter and accept the terms of academia as it exists. It easily fragments, makes esoteric, and corrupts knowledge that must serve to defend and build our communities and make us better people.

So can we find the wherewithal to enhance the virtues of community-based research and integrate it with advantages that universities afford?

As privileged producers of knowledge, we cannot assume that the established ways have been the best ways. We must work by a higher standard.

Chinese American History. A similar point can be made on an analytic level. In this presidential election year of 1992, we cannot be lured into the simplistic explanations of where our future lies with either political party. We cannot simply believe that conforming to one version of traditional, mainly Anglo American family values will suit Chinese Americans. Simply keeping our collective noses to the grindstone and lifting ourselves up without strong national vision has not worked in the past. Nor can it be believed that any rhetorical expression of a benevolent U.S. governmental "covenant" will hold up in difficult times, for they have not in the past.

Both ideological positions, ultra-conservatism and moderate-liberalism, have professed great affection for Chinese and Asian Americans as the "model minority." They have framed the debate that we inhabit. Conservatives hail Asians as the vanguard of the laissez-faire America that they live and breathe for. They claim our Confucian/family values are as good as their sacred Protestant work ethic and that we do not complain, and despite our being thought of as a racial group, we are not militant and demanding like African Americans. In fact, those people should be more like us, they claim.

Moderates and liberals also hail us for many of the same qualities. But they believe that social injustices are best corrected in concert with governmental programs. They are more willing to acknowledge continuing inequities and injustices, but they tend to think of them as the remnants of yet-to-be-fully modern people, those who are unenlightened, ignorant, and backward. If we can only get rid of localist prejudices, and if everyone becomes cosmopolitan, we can conquer racism, they believe.

To a large degree, we have bought into the limits of this ideological debate. The glass is either half full or half empty, but there is a fundamental faith that the glass is a good one and that it is perfectly adequate. Many of us believe that indeed we have made it, but we need to fight the remnants of ignorance and racism—while others of us believe that the "model minority" portrayal is largely a myth (after all, look at all the poor, largely invisible working class and immigrant Asians), and that we must lobby and agitate to get everyone on board. Their guiding analysis is "We need more government programs so that everyone will get a taste of the American dream." While both viewpoints have their moments, they are both thin of historical perspective.

I believe a more frank look at both the Chinese American past and the structural/symbolic role that Chinese and other Asians have played in United States society will yield a far more difficult and fundamental problem for these ideologies, and far more difficult challenges for community-minded activists.

A more careful examination of the 1882 Chinese Exclusion Law will reveal the accommodation of two seemingly conflicting traditions of United States life. We are certainly aware of the xenophobic and exclusionary portion of the law which stated that Chinese laborers were no longer allowed to enter the country. This main body of the law was the result of various regional movements against immigrant and racial others, organizing and uniting to gain political passage for exclusion. This nativist tradition has deep roots in the crazy quilt of American society. Such groups as American-born Protestants or Irish Catholics—or even Chinese—have indulged in the hallowed tradition of bashing those below them in order to prove how American they are. Groups who have been relegated to the status of outsiders or "others" in the class, racial, gender, language, and age pecking order of American society are often those who have been most anxious to prove their worthiness to the established powers that be. Certainly, it was no coincidence that many of the leaders of the anti-Chinese movement were the Irish, who were viewed by Anglo Americans as half-ape and half-thug. By being anti-Chinese, they were able to claim they were united with other Western European Americans in a common "whiteness."

We as a field have focused too much on the blatantly racist aspect of the Exclusion Law and have ignored analysis of the exemptions. We all know that merchants, scholars, diplomats, and students were entitled to continue entering and immigrating under this law, but we've rarely asked why this exemption existed. I believe it stems from another deeply-rooted American tradition, one that especially emanated from New York and other genteel, Eastern-establishment port cities. It was the tradition of Protestant pluralism, the basis of much of what we now call pluralism today. This tradition developed as an effective means for consolidating the many and various Protestant nationalities which settled in New York City. For example, in the 18th century, the Dutch and British were able to find common ground, as did many 19th-century German émigrés. This political accommodation also proved to become the basis of this nation's core cultural values.

Embedded in American Protestantism has been the Western-enlightenment faith in the superiority of Anglo-Saxon male rationalism and supreme rights of the possessive individual: that person who can be called the bourgeois man of property who is solely motivated by individual self-interest. This was Adam Smith's ideal. The pluralist inclusionary tradition came with the belief that all those who subscribed to this faith should become part of "We the People." Of course, the original architects of the constitution included neither African American slaves nor women in this democratic project. But in an interesting way, they were open to including the male Chinese court and merchant elite. After all, many founding fathers greatly admired China in the late 18th century for China's civil service, massive civic projects such as the Grand Canal, Confucian statecraft, and strong central government. This should not be mistaken for any love of the Chinese people. Indeed, many American elite shared the disdain of the xenophobes about Chinese workers and peasants. As the Pacific Coast-initiated Chinese Exclusion movement reached New York City and other centers of national power, exclusion was only granted with the Protestant pluralist caveat of still allowing Chinese male elites to enter freely.

We know that underlying both the nativist and pluralist traditions has been the measurement of the Anglo-Saxon American self above non-white others. But we tend not to realize that non-whites were perceived in a hierarchy.

In this year of the Columbian Quincentennary, all historians have made the understandable error of stating that these first "encounters" of America represented the coming together of three groups defined as races: Western European, indigenous native American peoples, and soon thereafter Africans. A fourth group has been omitted. After all, in Columbus' and other trader's imaginations, Cathay and the Indies always figured prominently in the driving motivation for their explorations. They wanted to trade on the perceived fabulous "riches" of the Orient. As a restless, self-defined enlightened people, these Westerners declared themselves to be the leading edge of progress and civilization, and Africans to be naturally backwards and primitive. Chinese? Chinese were once civilized but not stagnant. They were in between the lowest and the highest—at once to be praised for having strong traces of values that Westerners prized, but at the same time increasingly damned for resisting Western style modernization.

From the very beginning of the founding of this "New World," Asians in Asia and in America have been placed structurally and symbolically in the middle. We have been simultaneously respected and envied, disdained and feared. This, I believe, explains the historical roots of our current representation as a "model" and as the growing target of anti-Asian violence. And I believe that, notwithstanding the sincerity of the various ideological and activist positions, unless we acknowledge this fundamental character in the U.S. core history, we will be doomed to remain in this "in between" position between white and black, between the elite and the dispossessed. The Rodney King verdict and the Los Angeles rebellion involving African Americans, Latinos, Asians, and European Americans need to be understood in this context.

If this analysis of structural and symbolic position of Chinese and other Asian groups in U.S. society is accurate, then this historical analysis challenges us in the present day to devise appropriate long-term strategies. We cannot simply speak of the conservative, moderate, or liberal faith in ridding the society of the remnants of racism among "ignorant" individuals and groups, nor can we simply hope to enlarge the public pie to include more people. Nor can we trust that anti-Asian xenophobia, when it reaches the point of gaining opportunistic politicians enough votes, would not erupt once again onto the national landscape.

The only truly anti-racist tradition in the U.S. was not one animated by the realpolitiks of Protestant pluralism, but one generated by democratic social movements which have been agitated to open up the bounds of established society. In the 19th century, these movements stemmed from African Americans and European American women (and the likes of Wong Ching Foo) who sought to structurally and symbolically change the society to include them. They were at the forefront of what we can call a U.S. democracy movement.

Despite their substantial efforts and temporary victories during Reconstruction, the two apparently conflicting traditions of nativist xenophobia and Protestant pluralism found common ground in this post-Reconstruction Exclusion law and in the practice of "separate but equal." That coalition continued to dominate the character of this 20th century until it was finally challenged by the emergence of the post-"Brown vs. Board of Education" Civil Rights movement. And it was only then that the racial restrictions still written into the immigration laws were finally abolished. But as we all know, laws can be rewritten and cycles of mean-spiritedness have returned in the history of this country. We cannot mistake fool's gold for the real thing. We must keep our history and the larger experience of American history in mind when we strategize for the future. We have to be part of a democracy movement to push for basic changes in how this society thinks and acts about itself and "others," or else, as Chinese and Asian Americans, we risk losing our cultural souls. Cultural souls. No that's something that needs a long discussion, but let me briefly touch on it.

Ghosts. One of the ironies of this nation's fervent faith in "progress" and "being modern" is that it also creates a fear of, and a longing for, roots. Every time I see film maker George Romero's or any one else's "living dead" emerging from their graveyards to eat suburbanites regardless of race, gender, religion, creed, or age, I cannot but view it as the distinctly American compulsion to escape the past. In this world, memories of our ancestors are best kept buried. And when they pop up from the recesses of our psyches, we have to actively repress them.

In an aggressive commercial-culture constantly marketing newness, we are pressured to feel "old fashioned" and sentimental when we refuse to toss away past attachments and buy the latest. At the same time, Americans' search for identity, roots, and "authenticity" appears to be becoming more of a preoccupation. The huge interest in tracing one's genealogy, Afrocentrism, living history museums, visiting the land of one's ancestors, high school reunions, and popularized forms of history, such as Ken Burns' Civil War mini-series, attests to the apparently opposite desire to making the past come alive—to somehow connect.

While the ideology of European American modernism is used to counter localism and "old world" habits and superstitions, the countervailing grassroots search for meaning and steadying values seems all the stronger. Even if the pie of "progress" continues to expand, we're no longer so confident about the values it embodies. In our separate living spaces, we worry about electromagnetic radiation, environmental collapse, AIDS, homelessness and the "new" poor, sugar and other addictions, and the vacuousness of a technological materialism gone berserk.

In his 1944 visit to the United States, the Chinese sociologist Fei Xiaotong noted that the major problem he saw with the United States was that it was "land without ghosts." Although he greatly treasured the Western education he received, he mused:

> Our lives do not just pass through time in such a way that a moment in time or a station in life once past is lost. Life in its creativity changes the absolute nature of time: it makes past into present—no, it melds past, present, and future into one inextinguishable, multi-layered scene, a three-dimensional body. This is what ghosts are.... And, in the United States, a world without ghosts, life is free and easy. American eyes can gaze straight ahead. But still I think they lack something and I do not envy their lives.

Do we want to live with ghosts or not?

Sun Yat-Sen once spoke of overseas Chinese as being the "mothers of the revolution." He was speaking, of course, of the many tens of thousands of dollars raised from Chinatown community halls and laundry back rooms. But he was also speaking of their exposure to new ideas, especially those of deep structural change in society and notions of individualism and democracy that they brought back from being overseas. In this era in which the world has profoundly changed once again, the unique Chinese American historical experience challenges us to play a comparable role in United States and Asian events.

Is it possible to become a modern people in non-Eurocentric terms? Is it possible to live with ghosts and live in America? Can we resist the siren calls of material and individual success and help nurture the next democracy movement in this country? Will the history we research and write make us complacent? Or can our historical practice, both in terms of how we conduct our work and the content of the work we do, challenge us to be smarter, braver, and more eager to make a better world?

Chinese American History:
Achievements, Problems, Prospects

HIM MARK LAI
Chinese Historical Society of America, San Francisco, California

Interest in the study of Chinese American history and society began when Chinese Americans began establishing roots in this country and forming a Chinese American community. However, this interest was limited to a small circle until after World War II, and even then it did not become widespread until after the '60s. It is the purpose of this paper to examine developments in the field of Chinese American historical studies since the end of World War II, to appraise the achievements, to examine some problem areas, and to assess its future prospects.

A major political current during the post-World War II era has been the non-white minorities' demand for their rights as equal partners in American society. One phenomenon of this development has been the increase in interest in their history and society. In the case of the Chinese American minority, it had come out of World War II free of more oppressive provisions of the Chinese exclusion laws and with its social and economic status somewhat improved. During the ensuing decades, a Chinese American middle class consisting of professionals, technical personnel, and businessmen rooted in this country grew in strength and numbers. When its members played important capacities in the post-war expansion of the American economy, scholars began to sit up and take notice of their history and society. Within the Chinese American community itself, as this middle class grew and strived for equal status as partners in American society, it evolved a strengthened sense of community. Part of this process was increasing interest in the community's own historical experience as a valid part of its American heritage. These developments became major factors stimulating research and educational activities on Chinese American history and society.

For a decade after World War II, there was little scholarly activity on Chinese American history and society. But in 1957, Stanford Lyman, then a sociology doctoral candidate at the University of California, Berkeley, initiated a lecture series, "The Oriental in North America," at the University of California Extension in San Francisco. The subject matter in this first semester-length course on Asian American studies taught at a major university included the society and history of the Chinese, Japanese, and Filipinos in America. By the '60s Rose Hum Lee, S. W. Kung, Ping Chiu, and Gunther Barth had also published a few scholarly works on Chinese American society and history.

In the meantime, there were parallel developments in the Chinese American community. In 1963, Thomas Chinn, H. K. Wong, and others in San Francisco Chinatown founded Chinese Historical Society of America (CHSA) as the first community-based Chinese American historical group to be established after World War II. Four years later came the publication of Betty Lee Sung's *Mountain of Gold: The Story of the Chinese in America*, which introduced the Chinese American story to many readers all over the nation. During the late '60s, student pressure led to the founding of Asian American studies at San Francisco State College in 1969 and the first course in Chinese American history was offered as part of the curriculum. An Asian American Studies Center (AASC) was established at UCLA. By the early 1970s, Asian American studies program and courses were established in many colleges and universities throughout the nation, although the center of gravity remained on the west coast.

Reflecting the increasing ethnic consciousness among Chinese Americans, a number of community organizations interested in Chinese American history were founded; e.g., Hawaii Chinese History Center (HCHC) (Honolulu, founded 1971), Chinese Historical Society of Southern California (CHSSC) (Los Angeles, founded 1975), New York Chinatown History Museum (NYCHM; formerly New York Chinatown History Project, founded 1980), Chinese Historical Society of the Pacific Northwest (CHSPNW) (Seattle, founded 1980), Chinese Historical Committee of Stockton (founded 1985), Chinese Historical Society of Greater San Diego and Baja California (San Diego, founded 1986), Chinese American Historical Committee of Sacramento (founded 1987), and Chinese Historical Society of New England (Boston, founded 1992). Their activities were also often complemented by the activities of Chinese cultural groups such as the Chinese Culture Foundation (CCF) of San Francisco (founded 1965), Basement Workshop of New York (founded 1971), and Chinese Cultural Institute of Boston (founded 1980), as well as organizations of professionals such as The Association of Chinese Teachers (TACT) in San Francisco (founded 1969).

From the above we can see that over the past three decades, three principal groups were involved in activities connected with Chinese American history and society. These are the traditional social science disciplines, particularly history and sociology, and Asian American studies on the campus, and the historical societies and associated groups in the community. And comparing the situation 30 odd years ago with the situation today, there has been substantial achievements in the study of Chinese American history and society. Some of them are:

1. Compilation of Bibliographies and Increased Accessibility of Research Documents. During many previous decades, institutions had not systematically collected source materials on Chinese Americans. Often, such documents are widely scattered, and locating them is a challenging first task for the researcher. Thus, one of the early tasks in the Chinese American history field of study was the compilation of bibliographies to help facilitate the researcher and the building of collections. One of the earliest of these was Gladys C. Hansen and William F. Heintz, *The Chinese in California: A Brief Bibliographic History* (1970), based on the resources in the San Francisco Public Library. From Asian American studies programs came bibliographies of Asian American titles, of which Chinese American titles constitute a part. One of the earliest of these was *Asians in America: A Selected Annotated Bibliography* (Davis, CA: Asian American Studies, University of California at Davis, 1971, revised 1983). There has also been other bibliographies such as regional ones for the Pacific Northwest and for Hawaii, and specialized ones such as those listing masters theses and doctoral dissertations, Chinese newspapers and periodicals, and Chinese-language materials.

The demand for research materials led to a building up of Chinese American library holdings, usually as a part of Asian American collections. In 1978, Asian American Studies Library at University of California at Berkeley also established an archival collection on the Chinese in America, so that the library now has one of the most comprehensive collections of newspapers, documents and manuscripts relevant to Chinese American research. Other institutions also have primary documents of more limited scope; e.g., the Sacramento Chinatown documents in the University of California at Davis Library Special Collections, the Tom Leung papers in UCLA's East Asian Library, the Sam Cheung papers in the possession of the Chinese Historical Society of Southern California, the Ah Quinn diary in the San Diego Historical Society collection, etc. However, up to the '90s libraries were usually inadequately funded and underdeveloped.

A number of hitherto obscured and neglected documents were also rediscovered and made more accessible to researchers. Two published collections of primary documents are *"Chink!": Anti-Chinese Prejudice in America* (ed. Cheng-Tsu Wu 1972) and *The Sandalwood Mountains: Readings and Stories of the Early Chinese in Hawaii* (ed. Tin-Yuke Char 1975).

2. Development of Oral Histories as Source Material. In the absence of much detailed documentation on many events in Chinese American history, oral interviews often became important source materials. A pioneering application of oral history integrated with documentary research, as applied to Chinese American history, was Victor and Brett

Nee, *Longtime Californ': A Documentary Study of an American Chinatown* (1972), a work that used the words of the interviewees to narrate the social history of the San Francisco Chinese American community. The Nee's methodology has been adopted successfully by several histories such as *Island: Poetry and History of Chinese Immigrants on Angel Island, 1910–1940* (H. M. Lai, Genny Lim, and Judy Yung 1980), *A Place Called Chinese America* (Diane Mark and Ginger Chih 1982), and *Chinese Women of America: A Pictorial History* (Judy Yung 1986).

Asian American studies and/or the historical societies have also sponsored several oral history projects to record historical, sociological, and biographical information.

In 1978, UCLA's Asian American Studies Center collaborated with CHSSC on another project that resulted in the publication of *Linking Our Lives: Chinese Women of Los Angeles* (1984). Honolulu's Hawaii Chinese History Center has conducted field work in oral history which, integrated with documentary research, has resulted in a series of publications on *Chinese Historic Sites and Pioneer Families* for Kauai (1980), the Big Island of Hawaii (1983), and rural Oahu (1988). All three works were compiled by Tin Yuke and Wai Jane Char.

3. **Increase in Number of Historical Studies and Books.** As Chinese American history and society attracted researchers as a fruitful field of inquiry, an increasing number of papers were published in journals of the social sciences and humanities, as well as in *Amerasia* (1971), which became the scholarly journal for Asian American studies. Many historical societies publish newsletters. Some of the better known and more widely distributed publications which also included short historical items are CHSA's monthly *Bulletin* (initial issue 1966); CHSSC'S semi-annual *Gum Saan Journal* (initial issue 1977), and NYCHM's periodically published *Bao Gao Ban* (initial issue 1984), the publication of the New York Chinatown History Museum.

In 1983, CHSPNW became the first Chinese historical society to publish a collection of scholarly historical essays with its *The Annals of the Chinese Historical Society of the Pacific Northwest.* CHSA also began publishing an annual collection of historical essays *Chinese America: History and Perspectives* in 1987.

In the realm of scholarship, by the '70s and the '80s there were an increasing number of books on Chinese American history and society by scholars in the social sciences, such as Alexander Saxton, Stanford M. Lyman, Victor Low, Lucy M. Cohen, L. Eve Armentrout Ma, and Henry Shih-shan Tsai. A number of these were originally doctoral dissertations. The increased need for reference works in the field also led to the publication of older dissertations, such as those by Elmer C. Sandmeyer, Clarence E. Glick, Paul Siu, Stanford M. Lyman, and others. But by the 1980s books based on original research by Asian American studies scholars such as Ronald Takaki, Lucie Cheng, and Sucheng Chan were also being published.

Similarly, in the category of popular histories, by the '80s there were more detailed general histories targeted at the general public, such as works by Jack Chen (*Chinese of America, from the Beginnings to the Present*, 1980) and Loren W. Fessler (*Chinese in America: Stereotyped Past, Changing Present*, 1983). In addition to general histories, there are also an increasing number of historical pictorials, as well as scholarly and popular histories on regions such as Hawaii, Massachusetts, Washington, Seattle, New York City, Oakland, Stockton, San Jose, as well as special topics such as the maritime trade, the Rock Springs massacre, and the like.

Accompanying the increase in historical works was the greater availability of biographical literature on individual Chinese Americans as they wrote their life experiences for the edification of posterity. Many of the earliest came from Hawaii, where a Chinese American middle class was well established before the same phenomenon appeared in the continental United States, one of the earliest being Chung Kun Ai, *My Seventy Nine Years in Hawaii* (1960). A related field which has a great potential for developing more Chinese American historical materials is genealogical and family history research. CHSSC and AASC sponsored the first workshop in 1983. But it was in Hawaii that Chinese American genealogical research blossomed and flourished. These efforts have led to the publication of a number of Hawaiian Chinese family histories and genealogies. The first family history workshop was not held in San Francisco until 1989 in an one-day symposium sponsored by CHSA, CCF, and Cheng Society of America. By 1991, however, CCF, in conjunction with CHSA, has initiated a "Search for Roots" program in which participants researched their family histories under guidance, continued by visiting their ancestral villages in China, and then presented their findings in an exhibition.

In another discipline, archaeologists have excavated Chinese historic sites in the West as early as the '70s. The Great Basin Foundation's excavation at the old Chinatown of Riverside had resulted in a two-volume historical archaeological study, *Wong Ho Leun: An American Chinatown* (1987). However, in most cases, results of archaeological excavations have yet to be integrated with documentary information and incorporated meaningfully into Chinese American history.

4. Convening Conferences for Exchange of Ideas and Information.
Another achievement in the field is the periodic convening of conferences and seminars so that the expanding circle of researchers

and scholars can meet to present the results of their work and exchange information and ideas. In this respect, the field is one of the most active among the Asian American groups.

CHSA organized the first seminar on Chinese Americans in 1969 for educators in the San Francisco Bay Area, as a result of which *A History of the Chinese in California: A Syllabus* was published as a basic reference work. Two national conferences had been held in San Francisco in 1975 and 1980, with more than 36 and 80 presentations respectively. This 1992 conference, "Origins and Destinations," was the third, and it was jointly sponsored by CHSSC, UCLA's Center for Pacific Rim Studies, and California State University at Los Angeles' Institute for Asian American and Pacific Asian Studies.

There had also been other conferences with more limited scopes. In 1982, there was an exhibit and seminar in San Francisco to commemorate the centennial of the 1882 Chinese Exclusion Act; in 1986 there was a conference and event to commemorate the centennial of the expulsion of the Chinese from Seattle, and in 1988, the first conference on Chinese Hawaiian history was held in Honolulu to commemorate the bicentennial of the first arrival of the Chinese in the islands in 1788. The Association of Asian American Studies also holds annual national conferences which includes papers on Chinese American history and society. (The first conference was held in 1980.) Increasingly, Chinese American studies is also recognized in scholarly conferences of the traditionally established academic disciplines, such as American or Asian studies, with presentation of papers and sometimes separate panels on the subject. Such meetings served to increase the flow and exchange of ideas and advanced the state of knowledge in the field.

5. Sponsoring Exhibitions and Commemorations, Preservation of Historic Sites. In 1966, CHSA was first to establish a museum with a permanent exhibit devoted solely to the history of the Chinese of America. CCF also developed major exhibits, notably "Chinese of America, 1785–1980" (1980) and "Chinese Women of America, 1834–1982" (1982). The former became in 1985 the first exhibit on Chinese American history and society designed by Chinese Americans to be shown in China.

In New York, Basement Workshop's Chinatown Historical Society collaborated with the American Museum of Immigration, the Statue of Liberty National Monument to design the exhibit "Chinese in America: Images from a Neglected Past" in the mid-1970s. In 1978, Asian American Resource Center (AARC) revised this for exhibition in New York City as "Images from a Neglected Past: The Work and Culture of the Chinese in America." When New York Chinatown History Project succeeded AARC, one of its principal activities was also to research, design, and present exhibits on Chinese American history. In 1983, it designed the prize-winning exhibit, "Eight Pound Livelihood: Chinese Laundry Workers in the U.S."

There has also been other exhibits on Chinese in other regions such as the Sacramento Delta, Monterey Peninsula, Hawaii, San Diego, etc. Currently, CHSSC is part of an effort to develop a Museum of Chinese American History at El Pueblo de Los Angeles Historic Park.

Many historical societies also sponsored monthly lectures and field trips to Chinese American historic sites. CHSA and CHSSC are especially active in this regard. There were also commemorations of important events connected with Chinese American history. At the centennial of the completion of the transcontinental railroad in 1969, CHSA erected plaques at Sacramento, California, and at Promontory Point, Utah, dedicated to the Chinese railroad workers. In 1976, CHSSC dedicated a plaque to honor Chinese railroad laborers in Southern California who built the Southern Pacific Railroad and the San Fernando Tunnel.

Many individuals and historic groups were also active in organized efforts, with varying degrees of success, to preserve and restore Chinese American historic sites. Some examples are the Angel Island Immigration Detention Station, China Camp, the town of Locke, Chinese herb shop in Fiddletown, Hanford's Chinese temple, and San Jose's Ng Shing Gung.

These educational activities have substantially raised the awareness level of many Chinese Americans and the general public regarding the historic role of the Chinese in American society.

Problem Areas. Although considerable progress has been made in the study of Chinese American history and society in the past few decades, there remain a number of problem areas and gaps in the field of study which should be confronted to facilitate further developments in the field. I will give only a few examples:

1. Use of Chinese Language Materials. One of the concerns of Chinese Americans when they began pushing for recognition of the role Chinese played in America is that the Chinese point of view be presented. When one considers the fact that English-speaking American-born Chinese had always been a minority in the Chinese American community, then the use of Chinese language materials becomes that much more important in order to obtain the Chinese point of view. The use of these material are certainly necessary for understanding the internal dynamics of the Chinese community. Unfortunately, however, the great difference between Chinese and English language and Western culture becomes a gulf too wide for

most researchers in this field to bridge, and Chinese-language sources remain badly under-utilized—because of this, certain areas of inquiry have been sadly neglected.

Here, it is appropriate to say something of Chinese-language research, which has developed in parallel with research in the English language.

In a community that long had a preponderance of immigrants, it was not surprising that histories written in Chinese were published even before World War II, as part of handbooks on the Chinese in Hawaii. However, it was not until World War II ended that similar handbooks were published in the mainland Chinese community. By 1954, S. Y. Wu published the first Chinese American history in Chinese with his *One Hundred Years of Chinese in the United States and Canada*. But the most comprehensive and most detailed work is Pei Chi Liu, *A History of the Chinese in the United States of America* in two volumes (1976, 1981). The latest is Him Mark Lai, *From Overseas Chinese to Chinese American: The Development of the Chinese American Community in the Twentieth Century* (1992), which was written from the perspective of the American-born.

Historians writing in Chinese worked as individuals with little coordination and continuity in their research effort. However, due to their extensive use of community sources, particularly Chinese sources, their works are far richer in details of Chinatown events and personalities than any general history thus far published in English. These sources include newspapers and magazines, association publications, biographies and travel diaries, and other publications. The use of such sources adds a human dimension to Chinese American history that would have been difficult to convey by compiling statistics and quoting official documents, and is essential for areas of inquiry connected with the internal dynamics of Chinese American community development.

The rise in status of the Chinese minority in America after World War II has also aroused much interest in the study of the Chinese American history and society by scholars abroad. In both mainland China and Taiwan, this research is also tied closely to the respective area's policy toward overseas Chinese. When mainland China changed to an open policy in the late '70s and welcomed investments from Chinese abroad, this was reflected in the blossoming of studies on the overseas Chinese and by the establishment of overseas Chinese historical societies in a number of cities and overseas Chinese research programs in some universities and academies of social sciences.

During the past decade, there has been much research on the overseas Chinese, sometimes collaborating with institutions abroad. In 1979, Prof. Lucie Cheng of UCLA's AASC pioneered a project with Guangzhou's Zhongshan University to conduct field research and oral interviews in Taishan emigrant villages. Chinese researchers have also compiled bibliographies on the overseas Chinese in different countries. By the last half of the '80s a number of overseas Chinese histories have been published, including one on the history of the Chinese in America (1989). A number of works on the overseas Chinese written in the western languages have been translated into Chinese and been published. Local political consultative conferences have also published historical materials and memoirs, which included much material on overseas Chinese. In the past few years there has also been a major effort to compile local gazetteers. One of the fallouts from this has been the editing of chapters on the overseas Chinese and compilations of biographies of leaders and famous personalities.

On Taiwan, where the Nationalist regime has had strong ties to the overseas-Chinese communities since the republican revolution early this century, the Overseas Chinese Affairs Commission (OCAC) is deeply interested in developments among the Chinese abroad, especially those in the United States, which is considered one of the important bases of political support. However, due to OCAC's political objectives, its greatest interest is on current developments in contemporary overseas Chinese society. There is a limited amount of research by those in scholarly institutions such as the Sun Yat-sen Institute for Social Sciences and Philosophy of the Academia Sinica.

Hong Kong does not have any overseas-Chinese historical societies or institutes but it does have *Huaren Magazine,* which is unique as the only non-academic Chinese periodical outside China with articles dwelling on the historical experiences and contemporary condition of Chinese abroad in all parts of the world.

From the point of view of researchers in Chinese American history, the research efforts across the Pacific offer opportunities to examine in greater depth the many links between the Chinese in America and the ancestral land, and thus have a more complete overall view of Chinese American history.

2. Research on the Exclusion Era. When Dr. Stanford Lyman spoke at the seventh anniversary dinner of the Chinese Historical Society of America in 1970, one of the remarks he made was as follows:

> There is a period in Chinese American history we need to know something about. Strangely enough, it is the time period that we ought to know the most about, and we know least. And that is the time period from 1910 to the present. There is a curious tendency in the writing of Chinese history in America to concentrate on the period from 1850 to 1910. There's reason for that. It fits in with self-defense arguments. For it was in the period 1850 to 1910 that the outrageous and vilifying anti-Chinese movement took place, and was its heyday.

Since these remarks were made some 22 years ago, some progress have been made, but for the English reader, the bill of fare is still quite restricted. There are still many themes (e.g., influence of China politics, development of institutions, changes in the economy, the influence of American culture, etc.) which await more detailed research and integration into a general history of the Chinese in America.

3. Research on Other Communities and Biographies. For many decades, San Francisco was considered the political, cultural, and political center for the Chinese in America. Even today it is one of the major centers for the Chinese in America. Thus, more documentation is available from this location than any other locality, and many historians tended to center much of their history describing events in San Francisco to the neglect of communities in other areas. However, San Francisco, with its concentration of Chinese, is, in a manner of speaking, not typical, since the concentration of Chinese has a conservative effect and tends to help the population preserve its Chinese language and culture and help slow their adoption of mainstream culture. Thus, even though the San Francisco community no doubt plays a leading role among Chinese in America, there is a definite need to examine the other communities in America to get an more balanced interpretation of the course of development of the Chinese in America.

One important area often neglected is the history of the Chinese in Hawaii. At one point during the exclusion era, the Hawaii Chinese population was more than a quarter of the Chinese American population in the U.S. Due to the local environment which is somewhat different from that on the mainland, Chinese in Hawaii have a different history of development; they led the way in entering mainstream society. A study of this experience would be helpful in understanding historical developments among the Chinese on the mainland.

Also, researchers have almost exclusively focused on the Chinatown and the Cantonese merchant class. This has its historical reasons, since for many years, the Cantonese Chinatowns represented the bulk of the Chinese population in America and the merchant class provided the leadership. However, with the communities springing up in the suburbs and an increasing number of immigrants from other regions of China and other countries, historical information should be collected on the newer immigrant groups such as the Mandarin-speaking, the Taiwanese, ethnic Chinese from Indo-China, Cuban Chinese, Burmese Chinese etc. in order to have a more complete picture of Chinese American history. Also, there should be more research on other social groups such as labor, intellectuals, the American-born, and women.

A characteristic of many current Chinese American histories in the English language has been the fact that most Chinese on the stage of history appeared to be faceless and nameless. There are few identifiable heroes available as role models for the younger generation. While this may be somewhat acceptable for sociological and economic studies, it is grossly inadequate for historians dealing with people and events. Surely such personalities as Wong Ching Foo, Ng Poon Chew, Lew Hing, Kathryn Cheung, Walter U. Lum, Lue Gim Gong, and the like have contributed to the building of America and merit their places in history. One of the reasons for this inadequate coverage may be attributed to the lack of materials in the English language caused largely by the isolation of the Chinese community from the larger society. In order to remedy this, there should be a more concerted effort to develop more biographical materials by using oral histories and researching the Chinese newspapers.

4. Race Relations. Much of the history of the Chinese in America was influenced by its relations with white America. However, the Chinese existed in a multi-ethnic society, but so far there has been little work done on relations of the Chinese with other ethnic groups. It would be illuminating to probe such questions as cultural interchanges, intermarriages, social and economic relations. I suspect that research into these areas will bring forth some surprising findings.

Prospects. Today there is a greater acceptance of the fact that America is an multi-ethnic society. Many universities are requiring some understanding of other cultures other than western culture. More and more American studies are including histories of the minorities, and Asian studies have reached out to embrace study of the overseas Chinese. We can expect more scholars with Chinese-language skills to enter the field. In the Chinese American community also, there is increasing awareness of the importance of its own historical heritage and the need to preserve it and to educate the public.

Thus, the circumstances are favorable for more historical research. With the historical societies, Asian American studies, the traditional social sciences in this country and abroad each working in its field of specialization and sharing the fruits of their research, we may expect that an increasingly complete picture of the Chinese in America will emerge in the coming years, both as a history of the community by itself and as a integrated part of the history of the American people.

Chinese American History:
The Role of Historical Societies

MUNSON KWOK
Chinese Historical Society of Southern California, Los Angeles, California

Understanding an entity such as a "Chinese Historical Society" and its role in the local or regional community requires some delineation about the uniqueness of such an organization, of which many are proliferating wherever Chinese are congregating in today's North America. Furthermore, it is necessary to revisit the many motivating factors that have caused the creation of such Societies in this recent time span, only slightly greater than one generation, i.e., 30 years for the oldest established Society, the Chinese Historical Society of America (1962).

Good work in this respect has been done through the careful observations of Him Mark Lai in 1988 (11–29) and the perceptive interpretations of Wing Chung Ng in 1992 (177–210). Together, these works summarize most of the important factors in the initiation and the continued existence of such organizations.

These factors range from the increasingly middle-class members of long-time Chinese families, who express a pure curiosity and a desire to appreciate the history of pioneering ancestors (Lai 18); to those young individuals or recent arrivals of any economic strata, who have raised their ethnic consciousness and have accepted social activism (Ng 181). Thus, Chinese American history becomes not just a topic for significant research, but more importantly, a social tool for the improvement of society. We'll return to this thought later, when we examine motivation.

The need to know "what" a Society is and "why" it forms, i.e., the motivating factors for formation, is essential to our discussion today on the role of such groups in the larger fabric of our various communities and a Society's appropriate relation with academia. In particular, a clear knowledge of the original motivating factors—those elements which encourage continuing, successful operations; those aspects which have fulfilled or are meeting some community need; and especially the changes in those motivating factors in our changing social situations—is an important aspect in defining the role of a Chinese Historical Society in our modern, ethnically conscious society.

Throughout the presentations this weekend, I hope you will agree that we have seen ample indication of changes—rapid changes—occurring in our Chinese American world. Indeed, the very survival of our Chinese Historical Societies as we know them depends on our clear understanding of the rapid changes in Chinese America. It comes down to one of my favorite sound bites: James Burke's "if you don't know where you've been, you won't know where you're going."

Let me assure you that I don't believe I am being an alarmist. I do believe Chinese Historical Societies have an important role to play in a community and in Chinese American studies. But let me present an observation. In Los Angeles, there are over 60 historical societies, all joined together in the Associated Historical Societies of Los Angeles County. Are you amazed? Sixty. Now let me share the concern that many of these groups have. Most maintain some historic house or small local museum. Their membership has dwindled. Most members seem to be over age 60. Few young people seem to be involved. The groups are troubled. They admire my home organization, the Chinese Historical Society of Southern California, which I always say is a "full service" historical society with a wide range of activities. We have even had the chutzpah to try to mount this conference for you.

Many of our fellow Societies here are also "full service," the meaning of which I will try to outline in a few minutes. "How" the Societies do things, their activities and interests of the last 12 years help to define each Society's role. I perceive common trends toward institutionalization; toward strong contributions in community leadership; and toward embracing a wider range of activities in interests or issues not normally or strictly defined as Chinese American history. None of these developments are necessarily bad. In fact, these may be very good evolutions for our historical societies.

What makes us tick? Why does it work for us? Are we fated to end up like many of the L.A. societies?

I don't pretend to have the answers, nor can I see the future. I do hope to stimulate discussions which may help your local operations, and cast some directions for future conferences.

Chinese Historical Societies. What are the Chinese Historical Societies? Let's look not at groups affiliated with colleges or universities, but at groups that are basically community based. When Mark Lai did his 1988 survey, he identified seven groups (18–20); all but one continue to function, and most are represented here today. Some societies were and are: Chinese Historical Society of America (1962); Hawaii Chinese History Center (1970); Chinese Historical Society of Southern California, or CHSSC (1975); New York Chinatown History Project (1980, with antecedents to 1976), now very proudly the Chinatown History Museum; Chinese Historical Society of the Pacific Northwest (1980); Chinese Historical Society of Greater San Diego and Baja California (1986); a Chinese History Committee in the Sacramento area, and the Chinese Historical Committee of Stockton (1985). Now we must certainly include Chinese Historical and Cultural Project, from the Santa Clara Valley in California; the Taoist Temple Preservation Society of Hanford, California; Chinese Civic Association of Hawaii, and Friends of Museum of Chinese American History, in Los Angeles. Also, there is thought to be a Chinese Historical Society of New England (Lai 8/30/92).

We are beginning to see groups that do preservation or some history work, but may also concentrate on culture or other activities, such as the Chinese Consolidated Benevolent Association in Portland, Oregon; Orange County Historical and Cultural Foundation, or the Chinese American Council at the Bowers Museum. We see Chinese in Marysville, California, supporting the Bok Kai Temple and the once-a-year Festival. And a Committee in Riverside, California. There's the Phoenix (Arizona) Chinatown Archaeological Project, which brought that community together. I believe there is, as a result of the Hawaiian bicentennial, at least one active cultural/history group on Maui—I think in Kahalui—and there is the small group of pioneer Chinese of the Kwok Hing Society on the slopes of Haleakala, preserving some buildings and other sites. And there are groups that pursue their Chinese American history in an Asian American framework, such as the Wing Luke Museum in Seattle and the soon-to-be Oakland Asian Cultural Center.

I guess the main purpose of this litany is to give you a feeling for the mushrooming growth of this type of organization in the past 10–15 years, and the proliferation of historical groups wherever Chinese Americans are congregating in sufficiently large numbers. But we are already seeing groups that seem to be coming and going, like the Maui group, the Phoenix people, and the Riverside committee. Their focus seems to be on the one major effort of supporting a project, study, or anniversary; and there is no effective continuity or energy.

Nature of the Historical Societies. What are some of the unique characteristics of a Chinese Historical Society common to the major, continuing groups? Lai has already characterized them well (20). All the groups consist of volunteers. Few have paid staff, although some are affiliated with government projects or institutions. Most of the major organizations are educational, charitable non-profits; some have offices and equipment. Under these circumstances, Lai rightfully surmised that "the level of activity attained by each group is as much dependent on the continued participation of a core of active members as on available funding" (20). The directions of activities depend on the vision and interests of the core leaders (Lai 8/30/92).

Important to the Historical Society's role is its unique diversity of membership. It is quite clear that members have a common interest in some aspect of Chinese American history. In a large Chinese American community, the Historical Society remains one of the few

Chinatown-based organizations with a high percentage of non-Chinese members. Both the Chinese Historical Society of America and the Chinese Historical Society of Southern California average 25–30% of its members non-Chinese. Therefore, the Historical Societies provide a unique common ground for mutual understanding, and also an entryway into the broader community, external to an often still-insular Chinese community. With the discriminatory limitations of the past removed, a great number of the Chinese in America still find themselves reticent to comfortably enter this community at large; and Societies serve to facilitate that exposure.

Another unique aspect to membership was also noticed by Lai. The Chinese Historical Society provides a common ground for the professional and academic person to interact freely and easily with the amateur and layman (Lai 20). Without intimidation and without reservations on either side. The continued existence of ethnic studies usually depends on strong community support. Thus, a well-run Society can effectively channel community support, inputs, and knowledge into professional or institutional circles for program development or operations or any other agenda while the professional gains access to research opportunities, primary materials, and fulfills his obligation to provide educational outreach. These mutually beneficial opportunities are another example of the Historical Society serving as a very valuable bridging organization.

One other unique attribute of a Chinese Historical Society is that, in some local communities, it serves as an important center of intellectual focus, discourse, and education. In very small or close-knit Chinese communities, it may serve the equivalent of the salon, the community forum, the cultural center, the information clearing house. Thus, its range of interests and activities may go quite far afield from the narrow emphasis and confines of Chinese American history. Certainly, CHSSC, which was formed by a number of community leaders, has always featured some programs that just barely touch on Chinese American history. That group has had programs and projects on city planning, education, literature, general or regional history, topics in sociology, demographics, the arts, and even Chinese culture, such as the Moon Festival. In the case of the Moon Festival, involvement began by recalling and recreating some of the events of 1938 when a Chinese Moon Festival united the three Chinatowns of Los Angeles in a war relief effort for China. Those Moon Festival events were pivotal moments in history for Los Angeles Chinatown. The continued activity three years later helps to run a new generation of Moon Festivals for Los Angeles Chinatown in a purely cultural project. CHSSC shared in the creation of the culture center idea for Chinatown in 1985, and it has served always as an information service for Chinatown through its publicized phone numbers, one of which was in a AAA book edition some years ago and is still being used!

An unusual common feature of the early Societies is the use of the name "Chinese" instead of "Chinese American" or "American Chinese." That practice is almost idiosyncratic. Yet it is clear in all our minds that our missions deal with Chinese American history and studies, not Chinese studies or works on China. With the influx of a large number of immigrants, "Chinese" has a different meaning. CHSSC has been approached to publish works on China. There is now even a Chinese Historical Society for the Sino-Japanese War, based in Monterey Park, to remember the holocaustical events of that epoch much as the Jewish people keep alive the memories of Holocaust. The names of our groups seem not to accurately describe our mission; this may be a reflection of the uncertainty two or three decades ago about identity—the concept that there are Chinese in this country who never felt and don't yet feel "American"—and about the mission scope: how much of China's history must be included, especially when you are dealing with a sojourner's story? How we see ourselves remains a subject of hot debate today, and I don't propose to open that discussion here.

So what is a "full service" Society?

I know CHSSC best, of course, but this model fits Chinese Historical Society of America (CHS-A) and Chinese Historical Society of Greater San Diego, and many others. Let me warn you that I may seem to be using a lot of examples from CHSSC, but I don't mean to be biased and I do mean the cases to be somewhat generic. It's just that I know my home society and its activities best.

The "full service" Society presents, disseminates, publishes, studies, collects, preserves, researches, and promotes Chinese American history. Often, the emphasis is on a regional aspect: Hawaii, San Diego, Stockton, Los Angeles. Others specialize on one or a few aspects: the fine publications of Hawaii Chinese History Center (HCHC), the preservation work of the Taoist Temple Society. A wide range of services are provided by and for members and to others in a community. The string of verbs denotes a lot of charter. The functions are typical of many a historical society and certainly are not unique to a Chinese group. An organization must have a healthy and vigorous core group to cover this range of activities.

In presentations and dissemination, CHSSC holds periodic free meetings, usually monthly, at which speakers, panels, or shows address topics in Chinese American history. CHSSC also holds banquets or special receptions once or twice a year. During these events, a pioneer recognition program is given in the form of awards with descriptions of achievements or significant history. CHSSC conducts a special series of Centennial Awards, which supports the history that Los Angeles Chinatown came of age in the 1890s period. Some individuals and many institutions of today's Chinatown span the century. CHSSC conducts historical walking tours of Chinatown and offers a map of a self-guided tour. CHSSC also organizes tour trips for its members to Chinese historic sites, ranging across California and as far as Mexicali and Hawaii. CHS-A has had a rich tour program which has visited many of the Western States. Several groups have developed educational traveling exhibits. You have observed the wonderful San Diego exhibit this weekend.

Many of the organizations have been publishers for disseminating scholarly or educational materials. Several Societies have strong publishing programs. They include HCHC and CHS-A. San Diego and, I think, Stockton have developed materials for their schools. CHS-A has had the wonderful Bulletin series which was terminated. In its place, Him Mark Lai has led a group in producing the annual "Chinese America: History and Perspectives," a fine selection of pertinent scholarly articles. CHSSC has a semi-annual journal and has produced two books. It has worked with other L.A. Chinatown organizations (Chinese Chamber of Commerce and New Chinatown Corporation) to create historical articles.

In the 12 years since the last conference, the collective publication achievements by all the Societies have been excellent, in both books and journals. In my opinion, this is one of the singular important trends in that time period. The Societies have played an important, influential role in publishing key literature of the field.

One must realize that publication ventures by a volunteer group require significant resources and commitment. As illustrious as that publication record has been in trailblazing the field and expanding the realms of study, Dr. Tchen on Friday suggested the future in publication is muddy for the lay Chinese Historical Societies. On the one hand, publishing through the Societies is an excellent way to reach a faithful, somewhat limited lay audience; on the other hand, the incentive to do so is diminishing because of career prestige. As works on Chinese America become more readily accepted by mainstream publishers with wide professional distributions, Societies will need to find their market niche, which might be works focused on local, oral, or family history.

By the same token, one can ponder the fate of this Conference, which is traditionally co-produced by a lay group and an academic institution and includes presentations from both types of scholars. An advantage of the meeting seems to be its multi-disciplinary nature. The interactions between the two types of audience are clearly beneficial to both. The support of the academic community is essential, and I think that involvement will continue to be a willing one if the quality of the conference remains high.

Besides publishing, I think one other important achievement for the Societies during the 12 years is the conference held in Honolulu commemorating the bicentennial of Chinese immigration. Sponsored by HCHC, that meeting has been the only other major gathering for Chinese American studies. Due to its geographical location, however, there seemed to be less involvement of the mainland Societies.

To me, one of the most significant trends for community groups in the last decade is the development of museums. That evolution represents an institutionalizing of the functions of a "full service" society, namely, the disseminating, studying, researching, collecting, and promoting of Chinese American history. The coming of museums also reflects a certain confidence and maturity in both our Societies and our community and a willingness to invest in permanent places for Chinese American history. It also indicates that the community can now generate the resources to fulfill an expensive commitment. Twelve years ago, there was one small museum on Adler Place. Now, for CHS-A, there are bigger plans and a new location. We have displays or facilities in Seattle, Portland, New York, San Jose, and Hanford, among others. We have projects going in Los Angeles, San Diego, possibly Riverside, maybe at the Smithsonian and elsewhere. I see this institutional trend continuing for some years. It is an area of major commitment, effort and funding, and it is fitting that we had panels on museum and artifacts (archaeology) at this conference.

Let me dwell for a few moments on the idea of promoting Chinese American history and Chinese American studies. As community volunteer organizations, Chinese Historical Societies are in a special position to communicate, to develop interest in, and to create excitement about heritage and history. The Societies can work with other local groups to develop their histories or to foster a sense of local history with joint ventures. CHSSC has done that with the Chinese Chamber of Commerce, the New Chinatown Corporation, Chinatown Public Safety Association, the Consolidated Benevolent Association, Chinese American Citizens Alliance and others. CHSSC has done open, public programs, such as holding a day to invite historic photos to be copied. This Fall, CHSSC will be reviving this project concept by assisting the L.A. Public Library on "Shades of L.A.," searching for the photographic ethnic history of the City.

CHSSC has worked with other non-Chinese historical societies, with humanities-aligned professional groups such as architectural historians and archivists, with the county umbrella group and with the state group, the Conference of California Historical Societies, with which I know CHS-A is also affiliated. These liaison activities earn a respect and legitimacy for Chinese American history among the lay and professional groups at large, institutions in the community, and even business and corporate entities. These activities enhance mutual understanding and promote healthy multicultural exchanges. This outreach in itself can develop a reputation and sensitivity leading to external funding sources for future projects.

Societies should work with media. The CHSSC has participated in the L.A. History Project for public television on a segment presenting Chinese American history, serving as a resource and a script technical advisor. Numerous media appearances have been made by members on behalf of CHSSC in explaining or presenting Chinese American history.

Perhaps a most important area of promotion or advocacy of history for Societies is working with government and government institutions. This conference is a fine example of that cooperation, between two State academic institutions and a Society. Still, the best example for CHSSC is the close-knit partnership with UCLA's Asian American Studies Center, which spawned the Southern California Chinese American Oral History Project, 161 interviews, and a set of summary volumes for the Research Library. I know several Societies were formed to improve the educational materials in local schools. The CHSSC's most head-on encounters with government have been to lobby for the oldest remaining Chinese American structure in the County, an altar and shrine, to be an historic monument, and to argue, successfully, for a City Museum on Chinese American history. One side benefit from all this visibility was an exhibit on Chinese American history and archives in Los Angeles' historic City Hall rotunda during the City's birthday two years ago. And let us not forget that government can still be a helpful funding resource.

Motivating Factors. Now, let's look ahead. I am not a seer, but understanding how a Society relates to its community might provide some clues about its future. There are two basic ideas to summarize. An organization which serves no useful need of the community will and probably should diminish and maybe die. An organization is created and thrives because a sufficient number of people and resources support the interests and activities serving those perceived needs. Remember Him Mark Lai's core group. A group needs to exceed thresholds in numbers and energy (20). One needs to understand the motivating factors for formation and continued existence. Again, we can rely on the observations of Lai (11–29) and Ng (177–210).

Lai sees several causes for the early formation of Societies. They include the pure interest of scholarship and a rising sense of community and ethnic solidarity, as in the example of Hawaiian

Chinese of several native-born generations seeking an equal share in society (14). Lai views that the post-World War II movement toward the formation of Societies is driven by the same rise of a better-educated Chinese American professional and business middle class questing for an equal place in all aspects of American society.

Ng expands on the causes. The increased confidence and interests of Chinese Americans. The increased opportunities and fairness in a "host" country. A China closing its door and a vastly increased permitted immigration. All led to Chinese in America (and Canada) focusing on establishing life here (177). Ng also perceives that the advent of new social science theories and research methods stimulated much community-level work, and thus laymen became exposed to the efforts of scholars "The popular areas of investigation were the demographic profile, occupational characteristics, social mobility, organizational structure, leadership pattern, adaptation strategies, and the assimilation process" (180–81).

Both note that the rise of the civil rights movement and other upheavals of the 60s and 70s led to an intense rise of ethnic consciousness. Again, a quote from Ng: "this development kindled the interest of the Chinese in studying their own history in this country" (181). As we move to a younger generation, the quest for identity, the meaning of being a "Chinese American" or "American Chinese," often becomes more puzzling, and strong interest in Chinese American history is pursued.

Ng perceived one more development from these turbulent times: the radical viewpoint of student activists and scholars, that the Chinese of America were an exploited ethnic minority by the dominating white society. Ethnic history had to be actively discovered to define the group's rightful position in American history. A quote from Ng: "Within Chinese American history, history was seen more in terms of class relations and conflicts, and there was a strong antipathy towards traditional associations and elite establishment" (181). Needless to say, there would be some lively debates with and within the more conservative Societies. Yet as a whole, Chinese Historical Societies are viewed as the more liberal and open-minded of organizations inside a Chinatown.

Taking this sense of agenda one step further, one can consider history as a pragmatic tool for social or community improvement. Certainly, a motivation for the forming of CHSSC was the need for the proper definition of a local Chinese American history which would validate access to government services for a growing immigrant population in Chinatown. Another need was appropriate historical educational materials for teaching their young. My observations at the recent officers' installation of the Southern California Chinese American Lawyer's Association were instructive. Two keynote speakers extolled the importance of knowing the ethnic history well because it helped to develop precedence for arguments in law and because it gave perspectives for setting current social or political agendas. Following the L.A. riots, community leaders have formed the action group, Asian Pacific Americans for a New L.A., which has drawn a new generation of young activists. A portion of their draft vision statement reads, "We want a city where culture and history of each of L.A.'s diverse communities are truly understood and celebrated." History as a tool is coupled with a quite perceptible move away from ethnocentrism toward multiculturalism. I think Societies in each region can define or discover some social requirements that need the use of history.

What is a Chinese Historical Society's role here?

It would be difficult as a community organization to remain completely aloof from such pressures to meet social needs. However, to become totally activist would be incompatible to each Society's dedication to educational aims and probably uncomfortable to many members. What is probably emerging is a strong push toward local coalitions and joint efforts with other local community groups, in which a Society may choose its level of participation. Any participation at all is a novel step for a normal historical society to take, but such actions may be consistent with a group dedicated to ethnic history. What is also true is that history cannot be viewed in a vacuum, isolated from social forces and influences.

The Membership Challenge: Changing Demographics. Ng reminds us of trends regarding Chinese American demographics. The absolute number of persons with Chinese ancestry is rising, and the makeup of their backgrounds is changing. Namely, the dominance of the old-time American-Born Chinese (ABC) is rapidly diminishing from a high of 61% of Chinese Americans to half of that percentage due to the great new immigration since 1965 (Ng 185).

I need not remind you that most of the Societies formed in the 70s era were populated mainly by the American-Borns. The new Chinese immigrants, or their offspring, are being drawn in, but very slowly. For the Societies to continue as viable groups in the future, the membership of the New Chinese Americans must be encouraged. This means the group interests and activities, and the emphases on particular aspects of Chinese American history, are likely to shift with time.

Much of the work of Societies hitherto has had a pre-World War II tilt toward the achieving-pioneer suffering discrimination. For the future, one might foresee an increasing preoccupation with more recent time frames in study, an emphasis on history-in-the-making or "present history," and stories of the modern immigration. As the community grows in numbers and becomes complex, and as the professionals gain new theories and methods, there will be greater desires for interdisciplinary studies involving other humanities and social sciences.

Modern technology and communications have essentially removed most barriers to social mobility. The New Chinese will harbor super-regional or national viewpoints, and will expect examinations of interrelations and comparisons with other regions of the Pacific Rim. The paper by Wing Chung Ng this morning exemplifies what may become a typical scope of study someday (8/30/92).

So What Is the Role of a Chinese Historical Society? As long as there is a clearly defined Chinese American community and a clearly defined Chinese American identity, I believe there will be Chinese (American) Historical Societies. Continued involvement of academicians is important in maintaining the viability and influence of a Society in the field. That relationship will exist if, in turn, community support of ethnic studies is essential in maintaining these subjects in the schools. The roles of Societies must change, though, as their communities change. The successful Society will recognize these changes as they evolve. For the present, it seems beneficial and productive if a Society:

1. Preserves its unique attributes, e.g.:
    a. diversity of membership as a bridge between Chinese and at-large (white) communities.
    b. common ground for academicians and laymen.
    c. center for intellectual and educational endeavors.
    d. bridge between American-Born (ABC's) and the New Chinese Americans.
2. Develops institution or museum (but don't let it destroy your program).
3. Publishes, but seeks new types of products.
4. Becomes more proactive and visible in promoting Chinese American history and multi-ethnic understanding.
5. Anticipates expansion in the scope of historical interests
    a. in geography.
    b. in time frame.
    c. in subject matter.
    d. in the disciplines applied.
6. Demonstrates community leadership and participates in coalitions, collaborations, networks, and joint ventures, with community or academia, within the Chinese American community and beyond.

As you can see, there are a lot of things Chinese Historical Societies and like organizations can do now and in the future. I have put a lot of things on the table from which to choose. I have also suggested that we be aware of the changes in the community, and we move to be a constructive part of them. Good luck.

We thank Suellen Cheng for providing useful comments and referrals for this work.

Works Cited

Lai, Him Mark. "Chinese American History: Achievements, Problems, Prospects." Presented at Origins and Destinations: A Conference on Chinese Americans, Los Angeles, 30 August 1992.

Lai, Him Mark. "Chinese American Studies: A Historical Survey." In *Chinese America: History and Perspectives, 1988.* San Francisco: Chinese Historical Society of America, 1988.

Ng, Wing Chung. "A Comparative Discussion of Chinese Societies in San Francisco and Vancouver, B.C., 1946–1980." Presented at Origins and Destinations: A Conference on Chinese Americans, Los Angeles, 30 August 92.

Ng, Wing Chung. "Scholarship on Post-World War II Chinese Societies in North America: A Thematic Discussion." In *Chinese America: History and Perspectives, 1992.* San Francisco: Chinese Historical Society of America, 1992.

Chinese Seeking Justice in the Courts of the United States:
A Constitutional Interpretation

STANFORD M. LYMAN
College of Social Science, Florida Atlantic University, Boca Raton, Florida

On May 25, 1992, an editorial in a prominent Canadian newspaper proposed that the parliament of that country see fit to "make amends for... [the] racist actions of the state... [by voting a] formal apology and [granting a] financial compensation to the families of those [Chinese] who [had] paid the [head] tax," which was first enacted in 1885. That head tax had provided $23 million in revenue during its 38 years of operation (*The Toronto Star* 5/25/92). The editorial writer went on to observe that Canada's less than just treatment of its Chinese immigrants had included not only the onerous head tax, but also unwarranted wage discrimination, wholesale exclusion from 1923 to 1946, and denial of citizenship rights and the franchise until 1947.[1] In the building of the Canadian National Railway, their pay had been set at half of that given to white railroad laborers.

In the United States, no such proposal for redress has been put forward, either for its Chinese immigrants or for their descendants, though its record of ethnoracial prejudice and discrimination against this people is at least the equal of Canada's, and, despite advances in civil rights in recent years, bids fair to continue in various forms into

---

[1]The history of the "Chinese question" in Canada is, necessarily, beyond the scope of the present paper. Interested parties should consult the following works and documents: Report of the Royal Commission on Chinese Immigration 1885; Report of the Royal Commission on Chinese and Japanese Immigration 1902; Lower 3–16, 61–89; Angus 94–122; MacInnes 1927; Andracki 1978; Glyn-Ward 1921; Wickberg 1982; Chan 1983; Li 1988; Roy 1984, 13–34; 1989. For recent studies of Canada's Chinatowns, see Sedgwick 1973; Morton 1974; Yee 1988; Lai 1988. For interesting literary efforts, see Lee and Wong-chu 1991.

the future.[2] In this respect, it is worthy to note that in February 1992, the United States Commission on Civil Rights, in a report on "Civil Rights Issues Facing Asian Americans in the 1990s," in addition to recalling the long history of America's anti-Chinese and anti-Asian legislation, took care to point out the continuing effects of ethnoracial prejudice on the life-chances of these peoples, among many of which was one that echoed their earlier marginalization in both Canada's and the United States' labor forces, and suggested its persistence in the latter country: "The Commission has received allegations that Asian Americans are virtually shut out of construction unions in New York City and as a result are forced to take lower paying jobs restoring or repairing buildings" (Chun and Zalokar 200).

The construction of a marginalizing ethnoracial identity for America's Chinese is the topic to be investigated in the present paper. Throughout my discussion, I use the term "ethnoracial" in keeping with the issue as defined by Floya Anthias, viz., "...that race can only be considered as an analytically valid category if it is incorporated within the more inclusive, albeit highly heterogeneous, category of ethnos. The hallmark of this set of phenomena is inclusion and exclusion, difference and identity; the construction of entities, on the one hand, by way of some notion of a historical point of origin or essence and, on the other, the construction of a collective difference from an 'other'" (Anthias 21).

In this paper, it shall be argued that the agency in America that took as its charge the construction of the Chinese as an ethnoracial entity was the higher judiciary. Proceeding on the necessity of having to declare who belonged to the ethnoracial groups designated by the law as eligible for inclusion in the citizenry of the United States, the courts were led to classify individuals according to the ethnoracial groups to which they "belonged," and then to locate that categorization within or outside of the limited legislative classes of eligibles for naturalization in the United States. The categories of eligibility and ineligibility for naturalization, in turn, established the basis for a subsequent legislation of inclusion and exclusion with respect to property rights, the franchise, occupational opportunity, and primary and secondary human associations. The Chinese were the first people declared to be "aliens ineligible to citizenship in the United States." They were so designated as a resolution of the premier issue affecting the opening phase of post-Civil War America's judicial and civic discourse on the relationship of race and ethnicity to naturalization, a discourse that would subsequently stigmatize all

---

[2]For the Chinese situation in the labor market in the period in which union organization was beginning, see Hill 43–54; 31–82, esp. 37–45, and 132–200, esp. 172–183. See also Saxton 1971 and 1990, 215–218, 292–311; and Miller 145–204.

those who could be categorized in the same way. That discourse is unilaterally hegemonic in character and, in general, works to grant privilege to white males over all other kinds of human individuals or aggregates.

In an illuminating discussion of Asian American literature, Elaine H. Kim observes:

> Familiar representations of Asians always unalterably alien—as helpless heathens, comical servants, loyal allies, and, only in the case of women, exotic sex objects imbued with an innate understanding of how to please, serve, and titillate, extend directly to Asian Americans and exist in all cases to define as their dialectical opposite the Anglo man as heroic, courageous, and physically superior, whether as soldier, missionary, master, or lover. (148)

Although Kim and others[3] have pointed out that racist and culturally demeaning images of Asians are to be found in the works of such formerly popular Anglo authors as Bret Harte (1836–1902),[4] Jack London (1876–1916),[5] Earl Derr Biggers (1884–1933), who foisted "Charlie Chan" on America,[6] and Arthur Henry Sarsfield Ward (1883–1959), who, under the *nom de plume* Sax Rohmer, gave the occident its arch-enemy, "Dr. Fu Manchu",[7] as well as in the writings of earlier, now-forgotten writers (see Dooner 1880), the civic stigmatization of Chinese and, later, other Asian and Pacific Island peoples, was juridically established by and legitimated in the judicial casuistries of the courts of the United States.

That appellate judges and supreme court justices are mindful of the twin facts that, in their rulings, they are constructing, as well as construing, a civic discourse and in the process giving legitimating voice to the basic definition of the socio-corporeal entity that is before

---

[3]Ibid. 149. See also Kim 1982, 3–22 and Fenn 1–44, 73–131; Gardner 1–91, 148–199; and Chu 305–448.

[4]Frances Bret Harte. "Plain Language From Truthful James." Table Mountain, 1870. Reprinted in Fenn, op. cit. ix–x, with a discussion on 45–72. See also Bret Harte's *California: Letters to the Springfield Republican and Christian Register, 1866–67*, ed. by Gary Scharnhorst, Albuquerque: University of New Mexico Press, 1990. 27, 31, 113–115, 138, 154.

[5]See Clarice Stasz. *American Dreamers: Charmian and Jack London*. New York: St. Martin's Press, 1988. 53, 61–62, 73–74, 83–86, 129–131, 156–159, 206, 281.

[6]See Earl Derr Biggers. *Charlie Chan: Five Complete Novels*. New York: Avenel Books, 1981.

[7]See Cay Van Ash and Elizabeth Sax Rohmer. *Master of Villainy: A Biography of Sax Rohmer*. London: Tom Stacey Ltd., 1972.

them is doubtful. As long ago as 1913, Roscoe Pound, the father of sociological jurisprudence, pointed out that:

> ...the judge is hampered at every turn by the theory that he can only discover, that the principles of the unwritten law are invariable, and that application of a rule which has at least a potential logical pre-existence in the received system is his sole function. (775)

In treating with the laws governing eligibility for United States citizenship from 1870 to 1952, however, the courts discovered, occasionally to their openly stated consternation, that the principles underpinning the written law were ambiguous and that the application of a rule of that law evoked the possibility that it had no logical pre-existence, even no rational basis whatsoever. Nevertheless, their interpretations of the law—for they could not evade their responsibility to interpret the law and rule on its relation to the statutory code or to the Constitution of the United States—lent the imprimatur of "The Law" to an exclusionary division of humankind, privileging certain ethnoracial peoples, disparaging and disempowering others. Once having been excluded from citizenship, the hapless aliens could be made to bear additional burdens—all of the latter being justified by the rhetoric that defined and disenfranchised them in the first place.

The label "alien ineligible to citizenship in the United States" could be—and, in fact, was—employed to strip away economic, educational, social, and personal opportunities from those upon whose ethnoracial escutcheon it could be pinned. The significance of the Chinese in the social history of America's attempt to establish itself as a white republic is that—together with the Native Amerindians, who in 1831 were made into non-citizen, domestic, dependent nations;[8] the African-American slaves, who were deemed unworthy of citizenship altogether before their emancipation;[9] and the free men and women of color of the ante-bellum era, whose official civic status remained at best anomalous until the Thirteenth, Fourteenth, and Fifteenth Amendments to the Constitution had been adopted;[10]—they became the collective human situs on which post-Emancipation citizenship in the United States would be worked out (Lyman 149–159) The result was a multifaceted marginalization of this people, and, subsequently, of all others similarly labeled.

---

[8]*Cherokee Nation v. Georgia*, 30 U.S. (5 Pet.) 1 (1831); *Worcester v. Georgia*, 31 U.S. (6 Pet.) 515 (1832).

[9]*Dred Scott v. Sandford*, 19 Howard 393 (1857).

[10]See Franklin 58–120; Zilversmit 1967, passim; Smith 1967, passim; V. Jacque Voegeli 2, 17–18, 26–27, 77, 84–89, 166, 171; Curry 88, 216; Pole 148–176.

The concept and process of marginalization have been the topic of a recent critique by Janice E. Perlman (91–194, 242–263). According to her, the term has been applied virtually exclusively to the psychological state, as well as the sociocultural status of the urban poor, who have been unfairly and unwarrantedly stigmatized thereby. She goes on to offer a three-fold complaint: that the concept is embedded in an unanalyzed ideological context; that it is employed all too uncritically by social scientists who bring to bear on their studies of it as a phenomenon diverse methodologies and divergent and even contradictory theoretical perspectives; and that it owes its origins and persistence to the seminal, double-sided—and often misread—psycho-sociological formulations of Robert E. Park (881–893) and Everett Stonequist (see 1937; 1964, 327–345). It is not necessary for the present work that I answer each of Perlman's objections; for I am using the term in a special and limited sense that draws not only on the *sociological* aspects of the Park-Stonequist perspective, but combines that orientation with both the hierarchical-hegemonic corollary introduced by Dickie-Clark (1966) and the phenomenological (Gurwitsch 1985) and post-modernist (Ferguson, Gever, Trinh, and West 1991) outlooks that have revivified the concept and enhanced its usage for social critique.

Citizenship and Marginalization. From the moment of their first arrival in the United States, the Chinese have experienced and been subjected to an ambiguous welcome. Their merchant leaders were— for a brief moment—regarded as astute businessmen who might someday vote and serve in the legislature alongside other new immigrant entrepreneurs;[11] however, their laboring classes were spurned by virtually all parties in the debate over the "Chinese question." Exploited for their labor power by capitalist developers and refused entrance into the burgeoning workingmen associations that had begun to spring up among the Irish and other European newcomers, the Chinese workers were defended for a time by a few Protestant missionaries in search of new fields for soul-harvesting (see Speer 462–530, 554–681; Gibson 1877; Condit 1900) and, more altruistically, by a small coterie of civic-conscious attorneys seeking to advance the progress of American democracy. Even before the issue of their citizenship arose, immigrants from China had been made the objects of what would become nearly four decades of state laws seeking to restrict or halt altogether their entrance to America. These statutes were opposed in the courts and struck down, one by one, as state intrusions on the federal government's sole jurisdiction over

---

[11]See the editorial in *Daily Alta Californian*, May 12, 1851. The relevant portion of that editorial will be found in Lyman 1986: 235.

immigration.[12] In 1882, Congress enacted a law that forbade the coming of Chinese laborers for ten years. That law, despite care taken not to abuse their rights by certain federal court judges in California and the Northwest (Wunder 191–211; Mooney 561–637; Fritz 347–372; Przybyszewski 25–56), laid the basis for subsequent statutes establishing permanent exclusion, and its penumbra shadowed the establishment of a quota system in 1943 (see Chan 1991) and a "needs" and family reunification modification in 1965 (see Tsai 56–123, 151–166; Lai et. at. 46–55, 70–75, 79–83; Kwong 3–4, 21–29, 60, 77).

What proved most effective for marginalizing the Chinese in America were statutes and judicial rulings that excluded them from participation in the body politic. It is true, of course, that, as Jonathan D. Spence has recently observed: "The restrictive immigration laws levied against the Chinese—and at no other foreign nationals at the time—form a melancholy theme in late-nineteenth-century American history" (86). Even more tragic, however, was their formal exclusion from the benefits, rights, and opportunities of U.S. civil society that, at least in the casuistry of law and the rhetoric of public policy, were then accorded to all other newcomer Americans and, in theory but not practice, to the recently emancipated African Americans. For, if it is valid to hold, as Constitutional scholar Robert A. Goldwin asserts, that:

> The Constitution of the United States is unusual, and perhaps unique among the constitutions of the world, ... [in] that rights are inherent in individuals, not in the groups they belong to; that we are all equal as human beings in the sense that no matter what our color, sex, national origin, or religion, we are equal in the possession of the rights that governments are instituted to protect... (20)

Then it is necessary to point out that the Chinese were a people singled out by both the Federal and various state legislatures and municipal councils, as well as the judiciary, for exclusion from this individuating process. In the attempt to construct a new social order in the 35-year era after the Civil War had ended black slavery in America, when the need for settlers and workers had brought peoples from the farther reaches of the Eurasian continent to America, and while the aboriginal peoples were being conquered and sequestered on unpopulated waste-lands, neither Congress nor the courts seemed

---

[12]See, e.g., *People v. Downer et al.*, 7 Cal. 170 (1857); *Lin Sing v. Washburn*, 20 Cal. 534 (1862); *State of California v. The Steamship "Constitution" et al.*, 42 Cal. 578 (1872); *Inre Ah Fong*, 3 Sawy. 144 (1874); *Chy Lung v. Freeman*, 92 U.S. 275 (1875); *Chae Chan Ping v. U.S.*, 130 U.S. 581 (1889); *Ex Parte Ah Cue*, 101 Cal. 197 (1894).

ready to accept the full implication, the radical meaning, of President Lincoln's Gettysburg Address—viz., that the war had been midwife to a rebirth of an America dedicated to the principles of equality that had been laid down in the Declaration of Independence (Wills 90–147). The search for order in that era, as Robert H. Wiebe has shown, led to a reconstructed hierarchicalization of the peoples in and coming to America, and to a limitation on their civil rights—both justified by an emergent ideology "compound[ed] of biology, pseudo-science, and hyperactive imagination" (156). That hierarchy not only assured that those "alternately called Anglo-Saxon or Teutonic or Nordic always rested at the top" of its scale of deservedly privileged peoples, but also designated "all people of yellow, brown, or black skin as innately inferior" (ibid.). Seven years before the outbreak of the war to preserve the Union, the California Supreme Court had begun the degradation of the Chinese immigrants in that State by denying to them a basic right and protection of that civil association—the chance to testify in a judicial proceeding involving whites.

The First Phase: Exclusion of Chinese Testimony—*People v. Hall* (1854). It is altogether appropriate in 1992, as Americans, Spaniards, and Italians observe the quincentenary of Columbus' voyages to the Americas, that scholars and supporters of civil rights take notice of how, in 1854, the California Supreme Court invalidated the testimony of Chinese witnesses in judicial proceedings, by invoking, *inter alia*, the Genoese "discoverer's" intentions and conflating the ethnoracial physiognomy and cultural heritage of California's aborigines with those of the Aleuts, "Esquimaux," and the immigrants from the Empire of China.[13] The matter before the court concerned a homicide allegedly committed by "a free white citizen of this State" in the city of San Francisco. The only eyewitnesses to the killing were immigrant Chinese whose testimony provided the jury with information leading to the accused's conviction of a capital crime. Lawyers for the convicted man appealed the trial procedure, the verdict, and the sentence; they charged that the Chinese witnesses' testimony should have been excluded on the grounds that, State law having already provided that "No Black or Mulatto person, or Indian, shall be allowed to give evidence in favor of, or against a white man," the prohibition should have been understood to extend to Chinese since the latter are either descendants of the racial stock that in prehistoric times had provided California with its aborigines, or, alternatively, are to be understood as the judicial equivalent of blacks, i.e., a portion of that congeries of persons held to be non-white.

---

[13]The following draws on *People v. Hall*, 4 Cal. 399 (October 1854). Unless otherwise noted, all quotations are from this report.

Chief Justice Murray of the California Supreme Court agreed with the petitioner. In its decision, the Court put forth a tentative and much qualified juridical casuistry that combined a homage to Columbus with a conjectural history, and added to these a pseudo-scientific ethnology of Sino-Amerindian relations. It also designated the Chinese as judicially functional "Blacks," thus insuring their inadmissibility to the civic community. At the outset, the Court took notice of the fact that:

> When Columbus first landed upon the shores of this continent, in his attempt to discover a western passage to the Indies, he imagined that he had accomplished the object of his expedition... Acting upon this hypothesis, and also perhaps from the similarity of features and physical conformation, he gave to the [San Salvadorean] Islanders the name of Indians, which appellation was universally adopted and extended to the aboriginals of the New World, as well as of Asia.

Next, the Court observed that the understanding of California's law would in part be based on the recognition that it had been adapted from those of other States admitted to the Union much before California's accession in 1850. The adumbrating statutes had been enacted, so Chief Justice Murray claimed when "Ethnology ... was unknown as a distinct science, or, if known, had not reached that high point of perfection which it has since attained by the scientific inquiries and discoveries of the master minds of the last half-century." Murray announced the Court's willingness to accept the classificatory schema that had been developed by Baron Georges Leopold Chretien Frederic Dagobert Cuvier (1769–1832), "one of the most eminent naturalists of modern times," to the effect "that there were but three distinct types of the human species, which in their turn, were subdivided into varieties of tribes." Cuvier had not only presented the tripartite division of humankind as "Caucasian," "Mongolian," and "Ethiopian," but also had arrayed them in a descending order of physique and culture: Caucasians at the apex, the Mongolians less advanced, and the Ethiopians at the bottom (Banton 29–30).

It fell to Chief Justice Murray to commit the analytical error of confusing race as lineage with race as type (ibid. 28–64). For the aim of the first section of his judicial opinion was to place the Chinese within the category "Indian," making the latter term "generic," i.e., broad enough to embrace both the immigrants from Asia and the aborigines of America under the same classificatory heading, and to deny to both "Indians" and "Chinese" the right to testify in court proceedings involving whites. To accomplish these goals, he proposed that a probable assent should be given to the "ingenious speculations" about the human settling of Pre-Columbian America. "It has been supposed," he pointed out, "and not without plausibility, that this continent was first peopled by Asiatics, who crossed Behring's Straits, and from thence found their way down to the more fruitful climates of Mexico and South America." To lend even more plausibility to this hypothesis, Murray called attention to the geographical situation of the Aleutian Islands, that, he said, "From the eastern portions of Kamtschatka ... form a long and continuous group, extending eastward to that portion of the North American Continent inhabited by the Esquimaux." Murray now could assert that the existence of an island chain connecting Eastern Asia to Western North America made it at least possible for peoples from the former area to have crossed over to the land mass of the latter. But, he had already designated at least four distinct "tribes" along that route: Asiatics, Aleuts, Esquimaux, and California's aborigines. Were they related? If so, how?

Murray's tendentious ethnocultural conjectures gave him answers that were helpful but not judicially sufficient. First, he noted that the Aleutian Islands "are inhabited by a race who resemble, in a remarkable degree, in language and appearance, both the inhabitants of Kamtschatka (who are admitted to be of the Mongolian type), and the Esquimaux, who again, in turn, resemble other tribes of American Indians." These resemblances form the basis for his imputation of greater credibility to the proponents of the Behring Straits hypothesis.

> The similarity of the skull and pelvis, and the general configuration of the two races; the remarkable resemblance in eyes, beard, hair, and other peculiarities, together with the contiguity of the two continents, might well have led to the belief that this country was first peopled by Asiatics, and that the differences between the different tribes and the parent stock was such as would necessarily arise from the circumstances of climate, pursuits, and other physical causes...

However, such probabilistic reasoning, valuable as it was for promoting his thesis, did not satisfy Justice Murray's more exacting judicial mind. After all, he observed, it was always possible that "the light of modern science" would someday demonstrate that the Americas had not been "peopled by the inhabitants of Asia,"[14] or "that the Aborigines are a distinct type, and as such claim a distinct

---

[14]Indeed, 46 years later, the curator of the Brooklyn Museum put forward the heterodoxical thesis that aboriginal America—more specifically, the Paleolithic ancestors of the Zuni Indians—had been carriers of their civilization to Asia. See Lyman 1990, op. cit. 46–75.

origin."[15] If Chinese were to be placed under the legal rubric of "Indian," a sounder argument would have to be presented.

Murray approached the question anew, armed with his knowledge of juridical hermeneutics and legal semiotics. "...[T]he words of the Act," he announced, "must be construed in *pari materia*." That is, the prohibitory statute under investigation would have to be read as a whole, giving equal weight and dignity to such other terms of racial reference in it as "White" and "Negro." The latter terms were indisputably to be regarded as "generic," Justice Murray observed, lest "the most anomalous consequences ... ensue." In the event that the readers of this decision would not intuitively grasp precisely what those anomalous consequences were, the Chief Justice offered up a parade of horribles:

> The European white man who comes here would not be shielded from the testimony of the degraded and demoralized caste, while the Negro, fresh from the coast of Africa, or the Indian of Patagonia, the Kanaka, South Sea Islander, or New Hollander, would be admitted, upon their arrival, to testify against white citizens in our courts of law.

A generic designation for the terms "White" and "Negro" would go far toward accomplishing the "evident intention of the Act," Murray argued; for its purpose "was to throw around the [white] citizen a protection for life and property," a situation that "could only be secured by removing him above the corrupting influences of degraded castes." Moreover, generic designation was further indicated by the testimony statute's usage of the term "black" rather than "Negro;" for, as Chief Justice Murray took care to point out, "The word 'black' may include all Negroes, but the term 'Negro' does not include all black persons." Then, having laid the interpretive groundwork, the Chief Justice enlarged on his thesis, expanding its scope so as to embrace the exclusion of the testimony of Chinese, as well as that of Indians and Africans, in all proceedings involving whites. He ruled:

> The legislature, if any intention can be ascribed to it, adopted the most comprehensive terms to embrace every known class or shade of color, as the apparent design was to protect the white person from the influence of all testimony other than that of persons of the same caste.

---

[15]For the most recent anthropological account of the people whom Columbus encountered in the Caribbean, see Irving Rouse 1992. For a fine analysis of Eurocentric imagery of the Americas in Columbus's day, see Greenblatt 1991.

Aware of the vulnerability of ethnological theories, Chief Justice Murray had found an additional and more secure way to deny Chinese any opportunity to give evidence in a court proceeding where whites were parties to the action. Not only did he rule that the generic term "black" was to be understood as inclusive of all persons not white, regardless of color, but he also held that the "word 'white' has a distinct significance, which ... excludes black, yellow, and all other colors." Thus, he had forestalled any judicial consequences that might arise should his speculations about the ethnohistorical and physical-anthropological origins of America's aborigines be invalidated by future scientific investigations. "[E]ven admitting the Indian of this continent is not of the Mongolian type," he concluded on this issue, "...the words 'black person' ... must be taken as contradistinguished from white, and necessarily excludes [sic] all races other than the Caucasian."

In *People v. Hall*, black and white had been rendered mutually exclusive judicial categories, with the former term enlarged to embrace Chinese, Indians, and all other non-whites, while the latter term had been constricted to embrace only Caucasians. Chief Justice Murray indicated his antipathy toward the immigrant Chinese in his extraordinarily heated closing remarks, pouring forth an indictment of their culture, social organization, personality, and style of life, and virtually inviting their further persecution:

The anomalous spectacle of a distinct people, living in our community, recognizing no laws of this State, except through necessity, bringing with them their prejudices and national feuds, in which they indulge in open violation of law; whose mendacity is proverbial; a race of people whom nature has marked as inferior, and who are incapable of progress or intellectual development beyond a certain point, as their history has shown; differing in language, opinions, color, and physical conformation; between whom and ourselves nature has placed an impassable difference, is now presented, and for them is claimed, not only the right to swear away the life of a citizen, but the further privilege of participating with us in administering the affairs of our government.

In declaring Chinese ineligible to participate in any meaningful way in the judicial system of the State, Chief Justice Murray knowingly and intentionally drove the first nail in the coffin of their exclusion from America's civil society. As he stated, it was in the interests of "public policy"; for the "same rule which would admit them to testify, would admit them to all the equal rights of citizenship, and we might soon see them at the polls, in the jury box, upon the bench, and in our legislative halls." For the next two decades, other courts upheld his ruling, which remained in force until 1873, when the adoption of a superseding code of civil procedures for the State of California revoked its authority.[16]

Denial of Citizenship: The Race-Naturalization Question After Emancipation. Classification of Chinese and all other non-whites as blacks did in fact deny them the rights, duties, and privileges associated with United States citizenship before the adoption of the Thirteenth, Fourteenth, and Fifteenth Amendments. In 1857, U.S. Supreme Court Chief Justice Taney's decision in the Dred Scott case, without raising the Chinese issue, had, in effect, given a national imprimatur to the California Supreme Court's dictum about the civic status of blacks in *People v. Hall*.[17] After the Union victory in the Civil War, however, the Constitution was amended to prohibit slavery or involuntary servitude; to require that States not deny the equal protections of the law to all persons; and to assure birthright United States citizenship and the franchise to the former slaves and their American-born descendants. More significantly, in relation to the "Chinese question," the naturalization statute was revised in 1870; however, Senator Charles Sumner's attempt to strike the word "white" from its classificatory terminology of eligibles—admittedly an attempt to assure to Chinese immigrants the same right to seek United States citizenship as was then about to be granted to any dark-skinned newcomers from Africa—failed. Instead, the statute of 1870 added two common descent groups, "aliens of African nativity or persons of African descent," to the class of eligibles that since 1790 had only allowed naturalization to "free white persons" (Janisch op. cit. 180–208).

The Constitutional elevation of aliens of African nativity or persons of African descent to United States citizenship, together with a granting of the former slaves' right to the franchise, to jury service, witness competence, and property rights—although all too often dishonored in practice for the ensuing 80 years (see Waite 219–304)—bid possible fair to undermine the intended effect of Justice Murray's "generic" application of the term "black" to all who were non-white.

---

[16]See *Speer v. See Yup*, 13 Cal. 73 (1859); *People v. Awa*, 27 Cal. 638 (1865), entitling Chinese defendants to introduce Chinese witnesses in their own behalf; *People v. Washington*, 36 Cal. 658 (1869); *People v. Brady*, 40 Cal. 198 (1870); *People v. McGuire*, 40 Cal. 56 (1872); *In re Tiburcio Parrott*, 1 Fed. 481 (1880). For a detailed history of the legislative, judicial, and media campaigns in this matter see Hudson N. Janisch 208–228.

[17]*Dred Scott v. Sandford*, 19 How. 393 (1857). For discussions of this case, see Hopkins 1967; Kutler 1967; Fehrenbacher 1978; Fehrenbacher 1981; Stampp 68–109.

Indeed, in 1869, a mulatto defendant accused of robbing one of California's resident Chinese aliens successfully defended his newly acquired rights under the Civil Rights Act of 1866 and the Thirteenth Amendment to behave exactly as a white defendant was permitted, i.e., to disallow the testimony of the Chinese witnesses to his misdeed.[18] Justice Murray had asserted that while all Negroes were blacks, not all blacks were Negroes. Ergo, he had included Chinese under the rubric black while limiting the applicability of the term white to all persons not held to be black. The Thirteenth, Fourteenth, and Fifteenth Amendments had freed the slaves and elevated them, arguably in some jurists' minds,[19] to a civil equality with whites. But naturalization had been newly granted only to "aliens of African nativity and persons of African descent," not to "Negroes" or to "blacks," (and, of course, it continued in force for "free white persons"). Were Chinese—who had been ethnologically linked to Indians (not taxed and, under the Constitution, ineligible to citizenship), or, alternatively, generically to blacks (as slaves ineligible to citizenship; as non-white alien "persons of African nativity ordescent," ineligible to naturalization before 1870)—"Indians," "blacks," "whites," or of "African nativity or descent?" Or did they belong to some other class of humankind?

The available genealogical, ethnological, and juridical casuistries make any of these possible, but, at the same time, each is problematic. For example, Chinese in America might be descended from the same original stock that had also produced the Amerindians, but unlike the latter, the Chinese had been taxed. (Indeed, their virtually unprotested acquiescence[20] to the foreign miner's tax imposed unsuccessfully on all other non-Americans in California had the effect of providing the new State with its sole source of revenue for several years (Coolidge 29–38, 57, 60, 70, 431). The Chinese might be generically "black," i.e., among those not declared to be "white," but as one federal justice had implied,[21] they and some others might be "white," in that the latter term might be interpreted so as to encompass all those who are not "black." It is even possible, although no court case on the matter arose after the time that this thesis was advanced by some paleontologists, that Chinese are among the wide variety of persons who are of African descent, especially if one accepts one or another of the subsequently announced claims, viz., that all humankind descend from the Paleolithic Australopithecus of Southern Africa (see Diamond

[18]*People v. Washington*, 36 Cal. 658 (1869).
[19]See the dissent in *People v. Washington*, 36 Cal. 658, 672–687.
[20]See, however, *People v. Naglee*, 1 Cal. 232 (1850); *Ex Parte Ah Pong*, 19 Cal. 106 (1861); and *Ah He v. Crippen*, 19 Cal. 491 (1861).
[21]*In re Halladjian et al.* 174 Fed. 834 (1909)

34–37); or from the erstwhile inhabitants of Olduvai Gorge (Leakey
and Lewin 1977; Leakey and Lewin 1978; Leakey 97–184); or, from
"Lucy" or "Lucy's child," two more recent fossil finds from East
Africa (Johanson and Edey 255–376; Johanson and Shreve 211–290; see
also Brown). Still another possibility is that all humans are descended
from an autochthonous "Peking Man" (Jia and Huang 19–20, 30–31,
145, 279–289; Brown 19–20, 30–31, 145, 279–289); or, alternatively, as a
recent hypothesis has it, that "Peking Man" had no surviving
descendants, and that all humankind originated in Africa (see Gould
319–323).

In light of the changed civic status of America's ex-slaves after
1865, it would become necessary for courts to re-visit ethnological
theory more than once as part of their quest for a scientific grounding
for United States citizenship (see McGovney 129–161, 211–244; Gold
462–506; Gordon 237–258).

The issue was first joined in 1878, when a federal district court
chose to adjudicate the ethno-legal dispute over whether "Ah Yup, a
native and citizen of the empire of China, of the Mongolian race, ...
[could] be admitted as a citizen of the United States."[22] From the very
beginning, the court treated as undisputed fact that natives of China
were members of the "Mongolian" race. That race, however, had not
received legislative recognition in either the original or the revised
statutes relating to the naturalization of aliens. Hence, the court took
as its duty the answering of two questions: 1) Is a person of the
Mongolian race a "white person" within the meaning of the revised
naturalization statute of 1870? 2) Do the provisions of that statute
forbid the naturalization of all but white persons and persons of
African nativity or African descent? It is of some significance to note
that Circuit Judge Lorenzo Sawyer did not even think to raise the
possibility that "Mongolians" might be "persons of African nativity or
African descent," or, in keeping with the decision in *People v. Hall*,
to consider the possibility that Chinese might be "black." However,
Judge Sawyer did echo Justice Murray's opinion in ruling that, "As
ordinarily used everywhere in the United States, one would scarcely
fail to understand that the party employing the words 'white person'
would intend a person of the Caucasian race." Like Justice Murray,
Judge Sawyer did not question the etymology, validity, or
epistemological provenance of the term "Caucasian"—a designation
that in fact Johann Friedrich Blumenbach had introduced into the
technical language of anthropology little more than a century earlier
in order that he might be able to distinguish the unique craniology of
the peoples of western and central Europe. Blumenbach had been
struck by the resemblances of a skull found in the Caucasus mountain

---

[22]*In re Ah Yup*, 1 Fed. 223 (1878)

region of Russia to those of the Germans and speculated that that region might have been the original homeland of the Europeans (Gossett 37–38).

Judge Sawyer did take judicial notice of the fact that among three of the most prominent of the original group of European authorities on ethnology there had been no agreement on the precise number of human races making up the varieties of humankind. Blumenbach had listed five, a taxonomy of which Judge Sawyer quoted from Webster's dictionary: "1. The Caucasian, or white race, to which belong the greater part of the European nations and those of Western Asia; 2. The Mongolian, or yellow race, occupying Tartary, China, Japan, etc.; 3. The Ethiopian, or Negro (black) race, occupying all Africa, except the north; 4. The American, or red race, containing the Indians of North and South America; and 5. the Malay, or Brown race, occupying the island of the Indian Archipelago." However, Carolus Linnaeus had designated one less in his epidermal-pigmentary division of humanity ("1. European, whitish; 2. American, coppery; 3. Asiatic, tawny; and 4. African, black"); while the aforementioned Cuvier (Banton 29–30) had named only three: "Caucasian, Mongol, and Negro." Judge Sawyer acknowledged that "Others make many more," but the classificatory schemas of Blumenbach, Linnaeus, and Cuvier served his adjudicative purpose, for as he pointed out, the New American Cyclopedia's entry under "Ethnology" included the assertion that "no one of those classifications recognizing color as one of the distinguishing characteristics includes the Mongolian in the white or whitish race."

However, one issue in *Ah Yup* and *People v. Hall* was whether color was to be used as the index of eligibility for race and, therefore, for the extension of civil rights and citizenship. Moreover, if color were to be so used, how was it to be defined and determined? These questions would confound jurists until 1952, when the color issue was obviated from naturalization law.

In *People v. Hall*, such color terms as "white" and "black" had been used in a non-pigmentary sense—the former term to refer to members of the Caucasian race; the latter to refer to all persons— including Chinese—who were not white. The fact that prominent ethnologists employed what appeared to be terms referring to the hues of complexion to differentiate the varieties of humankind raised doubts about their applicability to a judicial proceeding where a different definition and usage of color terminology might be required. For example, a person with a "yellowish" shade of skin might be "black" because he or she is not white; "red" or "coppery," "American" because he or she is said to descend from a prehistoric common original stock; or "white" because he or she is neither "African" nor "American." Judge Sawyer's determination that Ah Yup was not white depended on how well he could articulate a color dictum that did not depend on a literally pigmentary usage of "white."

Judge Sawyer's approach took advantage of, and in fact derived its basic argument from, Senator Sumner's foiled attempt to have the word "white" struck from the revised naturalization statute. Ah Yup, Judge Sawyer averred, could not claim that "white" was meant to include persons of his race in the first instance because "I am not aware that the term..., as used in the statutes as they have stood from 1802 till the late revision, was ever supposed to include a Mongolian." Moreover, even more significantly, the judge pointed to the Congressional debates over the statute's revision "to show that it was universally understood in that body ... that it excluded Mongolians." After quoting extensively from the remarks of those who favored and those who opposed Sumner's amendment, Judge Sawyer concluded that "Congress retained the word 'white' in the naturalization laws for the sole purpose of excluding the Chinese from the right of naturalization." That inferred and uncriticized purpose—derived by Judge Sawyer from his own reading of the Congressional debates—was in effect deemed to be an acceptable motive for ethnoracially exclusive legislation by a democratically elected legislature.

Civil Rights and Hostile Intent: *Ho Ah Kow v. Nunan.*
Precisely because this judicial proceeding established the precedent of excluding Chinese—as well as others who could be tarred either with the brush of "Mongolian" status or stigmatized with the negation of their claim to be of white or of African nativity or descent (see Lyman 203–232)—it is worth inquiring into one of the issues that the learned judge did not address. Having determined that the legislative intent of the revised naturalization statute was "to exclude the Chinese" ("...as all white aliens and those of the African race are entitled to naturalization under other words, it is difficult to perceive whom it could exclude unless it be the Chinese"), Judge Sawyer did not inquire into whether such a purpose was *ultra vires*.

It has been noted by some legal scholars that naturalization statutes have rarely been subjected to challenges with respect to their constitutionality (Rossum 1300–1301; Karst 258–260).

Ah Yup was decided 10 years after the adoption of the Fourteenth Amendment to the Constitution. That amendment provided all persons, regardless of their citizenship status, with the equal protection of the laws; however, the amendment's wording allowed for its applicability to be limited to State rather than federal legislation (see Meyer 64–67). Had Judge Sawyer seen fit to extend the provisions and prohibitions of the Fourteenth Amendment to the national government—for example, by boldly declaring[23] that such Congressionally enacted civil rights acts as those of 1866, 1870, and 1875 were not only appropriate measures of enforcement of the postwar amendments but also laws that superseded those federal statutes that treated selectively and arbitrarily certain "persons" differently[24]—he might have deemed it appropriate to inquire into the Constitutionality of the naturalization statute's intent.

"To accomplish what *legitimate public* purpose had the naturalization statute been revised?" he might have asked. The asking of such a question is a *sine qua non* of judicial inquiry, especially when issues of arbitrariness, prejudice, and unlawful interest are alleged to be the intendment of a law.[25] That inquiry, in turn, entails a three-fold process: the discovery of the legislative intent; the determination of the extent to which the operation of the law realizes that intent; and the judgment as to whether that intent is within the scope of public law or of the powers granted to the legislative body that enacted it. A judicial ruling in 1879 by United States Supreme Court Justice Stephen J. Field, sitting, together with Judge Sawyer as a justice in the United States Circuit Court for the District of California, nicely illustrates this mode of reasoning, often utilized effectively with respect to State legislation and municipal ordinances, but rarely, if at all, applied to federal naturalization statutes.

The matter before the Circuit Court was a suit for the recovery of damages incurred by an alien Chinese plaintiff through the sheriff's enforcement of a San Francisco ordinance, enacted in June 1876, and requiring that "every male person imprisoned in the county jail ... shall immediately upon his arrival at the jail have the hair of his head 'cut or clipped to an uniform length of one inch from the scalp thereof.'"[26] The ordinance had been passed in response to the plaintiff's and hundreds of his countrymen's refusal to pay a fine for violating the city's nine-year-old and only occasionally and selectively administered ordinance requiring 500 cubic feet of air space for each

---

[23]Judge Sawyer, together with Judge Ogden Hoffman of the United States District Court for the Northern District of California, showed both courage and judicial acumen in extending the full force of the *habeas corpus* principle to individual Chinese immigrants subjected to exclusion from 1882 to 1891. See Fritz. in S. Chan, ed., *Entry Denied*, op. cit. 25–56.

[24]Ironically, in light of the argument being presented here, the long struggle over the so-called "incorporation doctrine" entailed the assertion that the adoption of the Fourteenth Amendment had made the provisions of the first eight amendments applicable to the States. See Baer 98–102. See also the discussion in Nieman 62–70.

[25]The following draws on Tussman and ten Broek 341–381.

[26]The following is from *Ho Ah Kow v. Nunan*, 12 Fed. 252 (Case No. 6,546), 1879.

person found sleeping or lodging in a rented room or apartment. The lodging house law, in fact, had been enforced only in San Francisco's Chinatown, and the Chinese convicted for violating it had refused to pay the fine, in effect staging a sit-in in the jail and making the latter institution potentially liable for violating the very same statute (Sandmeyer 51, 63, 75). The haircutting ordinance, however, threatened the Chinese alien immigrant convict with the severing of his queue, the mandatory badge of subjection to the Manchu Empire, the loss of which could result in execution for a remigrant to Qing China (see Spence 38–39, 48, 51, 213, 256). The plaintiff, Ho Ah Kow, petitioned the court for redress, but the defendant, San Francisco Sheriff Nunan, opposed his claim. Justice Field decided the matter in behalf of the plaintiff.

Relevant here is the manner and method of his decision and the contrast it presents with *Ah Yup* and other naturalization cases. Unlike Judge Sawyer's uncritical acknowledgment of Congress' intent in revising the naturalization statute, Justice Field's interrogation of San Francisco's assertion that its haircutting ordinance was merely one more instance of the city's lawful exercise of its police powers illustrates one method by which institutionalized racism can be uncovered by a detailed reading of the relevant facts and circumstances surrounding a particular legislative enactment. In reply to Sheriff Nunan's argument that the ordinance in question served the general purposes of securing improved sanitation and establishing appropriate discipline at the jail, Field, invoking the language of the Fourteenth Amendment, pointed out that, in fact, the evidence indicated that it "is special legislation on the part of the [Board of] Supervisors against a class of persons who, under the constitution and laws of the United States, are entitled to the equal protection of the laws." Field (1816–1899), who had resided in California for many years and served for six years (1857–1863) as its Supreme Court's Chief Justice,[27] but who was no firm friend of the Chinese immigrant (see Swisher 205–239; McCloskey 72–126), found it juridically impossible to acquiesce before the defendant's claim that San Francisco's Board of Supervisors had acted out of racially neutral and benevolent motives. He observed:

> When we take our seats on the bench, we are not struck with blindness, and forbidden to know as judges what we see as men; and

---

[27]Stephen Johnson Field, *Personal Reminiscences of Early Days in California*. 122–142. A manuscript edition of sketches taken down from Judge Field by a stenographer in San Francisco in 1877, to which other documents, commentaries, and memorabilia have been attached. MS photocopy in possession of the author.

where an ordinance, though general in its terms, only operates upon a special race, sect, or class, it being universally understood that it is to been forced only against that race, sect or class, we may justly conclude that it was the intention of the body adopting it that it should only have such operation, and treat it accordingly.

Field probed even more directly into the aim of San Francisco's law. Exploring the city council's debate over the adoption of the ordinance, he was able to show that the supervisors openly avowed the selective character of their proposed piece of legislation; to observe that "the ordinance is known in the community as the 'Queue Ordinance'"; and to conclude with certainty that "it is not enforced against any other persons [but the Chinese]." As to the Board of Supervisors' claim that the reserved police powers gave it the right to regulate sanitary conditions at the county jail, Justice Field made two objections: The first—necessarily outside the sociological scope of the present paper—was that "the Board of Supervisors had no authority to ... determine what special sanitary regulations should be enforced ... [for that] is a matter which the [State] legislature had ... seen fit to intrust ... to the Board of Health of the city and county..." The second, applying to each of the city's claims, viz., that its haircutting ordinance was both a sanitary regulation and a disciplinary measure, illustrates a method appropriate to effecting a sociological jurisprudence of minorities in the United States: how the classification made by a law may be examined to determine what relation, if any, it has to the officially proffered legislative intent and, if found to be unreasonably so related, the finding utilized to suggest a hidden and suspect purpose—in this instance, a purpose that violated two amendments to the United States Constitution.

Justice Field's employment of the purpose-classification methodology is exemplary and deserves direct quotation because of its unusual usage here, i.e., in cases involving a legislative body's invocation of a particular aspect of its police powers to justify regulations aimed at an ethnoracial minority:

The cutting off of the hair of every male person within an inch of his scalp, on his arrival at the jail, was not intended and cannot be maintained as a measure of discipline or as a sanitary regulation. The act by itself has no tendency to promote discipline, and can only be a measure of health in exceptional cases. Had the ordinance contemplated a mere sanitary regulation it would have been limited to such cases and made applicable to females as well as to males, and to persons awaiting trial as well as to persons under conviction...

In other words, the classification made by the ordinance was *underinclusive*, i.e., it encompassed too few, with respect to the elimination of, or control over, the unlawful mischief or unsanitary condition which the board of supervisors alleged to be its objective. However, it was also *overinclusive*, i.e., it included too many in its embracement, since, as Justice Field pointed out, "The ordinance was intended only for the Chinese in San Francisco" and only applied to the convicted members of that group who elected a jail sentence in lieu of payment of a fine. Although he did not write out the rest of the logic of his argument, Justice Field's reasoning seems to infer that, in the absence of any evidence to the contrary, it cannot be assumed *a priori*; that Chinese males convicted of violating the lodging house ordinance are the sole wearers of unsanitary coiffures, or that they are the unique carriers of a compulsion to undisciplinary conduct, either of which traits might require a prophylactic haircut to within one inch of the scalp. As Tussman and ten Broek seem to suggest in their seminal essay on the methods appropriate to determining whether an official statute or governmental order meets the requirements of the equal protections provision of the Fourteenth Amendment, the discovery of a classification that is both underinclusive and overinclusive might set off a warning bell to the judge or justice adjudicating the matter and send him or her in quest of a legislative intent that is *ultra vires* (op. cit. Tussman and ten Broek 352–361, 365–368, 373–381). In *Ho Ah Kow v. Nunan*, Justice Field rose to the occasion in no uncertain terms:

> The claim ... put forth that the measure was prescribed as one of health is notoriously a mere pretense. A treatment to which disgrace is attached, and which is not adopted as a means of security against the escape of the prisoner, but merely to aggravate the severity of his confinement, can only be regarded as a punishment additional to that fixed by his sentence.

And what hidden purpose might have moved San Francisco's Board of Supervisors to enact such a law? Justice Field's inquiry into that body's debate over the adoption of the ordinance led him to assert:

> The reason advanced for its adoption ... is, that only the dread loss of his queue will induce a Chinaman to pay his fine. That is to say, in order to enforce the payment of a fine imposed on him, it is necessary that torture should be superadded to imprisonment.

However, there is implicit in this designation of the actual purpose of the ordinance a further set of questions: 1) Is the newly discovered purpose for the statute one that is forbidden to lawmakers? 2) If so, what provision(s) of State law, or, more significantly, of the Constitution does this ordinance violate? 3) Can a regulatory ordinance that is general in its terms and that does not designate a particular class to be the object of its provisions nevertheless be deemed to be of the same type of legislation as that doomed by its open-faced and hostile class character?

Justice Field answered the first and second questions by declaring his assent to Ho Ah Kow's claim that the ordinance in question "is special legislation imposing a degrading and cruel punishment upon a class of persons who are entitled, alike with all other persons within the jurisdiction of the United States, to the equal protection of the laws." That particular ordinance, he went on to observe, had been enacted with no other objective than "to add to the severity of his punishment." It was, he continued, *inter alia*, an act of "wanton cruelty." Field compared queue-cutting, when carried out as a means to punish those who chose a stay in jail over payment of a fine, to the infliction "of the bastinado, or the knout, or the thumbscrew, or the rack, [which, he acidly observed,] would accomplish the same end." Yet, his comparative statement implied that none of these modes of regulation with respect to choosing between a fine or incarceration would be permitted.

In quotation marks, but otherwise uncited with respect to its source, Field invoked the language of the Eighth Amendment to the Constitution, which prohibits "cruel and unusual punishments." However, he rested his argument on the provisions of the Fourteenth Amendment, (making this decision, perhaps, a unique adumbration of the "incorporation" thesis that would be recognized more than seven decades later), and on the inherent repugnance of the statute itself. It was, he wrote, a piece of "legislation which is unworthy of a brave and manly people;" worse, "It is not creditable to the humanity and civilization of our people, much less to their Christianity, that an ordinance of this character was possible."

That queue-cutting by force of law was wanton cruelty did not make such an act *ipso facto* a violation of the Fourteenth Amendment. To bring the statute into conflict with the equal protection clause of that Amendment, Justice Field chose not only to show it to be a form of selective class legislation, but, more importantly, to assert that that amendment prohibits legislation that is both discriminatory and *hostile*. Tussman and ten Broek have took note of the cases in which "Laws are invalidated by the [United States Supreme] Court as discriminatory because they are expressions of hostility or antagonism to certain groups of individuals" (op. cit. 358). Although they do not cite the District Court's ruling in *Ho Ah Kow v. Nunan* as a lower court instance of this basis for a decision, examination of Justice Field's reasoning on this point reveals it to be an early forerunner of it. Having noted the more than unfriendly attitude toward the Chinese that prevailed in California—and, indeed, in a later part of the decision, indicating his own and other "thoughtful" persons' "hope that some way may be devised to prevent their further immigration"—Justice Field pointed out that "in our country hostile and discriminating legislation by a state against persons of any class, sect, creed or nation, in whatever form it may be expressed, is forbidden by the fourteenth amendment of the constitution." And he went on to observe that the protections established by that amendment are "assured to every one whilst within the United States, from whatever country he may have come, or of whatever race or color he may be..." In his discussion of hostile and discriminatory legislation, Field took particular care to point out that the prohibitions on every State's deprivation of any person's life, liberty, or property without due process of law, or denial to any person of the equal protection of the laws "applies to all the instrumentalities and agencies employed in the administration of ... [State] government, to its executive, legislative, and judicial departments, and to the subordinate legislative bodies of counties and cities." Moreover, perhaps recalling the restrictions on Chinese testimony effected in *People v. Hall*, Field ruled that the Fourteenth Amendment had ensured that, regardless of a person's race or color, "the courts of the country shall be open to him on the same terms as to all others for the security of his person or property, ... [and] that no charges or burdens shall be laid upon him which are not equally borne by others, and that in the administration of criminal justice he shall suffer for his offenses no greater or different punishment." Field, later, seemed to imply that, to a Chinese, loss of his queue was a deprivation of his liberty to practice his religion. However the deprivation be interpreted so long as it was of the kind prohibited by the Fourteenth Amendment, Field pointed out the Civil Rights Act of 1870 had established the liability of any one who subjects "any ... person within the jurisdiction [of the United States] ... to the deprivation of any rights, privileges, or immunities secured by the constitution and laws, [to a] suit in equity or other proper proceeding for redress."

The question of the ordinance's hostility to the Chinese was at the heart of the third question; for, on its face, San Francisco's haircutting statute appeared both broadly general and racially neutral. Tussman and ten Broek have called attention to the difficulties entailed in establishing the hostile purpose of a piece of Constitutionally challenged legislation that seems to bear neither a class character nor a written trace of animus toward those to whom it applies—difficulties that, no matter how great, they argue, must be surmounted if a logically and empirically sound adjudication of the matter is to be effected (366–367). Justice Field approached this issue by first claiming that "the class character of this legislation is none the less manifest because of the general terms in which it is expressed," and then went on to assert the Court's obligation "to take notice of the limitation given to the general terms of an ordinance by its practical construction as a fact of its history..." That history included not only an account of the Sinophobic antipathy that went into the making of the statute, but also, what Field emphasized, the fact that "the ordinance acts with special severity upon Chinese prisoners, inflicting upon them suffering altogether disproportionate to what would be endured by other prisoners if enforced against them." Field, having already reported on Ho Ah Kow's averment that "it is the custom of Chinamen to shave the hair from the front of the head and to wear the remainder of it braided into a queue; that the deprivation of the queue is regarded by them as a mark of disgrace, and is attended, according to their religious faith, with misfortune and suffering after death...," as well as having noted the plaintiff's claim that Sheriff Nunan "knew of this custom and religious faith of the Chinese, and knew also that the plaintiff venerated the custom and held the faith," could not but conclude about the law that "Upon the Chinese prisoners its enforcement operates as 'a cruel and unusual punishment.'" As such, both its purpose and its usage indicated unwarranted hostility toward those to whom it applied. Field pointed out that a court's failure to conduct the kind of investigation he had made into the prepossessing origins and selective application of San Francisco's seemingly general and apparently unprejudiced statute would allow "the most important provisions of the constitution, intended for the security of personal rights, ... [to] be evaded and practically annulled." And, lest the hostile disregard of the sacred customs of the Chinese indicated in the enforcement (but not the wording) of the municipal ordinance be regarded lightly, Field illustrated how a very similar law, though general and unprepossessing on its face, could be used against a perhaps better-favored minority group in the United States, some of whose customs also make them stand apart from the majority population. He observed:

> We have, ... in our community a large number of Jews. They are a highly intellectual race, and are generally obedient to the laws of the country. But, as is well known, they have peculiar opinions with respect to the use of certain articles of food, which they cannot be forced to disregard without extreme pain and suffering. They look, for example, upon the eating of pork with loathing. It is an offense against their religion, and is associated in their minds with uncleanness and impurity. Now, if they should in some quarter of the city overcrowd their dwellings and thus become amenable, like the Chinese, to the

act concerning lodging-houses and sleeping apartments, an ordinance of the supervisors requiring that all prisoners confined in the county jail should be fed on pork would be seen by every one to be leveled [sic] at them; and, notwithstanding its general terms, would be regarded as a special law in its purpose and operation.

Conclusion. Justice Field's decision in *Ho Ah Kow v. Nunan*, like the Supreme Court's decision seven years later in *Yick Wo v. Hopkins*,[28] stands out in the otherwise dreary history of Chinese litigants seeking equitable justice in the courts of the United States (see McCurdy 721–725, esp. 724). Although the addition of "person" to the due process and equal protection clauses of the Constitution's Fourteenth Amendment provided the basis for a great many Chinese aliens to seek redress for the violation of their personal and property rights (see Janisch op. cit. 233–1077; Lyman op. cit. 204–206), the denial of citizenship, affirmed in *Ah Yup* and remaining in force until 1943, stood as a bar to their integration into the American political community and civil society. Until 1943, when the right to naturalization was granted to Chinese aliens as part of a gesture to America's Kuomintang ally in the war against Japan, immigrant Chinese were officially marginalized in America's invidious hierarchy of races. They all too often were made to bear the burden of a juridical interpretation that had originated in the joint and separate employment of a conjectural ethnohistory, a dubious and contradictory ethnology, and, with rare and occasional exception, the judiciary's failure to discover and evaluate the real intent of the classificatory schemas that had begun to stigmatize them when they were first designated as generic "Indians" or as equally generic "blacks." Like blacks, Chinese had been tarred with the badge of slavery: namely, race discrimination; unlike blacks, they had not been emancipated in 1865 (see Lyman 63–86).

Works Cited

Andracki, Stanislaw. "The Immigration of Orientals into Canada with Special Reference to Chinese." Ph.D. dissertation, McGill University, 1958. New York: Arno Press, 1978.

Angus, H.F. *Canada and the Far East, 1940–1953.* Toronto: University of Toronto Press, 1953.

Anthias, Floya. "Race and Class Revisited—Conceptualizing Race and Racism." *The Sociological Review.* XXXVIII:1 (1990): 21.

---

[28]*Yick Wo v. Hopkins*, 118 U.S. 356; 1956

Baer, Judith A. *Equality under the Constitution: Reclaiming the Fourteenth Amendment.* Ithaca: Cornell University Press, 1983.

Banton, Michael. *Racial Theories.* Cambridge: Cambridge University Press, 1987.

Brown, Michael H. *The Search for Eve.* New York: Harper and Row, 1990.

Chan, Anthony B. *Gold Mountain: The Chinese in the New World.* Vancouver: New Star Books, 1983.

Chan, Sucheng, ed. *Entry Denied: Exclusion and the Chinese Community in America, 1882–1943.* Philadelphia: Temple University Press, 1991.

Chu, Limin. "The Images of China and the Chinese in the Overland Monthly, 1868–1875, 1883–1935." Ph.D. dissertation, Duke University, 1965. Ann Arbor: University Microfilms, 1970. 305–448.

Chun, Ki-Taek, and Nadja Zalokar et al. "Civil Rights Issues Facing Asian Americans in the 1990s." Report of the United States Commission on Civil Rights, Washington, D.C.: U.S. Government Printing Office, February 1992. 200.

Condit, Rev. Ira W., D.D. *The Chinaman as We See Him—And Fifty Years of Work For Him.* Chicago: Fleming H. Revell Co., 1900 (reprint, New York: Arno Press, 1978).

Coolidge, Mary Roberts. *Chinese Immigration.* New York: Henry Holt, 1909.

Curry, Leonard P. *The Free Black in Urban America, 1800–1850: The Shadow of the Dream.* Chicago: University of Chicago Press, 1981.

Daily Alta Californian 12 May 1851.

Diamond, Jared. *The Third Chimpanzee: The Evolution and Future of the Human Animal* New York: Harper Collins, 1992.

Dickie-Clark, H.F. *The Marginal Situation: A Sociological Study of a Coloured Group.* London: Routledge and Kegan Paul, 1966.

Dooner, P. W. *Last Days of the Republic.* San Francisco: Alta California Publishing House, 1880.

Fehrenbacher, Don E. *Slavery, Law, and Politics: The Dred Scott Case in Historical Perspective.* New York: Oxford University Press, 1981.

Fehrenbacher, Don E. *The Dred Scott Case: Its Significance in American Law and Politics.* New York: Oxford University Press, 1978.

Fenn, William Purviance. *Ah Sin and His Brethren in American Literature.* Peiping [Beijing], China: College of Chinese Studies cooperating with California College in China, 1933.

Ferguson, Russell, Martha Gever, Trinh T. Minh-ha, and Cornel West, eds. *Out There: Marginalization and Contemporary Cultures.* Cambridge: The MIT Press, 1991.

Franklin, John Hope. *The Free Negro in North Carolina, 1790–1860.* New York: W. W. Norton, 1971 [1943].

Fritz, Christian G. "A Nineteenth Century 'Habeas Corpus Mill': The Chinese Before the Federal Courts in California." *American Journal of Legal History* XXXII:4 (October 1988): 347–372.

Fritz, Christian G. "Due Process, Treaty Rights, and Chinese Exclusion, 1882–1891." In *Entry Denied.* Ed. S. Chan, op. cit. 25–56.

Gardner, John Berdan. "The Image of the Chinese in the United States, 1885–1915." Ph.D. dissertation, University of Pennsylvania, 1961. Ann Arbor: University Microfilms, 1970. 1–91, 148–199.

Gibson, Rev. Otis, A.M. *The Chinese in America.* Cincinnati: Hitchcock and Walden, 1877 (reprint, New York: Arno Press, 1978).

Glyn-Ward, Hilda. *The Writing on the Wall: Chinese and Japanese Immigration to B.C., 1920.* Vancouver: Sun Publishing Co., 1921 (reprint, Toronto: University of Toronto Press, 1974).

Gold, George W. "The Racial Prerequisite in the Naturalization Law." *Boston University Law Review* XV (1935): 462–506.

Goldwin, Robert A. *Why Blacks, Women and Jews Are Not Mentioned in the Constitution, and Other Unorthodox Views.* Washington, D.C.: AEI Press, 1990.

Gordon, Charles. "The Racial Barrier to American Citizenship." *University of Pennsylvania Law Review* XCIII:3 (March 1945): 237–258.

Gossett, Thomas F. *Race: The History of an Idea in America.* Dallas: Southern Methodist University Press, 1963.

Gould, Stephen Jay. *Wonderful Life: The Burgess Shale and the Nature of History.* New York: W. W. Norton, 1989.

Greenblatt, Stephen. *Marvelous Possessions: The Wonder of the New World.* Chicago: University of Chicago Press, 1991.

Gurwitsch, Aron. *Marginal Consciousness.* Ed. Lester Embree. Athens: Ohio University Press, 1985.

Hill, Herbert. "Anti-Oriental Agitation and the Rise of Working Class Racism." *Society* X:2 (January/February 1973): 43–54.

Hill, Herbert. "Myth-making as Labor History: Herbert Gutman and the United Mine Workers of America." *International Journal of Politics, Culture, and Society* II:2 (Winter 1988): 132–200.

Hill, Herbert. "Race, Ethnicity and Organized Labor: The Opposition to Affirmative Action." *New Politics* I:2 (Winter 1987): 31–82.

Hopkins, Vincent C., S.J. *Dred Scott's Case.* New York: Atheneum, 1967.

Janisch, Hudson N. "The Chinese, the Courts, and the Constitution: A Study of the Legal Issues Raised by Chinese Immigration to the United States, 1850–1902." J.S.D. dissertation, University of Chicago, March 1971. 208–228.

Jia, Lanpo, and Huang Weiwen. *The Story of Peking Man: From Archaeology to Mystery.* Trans. by Yin Zhiqui. Beijing: Foreign Language Press and Oxford University Press of Hong Kong, 1990.

Johanson, Donald, and James Shreve. *Lucy's Child: The Discovery of a Human Ancestor.* New York: William Morrow, 1989.

Johanson, Donald, and Maitland Edey. *Lucy: The Beginnings of Humankind.* New York: Simon and Schuster, 1981.

Karst, Kenneth L. "Citizenship (Theory)." Vol. I-II of *Encyclopedia of the American Constitution.* New York: Macmillan, 1986. 258–260.

Kim, Elaine H. "Defining Asian American Realities Through Literature." In *The Nature and Context of Minority Discourse*. Ed. Abdul R. Jan Mohamed and David Lloyd. New York: Oxford University Press, 1990. 148.

Kim, Elaine H. *Asian American Literature: An Introduction to the Writings and Their Social Context*. Philadelphia: Temple University Press, 1982.

Kutler, Stanley I. *The Dred Scott Decision: Law or Politics?* Boston: Houghton-Mifflin Co., 1967.

Kwong, Peter. *The New Chinatown*. New York: Hill and Wang, 1987.

Lai, David Chuenyan. *Chinatowns: Towns Within Cities in Canada*. Vancouver: University of British Columbia Press, 1988.

Lai, Him Mark. *Joe Huang, Don Wong, The Chinese of America, 1785–1980*. San Francisco: Chinese Culture Foundation, 1980.

Leakey, Mary. *Disclosing the Past: An Autobiography*. Garden City, N.Y.: Doubleday, 1984.

Leakey, Richard E., and Roger Lewin. *Origins: What New Discoveries Reveal About the Emergence of Our Species and Its Possible Future*. New York: E. P. Dutton, 1977.

Leakey, Richard E., and Roger Lewin. *People of the Lake: Mankind and Its Beginnings*. Garden City, N.Y.: Anchor Press-Doubleday, 1978.

Lee, Bennett, and Jim Wong-chu, eds. *Many-Mouthed Birds: Contemporary Writing by Chinese Canadians*. Seattle: University of Washington Press, 1991.

Li, Peter S. *The Chinese in Canada*. Toronto: Oxford University Press, 1988.

Lower, A.R.M. *Canada and the Far East—1940*. New York: Institute of Pacific Relations, 1941.

Lyman, Stanford M. "Asian American Contacts Before Columbus: Alternative Understandings for Civilization, Acculturation, and Ethnic Minority Status in the United States." In his *Civilization: Contents, Discontents, Malcontents, and Other Essays in Social Theory*, op. cit. 46–75.

Lyman, Stanford M. "Asians, Blacks, Hispanics, Amerinds: Confronting Vestiges of Slavery." In *Rethinking Today's Minorities*. Ed. Vincent N. Parrillo. Westport, Conn.: Greenwood Press, 1991. 63–86.

Lyman, Stanford M. "The Race Question and Liberalism: Casuistries in American Constitutional Law." *International Journal of Politics, Culture, and Society* V:2 (Winter 1991): 203–232.

Lyman, Stanford M. "The Significance of Asians in American Society." *Civilization: Contents, Discontents, Malcontents, and Other Essays in Social Theory*. Fayetteville: University of Arkansas Press, 1990. 149–159.

Lyman, Stanford Morris. *Chinatown and Little Tokyo: Power, Conflict, and Community among Chinese and Japanese Immigrants in America*. Millwood, N.Y.: Associated Faculty Press, Inc., 1986.

MacInnes, Tom. *Oriental Occupation of British Columbia*. Vancouver: Sun Publishing Co., 1927.

McCloskey, Robert Green. *American Conservatism in the Age of Enterprise, 1865–1910: A Study of William Graham Sumner, Stephen J. Field, and Andrew Carnegie.* New York: Harper Torchbooks, 1964 [1951].

McCurdy, Charles W. "Field, Stephen J. (1816–1899)." Vol. I-II of *Encyclopedia of the American Constitution*, op. cit. 721–725.

McGovney, Dudley O. "Race Discrimination in Naturalization." *Iowa Law Bulletin* VIII:3-4 (1923): 129–161, 211–244.

Meyer, Howard N. *The Amendment That Refused to Die.* Revised. ed., Boston: Beacon Press, 1978.

Miller, Stewart Creighton. *The Unwelcome Immigrant: The American Image of the Chinese, 1785–1882.* Berkeley: University of California Press, 1969.

Mooney, Ralph James. "Matthew Deady and the Federal Judicial Response to Racism in the Early West." *Oregon Law Review* LXIII:4 (1984): 561–637.

Morton, James. *In the Sea of Sterile Mountains: The Chinese in British Columbia.* Vancouver: J.J. Douglas, 1974.

Nieman, Donald G. *Promises To Keep: African-Americans and the Constitutional Order, 1776 to the Present.* New York: Oxford University Press, 1991.

Park, Robert E. "Human Migration and the Marginal Man." *American Journal of Sociology* XXXIII:6 (May 1928): 881–893.

Perlman, Janice E. *The Myth of Marginality: Urban Poverty and Politics in Rio de Janeiro.* Berkeley: University of California Press, 1976, 1979.

Pole, J. R. *The Pursuit of Equality in American History.* Berkeley: University of California Press, 1978.

Pound, Roscoe. "Legislation as a Social Function." *American Journal of Sociology* XVIII (May 1913): 755.

Przybyszewski, Linda C. A. "Judge Lorenzo Sawyer and the Chinese: Civil Rights in the Ninth Circuit." *Western Legal History* I (Winter/Spring 1988): 23–56.

Report of the Royal Commission on Chinese and Japanese Immigration, Sessional Paper No. 54, Ottawa: S. E. Dawson, printer to the King's most excellent majesty, 1902; reprint, New York: Arno Press, 1978. Part I, 1–326.

Report of the Royal Commission on Chinese Immigration, Ottawa: Printed by Order of the Commission, 1885; reprint, New York: Arno Press, 1978.

Rossum, Ralph A. "Naturalization." Vol. III-IV of *Encyclopedia of the American Constitution.* New York: Macmillan, 1986. 1300–1301.

Rouse, Irving. *The Tainos: Rise and Decline of the People Who Greeted Columbus.* New Haven: Yale University Press, 1992.

Roy, Patricia E. "A Choice Between Evils: The Chinese and the Construction of the Canadian Pacific Railway in British Columbia." In *The CPR West: The Iron Road and the Making of a Nation.* Ed. Hugh A. Dempsey, Vancouver: Douglas and McIntyre, 1984. 13–34.

Roy, Patricia E. *A White Man's Province: British Columbia Politicians and Chinese and Japanese Immigrants, 1858–1914.* Vancouver: University of British Columbia Press, 1989.

Sandmeyer, E. *The Anti-Chinese Movement in California.* Urbana: The University of Illinois Press, 1939.

Saxton, Alexander. *The Indispensable Enemy: Labor and the Anti-Chinese Movement in California.* Berkeley: University of California Press, 1971.

Saxton, Alexander. *The Rise and Fall of the White Republic: Class Politics and Mass Culture in Nineteenth-Century America.* London: Verso, 1990.

Sedgwick, Charles B. "The Context of Economic Change and Continuity in an Urban Overseas Chinese Community." M.A. thesis, University of Victoria, 1973.

Smith, Elbert B. *The Death of Slavery: The United States, 1837–1865.* Chicago: University of Chicago Press, 1967.

Speer, William, D.D. *The Oldest and Newest Empire: China and the United States.* Hartford, Ct.: S.S. Scranton and Co., 1870.

Spence, Jonathan D. *Chinese Roundabout: Essays in History and Culture.* New York: W. W. Norton, 1992.

Spence, Jonathan D. *The Search for Modern China.* New York: W. W. Norton, 1990.

Stampp, Kenneth M. *America in 1857: A Nation on the Brink.* New York: Oxford University Press, 1990.

Stonequist, Everett V. "The Marginal Man: A Study in Personality and Culture Conflict." In *Contributions to Urban Sociology.* Eds. Ernest W. Burgess and Donald J. Bogue. Chicago: University of Chicago Press, 1964. 327–345.

Swisher, Carl Brent. *Stephen J. Field, Craftsman of the Law.* Chicago: University of Chicago Press-Phoenix Books, 1969 [1930].

Tsai, Shih-shan Henry. *The Chinese Experience in America.* Bloomington: Indiana University Press, 1986.

The Toronto Star. "Waiting for Redress." 25 May 1992: A18.

Tussman, Joseph, and Jacobus ten Broek. "The Equal Protection of the Laws." *California Law Review* XXXVII:3 (September 1949): 341–381.

Voegeli, V. Jacque. *Free But Not Equal: The Midwest and the Negro During the Civil War.* Chicago: University of Chicago Press, 1967.

Waite, Edward F. "The Negro in the Supreme Court." *Minnesota Law Review,* XXX:4 (March 1946): 219–304.

Wickberg, Edgar, ed. *From China to Canada: A History of the Chinese Communities in Canada.* Toronto: McClelland and Stewart, Ltd., 1982.

Wiebe, Robert H. *The Search For Order, 1877–1920.* New York: Hill and Wang, 1967.

Wills, Gary. *Lincoln at Gettysburg: The Words That Remade America.* New York: Simon and Schuster, 1992.

Wunder, John R. "The Chinese and the Courts in the Pacific Northwest: Justice Denied?" *Pacific Historical Review* LII:2 (May 1983) 191–211.

Yee, Paul. *Saltwater City: An Illustrated History of the Chinese in Vancouver* Seattle: University of Washington Press, 1988.

Zilversmit, Arthur. *The First Emancipation: The Abolition of Slavery in the North.* Chicago: University of Chicago Press, 1967.

Awakening a 140-year Chinese American Community:
A Study of a Local Election

SYLVIA SUN MINNICK
Chinese Historical Society of America, San Francisco, California

Asian American political coalitions are soliciting qualified people to run for political offices. The nuts and bolts of political campaigns have puzzled many and, at times, it seems there are no answers to the many questions. How does a Chinese American break into the political process when the ethnic community has not been active? Are hurdles surmountable? Does ethnic and gender stereotyping still exist? Which is more important—timing or endorsements? The purpose of this paper is to add information on Chinese Americans involved in the political arena at the local level in the Central Valley.

Stockton has served as an important Chinese American center since the town's beginnings in 1850. Twelve years ago the 1980 census showed the Asians as only 9.1% of the population. That percentage grew to 22% by 1990, numerically about 49,000 of the city's 215,000 population. This rise is attributed to the influx of Southeast Asians and Filipinos. As the Asians with the longest history, the Chinese number 4,427, or almost 10% of the Asians.

Through history, Stockton Chinese's relationships with the dominant society remained symbiotic at best, separated by language, differences in culture, and focus in the economic market. By the 1920s, with an increasing number of family units, the adoption of western values, and the growing influence of Christianity, the Stockton Chinese began to be stake holders, particularly in owning properties and businesses. Other than going to the polls, they were not a part of the political process.

The sense of "duty" associated with casting a ballot occurred as early as 1898. That year, Joe Dye, a 21-year-old, second-generation Chinese American, underwent the rigors of a proficiency test in reading and writing skills and his knowledge of the state constitution. After satisfying the county clerk, Dye signed the Great Register, a log listing all official voters of San Joaquin County (Minnick 263).

Chinese Americans and other Asians began to seek careers in government by the 1950s, but usually only rising to the mid-management level. In City Hall today, there are 1425 employees, of which 25 are of Chinese descent, of which four are in management positions: the City Clerk, Personnel Director, Asst. Public Works Director, and Asst. Planning Director. Interestingly, these four are not native to Stockton.

Local civic commitment and participation tell a more pathetic story. Research shows that through the years, only six Chinese have ever served on boards and commissions, with Arizona transplant Dr. Dora Lee on the Parks and Recreation Board in 1970, followed by me on the Cultural Heritage Board in 1984. In 1988, three local-born became active in that level of local government—one on the Arts Commission and two on the Planning Commission. Stockton has 22 boards and commissions, which makes it possible to appoint 213 individuals. This year, there are only two of Chinese descent involved. We have made concerted efforts to get Chinese to apply, including making personal contacts, but to no avail. My point is that, while there are ample opportunities for the Chinese to take part in the political process of local government, they are much less interested than blacks and Hispanics.

Outside city government, two other Chinese entered a quasi-political arena. Frank Kim, a Chinese American, was appointed to the municipal court and later, through the election process, was promoted to the Superior Court. Judge Kim (a native of Marysville) ran unopposed and was never challenged throughout his career. He is now retired. Dr. Norman Wong (an orthodontist from San Francisco) served on the Stockton Unified School Board from 1971 to 1976. Wong, twice appointed, ran unopposed in the very first school district election in 1973 and resigned in 1976. He purportedly left the post when the school district underwent the throes of busing, to which he was adamantly opposed (Ingraham 6/16/92).

This minimal participation may stem from the lack of opportunities in the civic arena or even on priorities. However, I might also suggest that entering politics may not have occurred to them. For whatever reason, we should also consider "face saving" as a strong reason for non-involvement. Not wanting to put oneself "at risk" or under public scrutiny is a desire shared by millions. It certainly overshadows the sense of civic commitment. Why should the Chinese feel differently? One phenomenon is that the majority of those who forged forward locally are not native born.

In the late 1950s, when the city's *de facto* housing segregation vanished, many Chinese moved to the north part of the city but did not congregate in any one particular subdivision. By the late 1980s, only older Chinese, who encountered language barriers, and essentially were non-voters, remained in the Chinatown residential enclave.

The passage of a ballot initiative in 1984 changed the local election process for City Council members. This initiative's main purpose was to remove Council member Ralph White, a powerful black, who, for 12 years, held a tight rein in south Stockton. Several attempts to get other blacks (acceptable to the white community) to run against him failed.

Entitled Measure C, the initiative called for district voting in the primary. The two top contestants would face off citywide in the general election; thus, allowing the entire city to decide on Council members for each district. Large ethnic communities, such as those in Los Angeles, San Francisco, and Monterey, support district voting as a means for ethnic representation. They argue that city-wide voting works against minorities. This is a normal assumption, except when an ethnic group does not have the numbers to control a district. Measure C had additional provisions, such as a two-term limit and an odd/even district election cycle. As predicted, the Stockton blacks and Hispanic communities united their forces and sued to stop this change in the city charter. They never approached any Asian group to be a participant in their suit.

The Court, in 1988, ruled in favor of the city, citing that other blacks were elected even though they lived in predominately white districts. Thus, after five years, Stockton in 1989 called for an election of the entire City Council—six districts and a mayor elected at large. Thirty-six individuals—19 whites, seven Hispanics, five blacks, and five Asians (three Filipinos, one Japanese, and one Chinese)—ran for the seven seats.

Each district represents a minimum of 37,000 residents. Stretching from Interstate 5 to Highway 99, District 5 encompassed the old sections of downtown and Chinatown. The district had 11,566 registered voters. Its ethnic breakdown was 41.3% whites, 35.7% Hispanics, 15.7% blacks and 7.3% Asians. Partisan ratio showed 57% Democrats and 43% Republicans. There were four candidates for this council seat—two Hispanic males (an attorney and a Parks & Recreation commissioner), one white male who listed himself as a professional gambler, and me. All three males were native Stocktonians and all Democrats. I am a transplant and a Republican.

According to reporter Catherine Hedgecock of the Stockton Record, "District 5 is arguably the most important district in Stockton—encompassing the city's economic, historic, and civic center. Downtown Stockton sits smack in the middle of District 5, a narrow zig-zagging strip that reaches from tree-lined neighborhoods near Victory Park on the west to Highway 99 on the east (10/22/89).

The idea of a Chinese running for office brought a tepid response. Previously, one planning commissioner thought of throwing his name into the race, but that never happened. Five Chinese, all senior citizens, signed my nomination papers, and the process of getting the Chinese involved took on new meaning.

To every campaign, there are three segments—fundraising, endorsements, and getting the message across to the voters. This latter activity includes sending mailers, walking precincts, and phone banking. On the whole, the Chinese felt uncomfortable at the thought of either knocking on strangers' doors or making "cold" calls to get out the vote. Their reluctance centered on passivity as well as a self-perceived inability to articulate well. They truly performed on the first two segments: fundraising and endorsements. In retrospect, their methods and adaptations were a cultural "but, of course!"

From the start, most figured the Chinese community would be the largest contributor of my campaign. An accounting of donations from both the primary and general elections shows that of 538 entries, 215 (40%) came from Asian families, businesses, and groups. A further breakdown suggests that 31% were from the Chinese. Sixteen were from outside the area and most were family members or close friends.

I attended a regular Chung Wah meeting and announced my intentions. The elders did not give any formal endorsement or commit any funds. By election day, all 18 family and district organizations contributed $100 each. The amount was even across the board, so as not to upstage any one family group. Many asked, "What is a normal political donation?" or "How much do whites or Japanese give?" And they developed an informal formula: take the average white donation and reduce it by half. It was reasoned that the whites had been at this much longer. However, under no circumstances should the Chinese contribution be less than the Japanese one. Some wondered if a "lai shee," the traditional Chinese lucky money envelope, should be used. It was difficult for the community to understand why cash was not acceptable and why checks needed to be made out to a political committee.

Two other aspects to fundraising brought further education to the Chinese community. In giving a fund raiser, the Chinese organizers threw their heart and soul into planning the event. Since almost no one had ever attended such an affair, they did not know what to expect or what it entailed. But they reasoned, "How could it be any different from a normal celebration?" There was even talk about giving a pair of chopsticks and a rice bowl to those who showed up. That idea was quickly scratched. A plethora of Chinese delicacies, as served at birthday and wedding receptions, contrasted sharply to the western political events where attendees hovered over molded cheese balls. Decorations were very patriotic and colorful. Entertainment decidedly captured the Chinese flavor with music and traditional folk dance. The Asian distinctiveness was both expected by Chinese organizers and white attendees.

A fund-raiser to get Chinese attendance turned into a reasonably-priced traditional dinner, similar to a Chinese New Year banquet, but thematically programmed to give impetus to attendance. The fund-raiser was titled "A Bowl of Rice and Support for Sylvia," reminiscent of the late 1930s and early 1940s campaign to raise funds for war victims in China.

Endorsements equate with outward and financial support—literally putting one's name on the line. Retirees agreed to do so, but the professional and business members of the community were exceedingly hesitant. Reasons cited were fears that endorsements might negatively impact their businesses. A thought did occur, perhaps rightfully so, that if one did lend his name, other candidates might also pester for support. Also, because the Chinese community had been such non-participants, the appearance of a Chinese name suggested the endorser must have an interest in politics. There are elements of truth to these thoughts. Being sensitive to the Chinese community's preference, I chose not to produce mailers or newspaper ads with their names on them. The only time we used names was on the sidebar of the official stationery, giving a partial list of Chinese and white supporters.

A grassroots campaign uses lawn signs as a method to denote personal support. A sign on a property suggests that the entire household, their extended families, and possibly also the neighbors on either side of the home support the candidate. Distribution of lawn signs went out initially to mostly politically-active whites. When a small handful of Chinese displayed signs, others soon took to making the same statement on their front lawns. Those with several properties gave listings of their holdings where additional signs could be placed. As the general election gained momentum, signs appeared in Chinese restaurants and other businesses. The worry of negative business impact gave way to electioneering. The scattering of Chinese and other Asians throughout the city proved strategically beneficial. My lawn signs appeared in every subdivision and, seemingly, in every nook and cranny of the high-voting precincts.

As the candidate, I could not rely totally on the Asian support during the primary where district voting dominated. At this time also, some Chinese were not convinced that I would be a formidable contender. The key to winning the primary was personal contact. I personally walked door-to-door in 16 of the 22 precincts, oftentimes in 95- to 103-degree heat. For protection, a white friend, a retired undercover police sergeant, accompanied me. The reception was overwhelmingly warm. Old timers, Hispanics, Italians, and others would reminisce about Chinese kids they grew up with in school. They would then ask if the same people were still alive. I was surprised by the lack of continued ties, which further strengthened my belief regarding the Chinese isolation. Infrequently, was there a door slammed in my face, and when it occurred, it was generally in anger expressed over welfare aid to Southeast Asians.

In the primary, I received 53.4% of the votes cast with the nearest of the three opponents receiving 37% (summary 11/7/89). In the February special election run-off, I faced attorney Tony Gutierrez.

Gutierrez, a native son, was extremely popular and polls favored him. He had name recognition—he had previously run for both the Assembly and Supervisor seats. He received the endorsements of all the labor unions, developers, Hispanic groups, women's organizations, civic leaders, and both local legislative representatives, as well as support from both political parties' central committees. In the February 1990 citywide election, I captured 59.5% of the votes and was sworn into office on February 26th as the first Asian on the Stockton City Council (summary 2/6/90). If it were not for citywide election or for the fact that the Chinese were living in high-propensity voting precincts scattered throughout the city, the general election success would have been more difficult. Therefore, I am convinced timing and circumstances were extremely important elements in establishing an Asian representation.

My first term of office was nine months, which was considered a full term. In November 1990, I ran for re-election and had only one opponent—the professional gambler. There was no active campaign, and I received almost 70% of the votes. Numerous Chinese expected lawn signs, and rather than disappoint them, we used the leftovers from the first race (2/6/90).

Are the Chinese more interested in government? Some, but not all, have come to take a passive interest in local government. Council meetings are televised over the local cable television and some find the proceedings entertaining. Whenever a meeting hall is needed, particularly in the Chinatown area, the elders of the Confucius Church generously offer their facilities. In fact, the first town hall meeting, to address crime and drugs in the highest crime area in the city, was held at Confucius Hall. It brought together business-people and residents of all nationalities under one roof. Many of the "foreigners" finally got a peek into this bastion of the Chinese community.

The Chung Wah elders are now interested in pursuing redevelopment and commercial rehabilitation loans. They are not hesitant with complaints, information, or requests. While these may be positive signs that a 140-year-old community is beginning to be politically aware, this may not be the final analysis.

Knowing that my council seat was safe until December 1994, I recently challenged a 15-year incumbent Democrat for his supervisor's seat. But I pulled only 36% of the vote in a strong 81% Democrat Central/South city district. With district voting and without many of them living in the area, the Chinese, unfortunately, did not get as enthusiastic about the election. This is not to say there was no Chinese support; there was some. Chung Wah elders heartily endorsed the candidacy and even wrote letters to all the Chinese businesses and newspapers. Some were disappointed that they did not find my name on their ballot. I would suggest that their minimal participation and contributions in this election centered on disenfranchisement, rather than on issues or the candidate.

Moving away from the Chinese for a moment, as the candidate, I noted that in both the city and supervisor campaigns, several negative trends kept occurring. I suspect these to be partisanships, philosophy, and perhaps even prejudice in ethnicity and gender. While the offices were nonpartisan, the Democrats gave my opponents their full support. The local Republican central committee and leaders ignored me, even though I was an elected official in this last race. The unions had their own agenda and were not interested in any dialogue. Women's groups, (predominately white) endorsed my male opponents and never contacted me to give even minimal support. These social phenomena suggest that racism and sexism in the Central Valley still exist. Our local Asians need to realize their lack of political strength. Support from Chinese communities outside our area drew little response, other than from family or friends. One wonders that if I were a male, like Michael Woo or S.B. Woo, would there have been more interest, particularly from big cities such as Los Angeles and San Francisco?

In conclusion, while the Chinese community has had a minimal role in the political process historically, the local election of 1989–1990 afforded them an opportunity to promote Asian representation, and they did because I am Chinese. Does one conclude that their involvement will continue and perhaps grow? They are aware of government and politics, yet I sense that their passivity will prevent active participation. They will support another Chinese (note, not just any Asian) candidate when asked. It will take future generations to reach the degree of political activism that one finds in the larger urban communities.

Works Cited

Ingraham, Dr. J. Roland, Former superintendent of Stockton Unified School District. Personal interview. 16 June 1992.

Minnick, Sylvia Sun. *SAMFOW: The San Joaquin Chinese Legacy*. Fresno, 1988.

Semi-Official Election Summary, Primary Municipal Election. City of Stockton, 7 November 1989.

Semi-Official Election Summary, Special Election: Stockton Runoff. City of Stockton, 6 February 1990.

Stockton Record, 22 October 1989.

Chinese Merchant Wives in the United States, 1840–1945

HUPING LING
Social Science, Northeast Missouri State University, Kirksville, Missouri

The early Chinese American society has been widely known as a "bachelor society." From the beginning of the Chinese immigration, however, there existed a number of women who accompanied their husbands in their immigrant lives. The majority of these early Chinese immigrant women were merchant wives. According to the U.S. census, there were 1,784 Chinese women in the United States in 1860; 4,566 in 1870; 4,779 in 1880, and 3,868 in 1890; most of these women were merchant wives. Although the majority of the Chinese laborers came to America as "indentured laborers," they could not afford to bring their family with them; only the wealthy merchants were able to maintain their families in the new land. Especially after the passage of Chinese Exclusion Act in 1882, Chinese laborers were banned from immigration and the merchant class became one of the several exempted classes for entry to America. The records of the Immigration and Naturalization Service indicate that the majority of the Chinese women entering the United States between 1882 and 1943 were wives and daughters of Chinese merchants (RG 85).

Coming from a completely different society and having no ability to speak English, these early Chinese merchant wives went through a great deal of hardship in a new land. The forces responsible for their coming to America, the peculiar nature of their daily lives in a completely foreign environment, the kind of relationship with their family members, and the extent of their contact with the outside world have fascinated historians for some time. Although Chinese American studies has been a rapidly developing field and there has been a lot of work on Chinese Americans in general and on different aspects of their lives, the history of the lives of the Chinese merchant wives still remain unknown to a large extent.

Due to the lack of knowledge about these women, scholars and the public at large have tended to believe that early Chinese American communities were predominantly a bachelor society. It is this preoccupied concept that has led people to overlook or ignore the role of Chinese women in the early Chinese American society. In fact, the Chinese newspapers of the time and the Records of Immigration and Naturalization Service in National Archives contain abundant data on these Chinese merchant wives. From these sources, it is clear that there existed a subculture of Chinese women within the so-called Chinese bachelor society, which had considerable influence on the progress of Chinese communities in the United States.

Based on the original sources cited above and some secondary sources, this paper attempts to fill this void by focusing on Chinese merchant wives' life experiences. It first traces the Chinese merchant wives' motivation for emigration and the ordeal they experienced when they arrived in America ("There are no CATS in America"), then explores their lives and experiences after their entry to the United States. Finally, it discusses these women's contribution to the Chinese American society.

Chinese Merchant Wives' Motivation for Emigration and their Entry to America. A typical Chinese merchant wife in the late 19th and early 20th centuries was an illiterate woman with bound feet, growing up in a large family in a village near Canton. Her activities were defined according to the Chinese Confucian ideology of "Three Obediences"—a Chinese woman was expected to obey her father at home, her husband after marriage, and her son when widowed—and "Four Virtues"—chastity and obedience, reticence, pleasing manner, and domestic skill. Though without formal education, she was well-cultivated to be an obedient daughter, wife, and mother. She accepted the idea that she should follow and serve her husband whatever he was and wherever he went (Jiaji suiji, jiago suigo). This traditional ideology affected most Chinese merchant wives in making their decisions to come to America.

In many cases, the Chinese man migrated to America first, then worked and saved until he had enough money to travel back to China to bring his wife and children. This is true in the cases of Kwong Long and Gue Lim. Kwong Long, a Chinese merchant in New York City, went back to China in 1886 and returned with his wife and daughter after he worked in this country for some years (Entry 134).

Gue Lim, another Chinese merchant, petitioned the admission for his wife and children in 1900, and was rewarded the admission (Entry 132).

Generally, with sufficient funds, Chinese merchants could arrange for their families to join them.

In addition to maintaining family unity, many merchant wives were attracted by the economic opportunities in the United States. A second-generation Chinese American woman recalled her family history, in which her mother's marriage exemplified the common belief that America was a place full of gold, a "gumshan" (gold mountain):

> My father worked [in the United States] for a long time to save money for marriage. When he entered his middle age, he went to China to marry my mother, who was 20 years younger than him. The marriage was arranged by my mother's parents, and my mother was told that she would have better life in America. (Chang 6/10/92)

Some Chinese women even entered this country to take over businesses run by their husbands. Gin Far, the wife of a Chinese merchant in San Francisco, went back to China with her husband and her son. When her husband died in 1900, she desired to take over his interest in the firm in the United States, a respectable and responsible mercantile house, and so she applied to return to the United States with her six- or seven-year-old son. The Treasury Department authorized the Collector of Customs in San Francisco to admit her "as the surviving widow of a merchant with whom she formerly lived as his wife in this country" (Entry 132).

Like Gin Far, most of these Chinese merchant wives encountered interrogation and prolonged detention in the Customs Houses of the arriving ports, and later on Angel Island Immigration Station (1910–1940). Mai Shee, wife of Chinese merchant Lu Lian, arrived in San Francisco in May 1903, and was denied entry because the Customs had questioned the mercantile status of Lu Lian. Detained in the Customs facility known as "The Shed" on the San Francisco waterfront and deeply depressed, Mai Shee became very ill. Lu Lian applied for bail in order to have his wife treated by doctors. But the Customs refused his application, which caused great anger among the Chinese in San Francisco (*Chung Sai Yat Po* 5/30/1903).

Even wives of wealthy and influential merchants were not spared this humiliating treatment. Li Tom Shei, wife of Lee Lung, a successful Chinese merchant in Portland, arrived in Portland, Oregon, on April 3, 1900, with her husband and his nine-year-old daughter, Li A. Tosi. The Collector of Customs at Portland permitted Lee Lung to land without hesitation due to his established American residency and merchant status, but denied Li Tom Shei and Li A. Tosi's entry, due to the insufficiency of their papers. As a wealthy and influential merchant, Lee Lung appealed and launched a long battle against the Collector of Customs at Portland. His right of bail was pending the final determination by the Supreme Court of the United States. The

Immigration Record did not indicate if Li Tom Shei and Li A. Tosi were finally admitted. It was recorded that they had been detained in the Customs House at Portland at least from April 3 through August 18. It is not hard to imagine that Li Tom Shei, having led a sheltered life in China, must have gone through a difficult physical and psychological time during this ordeal (Entry 132, RG 85, Wash., D.C.).

Chinese merchant wives were, however, not always timid and passive victims. Some of them protested brutal treatment from immigration authorities. One merchant wife recalled her experience when she was interned on Angel Island: "While I was waiting in the immigration shed, Grandpa send a box of dim sum. I threw the box of dim sum out the window. I was still waiting to be released. I would have jumped in the ocean if they decided to deport me" (Yu 36).

Though not much help in their helpless situation, this form of resistance served as an emotional outlet for these detained women, and it reflected the cruelty and inhumane nature of the Immigration Station on Angel Island. To deal with the depressed and irritated detainees, the Immigration Station on Angel Island set up an isolation room, which is a three by three square feet tiny room without windows. The offensive inmates were locked in this tiny room for hours until they were "calm down."[1]

Some strong and resourceful Chinese women even fought against the immigration authority very effectively by making use of American immigration regulations. Gee Quock Shee was a good example of these courageous and capable women. She went to China with her husband, a Chinese merchant at San Mateo, in 1907. When she returned to the United States with the status of wife of merchant in February 1910, while her husband was still doing business in China, she was denied entry into the country because her husband was not presently in the United States. Defiantly, she provided the evidences that she had one half share in the business and that she had been actively managing the family business, Yee Hing & Co.; therefore, she was qualified to be a merchant herself. "If the law prevents me from being admitted as a wife of a merchant by reason of my husband not being in this country at the present time," she challenged McChesney, the immigration Inspector on Angel Island, "I therefore request that my application be withdrawn and renew it, having a status of a merchant myself." After investigation, the Immigration Service on Angel Island accepted her status as merchant and admitted her landing (Case 10385/5799, RG 85, San Bruno).

---

[1]For more details about Chinese immigrants' experiences on Angel Island, see Lai, Him Mark et al.

Defining Home, Work, and Community. Like other immigrant women, the early Chinese women mainly settled down at their ports of arrival. In the 19th century, San Francisco was the major landing port. In 1870, of 4,566 Chinese immigrant women arrivals, 3,873 remained in the San Francisco area; in 1900, of 4,522 Chinese immigrant women arrivals, 3,456 settled in San Francisco (U.S. Census Bureau Pubs.).

Beginning in the 1940s, New York had the second largest concentration of Chinese women in the continental United States. Out of a total of 20,115 Chinese women, there were 12,255 in California and 1,954 in New York (U.S. Census Bureau Pubs.).

In these urban settings, Chinese immigrant women, like their male counterparts, concentrated in the ethnic ghetto—Chinatown—and found themselves isolated and ignored by the rest of American society.

Physically, these Chinese merchant wives lived in four- to five-room apartments, possibly around the "Chinese Nob Hill" section on the 900 block of upper Clay and Sacramento streets and the area around Washington and Battery streets in San Francisco (Genthe 44, RG 85).

They often lived in seclusion, generally upstairs from a husband's business. Quarters were usually furnished with Chinese tables and chairs and decorated with Chinese ornaments.[2]

Due to the scarcity of women, the wives of merchants were closely guarded and highly valued commodities. Until she gave birth to a child, she was rarely to be seen outside her home. After she had children, her major responsibility was raising children. As a second-generation Chinese American woman noted about her mother, "My father traveled all over the world.... but his wife could not go into the street by herself" (Yu 38).

Though illiterate or poorly educated, most Chinese merchant wives brought a whole set of cultural values from China when they migrated to the New World. They struggled to preserve their cultural heritage while adapting to new ways of life in order to survive. In most merchant families, Chinese eating and dressing habits were maintained. As one Chinese girl noted: "The food [we eat] ... are rice, meat and fresh vegetables. In my family, my mother and I was dressed in Chinese costume, which was high collar and long sleeve" (in William Carlson Smith Documents MK-12).

Though some of them lived in poor or substandard housing with little furniture, they kept their places as clean as they could. The same Chinese girl wrote:

---

[2]See Genthe 44.

My home was a little house with two rooms, a parlor and a bedroom. In this house there were only two windows. Our kitchen and lavatory were outside of the house. The lavatory and bathroom were used by several families.... The furniture were old but they were kept clean by my mother who dusted them daily. We had very few pictures and decorations in the house. A few calendars and photographs were the only decorations in the house.... (ibid.)

As in eating, dressing, and housekeeping, Chinese merchant wives preserved their cultural traditions in child-rearing. Valuing traditional Chinese culture and customs, Chinese women taught their children, especially their daughters, as much as possible of the Chinese language and Chinese ways. As a Chinese girl in Hawaii said in the 1920s: "I have often made fun of the customs of my racial group. Some of the customs which I did not like were the serving of tea to visitors, forbidding to call the visitors by their first names; and the marriage customs" (ibid.).

Most early Chinese merchant wives had no formal education in China and knew little English. The children of Chinese merchant families learned and spoke English in public, while they spoke a Chinese dialect with their parents at home (Chang).

Since most well-to-do merchant families had house servants, their wives did not have to perform daily maintenance chores such as cooking, laundering, and cleaning. They usually filled their leisure time with needlework to be used as presents for relatives or as ornaments on caps for husband and children.

For many merchant wives, however, needlework seemed to be an important source of family income. These women sewed or mended clothes for Chinese bachelors at home. Low How See, one of the earliest Chinese women in San Francisco, worked as a seamstress. "I work in my room," she told the immigration official when she appeared in the Office of the Collector of Customs as witness for the entry of a Chinese woman. "My friends who know me will bring me work to do to my room" (Case 9514/536).

Some even ran a tailor's shop in which both husband and wife were involved. The oldest Chinese woman in Butte reminisced:

I made all my pin money sewing dozens upon dozens of [loose-fitting Chinese-style] suits for the merchandise stores. I was always busy. The suits even went to men outside of Butte: they would send in their orders. As soon as I made a dozen, I would start on another. Practically all of the women of the community sewed like I did, or mended. We had all we could do.

I made two kind of suits; washable ones for every day and woolen ones for special occasions. I never saw the men but my husband took orders at our store. He wrote down the measurements; I made the garments and sent them back through my husband. I saved several thousand dollars doing this until the [1911] Revolution. (Lee 193–94)

In addition to family sewing, many small-merchant wives also played important role in their family business. Some of them had a share in the business and became business partners of their husbands. Gee Quock Shee is a good example of a strong and capable early Chinese businesswoman. She was born in San Francisco in 1873 and was married to Yee Ho Wo in San Mateo, California, when she was 18 years old. After her son was old enough to be left alone, she joined the family business, Yee Hing & Co., a store selling general merchandise. With her being a woman, her name and interest were not mentioned in the business partners list, although she had an equal share of $500 in the company. Jointly having the largest share in Yee Hing & Co., she and her husband were the proprietors of the firm.

As a saleswoman and cashier, she played a crucial role in Yee Hing & Co. Everyday, she stood behind the counter looking after the business and took care of the money that came in, having her husband enter the money into books. Apparently, she functioned as a manager in the business and her husband a book-keeper. She was also in charge of monetary transaction of the firm. She went to San Mateo Bank regularly to do the banking business for the firm, though she was always accompanied by one of the other members of the company. Without formal education, she became a successful businesswoman, which impressed many people in San Mateo, including San Mateo Bank Cashier Henry W. Hagan and City Marshal M. F. Boland (Case 10385/5799, RG 85, San Bruno).

Meeting the Chinese immigrants' need for Chinese food and other goods, many Chinese ran grocery stores. Those stores were located mostly in Chinatown or oriental residential areas. Since most Chinese merchants possessed only small capital, they could not afford hiring extra help. In this type of small business, usually unpaid family members were fulfilling the demand of the labor needed for keeping the stores, and in most cases, these stores were husband-wife businesses. As wives of grocers, these women had to work side by side with their husbands, stocking, arranging, and selling goods, in addition to doing their daily maintenance chores at home. They usually knew very little English; sometimes barely enough to tell customers the price of their goods. Like Chinese girl Lily Chan's parents, "they did not know the English language, but they knew enough as to keep a store" (in William Carlson Smith Documents MK-2).

Their businesses were not good, and they could not make big money from keeping stores, for their clientele, mainly Chinese, were a minority. Their diligence, frugality, and shrewdness, however, enabled them to survive in the tough environment.

Isolation was a noticeable feature of life for Chinese merchant wives. Without knowledge of the English language and bound by Chinese tradition, the early Chinese merchant wives were excluded from larger American society and the male Chinese community as well.

Just as their male counterparts in the United States lived in an isolated environment, these Chinese women endured lonely, alienating, and even threatening surroundings. There were cases of Caucasian children yanking earrings from the pierced ears of Chinese women and pushing them into the mud or dragging them down by the hair. Most Chinese women of this period, having bound feet, could do little to defend themselves against such attacks.

Although her experience may not have been typical, the oldest woman in Butte, Montana's Chinatown provides insight into what life was like for some merchants' wives:

> When I came to America as a bride, I never knew I would be coming to a prison. Until the [1911] Revolution, I was allowed out of the house but once a year. That was during New Years when families exchanged... calls and feasts. We would dress in our long-plaited, brocaded, hand-embroidered skirts.
>
> ...The father of my children hired a closed carriage to take me and the children calling.... Before we went out of the house, we sent the children to see if the streets were clear of men. It was considered impolite to meet them. If we did have to walk out when men were on the streets, we hid our faces behind our silk fans and hurried by.... When the New Year festivals were over, we would put away our clothes and take them out when another feast was held. Sometimes, we went to a feast when a baby born into a family association was a month old. Otherwise we seldom visited each other; it was considered immodest to be seen too many times during the year. (Lee 252)

Though merchants' wives were the closest Chinese equivalent to the middle-class white women, Protestant women were struck by the former's situation and described the lives of merchants' wives as extreme examples of domestic confinement. Mission workers reported that Chinese women were so hemmed in by cultural prescriptions and by their own bound feet that "very few of them are allowed to go on the streets, and the vast majority never leave their rooms" (Pascoe 52).

Though leading a restricted life, early Chinese merchant wives managed to participate in social gatherings such as traditional festivals, family celebrations, and religious activities. Traditional festivals provided chances for Chinese merchant wives, especially in the early period, to go out to meet friends and relatives. The oldest woman in Butte, Montana's Chinatown recalled that during the Chinese New Year, long-confined Chinese women put on their best dresses and jewelry, visited each other, and exchanged information about their families and friends. She recalled: "The women were always glad to see each other; we exchanged news of our families and friends in China. We admired each other's clothes and jewels. As we ate separately from the men, we talked about things that concerned women" (Lee 252).

Other occasions, such as the celebration of a newborn, also provided opportunities for women to get together. "Sometimes," the same woman recalled, "we went to a feast when a baby born into a family association was a month old" (ibid.).

Like social gatherings, religious activities provided an emotional outlet for Chinese merchant wives. In Chinatown, one can find both Christian churches and non-Christian temples. The former were the products of missionary endeavors in both China and overseas communities; the latter represented another element of Chinese culture carried abroad. Moreover, unlike many Occidental people, the Chinese showed an affinity for syncretism, a remarkable acceptance of different religions, so that individuals often attended rites and celebration of more than one religion.

Protestant, rather than Catholic, churches were predominant in Chinatown. Except for the Chinese Catholic priests who wandered among early immigrants in the gold fields, the Catholic church paid little attention to the Chinese immigrants, preferring instead to minister to the large Irish populations, who entered California along with the railroads (Barth 164–66).

The Protestant endeavor was at its peak during the worst period of the anti-Chinese movement (1866–1904). In large Chinese communities, women had some opportunities to establish contacts with native-born women in various churches. When Suyuan Woo, a Chinese merchant wife in Amy Tan's novel, *The Joy Luck Club*, first arrived in San Francisco, the Refugee Welcome Society gave her two hand-me-down dresses. The society was composed of a group of white-haired American missionary ladies from the First Chinese Baptist Church. Because of these gifts, Suyuan Woo and her husband felt they could not refuse their invitation to join the church (Tan 20).

In churches and church-related activities like English classes, cooking classes, sewing classes, and social gatherings, Chinese women obtained the chance to peek at the American way of life, which certainly helped their adjustment to the new environment.

Apart from traditional festivals, friend gatherings, and religious activities, musical life in Chinatown also provided an opportunity to go out for fun. The 1920s brought substantial economic prosperity to the American society. Coinciding with such affluence, there was an upsurge in theatrical activity in San Francisco Chinatown, which had a special impact on the social life of Chinese women. The opera soon changed the evening life of Chinatown. "Before the opera came [in 1920s]," Ronald Riddle observed in his study, "the Chinese people stayed home in the evening and social intercourse was within the family.... After the opera came the young people began giving supper parties and inviting friends to each other's houses" (145).

Contrary to other ethnic women such as Irish American and Jewish American women, Chinese women were much less visible in the larger society and especially in the labor union movement. Obviously, the lower visibility of Chinese women in the union movement was largely a result of limited opportunities for Chinese women to work in factories outside of Chinatown. Besides, other internal barriers, including psychological constraints, cultural restrictions, and patriarchal and structural impediments, impeded political activism among Chinese American women (Chow 367–370).

Marriage and Family Structure. Immigrant experiences in a new country could very likely result in changes in family life and family structure for immigrant women. Like women in other immigrant groups, Chinese merchant wives also experienced changes in the institution of marriage and family structure.

The marriage of Chinese merchant family was often an arrangement between the families of bride and bridegroom, rather than a romantic union of two individuals. Most merchant wives were arranged by their parents to marry and had never seen their husbands before the wedding. The weddings were performed according to Chinese customs. A bride usually arrived at her groom's house in a sedan chair at about dark. She would worship the tablet of her husband's ancestor and serve tea for the guests. Following the ceremony, there was a feast to entertain relatives and friends. After the wedding, the husband would leave for America, leaving his wife behind to serve his parents until he had enough money to bring his wife and their children to the United States (Case 10434/6-10, RG 85, San Bruno).

Different from traditional Chinese family, which was a patriarchal and extended family, Chinese merchant families in the United States were patriarchal and nuclear families including a married couple and their children. Free of the supervision from in-laws and the service to in-laws and the brothers and sisters of her husband, the merchant wife experienced much less emotional stress and physical work than her counterparts in China, which was appreciated by many merchant wives. However, most merchant wives were still subjected to their husbands. A husband was the head of the family and made all decisions on family affairs alone.

Though living in patriarchal families, Chinese women were not always passive and oppressed parties in marriage. Some women ran away from unhappy marriages and found mates at their will. In the 1910s, an American-born girl from Portland married a Chinese merchant in Butte, Montana, at her parents' insistence. Her marriage became so intolerable for her that she deserted her husband, returned to Portland, and ran away with another Chinese. According to later reports, she was happily settled in Shanghai (Lee 253).

Others appeared at court to file for the dissolution of marriage. American-born Chinese woman, Xin Hao, was married to Chinese merchant Li Guang in 1907 in Idaho. A year after the marriage, the couple moved to San Francisco. Since then, the husband degenerated rapidly and abandoned his family. Xin Hao had to depend on her own parents for daily living. Finally, she went to court to request a divorce (*Sai Gai Yat Bo* 4/30/1910).

In a merchant family, the husband was usually much older than his wife. David Beesley's investigation, involving 27 married Chinese couples in a Sierra Nevada town, indicates that the average age of the women was 22, while the average age of the men was 31 (Beesley 174).

One reason for this large age-gap between married partners resulted from American immigration policies before 1943, which effectively reinforced the sexual imbalance among Chinese immigrants. According to Roger Daniels' research, from 1906 to 1924, an average of about 150 alien Chinese women had been legally admitted; from 1924 to 1930, none were admitted due to the 1924 immigration law that made it impossible for United States citizens of Chinese ancestry to bring in alien Chinese wives. In 1930, an act relaxed this ban: it provided for the entry of alien Chinese wives as long as the marriage had taken place before May 26, 1924: the date that the 1924 law had been enacted. Under this provision, about 60 Chinese women per year were admitted between 1931 and 1941 (Daniels 96–97).

The second reason was the enforcement of anti miscegenation laws in many states, which prevented Chinese men from marrying women outside their own ethnic group. Finally, the visible age difference between Chinese husbands and wives was also due to the financial disability of Chinese men. Many of them had to work for almost their entire lifetime to save enough money for a marriage. Therefore, American-born daughters of Chinese families were in demand as prospective brides.

The size of Chinese merchant families was usually small. The Immigration and Naturalization Service Records concerning Chinese merchant cases indicate that the average child rate of merchant families was 1.5 per family (RG 85, San Bruno).

On the contrary, a typical merchant family in China was a large-sized extended family. Traditionally, Chinese believed "more children and more fortune" (duozi duofu). How could Chinese merchants suddenly give up this traditional value after they migrated to America while still preserve other Chinese traditional values at the same time? Economic reason was probably an important one. Most petty merchants did not make enough money to support a big family. Moreover, the absence of grandparents and family support also made child-raising difficult in a strange country. It seemed a common practice for many merchants to send their young children to China to stay with grandparents and then bring them back when they reached a certain age (Cases 9508/107, 9508/651, 9512/21, 9515/63, 9515/64, 9518/76, 9576/688, 9578/775, 9579/43, 9579/622, and 9579/709, RG 85, San Bruno).

In this way, they could not only save expense on child-raising, but could also provide their aging parents in China company to relieve their regret that they could not be filial sons themselves.

In contrast to petty merchants, however, wealthy merchants usually tended to have big families. Isabelle C. Chang's father was a tea merchant from Hong Kong. He came to America around the turn of the century. He first arrived in San Francisco and later settled in Boston. He started as a bookkeeper and then operated his own business. He did very well and saved enough money to marry a young girl in China and to buy a house, which made him the first Chinese homeowner in Boston. Knowing that he did not have any relatives in America for immediate support, he wanted to produce as many children as he could for his future security. Being married in his middle age, he still managed to have nine children (Chang).

Conclusion. The majority of Chinese merchant wives led a restricted and secluded life, but significant numbers did not. Women of energy and ability stepped outside the traditional feminine spheres of home and child care to run businesses. Both traditional and untraditional women have all made a variety of contributions to their ethnic communities and to American life in general.

Chinese merchant wives have helped to maintain the cultural integrity and moral stability of Chinatown society. Cultivated by traditional Chinese ideologies, Chinese women transplanted their cultural values to the new land by preserving Chinese cultural practice at home and in Chinese communities, which further diversified American culture. The existence of respectable women also helped to decrease illicit conducts of the Chinese bachelors' society.

Chinese merchant wives have also helped to increase family income by either working at home or working as business partners in their family ventures. Their work was indispensable for their families' existence and for the survival of Chinatown communities. The sewing business, for instance, met the basic need of Chinese bachelors; while money made from sewing became a necessary part of family income. As Roger Daniels has pointed out, the fact that many married Chinese women engaged in the sewing business "illustrates an important and often unnoticed factor in Asian American economic success: that is, the contribution made by Asian American married women at a time when most married women in this country were not in the labor force" (Daniels 78).

Many Chinese merchant wives have stepped outside to participate in various social activities in the Chinese community. Gatherings of all sorts gave them a pleasure of diversity in their restricted lives. Special holidays or family anniversaries helped to brighten their daily routine. Chinese merchant wives found these social activities not only as an emotional outlet for themselves, but as practical means to establish or maintain contacts with other members of the Chinese American community and larger American society for their men as well.

In conclusion, these "forgotten" Chinese merchant wives who have played an important role in the life of Chinese communities can be rediscovered by a careful study of the Chinese press and the archival documents. Sources are available for the study of Chinese merchant wives. With the use of these available sources, much more can probably be uncovered.

Works Cited

Barth, Gunther. *Bitter Strength, A History of the Chinese in the United States, 1850–1870.* Cambridge, Mass.: Harvard University Press, 1964.

Beesley, David. "From Chinese to Chinese American, Chinese Women and Families in a Sierra Nevada Town." *California History* 67 (September 88): 174.

Case 9514/536, RG 85, Case 10385/5799, RG 85, Case 10385/5799, RG 85, Case 10434/6-10, RG 85, Cases 9508/107, 9508/651, 9512/21, 9515/63, 9515/64, 9518/76, 9576/688, 9578/775, 9579/43, 9579/622, and 9579/709, RG85, National Archives, Pacific Sierra Region, San Bruno.

Chan, Lily. "My Early Influences." 25 October 1926, in *William Carlson Smith Documents*, MK-2.

Chang, Isabelle C., Berkeley, CA. Personal interview. 10 June 1992.

Chow, Esther Ngan-Ling. "The Feminist Movement: Where Are All the Asian American Women?" In *Making Waves, An Anthology of Writings By and About Asian Women.* Ed. Asian Women United of California. Boston Beacon Press, 1989. 367–370.

Chung Sai Yat Po (Chinese Daily), 30 May 1903.

Daniels, Roger. *Asian America: Chinese and Japanese in the United States Since 1850*. Seattle: University of Washington Press, 1988.

Entry 132, "Chinese General Correspondence, 1898–1908," Record Group 85, National Archives, Washington, D.C.

Entry 134, "Customs Case File No. 3358d Related to Chinese Immigration, 1977–1991," Record Group 85, National Archives, Washington, D.C.

Genthe, Arnold. *Genthe's Photographs of San Francisco's Old Chinatown*. New York: Dover Publications, 1984.

Lai, Him Mark et al. *Island, Poetry and History of Chinese Immigrants on Angel Island*. San Francisco: Hoc Doi, 1980.

Lee, Rose Hum. *The Growth and Decline of Chinese Communities in the Rocky Mountain Region*. New York: Arno Press.

Pascoe, Peggy. *Relations of Rescue*. New York: Oxford University Press, 1990.

RG 85, Immigration and Naturalization Service Records, National Archives, Washington, D.C.

RG 85, National Archives, Pacific Sierra Region, San Bruno.

Riddle, Ronald. *Flying Dragons, Flowing Streams: Music in the Life of San Francisco's Chinese*. Westport, CT: Greenwood Press, 1983.

Sai Gai Yat Bo (Chinese World), 30 April 1910.

Tan, Amy. *The Joy Luck Club*. New York: G.P. Putnam's Sons, 1989.

U.S. Census Bureau Publications

William Carlson Smith Documents, MK-12."Life History." By a Chinese girl at McKinley High School, Honolulu, 20 November 1926.

Yu, Connie Young. "The World of Our Grandmothers." In *Making Waves, An Anthology of Writings By and About Asian Women*. Ed. Asian Women United of California. Boston Beacon Press, 1989. 36.

Expressing Self:
The Development of Personal Autonomy in Second-Generation Chinese American Women

YEM SIU FONG
University of Colorado, Boulder, Colorado

The interior life of Chinese women has long been a forbidden and unknown terrain for travelers; the tendency to internalize and endure their experiences rather than examine them, however, has cultural and historical roots (Lee 232).

Although the Chinese have been in the United States for over 100 years, the process of acculturation, assimilation, and defining one's cultural identity continues to influence socialization in Chinese Americans. While research since the 1960s have examined cultural conflicts, such as western individualism versus Chinese familial subordination, only recently have studies begun to focus on the unique issues facing Chinese American and Asian American women.

Chinese women in this country have been viewed stereotypically as exotic curiosities or subservient wives, quiet, docile, and submissive. Historically, they have had few legal property or economic rights, both in China and during their early history in the United States. Chinese women were subject to immigration laws that sought to exclude them and to Confucian patriarchal traditions in which they held no formal independent decision-making authority. It was not until the Civil Rights and women's movements that Chinese American women began to find their public voices. As writers, artists, political and social activists, they claimed their right to be heard and to be seen. This paper explores the search for expressing self for contemporary second-generation Chinese Americans, specifically focusing on the development of personal autonomy for these women who came of age during the 1960s and 1970s.

Ester Ngan-Ling Chow, who has researched issues of acculturation and feminism for Asian American women notes:

> Because they are also members of a racial and ethnic minority group, Asian American women develop their identification, self-esteem, and personality different from white women. In the midst of conflicting values, identity crises, and consciousness raising, Asian American women are in the process of building a new womanhood. (Chow 1985)

It is the intent of this paper to present a framework on the development of personal autonomy, recognizing the importance of race and gender in the bi-cultural setting. Findings presented are from original research conducted with 11 second-generation Chinese American women in 1990–91.

In this paper, the definition for personal autonomy is taken from Diane Meyers' book, *Self, Society, and Personal Choice*, where she defines personal autonomy as "discerning the desire of one's authentic self and acting in accordance with those desires." She further proposes that personal autonomy is influenced at three stages in the socialization process: self-discovery, self-definition, and self-direction (Meyers 1989). The hypothesis of the original study was that the western cultural stress on individualism leads to an increased desire to develop a sense of personal autonomy, in contrast to the traditional Chinese emphasis on outside authorities. As expected, the research found this to be true. What is central to this paper is how this transition occurred. In contrast to the experiences of earlier second-generation Chinese American women, the women in this research have had greater institutionalized opportunities to further develop autonomy, moving from the silent and invisible to the public support of expressing one's self.

Research Background. Eleven second-generation Chinese American women were interviewed as part of a University of Colorado-funded research project. These women were selected according to the following criteria, in order to capture a population of women whose China-born parents would have come from similar economic and class backgrounds: presently 30–45 years of age; pure Chinese descent; born in the United States or having come as an infant; parents originating from the rural villages of Guangdong Province, China. Guangdong was the homeland of the earliest Chinese immigrants. This very small sample included women raised on the west coast, eastern and southern United States, and the Rocky Mountain region. Six of the women were raised in or near Chinese communities, and two of the women had lived in black neighborhoods. The remaining women grew up in lower class, mostly white communities. Participants were contacted through associates in the ethnic studies field and/or were involved in social or political activism. As a result, all of the women were employed in professional jobs and were college educated. Eight of the women held M.A. degrees, one held a Ph.D., and the rest held bachelors degrees. The fathers of the respondents were launders, nurserymen, restaurant owners, and welders, while their mothers were launderers, restaurant workers, or seamstresses, as well as wives and mothers.

The interview methodology was chosen to provide in-depth case studies on each participant. Using an informal inductive approach, responses were compared and contrasted. Questions were developed which would demonstrate how each woman's sense of self had evolved, with particular attention to her upbringing, parental authority, school experiences, neighborhood and environmental factors, gender issues, and experiences with racial discrimination. Were the women encouraged to develop a positive sense of themselves, as females, as Chinese Americans? Did they receive praise and encouragement, necessary for self-esteem? Did they have positive role models? What role did their surrounding environment play in their evolution? Questions fit into the developmental stages discussed earlier: self-discovery, which includes childhood and early school experiences; self-definition, the middle school, high school, and college years; and self-direction, which includes adult life decisions, i.e. career, marriage, etc.

Summary of Findings. In the self-discovery stage, it was evident that most of the women had been raised in traditional Chinese, Confucian ways of behavior and subservience. All seemed to be very good little girls who were rarely praised for good behavior, and were often criticized or expected to always do better. Fathers provided the values and authority, while the mothers acquiesced, manipulated, or otherwise exerted influence. Almost all the women knew from an early age that they were valued less than males. They were essentially raised to be obedient, quiet, dutiful, and responsible—a reflection of the traditional "Four Virtues" ascribed to Chinese women in Confucian ideology. Conforming to expected behaviors was strongly stressed in the home and in school, both Chinese and public institutions. Authority figures were respected and not questioned. Individual self-expression was not encouraged within the family. One respondent summarized this:

> We were not encouraged to express ourselves, we were not encouraged to talk at the dinner hour or in front of our relatives. In the presence of adults we were always expected to be quiet and obedient. In Chinese school, that's reinforced that you don't question the teacher and never ask to express your opinion or anything. So we grew up that way and I think that was the "normal behavior" for kids in our neighborhood.

In this environment, the family was a close, protective unit. Fathers spoke some English, but the mothers spoke very little. Fathers were described as strict and disciplining. Mothers were too busy, some were very unhappy and even abused. The women did not leave the home to play and only ventured out on family outings, school, or church activities. Socialization was prescribed in a mostly restrictive, Chinese mode reflecting the values that the parents brought with them from China. The traditional Chinese family hierarchy is based on gender and generations. The young female is at the bottom of this hierarchy.

Second-generation daughters learned how to relate in the family and be caretakers by example. In the literature on development theory, feminist authors have examined the concept of the female self rooted in a sense of connection and relatedness to others (Gilligan 1982, Miller 1986). For males, development follows a more linear path, stressing separation and autonomy in their socialization process. Males learn to identify with authority and power structures and how to negotiate within them. Women learn that authority is held by the other, i.e. males. For these second-generation women, praise, encouragement, and positive identification with others generally were lacking in the home. Nine of the women who had brothers could cite examples of privileges given to boys but not the girls in the family. Choices were more limited for the daughters. As one respondent noted: "I don't remember having many choices or feeling I could ask for many things." Another said: "...we didn't think twice about it, we didn't manipulate, we didn't strategize, we didn't negotiate, we just accepted it."

When asked if their mothers were role models, or if they saw themselves as similar or different from their mothers, the women all had responses similar to this: "If anything, I try to make a point not to be like my mother." Mirrored back to these women were images of unhappy, hard working mothers with little overt control of power. Nonetheless, the daughters were aware of the manipulative and "behind the scenes" power mothers could wield. The immigrant mothers, along with the fathers, attempted to instill cultural values based on a patrilineal tradition. The importance of family, filial piety, and kinship were paramount to the survival of the Chinese family in a foreign host country.

In Feelie Lee's important doctoral research on Chinese American mothers and daughters (Lee 1982), she suggests a model of mother-daughter relationship based on functionality and relative power value. Daughters were raised to support the family unit, eventually marrying out. Through the sons, however, a mother could effect power, with the eventuality of dominance over a daughter-in-law and living with the son upon the husband's death. This Chinese model then is one of a lifelong mother-son bond, while the mother-daughter tie is expected to be short lived. Lee views this as a reverse of the American pattern of lifelong mother-daughter relationship ideally based on affection.

In addition to home life, public and Chinese school experiences reinforced authority, sex-roles, and racial stratification for these women. While public schools offered opportunities for verbal expression, European American teachers reinforced the stereotype of quiet and hardworking Chinese American students. All of the interviewees were good students, but only one would volunteer to answer questions in class. One woman noted: "I didn't want to have attention drawn to me. I was noticed for being different and it was usually negative attention."

During the self-definition years, these women began to experience more fully the conflicts between the familial culture and the dominant society, between always serving the group and the importance placed on individualism. Questioning of family authority, experiences of racial bias, and the realization, as one respondent put it, that "Americans had it all" occurred during adolescence and early college age. These women began to move from a position of silence and reliance on external authority to an understanding of their own inner truths.

In the seminal work, *Women's Way of Knowing*, four women psychologists interviewed 135 women from diverse ethnic, class, and age categories to explore the concept of how women learn. From this research, five stages of "knowing" were identified, silence being the stage where behavior and action are based on the "other" as authority. For Chinese American women, this meant that concepts of truth and power were held by males at home and white males in the American culture. As they sought to develop a more defined sense of self, trust in the male authority structure began to break down. This is exemplified in one woman's quote about when her father refused to pay tuition so that she could attend the college of her choice, instead of the local university where she would have to live at home:

> A lot of it built up as a child, that I was forbidden so many different things. I felt that if I did something on my own, I could separate myself and not feel so totally dependent on my father... I started to gain a real sense of—I don't know if I should say—power, but I felt that I had to do it on my own.

The authors further examine the importance of language and literacy, written and oral, as a means of learning and self-learning for women. Exterior dialogues is a precursor to inner speech and an awareness of one's own thought processes. Finding the powers of voice and mind are most often found through relationships with friends. For these second-generation women, silence was reinforced at home and at school and isolation from either a Chinese community or the dominant society occurred.

A sense of identity was further blurred in cultural conflicts and interactions with "others" outside the family. One interviewee felt this way: "As I got older and more aware and realized that the Americans had it all, I really tried to be more American and reject the Chinese part of me." All of the women recalled instances where they had been excluded or harassed for being Chinese, such as not being invited to parties or being uninvited to the prom because the boy's parents did not approve of their son dating a Chinese. One of the respondents raised in the south felt the additional discrimination of not being white when her family was never allowed to sit at the counter in Woolworth's. Her father would say that it was because the children must have been bothering the waitress. "He never said it was due to prejudice," she said.

When asked if they felt more Chinese or American growing up, responses were nearly evenly divided with six women identifying themselves as Chinese. There was no direct correlation between the racial makeup of their neighborhoods and feelings of being more or less Chinese. For two women who lived in the Bay area, but in black neighborhoods, being Chinese was more positively reinforced by teachers who encouraged them to be class leaders over their black classmates. The advantage for women raised in non-Chinese communities was that they learned to socialize in an "American" world more comfortably and at an earlier stage than women raised in Chinese environments. They learned to adapt socially through non-Chinese friends and neighbors while women in Chinatowns frequently felt inadequate outside of their boundaries. Conversely, women who did not live in Chinese areas felt uncomfortable and ignorant of Chinese custom and language as they became more "Americanized."

The double bind of subordination of the self to others, in family, and outside was most keenly felt during these years and in the years of self-direction. Major emotional and personal decisions such as dating, college, and marriage became the battleground for rejecting cultural, parental, and male authority. Most parents of these women did not approve of dating, believing that it was "not proper until you're ready to consider marriage" and that "every man is out to get your daughter." One Chinatown resident began to date on the sly, noting that "It was an American custom and everyone did it and it was fun. We just had to face the consequences every time we came home."

Eight of the 11 women were encouraged to go to college. Education being seen as important to survival and improving one's lot in America. Four of the women paid for college themselves. Parents all expected the women to marry after college. Women raised in or near Chinese areas married Chinese men, while those raised in non-Chinese communities married Anglo American men. One woman eloped at 19 to escape her family. Most of those marrying non-Chinese did so against their parents approval. One woman described going against her parents as one of the riskiest things she had ever done and notes: "I didn't think of it at the time, but it was such a big break, such a big thing to do, because I love my parents but I was going to do this (marry a non-Chinese). The only thing that could have potentially separated me from people I care about. Somehow my family has a far reaching influence on me."

These women were making these major decisions at a time in America when ethnic consciousness, civil rights, and the women's movement were in the foreground. Questioning all authority, expressing one's self, and finding validation in others all contributed further to the development of personal autonomy.

Conclusions. Clearly these second-generation Chinese American women developed personal autonomy in a Chinese American, non-linear, bi-cultural context. From being female, they learned to hone adaptability and relating to others. From being Chinese, subservience and gender roles meshed to further develop accommodation and adaptability skills. From their mothers, the daughters learned survival skills and to observe the informal power exercised by them. Feelie Lee suggests that "Chinese mothers historically have accrued considerable informal or unassigned powers and at the same time have maximized their opportunities in roles traditionally assigned to them." (Lee 91) Lee sees the female development of political and interpersonal skills as survival mechanisms in a "Confucian sanctioned male dominated world." (Lee 92)

Esther Chow's work on acculturation, which utilizes earlier research by Stanley Sue, describes four types of ethnic identity: traditionalist, assimilationist, pluralist, and ambivalent. These are based on the interplay of American and Asian values. She points out that the "central issue in the adaptation of Asian American women is the extent to which they retain their own cultural traditions, as opposed to assimilating culturally and structurally into American society" (Chow 1985). For these second-generation Chinese American women, the pluralist description is most apt. These women are no longer marginal. There is a high regard for both American and Asian values and an integration of the useful aspects of both cultures. She states: "This type, an outgrowth of continual reconciliation between two cultures has a dialectic element that includes conflict and contradiction as part of the dynamic process of acculturation; thus, each integration is only a temporary state leading to an affirmative and flexible identity." (Chow 244)

All of the women talked about their continued connections with their family. Their relationships with siblings, parents, and the importance of their own families was evident. At the same time, these women had successfully directed their lives as lawyers, writers, teachers, and professionals busy expressing themselves and interacting within both the dominant society and a connection with things and people Chinese. These second-generation women have integrated familial lessons—Chinese values, perseverance, survival skills—and have moved beyond subordination to acknowledgment of the self as uniquely Chinese American and individual, while still remaining strongly connected to others. Personal autonomy began to develop when outside authority was no longer believed to be the only choice. In the self-definition years, truth became personal and private. Through education, college experiences, and marriage, political and social awareness, knowledge, and trust in one's own abilities grew so that these women moved from silence to creators of knowledge, fully capable of expressing the self.

Works Cited

Armstrong, Jocelyn M. "Ethnic and Sex-Role Socialization: A Comparative Example Using Life History Data from Hawaii." *Sex Roles: A Journal of Research* 10 (1984): 157–181.

Beauvoir, Simone de. *The Second Sex.* New York: Vintage Books, 1974 (reprint of the 1953 edition published by Knopf.)

Belenky, Mary et. al. *Women's Way of Knowing: The Development of Self, Voice, and Mind.* New York: Basic Books, 1986.

Bond, Michael H., and Tak-Sing Cheung. "College Students' Spontaneous Self-Concept: The Effect of Culture among Respondents in Hong Kong, Japan, and the United States." *Journal of Cross-Cultural Psychology* 14 (1983): 153–171.

Chow, Ester Ngan-Ling. "The Acculturation Experience of Asian American Women." In *Beyond Sex Roles.* 2nd ed. by Alice G. Sargent. St. Paul: West Publishing Company, 1985. 238–251.

Chow, Ester Ngan-Ling. "The Development of Feminist Consciousness among Asian American Women." *Gender and Society* 1 (1987): 284–299.

Chun-Hoon, Lowell. "Jade Snow Wong and the Fate of Chinese-American Identity." *Amerasia Journal* 1 (1971): 52–63.

Fenz, Walter D., and Abe Arkoff. "Comparative Need Patterns of Five Ancestry Groups in Hawaii." *Journal of Social Psychology* 58 (1962): 67–89.

Fong, Stanley L. M. "Assimilation and Changing Social Roles of Chinese Americans." *Journal of Social Issues* 29 (1973): 115–127.

Fong, Stanley L. M., and Harvey Peskin. "Sex-Role Strain and Personality Adjustment of China-Born Students in America: A Pilot Study." *Journal of Abnormal Psychology* 74 (1969): 563–567.

Fujitomi, Irene, and Diane Wong. "The New Asian-American Woman." In *Asian-Americans: Psychological Perspectives.* Ed. Stanley Sue and Nathaniel N. Wagner. Ben Lomond, CA: Science and Behavior Books, 1980. 252–263.

Gilligan, Carol. *In a Different Voice: Psychological Theory and Women's Development.* Cambridge: Harvard University Press, 1982.

Jordan, Judith et. al. *Women's Growth in Connection: Writings from the Stone Center*. New York: Guilford Press, 1991.

Kim, Elaine H. *Asian American Literature: An Introduction to the Writings and Their Social Context*. Philadelphia: Temple University Press, 1982.

Lao, Rosina, Chong-Jen Chuang, and Kuo-Shu Yang. "Locus of Control and Chinese College Students." *Journal of Cross-Cultural Psychology* 8 (1977): 299–313.

Lee, Feelie. "Chinese American Mothers and Daughters: Bound and Unbound Feet." Unpublished Ph.D. thesis, Wright Institute, 1982.

Leong, Frederick T. L. "Counseling and Psychotherapy with Asian Americans: Review of the Literature." *Journal of Counseling Psychology* 33 (1986): 196–206.

Loo, Chalsa M. *Chinatown: Most Time, Hard Time*. Praeger Publishers, in press.

Meade, Robert D. "Leadership Studies of Chinese and Chinese Americans." *Journal of Cross-Cultural Psychology* 1 (1970): 325–332.

Meyers, Diana T. *Self, Society, and Personal Choice*. New York: Columbia University, 1989.

Miller, Jean Baker. *Toward a New Psychology of Women, 2nd ed*. Boston: Beacon Press, 1986.

Miller, Margaret. "Threads of Identity in Maxine Hong Kingston's Woman Warrior." *Biography* v. 6 no. 1 (1983): 13–33.

Mordkowitz, Eliott R., and Herbert P. Ginsburg. "The Academic Socialization of Successful Asian-American College Students." Paper presented at the 67th meeting of the American Educational Research Association, San Francisco, CA, 16–20 April 1986.

"1990 Annual Selected Bibliography." *Amerasia Journal* 16 (1990): 195–270.

Sue, Derald W., and Barbara A. Kirk. "Psychological Characteristics of Chinese-American Students." *Journal of Counseling Psychology* 19 (1972): 471–478.

Sue, Stanley, and Derald W. Sue. "Chinese-American Personality and Mental Health." *Amerasia Journal* 1 (1971): 36–49.

Sue, Stanley, and James K. Morishima. *The Mental Health of Asian Americans*. San Francisco: Jossey-Bass Publishers, 1985.

Sue, Stanley, and Nathaniel N. Wagner. *Asian Americans: Psychological Perspectives*. Ben Lomond, CA: Science and Behavior Books, 1980.

Wong, Jade Snow. *Fifth Chinese Daughter*. Seattle: University of Washington Press, 1950.

Yang, Julia. "Career Counseling of Chinese American Women: Are They in Limbo?" *Career Development Quarterly* 139 (1991): 350–359.

Yung, Judith. "Unbinding the Feet, Unbinding Their Lives: Social Change for Chinese Women in San Francisco, 1902–1945." Unpublished Ph.D. dissertation, UC Berkeley, 1990.

Yung, Judy. *Chinese Women of America: A Pictorial History*. Seattle: University of Washington Press, 1986.

On Contradiction: The Second Generation

MARJORIE LEE
University of California, Los Angeles, California

Astutely articulated by Mao Tsetung, *contradiction* is a bold, dynamic term that can unapologetically describe the metamorphic transformation of the second-generation American Chinese—women especially. It exists in the process of development of all things (Mao 91); it is the movement of opposites. Without life, there would be no death; without misfortune, there would be no good fortune; no east, no west; no first generation, no second. The struggle of opposites occurs, then, when there is hostility brought on by the presence of a new condition that disrupts prevailing conditions (Mao 125).

Such is the condition of the second-generation American Chinese between 1920 and 1950, who sought and struggled to make sense, opportunity, and significance of the two cultures they consciously and unconsciously embraced. Moreover, it is the women in this unique community who experienced more perplexing contradictions and, therefore, the most significant metamorphic transformations. Their contributions to their families, communities, and succeeding generations are evident in the historic legacies recounted and preserved in the *Chinese Digest*, *Chinese Press*, and *East Wind*—two newspapers and a magazine that channeled the heart and voice of American Chinese of the second and third generations into printed media.

Growing up in an era of blatant anti-Chinese sentiment and racism, legislative exclusion, and cultural oppression, the second generation found themselves alienated by a genuine lack of understanding from both sides of their bicultural spectrum. A deep sense of frustration pervaded the hearts and souls of American Chinese—born and reared in America, yet scarred by unmerited prejudice and cast off as heathen with moral and social disease.

In short, it was a gloomy epoch in time for the ABCs. As recounted by a Chinese American woman in the *Chinese Press* as late as 1941:

> In the United States, likewise we are regarded as foreigners; because of the color of our skin we bear a double yoke. Because our parents and grandparents were ground into the depths of degradation by fear and intolerance, many of the younger Chinese have grown up fearing the white man, and allow themselves to be beaten into feeling inferior—so much so, that the majority of them cringe and creep back further into the black depths of Chinatown, afraid to come out and prove that they can be a desirable element in American society.... (Anon 3)

The second-/third-generational study I conducted was an attempt to reach beyond the more prolifically researched immigrant experience into a neglected, but lively and significant, dimension of Chinese American Studies. Social historian Fred Cordova echoes the same sentiment in his research on second-generation Filipino Americans:

> We are the forgotten Second Generation, bridging the past with our present but remaining uncertain of our future, silent in our thoughts, private in our fears, deluded within our dreams, hidden in our pursuits, regretful over our failures, overlooked in our achievements, and omitted by our very own.... (Cordova 299)

The findings of my study are summarized in this paper to frame the context of this session's papers, which will provide a "her"-storical perspective and overview on the experiences of second-generation Chinese American women. Generational, cultural, and gender issues will be discussed within three major concerns endemic to these women: kinship relations, dual nationalism, and community orientation. Their resolution to taming the 'contradictions' will be reflected in the other papers to follow.

Defining Some Ambiguities. Before I continue, permit me to clarify two terms I elected to use for symbolic, academic, and expedient reasons. The first addresses the nomenclature for this esteemed group under discussion. For brevity and convenience, the acronym *ABC* ("American-born Chinese") will be used to refer to all Americans of Chinese descent. I will also use *American Chinese*, developed by sociologist Rose Hum Lee, who recognized the neglected, undervalued component of the "American" character and cultural transformation of ABCs. She writes:

> ...*Chinese-Americans* ...carries the connotation of the descendants of a racial and cultural group against whom prejudicial and discriminatory acts have been directed.... they are considered Chinese before they are Americans. This implies that they are second-class Americans and do not enjoy fully the rights and privileges accorded by the society to its citizens.... *American-Chinese* is used by those who are more enlightened and are attempting to correct the distorted areas of social relations between ethnic and cultural groups.... (R. Lee 113) [emphasis added]

Another term concerns the generational character of this group. While most studies designate "first-generation" as the foreign-born generation, it has been more commonly understood among the old-timers themselves to refer to the first generation born in America. For purposes of universal discussion within Asian American Studies and advocating for the important interrelationship between the first- and second-generations, "second generation" will be used to refer to the American-born.

Life for many of them was wrought with rebellion, racism, and conflict: against the old traditions of their immigrant parents; against the hostile and intolerant attitudes and actions by dominant American society; against the internal struggle within themselves to create harmony between the two cultures with which their names identified—American and Chinese.

Contradiction #1: Kinship Relations. Kinship relations in Chinese America at this time reflected the intensity of things American and things Chinese; a clash between self-determination and filial authority. The published autobiographies of Pardee Lowe and Jade Snow Wong illustrate the points of struggle between tradition and the "American" way. Personal choices endeavored to be made, yet in a way ever so delicately so as to retain some acceptable degree of parental respect and family harmony.

Filial piety, a common theme and powerful force of conflict throughout their autobiographies, is a strong Confucian ethic designed to maintain control and define the structure of authority and order within the family. The key ingredients are respect for authority, parental deference, and independence.

About the nature of authority, Pardee Lowe writes:

> For twenty-three years Father had sustained himself upon a myth: all Chinese children, especially his, were indestructibly, infallibly loyal to their parents. To him, far more than to others, our quiet acquiescence in his every wish and command brought a realization of strength that he was right, inevitably right. (Lowe 174)

On parental deference, Jade Snow concisely describes her childhood, "where respect and order ... were the key words of life" (J. Wong 2). Growing in her awareness and American dream to realize her individual aspirations—much against the wishes of her parents and the filial system of authority—she encountered intense struggle. While her father embraced both Confucian and Western values, he practiced them unevenly. Intellectually, he operated on Western values, yet emotionally, he drew his authority along Confucian ideals. Amidst this, Jade Snow fought the inconsistencies.

Moreover, her father insisted that "honor is owed to parents, before satisfying personal whims" (J. Wong 129), however, her strides to pursue independence typically marked the ABC choice:

> There were, alas, no books or advisers to guide Jade Snow in her search for balance between the pull from two cultures. If she chose neither to

reject nor accept in total, she must sift both and make her decisions alone. (J. Wong 132)

One of her conflicts is resolved as she chooses to attend college and fortunately succeeds in graduating and bringing honor to the Wong name:

For Jade Snow, the moment of triumph had come. She had proved that mama could raise her children to be a credit to the Wongs. She had shown her father and mother that without a penny from them, that she could balance her own budget and graduate from college not in debt. (181)

As a woman, Jade Snow experienced the oppressive nature of this traditional force far greater than Pardee Lowe. Of the newly arrived Wong baby in the family, she writes:

Forgiveness from heaven, because he was a brother, was more important to Mama and Daddy than dear baby sister Precious Stone, who was only a girl. But even more uncomfortable was the realization that she herself was a girl and, like her younger sister, [therefore] unalterably less significant than the new son in their family. (27)

Contradiction #2: Dual Nationalism. Dual nationalism has been a central issue among overseas Chinese everywhere. It was a central concern to the American Chinese during this period, and for many still today. The Ging Hawk Club of New York held an essay contest in 1941, in which contestants were asked to write on the subject, "Does My Future Lie in China or America?" It became a hotly debated topic after the winning essay was published in *Chinese Digest*, and its title alone aptly defines this term.

This dualism challenged and demanded strong loyalty, obligation, and commitment among overseas Chinese, and it brought much strife, confusion, and division among the ABCs, appealing to them along lines of allegiance and patriotism, their employment status and needs, and cultural identification. The winning essay, authored by William Dunn, concisely outlines these three major concerns. On patriotism, Dunn asks, "To which country do I owe the greater obligation? Which ties are more binding and why? Which country is it my desire to serve?" On employment, he continues: "Are the opportunities of obtaining remunerative employment better in China or America? Is it possible for me to find the work I am best fitted to do in America or in China?" Finally, Dunn anguishes over the issue of culture in this way:

Is my background different from that of the Chinese whom I shall contact in China, if I make my future there? Am I adaptable to a change in culture, environment, and language? (Dunn 3)

These concerns echoed among the ABC women as well, to which their responses were unequivocally supportive of both China and America. Their involvement and leadership in the 1937 war relief drive to aid China were critical and essential. In contrast, however, there is clear evidence in *East Wind* that these same women were undeniably American. Their last issue, which I found in Paul Louie's garage, describes five women who ventured on their own through a one-week bike tour along the New England towns—all by themselves, with the intent "to promote world peace, not by treaty or by statesmanship, but by creating in the hearts of the common people a deep mutual understanding (M. Wong 18). This is another indelible and passionate mark of the American Chinese.

Yet, the ensuing debate taken on by the Stanford Club questioned this dualism and was skeptical of their intent to be *bi*-cultural:

You tell us you owe allegiance to both America and China.... You express the desire to make America your home, but yet you want to help China. Do you really know what you want? (Stanford 11, 15)

The last question, to be sure, was one that haunted the ABCs throughout this period, but their quest to loosen the strangleholds of filial authority and America's sentiment of hostility brought them eventual emancipation and empowerment.

Contradiction #3: Emancipation and Empowerment. To make personal choices independent of one's family and to pursue plans for enabling and empowering—this is even yet the most significant mark of the ABC.

Kit King Louis, a sociologist of the 1930s who must be ABC at heart, describes the American Chinese in this way:

Those who seek and are willing to struggle for their opportunity and place in America, by competing with them in anticipation of earning recognition and employment on the basis of hard-earned merit. (Louis 253)

In the minds of these ABCs, there was a three-pronged plan to earn their place in America: integration—re-education—communication (M. Lee 127). Integration involved an encompassing plan to mainstream, to take on more assertive roles in the social and educational spheres of

America—not merely to become successful, but also to bring liberation and self-definition to American Chinese; independence and personal choices were their weapons. The *Digest*, *Press*, and *Wind* vividly sketched the panorama of ABC life, imbued not only in Chinatown, language school, or the family-run restaurant/laundry/curio shop, but also in tennis and golf, the picket line, the growing presence and voice of ABC women outside the family and in print.

Re-education involved educating the Americans, as well as their own Chinese American community; for their goal was to create better understanding and cooperation between the two communities. Consequently, it became essential to write, speak, and publicly address the needs and problems of the ABCs, as well as dispel myths and prejudices harbored among the other Americans. Such was the evolution of such organizations, such as the China Society of Southern California, Inc., founded in 1935 by Charles Leong, gifted and noted writer; the Chinese Women's Club of Los Angeles; the Square and Circle Club in San Francisco, and countless others from Arkansas to Baltimore.

Lastly, communication was necessary to build stronger bonds and ties within the ABC community, as well as to stimulate and strengthen their voice that needed to advocate for the empowerment and self-determination of American Chinese. Although the *Chinese Digest*, *Chinese Press*, and *East Wind* staff faced insurmountable obstacles, e.g., finances, staffing, circulation, they nevertheless endured the years because of their conviction and commitment to advocacy. Yes, they really did know what they wanted, and so did their loyal readers. What they wanted was the right to choose their own path, which may be either East or West, or perhaps even both.

Resolving the Contradictions: Chop Suey. An overseas Chinese graduate student, Homer Ch'i-Ch'en Loh, undertook his research on American Chinese in Philadelphia, and based on his findings, he concluded that ABCs were a blend of both the old and new worlds. Rather than marginalizing or diagnosing as schizophrenic, Loh instead vindicates ABCs in this way:

> What kind of men, then are Chinese-Americans? Marginal men? Possibly. But more accurately, they are "chop suey men," because they are not necessarily on the margin of two cultures. The term ... connotes two ideas:
>
> 1. Americans think they are Chinese and the Chinese think they are Americanized, just like chop suey, which Americans think is a Chinese dish, while the Chinese think it is an Americanized dish.

2. They have a bit of three cultures—the Chinese cultural heritage, the "chicken-chow-mein culture," and the American culture, just as chop suey has a bit of everything. (Loh 8)

Loh discovered a third culture on a social continuum among the American Chinese, one which more accurately depicted the breadth and complexity of their life experiences and cultural persuasions. Rather than embracing a marginal existence, ABCs chose to unite the extreme and subtle elements of Chinese and American cultures (Loh 179). And most importantly, the fluidity of this process is most important in resolving any potential struggling contradictions. While somewhat lacking in dignity and integrity, I've found Loh's typology to be the most accurate and 'palatable' in research to date. He echoes my sentiment in this way:

To be sure, no typology can ever be fully satisfactory, since some persons may represent hybrid types. The term, "chop suey men" itself embodies such a conception. (Loh 179)

An Epilogue on ABC Women. Jade Snow Wong understood the forces at work shaping the fate of Chinese American identity (J. Wong 53). In her own pilgrimage, she revealed the dynamic interplay and conflict between things American and things Chinese. The destination of her complicated quest to personhood was one which all we American Chinese search for today: self-determination.

Were it not for the two wars during these years, women like Jade Snow might not have had the open doors to grasp onto plausible and patriotic reasons to engage in non-family activities, seek employment outside of Chinatown, and even compete with their male siblings for a chance to go to college. Their coming of age was both auspicious and advantageous, freeing them from generational, cultural, and gender-specific contradictions of the old world (M. Lee 154).

The prerogative to make individual and personal choices was hers, and this should be our quest as well—not only for our own sake but for the generations that follow us into the American mosaic of life, liberty, and the pursuit of collective happiness.

Works Cited

Anonymous. *Chinese Press* 9 May 1941: 3.
Cordova, Fred. *Filipinos: Forgotten Asian Americans*. Seattle, WA: Demonstration Project for Asian Americans, 1983.
Dunn, Robert. "Does My Future Lie in China or America?" *Chinese Digest* 15 May 1936: 3.

Lee, Marjorie. "Hu-Jee: The Forgotten Second Generation of Chinese America, 1930–1950." M.A. thesis, Asian American Studies, University of California, Los Angeles, 1984.

Lee, Rose Hum. *The Chinese in the United States of America*. Hong Kong: Hong Kong University Press, 1960.

Loh, Homer Ch'i-Ch'en. "Americans of Chinese Ancestry in Philadelphia." Ph.D. thesis, Sociology, University of Pennsylvania, 1944.

Louis, Kit King. "A Study of American-Born and American-Reared Chinese in Los Angeles." M.A. thesis, Sociology, University of Southern California, 1931.

Lowe, Pardee. *Father and Glorious Descendant*. Boston: Little, Brown and Company, 1943.

Mao, Tsetung. *Selected Readings from the Works of Mao Tsetung*. Peking: Foreign Languages Press, 1971.

Stanford University Chinese Students Club. "Firecrackers." *Chinese Digest* 22 May 1936: 11, 15.

Wong, Jade Snow. *Fifth Chinese Daughter*. New York: Macmillan & Company, 1945.

Wong, Marilyn and Rita Quan. "A-hosteling We Will Go." *East Wind* (Summer 1948): 18–19.

Destination:
Nevada, the Silver Mountain

SUE FAWN CHUNG
Department of History, University of Nevada, Las Vegas, Nevada

In the late 19th century, the Chinese flocked to Yinshan, "Silver Mountain," the Chinese name for Nevada, for two main economic reasons: (1) mining, including its subsidiary occupations such as irrigation work, cooking, laundry, and woodcutting, and (2) railroads, including road work, construction, and maintenance. By 1880, their population of 5,416 constituted 8.7% of the state's total population of 62,266 and 20% of the state's 44% foreign-born population of 25,690 (U.S. Census 6/1880). Until recently, their greatest impact upon Nevada occurred in the late 19th century. Little is known about these Chinese in Nevada, and as a result, there are many misconceptions about their experiences and their accomplishments, which have not been fully appreciated.[1] This preliminary study of the Chinese in the Silver Mountain hopes to correct some of the misunderstandings. Although the setting is limited to Nevada, the experiences were not unlike that in many other parts of the American West.

The overwhelming majority of Chinese Nevadans in the late 19th century were men. The Census Manuscripts, especially for 1880, indicated that a substantial number were married and that some had wives and children living in or around the area. Statewide, in 1870 there were 2,817 men to the 306 women, and by 1880 this ratio changed from 5,102 men to 314 women, as illustrated in the table below. According to the Census Manuscripts for Nevada in 1880, approximately an average of one-third of the men were married—but they did not always live with their spouses. For example, in 1880 in the state capital of Carson City, of the 789 Chinese, 706 were men and of these, 267 were married, 18 were widowed, 391 were single, and 30 gave no information (Census Manuscript 1880). Among the 83 women there, 21 were married, 58 were single, and 4 gave no information. There were seven complete families,

---

[1]The major works are Chung 43–51; Loren B. Chan 266–314, and BeDunnah 1973.

that is, a listing of either two married adults, with or without children, or a parent with a child or children. The Census Manuscript for 1880 also listed three Chinese school teachers, suggesting that there were more than the 19 reported children, age 15 and under. In the mining community of Tuscarora, Elko County, the Census Manuscript enumerated only 224 Chinese, despite the popular belief that 2,000 Chinese lived there.[2] Of the 204 Chinese males, 63 were married, 2 were widowed, 133 were single, and 6 gave no information. Of the 20 females, 8 were married, 10 were single, and 2 gave no information. Of the 8 married women, 6 lived with their husbands, one lived with her five-year-old son, who was born in China, and the other lived with two female boarders. In comparison, in relatively isolated White Pine County, of the 115 Chinese, only 16 among the 102 men (including one child) were married. Of the 13 women there, five were married. Just five years earlier, in 1875, when a special state census was taken and when the Page Law, which severely limited the immigration of Chinese women, was passed,[3] White Pine County had an unusual ratio of 60 Chinese males and 20 Chinese females. Among these females, only seven were "courtesans," and the remainder were either married, living with their spouses, or "keeping house," probably for miners living in the general area (Nevada 1878). This data suggests that a small percentage of Chinese Nevadans planned or hoped to settle in the United States; that they were not sojourners, as they have often been described.

The census takers often missed Chinese women. The hardships of daily living in Nevada, including the extremes of the weather, the lack of water, the absence of family or clan support, and the isolation discouraged many Chinese immigrant women from remaining in Nevada. Those who came probably left within a short period of time. However, there were probably more women than the census data indicated. Although prostitutes were usually counted for taxation purposes, other women were undoubtedly missed due to lack of communication skills both on the part of the census taker and on the part of the Chinese; the traditional Chinese practice of women remaining secluded at home; the dangers of promiscuity, hostility and violence by Chinese and others, and the problem of kidnapping, which was not limited to prostitutes but also included innocent young girls.[4] By

---

[2]The number of buildings and stores in Tuscarora's two physically separated Chinatowns show that there had to be more Chinese living there. See the Sanborn Map of Tuscarora on microfilm.

[3]For more information on the Page Law, see Chan 1991.

[4]A typical example of the recurring problem of the kidnapping of prostitutes is seen in the Virginia City *Evening Chronicle* [hereafter abbreviated *VEC*], June 11, 1867. Winnemucca Chinese merchant Tong Ting's 10- or 11-year-old daughter was kidnapped by a Chinese, but later was found with the help of the

comparing the 12 marriage licenses taken out between 1874 and 1882 in Virginia City (location of the largest Chinatown in Nevada in the late 19th century), to the 1870 and 1880 Census Manuscripts, the majority of the newly married couples were omitted from the census. The names of only one couple, that of the prostitute You Gang and her husband Ah Yung, were in the 1880 Census Manuscript. The local newspapers announced the marriage of two other couples (Storey County 1982). One can assume one or two of the couples left the area, but some of the other names should have been included in the Census Manuscript. Thus the population in Table 1 is not accurate, but gives a representative profile of the number of Chinese in the state. Prior to 1930, the increasing and decreasing Chinese population reflected the trends of the state, which was greatly affected by "boom and bust" cycles.

Early Chinese Miners. The Chinese called California *Jinshan* (Gum Shan in Cantonese), or Gold Mountain, and Nevada *Yinshan* (Genug Shan in Cantonese), or Silver Mountain.[5] This was not surprising since the main lure to the American West was mining. However, it was irrigation work for mining that first brought the Chinese to that part of the Utah Territory, which would become the state of Nevada in October, 1864. As early as 1852, some Chinese ditch diggers were observed in the area, which later became known as Dayton, Nevada (Smith 162). Their reputation as industrious laborers persuaded John Reese, who led a group of Mormons from Salt Lake City into the Carson Valley, to hire 50 Chinese laborers from California in 1855 to dig an irrigation ditch from the Carson River to Gold Canyon, making mining possible in the area of present-day Genoa, the first non-Indian permanent settlement. These probable contract laborers were the first of many Chinese contract laborers in the Silver State, and this type of occupation would continue for the Chinese through the early 20th century. The contract laborers generally came from the same village or district or dialect grouping, and this may account for the dominance of one surname or home district in the scattered Nevada Chinese communities.

Winters were harsh during the two years of construction (1856–1858), so the Chinese probably returned to California each winter. The Mormons were so impressed by the hard-working Chinese that they allowed them to stay in the area to participate in mining when the irrigation construction ended. This initial group of Chinese was joined by

---

community, story quoted from the Winnemucca *Silver State* in the *Eureka Daily Sentinel* [hereafter abbreviated *EDS*], January 7, 1882. The family is not listed in the 1880 Census Manuscript.

[5]The characters were inscribed on the Chee Kong Tong, Carson City, altar pieces, now on display at the Carson City State Museum. Identical altar pieces were in the Elko "Joss House" altar.

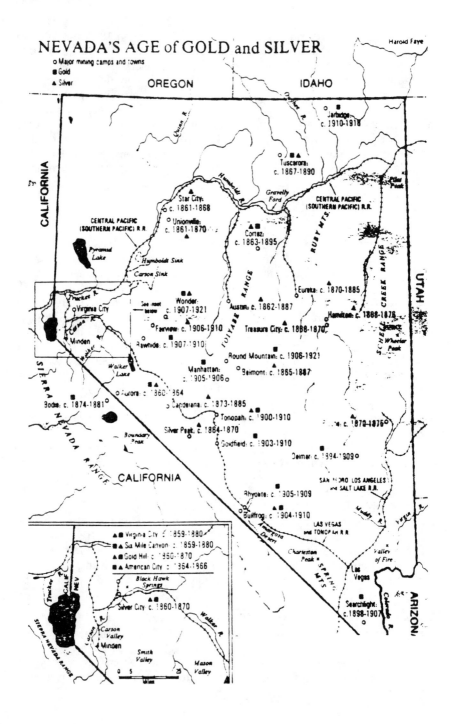

NEVADA'S AGE of GOLD and SILVER

o Major mining camps and towns
■ Gold
▲ Silver

Harold Faye

OREGON   IDAHO

CALIFORNIA

Jarbidge: c. 1910-1918

Tuscarora: c. 1867-1890

Star City: c. 1861-1868

Unionville: c. 1861-1870

CENTRAL PACIFIC (SOUTHERN PACIFIC) R.R.

Pyramid Lake

Humboldt Sink

Carson Sink

Gravelly Ford

CENTRAL PACIFIC (SOUTHERN PACIFIC) R.R.

Cortez: c. 1863-1895

Eureka: c. 1870-1885

See inset below

Virginia City

Minden

Wonder: c. 1907-1921

Fairview: c. 1906-1910

Rawhide: c. 1907-1910

Walker Lake

Bodie: c. 1874-1881

Candelaria: c. 1873-1885

Silver Peak: c. 1864-1870

Aurora: c. 1860-1864

Austin: c. 1862-1887

Treasure City: c. 1868-1870

Hamilton: c. 1868-1875

Round Mountain: c. 1906-1921

Manhattan: c. 1905-1906

Belmont: c. 1865-1887

Tonopah: c. 1900-1910

Goldfield: c. 1903-1910

c. 1870-1875

Delmar: c. 1894-1909

CALIFORNIA

Rhyolite: c. 1905-1909

Bullfrog: c. 1904-1910

SAN PEDRO LOS ANGELES and SALT LAKE R.R.

LAS VEGAS and TONOPAH R.R.

Boundary Peak

Charleston Peak

Las Vegas

Valley of Fire

Searchlight: c. 1898-1907

ARIZONA

■▲ Virginia City c. 1859-1880
■▲ Six Mile Canyon c. 1859-1880
■ Gold Hill c. 1850-1870
■▲ American City c. 1864-1966

Black Hawk Springs

Silver City c. 1860-1870

Carson Valley

Minden

Smith Valley

Mason Valley

0 5   25
Miles

114

others, bringing the total to approximately 200 and eventually the first "Chinatown" (its early name) was established in what was later to become known as Dayton, located just south of present-day Virginia City (Magnaghi 130). A newspaper article in Genoa's *Territorial Enterprise*, April 21, 1859, reflected the more positive attitude felt by some of the European American population in the area in regards to mining prospects: "...we hope that the 'good time coming' which has so long been in anticipation by the Celestials [Chinese] is near at hand."

These early Chinese miners followed the European Americans around the state to one "boom town" after another. This was in sharp contrast to their traditional lifestyle of settlement in one village or locality for generations. A few would become attached to a particular area and tenaciously remain despite the "boom and bust" cycles of the local economy. The Chinese in the placer mining town of Tuscarora, which experienced its boom in the 1870s, were just one of many examples.[6] Ah Lee Lake (surname Lee/Li), a wealthy merchant of Tuscarora and Chee Kong Tong leader, profited from the boom and remained in the area until the early 20th century. According to the 1910 Census Manuscript, Lee Lake was born in September, 1855, and immigrated in 1869. By 1884, he was the manager of the Quong Hing Lung & Company and had as partners, Lee Gung, Chin Fook, Chin Wing Yuen, and Lee Gee (Immigration and Naturalization File #113561/139). As a labor contractor, as some Chinese merchants were, he not only hired Chinese laborers, but also recruited European American laborers for work in the region. He moved with relative ease in the larger community, and when one of the prominent Tuscarora citizens, Arthur Primeaux, was on his honeymoon in San Francisco, Ah Lee Lake also was there, and he honored the newlyweds with an extravagant Chinese banquet. Upon his return from one of his numerous trips to China, he brought Postmaster James Beveride a quilted satin embroidered jacket (*TTR* 6/30/1897). Although Ah Lee Lake made many trips to China and San Francisco, he considered Tuscarora, and then Elko at the turn of the century, his home.

However, living in Nevada required an adventuresome and hearty person. The environmental conditions were very different from the humidity of South China, where the majority of Chinese immigrants were born and raised. Two deserts separate the state into two distinct parts. Northern Nevada, approximately 75% of the state, is part of the Great Basin Desert, with a base elevation ranging from around 4,500 to 6,200 feet, over 200 mountain ranges, and average temperatures that

---

[6]LuAnn Caressi, a master's degree candidate at UNLV, has been studying the Tuscarora and Eureka Chinese communities. Her thesis in history will be completed in 1995. I am indebted to her for much of the information on these communities.

range from nine degrees Fahrenheit in winter and 90 degrees Fahrenheit in summer in the Reno area. Southern Nevada is part of the Mojave Desert; is much lower in elevation, starting at 490 feet to 2,000 feet around Las Vegas to about 4,000 feet, and is much drier and hotter, with average temperatures ranging from 32 degrees Fahrenheit in the winter to 115 degrees Fahrenheit in the summer in the Las Vegas area. The harsh environmental conditions, often punctuated by floods and natural calamities; combined with the continual danger of fires breaking out in the towns and communities; along with the "boom and bust" economic cycles around the state required a independent, flexible, relatively mobile, and healthy person. The lack of medical care often meant that the Chinese had to travel to San Francisco for traditional Chinese medical treatment.

The lawlessness and rowdy nature of a predominantly single, male, European American population involved in mining and ranching—both highly mobile occupations—and the dangers of encountering a hostile Native American tribe also discouraged many Chinese from remaining in Nevada. In the 1860s, Quong Kee (b. ca. 1851; d. 1938 in Bisbee, AZ), a cook's helper in Virginia City, the first large Chinese settlement in Nevada, summarized his feelings about life there (Burgess 14–16):

> Me scaird all the time, plenty wild men. All the time in Virginia City some one get robbed—bang, someone dies in the streets. When the Vigilantes come, they brave men. They catch robbers and hang five in one day. Plenty excitement in Virginia City.

One of the major attractions to mining in Nevada was the ability to own property. Although land transactions were seldom recorded during these early years and oral agreements on land sales were made as late as 1900, the Chinese were active in land investments. As in all predominantly agricultural societies, land ownership was very important to the Chinese. As early as 1861, Virginia City's land records showed some Chinese busily buying and selling land (Ellison 261–262). In response to the large foreign-born population in the state, which in 1880 made up 44% of the total population, the Nevada Constitution, adopted in 1864, in Article I, Section 16, allowed "foreigners who are or may hereafter become *bona fide* residents of this state shall enjoy the same rights in respect to the possession, enjoyment, and inheritance of property as native-born citizens."[7] Reacting to the growing anti-Chinese sentiment in the American West, in February, 1879, the Nevada Legislature tried to restrict the Chinese from owning land by adding the

---

[7]The Article was reaffirmed in an 1884 Supreme Court decision, *State ex rel v. Fook Ling*, Preble 18 Nev 251, 2 Pac 754 (1884). Elmer Rusco elaborates upon this in his forthcoming article.

clause that foreigners, "except the subjects of the Chinese empire" may hold real property, but this was challenged by Fook Ling in 1884 when the state refused to sell him "non-vacant mineral lands belonging to the state..." (Nevada Statutes 1879). The State Supreme Court held that a resident Chinese had the right to own property as stated in the State Constitution and that the Legislature could not abridge this right. "The rights thus guaranteed by the constitution cannot be taken away," Chief Justice T. P. Hawley wrote. Nevertheless, yielding to prevailing anti-Asian sentiments and alien land laws, the Legislature, through a general election, repealed this constitutional provision in 1924, but those who already held property could continue to do so (Nevada Statutes 1921). Eventually, in 1947, in response to the post-war national sentiment favoring the Chinese, the law changed to allow the Chinese, whether residents or not, to own real property (Nevada Statutes 1947). In 1957, the Revised Code essentially revived Article I, Section 16, and in 1965, all restrictions and prohibitions related to any person of a specified race was voided. To own land was very important to the Chinese, so it was not surprising that when they could afford it, they bought land for mining, farming, and other endeavors.

Success in mining often led to discrimination. In 1859 working placers near Gold Canyon, a group of some fifty Chinese reportedly earned over $35,000 for their year's work (Miller 300). Some European American miners who had been mining in California were quick to recognize the danger of the presence of the Chinese, and they passed local mining laws similar to the ones in California to keep the Chinese miners out of their communities. This Gold Hill Miner's Resolution, passed in 1859, was typical of the early hostile attitude toward the Chinese in mining: "Sec. 11. No Chinaman shall be allowed to hold a claim in this district." (quoted in BeDunnah 5–7) However, this provision did not appear in rules adopted subsequently in Virginia City and other mining camps throughout Nevada.[8] Two companies of Chinese placer miners were observed in the Gold Canyon area in 1880, "making pretty good wages" (VEC 7/22/1880). More often, however, the Chinese ended up working in jobs supporting miners.

As the decades passed, the reputation of Chinese cooks was such that any mine owner who wanted to keep his miners on the job had to hire Chinese cooks. Mine owners also employed Chinese in other capacities, such as hauling wood, roadwork, and laundry work.

In Silver Peak, Esmeralda County, the *Engineering and Mining Journal* of July 13, 1869 reported that 100 men were employed at the mine and mill; of this number, 40 were Chinese and 60 were European Americans with the Chinese receiving $1 per day and board and the European

---

[8]Elmer Rusco is currently writing about the legal aspects of the Chinese Nevadan experience. See also Lord 91–92, 355–359; McMurtrie 31, and Kelly 476–480.

Americans, whose jobs often were dangerous or required specific skills, receiving $70 per month with board (Shamberger 11). The average bullion shipments from the mill was $200,000 per month.

The isolation of the area did not discourage one Chinese from remaining there for some 35 years.[9] The Chinese also found employment in mining towns throughout the state.

Carson City, which was the state capital and was located in the vicinity of the rich Comstock Lode, offered a insight into the variety of jobs held by the Chinese. In 1870, the 678 Chinese worked in 16 different types of jobs: servant, waiter, cook, farmer, clerk, merchant, paper hanger, shoemaker, tailor, laborer, lumberman, contractor, physician, "keeping house" (including housewives), prostitute, and laundryman (Braunstein). In 1880, the 789 Chinese held 60 different jobs: bootblack, dishwasher, gardener, packer, porter, rag picker, servant, waiter, cook, farmer, fisherman, herder, huckster, locksmith, mule packer, peddler, sailor, scissors grinder, trainer, baker, barber, blacksmith, butcher, carpenter, clerk, chair maker, cooper, dyer, fan maker, hairdresser, hostelry, jeweler, lumberman, merchant, miller, painter, restaurant owner or worker, shoemaker, tailor, teamster, watchmaker and repairer, weaver, wood dealer, laborer, bookkeeper, chemist, dealer, dentist, physician, pharmacist, gambler, joss house operator, opium den owner, student, teacher, housewife, "keeping house," ironer, laundry owner, laundryman. The variety of occupations indicated a relatively self-sufficient community with some members who interacted with the larger community. Elsewhere in the area, there were Chinese cowboys, sheepherders, railroad workers, and assayers as other main types of employment.

In Tuscarora, Elko County, there seemed to be a toleration, if not friendship, between the European Americans and Chinese. In 1870, European American miners hired 200 Chinese laborers to dig a ditch six miles across the mountain to enable the continuation of placer mining. A photograph of a group of European American miners and Chinese miners (Primeaux Collection); the fact that the Chinese band greeted the winning Tuscarora sports team after a victory out of town; the inclusion of the Chinese band in the Fourth of July Parade in 1898, and the close friendship between prominent European American and Chinese community leaders indicated a more cordial race relationship than that found in some Nevada mining communities. The isolation of the town contributed to the interdependence and interaction of all of the community members, and oftentimes the cordiality was shaped by the community leaders, which was the case for Tuscarora.

---

[9]Headstone now in the collection of the Central Nevada Museum, Tonopah, NV. I am indebted to the Museum's staff for their help in ferreting out unusual information on Nye and Esmeralda Counties.

By the end of 1870, most of the European American miners had moved out of Old Town in Tuscarora. As in California and elsewhere in Nevada, they sold or leased their "worked out" claims to the Chinese, who, in 1871, were estimated to number between 800 to 1,000. This probably was an exaggerated figure, but nonetheless, the Chinese reportedly took out close to a half million dollars in gold that year. (*Elko Independent* 1871). The population was large enough to be able to support two "joss houses" (a Hop Sing Tong and a Chee Kung Tong local headquarters), several stores, restaurants, laundries, gambling halls, underground opium dens, and houses of prostitution.

Each of the tongs probably hired its own physician, who at first treated only the Chinese community, but later expanded his practice to treat others in the town.[10] Like many other immigrant "brotherhoods," the tongs provided mutual aid services to its members, including the very important service of shipping the bones of the deceased back to China so that the spirit could rest in familiar surroundings.[11] When the placer mining gave out, the Chinese realized that hydraulic machinery would enable them to bring more ore out, so in 1884 they ordered the equipment from San Francisco and took out over $30,000 from Skinned Hill near Chinatown (*Tuscarora Times and Mining Review* 1885). This figure was the estimate from the local newspaper and may have been low since the Chinese, by 1880, had two assayers of their own. Like any boom town, the bust came in the 1890s, and by 1899 there were only 12 Chinese miners left in Tuscarora, almost all of whom were property owners, the last one dying in 1927 (Townley 11, 28).

Sometimes the Chinese were able to find isolated areas where they dominated the mining community. In Spring Canyon, just south of Unionville, Humboldt County, about 200 Chinese reportedly shipped $60,000 in gold dust in the fall of 1876 (Virginia City, *Territorial Enterprise,* 1877). The population was prosperous enough to support four Chinese stores. Like many of the smaller Chinese communities, the capital investment was small. For example, the Kia Hop & Company, which sold merchandise to the Chinese miners and was located there from 1891 to 1895, was owned by Lee Kia and Lee Sing Goy, each of whom had invested $1,000 in the business (National Archives File 13567/84). Four miles southwest, in American Canyon, Wong Kee (a common Chinese name in Nevada) headed a mining operation from 1885 to 1905 and employed as many as 900 men at one time, but by 1905, only 10 old Chinese men were still working Wong Kee's mine (Bragg 20–21). The

---

[10]This is a tentative hypothesis based primarily on an article about Dr. Chin Lee of Virginia City, *VEC*, January 12, 1878, but the same trend is seen elsewhere in the state.

[11]For more information about Chinese community organizations such as these, see Lai 1992, Chapter 2.

Canyon supported a Chinatown, which had a Joss House at its entrance and was guarded by a man who stayed there until his death in 1925 (Hansen 20–21).[12] Between Spring Valley and American Canyon, the Chinese reportedly took out $19 million in placer gold (Bragg, op. cit. 18). Although the area was basically abandoned by the 1910s, remnants remained until a flood destroyed all of the buildings in 1925. In nearby Barber Canyon, another Chinese miner in 1900 purchased a mine in an area that produced over a million dollars in placer mining, and in 1905, he discovered that it was a rich quartz mining site (Bragg, op. cit. 32). Placer mining continued to attract the Chinese throughout the late nineteenth and twentieth centuries, but because of the European American hostility, many Chinese miners were never counted in the Census, and their earnings were kept a secret or were only modestly reported.

Because the state had predominantly hardrock mining, which required large capital investments, the Chinese placer miners were not considered a major threat by the majority of European American miners. In 1870, at the peak of Nevada's mineral recovery, the total mining force in the state was 8,300 men, or about 20% of the state's total population of 42,491; but of the 3,152 Chinese in the state, only 240 men, or 8%, were listed as miners by the Census (U.S. Bureau of the Census 1870). Obviously, this count was far below what the general population and local reporters felt was true. By 1877, Nevada was out-producing California in gold and brought in a record $18 million to California's $15 million (Gregory 123). Moreover, the Chinese did become involved in capitalized mining. Chinese in San Francisco invested some $20,000 in an 1860s mining operation in Cortez (about 68 miles northeast of Austin) under the direction of a European American, Simon Wenban, who hired a Chinese foreman and Chinese miners to work the operation (Chan, op. cit. 283; Labbe 93–94, Angel 428–29). Wenban protected his Chinese workers, but only paid the miners $1.50 per day, millmen $2.50 per 12 hours, and woodcutters $2.50 per cord—far below the prevailing wage scale. Reputedly, the Chinese workers were very loyal to Wenban, but by the 1880s, the area was depleted and the miners had to move elsewhere. Some may have gone to Osceola, White Pine County, which was founded in 1877, and by 1882 boasted a total population of 1,500 with 400 mining claims.[13] Chinese laborers were hired to construct the 16-mile long West Ditch between 1884 and 1885 and the 18-mile, 19-feet long East

---

[12]One can assume that this "joss house" was a Chee Kong Tong local headquarters because all of the major Chinese communities in Nevada had a Chee Kong Tong branch. The pattern of one old man guarding the "joss house" (a Chee Kong Tong branch) until around 1930 was seen in Carson City as well.
[13]I am indebted to Sean Pitts of Ely for the information on Osceola. See also Paher 1970.

Ditch, which was completed in July, 1890. After digging the ditches, the Chinese were able to participate in the placer mining. However, the 1890 Census enumerated only 46 Chinese in the entire County. During its 20 years of prosperity, Osceola produced about two million dollars, including the largest gold nugget ever found in the state. By 1906, the mines were defunct and by 1920 the town was deserted. As in other "boom and bust" situations, the Chinese had moved elsewhere when the local economy faltered.

There were other types of mining in the state as well. For example, in Columbus, several hundred Chinese worked for the Pacific Coast Borax Company (of the "Twenty Mule Team" fame), obtaining borax and other minerals by heating marsh water in evaporation boilers. The Chinese maintained the roads, collected the wood for heating the boilers, and performed numerous other duties. Borax mining started to decline in 1875, but the production continued until the 1890s (Woodman 58).

Wood gathering and lumbering were other auxiliary occupations of mining that the Chinese tended to dominate. Not far from Osceola, White Pine County, the six Ward Charcoal Ovens, the largest ovens in Nevada designed and operated by Italian immigrants, were supplied with wood by Chinese lumbermen between 1876 and 1878; thus allowing the smelting of the local ore. Chinese lumbermen also worked in the Lake Tahoe area and other parts of the state, cutting down large trees for the railroad ties and other construction projects in the state.

Many times, however, the Chinese found a more stable job, such as cooking, and had the side occupation of mining; for example, Sam Wing (b. February, 1857, immigrated 1875) of Union Canyon, Nye County, a saloon-restaurant owner in the Reese River mining area, was also part-owner of the Bricklode Mine in Tonopah.[14] The Chinese merchant, Low Wing (surname Low/Lo) of Winnemucca, Humboldt County, also liked to "poke around" when business was slow (Chun 1993). However, the Chinese realized that wealth was not only in the mines, but also in service occupations, especially laundrymen and cooks.

Although the 1860 Utah Territory Census Manuscript enumerated only 22 Chinese males in Carson County (which included Virginia City, Truckee Meadows, Dayton, and Carson City), a pattern of settlement, which characterized almost all other Chinese Nevadan communities, became evident: relatives and fellow villagers tended to settle together in order to be protective and supportive of each other and to recreate some of the familiar traditions. Therefore, of the 14 Virginia City Chinese of 1860, five had the surname of Ling and worked as launderers, one of the

---

[14]Sam Wing is commemorated in a plaque in Union Canyon; his ownership in the Bricklode Mine in Tonopah is recorded in the *Nye County Deeds Book*.

major occupations of the Chinese in the American West.[15] Most of the Chinese lived in Chinatowns, but because of the nature of the laundry business—especially the necessity to be conveniently located in the immediate neighborhood—the Chinese laundrymen lived outside of Chinatown as well.[16] As the years passed and they realized that they needed to be organized, they formed an association which limited the density of laundries, as well as set fees for services (Caressi, op. cit.). The trade was labor-intensive, but it also required a certain capital investment for rent and equipment (Siu 1987). Innovative irons, heated by coals just above the flat ironing surface, attention to details, and reliability allowed them to dominate the laundry business.[17] Sam Kee of Eureka was one of many examples of a successful laundryman (*EDS* 3/12/1877). He immigrated in 1849 and lived in Oregon, British Columbia, Washington, Idaho, and Montana before settling in Eureka in 1869. He was the first to establish a laundry in Eureka when the boom began in the 1870s, and he eventually accumulated about $18,000. This enabled him to visit China three times, with one stay lasting two years; then he returned to Eureka, purchased a small building which housed a store and fan-tan games. During his affluent years, he became addicted to opium, and in 1878, he fell seriously ill. According to the local newspaper account, the *tong* to which he belonged sent him to San Francisco in August or September for medical treatment, but he died there in November, 1878 and was mourned by those who knew him in Eureka.

Laundry work in a mining town was usually the work of European American women, especially those whose husbands had died in the mines. Although most Chinese Nevadan women were involved in "keeping house" or prostitution, there were a few cases of Chinese women in the laundry business in mining towns. In the 1870 Census Manuscript, the only five Chinese women living in the notoriously lawless and rowdy town of Pioche, Lincoln County, listed their occupation as "laundry." Other Chinese launderers usually worked with their husbands; but this Pioche group, if they had worked together, would have been in a relatively large business for that time and place.

---

[15]Ronald James has written an article on the laundries of Virginia City, publication forthcoming.
[16]See map of Virginia City in 1880 as an example; from James, forthcoming publication.
[17]The irons can be seen in an exhibit at the Northern Arizona Museum in Flagstaff, AZ.
In one case a European American laundry was opened to compete with the local Chinese, but could not make it despite the $3,000 capitalization and in the end, mounds of clothes were heaped on the sidewalk for all takers when the laundry closed its door.

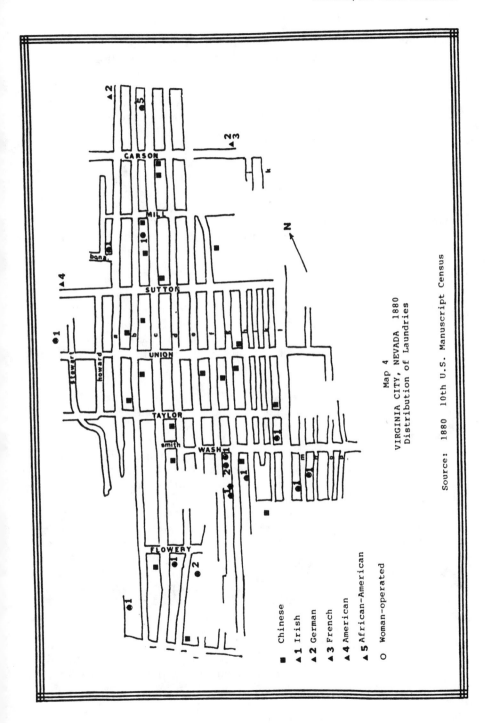

Map 4

VIRGINIA CITY, NEVADA 1880
Distribution of Laundries

Source: 1880 10th U.S. Manuscript Census

■ Chinese
▲1 Irish
▲2 German
▲3 French
▲4 American
▲5 African-American
O Woman-operated

Some Chinese miners, cooks, laundrymen, mule packers, prostitutes, merchants, and physicians in the Nevada mining communities were successful. A combination of luck and hard work in a relatively tolerant community helped in this success. This was indicated in the reported wealth of prosperous individuals in the Census Manuscripts, as well as in newspaper articles. The other main economic attraction brought even more Chinese men to the state.

Chinese Railroad Workers. The largest influx of Chinese into the state occurred because of the construction of the Central Pacific Railroad that would link the entire continent (Kraus 42–57). In a desperate effort to find reliable workers, Charles Crocker (1827–1888), the dynamic chief contractor of construction and one of the Big Four owners of the Central Pacific, against the advice of many, turned to the Chinese to fill the labor requirements. As a result, they became known as "Crocker's Pets." As S. S. Montague, in his annual report of 1865, stated:

> It became apparent ... that the amount of labor likely to be required during the summer could only be supplied by employment of the Chinese.... Some distrust was at first felt ... but the experiment has proven eminently successful. They are faithful and industrious and, under proper supervision, soon become skillful in the performance of their duty (Heath 12).

Eventually, the Chinese constituted 90% of the Central Pacific laborers. According to Central Pacific officials, over half of the Chinese hired were already in the Western United States, while the rest were recruited directly from China through labor contractors, most notably the San Francisco firms Koopmanschap & Company and Sisson, Walter, & Company (for whom Charles Crocker's brother, Clark, worked) (Barth 117). Some 5,000–12,000 Chinese railroad workers passed through Nevada between December 13, 1867 and May 10, 1869. Workers were needed to move tons of earth, level the track beds, build the grade, bridge rivers and canyons, and tunnel through granite mountains. The Chinese worked as masons, track layers, blacksmiths, and explosive handlers, to name a few jobs (Yen 111). The cold winters and deep snows of the Sierra Nevadas were in sharp contrast to the scorching heat and vast waterless stretches of sand and sage in northern Nevada.

The average working force of 11,500 men in the Sierra Mountains was reduced by mid-1868 to some 5,000 men. The main reasons for the smaller labor force were the comparatively flat terrain of Nevada and the fact that materials, such as timber ties which were in short supply in Nevada, could be shipped by train to Reno by mid-June, 1868 (Raymond and Fike 7). One of the major accomplishments of this later work force was the laying of 555 miles of track in less than ten months, between

July, 1868 and May, 1869 (U.S. Congress, Senate). Thus the common misperception that 12,000 Chinese laborers were left stranded in Promontory, Utah, in May, 1869 was erroneous.

One of the main criticisms of European Americans was the low wages paid to the Chinese railroad workers, but a closer examination of the situation suggested that the difference has been exaggerated. By 1866–1867, the average salary of the 11,500 Chinese workers salary was $35 for a 26-day month, the same as that paid to the 2,500–3,000 European American workers, but the critical difference was that at first, the Chinese paid their own board from their wages, while the Central Pacific paid an estimated additional $3 to $5 per day for the European American board (U.S. Pacific Railway Commission). An intermediary-broker received the salary from the railroad, deducted the cost of board, then paid the workers approximately $20 to $25 per month in actual wages (*San Francisco Alta California* 11/16/1867). In many cases, a European American clerk kept the accounts accurate, charging a monthly service fee of $1. The small salary represented much more than the average Chinese farmer made in Guangdong at this time, and it was combined with meals, often banquet-like, paid for by the railroad company. The daily availability of meat and the endless supply of hot tea, which meant that the Chinese suffered less from the cramps and dysentery that afflicted the other workers, made the arduous labor bearable for many of the Chinese. Every Sunday there was a freshly killed chicken (a rarity in Guangdong at this time). Rice, vermicelli, bean sprouts, bamboo shoots, various kinds of Chinese vegetables, four kinds of dried fruit, dried oysters, abalone and fish, dried seaweed, Chinese sausages, and peanut oil were imported directly from Hong Kong or Canton or were purchased from San Francisco merchants.

Life was very arduous for the Chinese railroad workers. The work day began at sunrise and ended at sunset, six days a week. Sundays were spent doing laundry, mending clothes, talking, smoking, and gambling among themselves. During the construction through Nevada, they lived primarily in tents, which was not uncommon temporary housing for many Nevadans of the time. One observer noted that the Chinese camps were organized in groups of three: two with 100 white tents each and one with 75. This was shelter against the wind and rain, but not against the heat and cold of the desert climate. James Harvey Strobridge (1827–1921), the able but arrogant construction superintendent who originally opposed the Chinese hiring on the grounds that they were not physically strong enough for the tasks, strictly prohibited opium smoking, gambling in gambling halls, or any type of indulgences that would prevent the Chinese from effective work. While in Nevada, he even prohibited them from celebrating Chinese New Year's because of the heavy work schedule (Griswold, op. cit. 306). When disputes broke out among the Chinese, as it did between the laborers of the *Sze Yup* and

Yeoung Wo district associations at Victory (eight miles east of Promontory, Utah), Strobridge and the Chinese headman quickly rushed in to restore order (*San Francisco Evening Bulletin* 5/8/1869, Myrick 19, Griswold op. cit. 112). Another staunch opponent to the use of Chinese labor was Thomas C. Durant, Vice-President of the Union Pacific Railroad; but by October 16, 1868, he had been convinced of the value of the Chinese laborers, and he hired 3,000 Chinese to work at Wells, Elko County, Nevada, thinking that Wells would be the meeting point of the two lines (Myrick 19).[18] The traits that were admired were expressed by Charles Crocker when he said: "Wherever we put them, we found them good and they worked themselves into our favor to such an extent that if we found we were in a hurry for a job... it was better to put Chinese on at once" (Griswold, op. cit. 112). The praise for their work was reiterated by a reporter for the *Alta California*, November 9, 1868, who wrote: "Systematic workers these Chinese—competent and wonderfully effective because [of their] tireless[ness] and unremitting in their industry." A belief in the efficiency of the Chinese workers led to the never-broken tracklaying record.

On April 28, 1869, as a result of a $10,000 wager between Crocker of the Central Pacific and Durant of the Union Pacific, 10 miles and 56 feet of track were laid some 3.5 miles from Promontory, Utah, within 12 hours using a crew of 4,000 men, most of whom were Chinese. On that day a San Francisco *Bulletin* reporter wrote: "In eight minutes, sixteen cars [of bolts, spikes, fish plates, and iron rails] were cleared, with a noise like the bombardment of an army."

Precise work and coordination were required. 3,520 rails, each 30 feet long, were laid at an average rate of 240 feet per one minute and fifteen seconds (McCague 307–308). All of the railroad leaders were extremely impressed and a sign was posted to commemorate the accomplishment. This feat has never been equaled.

On May 10, 1869, the Transcontinental Railroad was completed. Because of an accident caused by Chinese railroad loggers to the engine "Antelope" as it traveled through the Truckee River Valley toward Reno, the engine "Jupiter" had to be substituted at the last minute for the Golden Spike Ceremony (Best 72). At about 10:30 that morning, the Chinese began the final grading for the last two rails, the laying of the ties and rails, the driving of the spikes, and the bolting of the fishplates of the west rail. They also probably started a number of the spikes that were later ceremoniously "driven in" by the celebrities (Bowman 94). Two final rails were laid: one carried by a squad of Chinese workers under the direction of their boss, H. H. Minkler, for the Central Pacific, and another

---

[18]No rails were laid by the Union Pacific in Wells. The Chinese primarily did the grading work. The significance was that Durant had changed his mind and was willing to hire them.

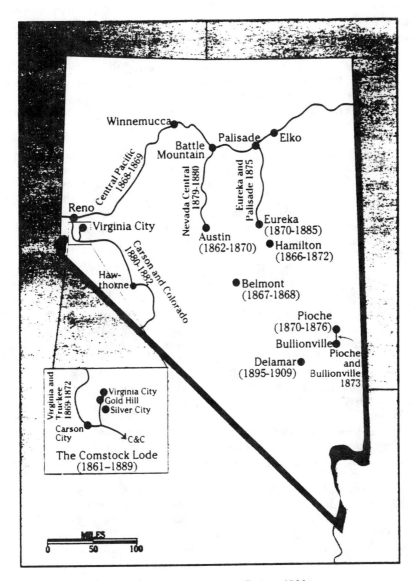

Bonanzas and Railroads (Before 1900)

Source: James W. Hulse, <u>The Silver State:</u>
<u>Nevada's Heritage Reinterpreted</u> (Reno, NV:
University of Nevada Press, 1991), p. 116

carried by an Irish squad under their foreman. When Leland Stanford and Charles Durant tried to hammer in the iron spikes, they missed and the Chinese had to finish the job (Griswold, op. cit. 329). After it was all over, there were the souvenir hunters; and whatever was taken, including a tie which the Chinese allegedly cut into pieces, had to be replaced by the Chinese workmen.

However, there was a common belief that few Chinese were present at the ceremony. According to one influential account:

> The bulk of the Chinese and other workers who had completed the line by May 1 had been shunted westward to improve certain points of the line, leaving only a few, perhaps a dozen, to do the grading, lay the ties and drive the few spikes of the west rail, lay the east rail for the ceremony, and replace the laurel tie. The bulk of the Union Pacific workmen had also been shunted to eastern points for line improvement. (Bowman, op. cit. 90–91)

This differs from the account of Union Pacific's Chief Engineer Major Grenville M. Dodge, who observed several hundred Chinese at the ceremony (Dodge 1966). Quong Kee (d. 1938), who was hired away from his assistant cook's job in Virginia City to continue cooking for the Central Pacific in Elko in 1870, was not on the tracklaying gang, but he fondly recalled being present at the ceremony (Burgess, op. cit. 14–16).[19] Andrew J. Russell, in his famous photograph with the caption "227 (plate number) East and West Shaking Hands at the Laying Last Rail," captured several Chinese at the ceremony, including a blurred Chinese man with his back toward the camera. At the completion of the ceremony, Strobridge, who now admired the Chinese, invited some of the Chinese workmen and foremen into his private train car for a dinner in their honor (Bulletin 5/13/1869). Thus, the commonly held belief that the Chinese were not present nor recognized for their contributions is erroneous.

Despite their hardships, some of the Chinese were very proud of their contributions to the American economy and national transportation system. Some of them were not forgotten by the "Big Four." Collis P. Huntington decided to honor 80 Chinese, known as "Gang No. 28" or the "Extra Gang," and he gave them lifetime jobs as a track maintenance

---

[19]Quong Kee's specialty was Irish Stew. His name appeared in the 1870 Census Manuscript for Elko. He eventually moved to Tombstone, AZ, where he opened the Can Can Restaurant and made friends with Wyatt Earp and Billy Clanton He was held in great esteem by the community. The Tombstone County Courthouse Museum has a special display about his life.

team at $1.55 per day.[20] By 1911, 63 of the original 80 were still working for the Southern Pacific (successor of the Central Pacific, March 17, 1884), and among them was We Woo, a resident of Lovelock's Chinatown. His 1914 funeral was an occasion for remembering the Chinese contribution to the construction of the Transcontinental Railroad (Lovelock Review-Miner 10/16/1914).

Contrary to popular opinion, the Chinese were not left stranded in Nevada and Utah. Many went on to work on other railroad projects in and around the state of Nevada (Myrick, op. cit.). Others were hired as maintenance men who constantly battled deterioration and erosion; replaced and repaired culverts, bridges, and ties; washed and maintained the cars and engines; installed and maintained new parts and equipment, and performed countless other tasks in what could be called "railroad towns." Ninety-five percent of the Chinese living in Lovelock and Winnemucca worked for the railroad in the 1870s, but by the end of the century, they turned toward other, more profitable, occupations, especially food and laundry services.[21] In fact, all of the restaurants in Lovelock, despite signs stating, "All White Help," which were put up during anti-Chinese movements between the 1870s and 1920s, were owned by Chinese (Chang interview 1992 and Yup interview 1993). These restaurants catered to the railroad passengers, the single ranchers, miners, those living in the surrounding area, and the local population. Just as the Lee clan was influential in the Tuscarora mining community, the Woo clan (although some ended up with other surnames, including Yup) from the Sze Yup District of South China dominated the Lovelock Chinese community.

A few Central Pacific railroad workers lived at relatively isolated stations or small towns which serviced the railroad lines. In a few cases, these Chinese lived in converted boxcars. Wallace E. Clay, who lived with the Chinese in Blue Creek, Utah, described a scene in the late 1800s that was commonplace in Nevada as well:

> When not "raising taps and tapping ties" those good Chinamen, among whom where "my very best friends," were many who probably got homesick for their wives and children in China, so they took me as a sort of pet and they gave me much Chinese candy and firecrackers and Chinese money... The antiquated box-car they lived in had been remodeled into a "work-car," in one end of which a series of small bunk beds had been built as a vertical column of three bunks, one above the other on both sides of the car-end from floor to ceiling so that around

---

[20]Phillip I. Earl has written about the "Extra Gang," in his collected works at the Nevada Historical Society, Reno. He has been extremely helpful in this project.
[21]For more information on the Winnemucca Chinese, see Beth Au, op. cit. The Lovelock Chinese has been studied by Rusco and Hart 1979.

eighteen Chinamen could sleep in the bedroom end of the car, while the other end of the car served as a kitchen and dining room wherein there was a cast iron cook stove with its stove pipe going up through the roof of the car and with all kinds of pots and pans and skillets hanging around the walls, plus cubby holes for tea cups and big and little blue china bowls and chop sticks and wooden table and benches. (interview in Conley 264)

Some stayed or returned to an area along the railroad line that pleased them. Like "Chinatown" which became Dayton, "Chinese Gardens" was one such location, later to be renamed Carlin.[22] Prior to December, 1868, the railroad workers had been sent ahead to prepare the land for tracklaying. In keeping with their agricultural background, some planted vegetable gardens in the Carlin Meadows on the Humboldt River and either stayed or returned to the area in 1869. They brought their wives and raised children there, so that when the Chinese Minister to the United States, Chen Lanbin, passed through Carlin in 1876 on his way to Washington, D.C., he observed 300 or more Chinese in the town, including wives and families, who greeted him (Chan, op. cit. 277).[23] The railroad brought many Chinese into Nevada and as a result, many stayed in or around the state.

Some of those who did not continue to work for the Central Pacific found employment with other railroad companies in the state, despite growing anti-Chinese sentiment. Census records indicated that in 1870, 246 Chinese were railroad workers and in 1880, the figure increased to 576 (Carter 85–86). Because of European American protests over the use of "cheap Chinese labor," beginning in 1871, the State Legislature enacted numerous prohibitions on the use of Chinese workers on railroads, road construction, and other similar types of work (*Nevada Statutes* 1871). In 1879, a law was passed banning the use of "Mongolian or Chinese labor on all railroads chartered by the state" (*Nevada Statutes* 1879). In 1881, the Legislature specifically prohibited Chinese workers from the construction of the Eureka and Colorado River Railroad Company (*Nevada Statutes* 1881). However, powerful railroad companies managed to ignore or circumvent these laws.

Chinese worked on the roadwork, construction, or maintenance of almost every railroad line in Nevada throughout the late 19th century. Several hundred Chinese began working for the Virginia and Truckee Railroad (V&T) on February 18, 1869, and despite harassment from European American miners in the area, the Chinese completed the line in

---

[22]The site and its background will be noted with the construction of a monument due to be completed in June 1994.

[23]Undoubtedly, the Chinese from the surrounding area joined the Carlin Chinese in welcoming the Chinese Minister.

November (Myrick op. cit. 137–138). The V&T opened for service in December 1869, then added a line and service to Reno by 1872. Maintenance work was done by the Chinese, all of whom had immigrated in 1880 or later, until the 1920s.[24] This line spurred the development and prosperity of Virginia City, Reno, and Carson City. However, with the economic declines of the 1890s, the fortunes of the V&T began to drop, and on May 30, 1950, it ceased operations altogether (Chan, op. cit. 300).

Other rail lines constructed primarily by the Chinese were the Carson and Colorado Railroad, which began on May 31, 1880, under Chinese labor contractor Ah Quong; the Bodie and Benton Railroad, in May 1881, which hired Chinese laborers through contractor Ah Sam; the Nevada-California-Oregon Railway (N-C-O) in late December 1880, which hired a small number of Chinese through contractor Ah Jack,; the Eureka and Palisade Railroad; and the Atlantic and Pacific Railroad (Myrick, op. cit. 166–210, 298–313, 341–383, 765). Working on these railroads was a difficult task because many of the workmen encountered hostility from the European American population, especially those who felt that they were discharged from their employment in favor of the Chinese (*VEC* 8/4/1880). Moreover, the pay was low and the laborers had to pay the $4 per person poll tax, which was collected directly from their wages (VEC 7/2/1880). Dissatisfaction sometimes led to a strike, which occurred in July, 1880 against the Carson & Colorado (bid). The workers demanded $1.50 per day plus board—a raise of fifty cents—but Superintendent of Construction Yerington steadfastly refused. The strike did not dissuade the railroad officials from continuing to employ Chinese, and a month later, the Reno *Evening Gazette* reported that 500 Chinese were employed on the Carson & Colorado. Once these railroad lines were completed, the Chinese performed maintenance and service work well into the 1920s, as was evident in the railroad town of Sparks, located near Reno, Washoe County.

Some of the Chinese railroad workers returned to China and helped to build China's much needed rail service. Ah Chin worked for the Southern Pacific in Nevada under the master mechanic Judge Hogan, later of McGill, White Pine County (McGill 7/17/1913). After he returned to China, he eventually became one of the foremost leaders in the railroad industry in China, and in 1913, he held the position of general superintendent of the King Yuen Railway Company. Ah Chin was just one of several Chinese who brought their skill and knowledge back to China.

However, due to the 1882 Chinese Exclusion Act and its indefinite extension in 1892, Chinese railroad laborers were in short supply and the

---

[24]Census Manuscript for Sparks (near Reno) indicated that almost all of the Chinese men in that town worked with the Japanese on railroad maintenance.

void was filled by Japanese, Asian Indian, and Filipino immigrants. For those who did not continue in railroad work, the lure of mining and its instant wealth or new economic opportunities in cooking, merchandising, or laundry was great.

The Chinese contributed to the development of the railroad by using its services as well. Freight going westward was cheaper than freight going eastward. The Chinese in Nevada and other American West towns and cities often shipped their foodstuffs by rail. In 1877, for example, 10%, or 18 million pounds, of the Central Pacific Railroad's revenue freight was Chinese tea and sometimes 60 cars of tea and other Chinese goods would pass through the station at Battle Mountain, Humboldt County, in a two-day period (ibid. 26). One of the largest Chinatowns in the area was the mining community of Tuscarora, Elko County, further east of Battle Mountain. It is probable that Tuscarora was the destination for much of this tea shipment.

Mining and railroad work, with their subsidiary occupations, played a major role in the motivation for the Chinese to travel and live in the Silver Mountain. As they settled down, they tried to recreate some of the traditions from their homeland while adapting to the new conditions in which they found themselves.

The lifestyles of the Chinese in Nevada was not unlike that of the Chinese in San Francisco's Chinatown, with a few exceptions. Since the Chinese population in Nevada was smaller and the European Americans were more dependent upon all of their community members, there was greater interaction between the two groups. Sometimes this led to lifelong friendships. This was the case for Ah Kim of Eureka, who had immigrated in 1850 and cleaned saloons for a profession (*EDS* 11/19/1881). He worked in Sacramento, then in 1860, he moved to Virginia City to work for Colonel John Van Buren Perry and Benny Irvin. When he moved to Eureka, he again linked up with Colonel Perry and earned the reputation of being respectable, as well as well-connected (his cousin Ah Ki worked with Nevada's Republican Senator William Sharon, 1875–1881). When Ah Kim died in November, 1881, he was mourned by numerous friends, and Perry saw that he was "decently laid away." Townspeople in places like Eureka and Carson City could form staunch anti-Chinese organizations but at the same time be very protective of the Chinese residents who had already lived there. The general message was "no more new immigrants," rather than "get rid of them all." Each county or town differed as to their relationships to the Chinese, and the prevailing sentiments were greatly influenced by the leaders of the community. When European American miners moved to a new boom town, the Chinese from that community probably also followed. It was not uncommon to go to a new boom town to find neighborhoods of residents from the same former "bust" town.

However, by 1890 to 1900, like the majority of the population, the Chinese began to leave Nevada. Some went to California or other western states, including the American territory Hawaii and the states bordering Nevada. Others went further east, especially to New York and the New England states, where they believed there was less discrimination against them.. Some returned to China permanently, but a few of these, accustomed to life in the American West, returned. A few drifted back to Nevada after wandering around other parts of the United States. A small, but significant, percentage spent most of their lives in Nevada, like Lee Kee of Austin, Lander County, a restaurant owner who had immigrated to the United States in 1849 and was 96 years old when the Census was taken in 1920.[25] Like Gold Mountain, Silver Mountain had its share of "long-time" Chinese.

Mining and railroad work brought the Chinese to the Silver Mountain. Like the European Americans who came for those reasons, some were successful, but most of them struggled or experienced wide fluctuations in their income in their search for that last "pot of gold." Nevada projected an image of a land of opportunity, and if one was lucky and healthy, had the kind of personality that could interact with the European American community, and was talented in some way or another, a modicum of success, as seen in the cases of Ah Lee Lake, Quong Kee, Ah Chin, and Lee Kee, was at the end of the rainbow.

Sources. The major source, Nevada newspapers, often were highly biased and derogatory, often distorting the situation in order to report a colorful story. Cultural biases and anti-Chinese movements influenced the reporting. However, sometimes a reporter consciously or unconsciously wrote something significant that gave some insight into the lives of Chinese Nevadans.

Another important source of information was the Census Manuscripts, available through the National Archives on microfilm for 1860 (Utah Territory), 1870–1880, 1900–1920 (see table below. Note: The 1890 Census Manuscript for Nevada was lost in a fire in 1921. For more information on this source, see Chan 1986). Unfortunately, there were numerous inaccuracies, but the data provided a general sketch of the population. The most problematic were the renderings of Chinese names. The Chinese gave their family (last) name first, then their *ci* (formal first name, usually consisting of two characters) or *hao* (familiar name, usually consisting of two characters) or nickname, usually prefaced by the familiar nomenclature "Ah." Although a person knew that his surname

---

[25]National Archives, *Census Manuscript*, 1920 [hereafter referred to as *Census Manuscript*], gives an incorrect immigration date (1824). In the 1910 Census, he was 87 years old when the census was taken and his date of immigration was given as 1849, which is more plausible.

or first name was not "Ah," he probably thought it was his "American" name and listed it as such. A common problem was in the reversal of names so that, for example, Low Wing (surname Low or Lo) of Winnemucca became known as Mr. Wing and his children have the surname of Wing (Au 1993). The local newspaper, the Winnemucca *Silver State*, referred to him by his *ci*, Low Hee Sing[26] when he presented Sun Yat-Sen with $3,500 raised by the local Zhigongtang (Chee Kong Tong, or Free Masons, as they were known), so it was difficult to ascertain that the two were one and the same person. Prior to 1900, census takers listed married couples and their children with different "last" names in many cases, thus the 1880 Census Manuscript for Virginia City reported a Ty Gung, 28, mother of the girl Ah Ing, 1. Age and occupation were additional errors made by the census takers. Since the Chinese calculated their age as one from their date of birth and added a year every Chinese New Year's, the reported age was not accurate until birthdates were included in the Census. Prejudice often led census takers to list Chinese women as prostitutes or harlots. Undercounting was a major problem and census takers omitted prominent Chinese, Chinese women, and children, as well as those who spoke English well.[27] Summaries in the official United States Census also differed from the Manuscript tally. For example, in White Pine County, according to the Census summary, the total of Chinese was: 292 in 1870, 107 in 1880, and 46 in 1890, but the Census Manuscript showed: 330 in 1870, 115 in 1880, and unavailable in 1890 The official census also differed from the final tally published in the local newspapers, so that, for example, the 1880 Census reported 5,416 Chinese in the state, but the *Eureka Daily Sentinel* (February 16,1881) listed the figure as 7,420. The Census Manuscripts of 1900 to 1920 gave additional information, including birthdate, marital status, education, immigration date, and net worth, so that a more accurate profile of individuals was available.

Other sources which provide information about the Chinese in Nevada are county records, including marriage licenses, land deeds, business licenses, and birth and death records; court and criminal records; United States Immigration and Naturalization files; and other

---

[26]A photograph of Low Hee Sing and Sun Yat-sen of May 1911 in Winnemucca was given to me by Him Mark Lai of San Francisco. Low was identified by his son, Charles Wing, of San Francisco, in 1993.

[27]The Chinese station master in Tuscarora was not included in the 1870 and 1880 Census Manuscripts. A Chinese man and his wife, both born in California, and their two-year-old son, born in Carson City, were interviewed in 1881 in the local newspaper, but did not appear in the 1880 Carson City Census Manuscript. These are just two of numerous examples.

local and national government documents.[28] Personal memoirs, oral histories, photographs, and other materials augmented these documents. The Chinese left very little writing of their own, but some can be found scattered in unlikely places. This kind of fragmentary data had to be used in conjunction with the other sources in order to recreate a picture of the Chinese experience in Nevada.

Population of the Chinese in Nevada, 1860–1990

Year	Total state population	Total Chinese in U.S.	Total Chinese in state	% of Chinese in state	Chinese males	Chinese females
1860	6,857	34,933	23	0.3	—	—
1870	42,491	63,199	3,152	7.4	2,817	306
1880	62,266	105,465	5,416	8.7	5,102	314
1890	47,355	107,488	2,833	6.0	2,749	84
1900	42,335	89,863	1,352	3.2	1,283	69
1910	81,335	71,531	927	1.1	876	51
1920	77,407	61,639	689	0.9	630	59
1930	91,058	74,954	483	0.5	440	73
1940	110,247	77,504	286	0.3	221	65
1950	160,083	117,629	281	0.2	205	76
1960	285,278	237,292	572	0.2	388	184
1970	488,738	433,469	915	0.2	567	348
1980	800,495	812,178	2,979	0.4	1,469	1,723
1990	1,201,833	1,645,472	6,618	0.6	3,180	3,438

Source: United States Bureau of the Census
Characteristics of the Population (title varies), 1860–1990

Works Cited

Angel, Myron ed. *History of Nevada*. Oakland, CA: Thompson and West, 1881. Reprinted., Berkeley, CA: Howell-North Books, 1958.

Au, Beth Amity. "Home Means Nevada: The Chinese in Winnemucca, Nevada, 1870–1950, A Narrative History." Unpublished master's thesis, Asian

---

[28]This study is part of a larger work to be published in 1995 by the University of Nevada Press as part of a grant from the National Endowment for the Humanities to the Nevada Humanities Committee. I am indebted to several organizations and individuals for their assistance in the archival materials, most notably Elmer and Mary Rusco, who have worked closely with me on this study of Chinese Nevadans; Phillip Earl of the Nevada Historical Society (Reno); Guy Rocha of the State Archives; Ronald James of the Division of Historic Preservation and Archeology; Robert Nylen of the State Museum, and David Millman of the Nevada Historical Society (Las Vegas). Robert Davenport and Eugene Moehring readily answered my questions on Nevada and the West.

American Studies, University of California, Los Angeles, 1993. Discusses the Low Wing family.

Barth, Gunther. *Bitter Strength: A History of the Chinese in the United States, 1850–1870.* Cambridge, MA: Harvard University Press, 1964.

BeDunnah, Gary. "History of the Chinese in Nevada, 1855–1904." Master's thesis in history, University of Nevada, Reno, San Francisco, CA: R and E Research Associates, 1973.

Best, Gerald M. "Rendezvous at Promontory: The 'Jupiter' and No. 119." *Utah Historical Quarterly* 37:1 (Winter 1969): 72–73.

Bowman, J.N. "Driving the Last Spike at Promontory 1869." *Utah Historical Quarterly* 37:1 (Winter 1969): 94.

Bragg, Allen C. *Humboldt County, 1905.* Winnemucca, NV: North Central Nevada Historical Society, 1976.

Braunstein, Mannetta. "The Carson City Chinese in Early Days." Unpublished research paper, UNLV Special Collections, 1992. Braunstein incorrectly separated "wash house" and "laundry" and reported 17 different occupations.

Burgess, Opie Rundle. "Quong Kee: Pioneer of Tombstone." *Arizona Highways* 25:7 (July 1949): 14–16.

Carson City Morning Appeal 14 March 1884.

Carter, Gregg Lee. "Social Demography of the Chinese in Nevada: 1870–1880." *Nevada Historical Society Quarterly* 18:2 (Summer 1976) 85–86.

Census Manuscript, 1880. This information is the result of data compiled by Mannetta Braunstein.

Chan, Loren B. "The Chinese in Nevada: An Historical Survey, 1856–1970." *Nevada Historical Society Quarterly* 25:4 (Winter 1982): 266–314.

Chan, Sucheng ed. Entry Denied: Exclusion and the Chinese Community in America, 1882–1943. Philadelphia, PA: Temple University Press, 1991.

Chan, Sucheng. *This Bittersweet Soil: The Chinese in California Agriculture, 1860–1910.* Berkeley, CA: University of California Press, 1986. Appendix, "Essay on Sources."

Chang, Frank, of Lovelock. Personal interview. 1992.

Chun, Mae Wing. Personal interview with daughter Mae Wing Chun. 1993.

Chung, Sue Fawn."The Chinese Experience in Nevada: Success Despite Discrimination." *Nevada Public Affairs Review* 2 (1987): 43–51.

Conley, Don C. Oral interview. In "The Pioneer Chinese of Utah." In *The Peoples of Utah.* Ed. Helen Z. Papanikolas. Salt Lake City, UT: Utah State Historical Society, 1976. 264. Reprinted in Anan S. Raymond, *op. cit.*, 49.

Dodge, Grenville M. *How We Built the Union Pacific Railway.* Ann Arbor: University Microfilms, 1966. Originally issued as United States Senate Document 447, 61st Congress, 2nd Session, 1910.

Elko Independent 23 April 1871, 22 October 1871.

Ellison, Marion. *An Inventory and Index to the Records of Carson County, Utah and Nevada Territories, 1855–1861.* Reno, NV: Grace Dangberg Foundation, 1984. 261–262. Examples of the activities of Ah Kay.

Eureka Daily Sentinel 12 March 1877, 30 June 1877, and obituary 28 November 1878. Information from LuAnn Caressi.

Eureka Daily Sentinel 19 November 1881. Details Ah Kim's life and death.

Glasscock, C. B. *The Big Bonanza: The Story of the Comstock Lode*. New York, NY: A. L. Burt Company, 1931.

Gregory, Cedric E. *A Concise History of Mining*. New York, NY: Pergamon Press, 1980.

Griswold, Wesley. *A Work of Giants* . New York, NY: McGraw-Hill Book Comapny, 1962.

Hansen, Walter. "Early Days in Buena Vista Valley of Nevada." Unpublished from Pershing County High School, n.d.

Hart, Philip D. "Chinese Community in Lovelock, Nevada: 1870 to 1940." In *Report of Archaeological and Historical Investigations at Ninth and Amherst, Lovelock, Nevada*. Eds. Eugene M. Hattori, Mary K. Rusco, and D. R. Tuohy. Carson City, NV: Nevada State Museum, 1979.

Heath, Earle. "From Trail to Rail." *Southern Pacific Bulletin* 15 (1927), Chapter 15, 12.

James, Ronald.Women on the Mining Frontier: An Overview of Virginia City, Nevada,. Forthcoming publication.

Kelly, J. Wells.*Second Directory of Nevada Territory*. San Francisco, CA: Valentine and Company, 1863.

Kraus, George. "Chinese Laborers and the Construction of the Central Pacific." *Utah Historical Quarterly* 37 (Winter 1969): 42–57.

Kraus, George. *High Road to Promontory: Building the Central Pacific Across the High Sierra*. Palo Alto, CA: American West Publishing Company, 1969. The best accounts of the Chinese participation in the construction of the Central Pacific Railroad.

Labbe, Charles. *Rocky Trails of the Past*. Las Vegas, NV: Charles Labbe, 1960.

Lai, Him Mark.*Con Huaren dao Huaqiao* [From Overseas Chinese to Chinese American]. Hong Kong: Joint Publishing, Inc., 1992.

Lingenfelter, Richard E. *The Hardrock Miners: A History of the Mining Labor Movement in the American West, 1863–1893*. Berkeley, CA: University of California Press, 1974.

Lord, Eliot.*Comstock Mining and Miners*. CA: Howell-North, 1959.

Lovelock Review-Miner 16 October 1914.

Magnaghi, Russell M. "Virginia City's Chinese Community, 1860–1880." *Nevada Historical Society Quarterly* 24:2 (Summer 1981): 130.

McCague, James. *Monguls and Iron Men, The Story of the First Transcontinental Railroad*. New York, NY: Harper & Row, 1964.

McGill Copper Ore 17 July 1913. I am indebted to Andrew Russell for this information.

McMurtrie, Douglas C. *Nevada Mining Laws*. Chicago, IL: The Black Cat Press, 1935.

Miller, B.F. "Nevada in the Making." *Nevada State Historical Papers* 4 (1923): 300. I am indebted to Donald Bennett for his help on Chinese miners in Nevada.

Myrick, David F. *Railroads of Nevada and Eastern California*. Berkeley, CA: Howell-North Books, 1962.

National Archives, Immigration & Naturalization File 13567/84.

National Archives, Immigration and Naturalization File #13561/139. Elmer and Mary Rusco searched the INS files for our project. The *Tuscarora Times Review* does not report this business formation until October 3, 1889.

Nevada Statues 1923, Resolution 14, 407

Nevada Statutes 1871, Chapter 18, Sections 11, 4.

Nevada Statutes 1879, Chapter 43, Section 1

Nevada Statutes 1879, Chapter 73, Section 2.

Nevada Statutes 1881, Chapter 67, Section 14.

Nevada Statutes 1921, Resolution 14, 416

Nevada Statutes 1947, Chapter 69.

Nevada, State of. Appendix to the Journal of the Senate and Assembly, 8th Session, 1875 Census, Carson City, 1878.

Ong, Paul Ong. "The Central Pacific Railroad and the Exploitation of Chinese Labor." *Journal of Ethnic Studies* 13 (Summer 1965): 119–124. Ong calculated that the Chinese were paid one-third of the wage rate of European Americans, thus differing from Ping Chiu's calculations of 64–90% less than European American wage rates; see his book, *Chinese Labor in California*, Madison, WI: University of Wisconsin Press, 1963.

Paher, Stanley. *Nevada Ghost Towns and Mining Camps*. Berkeley, CA: Howell North Books, 1970.

Patterson, Edna et al. *Nevada's Northeast Frontier*. Reno, NV: University of Nevada Press. Reprint of Western Printing & Publishers, 1969.

Primeaux Collection, Northeastern Nevada Museum, Elko, NV. I am indebted to Shawn Hall for his assistance on the Elko County Chinese.

Raymond, Anan S. and Richard E. Fike. *Rails East to Promontory: The Utah Stations*. Salt Lake City, UT: Bureau of Land Management, 1981.

Rusco, Mary K. "Counting the Lovelock Chinese." In *Report of Archaeological and Historical Investigations at Ninth and Amherst, Lovelock, Nevada*. Eds. Eugene M. Hattori, Mary K. Rusco, and D. R. Tuohy. Carson City, NV: Nevada State Museum, 1979.

San Francisco Alta California 16 November 1867 and 9 November 1868.

San Francisco Evening Bulletin 8 May 1869, 13 May 1869.

Shamberger, Hugh A. *The Story of Silver Peak, Esmeralda County, Nevada*. Carson City, NV, 1976.

Silver State 23 April 1905, 27 April 1905, and 2 May 1914. Ran a story about the American Mines of 20 years earlier; see also *Desert Magazine*, November 1958.

Siu, Paul. *The Chinese Laundryman: A Study of Social Isolation*. Ed. John Kuo Wei Tchen. New York, NY: New York University Press, 1987.

Smith, Regina C. et al. *Prehistory and History of the Winnemucca District: A Cultural Resources Literature Overview*. Reno, NV: Nevada State Office of the Bureau of Land Management, 1983.

State v. Preble, 18 Nevada 251, 252, 253 (1884).

Storey County, marriage license stubs, ST-013 for 1874–1879, ST-014 for 1879–1902, Nevada Historical Society microfilm. See also *VEC*, March 29, 1882.

Strate, Larry D. "Non-Resident Alien Rights to Nevada Minerals." *Hotel and Casino Law Letter* (UNLV) 2–4 (November 1983): 43–44.

Townley, John. "Tuscarora." *Northeastern Nevada Historical Society Quarterly* 2 (Summer/Fall 1971): 11, 28.

Travis, Norman J., and Edward J. Cocks. *The Tincal Trail: A History of Borax.* London: Harrap, 1984.

Tuscarora Times and Mining Review 22 March 1884, 17 April 1884, 28 May 28 1884, 23 July 1884, 19 May 1885.

Tuscarora Times Review 30 September 1897.

United States Bureau of the Census. *Characteristics of the Population: 1870.*

United States Congress, Senate. *The United States Pacific Railway Commission,* Senate executive documents, 51, 50th Congress, 1st Session, 1888, 2581.

United States Pacific Railway Commission, loc. cit.;

United States. *The Tenth Census* June 1880, vol. 1: Population: Nevada.

Virginia City Evening Chronicle 2 July 1880, 22 July 1880, 4 August 1880.

Virginia City. *Territorial Enterprise* 19 January 1877, quoting the *Winnemucca Silver State* 17 January 1877.

Woodman, Ruth C. *The Story of the Pacific Coast Borax Company.* Los Angeles, CA: Ward Ritchie Press, 1951.

Yen, Tzu-kuei. "Chinese Workers and the First Transcontinental Railroad of the United States of America." Ph.D.. dissertation in Asian Studies, St. John's University, New York. Ann Arbor, MI: University Microfilms International, 1977. 111.

Yup, Raymond, originally of Lovelock, now of Reno. Personal interview. 1993.

A Chinese Family in Honolulu, Hawai'i:
The Lum Choys

GREGORY YEE MARK
Ethnic Studies, University of Hawai'i at Manoa, Honolulu, Hawai'i

Whereas, In the opinions of the Government of the United States, the coming of Chinese laborers to this country endangers the good order of certain localities within the territory thereof: Therefore,

Be it enacted by the Senate and House of Representatives of the United States of America in Congress assembled, That from and after the expiration of ninety days next after the passage of this Act, the coming of Chinese laborers to the United States be, and the same is hereby, suspended; and during such suspension it shall not be lawful for any Chinese laborer to come, or, having so come after the expiration of said ninety days, to remain within the United States.

-Hawai'i Department of Foreign Affairs, 1896

The 1882 and succeeding Chinese Exclusion Acts had a profound impact upon the past and present Chinese community in Hawai'i. In 1900, after Hawai'i became a United States territory, American law applied to the islands. As a result, this set of restrictive, racist legislation applied to the Territory of Hawai'i and its Chinese population. The Chinese responded to these laws in numerous ways. From 1852–1900, an estimated 30,000 out of a total of 56,000 Chinese simply left the islands, and between 1900 to 1940, as with the U.S. mainland, many migrated to Hawai'i as paper sons. However, this paper studies two significant but yet very different responses via the case study of one turn-of-the-century Chinese Hawai'ian family: the quite common and cruel separation of families and the seldom-used merchant status exceptions.

Lum See Kwock, a.k.a. Lum Choy. On December 17, 1880, Lum See Kwock (his formal name), or Lum Choy, was born in a simple clay house in Sun Wui County's San How village. By 1880, many of his fellow villagers had migrated to the land of the Golden Mountain, Gum Shan, and the Sandalwood Mountains, Tan Heung Shan. He was an only child, and in 1896, at the age of 15 years, Lum left his mother and migrated to Hawai'i. According to his late son, Sai Wong Lum, Lum Choy was naive and did not know what to expect upon his arrival in Honolulu. His first job was digging graves, which paid him $5 per month. Lum believed this was a good wage because he had never earned so much money before in China. In comparison, during this period, most sugar plantations paid Chinese contract laborers approximately $15.50 per month.

A few months later, Lum Choy changed jobs and worked as a domestic worker for a wealthy *haole* family. For the Wright family, his duties were family cook, houseboy, and handyman. During some rare moments in his daily schedule, one of the Wright daughters taught him the rudiments of English. Lum was so determined to improve his English and learn more about the American way of life that he bought many books and thoroughly read each one. In addition, Mr. Lum interacted with many Native Hawai'ians, and he eventually learned to speak the Hawai'ian language.

At the age of 20, on April 24, 1901, Lum See Kwock returned to China, and the following year he married Lum Chu She. According to family sources, shortly after their marriage, a son was born, but he passed away soon after birth.

After only eight months of marriage, Mr. Lum had to leave his wife behind to return to Hawai'i and work at several service jobs. Apparently, in order to qualify for a return certificate, an overseas Chinese had to return to Hawai'i within one year. Family records indicate that in 1908, Mr. Lum worked as a waiter at the Young Hotel, which was located near Honolulu's commercial district. In 1909, Lum took a higher paying job as a bartender at the exclusive Commercial Club.

On October 30, 1911, almost immediately after the successful overthrow of the Manchus and the establishment of the Republic of China, he returned to Sun Wui. In 1912, Lum Chu She gave birth to their son, Lum Sai Wong. Unfortunately, in September 1912, after 11 months with his family, Lum Choy came back to Hawai'i—leaving behind his mother, wife, and baby son. Upon his return to Honolulu, he was able to work as a waiter at the Young Cafe.

It was during the post-1911 period that Lum Choy became very active in local Chinese organizations in Honolulu. Apparently, he was involved in three societies: Sze Yup or See Yup, Lum Sai Ho Tong, and the Quon On Society. The Sze Yup and Lum Sai Ho Tong were very prominent in the Chinese community. Today, they are still considered to be active and significant in the local community social structure. Lum Choy was very active in the Quon On Society, having served as one of its secretaries. On his Department of Labor Immigrant Service Return Certificate, dated March 6, 1917, Mr. Lum cited Quon On as his home address because he apparently viewed this society to be an integral and permanent part of his life.

By 1915/1916, Lum Choy was promoted to a steward at the Commercial Club, therefore receiving a pay increase as well. Thus, utilizing his replenished personal funds and fulfilling the requirements for his 1917 Return Certificate, he was eligible to return to his family.

However, to qualify for the Certificate, Lum had to guarantee that he would return to Hawai'i within one year and have at least $1000 in property in Hawai'i. His assets were a $375 interest in the Kwong Moy Lee Poi Co. and a $1008.27 savings account at Bishop Bank.

By 1917 Lum Chu She was 30 years old, living in China with her one son and caring for her husband's mother. On April 18, Mr. Lum departed from Honolulu on board the S/S Tenyo Maru. During his stay in China with his family, Chu She became pregnant with another child, but in 1918, the baby died one month after its birth. Unfortunately, Lum Choy was not able to be present for his baby's birth. In order to comply with the requirements for the Hawai'i Return Certificate, on April 27, 1918, Lum returned by himself to Honolulu on board the S/S Shinyo Maru.

Upon his return, Lum was able to continue his bartender job and he moved to 1166 Smith Street, which was located in Honolulu Chinatown. According to Lum Choy's children, from 1916 to 1924, he was a bartender at the prestigious Commercial Club. However, an Immigration Service report by Immigrant Inspector Edwin Farmer stated that Mr. Lum quit the Commercial Club in 1920 and then for the next two years did nothing. Then on August 12, 1922, he became partners with Mrs. Dung Ching She and opened the Sung Kee Co., which was a small storefront located in the heart of Chinatown at 1169 Maunakea Street. Its stock consisted of tobacco, oil, cigars and cigarettes, cloth, bags of rice, peanuts, fruit, canned goods, Chinese provisions, neckties, underwear, notions, and other articles. According to Inspector Farmer, the daily income was approximately $10, or a monthly average of $323.50 for the months of October and December in 1922 and January, March, May, July, and September in 1923. Generally, the store had about $1000 of stock on hand. Lum Choy's role in the store was to wait on customers and to maintain the financial records. Occasionally, Mrs. Dung, Sung Kee's co-owner, was there to assist store customers. There were no other salaried employees. To Lum, this small business represented much more than a meager income—it was the instrument to finally reunite his long-separated family.

Lum Chu She and Her Coming to Hawai'i. Lum Chu She or Lum Chee Shee was born on November 18, 1887. She was born and raised in Har Loo, a neighboring village to her husband's. According to her children, Chu She remembered the constant fear of night bandits and of villagers who were forced to hide food, prized possessions, and, of course, themselves. Her father was a farmer, and therefore from an early age, Chu She, her sister, and her brother worked in the fields. She never had the opportunity for a formal Chinese education and she could not read and write Chinese.

143

At the age of 15, Chu She and the 22-year-old Lum Choy were married. Most likely, they were married just weeks before his 1902 return to Hawai'i. As was the local custom, theirs was an arranged marriage, and when her husband departed for Honolulu, she was required to care for her mother-in-law.

Family Separation and Hardship. For the next 21 years, Lum Chu She cared for her mother-in-law, Lum Lai She, and shared with her husband a life that was separated by the vast Pacific Ocean and by what probably seemed like endless years. Their link was her letters to him (written by another person) and his letters to Chu She and the rest of the family. During their first 21 years of marriage, Lum Chu She and Lum Choy lived together as wife and husband for a total of two years. After their son Lum Sui Wong was born (April 1912), a family portrait was an important means to unite the family. This photograph superimposed a photo from China of Chu She holding infant Sui Wong with a photo from Honolulu of a formally seated Lum Choy. Thus, through creative photography, the Lum family finally become a "family."

The Lum family was one of thousands of Chinese American families that suffered untold hardships due to their family separations. For many like the Lums, their separations were for decades, and for others it was for a lifetime. Often, women were married as very young brides, destined to live their lives in painful marital solitude, caring for their husbands' families for years, and living occasionally or not at all with a man who, through time, became a virtual stranger.

A Resourceful Solution. In the case of Lum Chu She and Lum See Kwock, they endured a two-decade separation but were finally reunited as a family unit. On December 29, 1923, after a 30-day journey, Chu She and 12-year-old Sui Wong arrived in Honolulu on board the S/S President Taft. In a September 24, 1923 affidavit by Lum titled "Case of Chu Shee and Lum Sui Wong," Lum stated that:

> My occupation is merchant. I am a partner with Dung Ching Shee of the Firm Sung Kee, dealers in general merchandise, grocery, cigars, and tobacco on #1169 Maunakea Street, Honolulu. I am anxious to have my wife Chu Shee and our son Lum Sai Wong come to Hawai'i and live together so we may create a home.

Thus, the Lum family was brought together in the Territory of Hawai'i because See Kwock was able to change his occupational status from a laborer to merchant.

Upon closer examination, Lum See Kwock was able to circumvent and essentially manipulate the Chinese Exclusion Acts. In a document from the Office of the Treasurer, Territory of Hawai'i, it certified that the Sung Kee Co. was registered as a viable merchandise business on August 12, 1922. A little more than a year later on October 22, 1923, the U.S. Immigration Service granted Lum Choy mercantile status. Mr. Edwin Farmer, a Federal Immigration Inspector, stated in his investigative report that:

> The receipts of this store are very small and the stock of goods is very small—hardly enough to support two partners and not enough to keep two persons busy. About $10.00 a day is taken in, which is certainly not enough even of the kind of goods sold there to keep a salesman busy half the time and the keeping of the books would only occupy a little time each day. I am sure one man could do every particle of the work and then have plenty of time to spare. Yet he says the woman works there and receives a salary and Mr. Silva says the woman does a great deal of work. The applicant says he was formerly steward of the Commercial Club and quit there three years ago: that he did nothing for two years and then started in his present business.
>
> The circumstances of this case are peculiar and give rise to considerable doubt in my mind. But the evidence is favorable and the store, though small, is there, and the applicant is registered as a member of the firm, and has been there for a year. I am, therefore, constrained to recommend that he be granted a mercantile status.

Although, Inspector Farmer recommended that Lum Choy be legally defined as a merchant, he had his obvious doubts concerning the viability of Sung Kee Co. as a true business enterprise.

As a result of Lum's change of legal status and his money savings, the very next month, in November 1923, Lum Chu She and her son Lum Sai Wong set sail for Hawai'i. After the U.S. Immigration Service Board of Special Inquiry interrogated the three family members and other witnesses, mother and son were admitted into the United States. On February 7, 1924, Mrs. Lum Chu She submitted an application for a "Certificate of Identity" to the Immigration Service which documented that she was 36 years old and lived on 1269 Nuuanu Street, Honolulu, Territory of Hawai'i. Chu She recorded her occupation as housewife, and that she was admitted into the country as the "Wife of Lum Choy, merchant."

A short time later, the Sung Kee Company was forced to close its doors because of "poor business." Lum Choy returned to work at the Commercial Club. He never saw his mother again in China, but continued to send money back to the village for her support until she passed away. Chu She gave birth to three more children, Violet, Mae, and Henry, and she maintained a house that became a bustling neighborhood center. Chinese friends from all over Oahu came to visit Lum Chu She and they often sought her advice for their personal and financial affairs. Although it was widely believed that she was clairvoyant, she believed that she had a special gift and therefore never required a financial charge for her advice.

Lum Choy was equally charitable. He donated a great deal of his time to Honolulu Chinese societies. Also, many friends sought out his assistance because he was tri-lingual. He translated for them and read and wrote letters for them to loved ones in China. On October 7, 1945, Lum Choy passed away. In Honolulu, 16 years later on June 23, 1961, Lum Chu She followed her husband. Despite their 21-year separation, they were one of the more fortunate separated-Chinese families because they had a happy ending: they lived 22 years together.

The Chinese Did More Than Hard Labor in the Gold Rush

KAM L. WONG
Manhattan Beach, California

During the Gold Rush days, many Chinese came to America to perform hard labor, sending their earnings back to China. Most often, when they had accumulated enough money, they would go home. Some, after staying for many years, eventually settled in America, but they rarely settled in America during the Gold Rush years. This article relates the lives of Fee Lee Wong and his children in America, during the years of 1870 to 1921, and their contributions to America. Fee Lee Wong, my grandfather, passed away before I was born. Searching for information on his life was almost like searching for information on a stranger. There were many gold rushes in America. The key ones were California in 1849, Colorado in 1858, South Dakota in 1876, and the Yukon in 1897. For Fee Lee Wong, the setting was the South Dakota Gold Rush.

The Lure of the Gold Mountain. Many Chinese came to South America during the 16th century. By the 1800s, many of them moved north to the West Coast of North America to fish and to farm. The 1849 California Gold Rush greatly accelerated the influx of Chinese miners to California. By 1860, there were 30 to 50 thousand Chinese in California. By 1868, the Central Pacific Railroad Company alone employed 10,000 Chinese. By 1870, the farm labor force in California and the whole fishing industry along the West Coast in the U.S. were dominated by Chinese. Indeed, by then the U.S. became the "Gold Mountain," a lure that many Chinese could not resist.

By the mid-1800s, due to the fighting of rebel factions after the Taiping Rebellion, the floods, and the famine, many villages were devastated in southern China. The village of Bak-Sah, in the county of Toi-San, Kwong Tung, had fallen onto hard times in the 1860s. Fee Lee Wong and his brother were forced to leave their native village of Bak-Sah and resettle in the county of Yun-Ping. But life in Yun-Ping was also difficult. The two brothers finally resorted to renting their bodies via hard-labor contracts to work in the "Gold Mountain." The trip to the U.S. was not a pleasure trip. It cost $200 to $300 a person, consisting of ship passage and fees to the agent of $30 to $50. It took two to three months to cross the Pacific. One of the ships was unfortunate to have 20% of its passengers die. Nevertheless, the two brothers made it to the U.S. in 1870. By then, Fee Lee Wong was 24 years old.

147

The Gold Rush of Fee Lee Wong. It appears that Fee Lee Wong might have performed as a cook, as well as a laborer, in California from 1870 to 1876. By 1875, gold strikes in the Black Hills of South Dakota created a new gold rush. This time, even Californians headed for the Black Hills. Fee Lee Wong, serving as a cook, went with a group of Caucasians to the Black Hills. On the way, the group was attacked by either Indians or bandits, but they were able to fight the attackers off, and they arrived in the Black Hills some time in 1875 to 1876. Fee Lee Wong reached Deadwood in 1876, the year Wild Bill Hickok, a lawman and a scout for General Custer, was shot in the back in Saloon No. 10 in Deadwood.

The group staked some claims. Then the claims were distributed to the members of the group by drawing lots. At the beginning, someone suggested that the Chinaman, namely Fee Lee Wong, should not be allowed to take part in the drawing. However, others argued that since the group went through life and death together to get to the Black Hills, everyone should be treated equally. The result was that Fee Lee Wong received two claims. As luck would have it, gold was found on a claim next to one of Fee Lee Wong's. It was said that sometime between 1876 and 1882, Fee Lee Wong sold his claim for $75,000. At that time, gold was valued at roughly $20 per ounce. Presently, gold sells for about $340 per ounce. By equating the worth of a dollar through its gold equivalency, the $75,000 around 1880 would be equivalent to $1,275,000 in today's money. Most of the Chinese in America at that time would simply have taken the money and returned to China to live there happily ever after. However, Fee Lee Wong did not do that. Instead, he settled in Deadwood and raised his family there.

The Prominent Fee Lee Wong. Fee Lee Wong lived to become the most prominent Chinese in Deadwood during the city's prime years. Aside from the fact that he was rich, there were many other factors in his favor. He was believed to be the first Chinese to live in Deadwood and the first Chinese to raise a family there. His children went to the same schools as everybody else's. Thus, he and his family members were well-integrated into the society of Deadwood. His being a family man there provided a great deal of assurance to the non-Chinese in Deadwood that the Chinese would provide their share of the effort to tame the new frontier and not take the money and go home. Census records indicated that Fee Lee Wong spoke fluent English. This fact has a lot to do with the prominent position he attained. At times, the anti-Chinese sentiment around Deadwood would become explosive and lead to unreasonable violence against some Chinese. Fee Lee Wong quite often served as a go-between for the Chinese people and the non-Chinese society to resolve conflicts.

He made many good friends outside of the Chinese circle. Some of them were people in the high society of Deadwood, which included judges, city officials, and physicians. Certainly, there were continual discriminations of some sort against the Chinese. Apparently, through Fee Lee Wong's efforts, the Chinese were able to coexist in reasonable peace with the non-Chinese in that region. The following sections will provide some details on the lives of Fee Lee Wong and his children in a frontier town.

The Businessman and Physician. More than seven historians have written about or have mentioned Dr. Wing Tsue, which is the name the local non-Chinese called Fee Lee Wong. The name stemmed from the name of his store. In America, people traditionally name their stores after the owner's names. Of course, for the Chinese, doing such was taboo. Fee Lee Wong named his store Wing Tsue. The Deadwood people assumed that Wing Tsue was his name. I believe that people began to call him "Doctor" when they learned that he was selling Chinese medicines. By 1908, the Business Directory of Deadwood listed Wing Tsue as "Physician and Chinese Goods." It is possible that he was diagnosing sicknesses and prescribing medicines by that time. Dr. Howe, who was a western physician and served many terms as mayor in Deadwood, had high praise for Dr. Wing Tsue in his book on Deadwood doctors. Some people in Deadwood even claimed that Fee Lee Wong delivered babies. That would be hard to believe because even the professional "Chinese Physicians" did not deliver babies in the old days.

To understand what Fee Lee Wong did in Deadwood, it is necessary to know something about Deadwood. Prior to the Gold Rush, Black Hills was basically inhabited by a few Indians. After a few gold strikes, people from all over poured in, including Calamity Jane, a scout for General Crook. She stayed on and off in Deadwood and lived in the Chinatown section for a length of time. Deadwood was a town dominated by rough-and-tough miners and frontiersmen. At its prime, there were possibly 13,000 people living around Deadwood, including about 220 to 1,300 Chinese. This widespread estimate of the number of Chinese was due to the reluctance of Chinese to be identified—a reaction to the anti-Chinese sentiment. Thus, the low number of 220 reported in the 1880 Census record is most likely understated. At the time of the Census, many Chinese might have been working in the mines that were not easily accessible, and those responding to the census takers might not have reported everybody living in the households. The large number of 1,300 came from an estimate by an old-timer during a historical discussion held in 1967. If the high number is correct, this makes the Deadwood region the place with one of the largest concentrations of Chinese in America at that time (10%), far exceeding San Francisco. Thus, the Chinese population is a very important part of Deadwood. Fee Lee Wong might have realized that there was a bright future in Deadwood even for a Chinese, or he might simply have liked it there, as he really did not have bona fide roots in China, having resettled in another county before he came to America. In any event, he decided to make Deadwood his home.

Fee Lee Wong started his general store before 1878, as indicated in an entry in the postal money-order record book, before he went to China to bring a wife back to Deadwood. His wife, S.N. Ho, arrived in Deadwood with him in 1883. One interesting fact is that he had only one wife when many of the Chinese, especially the rich ones, would have several wives. Usually, the wives of the Chinese men in America at that time would stay in China. So, Fee Lee Wong's monogamy had nothing to do with the law in America. His store catered to Caucasians, as well as to Chinese, selling Chinese goods and Chinese foodstuffs, including herbal medicine. One of the medicines was opium. The local newspapers had reported that Fee Lee Wong was arrested for operating an opium den and mailing lottery literature. In the opium case, he was charged with causing public nuisance and was fined $25. There was no law against selling opium. In fact, in 1878, the County there passed a law to tax each opium den $300 a year. Gambling apparently was not a local offense, but a violation of U.S. mail regulations. One must realize that gambling and smoking opium were ways of life for many Chinese at that time.

There was a big fire in 1885 that burned 10 buildings in the Deadwood Chinatown. The fire was reported to be started in Fee Lee Wong's store. The city extended the water main into Chinatown and put a fire plug in front of the Wing Tsue store in 1886. Later on, Fee Lee Wong financed his own Fire Hose Team for fighting fires. He was a member of the Society of Black Hills Pioneers. Only people who came to the Black Hills before 1880 and their descendants could join this Society. For a Chinese to join such organizations in those times was a very rare event. He also bought many mining claims and real estate properties in and around Deadwood, including the three lots where his store was located. In the 1890s he built the only two brick-buildings in Chinatown on two of the lots. Now they are historical buildings being preserved in Deadwood, and the fire hydrant is still in front of the structures.

The Offspring. Fee Lee Wong had nine children. The children, who were born in Deadwood, went to regular schools there. The girls eventually went back to China and got married. The oldest son was an adopted son. He stayed in California, but never lived in

Deadwood. Fee Lee Wong gave each of his other sons $4,000 (either upon their graduation from high school or when they were ready to be on their own) for them to use to seek their future. The second son, H.Q. Wong, went on to study at the South Dakota School of Mines and Technology in 1907. Unfortunately, he contracted meningitis and had to drop out of the technical college. He then worked for the postal service and the immigration service in the U.S. The third son, S.Q. Wong, who was class president in his freshman year at Deadwood High School, received a B.S. degree in architecture from the University of Michigan in 1921. Besides having a very successful career in architecture and many other endeavors mainly in China, S.Q. Wong was commissioned as a Captain in the U.S. Marine Corps during the second World War when he was in his 50s. It is believed that he was the first Chinese to achieve that rank in the Marine Corps. He also received a Bronze Star for his bravery. The fourth son, T.Q. Wong, became a professional magician, owning his own troupe. His troupe performed all over the world, including shows at the 1936 Chicago World's Fair. Fee Lee Wong passed away in 1921 and did not get to see the fruits of the seeds he planted in his children, but he certainly would have been proud of them.

The End of the Black Hills Gold Rush. By the year 1910, the easily-accessible gold deposits were essentially all claimed by the miners in the Black Hills. The rise and fall of the population of Deadwood followed the number of new gold strikes, as did the population of Deadwood Chinatown. Officially, it was reported that there were 215 Chinese living in the Black Hills in 1900, and the number was down to 73 by 1910. During this time, Fee Lee Wong's family members also gradually left, and he himself left in 1919 to return to China. The last Chinese from the Gold Rush generation, who was once an employee of Fee Lee Wong, left Deadwood in 1932. All but one of Fee Lee Wong's grandchildren were born in China, but almost half of them returned to or are in the U.S. today. His grandchildren and great-grandchildren contributed to and are still contributing to the U.S. in a broad spectrum of professions.

Fee Lee Wong's life in Deadwood followed the rise and fall of the Chinatown in Deadwood. He did more than witness the birth and maturity of Chinatown; he helped shape its future. He also made contributions to the town of Deadwood. He proved that the American dream could be fulfilled for immigrants. Even a Chinese could succeed in an American frontier town. He greatly contributed in the area of race relations at a time when many Americans distrusted the Chinese and attempted to drive the Chinese out physically and legally. He did much to give the people in Deadwood a good impression of the Chinese. Fee Lee Wong contributed more than hard labor to

America. He joined the pioneering spirit of planting roots in the New World, and his descendants continue to contribute to America in many ways today.

The Western Military Academy in Fresno

FRANKLIN NG

FRANKLIN NG

Department of Anthropology, Cal State University, Fresno, California

In the 19th century, China found itself humiliated by a series of unequal treaties and territorial concessions. Defeated in a series of wars starting with the Opium War of 1839–1842, China lost its tariff autonomy, granted extraterritorial privileges, and opened its ports to foreign nations. Its subsequent debacle in the Sino-Japanese War of 1894 to 1895 only underscored its internal failures and external weaknesses. Coincidentally, this era marked the high tide of European imperialism, and China faced the grim prospect of division into spheres of influence controlled by the Western powers and Japan. Confronted with the danger of disintegration and collapse, how should China respond to the crisis? Chinese officials and observers heatedly debated the issue (see Spence 1990, Hsu 1983, Gray 1990).

At the end of the century, the views espoused by two groups received the most attention. The revolutionaries, who were led by Sun Yat-sen, favored an end to Manchu rule and the establishment of a Chinese republic. The reformers, who were led by Kang Youwei, wanted a constitutional monarchy based in part on the model of Meiji Japan (Schiffrin 1968, Wilbur 1976, Lo 1967, Gasster 1969). But for the ruling Empress Dowager Cixi, the positions of both groups were anathema. Holding power since 1861, she preferred the status quo and saw any major change as a threat to her position. Change might also undermine the foundations of Manchu rule in the Qing dynasty at some future date. Believing the reigning Guangxu Emperor to be too naive and overly sympathetic to the reformers, she staged a palace coup d'état and brought an end to his Hundred Days' Reforms Movement of 1898, which had been inspired by Kang Youwei. Thereafter, she kept him captive until his mysterious death on November 14, 1908, just one day before she also died (Kwong 1984, Wong 513–44).

The suppression of the Hundred Days' Reforms did not still the debate about the question of revolution or reform. Reflecting the concern in China, overseas Chinese were swept into the debate. Followers of Sun Yat-sen and Kang Youwei traveled widely in Southeast Asia, Japan, Hawaii, and the Americas, seeking support and money. They organized societies, printed newspapers, and mounted campaigns to publicize their ideas. Sun Yat-sen's supporters formed a Revive China Society (*Xingzhonghui*) in 1894 and later a United League (*Tongmenghui*) in 1905 for the purpose of overthrowing the Manchu dynasty. Kang Youwei's supporters, helped immensely by his protégé Liang Qichao, started a Chinese Empire Reform

Association or Protect the Emperor Society (*Baohuanghui*) in 1899 to restore the Guangxu Emperor to power (see Tsai 1983, 1986).

Those who sided with Kang Youwei and Liang Qichao found an ally in a California resident and self-styled military strategist named Homer Lea. Building upon his earlier ties with the Chinese community in San Francisco, Lea established a Western Military Academy (*Gancheng Xuexiao*) in 1903 to train Chinese cadets for the reformers. With its headquarters in Los Angeles, branches were started in many cities, including San Francisco, Fresno, Chicago, St. Louis, Philadelphia, and New York. In training the cadets, the organization awaited the day when it would help to return imperial control to the Guangxu Emperor instead of the Empress Dowager Cixi (Chong 70–72).

Homer Lea's personal connections were extensive, for he knew important reformers such as Wu Panzhao (Ng Poon Chew), Liang Qichao, and Kang Youwei. When Kang toured the United States in 1905, Lea accompanied him on the journey across the country to New York (*New York Times* 6/28/1905). Unfortunately for Lea, however, the Western Military Academy became the target of a state-wide controversy in California. George W. Jones, the District Attorney of Fresno County, believed that it was illegal for Chinese cadets to conduct military drills or to parade with arms. Because of his investigation, unfavorable publicity was focused on the activities of the organization in California and the rest of the country. This study examines the background of the Fresno branch of the Western Military Academy and its relationship with the Chinese and Caucasian communities.

The Chinese in Fresno. Fresno County is located in the central portion of the San Joaquin Valley of California. When the Chinese mined in the area during the 1850s, they initially congregated in the Millerton area. But anti-Chinese feeling here, as elsewhere in the state, forced the Chinese to move north to a site between Fort Miller and Millerton. When the Central Pacific Railroad completed its Fresno Station in 1872, the Chinese helped to lay the track. Later, when the county seat was changed from Millerton to Fresno in 1874, many Chinese also moved to new quarters along the railroad tracks. The Chinese even contributed their labor to help build the Fresno County Courthouse. At that time, the population of Fresno included 400 white persons and 200 Chinese (English 28, *Fresno Bee* 4/18/1956).

As in the case of Millerton, however, hostile sentiments surfaced against the Chinese. On August 5, 1874, a group of Fresno residents objected to the presence of the Chinese in the white section of the town. They circulated an agreement not to sell, lease, or rent any property to the Chinese on the east side of the railroad tracks (Vandor

330). From that point on, many Chinese referred to their neighborhood as being in the area situated "west of the tracks" (see Schrieke 36). Two years later, on September 23, 1876, the first edition of the *Fresno Morning Republican* editorialized on "The Chinese Question," warning that the continued entry of "Mongolians" would be a detriment to the prosperity of the county (Clough 5). In subsequent issues of the paper, articles frequently labeled the Chinese "Chinks" and called the Japanese "Japs" or "little brown men" (see *Fresno Morning Republican* 10/1, 9/20/1904; 6/29/1905). Chinese children were not permitted to attend the public schools in Fresno, so they went instead to a Chinese school (Clough 5).

Nevertheless, despite the prejudice and the discrimination, the Chinese community grew. Local writers and historians say that in the early 1890s, Fresno had the second largest Chinatown in the state (*Fresno Bee* 4/18/56; *Rehart* 6) A writer in 1904 claimed that Fresno's Chinatown was the third largest in the state, and one local resident stated that West Fresno's Chinatown once boasted a population larger than the city of Fresno itself (*Fresno Morning Republican* 11/20/1904; *Fresno Bee* 5/22/62). The U.S. and State censuses generally did not include accurate statistics for Chinatown, which was considered a tenderloin district with many transients, so it is difficult to determine the exact population for the Chinese (Rehart 6, English 32, Clough 5; see Chacon 371–99). One estimate in 1905 listed the population in the Fresno city limits as being 18,735, while the Chinese numbered 1,129 (*Fresno Morning Republican* 5/16/1905). The Chinese constituted an important portion of the migrant labor force in agriculture, too. In 1903, 3,000 Chinese laborers tended the grape vines; while in the 1904, the number was a smaller 2,000 persons. The reasons given for the difference were lower wages and the aging of the Chinese workers (*Fresno Morning Republican* 8/30/1905, Suhler 7).[1] Nonetheless, local historian June English estimated the Chinese population in Fresno County to be approximately 7,500 for 1918 (English 29).

Although the exact size of Fresno County's Chinese population is hard to gauge, it was a dynamic and vibrant community. Chinese from surrounding towns in the Central Valley, such as Hanford, Lemoore, Armona, Visalia, and Bakersfield, often participated in the activities of Fresno's Chinatown. The Fresno County business records indicate that for the period from 1899 to 1900, Chinatown was the home for three laundries, three restaurants, five saloons, and 59 merchants or traders (English 26–27). The associations typically found in most Chinese communities were also well represented. For example, there was a Sam Yup (*Sanyi huiguan*) Association building

---

[1]One former resident says there were about 1,000 to 1,500 Chinese families living in Chinatown in 1907.

in China Alley as early as 1887. In addition, a Kong Chow (*Gangzhou huiguan*) Society Temple, a Chinese Baptist Mission, and a Chinese theater were familiar landmarks. Moreover, fraternal organizations such as the Bing Kung Tong (*Binggong tang*), the Suey On Tong (*Ruian tang*), and the Bow On Tong (*Baoan tang*) provided important meeting places (*Fresno Bee* 5/22/41; 4/18/56; 5/22/62; Opper and Lew 48).

The Western Military Academy in Fresno. In a visit to Los Angeles in 1903, the reformer Liang Qichao met Homer Lea and encouraged him to train Chinese cadets (Chong 55–58, 68; Anschel 37–38). Fancying himself to be "a latter-day Bryon," as L. Eve Armentrout Ma has so aptly put it, Lea was all too glad to comply. He saw himself as being able to help reform China by placing troops and officers in the field against the Empress Dowager Cixi. In November, 1904, he established the Western Military Academy in Los Angeles and incorporated it with the State of California (Ma 59, 108–109). After several branches were opened in Chinese communities in different states throughout the United States, Fresno, California, also became the site for a branch of the Western Military Academy.

The Fresno branch was an outgrowth of the local chapter of the Protect the Emperor Society. It was more popularly known to outsiders as the Chinese Empire Reform Association or the Bow Wong Woy Chinese Reform Society (Ding 187, see Worden 1971).[2] The Fresno Bow Wong Woy (*Baohuanghui*) maintained an association hall on G Street in Fresno's Chinatown and furnished it with desks and chairs. On its walls were pictures of the reform movement and the charter members of the local association, along with a large picture of President Theodore Roosevelt. Several maps of China were conspicuously posted, and there were long rows of paper near the entrance bearing the names of members of the association. For 1904, the president was a well-known merchant named Fon Kee, and he led an organization that claimed between 300 to 350 members (*Fresno Morning Republican* 8/14/1904).[3]. A placard with pictures of its officers and directors showed 65 persons (*The Life, Influence and Role of the Chinese* xxxiv–xxxv).[4]

---

[2]Liang Qichao found no Baohuanghui in his trip through Fresno.

[3]The address was 1037 G Street, and Ben O. Young would be president of the Chinese Empire Reform Association in 1905 (*Fresno City and County Directory 1905,* 447).

[4]Key Ray Chong states: "By and large, training outside Los Angeles was clandestine, and the drill sessions took place in the evening or in remote places on the weekend" (Chong 72). In Fresno, the drills were daily at 8 p.m., but their activities were well publicized in the *Fresno Morning Republican.*

Indication that a local branch of the Western Military Academy was being started came in August, 1904. In an interview with the *Fresno Morning Republican*, John C. Tuck (Chen Qide) mentioned that the Chinese Empire Reform Association was expecting a general to come to Fresno from Los Angeles. The officer would drill the local Chinese, so that Fresno could send a company later "to fight and make China a civilized country with rulers who are ready to open the doors and let people from other countries come in and trade" (*Fresno Morning Republican 8/14/1904*). A month later, on September 10, 1904, the same paper reported that "Chinese across the tracks" were preparing to learn how to shoot "American bullets into the carcass of the Celestial dragon." The story noted that the Chinese Reform Association sought to reinstate the young emperor upon the throne of the Chinese empire (*Fresno Morning Republican 9/10/1904*). On October 5, 1904, the paper said that the soldiers of the Fresno Chinese Empire Reform Association had held their first drill the preceding night (*Fresno Morning Republican 10/5/1904*). Several weeks later, a photograph in the paper revealed 20 individuals dressed in uniform. The caption explained that "These are the Chinese lads who are learning American Army tactics" (*Fresno Morning Republican 10/23/1904*).

Reasons for Participation. The motives of the 26 Chinese who joined the "Chinatown militia," as the paper dubbed it, were several. First of all, some of them viewed themselves as modern and progressive. A number were also second-generation, born in the United States, and therefore American citizens (Crichton 5/5/1905). On August 13, 1904, John Tuck declared that some of the Chinese Empire Reform Association members planned to cut off their queues in "maybe one, two, or three weeks" (*Fresno Morning Republican 8/14/1904*). On September 3, 1904, Jeff Shannon Kit cut off his queue and dressed in a new American suit with trousers, coat, and a vest instead of Chinese garb. Born in Fresno's Chinatown on 1051 G Street, Kit believed his queue to be a useless appendage and had repeatedly vowed to get rid of it. But his mother had cried and pleaded with him to respect tradition. Nonetheless, Kit decided to go ahead, did not shave his head, and went to a barbershop for an American haircut (*Fresno Morning Republican 9/4/1904*, Opper and Lew 50). Lee Yee, a merchant, followed his example and also wore American clothes and footwear (*Fresno Morning Republican 9/7/1904*). By mid-October, seven other Chinese had discarded their queues (*Fresno Morning Republican 10/23/1904*).

The *Fresno Morning Republican* approved of the happenings in Chinatown. It saw the changes as a tendency for the "younger generation to break away from old things and take up the new things that it has found on these shores and in this city." The past few months had witnessed "the advance of civilization" upon Fresno's Chinatown. Not all of the Chinese cadets had cut off their queues, but they felt bound to at least wear wigs to hide their braids. The paper confidently predicted that, in time, others would cut theirs, too, once the hair on the shaved portions of the head grew long again (ibid.).

Closely related to the first reason may have been a second consideration, a desire to imitate their National Guard peers. During the first decade of the 20th century, to be a member of the California National Guard in Fresno was to enter into a fraternal order and a social circle. While weekly drills demanded an investment in time, there was ample opportunity for socializing and fun. Competition between Companies C and F led to spirited rivalry while the scheduled dances were gala affairs. Moreover, the local paper provided complete coverage with favorable commentary of all the activities of the Fresno units of the California National Guard. In joining the Fresno branch of the Western Military Academy, and banding together as Company D, the Chinese had a chance to partake of activities hitherto available only to others (*Fresno Morning Republican* 12/11/1904, Hudson 1952).

A third factor was a desire to do something patriotic and heroic. The visits of reformers Liang Qichao and Kang Youwei and revolutionary Sun Yat-sen from 1903 to 1905 to the United States, California, and Fresno excited the imagination of those who were still concerned about the homeland. In China itself, new armies and military schools influenced by Western teaching were regarded as important modernizing agents (Hatano 365–82). Furthermore, the distribution of Zou Rong's booklet *The Revolutionary Army* (*Geming Zhuzhun*) in 1903 inspired Chinese to attempt to control their own destiny and nurtured a martial spirit (Jung Tsou 1968, Schiffrin 330).[5]

Finally, the prejudice and discrimination that the Chinese encountered in Fresno and California may have encouraged them to build bridges with the Caucasian population. Socially isolated and segregated in the Chinatown section of Fresno, first-generation

---

[5]Chinese papers in the U.S. printed editorials, ballads (*geyao*), and Cantonese opera or drama (*yuesheng*) that focused on China's weakness and the need to save the country. See, for example, *Sun Chung Kwock Bo* (*Xin zhongguo bao*) or *New China Press* (Honolulu), February 18, 28, 1905. An interesting study is Pui-Chee Leung (Liang Peichi), *Nanyin yu yueou zhi yanjiu* (*A Study of Nan Yin and Yue Ou* . See also the *Gancheng Xuexiao ge* (Western Military Academy School Anthem) and *Baohuanghui ge* (Protect the Emperor Society Anthem) in *Baohuanghui Gancheng Xuexiao xiaoshi* (Historical Materials on the Protect the Emperor Society's Western Military Academy), in Archives, Asian American Studies Library, University of California, Berkeley.

Chinese were also by law denied the possibility of naturalization for U.S. citizenship. Aware of these differences in their social and legal status, the local Chinese may have welcomed opportunities to forge connections with other Fresno residents. All four of the aforementioned reasons may have been factors that motivated the members of the Fresno Chinese Empire Reform Association to enlist in Company D, a Chinese-organized military unit.

Activities of the Academy. From his headquarters in Los Angeles, Homer Lea probably selected the officers for the Chinese cadets in Fresno. No doubt he also consulted with the Fresno chapter of the Chinese chapter of the Chinese Empire Reform Association. William D. Crichton, a lawyer and former justice of the peace, was retained as an attorney for the Fresno association. He handled many legal affairs for the Chinese community and was a friend to the Chinese merchants. When his advice was solicited as to the choice of candidates to act as drill masters, one person he recommended was W. S. Scott (*Fresno Morning Republican* 10/23/1904, see Vandor 712–13). Scott had served as the first lieutenant and acting adjutant for Company C of the California National Guard in Fresno and therefore was experienced in the conduct of military drills and training (*Fresno Morning Republican* 6/4/1904). He had even been offered the post of captain in Company C, but he had declined, and resigned from the unit to attend to his own business (*Fresno Morning Republican* 6/30/1904). Crichton himself would also have a role as he would act as a legal adviser and general controller for the cadets (*Fresno Morning Republican* 9/16/1904).

Other officers for the Chinese unit included Curtis Neal and Ben O. Young. Neal was a second lieutenant for Company C and had served with Scott (*Fresno Morning Republican* 3/14, 6/4/1904). Lea promoted Scott to the rank of major and Neal was raised to the rank of first lieutenant. Offering Scott and Neal ranks that were higher than that which they held in the California National Guard was an inducement to elicit their involvement with the Western Military Academy in Fresno. Ben O. Young (Ouyang Xianzhou), publisher of the local Chinese paper and a member of the Chinese Empire Reform Association, held the rank of second lieutenant (ibid., Chapin unpublished manuscript).

In October, 1904, the Chinese cadets began their drills in earnest. They assembled daily in a Chinese opera house that had been converted into an armory. Dressed in khaki uniforms similar to those worn by American troops, they learned to march and to countermarch, to advance and to retreat. In the initial drills, Major Scott had difficulty communicating with the Chinese. Orders had to be shouted out, but the only results had been blank stares. An interpreter had to be used to explain the meanings of the various commands. To facilitate understanding of the different commands, a large sheet of paper was posted on the walls of the association. Instructions on the paper explained the proper execution for each order (*Fresno Morning Republican* 10/5, 10/23/1904).[6] The cadets also received Springfield rifles and dress uniforms for their use (*Fresno Morning Republican* 10/23, 12/11/1904).[7]

As news of the unit's activities spread, the local Chinese community became very proud of its Company D cadets. On February 13, 1905, they feted the Chinese soldiers with a sumptuous banquet at the Yet Far Low restaurant (*Fresno Morning Republican* 2/13/1905). Captain I. E. Wilson and Lieutenant T. Spivey of Company F, a unit of the California National Guard in Fresno, inspected the soldiers the next month and complimented the Chinese troops on their performance (*Fresno Morning Republican* 3/14/1905). That Company D was being accepted by the other chapters of the California National Guard is demonstrated by the extending of an invitation to a Chinese sergeant to speak before Company C (*Fresno Morning Republican* 3/11/1905).

Perhaps the two high points for the Chinese cadets were the arrivals of Kang Youwei and Homer Lea to Fresno. On March 12, 1905, Kang visited Fresno. His entourage included his private secretary, a valet, and a Chinese from Portland. They were greeted by 26 uniformed men of Company D. After inspecting the unit, Kang retired to the Hughes Hotel. He had not been feeling well, but that evening at a banquet, he delivered a speech to a packed audience in the Chinese Alley theater. He urged all the Chinese to cut their queues and to help uplift their race. Afterwards, Kang left for Los Angeles, accompanied by Ben O. Young as his interpreter (*Fresno Morning Republican* 3/14, 5/7/1905; *Sun Chung Kwock Bo* 3/25/1905). While in Fresno, Kang had met a girl named Haw Gum-lan, whom he later married (*Fresno Bee* 5/22/41).

Homer Lea's visit to Fresno in the next month on April 8, 1905, was eagerly anticipated by the Chinese community. As he was the head of the Western Military Academy, the local Chinese wished to welcome him in grand style. While touring the city, Lea expressed his

---

[6]The commands were perhaps translated in the same fashion as the "Bingshu zhaoyi shangwenjie xiawenyin" (translation of military terms), document, in the Powers Papers. Thus, "Right Face" was translated as *youmian* and to be pronounced in Cantonese with the Chinese characters *huli feishi*. "Left Face" was translated as *zuomian* and pronounced as *litian feishi*. "Forward March" was *jinqian qibu* and pronounced as *huohuo mazhi*.

[7]An attendance report for Company D is recorded on a form, "A Parade or Morning Report of W.S. Scott for April 1, 1905," Powers Papers.

wish to form a battalion in the Central Valley with companies at Hanford and Bakersfield or Visalia. Or, there might be two companies formed in Fresno and one organized from the other towns (*Fresno Morning Republican* 4/9/1905; *Weixin Bao* 4/19/1905).[8] But somewhat unexpectedly, Lea's inspection of the Chinese cadets caused a furor. In reviewing their drills, he had judged them and had decided to award four medals. Eager to show mastery of military skills, many cadets were disappointed that they had been passed over. They complained that Lea was not fit to evaluate their performance as soldiers. Only by Major Scott's intervention and patient explanations was the situation repaired and the cadets appeased (*Fresno Morning Republican* 4/14/1905). Several days later, Curtis Neal, one of the drill instructors, boarded a train for Los Angeles. The purpose of his trip was to meet with a Dr. Tom Leung (Tan Zhangxiao) and the Los Angeles branch of the Western Military Academy (*Fresno Morning Republican* 4/19/1905)[9].

A Controversy Unfolds. Nevertheless, Lea's difficulties were only beginning. While in Fresno to inspect Company F of the California National Guard, Lieutenant J. Alexander of the Adjutant General's Office learned about Company D of the Chinese cadets. He raised questions about the right of the Chinese to parade with arms, as it violated section 734 of the penal code of California. According to that provision, only the members of the National Guard and the soldiers of the United States could drill with the arms in public without a license from the governor. He hinted that Curtis Neal could be court-martialed for acting as an officer in an unlawful military organization while simultaneously holding a position with the California National Guard (*Fresno Morning Republican* 4/21/1905; *Chung Sai Yat Po* 4/22/1905).

W. D. Crichton, the legal adviser to the Chinese, responded quickly to Lieutenant Alexander's comments. He voiced the opinion that the lieutenant had "only lately been attached to the adjutant-general's office" and was suffering from a "swelled-head." Alexander was interfering "in a matter he knows nothing about." Crichton maintained that the reform association was organized under the laws of California for instruction in academic studies, language studies, and military science. He stated that the articles of incorporation were on file in the office of the county clerk for Fresno and that Governor Pardee had provided a license to carry arms (*Fresno Morning Republican* 4/22/1905).

---

[8]Hanford would have a school led by Sergeant William English (Glick 66).
[9]On Tom Leung, see Jane Leung Larson 151–98 and Louise Leung Larson 1990.

Also responding, W. S. Scott explained that, as an instructor for the Chinese, he did not feel that he was violating the law or was "any less of an American." He had served 13 years in the National Guard and was a veteran of the Spanish-American War. And, if duty called again, he "would enlist as a private and do my share toward protecting my country." But he did not feel that he merited criticism by officers of the National Guard for instructing a company of Chinese cadets (*Fresno Democrat* 4/21/1905).

Apprised of the situation, on May 4, 1905, California Governor George C. Pardee wrote to Crichton about Company D. He wondered whether the attorney had made the statement that the Chinese military company "has a license from Governor Pardee to carry arms." If so, he asked that Crichton produce a copy of the license permitting the Chinese military organization to bear arms (Pardee Papers 5/4/1905). Crichton immediately wrote back to the governor on May 5. Attempting to distance himself from a developing controversy, he denied that he was an attorney for the Chinese military academy. He was merely a lawyer for some of the Chinese merchants who were "in sympathy with it." It was Homer Lea who had given him the impression that a permit had been secured. He bemoaned that fact that the newspaper accounts had so "garbled" his comments that he "could hardly recognize the interviews." Wishing to avoid "any notoriety," he claimed that "I haven't anything to do with this thing as an organization, and hope never to have [sic]" (Pardee Papers 5/5/1905).

On the same day, Doctor Chester Rowell of Fresno also wrote to the governor. A supporter of Pardee's gubernatorial campaign in 1902, he tried to mediate in the situation. He opined that there was no need for "courtmarshaling [sic] anybody." Neither Scott nor the Chinese had any "improper motive" in their drills, and they would stop their training if there were any objections. Rowell explained that "the Chinese, quite a number of them native born to Fresno, were activated largely by the novelty of the affair." He did not believe that anyone had "purposely violated the law" (Pardee Papers 5/5/1905).

But Pardee was not pacified. He replied to Rowell that he had not issued any license for the Chinese to bear arms. Homer Lea was "much mistaken about this" (Pardee Papers 5/10/1905). He also relayed the same message to Crichton and asked that the Chinese in Fresno immediately desist from their drills with arms (Pardee Papers 5/10/1905). On that same day, the governor sent a letter to George W. Jones, the Fresno County District Attorney. Still upset, Pardee stated that he had been misrepresented as having issued a license for the Chinese military company in Fresno, but that "such is not the fact." He called upon Jones to investigate further into the matter so that "you may take such action as may seem proper for the enforcement of the law" (Pardee Papers 5/10/1905; see Vandor 1061).

Taking his instructions from the governor, Jones initiated an investigation of Company D. He learned that it was "under the direction" of the Chinese Empire Reform Association. The military company maintained an armory equipped with firearms and furnished its members with uniforms "in practically the same manner as troops of the United States are uniformed." He also discovered that the officers of the Chinese Empire Reform Association believed that a "General Lee [sic]" had procured the necessary permission as required by state law (Pardee Papers 5/17/1905; *Fresno Democrat* 5/16/1905; *San Francisco Call* 5/17/1905; *Chung Sai Yat Po* 5/15,16/1905).[10]

From the information that he had gathered, Jones understood that the company of "Chinese Imperial Guards" had been organized with the intent of overthrowing the government of China. As that government maintained friendly relations with the United States, he thought that the actions of Company D were violations of neutrality and international law. He therefore told the Chinese Empire Reform Association, the military company, its drill instructors Neal and Scott, and its attorney Crichton to halt their drills, parading, and bearing of arms unless legal permission had been obtained (*Fresno Morning Republican* 5/16/1905).[11] He pledged to the governor that if there were any further violations of the law, he would "take the necessary steps to prosecute all offenders" (Pardee Papers 5/17/1905). Homer Lea now entered the fray by writing to Jones. He protested the treatment and the "misunderstanding" regarding the military company. One year ago, a Western Military Academy had been organized in Los Angeles for academic and military instruction and had incorporated with the state. Subsequently, branches had been established in other cities situated in California. The Fresno branch of the academy had, in fact, filed incorporation papers with the County Clerk of Fresno. As Lea understood the laws of California, students of a military academy had "the right to use arms in the course of their education." Only if there was parading with arms in public was it necessary to have the consent of the governor. And, said Lea, Pardee had granted permission for the students of the Western Military Academy in Los Angeles to parade on January 1, 1905. Having made his case, Lea was "confident" that Jones would have "sympathy" with

---

[10]For an early Chinese view on the permit issue and Fresno, see *Sun Chung Kwock Bo* 5/16/1905.

[11]One wonders if Jones bore any resentment toward Chrichton. Several months earlier, Jones had been publicly embarrassed by the resignation of his deputy district attorney, S.C. St. John, who had left to join in a partnership with Chrichton's law practice (*Fresno Morning Republican* 11/30/1904).

the educational goals of the Chinese students (Pardee Papers 5/18/1905).

Receiving this new information, Jones launched a new investigation. He discovered to his surprise that articles of incorporation for the Western Military Academy had indeed been filed with the Fresno County Clerk on December 24, 1904, and had also been filed with the office of the Secretary of State on November 28, 1904 (Pardee Papers 5/22/1905). Replying to Lea, he said nothing about his finding. He obliquely criticized the academy by asserting that it had "no academic department" and that its emphasis was "wholly military in nature" and therefore was "in violation of the statute." But aware that this was much more complicated that he had first thought, Jones suggested that Lea "take this matter up with the proper state authorities and procure the necessary permission" (Pardee Papers 5/22/1905).[12] At the same time, he told the governor about his discovery—"this new phase of the question" (Pardee Papers 5/22/1905). In Fresno, Jones admitted that "I don't know what the outcome of the matter will be" (*Fresno Morning Republican* 5/24/1905).

Governor Pardee answered that he had given no such permission to the academy in Los Angeles to parade with arms. Homer Lea was "mistaken as to his facts, although I do not know how he can be." Consequently, the situation had not been changed at all by this new correspondence. Pardee reiterated that any attempt by the Fresno Chinese to continue their drills or to bear arms as a military organization would be "unlawful" (Pardee Papers 5/30/1905). It did turn out, however, that the Western Military Academy in Los Angeles had been incorporated in 1904 (Worden 126). Two days later, on June 1, 1905, in a letter to Jones, the governor's secretary tactfully conceded that Pardee had been "slightly mistaken." J. B. Lauck, the Adjutant General for California, had authorized the organization on December 18, 1904, to march in the Tournament of Roses in Pasadena on January 1, 1905. But the length of the permit was only from December 30, 1904, to January 3, 1905. So it remained true that branches in Fresno and elsewhere had "no permission or license to drill or parade with arms" (Pardee Papers 6/1/1905).

As the activities of the Western Military Academy in Fresno were reported in newspapers throughout the state and the country, accounts regarding other branches began to surface (*Berkeley Gazette* 5/20/1905; *Los Angeles Daily Times* 4/25, 6/1,2,3/1905; *New York Daily Tribune* 6/23/1905; *Chung Sai Yat Po* 6/21/1905). Charges by a R.A. Falkenberg drew additional attention. Evidently, he and Lea had

---

[12]Lea had accompanied Kang Youwei to New York and had asked Jones to write to him via the association in that city (Pardee Papers 5/18/1905).

both been recruiting and training Chinese for Liang Qichao and Kang Youwei. The two clashed over who was in charge, and Kang Youwei had decided to favor Lea (Powers Papers 4/7/1905; *San Francisco Chronicle* 4/3/1905; *Los Angeles Daily Times* 4/3,7,8,11/1905; *Chung Sai Yat Po* 5/5/1905). Disgruntled because he had been shunted aside by his rival, Falkenberg told the governor about other military companies in Oakland and Los Angeles (Pardee Papers 5/18/1905). Lea was intent on organizing the Chinese "in military affairs." He was even heard to have remarked, "I don't care what they say" and "they don't interfere with me." The Chinese informant had confided that the two military groups in Oakland and Los Angeles were "still running full blast." Falkenberg disclosed, however, that "our Japanese and Chinese Exclusion League is looking into this matter of defiance of laws" (Pardee Papers 8/30/1905).

Acting on this new information, Pardee notified the district attorneys of Alameda and Los Angeles to investigate. (Pardee Papers 9/8/1905). They confirmed that Chinese were uniformed and were training with Mauser rifles. In Oakland, the Chinese company had filed incorporation papers with Alameda County. In Los Angeles, the military tactics were taught as part of a Chinese school curriculum (Pardee Papers 9/14/1905, 10/21/1905). In compliance with the governor's wishes, the Oakland group disbanded (Pardee Papers 10/13/1905). In Los Angeles, the Chinese company purportedly had ceased drilling for about six weeks, "owing to lack of members or interest" (Pardee Papers 10/21/1905).

Homer Lea made the issue even more complicated when he tried to have an audience with General Frederick Funston, the commander of the California Department of the U. S. Army. When a Chinese and a Ralph Faneuf presented the dinner invitation, Funston was disturbed to see them wearing regular U. S. military uniforms. The incident provoked another flurry of articles, providing unfavorable publicity about the Western Military Academy (*San Francisco Call* 5/3/1905; *San Francisco Chronicle* 5/4/1905; *Chung Sai Yat Po* 5/4/1905).[13] Funston contemplated taking action, but learned that no federal laws had been violated and the state could handle the issue (*San Francisco Chronicle* 5/18/1905).

As the controversy unfolded in mid-May, 1905, the Chinese in Fresno decided not to oppose the governor and the county district attorney. They agreed to go out of existence until their legal status was settled (*Fresno Morning Republican* 5/16/1905; *Chung Sai Yat Po* 5/15,16/1905). A month later, in June, a Chinese was quoted as saying, "General Lea, he fix'um allight [*sic*]," indicating confidence

---

[13]The uniforms were patterned on those of the U.S. Army; see "General Orders No. 8 by Homer Lea," Powers Papers 11/1/1904, Powers Papers.

that Homer Lea could satisfactorily resolve the situation (*Fresno Morning Republican* 6/17/1905). In October, possibly not inclined to wait any longer, Pun Sing applied for admission into Company E, a California National Guard unit in Fresno. An American born Chinese belonging to the Baohuanghui, he was described as wanting to be "a soldier-boy." He had cropped his hair and parted it in the middle "according to the latest fashion." He spoke good English and his manners and habits were "fashioned after those of his American brethren." Some of the members of Company E reportedly were favorably disposed to the idea of accepting him (*Fresno Morning Republican* 10/13/1905).[14]

Despite the adverse publicity, Homer Lea did not drop the idea for a Western Military Academy. On October 7, 1905, he asked Governor Pardee to sanction the operation of the academy on land that it had purchased at Carlsbad in San Diego County. He pointed out that in June, 1905, he had discussed the education of Chinese as potential officers for China with President Theodore Roosevelt. The president had "expressed his approval" (Pardee Papers 10/7/1905; compare with *Los Angeles Daily Times* 6/28/1905).[15] The governor sought the advice of J. B. Lauck, the Adjutant General. The opinion rendered by Lauck was that educational institutions in the past had not been required to seek permission from the governor to arm their cadets. The sole exception was a public parade with arms as specified in section 734 of the Penal Code (Pardee Papers 10/9/1905). This time the governor relented, saying to Lea that "it is not my duty to issue licenses in such cases as that which you call to my attention" (Pardee Papers 10/13/1905).

Notwithstanding this different stance taken by Pardee, no further stories appeared about continued activities by Chinese cadets or the Western Military Academy in Fresno. An article in the *Fresno Morning Republican* on February 15, 1906, wondered what had happened to Company D. Most of the men in the group had disappeared from Fresno so that there was "scarcely a half dozen" left. A "good source" had indicated that most of them had sailed for China to help in the military instruction of a reform army. Ben O. Young had also disappeared, but a friend said he was out of town on business. In contrast, another source claimed that Young had gone to China. John Tuck explained the absence of most as attributable to work out of town, but he did not deny that some may have departed for China

---

[14]Only a week earlier, Chinese and Japanese arrested for gambling had been referred to as looking like "the Chinese Imperial Army" as they marched to the county jail (*Fresno Morning Republican* 10/8/1905).
[15]Lea asked for a letter of introduction to Roosevelt from the president of Stanford University (Stanford University Archives 5/10, 6/3/1905).

(*Fresno Morning Republican* 2/15/1906; compare with *San Francisco Chronicle* 2/13/1906).

Many years later, Ansel O'Banion, who had served as Homer Lea's deputy, commented that the first Chinese cadets from the Western Military Academy graduated in 1906. They then proceeded to China to help in the revolution against the Qing dynasty that would follow (Glick and Hong 214, Glick 223). O'Banion's account alludes to Lea's joining with Sun Yat-sen and the revolutionaries. As a result of the Falkenberg incident, Lea had become disenchanted with Kang Youwei and eventually joined with Sun (Huang 32–33 in Powers Papers; see Lu 417–19).[16] In one of the fascinating episodes in history, Lea would become a close friend and adviser of the father of the Chinese revolution in 1911. Because of this tie, the remains of Lea would be deposited with a marble tombstone at the Yangmingshan cemetery in Taiwan.[17]

For Lieutenant Curtis Neal, the drill instructor for the Chinese, repercussions would follow several months later in September, 1905. He would receive a widely publicized reprimand. Colonel Thomas Wilhelm, the Assistant Inspector General for the California National Guard, criticized Company C for having a low level of efficiency and performance. He suggested that this was due to Neal's neglect of his National Guard duties. Rather than "giving proper attention" to his unit, Company C, Neal had "given nearly all of his spare time to instructing an armed organization, known as "The Chinese Imperial Army Reform Association." Lieutenant J. Alexander and Colonel R. K. Whitmore, the regimental commander, endorsed Wilhelm's findings (*Fresno Morning Republican* 9/19/1905).

Yet, regardless of what Wilhelm, Alexander, and Whitmore may have thought about the episode, Fresno's members of the National Guard had their own opinions. A month later, in October, 1905, the soldiers of Company C disregarded Wilhelm's remarks and elected Neal to the higher rank of first lieutenant for their unit. Company C chose to award him a military commission and ignored the negative comments of the higher echelon (*Fresno Morning Republican* 10/7/1905). The following year, on February 1, 1906, the Chinese Empire Reform Association held a New Year's celebration. They invited six officers from Company C and warmly greeted Neal with cheers (*Fresno Morning Republican* 2/2/1906). At the same time, the Chinese community in Fresno harbored no hostility or ill will against

---

[16]A recent newspaper account is in *Shijie ribao* (World Journal), 10/17/1992.
[17]See "Dr. Sun's American Adviser Laid to Rest in Free China," *Free China Weekly* 4/27/69; *Lianhe Bao* (United Daily News) (Taipei) 4/21/69; *Zhongyang ribo* (Central Daily News) (Taipei) 4/19/69, and *Zhongguo shibao* (China Times) (Taipei) 3/5/1969.

District Attorney Jones. In August, 1905, they invited him and other government officials to a festive theater party and banquet in Chinatown. Jones had the opportunity to partake of birds' nest soup.[18]

Conclusion. The activities of the Western Military Academy constitute an interesting chapter in American-East Asian relations and the history of Chinese in the United States. At a time when reformers and revolutionaries tried to determine the fate of Qing China, the Chinese in Fresno joined in the debate. The organization of the Western Military Academy in Fresno demonstrated the interplay of local factors such as acculturation, social isolation, discrimination, and Chinese nationalism. By giving close attention to this local branch of the Western Military Academy, one can see how politics in China could have repercussions in one Chinese community in the Central Valley of California.

Notes. In preparing this paper, I am pleased to acknowledge support from the Chao Suet Foundation of San Francisco, the East Asian Studies Department at Stanford University, and the School of Social Sciences at California State University, Fresno.

Works Cited

"Dr. Sun's American Adviser Laid to Rest in Free China." *Free China Weekly* 27 April 1969: 4.

Anschel, Eugene. *Homer Lea, Sun Yat-sen, and the Chinese Revolution.* New York: Praeger, 1984.

Berkeley Gazette 20 May 1905.

Chacon, Ramon D. "The Beginnings of Racial Segregation: The Chinese in West Fresno and Chinatown's Role as Red Light District, 1870–1920s." *Southern California Quarterly* 70 (Winter 1988): 371–99.

Chapin, Frederic. "Homer Lea." Unpublished manuscript, Joshua B. Powers Papers, Hoover Institution, Stanford, California.

Chong, Key Ray. *Americans and Chinese Reform and Revolution, 1898–1922.* Lanham, Md.: University Press of America, 1984.

Chung Sai Yat Po (*Zhongxi ribao*) or *East-West News* (San Francisco) 22 April 1905.

Chung Sai Yat Po 4 May 1905, 5 May 1905, 15 May 1905, 16 May 1905, 21 June 1905.

Clough, Charles W., et al. *Fresno County in the 20th Century. From 1900 to the 1980s.* Fresno: Panorama West, 1986.

---

[18]Mayor W. Parker Lyon subsequently criticized Jones and the officials for being the guests of "Chinese gamblers" (*Fresno Morning Republican* 8/6, 9/8/1905).

Ding Wenjiang. *Liang Rengong xiansheng nianpu changpian chugao (Chronological biography and materials of Liang Qichao)*, vol. 1. Taibei: Shijie Shuju, 1958.

English, June. "Leaves from the Past: Chinese Pioneers of Fresno County." *Ash Tree Echo* 8 (January 1973): 28

Fresno Bee 22 May 1941, 18 April 1956, 22 May 1962.

Fresno City and County Directory 1905. Fresno: Fresno Directory, 1905.

Fresno Democrat 21 April 1905, 16 May 1905.

Fresno Morning Republican 14 March 1904, 4 June 1904, 30 June 1904, 14 August 1904, 4 September 1904, 7 September 1904, 10 September 1904, 16 September 1904, 20 September 1904, 1 October 1904, 5 October 1904, 23 October 1904, 20 November 1904, 30 November 1904, 11 December 1904, 13 February 1905, 11 March 1905, 14 March 1905, 9 April 1905, 14 April 1905, 19 April 1905, 21 April 1905, 22 April 1905, 7 May 1905, 16 May 1905, 24 May 1905, 17 June 1905, 29 June 1905, 6 August 1905, 30 August 1905, 8 September 1905, 19 September 1905, 7 October 1905, 8 October 1905, 13 October 1905, 2 February 1906, 15 February 1906.

Gasster, Michael. *Chinese Intellectuals and the Revolution of 1911: The Birth of Modern Chinese Radicalism*. Seattle: University of Washington Press, 1969.

Glick, Carl, and Sheng-Hwa Hong. *Swords of Silence: Chinese Secret Societies—Past and Present* . New York: McGraw-Hill, 1947.

Glick, Carl. *Double Ten: Captain O'Banion's Story of the Chinese Revolution*. New York: McGraw-Hill, 1945.

Gray, Jack. *Rebellions and Revolutions: China from the 1880s to the 1980s*. New York: Oxford University Press, 1990.

Hatano, Yoshio. "The New Armies." In *China in Revolution: The First Phase, 1900–1913*. Ed. Mary Clabaugh Wright. New Haven, Ct.: Yale University Press, 1988. 365–82.

Homer Lea to David Starr Jordan, May 10, June 3, 1905, University Archives, Stanford University.

Hsu, Immanual C.Y. *The Rise of Modern China*. New York: Oxford University Press, 1983.

Huang Jilu. "Guofu junshi guwen—He Mali jiangjun (Sun Yat-sen's Military Adviser—General Homer Lea)." Manuscript (n.p., n.d.): 32–33, in Powers Papers.

Hudson, James Jackson. "The California National Guard, 1903–1940." Ph.D. dissertation, University of California, 1952.

Kwong, Luke S. *A Mosaic of the Hundred Days: Personalities, Politics, and Ideas of 1898*. Cambridge: Harvard University Press, 1984.

Larson, Jane Leung. "New Source Materials on Kang Youwei and the Baohuanghui: The Tan Zhangxiao (Tom Leung) Collection of Letters and Documents at UCLA's East Asian Library." In *Chinese America: History and Perspectives 1993*. San Francisco: Chinese Historical Society of America, 1993. 151–98.

Larson, Louise Leung. *Sweet Bamboo: A Saga of a Chinese American Family*. Los Angeles: Chinese Historical Society of Southern California, 1990.

Leung, Pui-Chee (Liang Peichi). *Nanyin yu yueou zhi yanjiu* (*A Study of Nan Yin and Yue Ou*). San Francisco: Asian American Studies, San Francisco State University, 1988.

Lianhe bao (*United Daily News*) (Taipei) 21 April 1969.

Life, Influence and Role of the Chinese, The . Photograph, xxxiv–xxxv.

Lo, Jung-Pang ed. *K'ang Yu-wei: A Biography and a Symposium*. Tucson: University of Arizona Press, 1967.

Los Angeles Daily Times 3 April 1905, 7 April 1905, 8 April 1905, 11 April 1905, 25 April 1905, 1 June 1905, 2 June 1905, 3 June 1905, 28 June 1905.

Lu Fangshang. "He Mali dangan jianshu (A Brief Introduction to the Official Files on Homer Lea)." *Yenjiu Zhongshan xiansheng de shiliao yu shixue* (*Research on Historical Materials and Historiography about Sun Yat-sen*). Eds. Huang Jilu et al. Taibei: Zhonghua yinshua chang, 1975. 417–19.

Ma, L. Eve Armentrout. *Revolutionaries, Monarchists, and Chinatowns: Chinese Politics in the Americas and the 1911 Revolution*. Honolulu: University of Hawaii Press, 1990.

New York Daily Tribune 23 June 1905.

New York Times 28 June 1905.

Opper, S. Michael, and Lillie S. Lew. "A History of the Chinese in Fresno, California." In *The Life, Influence and Role of the Chinese in the United States, 1776–1960*. San Francisco: Chinese Historical Society of America, 1976. 48.

Pardee Papers, Bancroft Library, University of California, Berkeley. W. D. Crichton to George C. Pardee, 5 May 1905; A. W. Bradbury to George C. Pardee, 9 October 1905; Chester Rowell to George C. Pardee, 5 May 1905, 19 November 1902; Private Secretary to Governor to George W. Jones, 1 June 1905; J. D. Fredericks to George C. Pardee, 21 October 1905; John J. Allen to George C. Pardee, 13 October 1905; John J. Allen to George C. Pardee, 14 September 1905; J. D. Fredericks to George C. Pardee, 21 October 1905; R. A. Falkenberg to George C. Pardee, 30 August 1905; R. A. Falkenberg to George C. Pardee, 18 May 1905; George C. Pardee to Chester Rowell, 10 May 1905; George C. Pardee to George W. Jones, 10 May 1905; George C. Pardee to Homer Lea, 13 October 1905; George C. Pardee to John J. Allen, 8 September 1905; George C. Pardee to J. D. Fredericks, 8 September 1905; George C. Pardee to W. D. Crichton, 4 May 1905; George C. Pardee to W. D. Crichton, 10 May 1905; George C. Pardee to George W. Jones, 30 May 1905; George W. Jones to Chinese Empire Reform Association, 22 May 1905; George W. Jones to George C. Pardee, 17 May 1905; George W. Jones to George C. Pardee, 22 May 1905; Homer Lea to George C. Pardee, 7 October 1905; Homer Lea to George W. Jones, 18 May 1905.

Powers Papers. "General Orders No. 8 by Homer Lea," 1 November 1904; "A Parade or Morning Report of W. S. Scott," 1 April 1905; Kang Yu Wei to the

American People, announcement, 7 April 1905; Al H. Powers to Charles B. Engelke, 11 August 1942; Fresno County and City Taxes Assessed to Mrs. Frank H. Cole and Ethel B. Lea, document, 1943; H. B. Bemis to Ethel B. Lea Estate, 15 February 1944.

Rehart, Schyler. "Fresno's Turbulent Youth 1885–1901, Part I: A Rough Beginning." *Fresno Past and Present* 26 (Winter 1984): 6.

San Francisco Call 3 May 1905, 17 May 1905.

San Francisco Chronicle 3 April 1905, 4 May 1905, 18 May 1905, 13 February 1906.

Schiffrin, Harold Z. *Sun Yat-sen and the Origins of the Chinese Revolution.* Berkeley: University of California Press, 1968.

Schrieke, B. J. O. *Alien Americans: A Study of Race Relations.* San Francisco: R & E Research Associates, 1971.

Shijie ribao (World Journal) (U. S.) 17 October 1992.

Spence, Jonathan D. *The Search for Modern China.* New York: W. W. Norton, 1990.

Suhler, Sam, ed. *Interview with Mr. Allen Y. Lew.* Fresno: Fresno County Free Library, 1981.

Sun Chung Kwock Bo (Xin zhongguo bao) or *New China Press* (Honolulu) 18 February 1905, 28 February 1905.

Sun Chung Kwock Bo 16 March 1905, 25 March 1905.

Tsai, Shih-shan Henry. *China and the Overseas Chinese in the United States, 1868–1911.* Fayetteville: University of Arkansas Press, 1983.

Tsai, Shih-shan Henry. *The Chinese Experience in America.* Bloomington: Indiana University Press, 1986.

Tsou, Jung. *The Revolutionary Army. A Chinese Revolutionary Tract of 1903.* Ed. John Lust. The Hague: Mouton, 1968.

Vandor, Paul E. *History of Fresno County* (vol. 1). Los Angeles: Historic Record, 1919.

Weixin bao (Chinese Reform News) (New York) 19 April 1905.

Wilbur, C. Martin. *Sun Yat-sen, Frustrated Patriot.* New York: Columbia University Press, 1976.

Wong, Young-tsu Wong. "Revisionism Reconsidered: Kang Youwei and the Reform Movement of 1898." *Journal of Asian Studies* 51 (August 1992): 513–44.

Worden, Robert. "A Chinese Reformer in Exile: The North American Phase of the Travels of K'ang Yu-wei, 1899–1909." Ph.D. dissertation, Georgetown University, 1971.

Zhongguo shibao (China Times) (Taipei) 5 March 1969.

Zhongyang ribo (Central Daily News) (Taipei) 19 April 1969.

The Chinese Fishing Industry of San Diego

TOM HOM and
MURRAY K. LEE

Chinese Historical Society of Greater San Diego & Upper Baja California,
San Diego, California

Fishing was a familiar activity for many of the Chinese who came from the Pearl River Delta of Guangdong Province; therefore, it was understandable that the early Chinese immigrants would take up this activity in the bountiful waters along the California coast. Many of the Chinese, who left the gold fields and moved down the coast from San Francisco and Monterey in the late 1850s, found San Diego Bay to be an ideal base for further developing the California fishing industry. This was an industry that they would dominate until the 1890s.

The first Chinese fishermen in San Diego settled along the bay on Point Loma between Ballast Point and Roseville. Roseville, at that time at the mouth of the San Diego River, had ten shanties, drying racks, and salting tanks. Roseville also became the location of a Chinese shipbuilding industry, and there were many fine junks built there. In 1869, there were two fishing villages, the second along the waterfront of New Town, which consisted of two rows of unpainted redwood shacks at right angles to each other. Some were suspended over the water on stilts, because at that time, the harbor had not been dredged and the waterfront consisted of tidal mud flats. The Chinese kept their junks anchored nearby in deeper water, not far from the Pacific Mail and Steamship wharf. The area between 2nd and 4th Avenues, adjacent to the Stingaree red-light district, became San Diego's Chinatown. Although the harbor's edge has been altered considerably by dredging and filling,, the Chinese fishing village would have been in the area presently occupied by the San Diego Convention Center. Railroad construction along the waterfront in 1881 forced this fishing operation to be moved back to Roseville. By then, San Diego's Chinatown, with proximity to rail and ocean transport, was able to survive, at least until more recent times.

All varieties of fish and shellfish were taken by the Chinese fishermen, especially barracuda, mullet, sheepshead, shrimp, and abalone. Abalone, a highly prized catch, was dried and exported to China and other Chinese communities, since Americans had not yet acquired a taste for this delicacy. San Diego's abalone fleet became the largest on the west coast. The annual export of abalone reached 700 tons. The Chinese removed the meat and threw the shells away immediately, to lighten their load before returning to port. Later, when a market was developed for the shells in making jewelry, the fishermen kept them. Chickens, a by-product of the fishing industry, were raised on scraps and crushed shrimp shells. China Camp on San Pablo Bay in Northern

California is the only site where the remains of a once-productive Chinese shrimping industry can be observed.

The sea-going junks ranged from Cabo San Lucas, Mexico, in the south to Monterey in the north, while the sampans remained primarily in the bay. All the junks built in San Diego had at least two masts and were extremely fast and seaworthy, which proved useful in outrunning government authorities when necessary. The junks were built of California redwood with masts and rudders of ironwood from China. One large junk, the three-masted *Sun Yun Lee*, built in 1884, was 52 feet long, 16 feet wide, 4 feet deep, and almost 15 tons in gross weight.

The Chinese fishing industry was an important part of the San Diego economy. The fishermen supplied all the city's fresh fish needs with door-to-door selling; they exported through the Pacific Mail and Steamship Company wharf facilities, and they purchased lumber, food, and supplies. The industry also had an impact on Chinese workers throughout the West. The use of dried seafood products supplied by the fishermen to their fellow countrymen in the mining and railroad camps contributed to a more nutritious and varied diet than available to their white counterparts.

In 1888, there were 52 Chinese fishermen living and working in 22 shacks along the banks of Point Loma. At the peak of the industry, they sailed as many as 18 junks out of San Diego Bay, but by 1893, only one junk remained. The passage of the Scott Act in 1888, one of the many discriminatory laws aimed at the Chinese, was the beginning of the end for the Chinese fishing industry in America. The Scott Act canceled all outstanding certificates that had allowed reentry of Chinese who had temporarily left the United States. Twenty-thousand Chinese, who were visiting their families in China, were caught in these circumstances and were not allowed to re-enter the country. This law, in combination with the Geary Act of 1892 and its amendments, was used against the Chinese fishermen by preventing their legal re-entry into the country, when their boats had gone beyond the three-mile territorial limit to fish in foreign waters. As the fishermen departed, the industry soon stagnated. Eventually, it was taken over by other immigrants, many of whom had agitated for restrictions against the Chinese. The Chinese fishermen either went back to China or looked for other work in the area. Since farming was another familiar occupation for the men from the Pearl River Delta, they looked to Mission and Sweetwater Valleys to establish market gardening. By developing an irrigation system in these valleys and through door-to-door sales, they soon held a virtual monopoly in this business.

Works Cited

McEvoy, Arthur. "In Places Where Men Reject: Chinese Fishermen at San Diego, 1870–1893," *Journal of San Diego History* XXIII (Fall 1977): 12–24.

Nash, Robert A. "The Chinese Fishing Industry in Baja, California." Paper prepared at the Baja California Symposium IX, Santa Ana, California, 1 May 1971.

Richardson, William Clyde. "The Fishermen at San Diego." Unpublished Master's thesis, San Diego State University, Spring 1981.

Chinese Placenames and Their Significance

THOMAS A. MCDANNOLD
Department of Geography, Ventura College, Ventura, California

California placenames are a result of various cultural influences represented by groups such as Native Americans, explorers, trappers, soldiers, missionaries, miners, settlers, and most important for this study, the Chinese. As such, placenames become a rich source of information on inter-ethnic relationships. This is particularly the case when viewed as a situation where the presence of one group prompts the placename while another group formalizes the placename.

This type of inter-ethnic relationships can be seen in the Chinese placenames of California. A Chinese placename is the name given to a place associated with a Chinese presence. Of the 150,000 placenames in California, several hundred are clearly Chinese placenames.

Placenames usually conform to the principles of entity and use (Steward 8–11). In order for a place to be named, it must be perceived as an entity that is separate and identifiable from other places. Usually the named place has proven to be useful to the persons involved. Consider that those venturing into a new area need placenames that give a sense of location; therefore, the placename is a primary geographic reference system (Orth 1986). For example, China Gulch indicates a place geographically different than Trinity River.

A placename can be useful if it has a specific meaning that gives insight into the history or heritage of a place. Almost every placename has a meaning. Thus, it describes the site and records its human occupation or ownership (Steward 34–35). A placename such as China Mountain tells us that the area is considerably higher than the surrounding area and that the Chinese were found there.

Of particular note is the fact that Chinese placenames of California were recorded by those with a European heritage. These early European immigrants, venturing into a previously unknown area, commonly transferred the name of the local people to various natural features (Steward 67–68). This approach to placenaming was somewhat different from that of the Native Americans, who tended to describe only the physical character of a place (Gordon 227–28). It was also a method different from that of the early Spanish, who tended to corrupt the Native American placenames or simply renamed them (Herricks 271).

A tradition developed out of the European immigrant practice, to the point where the European Americans typically referred to places according to the people located there. Places within California, where Chinese were found, were associated with the them. As a result, the place was named accordingly, regardless of what the Chinese called the place. Thus, there are few placenames developed by the Chinese that received official status. An example which may be somewhat Chinese in origin is Nettie Won. This is the placename given to a pool of fresh water within San Mateo Creek where Chinese fishermen washed their nets. "Nettie" is thought to be pidgin English for net and "Won" is considered to be Cantonese for pond or small body of water.

Involved in this type of European American placenaming are certain principles, specifically rarity and repetition (Steward 74–84). The principle of rarity suggests that a placename most likely denoted the uncommon, rather than the ordinary. Therefore, in the early days, the presence of Chinese in an area might be unusual, prompting one to call it a "China," "Chinee," "Chinaman," or "Chinese" place. Later, as more Chinese were encountered, the principle of repetition came into play with "China" being the preferred form. This meant that the conventionalized vocabulary dictated that any place occupied by Chinese would automatically be named "China"-something. A review of Chinese placenames in California clearly reveals far more Chinese placenames that begin with "China" than any other term.

When the European Americans encountered a placename that was not in English, an effort to render it in English would be made, i.e. a phonetic transfer would be accomplished when an attempt was made to replicate the sound of non-English-spoken words using English.

This appears to be the case with Fong Wah Bar. A "bar" is a common gold-mining term meaning a deposit of gravel within a stream, often gold-bearing. However, "Fong Wah" signifies a Chinese presence. The Chinese who mined the area probably pronounced it as "Chong Wah" or "Chung Wah" (Lai 1992). At the time, the closest an English speaker could come was apparently "Fong Wah."

Placenames have a strong psychological significance. They can identify areas of cultural importance, as well as areas of political interest. In addition, a placename can carry legal weight in determining property, mineral, and water rights (Loy 12–13). As a result, placenames are symbols of social and political relationships, rather than an indication of past cultural conflict (Smith 139–154). Thus, placenames represent location in a cultural connotation.

Accordingly, the geography of Chinese placenames becomes concerned with the inter relationships among the land and its people—both those who the place was named after and those who officially recognized the placename (Loy 19; Zelinski 349). Thus, Chinese Harbor, located on Santa Cruz Island, suggests a place for safe ship anchorage where Chinese could be found, as perceived and named by European Americans.

Sources of official Chinese placenames in California include the National Gazetteer of the United States of America, topographic maps of the United States Geological Survey, nautical charts published by the National Oceanographic and Atmospheric Administration (NOAA), administrative and recreational maps published by the Department of Agriculture, Forest Service, aeronautical charts published by NOAA, and street maps of various city and county agencies.

Examples of the high level of significance attached to Chinese placenames are many. U.S. Geological Survey topographic maps that have Chinese placename titles include Chinese Camp, China Gardens, and China Mountain. There are over a dozen State Historic Monuments that bear Chinese placenames (Office of Historic Preservation 1990). In addition, over a half dozen Chinese placenames can be found in the national forests of the state (U.S. Department of Agriculture, Forest Service 1992).

Government agencies derive direction regarding placenames, as well as the placenames themselves, from the Board of Geographic Names (BGN). The BGN came about because of the surge in mapping and scientific reports associated with exploration, mining, and settlement in the West after the end of the Civil War. Established in 1890, the BGN was given authority to resolve questions concerning placenames with its decisions being binding on all federal government departments and agencies. In 1906, the BGN received authority to standardize all geographic names for federal use, including name changes and new names. Public Law 80-242 (1947) reorganized the BGN into its present form (Bedrossian 204).

The BGN requires that placenames be in standard English, except where Spanish or French names require distinguishing or diacritical marks. In addition, the placename may use the historical spelling or the form preferred by local citizens. However, the possessive apostrophe is avoided. Given these variations, the BGN requires that the official name, spelling, and application of a placename be given for only one geographic entity. As policy, the BGN will not initiate name changes except when the original name might be duplicated elsewhere, when it wishes to commemorate a person deceased for at least one year, or when the existing placename is derogatory (Bedrossian 204).

During the 1960s, the BGN began to eliminate names considered derogatory. An example, although beyond California, is that which occurred in Wyoming. The BGN accepted the proposal of a Chinese American tourist from Hawaii who found the name Chinamans Spring in Yellowstone National Park offensive. The name was changed to Chinese Spring (Lagerfield 21).

A BGN Committee of particular note is the Domestic Names Committee. It meets monthly and is responsible for standardizing placenames within the United States and areas under its sovereignty. The committee works closely with state geographic name authorities, state and local governments, and the general public to decide the choice, spelling, written form, and application of names for official use (Bedrossian 204). Forms to propose a placename or to change an existing placename can be obtained from the Executive Secretary, Domestic Geographic Names, U.S. Board of Geographic Names, c/o U.S. Geological Survey, 523 National Center, Reston, VA 22092.

The California Advisory Committee on Geographic Names (ACGN) provides advice to the Domestic Names Committee for approval/disapproval of name changes and proposals for unnamed geographic features within the state. The ACGN began as the California State Geographic Board in 1928. It supervised the selection of placenames, evaluated the merits of proposed names, rectified errors in existing nomenclature, and prepared and published catalogs and gazetteers. By 1961, the ACGN had become a part of California's Resources Agency. It was not until 1966 that it became the official advisory agency to the BGN and others on California placenames (Bedrossian 200–201).

Exploring Chinese Placenames. Placenames can be discussed in different ways. A common approach is placename density. This refers to the number of names per unit area. In California, there are approximately three Chinese placenames per one thousand square miles. To put this into a larger context, when all placenames of California are considered, there is one per one square mile. This is similar to the one placename per one square mile for the contiguous Unites States (Steward 7). Given the comparison, the density of Chinese placenames in California appears very low. However, when viewed cartographically, there is not a uniform distribution to the placenames as suggested by the density figure. Rather, Chinese placenames tend to cluster.

The clustering is directly related to several factors contributing to placename density. The first is variation in topography. The greater the land diversity, the more the need for placenames. Secondly, a cultural pattern of long term occupancy produces a higher concentration of placenames. This occurs because of a need for an increased discrimination of the environment (Steward 17–19). The result tends to be a recurrence of names in similar environments (Harris 1988). Chinese placenames clustering in Northern California and Eastern California represent places of great topographic diversity and an extensive, early-Chinese presence.

Another means of examining placenames is to differentiate between their generic and specific components (Steward 20). The generic part of a placename indicates the class of place while the specific restricts or modifies the meaning. For example, a frequently encountered Chinese placename on U.S. topographic maps is Chinese Cemetery. The placename's generic component is "Cemetery." The word "Chinese" is the specific and restricts the class of place to those interred as having Chinese ancestry.

Occasionally, the generic-specific components will be constricted through common usage. An example is the current placename Chinatown with no space between the words "China" and "town." The usual written form in the mid- to late-1800s was China Town. Further constriction has begun to produce the commonly spoken form, C-town. This form has not yet appeared on maps.

A third means of investigating Chinese placenames is to classify them by type (Steward 85–86). The placename may be descriptive, such as Ah Louis Store, an important center for the Chinese during the late 1800s. It could be associative like China Grade Loop Road, where the road that forms a loop is in proximity to China Grade, a steeply inclined street. The placename might convey an incident such as China Slide, where two Chinese gold miners were killed by a landslide. A placename can imply possession, as does Point Joe, a prominence of land extending into the ocean that was the home of a Chinese goat tender known as Joe. When a placename shifts to other places within an area, it often forms a name-cluster. An example is China Lake (a playa lake), City of China Lake (an urban area near China Lake), and China Lake Boulevard (a major street in the City of China Lake). There are a preponderance of Chinese placenames that are commemorative, such as China Ridge, named by loggers who recognized the effort made by the Chinese workers who constructed a rail line through a very rugged and steep mountainous area.

Additional types (McArthur vii; Marinacci 19–24) include those that are arbitrary, such as China Wall, a name given just about any pile of rocks constructed by humans. A placename may be dramatic, as with Our Chinese Colony, the name of a community's local Chinese settlement. Transported placenames are essentially a name that has meaning someplace else, such as Mei Ling Way, with Mei Ling being the maiden name of Chiang Kai-Shek's wife. Of course, the placename can be simply contrived, as was China City, a commercial development for tourists.

Others have used historic periods for deriving greater meaning from placenames (McArthur v–vi). Examples include the Native American Time, Period of Exploration, Pioneer Period, Indian Wars and Mining, Homestead Era and the Modern Period of Made-up Names or Historic Names. Classification of this type needs to be modified as the situation requires.

Although of application to Chinese placenames in California, a more useful system incorporates both geography and history. The spatial and chronological view clearly suggest a changing inter-ethnic relationship. The system is divided into the Early Days, the Urban Environment, and Community-Political Participation.

The following discussion serves as an example of the three-fold system. It is limited to recognition of the early presence of the Chinese, their experiences in the city, and a commemoration of outstanding leaders in the Chinese community. Each placename within a category has been officially recognized by a local, state, and/or national agency. All contain a generic and specific component.

The Early Days. The early period of Chinese in the state is often characterized as that of a predominantly male society whose members typically worked as fishermen, laborers, cooks, or miners. The following three placenames commemorate the Chinese presence, their contribution to the development of the state, and the level of official recognition.

China Camp, Marin County. Settled in the 1860s, China Camp was one of some 30 fishing villages around the shore of the San Francisco Bay. As the largest of the villages with some 500 occupants by the 1880s, it provided much of the dried shrimp exported to China. Shrimp was not an item found on the plates of most European Americans of the period. However, the overall impact of the Chinese fishermen was thought to be great. As a result, restrictions on the use of certain fishing technology, limitations on the time of year for fishing, and the outright ban on shrimp export caused all but a few to leave China Camp.

The significance of China Camp and the contribution of the Chinese was officially recognized when it was designated State Historic Landmark No. 924. A plaque at the site details aspects of the fishing village.

China Camp and 1500 surrounding acres became a state park in 1977. Remnants of the camp within the park include a shrimp-drying shed and related equipment, a store, floating houses that are now beached, and a pier. In addition, there are hiking and equestrian trails as well as fishing and camping opportunities.

China Garden, Kern County. China Garden, located on the Kern River, was the camp site for the Chinese who worked on the Edison Company Kern River project around 1903. They built flumes, provided general labor, and worked as cooks. Vegetables were grown at the site, using the abundant water from the adjacent river and the fertile soil of the terraces created by the river.

Today, it is part of the Greenhorn Mountain Ranger District of the Sequoia National Forest. When the Forest Service began to develop the Kern River for recreational use, they formalized the placename that had been in use for many years. China Garden Campground, its complete name, is considered a dispersed camping area requiring a camping permit. The four acres, along the tree-shaded Kern River, are a favorite place of recreational vehicle owners, those who enjoy a picnic, and rafting enthusiasts.

Chinese Temple, City of Oroville. Dating from 1863, Liet Sheng Kong, the Temple of Assorted Deities, consisted of a temple, storehouse, and theater. Only the temple survived a flood in 1907. Having fallen into disrepair, the structure and land were deeded to the city in 1937. Chinese and non-Chinese community members worked to restore the facility, with it opening to the public in 1949.

Initially, the complex consisted of a temple for Taoists (the original structure of 1863), Buddhists (constructed behind the Taoist temple in 1868), and a Confucian hall (built in 1874). Each temple is resplendent with appropriate artifacts. In 1968, a large display hall, memorial pavilion, and garden courtyard next to the temple were opened. Displays focus on the historic aspects of the area's gold rush. The authentic garden is one of the few public gardens in the United States. The typical living quarters of a Chinese miner were constructed and furnished behind the temple. It opened in 1971.

The temple, with all its reconstruction, authenticity, and expansion has served thousands of Chinese miners, laborers, worshipers, and residents of the area for many years. It continues to enlighten everyone who visits. Its significance is recognized by the local, state, and federal government: The city maintains the facility; it is State Historic Landmark No. 770, and it is listed on the National Register of Historic Places.

The Urban Environment. Chinese placenames within the city reflect not only a Chinese presence there but its lasting impact. This can be seen in the next four placenames. They stand as recognition of a well-developed community, complete with its own shrines.

China Lake, Kern County. By the late 1860s, Chinese were mining and processing borax from a playa lake in the Mojave Desert. The processed mineral, with many commercial and industrial uses, was sent to China. Because of the Chinese workers, the sometimes wet, most of the time dry, lake became identified as China Lake. A freight way station, linking the mines of the Inyo-White Mountains to Los Angeles, was located there by the early 1870s. It also became known by that name. In 1948, a post office was established in the area and was designated the China Lake Post Office by the U.S. Postal Commission.

During that time, a city developed within the Naval Reservation boundaries and officially became China Lake. Located about three miles southwest of the lake itself, it is a service and residential community serving the Center. One of its main streets is China Lake Boulevard. Contiguous to China Lake and outside of the military reserve is the community of Ridgecrest.

Chinatown of Riverside, City of Riverside. The Riverside Chinatown began at its present site in 1885, after the Chinese were forced to leave the downtown area. It had 350–400 permanent residents. During harvest season, the population would increase to 2000–2500, with the itinerant Chinese laborers living in tents next to the buildings. The last shop in Chinatown closed in 1938, with its last resident dying in 1974. After his death, the remaining structures were torn down.

The seven acres of Chinatown were declared historically significant by the County of Riverside Board of Supervisors on January 15, 1968. It was approved by the State Office of Historic Preservation as a State Point of Historic Interest on January 24, 1968. The City of Riverside designated the area Cultural Heritage Landmark No. 19 in 1974. Today, the eastern portion of the land is occupied by facilities of the Riverside County Office of Education. Landscaping and a commemorative plaque at the corner of Tequesquite Avenue and Pine Street mark the site.

Chinese Cemetery Shrine, City of Los Angeles. The Chinese Cemetery Shrine, with an inscription that reads September, 1888, is the oldest existing structure of the Chinese in the city. The shrine is located in its original site, present-day Evergreen Cemetery. It is the last remnant of a Chinese portion of the cemetery that existed there from the 1870s to the mid-1930s. The shrine itself continued as a ceremonial site for Ching Ming until the 1960s. Presently, it has two incinerators and an altar platform.

It was declared a Los Angeles Historic/Cultural Monument by the City Council in 1990 and was officially named the 19th Century Los Angeles Chinese Cemetery Shrine Historical Monument. This status gave it limited protection and provided sufficient time for the development of plans that would stop its eventual destruction.

During 1992, the Chinese Historical Society of Southern California purchased the shrine and the land upon which it sits. Plans for its renovation and community-based fund raising have been developed.

Los Angeles Chinatown, City of Los Angeles. The large Chinatown of Los Angeles that existed from the late 1800s to 1936 was destroyed so that a passenger railroad facility could be constructed in its place. The Chinatown of today arose from the destruction, and is located approximately a half mile northwest of the old Chinatown. It is centered on North Broadway.

New Chinatown, as it was known, held its grand opening on June 25, 1938. It was built on land owned by the Chinese, a unique condition at that time. Economically, it focused on tourist trade. Presently, it is the nucleus of a larger commercial and residential area serving recent Asian immigrants, members of the Chinese American community, and non-Chinese visitors.

The City of Los Angeles officially designated the area as Chinatown. The placement of a prominent street sign on Hill Street marks its northern boundary.

Community Involvement. Through time, perception of the Chinese by non-Chinese has changed, as represented by this category of Chinese placenames. Now, the Chinese tend to be viewed as individuals, many of whom are outstanding members of the community. Three placenames reflect the change.

Walter U. Lum Place, City of San Francisco. Walter U. Lum, born in 1879, was a first-generation Chinese American who grew up in San Francisco. Out of a concern for fair treatment, Mr. Lum and other Chinese reactivated the Native Sons of the Golden State in 1904. By 1915, the organization, which included Chinese Americans from throughout the state and beyond, changed its name to the Chinese American Citizens Alliance (CACA). Mr. Lum was elected its first Grand President, a position he held 15 times. The CACA is still an important civic, service, and social organization in the Chinese American community.

Through the years, Walter U. Lum held many positions where he continued to champion those of Chinese ancestry. He served as Camp Manager for the Mexican Chinese evacuated from Mexico to Texas during a time of civil unrest in Mexico. He also was Vice President and Managing Director of the Chinese-owned China Mail Steamship Lines. Most notably, he founded and ran the Chinese-language newspaper The Chinese Times, read in Chinese communities across the nation. Throughout his long career of community involvement, he tirelessly fought U.S. immigration practices and laws that discriminated against Chinese. He died in 1961.

The City and County of San Francisco designated Brenham Place as Walter U. Lum Place in the late 1980s. Chinese Affirmative Action, a political activist group, and Tom Shaw, CACA member and Supervisor of the district, helped bring about the name change.

Moon Lim Lee Safety Rest Area, Trinity County. Born in Weaverville in 1903, Moon Lim Lee helped his father in the produce business that eventually resulted in his own business, Lee's Supermarket of Weaverville. He almost single-handedly saved the Weaverville Joss House, being appointed trustee of the property by the Superior Court in 1938 and helped it become a state park in 1956. Moon Lim Lee served on many boards and committees that worked for the betterment of local communities and the highways of Trinity County. His continued involvement brought him to the attention of state officials; he was appointed by Governor Ronald Reagan to the California Highway Commission in 1967. He served as a commissioner for eight years. He passed away in 1985.

The rest area named in his honor by the State of California Department of Transportation is in a scenic portion of Highway 299. It is approximately one mile north of the junction of Highway 3 and Highway 299. A commemorative plaque, erected by the Rotary Club of Weaverville and Friends, identifies the area.

Wong Way, Riverside County. George Wong, as he was known to the community, was born in China in 1900. He arrived in the city of Riverside in 1914. By 1940, he had acquired six areas of property in Riverside's Chinatown. Although his ownership of the land was contested by the city, he prevailed. Mr. Wong, businessman, restaurant owner, collector of automobiles (with over 90 at the time of this death), was well-known throughout the area. He would often be seen driving through town in his Rolls Royce during the late 1920s. He lived on Brockton Avenue, the primary street of Chinatown. However, he insisted on calling it Chinatown Avenue, the placename used by the County of Riverside on a commemorative gate eventually constructed in Chinatown.

By the late 1950s, vacant land near Chinatown was beginning to develop. As a result, a one block-long street was created. By 1961, the Riverside City Council unanimously endorsed naming the street in his honor with one side of the sign to have the placename written in Chinese. Mr. Wong lived to see "his" street, for he did not pass away until 1974.

Currently, the street leads to a hilly area to the west with homes on the north side and commercial buildings on the south side. It terminates at a large shopping complex to the east. However, the Chinese language side of the sign is gone.

Conclusion. Many of California's placenames are directly related to the Chinese. Initially, it was the Chinese presence itself in a land unfamiliar to many of those who came to the state that prompted the placenames. The placenames acted as a geographic reference system.

There are no official Chinese placenames that were developed by the Chinese. However, there were some attempts by the European Americans to use the Chinese language as part of a placename. Formal recognition of Chinese placenames occurred at the local, state, and federal level. Starting in the 1960s, all have become concerned with eliminating derogatory placenames.

Chinese placenames can be examined using a number of strategies. A particular approach that employs a geographic-historic perspective suggests that the inter-ethnic relationship between the Chinese and the placename givers has changed. It has shifted from one focused on the Chinese as uncommon in an unknown land to that of a distinct community of people. Most recently, recognition of outstanding Chinese American individuals characterizes the relationship.

Works Cited

Bedrossian, Trinda L. "Geographic Names in California." *California Geology* September 1987: 199–204.

Department of Agriculture, U.S. Forest Service, 1992.

Gordon, Jeffery J. "Onondaga Iroquis Placenames: An Approach to Historical and Contemporary Indian Landscape Perception." *Names* September 1984: 218–233.

Harris, M.O. "Street Names in the Downtown Cluster." Bell Communications Research, Technical Memorandum No. TM-ARH-010066, 1988.

Herricks, Robert L. "Cultural Aspects of Placenames: New Mexico." *Names* October 1983: 271–287.

Lagerfield, Steven. "Name That Dune: The Power of the Board of Geographic Names Reaches Everywhere." *Atlantic* September 1990: 20–22.

Lai, Him Mark. Personal communication. 1992.

Loy, William G. "Geographic Names in Geography." Yearbook of the Association of Pacific Coast Geographers, 1989. 7–24.

Marinacci, Barbara, and Rudy Marinacci. *California's Spanish Place-Names: What They Mean and How They Got There.* Palo Alto: Tioga Publications, 1980.

McArthur, Lewis A. *Oregon Geographic Names, 5th ed.* Oregon: Press of the Oregon Historical Society, 1982.

Office of Historic Preservation. *California Historical Landmarks.* Sacramento: State of California: The Resources Agency, Department of Parks and Recreation, 1990.

Orth, D.J. *Principles, Policies, and Procedures, Domestic Geographic Names.* Reston, Virginia: U.S. Board of Geographic Names, 1986.

Simmons, Terry. "On the Political Significance of Place Names." Yearbook of the Association of Pacific Coast Geographers, 1977. 173.

Smith, Grant. "Density Variations of Indian Placenames: Spokane County and the State of Washington." *Names* June 1989: 139–154.

Steward, George R. *Names on the Globe.* New York: Oxford University Press, 1975.

Zelinsky, Wilbur. "Some Problems in the Distribution of Generic Terms in the Place-Names of the Northeastern U.S." *Annals of the Association of American Geographers* 45 (4) 1955. 319–49.

Dancing with the Dragon:
A Study of Ritual and Inter-Ethnic Community Relations

PAUL CHACE
Dept. of Anthropology, University of California, Riverside

An estimated 20,000 people come together for the annual celebration of the Bok Kai Festival in the City of Marysville. They watch a 150-foot-long dragon prance and swirl through the streets, and they hear the happy popping of several million firecrackers. The old Chinese Bok Kai Temple gong and the old temple banner, in the lead positions of the festival procession along the main street of this American city, are in the trustworthy hands of Boy Scouts, non-Chinese. They are followed by local Campfire Girls costumed as horses for the Chinese Year of the Horse, the Sons of Norway lodge members on a decorated boat, uniformed high school marching bands, fire trucks, Chinese American beauty queens waving from convertibles, the Marysville City Council riding in a vintage auto, a United States Congressman, and more.

This transplanted Chinese community ritual not only brings together the 12,000 diverse residents of this California Central Valley town, it attracts people from far and wide. These historic ritual activities in Marysville have served in bringing this community together in harmonious festivities throughout the years. By enjoying and participating together in these annual celebrations, the diverse people of Marysville demonstrate and validate their membership in this California community. While the ritual form of the Bok Kai celebration has its roots in old China and was locally initiated by the Chinese population in early Marysville, it has been adapted to this new community. From the Gold Rush up through World War I, the Chinese of Marysville constituted about 20% of the city's population of 5,000 people; thereafter, the number of Chinese residents has declined to less than 200 people. Still, for more than a century, these festivities have been conducted annually by the people of Marysville, Chinese and non-Chinese alike. Within Marysville, the annual re-creation of the festival tradition has functioned to promote and enhance inter-ethnic relations across the community.

My explanation for the festival's long-sustained success in promoting inter-ethnic relations is situated within the debate regarding the "diversity within the unity" of Chinese popular religion. In stretching the context for that debate to California, what becomes particularly apparent is that the ritual in Marysville is marked by "interpretive restraint." I define "interpretive restraint" as the purposeful withholding of symbolic meaning for traditional ritual performance. Although the concept is not of itself a functional explanation for action, often it is a logical and critical precondition for cooperative social action, such as that represented by the ongoing festival ritual (Chace 1992a). Because of an

189

effective public restraint on religious interpretation, this ethnically diverse urban population can celebrate together in this locally historic civic tradition. By participating together in this community ritual, the people of Marysville express their common humanity and their civic citizenship. Even while expressing their various ethnic identities, their differences are mediated through festive togetherness. These rites serve to reinforce the participants' identity as good citizens and supportive members of the civic community. In recent years, the principal public-justification for the festival simply is that it is a historically unique civic tradition. I would pose that Marysville's Bok Kai Festival ritual is traditional Chinese folk-ritual transplanted; however, the festival celebrations have evolved over a century to reflect the diversity of the community's inter-ethnic social relations.

This account of the Marysville ritual festivities is focused upon describing the breadth of inter-ethnic community participation and documenting interpretive restraint. After outlining my theoretical orientation, the events of the Bok Kai Festival are described. In the concluding discussion, the different organizations behind the festival are noted, along with the importance of interpretive restraint in the sustained success of this civic tradition of festive social solidarity.

My description of the ritual festivals is based upon observing the festivals since 1990, viewing videotapes of most of the festivals since 1984, and assembling accounts for all the festivals over the past century. Only a few short articles on this California Chinese community and the festivals previously have been published (Lee 1943, Eberhard 1962, Wells 1962, Ibanez 1967, Williams, Wong and Wong 1976, Chan 1984, and Cheng 1989). The primary source materials describing these annual public festivities, since these civic rites were initiated in 1872, are publicity and accounts in the community's newspapers (Chace 1992b).

Background and Theory. Scholars long have been concerned with Chinese popular religion and its ritual, particularly as they served to promote earthly social harmony and community solidarity. Most recent studies have been focused on Hong Kong or Taiwan, since religion was suppressed in mainland China from 1949 to 1979 (Ahern 1981; Ahern and Gates 1981; Anderson 1970, 1977; Blake 1981; Brim 1974; Burkhardt 1958; Faure 1986, 1989; Feuchtwang 1992; Gates and Weller 1987; Jordan 1972; Lagerwey 1987; Madsen 1984; Pas 1989; Sangren 1984, 1987a, 1987b; Saso 1990a, 1990b; Siu 1989; Taylor 1990; Topley 1968; Wang 1982; Ward 1985; Watson 1985, 1988; Watson and Rawski 1988; Weller 1987; Wolf 1974; Yang 1961, and many others). Studies of the extension of Chinese popular religion into California, in contrast, have received only relatively brief attention (Armentrout Ma 1988; Bowman 1988; Chace 1987, 1989, 1991, 1992a, 1992b; Chinn 1969; Culin 1887; Eberhard 1962; Hoy 1939, 1948; Ibanez 1967; Lee 1943; Lydon 1985; McDonald and McDonald 1986;

Minnick 1985; Wells, 1962; Wey 1988; and Williams, Wong and Wong 1976).

A major debate among social scholars concerned with Chinese religion has been the "diversity with unity" issue. What significance should be attached to the apparent diversity of ritual practices and beliefs within the unity recognized as Chinese popular religion? This issue was raised to debate initially at a 1971 conference on religion and ritual in Chinese society (see particularly Freedman 1974, Smith 1974, Wolf 1974, and Watson 1976). This debate recently has resolved into three distinctive perspectives. Watson (1988: 4) has emphasized "diversity," that the proper performance of rites took precedence over belief; "it mattered little what one believed ... as long as the rites were performed properly." In contrast, Rawski (1988: 21) has emphasized the "unity" of beliefs through the literary tradition of China's civilization and state, with its ancient texts on rites, which has penetrated any regional folk religion; "Chinese peasant culture was embedded in a complex literate civilization with a long historical tradition." Some have gone further in their view of "unity" (Sangren 1987a, 1987b), as does Feuchtwang (1992), who argues that "the separation of belief from [ritual] performance is inappropriate" and that Durkheimian "collective representations" articulate "both thought and action." Also with the unity perspective, scholars (Taylor 1990; Watson 1985; and Topley 1968) have demonstrated how the state's unified religion adopted certain diverse popular cults and transformed them into the officially unified religion.

Utilizing a third perspective focused on "varying social relations," Weller (1987: 5–6) has offered a systematic structuralist view in his recent book, *Unities and Diversities in Chinese Religion.*:

> Both the unity and the diversity hypotheses suggest that there is a shared body of culture (or at least religion), but they differ in the social group with which they associate it. One view associates culture with society as a whole, while the other associates culture with groups within the society. Phrased in this form, the two hypotheses cannot be reconciled.... It is not possible to provide a catch-all characterization of religion in a complex society as unified or diverse. Instead the variation (or lack of it) relates to the varying social relations of the people involved.

Theoretically, with Weller's "varying social relations" approach, distinctive social relations generate differences in religious beliefs and practices. For Chinese immigrants in California the complexities of social relations included a polity dominated by Anglo American society, with a different language and a different world view. Further, while American society supported religious diversity in principle, Christianity remained hegemonic. It follows that Chinese popular religion, as it evolved in California, where the distinctive social relations involved domination and hegemony, should generate new and unanticipated variations in ritual practices and beliefs.

Weller's (1987) "varying social relations" perspective was based upon an empirical Weberian view of religion and culture (but not on Weber's own writing on Chinese religion). Hughey (1983), in his book *Civil Religion and Moral Order*, called for the same approach in understanding social order, although he structured his argument differently in order to assert its universal application. With Weberian reinterpretation, Hughey demonstrated the importance of the flexible Weberian approach for interpreting ritual and religious beliefs within any social community. Hughey emphasized that varying social relations between individuals exist throughout even small communities, with concomitant variations in their understandings and meanings for ritual symbolism. Hughey illustrated the importance of empirically investigating variations between social relations and concomitant variations in religious beliefs and meanings of ritual symbolism. He emphasized the importance of both the interrelationships between these aspects of culture and their real variations within even a single social community. This third theoretical orientation of "varying social relations" is essential for appreciating the annual ritual festivities in the multi-ethnic urban center of Marysville.

The Historic Bok Kai Temple at Marysville. Marysville was a boom town of California's 1850s gold rush, and the Chinese emigrants in early Marysville probably constructed an initial Bok Kai Temple soon after establishing their settlement there. The small early temple was removed to a brick building renovated in the spring of 1869. Apparently, the acquisition of this leased building was accomplished by the people of the *Sze Yup Hui Kuan*, who were linked to Hong Woo & Co. This company was the biggest and wealthiest Chinese business-house in early Marysville and was connected with one of the largest firms in San Francisco (Chace 1992b).

The Bok Kai Temple became a community temple and was further enlarged early in the year of 1880. This is the temple that still stands in Marysville, along the north bank of the Yuba River. The title to the temple property at this point was secured, it appears, in the names of the four leaders of the existing Chinese community groups. These four men would have represented Marysville's initial consolidated Chinese community association, a *Chung Wah Hui Kuan*. This enlarged Bok Kai Temple was dedicated with a big civic festival. Everyone in Marysville, including the non-Chinese, was invited and welcomed to the celebration. The Marysville newspaper described the new temple dedication ritual and the many Anglo onlookers. The final event of the festivities, the competition to catch the rings from the temple's lucky bombs, was viewed by a crowd of spectators numbering half the city's total population. The turnout would have been even greater except for stormy weather (Chace 1992b).

In Marysville, the annual rites honoring Bok Kai, the principal deity in the community temple, usually have been focused around the second day of the second month on the traditional Chinese calendar. This is now said to be Bok Kai's birthday. Within the temple, Bok Kai is represented by a small, but elaborate, figure placed in the prominent central altar position. Bok Kai is flanked by six other Chinese deities represented as handsome polychrome figures. Tour guides explain to non-Chinese visitors at the temple: "These figures are like the saints in the Catholic church." An elaborate jade tablet set in a carved gilt frame is situated in front of the altar and it, some say, also represents Bok Kai. In Marysville, the English-language newspapers have informed readers that in Chinese mythology, Bok Kai is considered the God of the North or Dark Northern Heaven. Bok Kai also is presented to the community as the "Chinese God of water" or rarely as the "God of water and flood control," but typically without further interpretive commentary. With further restraint, for the English-language media in recent years, the announced festival theme simply is the celebration of the new Chinese year, and the festival theme features the current year's animal in the Chinese zodiac. Thus, for 1990, the festive activities celebrate the new Chinese Year of the Horse.

Activities at the Bok Kai Temple. The temple is filled with ardent worshippers throughout the festival weekend. The altar tables are quickly covered with the offerings of golden-colored roasted piglets, roasted ducks, oranges, buns—even cartons of Chinese takeout-food (dutifully opened for ancestors), bottles of wine, bright flowers, and bottles of oil. At the busy sales desk just inside temple doors, prepared bundles of incense-candles-paper money are sold to visitors. The censers before the altar quickly become filled with offered multitudes of sweetly burning incense sticks and bright candles. The paper money is set aflame and deposited in the nearby stove. The clacking of the wooden casting blocks and the rattling of fortune sticks is continuous as devotees make their prayers and beseech knowledge of their future fortunes. Outside the temple doors at a card table, the temple manager provides assistance to worshippers interpreting the printed paper fortune slips. Sometimes he also reads the points of a devotee's hand or the points of their face. Lucky keepsakes and talismans are sold to temple visitors. Worshippers come from Sacramento, Modesto, San Jose, San Francisco, and even from Hong Kong, Singapore, and Thailand. The busy ladies at the frantic sales desk estimated that 3,000 to 5,000 people now visit this venerated old temple during the festival weekend.

The Parade-Procession. The big Saturday parade is billed as "California's Oldest Parade." In recent years, the parade features about 130 units, including about a dozen floats, along with community dignitaries, beauty queens, high school marching bands, drill teams, military units, fire trucks, the Budweiser Clydesdale draft horses and beer wagon, the Wells Fargo stage coach, antique automobiles, American Indians, uniformed Boy Scouts, Girl Scouts, Campfire Boys and Girls, 4-H'ers, tractors, clowns, horse units, and numerous politicians ([Nall] 1990; Chace 1992b). Besides the members of the Marysville City Council, the parade includes the elected civic representatives from three other nearby cities, the County Supervisors, the local State Assemblyman, and the United States Congressman, plus the Commanding Officers of nearby Beale Air Force Base. The elementary school children of the Linda community, just outside Marysville, march under a 200-foot-long cloth dragon they created for the parade. Many parade units are decorated with a horse motif, as appropriate for the Chinese Year of the Horse theme. (Similarly, for the Chinese Year of the Ram in 1991 and the Year of the Monkey in 1992, many of the parading units followed the zodiac animal theme in their costumes and decorations.) Chinese red paper-lanterns are strung along the parade route, and yellow festival-banners hang from lamp posts along all the major streets of the town. Along with numerous U. S. flags, many large and small flags of the Republic of Taiwan fly from the Chinese society halls and certain buildings along the parade route. Immense throngs gather along the 12 downtown blocks of the parade route, and the beginning of the parade is prefaced by the shrieking sirens from Marysville police officers on motorcycles and in a police car passing down the street.

Leading the parade off are hundreds and hundreds of noisy firecrackers, multiple packets of exploding crackers tossed every few paces by a native Marysville Chinese American. Over the public address system the parade announcers proclaims, "The firecrackers ... are used to scare off the evil spirits so that the Bok Kai Festival and the Year of the Horse may begin with good fortune" ([Nall] 1990). Immediately following comes a small, wheeled scaffold with two gongs; it is pulled by two trustworthy Boy Scouts in uniform, while two Girl Scouts bang dutifully at intervals on the gongs. (All four scouts are Anglos.) Above the reverberations, the announcer reads over the public address system, "The ceremonial gong traditionally marks the beginning of the Bok Kai parade. It alerts Bok Kai, the Water Deity and also the God of the North, that the festivities which honor him are beginning" ([Nall] 1990). Next, other Boy Scouts carry the very old Bok Kai temple banner with its antique metallic embroidery and Chinese characters, and a new festival banner. The banner carriers are followed by the Beale Air Force Base Color Guard with their tall flags. The new bright-red Bok Kai Festival banner with golden Chinese characters was bought in 1988, the announcer says, by the Marysville Merchants Association. No interpretation is provided for the Chinese symbolism on the two banners or for the flags.

The honored Grand Marshal for the parade (in 1990), sitting on the rear of a shiny new convertible, is the current President of the Marysville Chinese Community [Inc.] and the Suey Sing Society of Marysville. Autos also carry the leaders of the Hop Sing Society. The young men of the Marysville Hop Sing Society dance with their three colorful lion costumes, "to bring good luck," the announcer says; and the Hop Sing Society from San Francisco energetically entertains with four more lion dance troupes. Chinese dignitaries from the Grand Lodges of the Hop Sing Tong and the Suey Sing Tong in San Francisco are prominent, as are officials from the Republic of Taiwan. Groups from other Chinese communities in colorful parade attire also participate: the Sacramento Mandarin Drum & Bugle Corps, the St. Mary's School Chinese Drum and Bell Corps of San Francisco, the Kin Kwo High School Bell and Drum Corps from San Francisco, and the Marin County Chinese Cultural Group Lion Dance Troupe. Marysville's own magnificent dragon brings up the rear of the parade and dances respectful bows at four locations: the Bok Kai Temple, the Suey Sing Hall, the Hop Sing Hall, and the Officials' Reviewing Stand with its honored guests. The teaser leading the dragon is of Chinese ancestry, but the legs dancing under the dragon, the parade announcer proclaims, are "the men and women of the 9th Avionics Maintenance Squadron from nearby Beale Air Force Base" ([Nall] 1990). To conclude the two-hour-long procession, a 15-foot string of firecrackers is strung up and exploded in front of the reviewing stand.

The official Bok Kai Festival Hostess, in a red silk gown, graces the Marysville Chinese Community float and then joins the other honored guests on the reviewing stand to view the other parading units. The Bok Kai Hostess from the prior year waves from a convertible. [Notably, the Marysville Chinese community crowned its first festival Queen in 1947. This is the earliest adaptation of the American beauty queen custom into Chinese American festivals (Chace 1992b).]

Many units in this annual community-parade are regular entries, but diverse groups often join in. The parade has expanded in recent decades with increasing numbers of community organizations and ethnic groups participating: the Marysville Charros Association, the [Hispanic] *Organizaciones Unidas*, the Filipino Community Association, the local Sons of Norway Lodge, the Yuba-Sutter Scottish Cultural Society, the Democratic Central Committee, the Sutter County Young Republicans, various 4-H Clubs, packs of Cub Scouts, the Marysville Lions Club, the Marysville Elks Lodge, the Shriners, the Presbyterian Church Pioneer Girls, the Latter Day Saints Church float, the Yuba City HOG Motorcycle Club, the local chapter of the American Red Cross, etc.

A century ago, these festival processions were equally colorful, and they attracted the diverse townspeople as spectators, if not as participants. The early processions regularly featured great silken banners, several loud Chinese bands, and often an entire Chinese opera troupe in their magnificent stage costumes. By the 1880s, the festival procession usually was headed by the Anglo community's governmental authority, either the marshal or the chief of police, with American flags gaily flying from the four corners of his buggy. Sometimes the Anglo community's New Pacific Brass Band was contracted for the march. The Chinese community temple leaders for the 1890 festival purchased a great 150-foot-long dragon to include in the procession, and in subsequent year, this spectacular attraction resulted in many throngs of visitors. Anglo friends in carriages preceded the great dragon in some processions. Often, Anglos drove buggies and wagons carrying Chinese in the early parades. The local schools declared a holiday for these colorful town affairs, and many rural farmers from the surrounding regions, both Anglos and Chinese, came into town for the celebrations (Chace 1992b).

Other Festival Events. Additional elements were added to the early festivals to expand the community's enjoyment and participation, and the planned festivities soon required two days. Chinese opera companies entertained, sometimes they were sponsored and performed for the public free of charge. Many Anglo visitors entered and enjoyed the theatrics even if they did not fully understand the dialogue. Free evening shows of fireworks first were added by the Chinese merchants in the 1890s, which resulted in great numbers of Anglo visitors staying in town for the entire celebration (Chace 1992b).

While feasting always has been an important part of the ritual, at the turn of the century, the Chinese associations began inviting their American attorneys and local court officers to dine with them in formal festival banquets. These inter-ethnic banquets in the Chinese association halls soon expanded to include the city mayor and many prominent business and professional leaders (Chace 1992b). These inter-ethnic community banquets remain as an important element.

In this century, many additional elements have been scheduled into the festivals. These activities have included martial arts tournaments, basketball games, and boxing matches. Anglo entrepreneurs began staging evening social dances for festival visitors in the early 1900s. Formal benefit balls occurred at the municipal auditorium, beginning in the 1930s festivals, which received wide Chinese American and Anglo American support (Chace 1992b). Chinese puppet shows, piano concerts by a Chinese artist, fashion show luncheons, and art exhibits, as well as bicycle races and running events, have been organized in recent festivals.

The Firing of the Bombs. The firing of the temple's lucky bombs is the traditional finale for this ritual for civic prosperity and good fortune. This activity has occurred since 1872. A procession of Chinese elders marches with solemnity from the old temple, with firecrackers popping, a clanging gong, the old jade tablet representing Bok Kai draped with streaming red ribbons, and a white tureen with smoldering incense sticks. Stout younger men lugging the heavy box of bombs follow directly behind the elders. These processioners walk the one block to the intersection opposite the two Chinese society halls. Marysville City police, fire, and street maintenance personnel cooperatively rope off the intersection around which 500 to 1,000 spectators assemble.

To initiate the event, the Bok Kai tablet is placed upon a table looking north over the activities. The censer pot with curling incense is set directly in front of the tablet. Then, to the accompaniment of particularly rapid banging on the gong, the senior leaders stand in front of the table and respectfully bow three times. One of the elders then auctions the rights to the traditional most lucky Ring Number Four. This is done in the Toishan Chinese language, but using the speaker system in the Police Commander's cruiser. (This cooperative use of the Police Commander's speaker first occurred in 1990, but this cooperation has occurred in each festival since.) Otherwise, the activities proceed without a public announcer or other commentary.

The six-inch-long handmade bombs, each with a three-inch ring set over the top, are placed into a three-foot-tall log mortar and are fired off one by one, to the constant sounding of the nearby gong. The beribboned ring of each bomb flies 50 to 75 feet into the air. The lucky ring falls from the sky, it is said, specifically to the one to be blessed for the year. About 15 young men within the intersection jump mightily to catch the lucky ring, and they scrimmage forcefully to snatch the prize if it falls among them to the pavement. Several packets of popping firecrackers are exploded between each bomb firing. This booming-popping-gonging activity, punctuated with competitive leaps and scrambles, lasts for an exciting hour.

After all the bombs have been fired, the elders march back to the temple with the Bok Kai tablet, followed as before by the younger men carrying the big empty bomb box. The tablet is replaced solemnly at the altar, and the men bow. The large ceremonial gong inside the temple is sounded with a booming reverberation, and the affair is concluded with the blasts of several packages of firecrackers thrown out in front of the temple doors.

Organizing the Festivals. The elders within the Marysville Chinese community have organized the ritual activities of the Bok Kai celebration for over a century, and they have regularly informed and invited the wider community to the public festival activities through the local

English-language newspapers (Chace 1992b). The consolidated Chinese-community association is responsible for the temple and takes the lead role in the annual ritual honoring Bok Kai. Other groups within the Chinese community join in, sponsoring their own organization banquets and celebratory activities. Various non-Chinese organizations similarly stage events during the festival schedule and join in the celebration, particularly in recent decades.

As the Chinese American population declined in Marysville in the years following World War II, it became necessary to restructure the organization behind the festival. The elders of the Marysville Chinese-community association approached and enlisted the Marysville-Yuba County Chamber of Commerce in 1965 to help sustain this uniquely local annual civic celebration. The Chamber organized numerous non-Chinese merchants and volunteers to assist in planning the prideful civic boosterism activities of the festival schedule. The Chamber's annual festival committees, however, always included one or more prominent local Chinese Americans who served as liaison officers with the Chinese community leadership and helped ensure that all activities were concordant with the traditional celebration and temple ritual. This organizational arrangement lasted for two decades, but since 1987, the festival committee of community volunteers has been organized independently of the Chamber (Chace 1992b).

Many Marysville people recognize the local importance and landmark status of the old Chinese temple. A group of local folk, primarily non-Chinese citizens, embarked in the early 1970s to have the Bok Kai Temple recognized as a historic landmark. The still active temple building soon became a California State landmark, and the temple was officially listed on the National Register of Historic Places in 1976. These efforts were necessary, in part, because the declining economy within the local Chinese community no longer provided for the maintenance and repairs of the temple building. An extensive building restoration project was organized through the Marysville Kiwanis Club and was carried out through the 1970s. Later, it was the Marysville Lions Club that repainted the temple as a community service project in 1986. The broader community of Marysville citizens, non-Chinese and Chinese alike, has adopted the old temple as a Marysville landmark. The Bok Kai Temple, however, has remained the property of the consolidated Chinese-community association and still serves as a revered Chinese temple for worship.

Civic Ritual, Tradition, and Interpretive Restraint. The annual civic rituals of Marysville's Bok Kai Festival have been practiced for over a century, but they have been presented to the community with an interpretive restraint on the religious symbolism. The festival activities are marked by a pronounced lack of interpretive texts in the festival committee's press releases, in general newspaper stories, in newspaper advertisements, in the parade announcers' scripts, and even in street conversations. Indeed, for the great majority of participants, the festival is not understood as a religious activity, it is a historic civic tradition.

In recent years, the festival had come to represent a joyous California community celebration, historically rooted in traditional Chinese culture, although those of Chinese ancestry now constituted only a tiny fraction of the local population. This festival serves, as it has in the past, to draw the wider urban community together by the utilization of traditional activities and symbols. The symbolism, by the very nature of symbols, remains open to interpretation, particularly since religious interpretations remain restrained.

From the earlier perspectives of ambitious Chinese business leaders in decades past (and their consolidated community association) and from the perspective of current Anglo American businessmen (and their chamber of commerce), this community festival can be appreciated from the standpoint of good business and civic boosterism. The festival events promote the town and its enterprises. Hotels and motels usually are filled with visitors throughout the festival schedule. Street vendors and retail stores sell commodities which cannot be considered religious, such as chocolate fortune cookies. Many downtown shops have festival promotions in their front windows, and numerous businesses purchase advertisements in the community newspapers promoting the festival. Since the festival is included in the civic boosterism schedule, many non-religious local groups seek to be represented and to be seen publicly in the festival parade.

Different participants are attracted even to the focal events, but relatively few are concerned with a religious perspective for the Bok Kai festivities. Approximately 20,000 people view the Saturday parade, but probably less then 20% appear to be of Asian ancestry. Of the 123 units composing the parade in 1990, only 16% were constituted with most participants of apparent Chinese ancestry. There were around 2,100 parading participants that year, and, very approximately categorized by ancestry, they appeared about 13% Asian, 83% European, 2% black, 1% Hispanic, and 1% American Indian. In contrast, about 500 to 1,000 people come out to observe and participate in the firing of the bombs on Sunday, and somewhat over half are of Asian ancestry. Of the several thousand visitors to the temple over the weekend, more than 95% appear to be of Asian ancestry.

Over the years, there never has been a hint that the ancillary festival events were staged to entertain, amuse, and entreat the Chinese gods, who by tradition should have been present (Chace 1992b). The Chinese opera performances, the piano concerts, the puppet shows, the school poetry writing and art contests, the queen (or hostess) competitions, the parade float contests, the martial arts tournaments, the mile runs, and the bicycle races all simply were advertised and described as festival events for participants and competitors. For the Marysville community, these are contests, competitions, and entertainment; they serve winners, participants, and spectators, as well as event sponsors and advertisers. They further promote the community, its leaders, and its commerce. Overall, the different peoples in the diverse festival events, from bicycle racers to parading Cub Scouts to those purchasing temple incense, had various motivations, values, and beliefs. However, they participate together and socially cooperate in the enjoyment of the various festival activities.

The Bok Kai Festival is publicly interpreted to the broad English-language community primarily in terms of civic history and local tradition. The official festival poster displayed with the schedule of community events in 1990 was titled, "—1990 YEAR OF THE HORSE— *BOK KAI FESTIVAL* OF HISTORY & THE ARTS." Community newspapers focus almost exclusively on the public activities of the festival. Reference to Bok Kai, as the Chinese God of water, being honored is mentioned only very briefly in newspaper feature stories.

The worshipful ritual occurring at the temple is not announced or is politely ignored. In fact, to the immense crowd gathered for the parade, the announcers indicate that public tours of the old landmark temple occurred earlier in the month and could be arranged at a later date. Thus, it is politely implied that the temple is not available for general public visitors. Actually, the small temple room is jammed continually both Saturday and Sunday with the many worshippers making offerings and prayers. No public comment is made about the symbolic tablet representing Bok Kai being brought out to oversee the firing of the bombs. Similarly, the firecrackers, gongs, lion dancers, dragon, bombs, incense, paper money, roasted piglets, etc., as well as the music, sports, and other festival ritual are not publicly interpreted as religious. With interpretive restraint, community harmony is maintained and positive inter-ethnic relations are promoted.

In recent decades, the historic Marysville tradition of the parade has been emphasized as the core event of the festival. For most of the Marysville community, what was once a ritual procession has become a civic parade. Participation is encouraged from distant Chinese American communities through their youth marching corps and lion dance troupes. The temple devotees, for their part, accede the symbolic procession banners and gongs to the disciplined hands of local Boy and Girl Scouts and the Marysville dragon to be carried by a local Air Force squadron. A variety of local ethnic organizations proudly join in this civic parade. The auto dealerships in the region provide VIP cars for the parading dignitaries. Viewed as a civic tradition, the historic Bok Kai Festival now generates wide community participation. Organized entirely by civic volunteers, the events are co-sponsored by the

Marysville Chinese Community [Inc.], the City of Marysville, and the Yuba-Sutter Asian Cultural Exchange, plus local commercial sponsors, the Yuba-Sutter Regional Arts Council, and the California Arts Council. Similarly, the chamber of commerce, merchants, public utilities, political leaders, and many diverse community groups lend their support and involvement. The Bok Kai Festival is a community celebration.

Conclusions. The Bok Kai Festival obviously is symbolically interpreted as a unique Marysville historic tradition, and the festival has served to bring together the broad community, non-Chinese and Chinese alike. The festival activities have been developed locally to promote and enhance inter-ethnic relations. The celebrations utilize traditional symbols, but also employ restraint in interpreting those symbols. The festival activities and symbols remain open to interpretations from diverse perspectives. With this tradition and with restraint, the urban community can celebrate happily together in social solidarity. The diverse people of Marysville have learned, over the many years, to dance with the dragon.

Further, this description of Marysville's Bok Kai Festival more clearly resolves the debate about the "diversity within the unity" of Chinese popular religion. One might ask if the ritual activities at Marysville are properly performed. Arguably, they are proper; dissenting views are not expressed, while broad support and participation is evident from Chinese American participants. To this extent, the "diversity" perspective is supported, that proper performance is more important than the participants' various beliefs. As an urban community study, the variety of motivations and beliefs among participants probably do not represent an unusual case of variance. There obviously is little unity in the beliefs of participants, and the "unity" perspective is not sustained. Clearly, in the "diversity within the unity" debate, it is the "varying social relations" perspective which provides the more parsimonious view to best explain the evolved Marysville ritual. Under the polity and hegemony of American cultural patterns, the introduced Chinese traditional ritual has evolved. The distinctive social relations of the Marysville community have generated differences in ritual practices and understandings. Thus, local social relations, along with interpretive restraint, are primary for appreciating Marysville's long sustained Bok Kai Festival.

Acknowledgments. In initially directing my attention to this festive ritual tradition, the ongoing guidance of Munson Kwok is acknowledged. An especially warm appreciation is owed to Brock Bowen, Robert Jackson, Bing Ong, Kathleen Lim, Janice Soohoo Nall, and the many other friendly people of Marysville who graciously responded to my many inquiries. For their encouragement and critical assistance in this project, my personal thanks go to my UCR dissertation committee of Eugene Anderson, Michael Kearney, and David Kronenfeld. I alone, however, shoulder the responsibility for the interpretation presented of this traditional community ritual.

Works Cited

Ahern, E. M. *Chinese Ritual and Politics*. Cambridge: Cambridge University Press, 1981.

Ahern, E. M., and H. Gates, Eds. *The Anthropology of Taiwanese Society*. Stanford: Stanford University Press, 1981.

Anderson, E. N., Jr. "The Changing Tastes of the Gods: Chinese Temple Fairs in Malaysia." *Asian Folklore Studies* 36(1): 1977, 19–30.

Anderson, E. N., Jr. *The Floating World of Castle Peak Bay*. Washington: American Anthropological Association, 1970.

Armentrout MA, L. E. "Chinese Traditional Religion in North America and Hawaii." *Chinese America: History and Perspective, 1988*, 1988. 131–147.

Blake, C. F. *Ethnic Groups and Social Change in a Chinese Market Town*. Asian Studies at Hawaii, No. 27, University Press of Hawaii, 1981.

Bowman, P. "Restoration of a Taoist Temple." *Chinese America: History and Perspective, 1988*, 1988. 148–152.

Brim, J. A. "Village Alliance Temples in Hong Kong." In *Religion and Ritual in Chinese Society*. Ed. A. P. Wolf. Stanford: Stanford University Press, 1974. 93–103.

Burkhardt, V. R. *Chinese Creeds & Customs*. Three volumes, [Hong Kong] 1958.

Chace, P. G. "Interpretive Restraint and Ritual Tradition: Marysville's Festival of Bok Kai." *Journal of Contemporary Ethnography* 21(2): 1992a, 226–254.

Chace, P. G. "Returning Thanks: Chinese Rites in an American Community." Ph.D. dissertation in Anthropology, University of California, Riverside, 1992b.

Chace, P. G. "The Oldest Chinese Temples in California, A Landmarks Tour." *Gum Saan Journal* 14(1): 1991, 1–19.

Chace, P. G. "The Turtle Dove Messenger, A Trait of the Early Los Angeles Chiao Ceremony." *Gum Saan Journal* 12(2): 1989, 1–9.

Chace, P. G. "Viviparus, The Chinese Field Snail, A Historical Archaeology Enigma." *Pacific Coast Archaeological Society Quarterly* 23(2): 1987, 69–79.

Chan, S. "Chinese Livelihood in Rural California: The Impact of Economic Change, 1860–1880." *Pacific Historical Review* 53(3): 1984, 273–307.

Cheng, A. "Chinese Gods—Borne to the U. S. A." *Sinorama* 8 (August 1989): 116–125.

Chinn, T. W. [ed.] *A History of the Chinese in California, A Syllabus*. San Francisco: California Historical Society of America, 1969.

Culin, S. *The Religious Ceremonies of the Chinese in the Eastern Cities of the United States*. Philadelphia: Privately printed, 1887.

Eberhard, W. "Economic Activities of a Chinese Temple in California." *Journal of the American Oriental Society* 82 (1962): 362–371. Reprinted in *Settlement and Social Change in Asia by Wolfram Eberhard, Collected Papers, Volume One,*. Hong Kong: Hong Kong University Press, 1967. 264–278.

Faure, D. "Folk Religion in Hong Kong and the New Territory Today." In *The Turning of the Tide, Religion in China Today*. Ed. J.F. Pas. Oxford: Oxford University Press, 1989. 259–270.

Faure, D. *The Structure of Chinese Rural Society: Lineage and Village in the Eastern New Territory, Hong Kong*. Hong Kong: Oxford University Press, 1986.

Feuchtwang, S. *The Imperial Metaphor, Popular Religion in China*. London and New York: Routledge, 1992.

Freedman, M. "On the Sociological Study of Chinese Religion." In *Religion and Ritual in Chinese Society*. Ed. A. P. Wolf. Stanford: Stanford University Press, 1974. 19–41.

Gates, H., and R.P. Weller. [eds.] "Symposium on Hegemony and Chinese Folk Ideologies." *Modern China* 13 (1 and 3): 1987, 3–109, 259–371.

Hoy, W. "Native Festivals of the California Chinese." *Western Folklore* 7(3):1948, 240–250.

Hoy, W. *Kong Chow Temple*. San Francisco: California Chinese Pioneer Historical Society, 1939.

Hughey, M. W. *Civil Religion and Moral Order, Theoretical and Historical Dimensions*. Westport, Connecticut: Greenwood Press, 1983.

Ibanez, R. [ed.] *Historical Bok Kai Temple in Old Marysville, California*. Marysville: The Marysville Chinese Community [Inc.], 1967.

Jordan, D. K. *Gods, Ghosts, and Ancestors: The Folk Religion in a Taiwanese Village*. Berkeley: University of California Press, 1972.

Lagerwey, J. *Taoist Ritual in Chinese Society and History*. New York: Macmillian Publishing Company, 1987.

Lee, J. "Some Chinese Customs and Beliefs in California." *California Folklore Quarterly* 2(3)1943: 191–204.

Lydon, S. *Chinese Gold, The Chinese in the Monterey Bay Area*. Capitola: Capitola Book Company, 1985.

Madsen, R. *Morality and Power in a Chinese Village*. Berkeley: University of California Press, 1984.

McDonald, D., and G. McDonald. *The History of the Weaverville Joss House and the Chinese of Trinity County, California*. Medford, Oregon: McDonald Publishing, 1986.

Minnick, S. S. *Samfow: The San Joaquin Chinese Legacy*. Fresno: Panorama West Publishing, 1988.

[Nall, J. S.] "Parade Script, Announcers Packet, 1990, The 110th Bok Kai Parade, Year of the Horse, March 3, 1990, California's Oldest Parade." Typescript, 28 pages, printed for the parade announcers, 1990.

Pas J. F. [ed.] *The Turning of the Tide, Religion in China Today*. Oxford: Oxford University Press, 1989.

Rawski, E. S. "A Historian's Approach to Chinese Death Ritual." In *Death Ritual in Late Imperial and Modern China*. Ed. J. L. Watson and E. S. Rawski. Berkeley: University of California Press, 1988. 20–34.

Sangren, P. S. "Great Tradition and Little Traditions Reconsidered: The Question of Cultural Integration in China." *Journal of Chinese Studies* 1(1):1984, 1–24.

Sangren, P. S. "Orthodoxy, Heterodoxy, and the Structure of Value in Chinese Rituals." *Modern China* 13(1):1987a, 63–89.

Sangren, P. S. *History and Magical Power in a Chinese Community*. Stanford: Stanford University Press, 1987b.

Saso, M. R. *Blue Dragon White Tiger, Taoist Rites of Passage*. Washington, D. C.: The Taoist Center, 1990b.

Saso, M. R. *Taoism and the Rite of Cosmic Renewal, 2nd Ed*. Pullman: Washington State University Press, 1990a.

Siu, H. F. "Recycling Rituals: Politics and Popular Culture in Contemporary Rural China." In *Unofficial China, Popular Culture and Thought in the People's Republic*. Ed. P. Link, R. Madsen, and P. G. Pickowicz. 121–137. Reprinted (1990), with alterations, in *The Yale-China Association China Update* 10(2):1989 1–8.

Smith, R. J. "Afterword." In *Religion and Ritual in Chinese Society*. Ed. A. P. Wolf. Stanford: Stanford University Press, 1974. 337–348.

Taylor, R. "Official and Popular Religion and the Political Organization of Chinese Society in the Ming." In *Orthodoxy in Late Imperial China*. Ed. K. C. Liu. Berkeley: University of California Press, 1990. 126–157.

Topley, M. "Chinese Religion and Rural Cohesion in the Nineteenth Century." *Journal of the Hong Kong Branch of the Royal Asiatic Society* 8:(1968) 9–43.

Wang, S. H. "Ethnic Communities in Cheung Chau, Hong Kong." In *Ethnicity and Interpersonal Interaction, A Cross Cultural Study,*. Ed. D. Y. H. Wu. Singapore: Maruzen Asia, 1982. 181–198.

Ward, B. E. "Regional Opera and Their Audiences: Evidence from Hong Hong." In *Popular Culture in Late Imperial China. Ed.* D. Johnson, A. J. Nathan, and E. S. Rawski. Berkeley: University of California Press, 1985. 161–187.

Watson, J. L. "Anthropological Analyses of Chinese Religion." *The China Quarterly* 66:(1976) 355–364.

Watson, J. L. "Standardizing the Gods: The Promotion of T'ien Hou ('Empress of Heaven') Along the South China Coast, 960–1960." In *Popular Culture in Late Imperial China*. Ed. D. Johnson, A. J. Nathan, and E. S. Rawski. Berkeley: University of California Press, 1985. 292–324.

Watson, J. L. "The Structure of Chinese Funerary Rites: Elementary Forms, Ritual Sequence, and the Primacy of Performance." In *Death Ritual in Late Imperial and Modern China. Ed.* J. L. Watson and E. S. Rawski. Berkeley: University of California Press, 1988. 3–19.

Watson, J. L., and E.S. Rawski [eds.] *Death Ritual in Late Imperial and Modern China*. Berkeley: University of California Press, 1988.

Weller, R. P. *Unities and Diversities in Chinese Religion*. Seattle: University of Washington Press, 1987.

Wells, M. K. *Chinese Temples in California*. M. A. thesis, University of California [Berkeley]. Reprinted (1971), San Francisco: R and E Research Associates, 1962.

Wey, N. "A History of Chinese Americans in California." In *Five Views: An Ethnic Sites Survey for California*. Sacramento: State of California, Office of Historic Preservation, 1988. 103–158.

Williams, G. M., D. D. Wong, and B.L. Wong. "The Chinese Temples of Northern California." In *The Life, Influence and the Role of the Chinese in the United States, 1776–1960: Proceeding/Papers of the National Conference Held at The University of San Francisco, July 10, 11, 12, 1975*. Eds. T. W. Chinn and D. W. Chinn. San Francisco: Chinese Historical Society of America, 1976. 293–296.

Wolf, A. P. "Introduction." In *Religion and Ritual in Chinese Society*. Ed. A. P. Wolf. Stanford: Stanford University Press, 1974. 1–18.

Yang, C. K. *Religion in Chinese Society, A Study of Contemporary Functions of Religion and Some of Their Historical Factors.*. Berkeley: University of California Press, 1961.

Minorities Within a Minority

MEHDI BOZORGMEHR and
CLAUDIA DER-MARTIROSIAN
Department of Sociology, University of California, Los Angeles

Ethnic and cultural diversity are currently the buzzwords in multi-ethnic American cities. The recent riots in Los Angeles have further heightened public sensitivity to the status, needs, and concerns of various ethnic and racial groups in American society. Although ethnic diversity is a historical phenomenon, the new tide of immigration to the U.S. has extended its range and scope. By 1990, the total foreign-born population of the U.S. had increased to 21.6 million (U.S. Bureau of the Census 1992), a much higher figure than the highest previously recorded figure of 14.2 million in 1930 (Jasso and Rozenzweig 1990). The increase in volume of immigration is accompanied by heterogeneity in the new immigrants' countries of origin. Unlike the early immigrants, new immigrants originate from many more countries. In contrast to the turn of the century unskilled immigrants, many new immigrants are skilled workers. The change in volume, source, and quality of immigration to the U.S. is, in part, an artifact of changes in the American immigration policy since 1965. The 1965 Immigration Act raised the quota to 20,000 per year for each country in the Eastern Hemisphere with an annual ceiling of 170,000. Subsequently, the sources of immigration have shifted from Europe to Asia, Latin America, Africa, and the Middle East.

The recent scholarly and popular emphasis on diversity is partly a response to the reality of new immigration, and partly a belief in cultural pluralism instead of assimilation. In the overview of a book synthesizing the vast literature on immigrants in America, Portes and Rumbaut (25) write that "the emphasis throughout is on diversity in both the immigrants' origin and their modes of incorporation into American society." These authors emphasize inter-ethnic differences among immigrants, which result in divergent adaptation processes in the U.S. Portes and Rumbaut argue that, upon arrival, nationality groups have a strong awareness of their ethnic identity, but are unaware of the broader category under which they are placed in America. Thus, outsiders refer to Mexicans, Cubans, and other Latin and Central Americans as Latinos or Hispanics. Similarly, Chinese, Japanese, Koreans, and others are considered Asians or Asian Americans, despite major linguistic and cultural differences. Mittleberg and Waters (1992) adopt the concept of "proximal host" to refer to the category or group in which the immigrants are most likely to be classified or absorbed. Portes and Rumbaut (137) remind us that "national experiences are too divergent and national loyalties too deeply embedded to yield to this supranational logic." These scholars, however, do not raise this question at the intra-ethnic level among ethnic groups of different national backgrounds, e.g., Chinese, Jews, or Armenians.

Subethnicity or Intra-Ethnic Diversity. The presence of sub-groups within an ethnic group (e.g., Chinese, Jewish, Armenian) creates subethnicity. At the broadest level, these subgroups corre-spond to nationalities or countries of origin. Each subethnic group has a different national loyalty and cultural heritage. Each subethnic group may also have a different socioeconomic profile upon arrival, affecting their adaptation. Many factors such as the level of economic development of the country of origin, causes of migration, and migrant selectivity affect the post-migration social and economic adaptation of the subgroups. Thus, aggregation at the group level could mask the unique experience of each subethnic group (Der-Martirosian, Sabagh, and Bozorgmehr 1993; Yancey, Erickson, and Juliani 1976).

Subethnicity results from the successive influx of the same ethnic group from different countries. Populations with a long history of migration such as the Chinese are scattered around the world. The reunification of these populations through subsequent migration creates subethnicity. Subethnic groups could be the majority population in the country of origin (e.g., Chinese in China, Taiwan, or Hong Kong), or a minority (e.g., Chinese in Vietnam or Thailand).

The timing of migration is immaterial in the creation of subethnicity; immigrant waves originating from different countries could coincide or be spaced apart. If the migration is old, it could result in second and subsequent native-born generations. The Jewish immigration to the United States has spanned over three centuries (Goldsheider and Zuckerman 1984; Sklare 1971) and represents a historical example of subethnicity. The Chinese and Armenian immigration to the United States represent more contemporary examples of subethnicity. Compared to the Chinese, however, the Armenians and the Jews come from a broader range of countries, thus accentuating dissimilarities among the subgroups. In light of these divergent backgrounds and immigration histories, it is a simplification to discuss merely Armenian, Chinese, and Jewish ethnicity and identity and ignore subgroup differences.

Immigrants acquire new identities in the host society. When ethnicity is synonymous with nationality, nationality is the primary identity. For ethnically homogeneous immigrant groups such as Koreans (Min 1991), ethnicity and nationality are one and the same. Korean immigrants in the U.S. considered themselves Koreans in Korea, and continue to do so after immigration. If there is any change in ethnic identification, it is in adopting a hyphenated (i.e., Korean-American) identity. This pattern, however, does not hold for ethnically diverse groups such as the Chinese. For instance, the indigenous Chinese in Taiwan consider themselves Taiwanese, further distinguishing their Taiwanese or Chinese origin. After immigration, however, Americans refer to immigrants from Taiwan in more commonly understood ethnic labels (i.e., Chinese). Thus, the Taiwanese in the U.S. become the Chinese from Taiwan. On the other hand, the Taiwanese identity is reinforced through interaction with other Chinese who are well-aware of nationality distinctions among themselves.

Conversely, ethnic identity is the primary identity for groups who were minorities in the country of origin. For instance, the minority Chinese in Vietnam identify themselves as Chinese. After immigration to the U.S. and contact with both the ethnic Vietnamese, as well as other Chinese, some members of this group identify themselves as Chinese-Vietnamese. Thus, irrespective of pre-migration majority or minority status, Chinese subethnic groups develop a new ethnic identity in combined ethnic and nationality terms.

Since the relevant research is lacking on the Chinese, we turn to other groups for whom there is evidence. Our research on Iranians in Los Angeles supports the above propositions. With 98% of the total population Muslim, pre-revolutionary Iran was a religiously homogeneous society. As a result of the Islamic revolution, however, Iranian immigrants in Los Angeles are disproportionately drawn from the ranks of religious minorities. In addition to Muslims, there are sizable numbers of Jews and Christian Armenians among Iranians. These ethno-religious minorities in Iran considered themselves, and were thought of by others, simply as Jews or Armenians. Since Los Angeles contains the largest Armenian and the second largest Jewish population in the U.S., Armenian and Jewish Iranians coexist with non-Iranian co-ethnics. Thus, general minority designations in Iran, i.e., Jewish or Armenian, are no longer distinctive in the U.S. Furthermore, encounters between co-ethnics from different countries highlight their cultural and other differences. Therefore, after immigration to the U.S., the first hyphenation that follows Armenians or Jews from Iran is not American, rather, it is Iranian. Instead of assimilation or acculturation (becoming like Americans), subethnicity is reinforced. Armenians from Iran are considered by other Armenians, and consider themselves, Armenian Iranian. The same pattern applies to Iranian Jews (Bozorgmehr 1992).

Subethnicity is often overlooked in the literature because the objective component of ethnicity is emphasized at the expense of the subjective part. According to Barth (1969), ethnicity is both subjective and objective. The objective dimension is socially constructed by the outsiders (e.g., members of the host society), who often cannot differentiate among immigrants originating from a particular world region. For instance, regardless of the country of origin, immigrants from Asia are simply referred to as Asians. Under these circumstances, it is not surprising that outsiders are unable to distinguish complex intra-group diversity among the Chinese.

In turn, ethnic labels are sometimes internalized by group members. Ironically, the subjective side of ethnicity can further reinforce this lumping effect, since immigrants often give easily recognizable answers to questions about their origin. When asked about their ethnic background, many Armenians simply answer Armenian without providing additional information about their country of origin. Immigrants are cognizant of intra-group differences only among themselves. Yet, to enhance group solidarity, members often downplay subgroup differences. For instance, Jews disregard nationality differences in an effort toward unity. Since outsiders are oblivious to subtle intra-group differences, and insiders consciously overlook them, little research has been conducted on subethnicity.

The scant historical literature available on Jewish subethnicity suggests that it was the basis of the social organization of this minority at the turn of the century in New York City. In the late 19th century, German Jews in New York City had more social contacts with American Jews than they had with other Germans. The influx of lower-class Russian Jewish refugees, however, caused German Jews to maintain distance from these co-religionists. German Jews even tried to halt the new wave of Jewish immigration. German and Russian Jews lived in uptown and downtown sections of New York City, respectively, had their own schools and hospitals, and rarely inter-married. Only in charity was there some cooperation between German and Russian Jews. This initial strained relationship subsided in the early 20th century (Rischin 1962, 1986). Nevertheless, in a study of post-W.W.II European refugees in New York City, Gaertner (1955) notes that Jewish refugees still fared better than other refugees, due to the assistance of co-religionists.

Subethnicity resurfaces with each new wave of Jewish immigration to the U.S. Despite several decades of coexistence, the majority of Jewish Cuban exiles in Miami have not been integrated into the sizable non-Cuban Jewish community of the city (Boswell and Curtis 1983). Subethnicity is a formidable barrier toward broader Jewish community despite conscious efforts of some recent Jewish immigrants. According to Gold:

Initially hopeful about developing ties with American Jews, many [Soviet Jewish] émigrés discovered that the cultural, linguistic, and moral gulf between themselves and the host community was difficult to cross. (78)

This finding is not unique to Russian Jews. Gold's research on Israeli Jews in Los Angeles reveals similar findings:

Israelis are often united by the nature of their relations with American Jews.... Such links not withstanding however, on the group level, Israeli immigrants are unified by their shared feelings of distance from and incompatibility with American Jews. They are rooted in the two groups differing cultural, linguistic, ideological, and religious outlooks. (Gold forthcoming)

Our study of Iranian Jews in Los Angeles shows little overlap in their ethnicity with non-Iranian co-religionists (Bozorgmehr 1992). Iranian Jews rarely have non-Iranian Jewish social and economic ties (Bozorgmehr 1992). In sum, existing studies suggest that Jewish immigrant groups have received assistance from co-religionists in the U.S., while maintaining their distinctive subethnic identity.

The above discussion calls into question the conventional wisdom that each new wave of co-ethnic immigration has a reinforcing, or even resurgent, impact on ethnicity. In the Chinese case, where there is substantial new immigration from various countries of origins, it cannot be assumed that the Chinese ethnicity is reinforced. This assumption is unwarranted since Chinese subethnic groups are culturally, socioeconomically, and even linguistically distinctive from one another. Moreover, the causes, history, and pattern of migration of each subethnic group also differs from one another.

Chinese Immigration to the United States. The periodization of Chinese immigration to the U.S. varies arbitrarily in number of waves from two to four, depending on the source. Since Chinese immigration ebbed and flowed according to the U.S. immigration laws, the periodization is defined in legalistic terms. Over time, diversification in the origins of Chinese immigrants has shaped the diversity of this minority group in America.

It is commonly agreed upon that the first wave of Chinese immigration began in mid-19th century and, for all practical purposes, came to a halt by the Chinese Exclusion Act of 1882. This wave or phase is known as the period of free immigration (Wong 1979). Most Chinese immigrants in this wave originated from the Cantonese provinces of Kwangtung and Fukien in South China. Light (81) writes that "in the United States, Cantonese immigrants early organized themselves into district associations, each of which recruited its membership from a particular Kwangtung district." The following six districts made up the Cantonese provinces: Sam Yup, Sze Yup, Heungshan, Tungkun, Kok Shan, and Fayuan (Wong 1979). Two major dialect groups existed in the Kwangtung region, resulting in strained relations between the speakers of each dialect in the U.S. In sum, the differences in linguistic, clan, and regional communities among the Chinese defined the boundaries of each subethnic group.

As might be expected, the period of Chinese exclusion (1882–1943) did not result in any sizable immigration to the U.S. In light of halted immigration, native-born Chinese (40,260) outnumbered the foreign-born in 1940 (37,242) (Wong 29). The next major wave of Chinese migration began about a century after the first, with the outbreak of the Chinese Revolution of 1949. This second wave consisted of well-educated and skilled refugees who came from different parts of China and Taiwan.

The repeal of exclusionary policies against the Chinese during World War II was symbolic, resulting in a token quota of 105 persons per year (Wong 1979). The passage of the 1965 immigration law, however, spurred another wave of Chinese immigration. Under the third and sixth preferences of the new immigration law, professionals (e.g., doctors and engineers) and skilled workers were eligible to immigrate to the U.S. Automatically, each country's quota was set at 20,000 annually. Thus, 40,000 Chinese from Hong Kong and Taiwan became eligible to immigrate to the U.S. annually. When the U.S. finally recognized the People's Republic of China (P.R.C.) in 1979, another 20,000 Chinese were able to immigrate to the U.S. per annum.

The third wave consists mainly of Chinese urbanites from China and Chinese from Taiwan and Hong Kong, many of whom are of mainland origin (Kwong 1987; Zhou 1992; Zhou and Logan 1989). The third wave of Chinese immigration also includes Chinese refugees from Vietnam, a subject we will return to later in this paper. Furthermore, this wave includes the new anticipatory exiles from Hong Kong before China's takeover in 1997 (Gibson 1990). As a result of this heterogeneous wave, Portes and Zhou write that:

> Post-1965 Chinese immigration is bi-modal, featuring a stratum of highly-educated professionals alongside large numbers of immigrants brought through family connections who know little English and have only modest educational credentials. (512)

Chinese in the United States. As a diaspora, Chinese are scattered across the globe. The number of overseas Chinese was estimated between 26 and 28 million in 130 countries circa 1980 (Poston and Yu 1990). Overseas Chinese are persons of Chinese ancestry living outside mainland China and Taiwan. The vast majority of overseas Chinese live in Asia, more specifically in Southeast Asia. About 2.5 million (less than 10%) of the overseas Chinese lived outside Asia circa 1980 (Poston and Yu 1990). Over a third of these (894,453) were enumerated in the 1980 U.S. by reporting Chinese ancestry.

Table 1 presents data from the 1990 U.S. Census on the number of persons born in China, Hong Kong, and Taiwan, three major sources of Chinese immigration. According to Table 1, there were 543,208 persons from China; 253,719 from Taiwan, and 152,263 from Hong Kong, totaling 949,190 in the U.S. in 1990. Given the preponderance of the Chinese in China, Hong Kong, and Taiwan, it is safe to assume that the vast majority of this nearly one million individuals are Chinese. Together, these three populations made up 4.4% of the total 21.6 million foreign-born persons in the U.S. in 1990. Even excluding Chinese from other countries, the Chinese from the above three countries constitute the largest Asian immigrant group in the U.S.

Table 1 further shows the breakdown of the foreign-born persons from China, Hong Kong, and Taiwan by the two largest states of residence, California and New York, respectively. Around 40% of each of the three foreign-born populations resided in California, whereas 24% of those born in China, 21% of Hong Kong nationals, and merely 11% of Taiwanese lived in New York. Clearly, California far surpasses New York as the favored destination of these three nationalities, especially for the Taiwanese. By contrast, California was home to 31% of all foreign-born persons, and New York to 14%. With the exception of Taiwanese in New York, the Chinese are highly concentrated in both California and New York.

Table 1. **Size of Foreign-born Population from China, Hong Kong, and Taiwan in the United States, California, New York, and Other States: 1990**

Residence	China-born	% of U.S.	Hong Kong-born	% of U.S.	Taiwan-born	% of U.S.
California	216,324	40	66,427	44	106,914	42
New York	129,782	24	32,228	21	27,648	11
Other states	197,102	36	53,608	35	119,157	47
Total U.S.	**543,208**	**100**	**152,263**	**100**	**253,719**	**100**

Source: U.S. Bureau of the Census (1992)

Although the geographical distribution of the Chinese subgroups are somewhat similar, their social and economic characteristics are less so. The data in Table 2 illustrate the differences in socioeconomic characteristics of the three major Chinese subgroups in 1990, using the total U.S. foreign-born population as a reference. There were about

529,837 immigrants from China, 147,131 from Hong Kong, and 244,102 from Taiwan in the U.S. The Taiwanese are the most recent immigrants of the three subgroups, over a third of whom immigrated during 1985–90. The Taiwanese are also the most educated of the three subgroups. Remarkably, almost two-thirds of the Taiwanese held a bachelor's degree or higher, compared to less than half and a third of persons born in Hong Kong and China, respectively. Not surprisingly, after India, Taiwan ranked second on this indicator of educational achievement; Hong Kong ranked fourth and China tenth (Bureau of the Census 1993a). College and university students partially account for the high levels of education of all three Chinese subgroups. There were 45,130 foreign students from China, 37,430 from Taiwan, and 14,020 from Hong Kong in the U.S. institutions in 1992–93. Indeed, China was the top country of foreign student origin in the U.S. (Institute of International Education 1992/93).

Table 2. **Social and Economic Characteristics of the Foreign-born Population from China, Hong Kong, and Taiwan in the U.S., and Total U.S. Foreign-Born Population: 1990**

	China-born	Hong Kong-born	Taiwan-born	U.S. foreign-born
Total persons	529,837	147,131	244,102	19,767,316
Immigrated 1985–90	30.4%	24.9%	33.5%	22.8%
Completed 4 yrs. or more of college*	30.9%	46.8%	62.2%	20.4%
In managerial professional specialty jobs**	28.9%	40.9%	47.4%	22.2%
Median household income, 1989	$30,597	$42,033	$38,966	$28,314

*Persons 25 years and over
**Employed persons 16 years and over

Source: U.S. Bureau of the Census (1993b)

The higher education of Taiwanese as compared to the other two subgroups translates into their heavier concentration in the top managerial and specialty occupations. Finally, the median household income varies considerably between immigrants from China and the other two subgroups ($30,597 for China, $42,033 for Hong Kong, and $38,966 for Taiwan). The data in Table 2 clearly indicate that aggregating the socioeconomic characteristics of persons born in China, Hong Kong, and Taiwan into a Chinese category would conceal salient differences among these subgroups.

Chinese Subethnicity in the United States. As a result of a century and a half of immigration, spanning three distinctive waves, the major Chinese communities in the U.S. are highly diverse. For example, in New York's Chinatown, one of the oldest in the nation, the Cantonese from China and Chinese from Hong Kong made up the bulk of the population before the 1970s. Now, New York Chinatown contains "Chinese from all parts of the world" from Southeast Asia and even from several Latin American countries. These Chinese bring different dialects, cultural traditions, and occupational specializations. They tend to settle in distinctive parts of the Chinatown, corresponding to their countries of origin (Kwong 39–42). Interestingly, many of the new educated and skilled Chinese immigrants have settled in New York Chinatown. The attraction of Chinatown is apparent for immigrants who are not proficient in English. But Chinatown also has attracted investors from Taiwan, and especially Hong Kong, whose information about mainstream channels for investment is limited (Portes and Zhou 1992; Zhou 1992). Similar patterns of national-origin diversity exist in other Chinatowns (Lai 1988; Lyman 1986), including San Francisco's Chinatown (Nee and Nee 1972), as well as Chinatown and Monterey Park in Los Angeles (Fong 1989; Horton 1992; Wong 1979). Yet, to our knowledge, there is no systematic study of subethnicity in major Chinese ethnic communities.

Waldinger and Tseng (1992) have argued for distinguishing the New York from the Los Angeles Chinese communities. They treat this regional distinction as a form of "intra-group diversity." Waldinger and Tseng argue that although both communities started from similar beginnings, the new post-1965 immigration has resulted in major differences in the country of origin and, concomitantly, social class of the Chinese in New York and Los Angeles:

> Whereas Los Angeles has become the favored destination of middle- and upper middle-class immigrants, many of them from Taiwan, New York has received a heavily proletarian population, originating in the P.R.C. and Hong Kong. These initial differences in characteristics of arrivals have led to divergent trajectories of ethnic incorporation. In Los Angeles, the Chinese have engaged in "leapfrog migration,"

settling in middle-class suburban areas; in New York, by contrast, the Chinese population remains tied to the inner city, with a heavy concentration in traditional Chinatown. (Waldinger and Tseng 3)

Other important differences between the two communities correspond to differences in entrepreneurial activities and politics. The Los Angeles Chinese ethnic economy centers around more skilled activities than the low-skilled garment and restaurant Chinese industries in New York. Since recent Chinese immigrants, especially from Taiwan and Hong Kong, have settled in suburbia (e.g., Monterey Park), they have experienced ethnic conflict with established residents (Fong 1989; Horton 1992; Waldinger and Tseng 1992). As such, the Chinese have organized collectively against white racism for political purposes. This collective organization has further contributed to the homogeneous image of Chinese, masking important subgroup differences and experiences. Internal divisiveness, however, characterizes the Chinese American political life, depending on the country of origin, loyalty, and ideology (Holley 1985).

Since Waldinger and Tseng are mainly interested in regional, as opposed to national-origin differences among the Chinese, they present little data on subethnic differences. Nevertheless, they report data from the 1980 U.S. Census and from the 1986 U.S. Immigration and Nationalization Service (INS) which show that there are major differences in selected socioeconomic characteristics of the foreign-born Chinese from Hong Kong, P.R.C., Taiwan, and other Chinese in New York and Los Angeles. Thus, Waldinger and Tseng (2–3) cogently sum up that "Intra-ethnic diversity ... calls into question the notion that members of a single ethnic group follow a common pattern of adaptation."

According to the 1990 census, New York City and Los Angeles County had an identical number of Chinese (around 240,000). While the Chinese population of New York City nearly doubled from 1980 to 1990, the Chinese population of Los Angeles County increased by more than two and half times from 94,000 in 1980 (Sabagh 1993). In 1980, the Japanese were the most numerous Asian group in Los Angeles County. By 1990, however, the Chinese had replaced the Japanese as the largest Asian group. Sabagh (107) observes that "the Chinese were the most rapidly growing Asian group in this period (161% increase)." As such, the Los Angeles metropolitan region provides an ideal setting for examining Chinese subethnicity.

Chinese Subethnicity in the Los Angeles Metropolitan Region. Chinatown; Monterey Park and Alhambra, Westminster and Garden Grove are the three largest Chinese concentrations in the Los Angeles metropolitan region. The Los Angeles Chinatown is the oldest Chinese center in this area. Since the 1970s, Chinese have accounted for the largest number of immigrants into Monterey Park (Fong 1989), now spilling over into Alhambra. The following factors are enumerated to account for this influx: political instability in Taiwan and Southeast Asia in general (Wong 1979), the 1965 U.S. Immigration Act, United Nation's recognition of P.R.C., and the instrumental role played by a Chinese developer, Fredric Hsieh, who publicized Monterey Park as the "Chinese Beverly Hills," especially to the Taiwanese (Fong 1989). Chinatown neither had the residential space nor the amenities to attract affluent and educated immigrants from Hong Kong and Taiwan. Aptly called the "nation's first suburban Chinatown" (Arax 1987), Monterey Park offered these amenities, as well as proximity to Chinatown (Klein 1991). Westminster and Garden Grove are home to the Chinese-Vietnamese. Thus, the patterns of Chinese settlement in the Los Angeles metropolitan region roughly correspond to the country of origin.

In an early comparative study of Chinatown and Monterey Park, Wong writes:

> In terms of Chinese ethnicity, Chinatown is characterized by ethnic continuity and solidarity; and Monterey Park is characterized by ethnic fluidity and conflict. This is not surprising since Chinatown is mainly composed of immigrants who face the same situations with a shared world view. Monterey Park, on the other hand, houses a far greater diversity of Chinese in terms of educational achievement, occupations, cultural identity types, nativity, and other social [and] economic characteristics. (298)

He further observes that the Chinese in Monterey Park come from the ranks of entrepreneurial and white collar professionals, joined by wealthy immigrants from Hong Kong, Republic of China, and elsewhere. Wong writes:

> From the perspective of multiple Chinese identity types, we shall attempt to explicate the subcommunity's sources of ethnic identity and conflict ... but first, in order to correctly understand the dynamics of the Chinese populace, the various subgroups must be distinguished by cultural identity types. Since membership in an ethnic group is a matter of social definition, a symbolic interplay between self and others, the term "Chinese" can and does refer to different people depending upon the uses, especially during situations of conflict. In Monterey Park, the multi-dimensional levels of Chinese identity are mainly differentiated by linguistic (Cantonese and Mandarin), kinship relationships (from bloodline to clan association), political (Communist and anti-Communist), geographical origins (e.g., Hong

Kong, Republic of China, Singapore), and cultural preference patterns. When desired, a Chinese can invoke any or all of these differentiated attributes as a basis for aligning or separating himself from other Chinese. Conversely, he can ignore these differentiated attributes when so desired that there prevails unity of interest and identity. (260, 268)

Accordingly, in the late 1970s, Wong laid out a research agenda to specify which of these attributes, if any, are the basis of ethnic identity of the Chinese, and under what conditions these attributes are invoked or suppressed. Wong found that:

In most situations, the most salient division is drawn between cultural preference identities. Within this Chinese/American identity continuum, there are five ideal type identities: traditionalist, acculturationalist, marginal man, bi-culturalist, and Asian American. (268–269)

Wong offered no discussion of Chinese subgroups, however, not even under traditionalist category. Instead, Wong speculated:

Exactly what new forms of Chinatown social structures will evolve is presently uncertain, but what is certain is that it will not remain the same. In terms of ethnicity, the traditional bases of intra-ethnic identification (e.g., surname, regional origins, dialects) may decline in prominence as the secular character of Communist thought and cosmopolitan immigrants take hold in Chinatown. (300)

But according to MacMillan (B1), "in the last decade, an influx of Chinese from several Southeast Asian countries and their investments have dramatically altered the once sleepy Cantonese community."

Referring to Los Angeles Chinatown in the past, the director of the Los Angeles Chinatown Service Center, Deborah Ching, was quoted as saying:

The cultural style was fairly homogeneous.... Now people of several different nations, tied together only by Chinese ancestry, live side by side, often uneasily and divisively, in the one-square-mile community north of City Hall.... Now there are Chinese from all over the world. It's changed the face of Chinatown (in McMillan B1–2).

In light of the absence of research on all Chinese subgroups, we turn to a case study of the Chinese-Vietnamese. By serendipity, the Chinese-Vietnamese are perhaps the best-studied Chinese subgroup, since there is extensive research on Vietnamese refugees, including the ethnic Chinese.

The Chinese-Vietnamese: A Case Study. According to the ethnicization model, national identities over time have replaced the initial religious, regional, and linguistic divisions among immigrants. Espiritu (1989) argues that the ethnicization model ignores twice minorities. For example, the "Viet Hoa" or ethnic Chinese, who were once a minority in Vietnam, are a twice minority in the U.S. Twice minorities have been subjected to societal designation and external threat. Minorities in the country of origin responded to external threat by mobilizing along ethnic lines. Thus, Chinese-Vietnamese were not fragmented and weak upon arrival in the U.S.; they arrived as a cohesive and identifiable ethnic group. Bhachu (1985) has argued that the "twice migrant" status facilitates adaptation because twice migrants are able to mobilize politically and can draw on the resources of established co-ethnics. For instance, Woon (1985) has shown that Chinese-Vietnamese have relied on Chinese Canadians for sponsorship, jobs, services, and housing. Conversely, Chinese-Vietnamese have maintained their distance from the Vietnamese, due to strained historical relationship in Vietnam.

The fall of Saigon in 1975 resulted in massive emigration of the Vietnamese, mostly to the U.S. The Vietnamese label, however, is misleading because this refugee group consists of two major ethnic-subgroups. Although the pre-1979 wave consisted of predominantly ethnic Vietnamese, Chinese from Vietnam make up a greater proportion of the most recent Vietnamese refugees. Tran (1988) estimated that Chinese-Vietnamese comprise about a third of the Vietnamese in the greater Los Angeles area.

Many Chinese-Vietnamese never learned to speak Vietnamese inside "Cholon," the Chinese community of half a million in Vietnam. Like the early Chinese immigrants to the U.S., the Chinese in Vietnam originated from the Guandong (Kwangtung) province, directly north of Vietnam. Cantonese, Chao-Zhou, Hainanese, Fujianaese, and Ha'kanese were the major regional/dialect Chinese-Vietnamese groups. The Chinese in Vietnam maintained highly organized communities based on dialect and region. An entrepreneurial class, Chinese occupational specialization was organized by these dialect groups in Vietnam (Gold in press). This background suggests that subethnicity is multi-layered, whose origins may be traced to the pre-migration phase.

The persecution of Chinese in Vietnam in 1978–79 resulted in large-scale exodus of this minority. The following reasons account for the expulsion of Chinese from Vietnam: doubtful loyalty, removal of a capitalist class, and governmental revenue in the form of a fee for exit visas (Gold in press). Arriving as post-1978 boat people, however, recent Chinese-Vietnamese refugees are of humble origins.

The ethnic Chinese maintain distinctive communities from other Vietnamese in the U.S. Many Chinese-Vietnamese have even changed their names to Chinese. Ethnic Chinese appear to adapt slower economically than do the Vietnamese to the U.S. (Desbarats 1986; Rumbaut 1989). Many, however, have been able to reestablish themselves in self-employment. Although the Chinese constituted only 3% of Vietnam's population, they dominated the country's internal trade. Despite a tradition of entrepreneurship, Chinese-Vietnamese refugees were unable to bring capital with them to the U.S. They reestablished themselves in business, partly through assistance from other Chinese.

The Chinese are often engaged in internal and international trade. Thus, the Chinese social and economic networks extend across the globe, but especially throughout Southeast Asia. This network has been strengthened recently due to the significance of the Pacific Rim in international trade. In the words of a journalist, "in effect, entrepreneurs are forming an ethnic Chinese rim around the Pacific Basin" (Gibson 1990). International co-ethnic linkages and a tradition of entrepreneurship account for the prevalence of large enterprises on the West Coast by the Chinese-Vietnamese.

The current proclivity of the Chinese-Vietnamese toward self-employment is partly due to their pre-migration tradition of entrepreneurship. Gold reports some very interesting findings from his research in Little Saigon. Community leaders estimate that up to 40% of entrepreneurs in Orange County's Little Saigon are Chinese-Vietnamese (Gold in press). Little Saigon was mainly built by Chinese-Vietnamese real estate developers using overseas Chinese capital. Capital provided by affluent Chinese investors from Taiwan and Hong Kong is an important source of start up money used to open businesses. Chinese work with co-ethnics because they are perceived as trustworthy and honest, not a credit risk. Initially hired by established Taiwanese because of common language, some Chinese-Vietnamese later became partners. Others received favorable terms in leasing commercial real estates from Chinese landlords. In the words of a Chinese-Vietnamese journalist:

> And the Chinese, we help together. Say I am Chinese, I come from Vietnam. Example, you are Chinese and you come from Taiwan or maybe Singapore, or maybe Hong Kong. I need money—I need you to help support my business. How come you help me? I like to tell you. Because I, I have good experience and I have good credit. You have the money, but you don't know how to run a business. So you check on my credit and ask the other people. I want to buy this restaurant. You

help me, maybe you become partner, because you believe in my ability. Maybe you are partner, or maybe I give you interest in six months. It works because we are all Chinese. (in Gold in press)

The Chinese-Vietnamese have played a critical role in urban restructuring through revitalizing the Los Angeles Chinatown. There is a glaring difference between the "old Chinatown" and the newly built Saigon Plaza with many business names in Vietnamese in addition to Chinese. In addition to the new businesses, the Vietnamese script appears on many established ones in Chinatown. Yet Chinatown is not a misnomer. According to the president of the Los Angeles Chinatown Chamber of Commerce, Chinese-Vietnamese own and operate about a third of Chinatown's estimated 1,400 businesses, aptly nicknamed "Little Cholon" (Gold in press). A similar development is taking place in other North American Chinatowns in Seattle, San Francisco, Oakland, Toronto, and Vancouver. Parallel but suburban revitalization is underway in Monterey Park and Little Saigon in the Los Angeles metropolitan area, as well as Tully Road in San Jose.

The Chinese-Vietnamese own some of the major groceries and restaurants in L.A. Chinatown and Monterey Park. Gold (1992) has characterized this process as an example of the well-known phenomenon of ethnic succession, but subethnic succession is probably more appropriate. Gold sums up: "However, even among the ethnic Chinese, cooperation exists within groups of common regional/linguistic or familial origins, and not at the level of the broader Chinese-Vietnamese population" (1992: 192).

According to the president of the Los Angeles Chinatown chamber of commerce: "Occupational specialization is organized by dialect-groups: Hainan-origin groups own grocery stores; Chao Zhou refugees are restaurateurs, Ha'kanese are herbalists, and so on" (in Gold 1992: 15).

Preliminary evidence on the Chinese-Vietnamese entrepreneurship suggests that Chinese subethnic groups can pool class resources (capital, education, knowledge of English, occupational skills) and ethnic resources (tradition of entrepreneurship, social ties) to establish a viable ethnic economy and be economically self-sufficient. Immigrant or ethnic groups are often more endowed in one type of resource than the other (Light 1984). The presence of subethnic groups enhances the overall resource capacity of the ethnic group, thereby increasing their rate of self-employment. The entrepreneurs can in turn hire co-ethnics, thus lowering unemployment and welfare dependency. Assuming that these practices are not exploitative, subethnicity confers advantages to the broader ethnic group. The catch is to overcome the initially divisive role of subethnicity in economic activities and other aspects of adaptation. The former Los Angeles Councilman and mayoral candidate, Michael Woo, offers an optimistic prognosis:

> We are seeing an increasing level of interaction between the Hong Kong [immigrants] and the Taiwanese here. The business people are guided more by pragmatism than cultural differences, which they learn to overcome. In the 1990s we will see more cohesion." (in Gibson A29)

Conclusion. In this paper, we provided a theoretical framework toward a better understanding of intra-group diversity, and a necessary first step toward research on this under-studied subject. We reviewed the literature to show the historical and contemporary significance of subethnicity. In addition to the Chinese, the Jews and the Armenians are a diverse ethnic group which consist of various national subgroups.

The extent of Chinese intra-group diversity has increased dramatically over time. In the previous century, diversity was delimited to different districts of southern Chinese provinces. In other words, there was diversity in dialects, clan, and districts. The new Chinese immigration is far more diverse, originating in different countries. Moreover, the turn-of-the-century differences did not result in important socioeconomic differences among rural-origin subgroups, with their concomitant effects on adaptation to American economy and society. The new Chinese immigrants, however, vary considerably in education and occupation in their respective countries of origin. Ironically, Chinese are one of the few ethnic groups in the U.S. who simultaneously originate in one of the last bastions of socialism (P.R.C.) and some of the most tenacious capitalist economies in the world (Hong Kong and Taiwan). These pre-migration experiences invariably affect post-migration adaptation to U.S. society and economy. Thus, subethnicity among the Chinese is more critical now than ever.

Chinese Americans consist of the foreign-born from China, Hong Kong, Taiwan, and other countries, as well as native-born descendants of the earlier Chinese immigrants to the U.S. Since the causes of migration, migration histories, background characteristics, national loyalties, cultural heritages, and adaptation experiences of these subethnic groups differ, it is a simplification to aggregate them together as Chinese. Yet, these subethnic groups share a common Chinese ethnic identity. As such, their social, economic, and political ties cut across subgroups, often facilitating their adaptation. Thus, it is also inappropriate to separate the subgroups altogether. Instead, we propose that future research on Chinese Americans should take into account the social, economic, and political roles minorities play within this minority.

We thank Ivan Light, Mia Tuan, Yah-Min Kan, and Cao Hong for their helpful comments on the conference draft of this paper.

Works Cited

Arax, Mark. "Monterey Park: Nation's 1st Suburban Chinatown." *Los Angeles Times* 6 April 1987: A1.

Barth, Fredrick. "Introduction." In *Ethnic Groups and Boundaries*. Ed. Fredrick Barth. London: George Allen and Unwin, 1969.

Bhachu, Parminder. *Twice Migrants: East African Sikh Settlers in Britain*. London: Tavistock, 1985.

Boswell, Thomas, and James Curtis. *The Cuban-American Experience*. Totawa, NJ: Rowan and Allenhead, 1983.

Bozorgmehr, Mehdi. "Internal Ethnicity: Armenian, Bahai, Jewish, and Muslim Iranians in Los Angeles." Unpublished Ph.D. dissertation, University of California, Los Angeles, 1992.

Der-Martirosian, Claudia, Georges Sabagh, and Mehdi Bozorgmehr. "Subethnicity: Armenians in Los Angeles." In *Immigration and Entrepreneurship*. Eds. Ivan Light and Parminder Bhachu. New Jersey: Transaction, 1993.

Desbarats, Jacqueline. "Ethnic Differences in Adaptation: Sino-Vietnamese Refugees in the United States." *International Migration Review* 20 (1986): 405–27.

Espiritu, Yen. "Beyond the Boat People: Ethnicization in America." *Amerasia* 15 (1989): 49–67.

Fong, Timothy. "The Unique Convergence: Monterey Park." *California Sociologist* 12 (1989):171–193.

Gaertner, Miriam. "A Comparison of Refugee and Non-refugee Immigrants to New York City." In *Flight and Resettlement*. Ed. H.B.M. Murphy. 1955.

Gibson, Robert. "Network of Chinese Rim Pacific." *Los Angeles Times* 22 July 1990: A1.

Gold, Steven. "Chinese-Vietnamese Entrepreneurs in California." In *The New Asian Immigration and Restructuring in California*. Eds. Edna Bonacich, Lucie Cheng, and Paul Ong. Philadelphia, PA: Temple University Press, in press.

Gold, Steven. "Patterns of Economic Cooperation among Israeli Coming Immigrants in Los Angeles." *International Migration Review* forthcoming.

Gold, Steven. *Refugee Communities: A Comparative Field Study*. Newbury Park, CA: Sage, 1992.

Goldscheider, Calvin, and Alan Zuckerman. *The Transformation of the Jews*. Chicago, IL: University of Chicago Press, 1984.

Holley, David. "Chinese in Tug of War for Loyalty." *Los Angeles Times* 21 July 1985: P1.

Horton, John. "The Politics of Diversity in Monterey Park, California." In *Structuring Diversity*. Ed. Louise Lamphere. Chicago, IL: University of Chicago Press, 1992.

Institute of International Education (IIE). *Open Doors: Annual Report on International Education Exchange*. New York: IIE 1992/93.

Jasso, Guillermina, and Mark Rozenzweig. *The New Chosen People: Immigrants in the United States*. New York: Russell Sage Foundation, 1990.

Klein, Karen. "Cultural Diversity Springs from Asian Influx." *Los Angeles Times* 13 October 1991: K2.

Kwong, Peter. *The New Chinatown*. New York: Hill and Wang, 1987.

Lai, David. *Chinatowns*. Vancouver, BC: University of British Columbia Press, 1988.

Light, Ivan. "Immigrant and Ethnic Enterprise in North America." *Ethnic and Racial Studies* 7 (1984): 195–216.

Light, Ivan. *Ethnic Enterprise in America*. Berkeley and Los Angeles: University of California Press, 1972.

Lucerne, Switzerland: UNESCO.

Lyman, Stanford. *Chinatown and Little Tokyo*. Millwood, NY: Associated Faculty Press, 1986.

McMillan, Penelope. "Newcomers Changing Face of Chinatown." *Los Angeles Times* 28 January 1990: B1.

Min, Pyong Gap. "Cultural and Economic Boundaries of Korean Ethnicity: A Comparative Analysis." *Ethnic and Racial Studies* 14 (1991): 225–41.

Mittleberg, David, and Mary C. Waters. "The Process of Ethnogenesis among Haitian and Israeli immigrants in the United States." *Ethnic and Racial Studies* 15 (1992): 412–435.

Nee, Victor, and Brett de Bary Nee. *Longtime Californ*. New York: Pantheon, 1972.

Portes, Alejandro, and Min Zhou. "Gaining the Upper Hand: Old and New Perspectives in the Study of Ethnic Minorities." *Ethnic and Racial Studies* 15: 491–522.

Portes, Alejandro, and Ruben Rumbaut. *Immigrant America: A Portrait*. Berkeley and Los Angeles: University of California Press, 1990.

Poston, Dudley, and Mei-Yu Yu. "The Distribution of the Overseas Chinese in the Contemporary World." *International Migration Review* 24 (1990): 480–508.

Rischin, Moses. "Germans versus Russians." In *The American Jewish Experience*. Ed. Jonathan Sarna. New York and London: Holmes and Meier, 1986.

Rischin, Moses. *The Promised City: New York Jews, 1870–1914*. Cambridge, MA: Harvard University Press, 1962.

Rumbaut, Ruben. "The Structure of Refuge: Southeast Asian Refugees in the United States, 1975–1985." *International Review of Comparative Public Policy* 1 (1989): 97–129.

Sabagh, Georges. "Los Angeles, A World of New Immigrants: An Image of Things to Come?" In *Migration Policies in Europe and the United States.* Ed. Giacomo Luciani. Dordrecht, Netherlands: Kluwer Academic Publishers, 1993.

Sklare, Marshall. *America's Jews.* New York: Random House, 1971.

Tran, Anh. "Adaptation Strategy of Chinese-Vietnamese in the U.S., 1975–1987." Unpublished paper, Asian American Center, University of California, Los Angeles, 1988.

U.S. Bureau of the Census. "Census Bureau Finds Significant Demographic Differences Among Immigrant Groups." Press release. Washington, D.C.: U.S. Department of Commerce, 1993a.

U.S. Bureau of the Census. *1990 Census of Population: The Foreign-Born Population in the United States.* Washington, D.C.: U.S. Department of Commerce, 1993b.

U.S. Bureau of the Census. *The Foreign-Born Population by Place of Birth for the United States: 1990.* Ethnic and Hispanics Branch, 1990 Census Special Tabulations. Washington, D.C.: U.S. Department of Commerce, 1992.

Waldinger, Roger, and Yenfen Tseng. "Divergent Diasporas: The Chinese Communities of New York and Los Angeles Compared." Unpublished paper, 1992.

Wong, Charles Choy. "Ethnicity, Work, and Community: The Case of Chinese in Los Angeles." Unpublished Ph.D. dissertation, University of California, Los Angeles, 1979.

Woon, Yuen-Fong. "Ethnic Identity and Ethnic Boundaries: The Sino-Vietnamese in Victoria, British Columbia." *Canadian Review of Sociology and Anthropology* 22 (1985): 534–558.

Yancey, William, Eugene Erickson, and Richard Juliani. "Emergent Ethnicity: A Review and Reformulation." *American Sociological Review* 41:(1976) 391–403.

Zhou, Min, and John Logan. "Returns on Human Capital in Ethnic Enclaves: New York City's Chinatown." *American Sociological Review* 54 (1989): 809–20.

Zhou, Min. *Chinatown: The Socioeconomic Potential of an Urban Enclave.* Philadelphia, PA: Temple University Press, 1992.

Monterey Park and Emerging Race Relations in California

TIMOTHY P. FONG
University of California at Davis, California

The two days of rioting in South-Central Los Angeles following the acquittal verdict in the Rodney King police-brutality case has served as the lightning rod for a renewed national re-examination of race-relations issues. Unfortunately, except for a precious few exceptions, the mainstream debate has remained provincial and has been slow to move beyond the simplistic analysis of black versus white, minority versus majority, relations.

Clearly, race relations in major metropolitan areas throughout California and the United States have been going through a period of transition. The explosion seen in Los Angeles was just one—although the most dramatic—example of this fact. This transition has been fueled by the continuing influence of the civil rights movement in the United States, increased immigration from Latin America and Asia, and the globalization of the economy featuring the prominent emergence of East Asian nations.

This period of transition began in earnest in the early 1970s and can best be characterized in three ways. First is the proliferation and intensification of racial conflict between whites and people of color in this country. Second is the growing competition among people of color fighting for political power and limited resources. Third is the rising inter- and intra-racial conflicts brought forth in large part by the influx of immigrants from Pacific Rim countries with broadly diverse class backgrounds.

With this introduction in mind, this paper will focus on recent events in Monterey Park, California. Dubbed by the media as "The First Suburban Chinatown" and "The Chinese Beverly Hills," Monterey Park is the only city in the continental United States with a majority Asian population. According to the 1990 Census, Asians make up 56% of the city's population, followed by Hispanics with 31%, and whites with 12% (U.S. Bureau of the Census 5/13/91).

Monterey Park is located just eight miles east of downtown Los Angeles and is a community of 60,000 residents. Throughout the 1980s, Monterey Park was the center of a highly publicized anti-Chinese backlash that came on the heels of an economic boom.

This paper is intended to show what was generally seen by the media and many outsiders as a "racial" conflict in Monterey Park was, in fact, very much a class conflict between residents and developer interests struggling over control. This presentation will describe and analyze events leading up to the recent April 1992 city council election in Monterey Park to show how racial politics was used as a mask to hide the fundamental class basis of conflicts. Many in Monterey Park see the 1992 election as evidence of a positive realignment of city politics and a sign that the tactics of division and false ethnic solidarity may be over.

In Monterey Park, the parallel emergence of both a populist growth-control movement and a nativist anti-Chinese, anti-immigrant movement created a complex controversy. There was certainly a "re-articulation" of a racist agenda under the guise of community control, slow growth, and official English that took place in Monterey Park. This served to propel tensions to new heights and distract from legitimate concerns over uncontrolled development in the city.

At the same time, pro-growth interests in Monterey Park played their own "race card" and purposely usurped the messages of racial-harmony advocates who emerged to fight growing anti-Chinese and anti-immigrant sentiments. It was the developers' hope that they would be able to undermine their opponents and promote their own policies for the city. Many calls for ethnic unity were often merely covers for the class interests of developers and speculators in the community. While class and inter-ethnic conflicts were apparent in Monterey Park politics, recent events also show strong intra-ethnic conflict within the Chinese community, between American-born and foreign-born.

Research by Victor and Brett de Bary Nee in San Francisco (1972) and Bernard Wong in New York (1979) have shown similar splits along class and nativity in those Chinese communities. In both studies, the two primary factions are the "traditional elite," predominantly older Chinese businessmen associated with the Chinese Consolidated Benevolent Association (CCBA), and the "social service elite," made up of primarily American-born Asian professionals and students (Nee and Nee 1972, Wong 1–22).

Generally speaking, the "traditional elite" and the "social service elite" differ considerably in their interactions with the larger society. First, members of the traditional elite have historically been described as isolationists. This means they prefer as little interaction with, and help from, the larger society as possible. If interaction must take place, they prefer a low-keyed accommodation over conflict. Members of the social service elite, however, tend more to be conflict-oriented in their interactions with the larger society. Taking their cue from the civil rights movement, they prefer to use direct action strategies to achieve their goals and to assert their power.

Second, members of the traditional elite are described as conservative because of their staunch anti-communist position and desires to maintain the status quo in Chinatown communities.

Members of the social service elite, on the other hand, are mostly born and raised in America, and are much less antagonistic toward the People's Republic of China. In addition, they see themselves as change agents directly challenging the status quo of the structures in Chinatown, as well as in the broader society.

Third, members of the traditional elite believe themselves to be cultural managers. This means that they maintain strong traditional values of filial piety and they support programs such as Chinese-language school, Chinese New Year's parades, and Chinese festivals. Through these activities, they hope to retain cultural identity and to secure community control. Members of the social service elite, on the other hand, hold to a larger ethnic identity—that of Asian American. In this case, ethnic group identification is intended to promote solidarity in order to enhance the group's political and economic power, rather than for cultural maintenance. In short, the social service elite has taken on the role of an interest group.

More recent work by Peter Kwong on New York's Chinatown (1988) and Richard Thompson on Toronto's (1979) acknowledged these two polarized camps, but also added an extra player: the new overseas Chinese "entrepreneurial elite." While both described the impact of the new overseas Chinese elite on the Chinese community, neither focused on the new elite's interactions with the larger society (Kwong 25–27, Thompson 306–322).[1]

Events in Monterey Park will show that members of the new entrepreneurial elite are a unique hybrid and are rather fluid in their interactions with the broader society. They are *not* isolationists and do not shy away from asserting themselves—economically, culturally, or politically. They see themselves very much as change agents in the forefront of creating a world financial capital in Monterey Park that will serve as the "Gateway to the Pacific Rim." Furthermore, the new entrepreneurial elite works in Monterey Park to uphold ethnic group identity for *both* cultural maintenance and economic and political ends.

The distinctions between the traditional, social service, and entrepreneurial elite help to frame this discussion of Monterey Park. This introduction also serves as a reference for an analysis of the complex controversies that emerged in Monterey Park.

An Overview of Demographic Change. Monterey Park was incorporated in 1916 and has a long history of population growth and change. Three distinct demographic periods can clearly be identified.

---

[1]Thompson saw the "social service elite" as Hong Kong-born, rather than native Canadian-born. However, both remained similar in most every other aspects.

The first period, from incorporation until World War II, saw Monterey Park as a small, rural community made up predominantly of farmers and chicken ranchers. For a short time in the 1920s, enterprising realtors began grand plans to transform the hills surrounding Monterey Park into an exclusive, upper-class suburb. However, the stock market crash of 1929 abruptly ended development interest in Monterey Park, and the city remained stagnant for nearly 20 years.

The end of World War II to 1970 marks the second period in Monterey Park's demographic history. During this time, many new people, mostly war veterans taking advantage of G.I. loans, settled in Monterey Park. The number of residents expanded from 8,500 in 1940 to 20,000 in 1950, to almost 38,000 by 1960. Beginning in the late 1950s, Monterey Park began drawing in Chicanos from adjacent East Los Angeles, Japanese Americans from the Westside of Los Angeles, and Chinese Americans from nearby Chinatown. By 1970, Monterey Park's population was just over 49,000 (Community Development Department 5).

At this time, whites were just barely over 50% of the population, followed by "Hispanics" at 34%. Japanese Americans outnumbered Chinese Americans 4,627 to 2,202, but together, Asians made up 15% of Monterey Park's population (Community Development Department 3).

The third period is dominated by the coming of immigrant Chinese, beginning in the early 1970s. Its salient feature is the unprecedented influx of newcomers primarily from Taiwan and Hong Kong who found homes in Monterey Park. These Chinese immigrants constituted a diverse group of young professionals who came to the United States for an education, but who decided to settle in this country after receiving their degrees. In the mid- to late-1970s, a second wave of Chinese immigrants started arriving in Monterey Park. This group included established professionals, business people, developers, and speculators who were looking for a safe shelter for their families and their money during a time of escalating political turbulence throughout Southeast Asia.

The 1980 Census recorded for the first time that Monterey Park was a "majority minority" city. In 1980, Chicanos were 39% of the city's population of 54,000, followed quickly by Asians, who mushroomed to 35% of the population. At this time, the Chinese, because of the new immigrants, slightly outnumbered Japanese 8,082 to 7,533. The Census showed that only 25% of the population of Monterey Park in 1980 were white (ibid.).

Electoral Politics In Monterey Park: An Overview. From the late 1950s through the late 1960s, middle-class Chicanos, Japanese

Americans, and Chinese Americans moved to Monterey Park and were generally warmly received. It was not until the early and late 1970s, when relatively affluent Chinese immigrants began settling and investing in the community, that tensions started to rise. The shifts in race and ethnic relations in Monterey Park are what makes the study of this community so dynamic and compelling.

Upon close examination, an analysis of election results in Monterey Park have not shown signs of consistent racial polarization. For example, Asians have been elected to Monterey Park's city council long before they were the majority of the population. Korean American Alfred Song was elected to city council in 1960, Japanese American George Ige was elected in 1970 and again in 1974, Filipino American G. Monty Manibog was elected in 1976, 1980 and again in 1984. Lily Chen received the most votes of any city council candidate in Monterey Park's history when she became the first Chinese American elected to city council in 1982.[2]

Monterey Park's most tumultuous period began in late 1985, when a small group of Monterey Park residents, with the aid of U.S. English, a Washington D.C.-based organization, submitted a petition to the city clerk requesting that a measure be placed on the local ballot that would declare English the official language of the city. This action was largely in response to rapid development and an increase of Chinese-language business signs dominating the city's main commercial thoroughfares. When the initiative was stopped by the city attorney and city council for, ironically, improper wording, the official English supporters charged that the city council was bought out by Chinese developers.

These accusations fell on receptive ears. As early as 1982, when Lily Chen was elected, development and land-use policies were very important issues. In a special June 1982 election, two control growth propositions overwhelmingly passed in Monterey Park. The city council openly opposed the two propositions, and between 1982 and 1986, a number of building variances were passed that enabled several large development projects to continue even though they were not built in accordance to city codes. As development in Monterey Park continued, so did the tension and frustration.

When the 1986 city council elections came around, the increase of Chinese population, official English initiative, and development issues were on residents' minds. Three challengers took aim at three city council members up for re-election and ousted them from office. The

---

[2]The results of the April 13, 1982 City Council elections: Lily Chen (4,765), David Almada (3,509), Rudy Peralta (3,506), Harry Couch (3,220), Irv Gilman (3,035), Sonya Gerlach (2,275), and Bill Feliz (730). Source: Monterey Park Office of the City Clerk.

city council candidate who stayed away from the official English issue, Chris Houseman, received the highest number of votes, while the person most identified with official English, Frank Arcuri, received the smallest.[3]

Tensions Rise. However, immediately after assuming office, two newly elected city council members, Barry Hatch and Patricia Reichenberger, pushed for the passage of Resolution 9004. Though both Hatch and Reichenberger supported official English, they did not focus their campaign on the issue. Resolution 9004 recommended, among other things, that English be the official language of the United States of America (Monterey Park City Council 6/2/86).

In protest, an ad hoc group of Asians, Chicanos, liberal whites, and some developer interests formed the Coalition for Harmony in Monterey Park (CHAMP). After 12 weeks of protests, CHAMP finally forced the city council to rescind Resolution 9004 (Monterey Park City Council 10/27/86).

Despite backing down on this issue, the new city council continued to take other controversial actions which many critics labeled "anti-Chinese." These included a broad moratorium on construction, the firing of the City Planning Commission that had approved many Chinese commercial projects, and the rejection of plans by a Taiwanese group to build a 43-unit senior housing project.

Because of the actions taken by the new Monterey Park city council, a pro-growth faction from within CHAMP split from the group and started taking action into their own hands. ABC gathered 4,600 signatures from registered voters, demanding a recall of two city council members deemed the most divisive: Barry Hatch and Patricia Reichenberger. In response, the two council members and their support organization, the Residents Association of Monterey Park (RAMP), countered that the recall effort was spearheaded by disgruntled developers and defeated council members. RAMP members were quick to point out that one of the co-chairs of ABC was Kevin Smith, whose father was one of the most active real estate developmenters in Monterey Park.

The recall was in reality a thinly veiled attempt by developer interests to regain power in City Hall. According to ABC's own records, 90% of their contributions came from developer-associated individuals and companies. Of the individuals and companies listed,

---

[3]The results of the April 8, 1986, City Council election: Chris Houseman (4,959), Barry Hatch (3,993), Patricia Reichenberger (3,782), Lily Chen (3,139), David Almada (3,031), Rudy Peralta (2,590), Frank Arcuri (1,993). Source: Monterey Park Office of the City Clerk.

44% were from outside of Monterey Park (Association for Better Cityhood 10/86–6/87).

During the recall campaign, ABC was even further discredited when a disgruntled campaign worker publicly announced that he was paid to spread fear of personal persecution and deportation into Asian and Latino voters in order to gain support for the recall (Walker 6/11/87).

The results of the June 16, 1987 special recall election was an overwhelming defeat for ABC. Barry Hatch received 5,136 votes against the recall, compared to 3,211 votes in favor of removing him from office. Patricia Reichenberger gathered 5,163 votes against the recall and received only 3,222 in favor. The turnout for this special election was 35.5% of the city's registered voters, the highest turnout for a special election in Monterey Park history (Monterey Park Office of the City Clerk 6/16/87).

The 1988 and 1990 City Council Elections. Following the defeat of the recall attempt, Monterey Park residents hoped for a much deserved period of calm. For a short time, calm did prevail. In April 1988, another city council election was held for two available seats. The candidate who received the most votes was a Chinese American woman, Judy Chu—psychologist, community organizer, and wife of CHAMP leader, Michael Eng. Betty Couch, a housewife and long-time RAMP activist, placed second in the election. Both Chu and Couch ran campaigns focusing on controlling growth and bringing a calming influence to the recent chaos and personal vindictiveness that had been so much a part of the city's politics.[4]

This particular election was closely monitored by the Asian Pacific Voter Registration Project, in cooperation with the San Antonio-based Southwest Voter Registration Project, and a team of researchers from the University of California, Los Angeles, led by sociologist John Horton. An exit poll collected 1,390 usable questionnaires—17% of the 8,148 residents who voted—and it showed interesting results (Horton 578–92, see table below).

The research confirmed the fact that while Asians were a majority of the population, approximately 51% at the time, they made up only 36% of the registered voters. Of the total number of registered Asian Voters, 58% were of Chinese ancestry and 37% were Japanese Americans. The poll also found that 73% of the Chinese who answered were born outside of the United States. Not surprisingly, the

---

[4]The results of the April 12, 1988 City Council election: Judy Chu (3,594), Betty Couch (2,874), George Rustic (2,486), Fred Balderrama (2,129), Cam Briglio (1,489), Marie Purvis (897), Frank Arcuri (622), Victoria Wu (530). Source: Monterey Park Office of the City Clerk.

research showed a pattern of voting based on ethnic lines for the major candidates. This was particularly true for top vote-getter Chu, who captured 89% of the Chinese votes and 75% of the Japanese American votes. But the most interesting finding from the research was the relatively high percentage of cross-ethnic voting. Chinese American candidate Chu received 35% of the Latino vote, as well as 30% of the white vote.

Candidate Preference by Ethnicity, City Council Elections, Monterey Park, April 12, 1988

Candidate	Chinese	Japanese	Latino	Anglo
Chu	89	75	35	30
Couch	12	28	19	45
Rustic	8	22	15	45
Balderrama	17	21	63	17
Briglio	15	19	19	14
Purvis	1	8	12	14
Arcuri	2	2	8	11
Wu	22	2	1	1
Voter Characteristic				
Female	46	55	56	52
Age 45 or older	42	71	61	77
Foreign-born	73	6	15	9
College Degree	71	42	28	41
$50,000+ income	51	46	31	33
Party Affiliation				
Democrat	24	60	80	59
Republican	45	30	16	35
Independent/None	30	10	4	6
Respondents	397	247	216	266

Note: Voters could cast up to two votes. Percentages are rounded off and do not add up to 100.

Source: Southwest Voter Research Institute, Moterey Park, CA, Exit Poll, April 12, 1989, for the Asian Pacific American Voter Registration Project.

Two years later, when the 1990 city council election came around, many saw this as an opportunity for the community to re-evaluate the choices it had made just four years before. Previously arrogant in their belief that they had been swept into office by a mandate of the people in 1986, the incumbents were not so secure this time. Patricia Reichenberger began retracting her initial support for official English in order to broaden her constituency, while Barry Hatch continued to make rude and antagonizing statements against new immigrants. Because of his embarrassing behavior, Hatch saw many of his supporters, including RAMP, back away from his campaign. Chris Houseman, the leading vote-getter in the 1986 election, quietly let the deadline for submitting candidacy papers to the city clerk's office slip by and did not run for re-election.

On the other hand, Samuel Kiang, a Hong Kong-born, U.S.-trained engineer and lawyer, had announced in August 1989 that he would run for city council. Kiang, who had never been involved in electoral politics before, said he made his decision largely because of his dissatisfaction with the performance of Barry Hatch. He was strongly supported by the money and people of C-PAC, the Chinese American Political Action Committee, a group headed by former Monterey Park council member, Lily Chen. With C-PAC's help, Kiang raised $42,844 and spent $43,899 in campaign contributions, well above any of the other candidates (Citizens for Sam Kiang 3/90–5/90).

Together, Kiang and C-PAC ran an aggressive door-to-door and absentee ballot campaign. These efforts were rewarded, as Kiang received the highest number of votes of the six city council contenders.

Kiang collected 3,880 votes, 1,157 of which came from absentee ballots (out of 1,773 sent out). Fred Balderrama, who at the time was the president of the Monterey Park Chamber of Commerce, was second with 3,390 votes. In what many in the town considered the election's biggest surprise, Marie Purvis, a former Monterey Park Chamber of Commerce president who fared poorly in the 1988 election, came in third with 2,992 votes. RAMP-endorsed candidates David Barron and Patricia Reichenberger placed fourth and fifth, with 2,666 votes and 2,473 votes respectively. Barry Hatch came in last with only 1,907 votes (Monterey Park Office of the City Clerk 4/10/90).

Because Hatch managed to alienate himself from the community, he also discredited the RAMP group that had helped him get elected in 1986 and had supported him against the recall attempt in 1987. Despite RAMP's refusal to endorse Hatch in 1990, he was still identified with RAMP, and the RAMP slate lost. However, while voters voted against RAMP candidates in 1990, they overwhelmingly supported RAMP-sponsored Proposition S on the same ballot. Proposition S was an initiative that extended the limitation of no more than 100 new housing units per year approved in Proposition K (1982) for another 10 years. The proposition passed by a 4,189 to 1,014 margin (ibid.).

The new pro-growth oriented city council majority elected in 1990 has spent little time setting new priorities for the city. While all of the new council members campaigned on managing growth, recent actions have shown them being less restrictive toward development.

Several variances have been passed allowing property owners to build above and beyond the limits allowed by city ordinances. In addition, while the previous council majority was keen on finding "American" stores to come into Monterey Park, the new council is entertaining proposals to build a large hotel complex and Taiwanese department store to serve as magnets for even more foreign investment into the city (Chang 11/18/90, *Monterey Park Living* Spr. 91).

Intra-Chinese Conflicts and the 1992 Election. With the election victories of both Kiang and Chu, Monterey Park was touted as the first city on the United States mainland to have two Chinese Americans serving on the city council concurrently. While the emergence of Asian American power and politics in Monterey Park seems inevitable, recent events continue to show that calls for ethnic unity are often covers for class interests, and they continue to be resisted. This can best be understood by looking at a bizarre twist in Monterey Park that took place during the summer of 1991. In late July, a group of about 100 Chinese American seniors, many of whom did not speak English, held a protest march in front of the Monterey Park City Hall demanding a recall of Judy Chu because she was "anti-Chinese" (Chang 7/28/91, Cheng 8/2/91).

The issue originally stemmed months earlier from complaints by non-English speaking residents in Monterey Park who wanted the city to provide bilingual emergency services. In May 1991, the Monterey Park City Council approved a city staff-proposed preferential hiring plan that would eventually lead to having bilingual 911 dispatchers fluent in Mandarin, Cantonese, or Spanish on every shift. But the plan was rejected by the city's Personnel Board in July 1991, after it was heavily lobbied by a number of unions representing Monterey Park city workers.

The Board said they rejected the proposed hiring plan because it discriminated against people who spoke only English and those who were bilingual in languages other than the three desired in Monterey Park. Angry at the rebuff, newly-elected council member Kiang immediately called for a change in the city code, which would allow the city council to override the Personnel Board's decision.

At the same time that the proposed hiring plan was being considered, Chu voted with council members Couch and Purvis to fire City Manager Mark Lewis, a supporter of the preferential hiring plan. Ironically, the reason given for Lewis' dismissal was that there had been improper hiring and promotional practices unrelated to the recent bilingual issue. In addition, Chu did not support Kiang's call for an override of the Personnel Board's decision and offered her own compromise proposal instead.

Kiang charged that Chu's vote against Lewis meant that she was opposed to the programs Lewis had supported—specifically the plan to give preference to hiring bilingual 911 dispatchers. Lewis was popular among immigrant-Chinese residents and the Chinese-language press because he often clashed with Barry Hatch over policy issues. Lewis also encouraged more open economic-development planning, supported increased community-services programs, and pushed for aggressive affirmative-action hiring practices. Because of his positions, one Chinese-language newspaper reportedly dubbed Lewis, "the Yellow Savior" (Hong 8/2/91).

The July protest march against Chu was organized by Abel Pa, president of Southern California Chinese Radio Broadcasting, Inc. Pa acknowledged that the protesters were from "all over Los Angeles County," indicating that the mobilization was not a spontaneous response by Chinese residents in Monterey Park. Former mayor Lily Chen, who is said to be extremely jealous of Chu, and Sam Kiang, who had clashed with Chu earlier over differences on development issues, were rumored to have wanted to discredit and embarrass Chu in the eyes of the Chinese community in an effort to strengthen their own political base (ibid.).

Chu called a press conference and vehemently denied that the firing of Lewis and the bilingual hiring plan were related. She reminded the reporters that she had voted in favor of the bilingual 911 dispatcher hiring plan. Charges that the American-born Chu is "not Chinese enough" are often stated in the Chinese-language newspapers. The *Chinese Daily News* cited a "concerned resident" named "Lum" saying that Chu had plans to run for statewide office after her term on the Monterey Park City Council expires in April 1992. The resident believed that Chu's recent votes indicate her desire to broaden her constituency. "Chu needs to support white society issues and laying off the city manager is one of them," Lum said (*Chinese Daily News* 7/22/91. Translated by Susan Chow).

While Monterey Park's immigrant-Chinese population superficially appears to be cohesive because of their overall presence in the city's economic, social, and cultural life, they still do not dominate the city's political life. This can be seen in the most recent April 1992 city council election, in which Judy Chu was re-elected to office and again received the highest total number of votes. Chu was expected to face stiff competition for most votes from Bonnie Wai, who, like Samuel Kiang, is an American-trained attorney born in Hong Kong. Also like Kiang, Wai is fluent in English, Cantonese, and Mandarin, and was strongly supported by Kiang, Lily Chen, C-PAC, and Chinese business interests.

But speculation that Monterey Park would be the first city in the continental United States to have an Chinese American majority on the city council did not materialize, as Rita Valenzuela, a political newcomer with long-time ties in the community, finished second in the voting. Highly favored Wai finished a distant third in Monterey Park's first city council election utilizing tri-lingual ballots (English, Spanish, and Chinese). Two other Chinese candidates, Raymond Wu and Charles Wu (no relation), fell eighth and ninth in a nine-candidate race. Many in Monterey Park anticipated the April 1992 election to be an important test that pit Chu's liberal, multi-ethnic coalition against an increasingly organized immigrant-Chinese voting block that is generally considered conservative, nationalistic, and ethnocentric.

Rather than ethnic polarization, coalition building seemed to be the dominate theme of the 1992 race. This is evidenced by RAMP's endorsement of Judy Chu for city council. Chu's consistent moderate positions on growth and development issues during her first four years in office genuinely impressed RAMP members and leadership. Anxious to emerge from the embarrassment of the 1990 city council election, RAMP leadership very much wanted to move beyond its negative reputation as a "racist," "no-growth" organization. RAMP also endorsed Rita Valenzuela for council, and threw their support behind Proposition T, a measure that would actually allow for an *increase* in the height of commercial buildings in the city.

According to the Monterey Park Office of the City Clerk, Chu's first place total of 3,405 votes included 1,220 absentee votes, the most of any candidate. Valenzuela picked up 2,655 votes, while third-place finisher Wai received 1,770. Perhaps the biggest surprise in the election was the respectable fourth-place finish by outspoken official English advocate Frank Arcuri, who gathered 1,341 votes. Though Arcuri toned down his harsh rhetoric, he was the only council candidate that did not submit a Spanish or Chinese translation of his personal statement for the Sample Ballot and Voter Information Pamphlet that was sent to all registered voters. Arcuri's showing indicates that a solid anti-Chinese voting block is still present in Monterey Park. Latino candidate Andy Islas came in fifth with 1,035 votes, followed by John Casperson and Francisco Alonso with 874 and 773 votes respectively. Eighth-place Raymond Wu received just 542 votes and last-place Charles Wu received just 310 votes. Monterey Park also passed its first pro-growth initiative, Proposition T, 2,831 in favor to 2,340 against (Monterey Park Office of the City Clerk, "Monterey Park General Municipal Election, April 14, 1992").

Slowly, but surely, Monterey Park voters turned away from the politics of division and isolation advanced by the most ardent anti-immigrant, nativist elements in the community. At the same time, calls for ethnic unity were recognized as a cover for the class interests of a pro-growth faction in town. Both the tactics of division and those of false unity were rejected by the community.

The question remains: Will the political and economic future of Monterey Park continue to be marked by splits along class, ethnic, and national origin lines, pitting development and community interest against one another? It remains to be seen whether the new entrepreneurial-elite leaders will continue to exercise an ethnic "them-versus-us" strategy as we have seen in recent years, or work toward reaching out to other groups to build coalitions.

Conclusion. The description and distinctions between the traditional, social service, and entrepreneurial elite helps to explain the rivalries between Lily Chen, Samuel Kiang, and Judy Chu. Chen and Kiang clearly represent the new entrepreneurial elite in Monterey Park and their interests. Though Chen is employed as a social service administrator for the county of Los Angeles, her term on the council was marked by several major development controversies and an unabashed ambition for higher office. Since her city council defeat in 1986, Chen has been appointed a member of the California State World Trade Commission and has made an unsuccessful bid for Congress in 1988.

Kiang has positioned himself as a staunch advocate for the immigrant Chinese and has been actively seeking a political issue to rally his constituents. However, his clumsy mishandling of the bilingual services and Mark Lewis episodes failed to generate much excitement among immigrant Chinese residents in Monterey Park and only served to deeply antagonize non-Chinese. The disappointing third-place finish of Kiang's protégé, Bonnie Wai, shows his support base has dwindled.

On the other hand, American-born Chu represents a new hybrid version of the social service elite. Galvanized into direct political action during Monterey Park's official English controversy, she was not hesitant to clash with Barry Hatch after she was elected to city council in 1988. At the same time, when she rotated into the position of mayor, in April 1990, one of her priorities was to encourage "harmony" programs intended to encourage more interaction among all residents. Among the programs she organized were a renewed emphasis on Neighborhood Watch, a strengthening of the sister cities ties with Taiwan and Mexico, and the initiation of a "Harmony Week" of activities promoting an appreciation of ethnic diversity in the city.

Like the traditional elite described above, Chu has tended to take a low-key and accommodating profile when dealing with non-Chinese. But unlike the traditional elites, her primary support is not based along ethnic lines. While Chu's positions and strategy may be considered cooperation in the highest order, Peter Kwong argues for the same approach in his analysis of New York's Chinatown. In Kwong's *New Chinatown*, cross-ethnic coalitions were specifically stimulated by the uncontrolled land speculation in New York's Chinatown that has quickly spread to neighboring communities (172–173).

This paper has clearly shown that in Monterey Park, race and ethnicity issues have been used as political organizing tools and weapons. But what sets Monterey Park apart is the new class dynamics and the diversity of the Chinese living in the community within a rapidly shifting global economy. In short, the changes in race and ethnic relations in Monterey Park can be explained in terms of shifts in the primary sector of the broader economy. Monterey Park demonstrates on a community level that race relations have entered an era of transition.

This era of transition is most clearly seen in the fluidity of power relations between (and among) races and classes. Old theoretical dichotomies of black versus white, minority versus majority do not adequately address the rising inter- and intra-ethnic differences brought about in part by the infusion of highly affluent Asians from the Pacific Rim since 1965.

This globalization and long-term partnership with Asian people and nations are facts that will not go away. The worst case scenario in this era of transition would be the emergence of economic and social nativism. Our challenge is to develop a better understanding of this international, multiracial, multicultural, and dynamic class reality. Only through honest understanding can responsible public policy be successfully implemented to insure economic growth, environmental integrity, and social justice.

Works Cited

Association for Better Cityhood. "Recipient Committee Campaign Statement." Government Code 84200-84217 (statement covers period from 10/86–6/87).

Chang, Irene. "Embattled Chu Airs Bilingual Hiring Plan." *Los Angeles Times* 28 July 1991.

Chang, Irene. "New City Council Majority Takes a Softer Line on Growth." *Los Angeles Times* 18 November 1990.

Cheng, Edward. "Councilwoman Judy Chu Draws Ire of Chinese American Community." *AsianWeek* 2 August 1991.

Chinese Daily News 22 July 1991. Translated by Susan Chow.

Citizens for Sam Kiang. "Recipient Committee Campaign Statement." Government Code Sections 84200-84217 (statement covers period from 3/90–5/90).

Community Development Department, "Monterey Park, California Community Profile." City of Monterey Park, August 1978: 5.

Community Development Department. "City of Monterey Park Population & Housing Profile." City of Monterey Park, November 1984: 3.

Hong, Howard. "Chinese Split Signals Power Play in Monterey Park." *Asian Week* 2 August 1991.

Horton, John. "The Politics of Ethnic Change: Grass-Roots Responses to Economic and Demographic Restructuring in Monterey Park, California." *Urban Geography* 10 (1989): 578–92.

Kwong, Peter. *New Chinatown*. New York: Hill and Wang, 1988.

Monterey Park City Council, Minutes, 2 June 1986.

Monterey Park City Council, Minutes, 27 October 1986.

Monterey Park Living. "Proposed North Atlantic 'Gateway' in Sight." Spring 1991.

Monterey Park Office of the City Clerk. "City of Monterey Park Special Election, June 16, 1987."

Monterey Park Office of the City Clerk. "Monterey Park General Municipal Election, April 10, 1990."

Monterey Park Office of the City Clerk. "Monterey Park General Municipal Election, April 14, 1992."

Nee, Victor and Britt de Barry Nee. *Longtime Californ': Documentary Study of an American Chinatown* New York: Pantheon Books, 1972.

Thompson, Richard. "Ethnicity Versus Class: An Analysis of Conflict in a North American Chinese Community." *Ethnicity* 6: (1979): 306–322.

U.S. Bureau of the Census. "Monterey Park City, California." 1990 Census of Population and Housing Summary Tape File 1, 13 May 1991.

Walker, Richard. "Allegations Fly in Recall Campaign." *Monterey Park Progress* 11 June 1987.

Wong, Bernard. "Elites and Ethnic Boundary Maintenance: A Study of the Roles of Elites in Chinatown, New York City." *Urban Anthropology* 6 (1977): 1–22.

The Tom Leung Papers:
New Source Materials on the Chinese Empire Reform Association

JANE LARSON
Portland, Oregon

Tom Jernghow (Tan Zhangxiao) (1875–1931), usually known by his professional name, Tom Leung (Tan Liang), was a prominent Chinese herbalist in Los Angeles and a leader of the local Baohuang Hui (Empire Reform Association or Protect the Emperor Society) in the early 1900s.

The Baohuang Hui was founded in Victoria, Canada, in July 1899 by Kang Youwei (1858–1927), philosopher and leader of the 1898 Hundred Days of Reform. This was a massive program to modernize Chinese government and society, ordered by Emperor Guangxu in June 1898, which failed in September when he was imprisoned by Empress Dowager Cixi. Kang and many of his disciples fled China, and they formed the Baohuang Hui as an overseas Chinese organization with the goals of restoring the Emperor to his throne and establishing a constitutional monarchy.

In the U.S., the Baohuang Hui was the most powerful political organization of Chinese Americans from 1900 to 1908, with thousands of active members and many others who read Association newspapers, took part in Association-sponsored political rallies and movements, and patronized Association-owned businesses. Through the Baohuang Hui, Chinese in the U.S. raised funds for political and military actions in China, and they financially supported reformer-organized projects for Chinese economic development. Their main rivals were the revolutionaries led by Sun Yat-sen, but many of their activities and Kang's theories of political and economic reform eventually contributed directly or indirectly to the revolutionaries' cause.

Tom Leung was born in Gum Jook (Gan Zhu), Sun Duck county (Shunde Xian). His father was Tan Zizhong, who was a jin shi scholar and official. In spite of his family's opposition, Tom Leung himself became a student of Kang Youwei at Kang's Guangzhou school, Thatched Hut Among 10,000 Trees, during the 1890s, where he learned about Kang's theories of Confucianism as a philosophy of reform.

Tom first came to the U.S. in 1899 to assist his cousin, Tom Foo Wing (Tan Fuyuan), with his successful herb business in Los Angeles. In 1901, Tom returned to China for his wife and re-entered the U.S. in 1902.

Over the years, Tom Leung was in close contact with his teacher, Kang, as well as with Liang Qichao (1873–1929), Kang's most famous follower, and many other Baohuang Hui leaders all over the world. It is not known what official position, if any, Tom held in the L.A. Association, but he devoted much of his time to its activities during his first years in the U.S. It is known that he was responsible for the operation of a Chicago restaurant run by the Baohuang Hui, the King Joy Low (Qiongcailou), and that he was later accused of not repaying $160,000 in loans from the restaurant, a scandal which never seems to have been resolved.

Family memories of Tom Leung are recorded in *Sweet Bamboo: A Saga of a Chinese American Family* by his daughter, Louise Leung Larson, 1990. Tom Leung is pictured as thriving in American society, not only as a prosperous businessman whose patients were almost exclusively non-Chinese, but in his hearty embrace of the American lifestyle and customs. He returned to China only once, for a year in 1921 when he took a concubine; unsuccessfully sought a school for his sons to attend, and visited (and gave money to) Kang Youwei in Shanghai.

Tom Leung presciently kept letters and other documents he had received from Baohuang Hui members over the years. Leung died in 1931; 20 years later, his children left the family home at 1619 W. Pico in Los Angeles and moved to separate households. Not being able to read Chinese, they left the letters behind. Louise Larson's husband, Arnold Larson, was an amateur historian and was fascinated with his wife's family background and with Tom Leung, whom he never met. He salvaged the letters from the vacant house and Louise eventually gave them to the UCLA East Asian Library.

The collection includes nearly 200 letters, poems, and official documents and business records relating to the Chinese Empire Reform Association. It is available on microfilm. An index lists each letter by number, with writer, receiver, and date (when available). The materials date from 1899 to 1912. Included are nearly 40 letters and poems from Kang Youwei, as well as important Association documents, such as the charter of the Los Angeles chapter which was drafted by Liang Qichao when he was in the U.S. in 1903. Other letter writers include Liang and hundreds of Association activists such as Xu Qin (Chuy C. Kain), Kuang Shuomin, and Ye En (Yip On). Mentioned in the letters are many other Association activists, including Tan Shubin (Tom She Bin) who founded the San Francisco Baohuang Hui in 1899 and Tang Qiongchang, manager of *Mon Hing Bo* (*Wenxing Bao, Chinese World*), of San Francisco. Some are group letters from Kang, Liang, or others to members of the whole Association or of a chapter; these report on the political situation in China, give guidance to members (what to read, why there is hope for the future of reform, etc.), and make a plea for donations to support the cause. Some letter writers are Tom Leung's relatives, who were involved in the reform movement or had investments in Baohuang Hui businesses. Most of the writers are from Nanhai, Xinhui, Shunde, and Xiangshan counties in Guangdong and were students of Kang Youwei or were their relatives.

The collection is especially valuable because no Association newspapers are available from this early and most active period of the Association, with its widespread and diverse activities in China, the U.S., Canada, South and Central America, Japan, Korea, Macao, Singapore, and England. In the collection, there is extensive documentation from many different sources of Baohuang Hui military ventures in China, its newspapers and schools all over the world, the Western Military Academy which trained cadets and was headquartered in Los Angeles, and major political movements in the U.S. to further the reform cause. Of special interest are the documents concerning the many Baohuang Hui commercial ventures, including King Joy Low in Chicago and the Wah Yick Bank in New York. Other topics in the letters: the 1900 Datong Uprising, staged to bring the reform-minded Emperor back to power, and supported financially by overseas Chinese; the American Homer Lea who was involved in Baohuang Hui military activities in the U.S.; the movement to send students abroad to study law, business, and other subjects useful for reform; and the evolution of Kang's ideas about modernization and Western political values, and his reactions to American society and politics. Thus, one can get an intimate view of internal Association workings and of the members' visions, strategies, and problems. Factionalism and corruption were to quickly erode Baohuang Hui influence in the U.S. after 1908, and the letters reveal conflicts already rife in the Association soon after its founding.

Research on the Collection. Since the mid-1980s, the author has been overseeing the translation of the letter collection, working primarily with Charles Liu, who is a Chinese-language professor at Portland State University. Also assisting with translation has been Li Shian, a Chinese historian from Guiyang Normal University who taught a course in "Historical Documents" and now lives in Portland. The author polished the English and attempted to date and briefly annotate each letter as it was translated. An index card was made for each person and organization who wrote or was mentioned in the letters, listing the numbers of the letters in which the names appeared, with the cards organized alphabetically by name in pinyin. The letters are often difficult to translate because they are written in classical Chinese; Kang's handwriting in particular is hard to read; the envelopes (which might bear postmarks) are almost all missing; and dates, when given, use the lunar calendar and almost always lack the year (historical clues were used to guess at the years the letters were written). Non-Chinese names are often in Cantonese transliteration and many alternate names are used for such individuals as Kang and Liang, requiring familiarity with the history of the Baohuang Hui and the personalities of the times.

I went to China in November-December 1990 and worked in Beijing with Ruan Fangji and Huang Chunsheng of the journals *Lishi Yanjiu* (Historical Studies) and Wu Jie of *Social Sciences in China* to transcribe 10 representative documents (including the three quoted) into modern Chinese, translate and annotate them. Tang Zhijun, of the Shanghai Academy of Social Sciences Institute of History, and probably the foremost scholar of Kang and the reform movement, read the 10 transcribed letters and made corrections based on his experience in reading Kang's handwriting. In January 1992, the 10 letters were published, with an introduction by Ruan Fangji, in *Jindaishi Ziliao* (Modern historical materials, Ruan et al. 1–18).

Because of the historical significance of this collection, the Guangdong Academy of Social Sciences in Guangzhou, led by historian Fang Zhiqin, is transcribing the letters into modern, simplified, and punctuated Chinese and annotating them for publication as a book in 1993. Stimulated by the availability of this newly discovered collection, Ruan Fangji in Beijing and the Kang Liang Study Society in Guangzhou also are organizing an international conference on the Baohuang Hui in October 1993.

Excerpts from Three Documents. Excerpts of three documents will show the diversity of this collection and the inside view it offers of an overseas Chinese political-movement which was to have a profound influence on the modernization and politicization of China.

The first letter excerpted, #513, is to Tom Leung from Chen Guoyong, a leader of the reform association in Yokohama, Japan, and was written in May 1900. The year 1900 was a time of growth and debate within the Association when as many as an eighth of the entire Chinese population in the U.S. were Association members (Ma 51).

In January, Empress Dowager Ci Xi attempted to depose Emperor Guang Xu by issuing an imperial edict to make her great-nephew Pu Jun the legitimate heir of the previous Emperor Tongzhi. This brought immediate opposition within China and from abroad, and overseas-Chinese, organized by the Baohuang Hui, flooded Beijing with telegrams of protest. The Empress Dowager had to back down although the Emperor was never to regain power after the Hundred Days of Reform.

This was also the time of the Boxer disturbances, and the chaos in China led to a series of uprisings organized by reformers and revolutionaries. The reformers hoped that the Western powers, in their opposition to the Qing which had joined the Boxers in attacking foreigners, would lead to the overthrow of the Empress Dowager and the restoration of Guang Xu as Emperor. The letter refers to plans for a joint uprising of Tang Caichang's Independence Army and secret society recruits of the Ge Lao Hui (Society of Brothers and Elders), which was to take place simultaneously in four provinces on August 9, with the aim of restoring the Emperor to his throne. In addition, the letter refers to recruiting assassins to kill the "evil clique" or powerful imperial government officials who opposed reform, such as Qing Grand Councilor Rong Lu. The failure of both of these efforts eventually sealed the Baohuang Hui's fate and ended its experiments with violence. Chinese reformers sent many students abroad to study subjects of use to China's modernization. Tom Leung helped a number of students who came to Los Angeles, housing them and/or giving them money to pursue their studies. From the letter, it appears, just as it does today, that convincing students to return to China was sometimes difficult.

Also referred to in the letter is an unusual American, Homer Lea, who, after leaving college, used his considerable knowledge of military strategy (without the benefit of experience) to convince the Baohuang Hui leaders that he could train and organize an army of Chinese Americans to fight the Empress Dowager. He involved other Americans with military background and they began the Western Military Academy, first in Los Angeles and then in many other U.S. cities. There is also information that Lea was sent to China in 1900 to lead the August uprising, but no evidence that he actually took part.

Let us now hear the writer, Chen Guoyong, tell Tom Leung of his opinions on some of these issues:

> Today the Baohuang Hui is our only hope to save China from perishing. The overseas Chinese are indignant. The last month of the lunar year, they dispatched more than a hundred telegrams to Beijing to oppose the adoption of an heir [as the legitimate successor to the

Tongzhi emperor].[1] This shows that Heaven will not let China perish by keeping several million Chinese overseas for the purpose of restoration of the Han mandate! In the last few months, the Baohuang Hui has gained a lot of strength and momentum. The foundation has been set up gradually. So far, we have delayed making any moves [to carry out an armed uprising]. This is because of two important factors. We need to raise more funds and find qualified people. That is why we have to wait.

In your letter you mentioned that Mr. Ye and Mr. Zhang are well versed in English and Mr. Zhang is now studying naval and military sciences. These kinds of talented people are rare. Since you have established a good relationship with them, maybe you can persuade them to return to China to help with the armed uprising to save the emperor. When the uprising meets with success, their achievements would be great.

Now we are seeking useful, talented people. Moreover, since they [Ye and Zhang] have a good command of the English language, they will be good candidates for diplomatic posts in the future. I think there must be a lot of talented overseas Chinese like these two persons. Please be on the lookout for them and see if you can arouse their righteous indignation [against our enemy] and enlist their services for us. This is what the Elder [Kang Youwei] repeatedly admonished us to do.

According to your letter, Kan Ma Li [Homer Lea] is really a talented and rare person.[2] Today, we have to utilize strength from abroad. Lea not only understands military matters but also has a mind to help us. Why don't you simply tell him what our party is doing and ask him whether he can recruit American soldiers to help us when the

---

[1] The historical name of this incident is "Establishing an Imperial Family in the Year of Ji Hai" and took place on January 24, 1900 (25th year of Guangxu's reign, 24th day, 12th month).

[2] Homer Lea (1876–1912). According to Ma, p. 59: "In 1900, ...he and his friends organized a drill squad and let it be known that he wanted to fight the Empress Dowager. Hearing of this, a local Pao-huang hui leader (probably Tan Jiqian, whose letter of introduction for Lea to Kang Youwei was printed in the B.A. thesis of Frederic Chapin, 'Homer Lea and the Chinese Revolution,' Harvard, 1950) invited him to join that organization and sent Lea from his family's home in Los Angeles up to San Francisco with Reverend Wu P'an-chao.... In San Francisco, Lea was initiated into the Pao-huang hui and the Chih-kung t'ang, and then was packed off to China with money, collected by the San Francisco Pao-huang hui, which he was to deliver to K'ang Yu'wei. Later, Lea became allied with Sun Yatsen, and in 1912 he temporarily was appointed as a high-level military advisor to the general president when Sun returned to China. He died in 1912 in Los Angeles, and his ashes were taken to Taiwan in 1962."

opportunity arises.[3] If our cause succeeds, they will be rewarded with rights in China, such as mines and railroads. If he agrees, ask him to see the Elder to discuss it when he has a chance to travel here. What I am afraid of is that he might have set out on his journey before this letter reaches you.[4]

Now the arrangements and deployments in China will soon be completed and many people of exceptional ability from all parts of the country have come to pledge allegiance. Our vision is that when the righteous troops rise against the enemy, it will be as easy as crushing dry weeds and smashing rotten wood. I am sure of that.

As for recruiting assassins who are willing to die to kill the evil clique members, this is extremely difficult.[5] Since last year, we have paid a lot of attention to this and spent considerable money for recruitment but, so far, we have not gotten any results.

At present our Association has been established in all cities, all extremely enthusiastic. However, the Association has not been established yet in your flourishing city [Los Angeles, which according to a June 1900 letter from Kang Youwei was then being set up]; for this we have to depend on you for the your inspirational efforts. I hope you can make it happen as soon as possible. When things are in good shape, I also hope you will write us frequently and tell us about it. Among those who have courage and uprightness, a sense of loyalty, and moral indignation, there must be a lot of people in your city who are earnest about supporting the emperor and the country. How could they be willing to lag behind the others? I hope you will often encourage them and arouse them with words of loyalty and righteousness. Each person we recruit will add to our strength and each dollar we raise will add to the usefulness of our funds. As the

---

[3]Ma, p. 59, says that Lea did recruit American volunteers, but that none seems to have gotten to China for the 1900 Tang Caichang uprising.

[4]Letter #514 to Zhangxiao, also from Chen Guoyong, dated July 25, 1900 (?): "Kan Ma Li, the American, arrived in Yokohama on July 11. I have met and talked with him. By instruction of the Association in San Francisco, we gave him $200 as a gift. He left for Hong Kong and Macao by the same ship the next day. Then he will go to see Kang Nanhai. We have provided him with an introductory letter." Kang was then in Singapore, and there is no evidence that he met Lea.

[5]The "evil clique" according to Tang Zhijun were: Rong Lu [1836–1903, Manchu Plain White Banner and Qing Grand Councilor], Gang Yi [1837–1900, Manchu, Blue Border Banner, Qing Grand Councilor], and [Governor General of Hebei: Yulu, a Manchu, held this position 1899 to 1900, according to Edward Rhoads]. Hsiao, p. 238, says that Kang said that Rong Lu, Prince Qing, and Li Hongzhang were members of the evil clique, while Zhang Zhidong and Liu Kunyi wavered between the pro-empress dowager and pro-emperor parties.

Analects of Confucius say, "Mount Tai never refuses any addition of soil; the [Yellow] River and the sea never refuse water from the smallest stream." It is time today to unite the masses in order to accomplish great things. Anyway, this will necessarily render some help to our country, to their own country. The Association has a lot of work to do. Nevertheless, the main task overseas ought to be the recruitment of key personnel and fundraising, as I said above. It's an immense responsibility and you have to do your best. It has been heard here that people in San Francisco are lost and disorganized. Maybe they are intimidated by the threats of the Chinese Consul [He You]. Another reason is that Ren Gong [Liang Qichao] has not arrived yet [he was to come to the U.S. in 1903 when he had great success in stimulating Baohuang Hui activities]. Furthermore, this is also due to the fact that so many candidates for president [of the Baohuang Hui chapter] in the city have been nominated that no agreement can be reached.

The situation in our country is dangerous and I cannot tell you all about it. Chen Guoyong bows his head.

The next letter, #509, is dated July 5, 1901, and is from Kang Youwei, written in exile from Penang, an island off the coast of the Malay Peninsula that was part of the British Straits Settlements; it is addressed to Tom Leung. The August armed uprising (also known as the Hankou uprising, because that was where the plot was uncovered) had failed because it was uncovered by Qing officials and its failure must have had some effect on Association fundraising efforts. Kang decries the money wasted on Homer Lea, presumably for his military aid to the uprising. He takes aim at the overseas Chinese whose unrealistic expectations and enthusiasms are matched by their inability to raise funds. With the failure in Hankou, the Qing government sent officials to investigate Baohuang Hui activities abroad, particularly in Macao, where it became necessary to close the Association newspaper, Zhixin Bao, or "China Reformer," and to carry on Association activities in secret. About the same time, Qing officials in the U.S. were attempting to stop Baohuang Hui leaders from entering the country to recruit new members. Two such leaders were Liang Qitian, who was sent to the U.S. in 1900 and whom the Chinese minister Wu Tingfang tried to get the U.S. Department of State to expel, and Xu Qin, who came to the U.S. in 1901 to take over from Liang, and whose family in Guangdong was threatened with arrest by He You, the Qing consul in San Francisco. In spite of the persecution, both Liang and Xu were highly successful in arousing Chinese American involvement in Baohuang Hui and many branches were formed as a result. Kang's rather scolding, harsh letter in a pessimistic tone contrasts with others of his in the collection—which seem far more optimistic and display much admiration for western things.

What kind of work do we do now? It must be kept secret. If there is a leak, some people involved might be killed. Commissioners [or "Committee members"; i.e., Qing officials] have been sent to Hong Kong and Macao to secretly investigate us. Only a few comrades know what we are doing. But our failures are still due to leaks. As a result, large quantities of funds went down the drain and many good and useful people died. The Hankou Incident is a good example. Ever since fall and winter, everything which we planned to do has been known [in advance] by local officials who in turn immediately enforced martial law and arrested our people. The situation has been extremely dangerous. This is not like two nations who fight each other and openly prepare armaments and dispatch generals and officers. But your letter sounds as if we have established a new nation. How can you be so ignorant! We clearly understand that, only when we have the popular support of all the cities, can we raise large sums of money. However, the situation and human relations have become clear after two years of campaigns. People always give up whenever we have a slight frustration or minor failure. After the failure in Hankou and arrest of Mr. Luo and Tang, few people have contributed money.[6] Even if all cities enthusiastically donate, it will not be much. As for the Hankou Incident, we were completely dependent on [Qiu] Shu Yuan going all the way to donate funds.[7] Unfortunately we have few people in each city who are like him. Many people do not understand this and many have recommended Westerners to come. For example, it has cost us several thousand dollars for Kong Ma Li [Homer Lea], who was of no help to us. If we recruit people from all the cities, then the sum of money we raise in each city will not be enough to support the personnel in charge of those cities, to say nothing of our activities. People like Kong Ma Li and Rong Chun Fu [Yung Wing] all do things

---

[6]Luo is probably Luo Botang, who, according to Letter #501, is a San Francisco Association member and Tang is probably Tang Qiongchang, who was founder of the powerful Translators Lodge and manager of "Chinese World" or *Wen Xing Bao* in San Francisco. Their families were arrested by Guangdong authorities, perhaps as a result of the Datong Uprising (Lo 183).

[7]Qiu Shuyuan was a wealthy rice merchant who lived in Singapore. In 1900, he was chosen by Kang Youwei to be chairman of the Bao Huang Hui of the British colonies of Southeast Asia. The same year, he contributed 250,000 yuan in financial aid to the Independence Army uprising. He was the principal donor of funds for this uprising and warrants were issued for his arrest by the Qing after the uprising failed.

in the Western style.[8] They just ask for thousands and millions of dollars from our association. They suggest that such and such arms should be purchased for several million and such and such a steamboat worth several million should be purchased, etc. They do not know that our Association is about as big as the blood of a mosquito and as small as the urine of an ant. The money you raise from different cities amounts to thousands of dollars to a few hundred. How can it be sufficient when you use the blood of many mosquitoes to feed an elephant? Kong Ma Li's words are merely like someone talking in his sleep. People in foreign countries [refers to Association members abroad] do not know the straitened circumstances in China. They cannot donate enough funds but have great expectations. It's ridiculous. If you look at those countries which have donated funds, even Canada hasn't raised any more money than before though they are very enthusiastic. Because their financial sources are limited, they cannot do any better.

In Macao, commissioners are sent from various provinces to secretly watch our members.[9] Some of us have been arrested repeatedly and our news has been leaked time and again. Therefore I purposely issued an order to halt activities and told *Zhi Xin Bao* to stop publishing.[10] This is actually against my will but I cannot help but act. When it seems from the outside that all activities have stopped, we will secretly start again. All this cannot be told to anyone else. You must keep it secret, and try to clear up the doubts in our people's minds. Thus, when anyone asks about the Macao situation, he should

---

[8]Yung Wing, a native of Xiang Shan, Guangdong, was the pioneer Westernized Chinese who was the first Chinese student in the U.S. (graduated from Yale College in 1854, Tsai 120), later was the head of the Chinese Educational Mission (1872–81) in the U.S. and became Chinese minister in Washington, D.C. Yung was one of the first to support the 1898 reforms, and in the U.S., he was a member of Bao Huang Hui and was active in the Hartford, Connecticut, community, where more than 100 Chinese resided (Ma 90). He was increasingly supportive of revolutionary activity, and around 1908, he deserted Kang Youwei and recruited Homer Lea as a secret agent for Sun Yatsen (Ma 129).

[9]In Letter #533, He Tingguang, manager of *Zhi Xin Bao* in Macao, reports about the same time as Letter #509: "Ever since our failure in Hankou last year, many comrades who participated have managed to escape and have arrived here one after another. He was one of those on the wanted list."

[10]*Zhixin Bao*, "China Reformer," was a newspaper sponsored by the reform faction and was first published in February 1897 in Macao and run by Kang Guangren, He Tingguang, Xu Qin, and others. Its circulation was very small after 1898, and with the increased Qing government pressure on Macao after the 1900 Hankou Uprising, it stopped publication in 1901.

be told that activity is halted. This is to avoid suspicion by the Committee Members. If we cannot establish ourselves in such a small place, how can we possibly establish a nation as you thought. Therefore, if anyone talks about Macao, do not believe that person. Just tell him that all the information was leaked and the Committee Members are watching. You already know that our letters have been opened before they reach us. So you cannot tell the truth in your letters. Because of our letter to Hankou last time, more than 2,000 people were killed. Such slaughter is still continuing at present. You cannot raise much money in San Francisco, but countless good people were killed in China. So recently we have everything done in Penang and I personally am in charge. As for Macao, it doesn't matter whether we continue our activities there or not. You should tell all foreign cities about the difficulties we encounter in China. Many people died and many chances were missed. However, tell them not to worry. From now on, money and letters should be sent to me at Penang Island.

It is very nice of you to defend Jun Li.[11] You can do the same when other incidents occur. Today our goal is to establish the Association in new cities. If we establish new branches, we will have new sources of funds. In those old places we cannot do anything other than make trouble for ourselves even if we have the most talented speakers like Su [Qin] and Zhang [Yi].[12] Jun Mien [Xu Qin] is scheduled to arrive now.[13] You can work closely together with Jun Mien and Jun Li to develop new branches and raise funds. I have high hopes for you. I wish you peace.

We close with a poem by Kang Youwei, written in September 1905 during his first trip to the U.S. when he was staying at Yellowstone Park. Tom Leung was one of Kang's main hosts during his time in the U.S., especially in Los Angeles, where Kang was from March 16 to May 18, 1905. While in Los Angeles, he was welcomed by a huge banquet hosted by the local Association chapter; he met with Homer Lea and R.A. Falkenberg of the Chinese Imperial Reform Army, and he lived in a house at Westlake Park.

---

[11]Jun Li, namely Liang Qitian, was Liang Qichao's relative and Kang's student. He was sent to the U.S. in 1900 to gain support for the August uprising (Lo 184). According to Ma 51: "Chinese minister Wu T'ing-fang tried but failed to get the United States to expel Liang Ch'i-t'ien, claiming Liang's presence was in violation of Chinese Exclusion [Liang Qitian]."

[12]Su Qin and Zhang Yi were counselors of the Warring States (475 B.C. to 221 B.C.) and were celebrated for their eloquence and quick-tongued argument.

[13]Jun Mien, namely Xu Qin, who came to the U.S. to take over recruiting for Bao Huang Hui from Liang Qitian.

Flat are the great plains of America, where there is little good scenery to see.

Of the whole land, which I have traveled, Los Angeles is the most excellent:

Close to the ocean and the mountains, it is neither too cold nor too hot;

Many are the flowers and various the fruits, and all the houses and buildings are newly repaired;

Big as one's fist are the fragrant oranges, which are sold throughout America.

A house is rented, facing the West Lake, its blue green waters so beautiful.

Day after day I walked around, leaning on my cane and roamed the islands across the wooden bridge.

All over the slopes, flowers flourished, and the meadows served as a carpet for me and my books.

For two months in spring I had a short sojourn here, recuperating and forgetting the worries of one in exile.

On the east coast there is just Hartford[14] where the groves and houses can be compared to [those in Los Angeles],

Yet there are no hills and I am afraid of the cold; it is not a good haven for me.

Tan, my disciple, you who did so well choosing the present place for me, you are the originator of teaching military tactics. Don't forget me when you travel in your dreams, in our old mansion the blossoms are fine.

Los Angeles' scenery is the best in America. I toured there in the 2nd and 3rd lunar month of spring [March and April]. My student, Tan Liang [Tom Leung] and other Baohuang Hui members rented a house beside the West Lake for me. Everyday I walked around with the help of my stick and sometimes I lay down on the grass among the flowers. Recalling the house where I stayed, I composed this poem for Tan Zhangxiao.

---

[14]Although the characters used are for "Harvard," Kang Youwei traveled to Hartford, Connecticut, in July 1905 to see the home of his daughter, Kang Tongbi, and visit Yung Wing; according to Worden, "A Chinese Reformer in Exile" 177, Kang found it the "cleanest city he had ever been in." There is no evidence he visited Harvard when he was in the Boston area.

GLOSSARY
(In order of first appearance)

Romanization	Chinese	*Social Sciences in China* 中國社會科學
Tan Zhangxiao	譚張孝	Tang Zhijun 湯志鈞
Tan Liang (Tom Leung)	譚良	Fang Zhiqin 方志欽
Baohuang Hui	保皇會	Tang Caichang 唐才常
Kang Youwei	康有為	Ge Lao Hai 哥老會
Gan Zhu (Gum Jook)	甘竹	Mr. Ye 吐
Shunde Xian	順德縣	Kan Ma Li 堪罵李
Tan Zizhong	譚子中	Rong Lu 祿
Jin shi	進士	Gang Yi 剛毅
"Tatched Hut Among 10,000 Trees"	萬木草堂	He You 何祐
Tan Fuyuan (Tom Foo Wing)	譚富園	Liang Qitian (Jun Li) 梁啟田 (君力)
Liang Qichao	梁啟超	Wu Tingfang 伍廷芳
Qiongcailou (King Joy Low)	瓊彩樓	Qiu Shu Yuan 邢救園
Xu Qin (or Jun Mian)(Chuy C. Kain)	徐勤 (君勉)	Kong Ma Li 孔馬哩
Kuang Shoumin	鄺壽民	Rong Chun Fu 容純甫
Ye En (Yip On)	葉恩	Luo Botang 羅伯堂
Tan Shubin (Tom She Bin)	譚樹彬	Tang Qiongchang 唐瓊昌
Tang Qiongchong	唐瓊昌	"Translators Lodge" 洋文政務司
Wenxing Bao (*Chinese World*)	文興報	*Zhixin Bao* 知新報
Li Shian	李世安	Kang Guangren 康廣仁
Ruan Fangji	阮芳紀	He Tingguang 何廷光
Huang Chunsheng	黃春生	Su Qin 蘇秦
Lishi Yanjiu (*Historical Studies*)	歷史研究	Zhang Yi 張儀
Wu Jie	吳洁	

Works Cited

Chapin, Frederic L. "Homer Lea and the Chinese Revolution." Undergraduate thesis, Harvard University, 1950.

Chin, Doug and Art. Uphill: *The Settlement and Diffusion of the Chinese in Seattle*. Seattle: Shorey Book Store, 1973.

Chong, Key Ray. *Americans and Chinese Reform and Revolution, 1898–1912: The Role of Private Citizens in Democracy* Lanham, New York, and London: University Press of America, 1984.

Fang Zhiqin. "Weixin Fansi Lun, Theory of Re-assessing Reform." In *Wu Xu Bianfa Yundong Yanjiu Lunwen Ji*, Guangdong Kang Liang Yanjiu She.

Frederic Wakeman, Jr. *The Fall of Imperial China*. New York: The Free Press, 1975.

Hsiao, Kung-chuan. *A Modern China and a New World: K'ang Yu-wei, Reformer and Utopian, 1858–1927*. Seattle and London: University of Washington Press, 1975.

Leung Larson, Louise. *Sweet Bamboo: A Saga of a Chinese American Family.* Los Angeles: Chinese Historical Society of Southern California, 1989.

Levenson, Joseph R. *Liang Ch'i-Ch'ao and the Mind of Modern China*. Berkeley and Los Angeles: University of California Press, 1967.

Ma, L. Eve Armentrout. *Revolutionaries, Monarchists, and Chinatowns: Chinese Politics in the Americas and the 1911 Revolution*. Honolulu: University of Hawaii Press, 1990.

Rhoads, Edward J.M. *China's Republican Revolution: The Case of Kwangtung, 1895–1913*. Cambridge: Harvard University Press, 1975.

Ruan, Fangji, Huang Chunsheng, and Wu Jie, with materials provided by Tan Jingyi [Jane Leung Larson]. "Guanyu Baohuanghui shijianshougao [Ten original documents concerning the Baohuanghui]." Jindaishi Ziliao, [Modern historical materials 80 (January 1992): 1–18.

Shanghai Shi Wenwu Baoguan Weiyuanhui (Shanghai Cultural Artifacts Protection Society), Kang Youwei Yu Baohuanghui, (Kang Youwei and the Baohuanghui) Shanghai: Renmin Chubanshe, 1982.

Tsai, Shih-Shan Henry. *The Chinese Experience in America, Bloomington and Indianapolis*. Indiana University Press, 1986.

Worden, Robert Leo. "A Chinese Reformer in Exile: The North American Phase of the Travels of K'ang Yu-wei, 1899–1909." Ph.D. dissertation, Georgetown University, Washington, D.C., 1972.

Re-Center the Chinese in History:
Using Chinese-Language Resources for Research

HAIMING LIU

Comparative Culture, University of California, Irvine, California

In the past few years, I have been working on a collection of family papers left by Sam Chang, a pioneer Chinese farmer in Southern California. Letters are the major portions of this collection, though it also includes pamphlets, placards, flyers, posters, farming notes, poems, essays, and personal reflections on cultural and political events both in China and the United States. Of the 2,000 letters, half were addressed to Sam's children and siblings; the other half went to other relatives and friends. Sam wrote the drafts of those letters on several dozens of student notebooks; and he kept them until his death in 1988. There are another 300 incoming letters from his family members and friends in the collection. Though Sam Chang's family history may not reflect every aspect of Chinese American life, few first-hand materials are as comprehensive and systematic as those letters about the Chinese American experience. In this paper, I wish to discuss the importance of using personal letters for Chinese American studies, based on my research on the Sam Chang Collection.

Few of the existing Chinese American scholarships have been based on personal letters. In fact, few were based on Chinese-language resources, except for Henry Tsai's *China and Overseas Chinese in the United States, 1868–1911*, published in 1973, though the primary source for this book was the Qing government documents rather than records left by the Chinese immigrants themselves (Tsai 1983).

Most Asian Americanists have not studied/used letters or other Chinese language sources because of inadequate Chinese-language ability and lack of access to resources. A few scholars, however, assumed that early Chinese immigrants failed to leave any records about their experience because they were too busy making a living and most of them were illiterate (Barth 1965).

This is not true. Him Mark Lai's *A History Reclaimed: An Annotated Bibliography of Chinese Language Materials on the Chinese of America* demonstrates that Chinese-language materials are abundant in public institutions in Northern California (Lai 1986). Many studies on Chinese Americans published in China also confirmed this fact. A Ying's edited book, *An Anti-American Literary Collection on the Exclusion of Chinese Laborers*, for example, included the novel, *Bitter Society*, which is actually based on personal stories and testimonies by the returned overseas-Chinese laborers (Ying 1959).

Using personal letters or other original records for research is to emphasize the importance of studying Chinese America from the perspective of Chinese immigrants themselves. Such perspective requires scholars to describe not only what has happened to Chinese Americans, but also what they have achieved and how the Chinese perceived American society. Correspondence is not a one-way communication. Information, ideas, and feelings are to be exchanged back and forth across the Pacific. Sam Chang's extensive correspondence with his family and friends has left us a gold mine of first-hand material which reflects the attitude and perceptions of the Chinese about their life in the United States. Personal letters are one of the few documents that allow us to penetrate the meaning of immigration experience to the individual Chinese.

For example, though the Chang family was doing well in their herbal and farming business, the letters demonstrate that Sam Chang was pessimistic about the future of his children, as he was fully aware that the Chinese were treated as an inferior race in the United States. As historical data to document personal insights and feeling, personal letters are probably also more objective than memoirs or interviews, since the latter often reconstruct the past events based on memories and feelings and are often meant for the public to read. However, similar to memoirs or interviews, letters reveal personal perceptions which enable us to find out the subjective meaning of Chinese American experience. As valuable historical data, personal letters enable us to find out the subjective meaning of human migration and place the immigrants themselves into the center of history.

Early studies of Chinese experience in this country failed to provide a balanced representation of Chinese Americans because they often treated them as objects rather than subjects in their studies. For instance, Stuart Miller's *The Unwelcome Immigrant: The American Image of the Chinese, 1785–1882* is an important book on racial discrimination against the Chinese. It pointed out that racism had existed in America long before the Chinese arrived, and that anti-Chinese sentiment was a national, rather than a Californian, phenomenon. But by studying Chinese image in the writings of American missionaries, diplomats, and mass media, Miller's study is, in fact, a book of American culture history. And so is Alexander Saxton's *The Indispensable Enemy: Labor and Anti-Chinese Movement in California*. Though it is a powerful critique on racism, it is more of a Caucasian union history rather than an Asian American history.

To re-center the Chinese in history, we need to treat them as participants in social and economical activities. In our immigration studies, for example, use of aggregate statistic data and investigation of structural determinants such as timing or political economy are important, as they offer a general picture about causes of immigration. But the average immigrant was not a helpless victim pushed and pulled by various social forces. Most immigrants were actively involved in the migration movement by making decisions on their own. Such decisions were based on personal evaluation of the social conditions in both the sending and receiving countries. When early immigrants wrote home to influence the potential immigrants, their letters could encourage or discourage the potential immigrants. So letters themselves were a vital part of the chain migration process. Using letters as historical data helps us to understand immigrants as decision-makers in the immigration movement.

Immigrants' letters are a valuable source for studying the process of migration. After human migration achieves its momentum, ties of family, kinship, friends, and townspeople form the social network to keep the movement going, which is usually referred to as chain migration. Personal letters are instrumental in chain migration because they provide the link between the immigrants and their social network, and they inform the potential immigrants about the local conditions of the receiving country, and they advise them how to travel, what kind of jobs are available, where to find friends and residence, and what decisions to make.

In some cases, personal letters were published because of public interest. For example, in studying Norwegian immigration, Theodore Blegen noted that Norwegian immigrants' letters were referred to as "American letters" in the home country and they aroused enthusiastic public interest because many Norwegians wanted to find out about the new world. Some of the letters were printed as soon as they were received and thus, "American letters" became "Newspaper letters" (Blegen 1975). Similar phenomenons also occurred in 19th-century Welsh and Sweden. In studying the Welsh immigrants, Alan Conway noted that immigrants' letters were published in the press. Some immigrants even wrote letters directly to a newspaper or periodical and enjoyed seeing their adventure in print (Conway 4, Barton 5). In my own observation, Sam Chang's collection was not correspondence between two individuals, but was a network communication comprising more than a dozen people, and he constantly offered advice and suggestions on when, how, or if they should come to America. When Sam Chang's letters have enhanced our understanding of the migration process, they transcend one family history.

Many letters of Sam Chang contained advice and suggestions to his relatives and friends on whether they should come to America or not. In a letter of 1922, for example, Sam advised his second brother not to come because everything was expensive there, though one could earn higher wages. Following Sam Chang's advice, his second brother did not come. A letter like this enables us to understand why some family members left, while others stayed behind. Other data probably cannot provide an answer to a question like this.

While sharing opinions and advice to their relatives or friends in the letters, immigrants expressed their perception about America and their life in American society. For example, Sam Chang believed that life of the Chinese in America represented downward, rather than upward, mobility in terms of their social status. Racism did not allow the Chinese to pursue a decent profession in America. On May 24, 1922, he wrote to his son:

> If you want to achieve great things, America is not the right place. But if you want to make good money to help your family out of financial difficulty, no other country's money is worthier than the American dollar.

He encouraged his son to complete at least high school education in China before he came to America for more advanced degrees. With a solid Chinese cultural foundation, his son would be able to return to his home country if he failed to find a good job in America.

Sam Chang also tried repeatedly to persuade his third younger brother Elbert, who was brought up in America and had a medical degree from Georgetown University, to stay in China when he had a position in Beijing Union Hospital (Xie-he Hospital), a medical institution sponsored by the Rockefeller Foundation. Sam wrote to his son about Elbert, November 16, 1924:

> If he comes to America, his financial income would depend on his practice. In America, the racial difference is great. The white is regarded as the most superior race. Very few white people would go to a Chinese doctor. The patients would either be the low class people or have very difficult symptoms. It will be hard to make a profit.

On January 4, 1925, he wrote to his son again:

> If your uncle comes back to America, he might make a little bit more money. But his reputation and social rank will be low; and his knowledge will be wasted. As a result, he will become a low class citizen without fame. He will never become a respected man as America is the most racist society and very prejudiced against the Yellow race of people.

Sam Chang's letters enable us to gain insight into personal feeling of immigrants about racism in American society. Without using personal records such as letters or diary, we can hardly penetrate the meaning of immigration experience to the individual Chinese. The above letters also tell us why many Chinese immigrants traveled back and forth between the Pacific and pursue education and jobs in both China and America. Racial environment was an important consideration in their immigration plan.

In my research on Sam Chang Papers, I have been most impressed by his conscientious effort to preserve a record of Chinese activities in America. In addition to letters, Sam Chang's Papers also included his farming notes. Though Sam became a farmer only after he arrived in America, and did not begin his farming career until 1917–18, he was sensitive to the role the Chinese had played in agri-business of Southern California. His intellectual background enabled him to make a careful observation and record of Chinese asparagus-farmers during that period. In the early years of his farming career, he also kept a detailed note of his own farming experience in a student notebook. He attempted to write a book or an article on agriculture. In the notebook, he listed several subjects he intended to write about, which included the current situation of Chinese American farmers, the gambling hobby among Chinese American farmers, agricultural policies in China as compared to other countries, or the new alternatives of developing agriculture in China. Sam's farming notes provided a valuable, first-hand account of Chinese agri-business activities in Los Angeles area from a Chinese perspective. Among other things, his notes contained a detailed description about the Asian-produce market in Los Angeles at the turn of the century. In the notebook, Sam Chang wrote:

...Los Angeles agriculture markets are famous in American West. It has three big markets: one on the 6th Street, one on the 8th Street, and one on 9th Street. The one on the 8th Street is the largest one where many import and export trade is done. The one on the 6th Street is smaller. And the one on the 9th Street is the smallest. This one is operated by the Chinese and Japanese. As the whites often discriminated the Yellow race people in the last ten years, the Yellow race could not tolerate this so they opened their own market. The 9th Street market opens 2:00 a.m, three to four hours earlier than the markets on the 8th and 6th Street, so that the peddlers or truckers will be able to deliver them to various restaurants for use before the breakfast time. The markets on the 8th and 6th Streets have more wholesale business and need to deliver their goods to the railroad station. They open at 5:00 or 6:00 a.m. Chinese asparagus farmers mainly sell their products to the 9th Street market.

The market on the 9th Street in Sam Chang's description was also referred to as the City Market Wholesale Produce Terminal of Los Angeles and, as Sam Chang recorded, had a bitter history of racial conflicts between the Chinese and the Caucasians. According to Charles Choy Wong, before the City Market was established, there had been a Union Wholesale Terminal Market on the 6th and Alameda Streets. When disputes erupted on the future development of the Market, one group of merchants stayed and another group left to build the City Market place at the 9th and San Pedro streets in 1909. Of these two markets, the City Market was the dominant one.

It was created through the cooperative efforts of Chinese, Caucasians, and Japanese. The Chinese were led by Mr. Louis Quan who, by virtue of his better English-speaking ability and business acuity, promoted a Chinese stock company of 373 stockholders and raised $82,000, or 41% of the City Market ownership (Wong 65).

In Sam Chang's writing, the market on the 9th Street, however, became the smallest one. It was possible that by 1922, the Caucasian businessmen took out their shares and set up the third market on the 8th Street because of conflicts with Asian farmers. According to Isamu Nodera, the Caucasians owned slightly more shares than the Chinese. But there were only 45 Caucasian shareholders. In comparison, there were 373 Chinese shareholders (Nodera 101).

With a smaller number of holders and a larger share of the market, it would be easy for the Caucasian to split and set up another market.

In Sam Chang's writing, we can see a decline of Chinese dominance in Los Angeles agri-business marketing system at the beginning of the 20th century. With more capital, and through racist behavior, the white businessmen gradually squeezed out their Asian counterparts and dominated wholesale agri-business, which was mainly done in the market on 8th Street. According to Sam Chang, the whites received big orders from the East Coast and Mexico. The Asian market on 9th Street was the smallest one and mainly dealt with local trade. The Asian businessmen also had to start work several hours earlier than the white counterparts. But at least the Asians still possessed their own market, which reflected the historical dominance of the Chinese in agri-business and demonstrated the efforts of the Asian merchants in protecting and expanding their business interest and opportunities.

In the asparagus business, however, the Chinese farmers were still the dominant force. Sam Chang continued to write:

> The quantity of our asparagus production is controlled and the daily fresh products usually supplies the local market. The price of fresh asparagus is made by the Chinese in consideration of the price of asparagus samples imported from other places. The local asparagus price will be 2 to 3 cents per pound higher than the asparagus price supplied from other places. The price is not necessarily determined before the sale is made, as the payment is on weekly rather than on

daily basis. As growing asparagus is a hard work and labor is also difficult to get by, there are few Western asparagus farmers. So the Chinese grow 80% of asparagus in Los Angeles. The Chinese are hard-working and can handle it. Four acres of my farm began to produce asparagus which were sold at 14 cents per pound in the last four years from 1919 till 1922. According to this price, if you can control the cost under 10 cents per pound, a little profit will be made. I really hope more Chinese will come to buy land and grow asparagus so that such profit will not go to the pockets of other people. Los Angeles is now among the five top metropolitan areas in America and will become the most famous city in the world in the future. The land price will rise drastically.

By emphasizing the golden land investment opportunity in this area and presenting a detailed description of the marketing system in Los Angeles, Sam Chang intended to invite more Chinese to come and make land investment in Southern California. This intention showed his concern for the economic interest of the Chinese as an ethnic group and also demonstrated an important quality of the Chinese business community at the that time. Agri-businessmen like Sam Chang were seriously considering a long-term settlement in America rather than a transient opportunity of making fast cash.

With a few example letters listed here, I want to show what we can benefit from the study of personal letters. The significance of Sam Chang Papers go beyond one family history, as this collection covers a period from 1920 to 1950, decades where very little is known about Chinese Americans. These personal documents enable us to understand Asian immigrants as real human beings instead of faceless masses. As Ronald Takaki pointed out:

> They are entitled to be viewed as subjects—as men and women with minds and voices. By "voices" we mean their own words and stories as told in their oral histories, conversations, speeches, soliloquies, and songs, as well as in their own writings—diaries, letters, newspapers, magazines, pamphlets, placards, posters, flyers, court petitions, autobiographies, short stories, novels, and poems. (Takaki 7–8)

In immigration studies, while aggregated data, demographic statistics, and structural determinants such as economic cycles and social ecology allow us to make hypothetical assumptions about intentionality of immigrants in their decision making, records left by immigrants themselves, such as personal letters, will let us gain insight into the personal motivations and aspirations. Those documents help us to answer specific questions, like why those individuals chose to migrate while the majority from their hometown did not. After all, migration is often an individual decision and immigrants were active individuals making decisions on the basis of an evaluation of the situation at home and abroad.

Though there is also a growing tendency of using Chinese-language materials for research in Chinese American studies, official or English-language sources such as newspaper articles are still the basis of most studies. And few studies on personal letters have appeared so far. Hence, the most lively, most interesting aspects of Chinese American life may be still missing. As the Chinese in the United States have had a history exclusive from the mainstream society, Chinese language is not only the major means for communication, but also the major expressive form in commercials, flyers, pamphlets, newspapers, and magazines. A true presentation of the Chinese experience is almost impossible without using Chinese language materials.

In contrast to Chinese American studies, personal letters have been a primary source and an important subject in many immigration studies. A classic example is William Thomas and Florian Znaniecki's multi-volume book, *The Polish Peasant in Europe and America*, published in 1918. The book was essentially based on immigrants' letters (Thomas and Znaniecki 1984). In the more recent decades, scholars have not only used letters as the primary source for research, but have also translated and published them. Theodore Blegen's *Land of Their Choice*, Alan Conway's *The Welsh in America*, Charlott Erickson's *Invisible Immigrants*, Arnold Barton's *Letters from the Promised Land*, Samuel Baily and Franco Ramella's *One Family, Two Worlds*, Walter D. Kamphoefiner's *News from the Land of Freedom: German Immigrants Write Home*, and Josephine Wtulich's *Writing Home* were all studies and translations of various European immigrants in the early 19th century.

These studies are fruitful attempts to explore the subjective meaning of human migration. Sam Chang's Papers indicate that similar records may exist in many Chinese American families. We should encourage them to make such records available to scholars who wish to link their research directly to the Chinese community. A community oriented and supported research is essential for an accurate interpretation of Chinese American experience. As the validity of the research depends on perceptions of the people you do research for, it is time to consider studying personal records as a priority in our research agenda.

Works Cited

Baily, Samuel, and Franco Ramella, eds. *One Family, Two Worlds: An Italian Family's Correspondence Across the Atlantic, 1901–1922.* New Brunswick: Rutgers University Press, 1988.

Barth, Gunther. *Bitter Strength: A History of the Chinese in the United States.* Cambridge, Mass.: Harvard University Press, 1965.

Barton, Arnold ed. *Letters from the Promised Land: Swedes in America, 1840–1912.* Minneapolis: University of Minnesota Press, 1975.

Barton, Arnold. *Letters from The Promised Land: Swedes in America, 1840–1914.* Minneapolis: University of Minnesota Press, 1973.

Blegen, Theodore ed. *Land of Their Choice: The Immigrants Write Home.* Minneapolis: University of Minnesota Press, 1955.

Conway, Alan ed. *The Welsh in America: Letters from the Immigrants.* Minneapolis: University of Minnesota Press, 1961.

Erickson, Charlotte ed. *Invisible Immigrants: The Adaptation of English and Scottish Immigrants in Nineteenth-Century America.* Coral Gables, Florida: University of Miami Press, 1972.

Kamphoefner, Walter, Wolfgang Helbich, and Ulrike Sommer, eds. *News from the Land of Freedom: German Immigrants Write Home.* Ithaca: Cornell University Press, 1991.

Lai, Him Mark. *A History Reclaimed: An Annotated Bibliography of Chinese Language Materials on the Chinese of America.* Los Angeles: Asian American Studies Center, UCLA, 1986.

Nodera, Isamu. "A Survey of the Vocational Activities of the Japanese in the City of Los Angeles." M.A. thesis, University of Southern California, 1936. 101.

Takaki, Ronald. *Strangers from a Different Shore: A History of Asian Americans.* Boston: Little, Brown and Company, 1989.

Thomas, William, and Florian Znaniecki. Edited and abridged by Eli Zaretsky. *The Polish Peasant in Europe and America.* Urbana and Chicago: University of Illinois Press, 1984.

Tsai, Henry. *China and Overseas Chinese in the United States, 1868–1911.* Fayetteville: University of Arkansas Press, 1983. Note: However, Him Mark Lai has used Chinese-language sources extensively in his publications, though English-language materials were also his major sources.

Wong, Charles Choy. "Chinese Grocers in Southern California." In *The Journal of Ethnic Studies* 8#2 (Summer 1980): 65.

Wtulich, Josephine ed. *Writing Home: Immigrants in Brazil and the United States, 1890–1891.* New York: Columbia University Press, 1986.

Ying, A, ed. *An Anti-American Literary Collection on the Exclusion of Chinese Laborers.* Beijing, China, 1959.

Chinese American Jazz
and Asian American Experiences

WEI-HUA ZHANG

Music Department, University of California, Berkeley, California

From the late 1960s, an indigenous movement to develop a distinct Chinese American identity as part of a broader Asian American movement followed the lead of the black civil rights movement (Houn 28, Jang 1988: 33). As a political movement, it owed its genesis to and derived its inspiration, agenda, and tactics from the latter. However, its content was rooted exclusively in Chinese American and Asian American experiences. Its objective was not only to reconceptualize Chinese American identity, but also to demand a rightful place in the United States for all Chinese Americans (Wang 1991). College students pressed for the establishment in universities of Asian American studies programs, through which they could learn about their past, as well as the present conditions of Asians, including the Chinese in America. A Chinese National Movement to unite the American-born and the new immigrants was also under way.

Chinese American arts, which blossomed out of this social background, manifested a keen social awareness and Asian sensitivity. Young, talented artists thrived, such as Maxine Hong Kingston and Amy Tan in literature, Frank Chin in drama, and Wayne Wang in film. In this fertile field, a new style of Asian American expression emerged: Chinese American jazz; and this will be the focus in this paper.

The significance of Chinese American jazz is that it is a new creation, a new genre. It is different from the traditional music that Chinese immigrants brought with them as their cultural heritage, even though I will demonstrate that traditional music has been adapted in content and performing style. Chinese American jazz is also different from musical compositions by other western-trained Chinese musicians that show some Chinese musical elements, because not all compositions of this category attempt to express a specifically

American experience. It is also different from the products of Chinese American musicians who happen to play jazz, country music, rock, or other indigenous American music, but who do not consciously express their Chinese identity. Finally, Chinese American jazz is significant in that it is the expression of a migrant people who are now rooted in this country and realize that they are Americans and not sojourners anymore. This parallels the African American experience as LeRoi Jones describes it in *Blues People,* since Chinese American music began only when the musicians spoke in an American musical language and used America as a reference.

The San Francisco Bay Area has one of the largest Chinese concentrations in the country and because of historical reasons, it also plays a leading role in developing this new cultural expression.

Even though documents are rare, there is no question that the early Asian immigrant laborers brought their traditional musical culture with them. *Songs of the Gold Mountain,* an anthology of the poetry of early Chinese laborers, including poems carved on the walls of cabins in Angel Island, belongs to this category. The forms were traditional, but the content related to experiences in the New World and the expression revealed an Asian American sensibility (Hom 1986).

Later on, these Asian immigrants did actively join the American entertainment business. Riddle reports that "the Cathay Club, the oldest music club in Chinatown, was founded in 1911 by teenagers as a marching band with a totally Western repertoire. From its beginnings until 1963, when it ceased its band activities, the club provided music for virtually every holiday and festive occasion in Chinatown" (Riddle 244). In 1919, a Chinese- instrument ensemble was formed to add some novelty to the program. The group participated in a national tour of vaudeville houses on the Orpheum Circuit and was billed as A Chinese Band, The Chinese Military Band, and The Chinese Jazz Band.

During the swing era in the 1930s, when jazz became the most popular music in America, many Asian American musicians were engaged in playing jazz in Hawaii and the mainland. "Japanese American big bands were quite popular and continued so, even during their incarceration during W.W.II in concentration camps; and Filipino musicians formed dance bands and combos, as taxi dance halls flourished both in urban and rural areas of Filipino concentration" (Houn 28).

Arthur Dong's film, "Forbidden City," (1990) is a rare documentation of the popular night club with the same name situated in San Francisco's Chinatown, which lasted from 1938 to the 1960s. Interviews with surviving performers and owners, pictures, and posters reveal the glamour and bustling popularity of the club. The club was visited by Duke Ellington and other celebrities in American popular music. Performers testified that as second-generation Chinese Americans growing up listening to American popular music, they wanted to learn and imitate that style and to participate in American culture. According to Alex Hing, whose parents were both performers at the club, the Chinese American nightclub had its heyday in the 1940s in San Francisco. At the height of the era, San Francisco's Chinatown sustained six nightclubs which featured all-Asian revues (Hing 1990).

Since the 1980s, a Pan-Asian American Arts movement has gained ground and has flourished significantly in the West Coast. The Kearny Street Workshop has played a definitive role in its development. Formed in 1972 to serve the Chinese American community through the arts, the workshop has provided a base for Asian American artists to develop their skills and to improve community conditions. Under its umbrella, poets, photographers, muralists, printmakers, and musicians have worked collectively to reach a wider audience with lasting works of art that reflect the lives, hopes, and dreams of the community. Poet George Leong developed the Asian American Writer's Workshop. In Los Angeles, Mako founded the East/West Players to develop Asian American Theatre.

The Kearny Street Workshop has played an important role is the development of Asian American music. In 1981, The Asian American Jazz Festival got started with sponsorship by members of the Kearney street Workshop, and the festival celebrated its eleventh anniversary in 1992. A list of the ten years' programs of the Festival demonstrates the growth of Asian American involvement in jazz. A partial discography already lists 35 albums recorded by Asian American jazz musicians (program notes Tenth Anniversary Asian American Jazz Festival).

Mainly consisting of Japanese Americans and Chinese Americans, there are also Filipino Americans who have performed in the Festivals. Russel Baba and the United Front, which included Mark Izu and Anthony Brown, performed in the first Festival in 1982 and again in the tenth Festival in 1991. These musicians all strongly felt the need to reestablish their Asian heritage and identity. They explored Asian philosophies, musical concepts, and aesthetics, as well as the learning of Asian musical instruments. Many Japanese Americans studied *gagaku* (Japanese court music), taiko drumming, *koto* (Japanese plucked zither), and *shakuhachi* (Japanese flute). Robert Kikuchi-Yngojo went back to the Philippines to study *kulintang* (bronze pitched kettle-gongs). Mark Izu learned the Chinese wind instrument, *sheng*. And Jon Jang studied the kulintang and the Chinese Yangqin.

Jang is the most prominent Chinese American jazz musician in the Bay Area, and is also an eloquent spokesman for the Pan-Asian Arts movement. In the following, I will study his work in relation to his personal experiences as a representative. Jang was born in Los Angeles on March 11, 1954, of a Chinese intellectual family. Jon Jang's father came to the U.S. from Canton, China, when he was 18 years old, and earned his Ph.D. degree from the University of Minnesota in 1943. He worked for a large company as a senior chemical engineer. Jon was brought up in Whittier, a conservative white town in Southern California. On a business trip to the midwest during 1956, Jang's father was killed in a plane crash. This catastrophe changed Jang's life.

After the death of Jang's father, the family moved to Palo Alto, where his mother bought a house. Jang's mother wanted all of her three children to go to Stanford University to become chemical engineers, to "follow in their father's footsteps," but Jon was not interested in this destiny.

Like the youths of his time, he listened to rock-n-roll in the 60s. He joined a band, playing keyboard (an electric keyboard organ called farfisa organ, popular in the 60s) because "white kids played either guitars or drums, so I had to play either bass or piano." Jang was also active in sports, especially wrestling and basketball. He did everything with a ferocious intensity and wanted to reach a certain height. Realizing that he lacked the necessary qualities and condition to be a top level wrestler, and because the competitive mentality it takes to be a wrestler is in conflict with being a musician, he finally gave up wrestling. He shifted his entire energy and intensity to the study of music.

During his high school years, Jang felt alienated from the Palo Alto white middle class environment. In a history class, a reading of *Blues People* by Amiri Baraka helped lead to his exploration of such progressive black jazzmen as Max Roach, Elvin Jones, and Cecil Taylor. Music also was a way for Jang to cope with his alienation. Jon states: "It was the 'hot' creative music of 'Trane, Mingus, Rasahaan, and Shepp that liberated me,... The sound of 'Trane's music made revolutionary justice as real to me as the sound of words of a speech by Malcolm X" (Jang 1988).

After a year at U.C. Berkeley, Jon dropped out to begin his first private piano lessons in classical music. He had a very tight schedule, practicing piano in the early morning and late afternoon, while working for a Japanese American gardener during the day. The piano teacher was strict. Jon worked on exercises and pieces of various European classical periods. After one year, he could play Mozart sonatas and after two years, he could execute scales at a rapid tempo of 160 beats per minute. While trimming bushes at a big mansion with Jackson, Jon heard the story about the Japanese internment during W.W.II for the first time. The bitter experience of land and farm taken away explained the repressed silence of Jon's Japanese friends. The story left a deep impression on him and inspired his later composition, "Reparations Now!."

After only a year-and-half of piano lessons, he applied to Oberlin Conservatory and was accepted with a three-year scholarship. Despite the scholarship, he had to work at four jobs to survive. Feeling increasingly alienated from European classical music, he was drawn to the conservatory's African American music program, then being developed by composer Wendell Logan. In a way, the Oberlin Conservatory experience had a negative effect on Jon. As he explained in an interview: "In the conservatory, I was one of the three Asian Americans and I was playing jazz. I started to play the piano at a really late age of 19 while many of the other students had started at the age of 3 or 4, and they had all kinds of training which I didn't have. I had a lot of pressure to fit in at the conservatory, so I really didn't feel I had a place there. As a Chinese American I have many conflicts, many feelings of who I am and their music wasn't really meaningful to me" (Jang 1991). Consequently, after he earned his Bachelor of Music from Oberlin in three years, Jon quit music and worked as a deliverer at Stanford University for a while.

Jang's musical aspirations were reawakened at the first Asian American Jazz Festival held at Fort Mason, San Francisco, in 1981. There he realized that a few Asian musicians were doing the kind of progressive collective improvisation that he had previously found only in African American groups. What was significant about their music was that the creative impetus came from Asian American artists who had an Asian American consciousness. Because of the Asian American Jazz Festival, Jang became involved with the Asian movement.

Jang was drawn to the music of John Coltrane in high school. He feels that McCoy Tyner, Coltrane's pianist, is a model for using Asian instruments, pentatonic scales, and bass drones. In Jon's words, "What's going to make my music more human is to address the question of the specificity of my experience as an Asian American; part of this is to develop an Asian American cultural expression.... Fred and I are pioneers in the sense that there wasn't music beforehand that Asian Americans and African Americans share artistically" (Jang 1987).

Emphasis on collective improvisation is a strong characteristic of Jang's music. He said: "In composing, I have some musical ideas but I think it is most important to consolidate everybody's ideas and blend them into one. To me the collective improvisation is really powerful. Music is a way of expressing the truth of humanity, and people want to hear the truth" (ibid.). In his compositions, there is always plenty of room for individual musicians to improvise, and the result is a lush orchestration with maximum input from his fellow musicians.

His approach to Chinese music is to use Chinese melodies as themes in his compositions. For example, "Butterfly Lovers' Song" is based on a theme from a Chinese regional opera and "Bruce Lee" is based on a Taiwanese folk song, "High Mountain Green." He feels that since these melodies are so beautiful, they are fertile sources for development. His creative revolutionary arrangements transform them into powerful political works.

Jang has a long history of involvement with social organizations. In the late 1970s, when he worked at Stanford University, he experienced racism. He was a labor union organizer even though he was one of only a few Chinese workers in the union. In the 1980s, he was active in the Chinese National Movement, specifically bringing together the Chinese immigrants and the American born. He was involved with the Chinese Progressive Association and taught the citizenship class for a year in 1989. Though Jang claimed that he was never a Marxist, he was a member of the radical revolutionary organization known as the League of Revolutionary Struggle, which no longer exists.

In order to expand the creative control of Asian American musicians of their own music and to break up the citadel of the recording industry, Jang developed Asian Improv Records with other Asian American musicians. Using as its model the "self-reliance" movement of black artists of the 1970s, Asian Improv Records provides a record label for Asian American musicians to produce their own records. There are about 10 albums produced and Jang hopes that their efforts might inspire others to follow.

In 1990, Jang received a three-year Artist in Communities residency from California Arts Council. Therefore, he is working more closely with the community. He has started a jazz workshop in the heart of San Francisco's Chinatown at Cameron House, which is a non-profit organization providing sanctuary, counsel, and activities for Chinese immigrants since the last century. As part of the program, Jang also gives free jazz piano lessons to community members. His class was immediately full.

Jang's teaching career is not only limited to the community. In the spring of 1992, he was invited by the Ethnic Studies Program at U.C. Berkeley to offer a course on Asian American Creative Music/Jazz. This is the first time such a course has ever been offered in this country. I think this pioneer work will be followed, as the study of cultural expressions of ethnic groups attracts attention more and more. Jang is also invited by the Central Conservatory of Music in Beijing, China, to give master classes on jazz piano.

I would now like to talk about Jang's three compositions and play musical examples. The first one is "Reparations Now!."

In the early 1980s, the redress movement became strong in the Japanese community in the Bay Area. Jang lived in San Jose at that time and was close to the Japanese community there. Since this is part of the civil rights movement for Japanese Americans and all Asian Americans, Jang became deeply involved. Jang recalls that during the 45th anniversary of the 9066 Executive Order (for the internment of Japanese Americans in 1942), a candle light vigil was held in San Jose. The parade walked around two street blocks with the San Jose Taiko group among them playing taikos to accompany the parade. The expression was very powerful. The success of the Japanese American redress movement is equivalent to the victory of the African American civil rights movement and the drum beat is a metaphor for the triumphant battle.

"Reparations Now" has four movements, with the subtitle of "An Asian American Koncerto for Jazz Orchestra and Taiko." The first movement, Redress Blues, is dedicated to Akira "Jackson" Kato, the nisei (second-generation Japanese American) gardener. Jang heard the "blues" in Jackson's story about homes and lands taken away during W.W.II. The second movement, Ganbaro, means "preservation and self-determination" in the Japanese language.

The third movement, "Reparations Now," uses a taiko rhythm as a principal motif. This rhythm conveys the feeling of a horse's gallop. The baritone saxophone plays an ostinato in the same rhythm, and the syncopated 16th notes in the second half of the motif express an urgency and impatience for the demand Reparations Now.

The fourth movement was added later to celebrate the victory of the redress movement, since the Reagan government passed an ordinance in 1988 to pay compensation to the interned Japanese. Tanko Bushi is originally the Japanese coal miners' dance music that most Japanese would want to move with. Jang divides the movement into two parts: the first one opens with the dirge, or hymn-like simplicity of a folk song and then moves to the second part, a hilarious, humorous, and happy celebration. This reminds one of the common practice of New Orleans funeral band procession music, which plays a slow dirge to the cemetery and a fast jubilant music on their return. (ex. 1 Jang uses a Japanese mode to unify the themes of all four movements and gives them an Asian sound.)

The second piece I want to introduce is a piano piece, "The Butterfly Lovers' Song." The theme of this music was from a regional Shaoxin opera, "Liang Shan-bo and Zhu Ying-tai," which is a household favorite in China. The tragic love story during the Chinese feudal society has evoked much compassion. After the death of the two lovers, their spirits metamorphose into a pair of butterflies to symbolize their protest to the society and their pursuit of freedom. This music was introduced to Jang by Mabel Tang of the Chinese

Progressive Association, and Jang was asked to perform this piece during the celebration of the Association's 16th anniversary in 1990. Since then, this piece has stayed in Jang's repertoire and has become a favorite among his Chinese audience. (ex. 2 The example demonstrates how Jang uses specific pianistic techniques such as tremolo to imitate the "yangqin" and how he transforms the theme into an African American style.)

The third piece I will mention is "Tienanmen!." These are the composer's own words in the program notes: "Similar to Duke Ellington's greatest work, 'Black, Brown and Beige,' which extolled the contributions of African American people, 'Tienanmen!' expresses American-born Chinese and Chinese struggle for democracy and freedom." This piece has an introduction and five movements: "Tears From the Peaceful Gate," "Great Wall, Gold Mountain," "I Feel The Thunder In My Heart," "Come Sunday, June 4, 1989," and "Fifth Modernization: Democracy 1st Amendment: Freedom of Expression." In addition to Jang's nine-piece Pan Asian Arkestra, two Chinese traditional musicians are featured. Zhang Yan is a virtuoso *guzheng* master and Liu Qi-Chao is versatile on *sheng, erhu,* and *suona.* (Ex. 3 The musical example shows how Jang blends the traditional Chinese instruments with the jazz orchestra.)

In this piece Jang attempts to create an epic which sets the history of early Chinese immigrants into the long historical river of China by using the railroad workers' song as emblem for the former and "Mengjiang Nu Crying at the Great Wall" as a symbol for the ancient China. In another direction, Jang is looking ahead for the future of a democratic China and the possible connection and contribution of Chinese Americans to their ancestral land. "That dream is the struggle of a generation of Chinese, who, like a larva waiting to be transformed, yearn for the strong and beautiful wings of a butterfly." This quote from Shen Tong, the Chinese freedom fighter, ends the program notes and it seems to be Jang's wish as well.

Although still far from commercially successful, Jang's national and international reputation is rising, and his music has made a profound impact on the community. One response from the audience reads:

> ...Over the past three years, in my attempt to figure out where I stand in relation to my Asian identity, I have become increasingly interested in the ways in which Asians born in North America assert themselves, speak out against stereotyped images that aim to suppress and silence Asian voices: the stereotypes of meek, quiet, studious, hardworking people, men, depicted as asexual, women as exotic. It is really inspiring for me to see individuals such as Fred Ho and Jon Jang step out and signify through their art: "Hey! Take me seriously! I am a

real human being! I care about such-and-such social and political issues!" (P.C. Waxer 10/29/91)

The history of Asian immigrants in this country is a history of oppression. The exclusion law for Chinese before 1947 and the concentration camp experience of the Japanese during W.W.II are vivid examples. The race discrimination situation for Asians is hardly better than for African Americans, and this reality spurs committed artists like Jon Jang and Fred Ho to take a stand. In the forefront of the Asian American movement, together with artists of other Asian descent in theater, dance, and other musical forms, they attempt to forge a new Asian American cultural expression. To incorporate their common experience in the new world, they took something in from their host culture, the music expression of the African Americans who have endured similar oppressions in this country. Yet, it is not borrowing, since it is the music with which they grew up, such as rock, big band, and jazz. Blending them with their own and other Asian traditions, their music is meant to bring unity to all generations of Asians and new immigrants, and to connect with other groups that share similar goals. They consciously take the African American movement of the 1960s as a catalyst to alleviate inequality and stimulate social and political change.

Above all, the image and conviction expressed in Jang's work is a positive and truthful one which a young generation of Asian Americans can relate to and be proud of. Their use of traditional culture is not to explore its exoticism so their wares can sell. They are searching for their roots and attempting to inherit the values, ethos, and teachings of an ancient civilization in order to cherish a new cultural identity in this country. The group of Asian Americans to which their music especially appeals is going to be significant in all fields of society, and therein lies the future of Jang's music.

Works Cited

Hing, Alex. "Forbidden City, U.S.A." In *Gidra, 1970–1990. The XXth Anniversary Edition*: 1990. 26–27.

Hom, Marlon. *Songs of the Gold Mountain*. Berkeley: University of California Press, 1986.

Houn, Fred Wei-han. "Asian American Music and Enpowerment." *View on Black American Music, 1985–88* 3 (1988): 27–32.

Jang, Jon. "We All Don't Sound Alike." *View on Black American Music, 1985–88* 3 (1988):33–38.

Jang, Jon. Interview by the San Francisco KQED Public Television Station in the "Creative Mind" series. 7 July 1991.

Jang, Jon. Interview by the University of California at Berkeley KALX Radio
Station. 22 February 1987.
Riddle, Ronald. "Music Clubs and Ensembles in San Francisco's Chinese
Community." In *Eight Urban Musical Cultures: Tradition and Change*. Ed.
Bruno Nettl. Champaign, Ill.: University of Illinois Press, 1978.
Wang, Ling-chi. "Roots and Changing Identity of the Chinese in the U.S."
Daedalus 120/2 (1991): 181–206.

Chinese American Music in Southern California

WEN-HSIUNG YEN
Department of Ethnomusicology and Systematic Music,
University of California, Los Angeles

This paper surveys Chinese American music in Southern California, including instrumental music, choral music, theatrical music, and other genres.[1] The first part of this paper focuses on historical developments, including a survey of the literature, educational institutions, cultural organizations, and performance troupes from abroad, mainly from Taiwan since 1949. The second part will deal with the social context of music, emphasizing the political, social, and religious implications. In particular, this paper will focus on the relationship between music and political function, ritual purpose, and social demand.

Survey of the Literature. Ronald William Riddle was one of the scholars who was involved with Chinese American music in the United States. He published several articles and monographs on Chinese American music, including "Music Clubs and Ensembles in San Francisco's Chinese Community" in *Eight Urban Musical Cultures Tradition and Change* and Chinatown's Music: A History and Ethnography of Music and Music-Drama in San Francisco Chinese Community.[2] In this article, he states that "Studies of social and cultural aspects of overseas-Chinese communities have rarely touched upon the phenomenon of organized music-making by amateur groups" (223). The repertoire of Chinese instrumental ensembles includes Chinese traditional classical music, Chinese modern classical music, Chinese and American dance band music, Western classical music, and contemporary music.

The Los Angeles Chinatown Corporation, the Chinese Chamber of Commerce of Los Angeles, and the Chinese Historical Society of Southern California sponsored Chinatown's 50th Anniversary. They

---

[1] This paper is a preliminary study and is based on field work consisting of interviews and 20 years of personal experience as an insider. The initial title was "Chinese American Music in Southern California: Historical Development and Social Context." Chinese music, though thought to be the same as Chinese American music, is, in fact, quite different. Chinese American music has been acculturated to reflect both the Chinese and American culture rather than just the Chinese. Chinese American music is characterized by a style that fuses Chinese and American musical elements; and this fusion has resulted in unique stylistic features.

[2] Ronald Riddle's "Music Clubs and Ensembles in San Francisco's Chinese Community" is a good survey on Peking opera and instrumental ensemble in the Bay Area.

published a booklet which included several articles describing the historical development and past activities of Chinatown. The articles, written by the members of the Historical Society of Southern California, are "Chinatown Landmarks" by Cy Wong, "Pioneer Families Share Their History" by Ella Yee Quan, "The Golden Years of Los Angeles Chinatown: the Beginning" by Suellen Cheng and Munson Kwok, "Los Angeles Chinatown 1958–1968" by Beverly M. Hom and Lillian Fong, "Chinatown—the Present" by Karen Lew.

From this booklet, Chinese musical life can be seen by looking at some photographs which date back to 1938. The instruments shown in the booklet include a trumpet, two cornets, and a snare drum (32). Further in this booklet, one can see a musical band performing at the Grand Opening Ceremony of the new Chinatown (46). There are eight players in the picture; the conductor stands in front of the band holding the trumpet in his left hand. The musicians are wearing dark uniforms with boat-shaped hats. There are two trumpets on the right side, a clarinet and a Sousaphone on the left, and a military drum on the platform. The ceremony was evidently being held on Hill Street in the afternoon, as the shadows suggest. The long banner with 10 Chinese characters meaning "Grand Opening Ceremony of New Chinatown" visible in the picture is still seen today in Chinatown. Similarly, the plaque with four Chinese characters on the gate can be translated as "The Gathering of Outstanding Chinese" also still exists. On the right corner, one can see the national flag of the Republic of China, and on the left corner, one can see the flag of the United States. In the booklet, one article mentions Peter Soo Hoo, Sr. as an important music maker who formed an orchestra and a glee club.

New Chinese Immigrants. According to historical records, Chinese laborers came to California from the Guangdong province to construct railroads. These men lived in Chinatown, and for entertainment, they attended Cantonese operas performed by troupes from Guangdong and Hong Kong. The Chinese American community in California was established during the mid-19th century. From 1870 to 1890, this theater gave nightly performances starring local amateur musicians.

Being a small ethnic minority in Western society, Chinese Americans were also greatly influenced by the Western musical tradition. For example, the Protestant missionaries' church hymns were favored by new settlers, particularly the younger generation. The popular symphonic-music brass bands and dance orchestras of the West dominated in older society during the first part of the 20th century.

H. M. Lai, in the foreword of Riddle's book *Flying Dragons, Flowing Streams* stated that during the first part of the 20th century, a form of chamber music, now known as Cantonese music, developed from the music used to accompany Cantonese opera performances. Western instruments such as the violin and saxophone were introduced into the Cantonese musical ensemble. Chinese composers began to adopt some Western techniques. Arrangements of classical and folk instrumental orchestral compositions, as well as Chinese popular songs and music, also became popular in the San Francisco Bay area (see Lai 5).

With regards to Chinese music in present-day educational institutions, the following questions are considered:

How many educational institutions in Southern California provide a Chinese American music program as part of their curriculum? Are these classes well-attended by students? What is the student's main interest in taking this kind of music? Who is in charge of this instruction? What is the instructor's special field? How does the group select its repertoire? Do performers keep or discard traditional elements, and if so, how? How do audiences react to the music when the group performs?

In 1936, the Federal Theatre Project of the Work Progress Administration published *Chinese Theatres in America* by Peter Chu, Lois M. Foster, Nadia Larova, and Steven C. May.

Music in New Chinatown. The old Chinatown was located in the Union Station area. Because of the construction of the railroad and station, Chinese people were forced to move to the new Chinatown in the 1930s.

Peter Soo Hoo, Sr. was an important figure in the introduction of Western music to the Chinese community. He graduated from the University of Southern California as an electrical engineer and was the first Chinese to be employed by the Department of Water and Power. He played the trumpet and, with family members and friends, formed one of the first western-style Chinese bands which participated in the Labor Day parade in Los Angeles and a parade in San Diego. He also played for local Chinese dances. Soo Hoo also organized the first Chinese orchestra of Western instruments, which played in Los Angeles theaters such as the Chinatown Orpheum Theater. In 1935–36, Soo Hoo formed a glee club that sang at the San Diego World's Fair in 1935–36. He also organized a Chinese Boy Scout drum and a bugle corps.[3] His son, Peter Soo Hoo, Jr., whom I met through Ella Yee Quan, told me that the band had about 25 players. His uncle, Monroe Leung, was a drum player and his cousin, Joe Tang, was a clarinet player. At the grand opening of new Chinatown in 1938, Peter Soo Hoo, Jr. was a 12-year-old boy. The spectacle was held with dragon and lion dances, fireworks, and both Western and Chinese bands. He knows about the Chinese band, but the number of members of the group and its repertoire must be investigated through Soo Hoo's family and his close friends.

---

[3]We can see a lion dance with drum and gong team and a Western-type marching band in *The Golden Years 1938–1988,* The Los Angeles Chinatown Corporation, June 25, 1988.

The number of Chinese immigrants rose sharply after the passage of the Immigration and Nationality Act in 1965. I prepared a chart which indicates the population of Los Angeles County from the 1990 Census. We can see that in some cities, the Asian population is very high Music and language are vitally important parts of the society—that of the new world functioning as a symbol of assimilation and adaptation and that of the old as a means of preserving cultural identity (see Table 1 below).

Chinese American culture is a very important part of "the melting pot culture" in the United States, particularly in California, with respect to acculturation factors, historical construct, social maintenance, and individual creation and experience. The Chinese music, dance, theater, and other related art forms were brought by Chinese people who came from Taiwan, Hong Kong, and mainland China. The genre of Chinese music includes traditional classical instrumental music such as pipa, qin, erhu, sheng, cheng, and various percussion instruments.

Table 1. **Asian Population in Some Citites in Southern California**

	City Population	Asian or Pacific Islander Population
Los Angeles County	8,863,164	954,485
City of Los Angeles	3,484,793	341,721
Monterey Park	59,096	34,152
Alhambra	82,106	31,313
Cerritos	53,223	24,046
Rosemead	51,617	17,725
Hacienda Heights	52,354	14,283
San Gabriel	37,120	12,044
Arcadia	48,277	11,321
Pasadena	131,591	10,678
Temple	30,549	5,890
South Pasadena	23,936	5,086
San Marino	12,959	4,189

Source: 1990 Census of Population of California

Music in Educational Institutions. The Institute of Ethnomusicology at UCLA was established in 1955. Robert Stevenson edited the Directory of UCLA Ethnomusicology Graduates in 1977; it includes five Ph.D. dissertations and several MA theses on Chinese music: David Ming-Yueh Liang's Master's thesis, "Chinese Chin: Its History and Music" and Ph.D. dissertation, "The Art of Yin-Jou Techniques for the Seven-Stringed Zither" (1973); Frederic Lieberman's dissertation, "The Chinese Long Zither Chin: A Study based on the Mei-an Chin Pu;" Marjory Liu's dissertation, "Tradition and Change in Kunqu Opera;" Nora Yeh's thesis, "The Yueh Chu Style of Cantonese Opera with an analysis of 'The Legend of Lady White Snake'" (1972); Wen-hsiung Yen's thesis, "The Chinese Sheng and its Music: Theory and Practice" (1971).

Later dissertations include I-To Loh's "Tribal Music of Taiwan: with Special Reference to the Ami and Puyuma Styles" (1980) and Nora Yeh's "Nanguan Music in Taiwan: A Little-Known Classical Tradition" (1984).

"Musical Cultures of the World," taught at UCLA, is a survey that teaches the role of music in society and its relationship to other arts. The content of world music is focused on people, land, custom, religion, and musical life. The musical material includes scale structure, instruments, musical forms, tuning systems, and performance standards. Each year is divided into A, B, and C sections for each quarter, and the C section is music related to south Asia, Southeast Asia, and the Far East. Chinese music is always taught as an important part of this instructional course.

Tsun Y. Lui, a pipa and qin master, came to UCLA in 1960. He taught Chinese music and instrumental ensemble until he retired in 1991. The classes, "Music of China," "History of Chinese Opera," and "Studies in Chinese Instrumental Music," were listed in the 1990–91 UCLA general catalog.

The Chinese Student Association at UCLA formed a Chorus on Campus in May 1970. I was invited to conduct, and I presented a concert at Schoenberg Hall in December 1974. My new compositions, "Sheng Mu Song" (Ave Maria) and "Song of a Chinese Student" were included in the concert program. Chinese folk songs were introduced and sung by the Chinese-language school students.

New Compositions on Campus. The Department of Music, UCLA and *Modern Tunes* presented a concert by Ting Lien Wu, a doctoral student in composition on April 9, 1985 at Popper Theater, Schoenberg Hall. The program included "Three Chinese Poems" (1982), "Dream in the Dusk" (1982), "Mistake" (1979), and "Improvisation No. 1 for 12 players" (1985).

Wen-hsiung Yen organized his first concert at Schoenberg Hall, UCLA in 1974. Since then, nine public concerts have been held at universities and colleges in Southern California, including UCLA (1974, 1982), University of Southern California (1976, 1980), California State University of Los Angeles (1986, 1989, 1991), Woodbury University (1987), and Pasadena City College (1992). The invitation of The Chinese Music Orchestra of Southern California to "China Night" included California Institute of Technology (1980, 1981), UCLA (1980), California State University, Northridge (1986). New compositions and folk song arrangements were presented in concerts. The following are some examples:

1. For chorus: "Reminiscence of the Sun-Moon Lake in Taiwan" (words by Stephen K. Yee, music by Wen-hsiung Yen, sung by The Voice of Los Angeles Chinese Chorus, conducted by Hsin-hsin Yen, 1986); "The Green Mountain of Taiwanese Folk Song" (arranged by Wen-hsiung Yen, sung by The Yue You Chorus, conducted by Wen-hsiung Yen, 1989); "Ode to My Home Land " (words by Stephen K Yee, music by Wen-hsiung Yen, sung by The Yue You Chorus and Southern California Chinese Catholic Choir, conducted by Wen-hsiung Yen, 1992).

2. For vocal solo: "Pondering on the Lake Bank" (words by Chi-Ching Wang, music by Wen-hsiung Yen, sung by Sophia Lai Kan, 1986); "Picnic Near the Pond" (words by Yu-Hsin, music by Wen-hsiung Yen, sung by Sophia Lai Kan, 1986); "The Little Stream" (Yun Nan Folk Song, arranged by Wen-hsiung Yen, sung by Sophia Lai Kan, 1986); "Thinking of Love" (Taiwanese folk song, arranged by Wen-hsiung Yen, sung by Sophia Lai Kan, 1986); "Yu Mei Ren" (words by Li Hou-Chu, music by Wen-hsiung Yen, sung by Theresa Cheng, 1991); "Wang Zhao Jun" (arranged by Wen-hsiung Yen, sung by Theresa Cheng, 1991).

3. Music for Instrumental Ensemble: Wen-hsiung Yen's "San Yang Kai Tai" (1980), "The Spring Dance" (1986), "Oh! Susanna and Mei Zai Zhong Hua" (1989), "Plum Flower Are Tracing in the Sunshine" (music arranged by Wen-hsiung Yen, 1992).

Chinese Music Groups in Southern California. There were only five to seven chorus groups in Southern California from 1970 to 1980. Between 1980 to 1990, the number increased to more than 10. They were: Zhong Hua (the Chinese Choral Society), Lo Sheng (the Voice of L.A. Chinese Chorus), Ai Yue (the Philharmonic Chorus), Shao Yin (the Melodia Sinica), Yue You (the Chinese Choral of Southern California), Ya Yin (the Arcadia Women Chorus), Nan Wan (the South Bay Chorus), Hua Sheng (the Chinese Voice Chorus), Rui Sheng (the Lucky Voice Chorus), and Mu Xing (the Jupiter Chorus). Their conductors were generally professional musicians, and the membership varied from 20 to 50 or more.

The Voice of L.A. Chinese Chorus was formed in 1980 and made its first public performance in 1981. In 1990, the group held its eighth concert at San Gabriel Civic Auditorium. In addition, The Huo Guo (The Festive Singers) was a small choral group with emphasis on harmonic effection. The members numbered less than the other chorus. They recently presented the Hakka Music Culture of Taiwan.

The Chinese Choral Society was established by Peter Kwong, a motel businessman, and conducted by Professor Kwan Lin, a well-known tenor singer who had studied vocal music in Italy. He had worked at the Chinese Broadcasting Corporation in Taiwan before he came to California. Lin formed the Jupiter Chorus in 1988. Many members of his family are singers, including his wife and daughter-in-law. He always invited a few professional guest vocalists to participate in his once-a-year concert.

The Chinese Cultural and Arts Festival was started in 1989; it organized many performance groups in Southern California and provided financial support to each group with the Overseas Chinese Affairs Commission of The Republic of China, the Philharmonic Chorale (1987), and the Jupiter Chorus (1988). Only two choral groups participated at the 1990 Chinese Cultural and Arts Festival. In 1991, more choral groups attended the Chinese Cultural and Arts Festival; and the Chinese Choral Society, the Jupiter Chorus, the Yue You Chorus, the Arcadia Women Chorus, and the Festive Singers Chorus had their public performances. In 1992, the participating groups were almost the same as in 1991, but the Southern California Chinese Catholic Choir joined the Yue You Chorus to sing a new composition, "Ode to My Home Land," words by Stephen K. Yee, music by Wen-hsiung Yen.

The Yue You Chorus was formed in 1987 by Wen-hsiung Yen. At first, it rehearsed at the Chinese Culture Center in Chinatown. During 1988, the chorus moved to the Happy Tune Music Store in Monterey Park. Since 1989, the Chorus has practiced at Arcadia Mormon Church. Their repertoire was Chinese folk songs and Chinese arts songs. Taiwanese folk and popular tunes were also included.

The most important organizations supporting Chinese music, dance, and theater in California are: Southern California Council of Chinese Schools(1975), the Chinese Historical Society of Southern California (1975), Chinese Culture Service of Los Angeles (1978), Chinese Cultural Center of Chinese Council of North America Affairs (1985), Buddha's Hsi Lai Temple (1988), the Joint Association of Chinese Social and Cultural Organizations in Southern California (1987), Chinese American Dance Association (1987), and Chinese American Musicians Association of Southern California (1990). They not only provided a place for meeting and performing, but also organized the events and gave financial aid.

The Third Confucius Commemorative Day Ceremony, with all its related activities, was held October 26, 1984 (the first and second were held in San Francisco in 1982 and 1983). The content of the ceremony included essay content on Confucianism, outstanding-teachers' awards, a Confucian cultural heritage exhibition, a conference on Confucianism, and a special journal publication. The Confucius Commemorative Day Ceremony was a big event which attracted many hundreds of politicians and leaders from state and local communities—some important personalities were even invited from Taiwan. More than 200 sponsoring community organizations participated, and many thousands attended the activities. The Chinese traditional instruments, such as bian-zhong (a set of bells), bian-qing (a set of stone chimes) yao-gu (shaken drum with two beating beads), te-zhong (the big sonorous bell), and many worship utensils and equipment were shipped from Taiwan. Ceremonial experts such as Pien-Li Chung and Huang-hsin Hsia were also invited to guide the ritual and ceremonial music. Members of the Chinese Music Orchestra of Southern California participated in the ritual music. The number of musicians reached 30, and a group of Ba-yi dancers and over a hundred of the Chinese school students participated. The music was played and sung by local musicians, both Chinese and American. The Confucius Commemorative Day Ceremony had many political, religious, social, musical, and educational purposes. Yuen-Sang Wong, in his article, "My Impressions of the Confucius Commemorative Day Ceremony," stated that, "Confucian teaching has depth and scope, is simple and popular, solid and timeless, and applicable anywhere." These activities led not only Chinese people to respect Confucian thought, but also Americans, Japanese, Koreans, and Vietnamese.

Overseas Influence on Chinese American Music. The Overseas Chinese Affairs Commission has consistently striven to strengthen both Chinese language education and cultural activities outside of China. An "Overseas Chinese Arts Festival" has been arranged for more than a dozen cities in the world with large populations of overseas Chinese, such as New York, San Francisco, and Los Angeles. This event has been held since 1989, and it links artistically talented, overseas-Chinese individuals and performing troupes. The purpose of the Chinese Arts Festival was to promote Chinese cultural exchange, particularly in the fields of music, theater, dance, and the arts. For example, there were 38 events in Southern California between April and June of the 1992 season. The performance arts included five Chinese opera clubs and one Cantonese club, three Chinese instrumental groups, and five choral societies.

Chinese Performance Troupes that Have Visited Southern California. The Central Traditional Orchestra made its premiere U.S. concert tour in 1984 and performed at the Olympic Arts Festival. The Central Traditional Orchestra is considered to be among the highest-ranking musical performing organizations in China. The orchestra was formed by 18 outstanding musicians, among whom are Lufeng Ding on erhu, Tiechui Wang on di, Zhengyin Xu on pipa, Huizhong Wang on sheng, and Yuxia Wu on pipa. The repertoire included "Prince Qin Storms the Enemy Lines," "Flowers and Moonlight on the River in Spring," "Dance of Yao," "Dark is the Night," "Jiang Jun Ling" (the

General's Order), "Thunder after Drought," "Peace and Joy," "Rain Drops on the Plantain," "Butterflies Among Flowers," "Pluming Bloom: Three Variations," "Ducks Quarreling and the Tiger Gnashing its Teeth," "Spring Has Come to the Yi River," "A Southern Xinjiang Dance," "Song of Joy," and "Tanci Three-Six."

Since the Olympic Art Festival held in Los Angeles, several traditional musical ensembles, Chinese zither groups, the Peking Opera, Taiwanese folk opera, a western symphonic orchestra performing Chinese composition, and choral groups from Taiwan and mainland China have visited the United States. Among the groups were the Han-Tang Classical Music Institute, led by Mei-er Chen and performing in several famous universities such as Harvard University, University of Michigan, UCLA (1986); Xiang Yin (Homeland Sound goodwill troupe (1990); Fu Xing Theater Troupe, led by Lan-jing Yen (1987; Taipei Municipal Teacher's College Alumni Chorus, led by Tian-Fei Xu (1988); Ya Yin (Elegant Music), led by Xiao-Chuan Kou; He-zi Qin Xuan Cheng troupe, led by Roung Shen Dong (1989); Taipei and Taichung Chen-hsing Chinese Zither Orchestra, led by He-ming Chung, Der-Dong Wei, and his brother, Der-Liang Wei (1989); the Symphony Orchestra of National Taiwan Normal University, conducted by Chang Tah-sheng (1991); Chinese Zhong Hua Peking Opera troupe (1991); Taipei City Symphony Orchestra, conducted by Chiu-sen Chen (1991); Hsin Ho Hsin Taiwanese Opera Troupe, led by Qing-Liu xiang (1991), and the Mystique of Tibet Zaxi-Luge, led by Puchong (1992).

These performing troupes bring to the overseas Chinese communities good will, political messages, and cultural exchange with their musical performances. The sponsors and audiences are different. The government officials and local community leaders have been invited to express their welcome. Because these visits were of cultural exchanges, the troupes have selected their repertoire according to audience preference. The events have been held on national holidays such as the Double Tenth (the Tenth of October) of the Republic of China.

Evergreen Chorus was established in 1989 by several senior citizens who are Chinese immigrants. Their average age is 68 years . They have been invited to sing in holiday rallies and ceremonial gatherings. The conductor is Zhou Sheng, who is from Taiwan, where he was a singer and had worked for a television station.

Another musical group is called Song Bo Chinese Opera Club, which was formed in 1986. The co-founders were Ping Wang, Wentsai Yang, and Zhang-pan Tsai. This group gathers at the Langley Center, a public facility in Monterey Park for rehearsal. Since 1988, the group has performed regularly in public. They raised about $44,000 for earthquake victims in San Francisco and some disabled groups.

Repertoire. The repertoire of Chinese instrumental music, including "Melody of the Four Seasons," "The Moon is High," "Martial Arts," "Raging Water," "Blossoming of Snowpea Flowers," "Bow Dance," "Plum Flowers Are Tracing in the Sunshine," "Colorful Clouds Chasing the Moon," "The General's Order," "Celebration of the Prosperous Harvest," and "Dance of the Awakening Lion," are played as an ensemble by the Chinese Music Orchestra of Southern California, the Spring Thunder Chinese Music Association, and the Cheng-Hsin Chinese Zither Orchestra of Los Angeles.

The Asian Philharmonic Symphony Orchestra, in its second annual concert, presented "The Great Music of China," which included "Chang O the Moon Goddess Fleeing for the Moon" by Tsang-Houei Hsu, "Little Sisters of the Grassland" by Zuqiang Wu Yen Qiao Wang and Dehei Liu, "Reflection of the Moon in Er-Chuan" by Yanjun Hua and arranged by Zuqiang Wu, and "Kotzuhsi Fantasia Suite No. 1" by Wei Li. The concert was conducted by Ming-Tsung Fang and was held at the San Gabriel Civic Auditorium on July 14, 1990. On October 19, 1991, the Orchestra held its third annual concert. They introduced "Five Pieces for Hu-qin," arranged by Gang Chen. The hu-qin soloist was Jiebing Chen. Miss Chen used the banhu, jinghu, gaohu, and erhu to play this rearranged piece from a northeastern Chinese folk melody, an excerpt from the Peking Opera, a Cantonese melody, and a new composition. The "Four Seasons of Formosa" was arranged by a Japanese musician, Misaaki Hayakawa. The popular tunes were "Spring: Loving the Year Round," "Butterfly Nectar," "Plum Blossom Country," "Summer: the Ploughman's Song," "Dumplings Meat Dumplings!," "In the Cold Pouring Rain," "Autumn: Formosan Evergreen," "Midnight Sorrow," "Autumn Melancholy," "Winter: Bittersweet Flowers," "Dockside Farewell," and "The Rain-soaked Bird." Of these 12 songs, some are folk songs and the rest are Taiwanese popular songs.

The most active Chinese instrumentalists are Pui-Yuen Lui (pi-pa, Qin), Yu Xue-Hong (sheng), Zhang Yi-cheng (di, xun), Li You (erhu), Li Chi (er-hu), Yao-hwa Gao (erhu), David Liu (Cheng and di), Xiao Wu (pipa), Zhiming Han (Yangqin), Cynthia Hsin-Mei Hsiang (cheng), Mei-Ye Ma (pipa), Lang C. Chu (cheng), Rene Wu (erhu), Shu-feng He (pipa and cheng), and Jin-Sheng Jin (erhu). They all have had solo roles during the past two years in Southern California. Those listed here are artists I know of, some have performed with Chinese Music Orchestra of Southern California, some are through mass media.

The repertoire for Chinese instrumental solo pieces such as "Galloping," "Here He Comes" ," Horse Racing", 'Reflection of the Moon on the er-Chuan Lake" ,and "Galloping through the Meadows" are often played by erhu solo artists. "Encountering Hurricane", "Song of Returning Fisherman", "Spring, the Innocence", "The Dance of Yi Tribe" are for cheng solo. The most popular pipa solo piece is "Ambush".

The Chinese American Musicians Association of Southern California was established by Wen-hsiung Yen in 1991. The aim of the Association was to combine the Chinese Music Orchestra of Southern California and the Chinese Choral Society of Southern California as a cultural and musical association, which would preserve Chinese musical culture and unite professional and non-professional musicians. These two musical groups performed for Harmonic Week in Monterey Park in October 1990. The Church of Jesus Christ of Latter-Day Saints in Arcadia also invited these groups to perform to celebrate the Chinese New Year in 1991. The repertoire included the instrumental ensembles "Sights and Sounds of Spring," "Jubilation All Around," and "Rosy Clouds Chase the Bright Moon," played by the Chinese Music Orchestra of Southern California, conducted By Wen-hsiung Yen. "Happy Encountering" for di solo and "Resentment in the Palace" for xun (ocarina) solo were played by Yi-cheng Zhang, accompanied by his wife, He Ning, on piano or synthesizer. "Reflection of Moon on the Er-chuan" and "Galloping through the Meadows" for erhu solo were played by Jin-sheng Jin, and accompanied by his wife, Yuan-pei Wang, on yang-qin (the dulcimer).

Patriotic Songs for Political Gathering. On October 7, 1989, Taiwan Benevolent Association of California and Yong Ho Sister City Committee jointly sponsored the flag-raising ceremony in Borents Park, just next to Monterey Park City Hall. The rally was to celebrate the Double Tenth, a national holiday of the Republic of China. The participants totaled about 2,000 immigrants, mainly from Taiwan. The celebration included a dragon and a lion dance with drums and gongs, Kung Fu demonstration and choral singing. As the president of Taiwan Benevolent Association of California, I arranged three patriotic songs: "Gou Qi Ge" (The Song of the National Flag), "Mei Hua" (the Song of Plum Flower), and "Zhong Hua Ming Gou Song" (the Praise Song of the Republic of China). All participants were asked to sing together.

Chinese music, particularly popular songs and patriotic songs, can be heard on Chinese-holiday gatherings—especially Chinese New Year banquets and national holiday ceremonial events in restaurants or on the street. On the other hand, instrumental music is performed at the moon festival sponsored by the Chinese Historical Society of Southern California, and Los Angeles City Cultural Affairs, and Chinese Chamber of Commerce Association. The Lotus Festival sponsored by the Department of Recreation and Parks of Los Angeles has always attracted many thousands. The Chinese Music Orchestra of Southern California has participated and has performed from 1977 to 1981. "Oh! Susanna" and "Oh! Beautiful China" were rearranged for an ensemble form. This piece always receives a warm response from audiences since most are familiar with "Oh! Susanna."

The melody of "Oh! Susanna" is an American favorite. Its words and music were composed by Stephen Foster in the mid-19th century. "Oh! Susanna" became a favorite with the forty-niners and it was called the "theme song" of the California Gold Rush. Professor Wen-hsiung Yen rearranged this melody with one of the popular arts songs called Mei Zai Zhong Hua ("Oh! Beautiful China") for a Chinese traditional instrumental ensemble. The structure of the new piece is in D scale in a duple meter and four beats alternating with drums and gongs. The music has four sections with spirit and delight.

The repertoire of patriotic songs include "Mei-Hua" (the Song of Plum Flower), "Zhong Gou Ren" (a Chinese), "Zhong Hua Ming Guo Song" (To Praise the Republic of China). Some Chinese folk songs and Taiwanese folk songs are included; among them are "Wang Chun Feng" (a Hope with Spring Wind), and "Gao Shan Qing" (the Mountain is High and Green). The entertainment usually comes after the banquet or during the banquet. The artists are sometimes professional singers, movie stars, or singing figures. Vocal presentations are accompanied by the piano, synthesizer, or karaoke equipment. The tunes of the Peking Opera can also be heard occasionally at a dinner party. The language for these kinds of gatherings is Mandarin Chinese, but Cantonese and Taiwanese are used, too. For Cantonese and Mandarin speakers, an interpreter or a translator is needed for a political rally or at a large dinner party.

Musical Drama. There are more than 300 forms or styles of regional theatre in China. There are several forms or styles of musical theaters which have performed in Southern California Peking opera, Cantonese opera, Kun Qu, He-nan Bang, and Taiwanese opera. Characters in a Peking opera are primarily categorized, not by vocal range, as in the European opera, but by the character of person represented. There are four characters: the sheng, tan, ching, and chou. The elements of the Peking opera are singing, acting, speech, dancing, etc. The Peking opera is combination of arts such as poetry, vocal music, instrumental music, dancing, lighting, scenery setting, acrobatic movements, speech, and dialogue. The er-huang generally occurs in a more serious section and the xi-pi is livelier and merrier. The musical accompaniment is divided into wen-chang (the string instrument section) and wu-chang (the percussion section). The qing hu is the major instrument accompanying the principal singer. The other instruments include yue-qin (a two-string fiddle), san-xian (a three-string lute with a long neck), a so-na (the oboe), and wooden block, gong and cymbals.

Mei Lan-fang, a famous Peking Opera star, was invited to perform in the United States in 1930. Mei took New York's Broadway by storm and scored a triumphant artistic success. Mei Lan-fang and his troupe were received enthusiastically in Los Angeles, Chicago, and New York.

Irmgard Johnson wrote an article, "An Interview with the Son of Mei Lan-fang in Chinoperl" (1979–1980 no. 9 page 116).

The Chinese Opera Club of Los Angeles (COCLA) was first formed in 1963, according to Nancy Yuan, an actress of COCLA. The aim of COCLA is to promote the study and performance of traditional Chinese opera. In July 1965, a well known movie star, Lisa Lu, played the main role in the first performance at the University of Southern California. Since then, the group has given a public performance once a year. The repertoire of 1990 was Wang Jiang Ding at the East Los Angeles College, Monterey Park; the repertoire of 1992 was Romance of the West Chamber at Rosemead High School, Rosemead.

There was a group of the Peking opera in Chinatown before 1970. I made a field recording of rehearsal of the group when I was a graduate student at UCLA. *New Grove Dictionary of American Music* states that in the 1980s, music clubs organized by generations of northern Chinese continue to nurture and promote Peking opera. At that time, there were three clubs in Los Angeles, four in New York, and two in Washington, D.C.

There are at least 10 Chinese operas in Southern California, for example: the Chinese Opera Club of Los Angeles, the Da Han Tian Sheng Chinese Opera Club, the Chinese Opera Club of Southern California, the Song Bo Chinese Opera Club, the Overseas Chinese Opera Club, one Cantonese opera club, and one Kun-Qu club. Although there are more than 10 groups by name, some groups are very small, without enough instruments and costumes.

Seven Chinese opera groups attended the 1990 Chinese Arts Festival. They were the Chinese Peking Opera of Southern California, Hong Hong Guandongnese Opera Troupe, Chinese Opera Club of Los Angeles, Jiu Gu Chuan Sheng Opera Club, the Da Han Tian Sheng Opera Club, the Overseas Opera Club, and the Song Bo Opera Club. In 1991, Chinese Arts Festival, only five groups participated. They were The Yu Qu Opera troupe (the sponsor is the He-Nan Province Association), the Da Han Tian Sheng Opera Club, the Angel Apartment Chinese Opera Club, the Song Bo Opera Club, and the Chinese Peking Opera Club. Some groups only sang without any acting, such as the Song Bo and the Angel Opera group. In the 1992 Chinese Arts Festival, five groups participated: the Zhong Hua Guo Qu She, the Da Han Tian Sheng Opera Club, Chinese Opera Club of Los Angeles, Kai Xuan Musical Club (Cantonese Opera), and the Angel Opera Club. Each year, they have their different repertoires. Since the leading roles are difficult to perform, some principal actresses or actors were invited to perform in other groups. For example, Wendy Chang is the leading female role in the Da Han Tian Sheng group and the supporting role in the Chinese Opera Club of Los Angeles.

The Chinese Dance Festival was first held in June 1988 at Cypress and Pasadena. Its purpose was to promote Chinese cultural exchange and friendship by bringing together those who had a keen interest in Chinese dance.

The Chinese American Dance Association sponsored the 1992 Chinese Dance Festival at San Gabriel Civic Auditorium on June 19, 1992. The 10 dance groups that participated in this event were: Chinese American Dancing Group led by Jaw John Chang, Elegant Arts Institute led by Angela Lai, Fullerton Chinese Dance Club led by Cici Yuan, Hwa-Yi Chinese Ethnic Dance Co. led by Frank Que, I Tien Yu Dancing Center directed by Tien -Yu I, Los Angeles Chinese Folk Dancers led by Olivia Liou Ming, Yuan Chinese Classic and Folk Dance Troupe led by Sister Joan Chiang, Orange County Chinese Cultural Club led by Lyda Chee, Yen Yen Dance Group led by Donna Chen and Ling-Mei Lein, and Yi-Wu Dance Group led by Teresa Y. Chao. The Chinese Cultural Center of CCNAA office in Los Angeles has supported 68 events on Chinese performing arts from 1989 to 1992 (see Table 2). Among them were 34 musical concerts, 28 musical dramas and dramas, and six dances.

Table 2. **Analysis of Chinese Arts Festival of Southern California on Chinese Performing Arts, 1989–92**

Music	1989	1990	1991	1992	Total
Vocal	1	4	6	4	15
Instrumental	3	0	0	2	5
Variety	2	2	7	3	14
Musical Drama and Drama					
Peking Opera	5	6	4	6	21
Regional Opera	1	1	1	1	4
Modern Drama	2	0	1	1	3
Dance					
Performance	1	0	1	2	4
Competition	1	1	0	0	2
Total	15	14	20	19	68

Source: Chinese Cultural Center CCNAA Office in Los Angeles

Conclusion. The result of this research contributes to many fields of study in anthropology, linguistics, history, folklore, religion, and social sciences. The Chinese preserve their traditional musical culture by creative performances. To improve society, we need to work with other nationalities in order to reach a harmonic way of life. Many people feel that most youngsters are not interested in traditional Chinese musical theater and instrumental music, but we still see many American-born boys and girls learning Chinese folk dances or Chinese zheng or erhu and other instruments. We are also very happy to know many American friends who are interested in listening to and studying Chinese traditional music. For them, Chinese American music has an important role in the modern society.

Acknowledgments. The author of this article wants to thank his mentors at The Department of Ethnomusicology and Systematic Musicology, UCLA, Professor Nazir Jairazbhoy, Professor James Porter and Professor Timothy Rice for their constantly encouraged and valuable criticisms or suggestions.

Works Cited

Han, Kuo-Huang. "Chinese Music in America." In *East to West: Essays on Chinese Music.* Taipei: 1981. 79.

Jairazbhoy, N.A. and S.C. Devale, Eds. "Asian Music in North America." *Selected Reports in Ethnomusicology, VI.* Los Angeles: 1985.

Lai, Him Mark. "Cantonese Music." *East-West* 26 May 1971: 5.

Lieberman, F. *Chinese Music: An annotated Bibliography.* New York: 1970, second edition, 1979.

Los Angeles Chinatown Corporation. *The Golden Years 1938–1988.* Los Angeles: 1988.

Nettl, Bruno, ed. *Eight Urban Musical Cultures Tradition and Change.* University of Illinois Press, 1978.

Riddle, R. "Recent Trends in the Musical Life of America's Urban Chinese." *Chinese Historical Society of America Bulletin* XIV /3 (1979): 3.

Riddle, R. "The Cantonese Opera: A Chapter in Chinese American History." In *The Life, Influence, and the Role of the Chinese in the United States, 1776–1960.* Ed. T. Chinn. San Francisco: 1976. 40.

Smith, B.B. "Chinese Music In Hawaii." *Asian Music.* Vi/1–2 (1975): 225.

Yee, Sue, and Barbara Jean Lee, edited 1990. *Chinese Moon Festival.* Los Angeles: The Chinese Cultural and Community Center of Greater Los Angeles and the Chinese Historical Society of Southern California, 1990.

Yen, Wen-hsiung. *Chinese Musical Culture and Folk Songs.* Taipei: Zhong Wen Book Co., 1979.

Yen, Wen-hsiung. *The Yearbook of Chinese American Musicians Association of Southern California.* Los Angeles: 1990, 1991.

Zheng, Su de San. "Music and Migration: Chinese American Traditional Music in New York City." In *The World of Music.* International Institute for Comparative Music Studies and Documentation Vol. xxxii. No. 3 (1990).

Who Is Amy Ho and
Why Is She a Fortune Cookie?

LORRAINE DONG

Asian American Studies, San Francisco State University
San Francisco, California

Born in Taiwan on July 16, Year of the Dragon, Amy Ho is the daughter of Henry Ho, a Chinese businessman, and Pauline Ho, an American photojournalist.[1] Except for a few words, Amy cannot speak Chinese, but she does speak English fluently. She has lived in Australia, Thailand, London, and New York, and is currently attending a New Hampshire boarding school called the Alma Stephens School for Girls. Amy is introduced as a 13-year-old teenager, "short and athletic-looking," with "jet-black hair chopped off in a spiked punky style" (1:1).[2] Black is her favorite color, so her usual attire consists of black pants, black T-shirts, and a black beat-up motorcycle jacket. Amy sings, as well as writes songs and plays the guitar, and she enjoys listening to a wide assortment of music ranging from rock-n-roll and heavy metal to folk and Broadway musicals. Her hobbies include carpentry, pottery, photography, calligraphy, and modern dance. Athletically, she is active in ice-skating, swimming,

---

[1]It is unclear what Pauline Ho's ethnicity is because her physical features are never described. She does speak Chinese to her husband, but that does not necessarily mean she is of Chinese ancestry. The Year of the Dragon falls on 1976.

[2]In Wyeth, Sharon Dennis. *Pen Pals 1, Boys Wanted!* New York: Dell Publishing-Bantam Doubleday Dell Publishing Group, Inc., 1989. To date, there are 18 volumes of Pen Pals and two volumes of Super Special Pen Pals, all published by the same publisher, dating from September 1989 to August 1991. For the sake of simplicity, citations from the Pen Pals series will be followed by the volume number, a colon, and then the page number(s) in parentheses. Two "super special" volumes have been published and citations from these will be preceded with "SS."

jogging, calisthenics, soccer, basketball, and softball. Academically, she excels in math. And, last but not least, Amy proclaims herself to be "the fearless crusader for female equality" (SS2:110) and has appeared on front covers every month from 1989 to 1991. Who is this supergirl and what is her influence on Chinese American as well as non-Chinese American girls?

The late 1980s saw the rise of Asian American characters in pre-adult literature written by non-Asian Americans. Three such characters were conceptualized during this time period. They can be found in two popular reading series targeted for the eight- to twelve-year-old pre-teen female audience. These series are sometimes categorized in the bookstores as "intermediate" children literature. The first to emerge was a Japanese American named Claudia Kishi, created by Ann M. Martin. Claudia belongs to The Baby-Sitters Club series that inaugurated in 1986. Six years later, this series has published over 50 volumes, not counting the Little Sister, Super Special, and Mystery series that are spin-offs of the Baby-Sitters Club. In 1989, a new Asian American regular was introduced into the series. She is Emily Michelle Thomas Brewer, a two-year-old Vietnamese orphan adopted by the family of Kristy Thomas, president of the Baby-Sitters Club. Also, in that same year, a new pre-adult series surfaced with a regular Chinese American character. She is Amy Ho of the Pen Pals series, written by Sharon Dennis Wyeth. A total of 20 Pen Pals books (two of which are super specials) have been published. Both series have averaged about a book a month during their publication period.[3]

Of the three Asian American girls, two have many similarities. Claudia Kishi and Amy Ho are 13 years old, come from middle/upper-class families, live and/or go to school in American suburbia, have parents who are very concerned about their education, and belong to a very close-knit group of four girls, of which they are the only Asian among three Caucasian girls. The series deals with typical adolescent issues and adventures, such as friendship, money, clothes, curfews, school, parents, and dating. Widely read by teenage girls throughout the United States, it is important to analyze the impact these Asian American characters might have on its intended audience.

This paper focuses on one of these characters, Amy Ho. Due to time constraints, the analysis will cover only two features manifested in the character: her Chinese American identity and her independence and identity as a member of the female gender. Both reveal that

---

[3]It appears the Pen Pals series has ceased publication with Volume 18 (August 1991), whereas the Baby-Sitters Club series is still going strong as of September 1992 with Volume 57.

Sharon Dennis Wyeth has failed in Amy Ho to create a role model conducive for modern Chinese and non-Chinese American girls to emulate.

"My name is Amy Ho and I am Chinese-American [sic], but my family has lived all over the world because of dad's business" (1:66). This is how Amy begins to introduce herself in her first pen pal letter to Simmie Randolph III.[4] Just how she is depicted as Chinese American reveals either Wyeth's ignorance of the Chinese American experience or her profound understanding of what growing up in a Eurocentric environment can do to a Chinese American psychologically, culturally, and ethnically. Upon careful scrutiny, it appears that the former is more likely the case, compounded by the author's Eurocentric interpretation of a Chinese American.

Amy is the only character identified as a hyphenated American. No other ethnic minority is mentioned in the series except for two African American characters, Gina Hawkins and Themba Somali, and a Greek American, Nikos Smith.[5] This sets the premise of the series in which everything is based on and judged by Eurocentric values. Other than her family, there are no other Chinese or Asian American contact in Amy's life. All the boys described and talked about, as well as almost all the heroes and musicians whom Amy admire, are Caucasian. Beauty is consistently described with physical attributes such as golden blond, silky/sandy brown or bright red hair, with big blue, green, hazel, gray, or violet eyes.[6] Amy is simply described with dark eyes, dark eyebrows, and straight dark hair. Only two other adjectives are used to modify this "darkness"—"jet-black" or plain old "black," and every once in awhile the eyes would be

---

[4]The basic premise of the Pen Pals series is centered on four teenagers named Shanon Davis, Palmer Durand, Amy Ho, and Lisa McGreevy, who share the same suite at Alma Stephens. Maxine Schloss joins this group in Volume 13. They are bored with their all-girl environment and they begin writing to pen pals from the neighboring all-boy Ardsley Academy.

[5]Gina Hawkins calls herself an "African-American [sic]," but Themba always considers himself to be a foreigner, even though he was only five years old when he arrived from South Africa (12:92). In the end, Themba returns to South Africa when his father is appointed the director of a theater project there (12:122). Nikos Smith was born in Greece, came to the United States at age two, and grew up in New Orleans. Other than the mention of Nikos' birthplace, no mention is made of his Greek ancestry nor is he ever referred to as a hyphenated American.

[6]Gina Hawkins, the African American girl, is described as having light brown skin (8:17), golden brown eyes (8:17; 12:6), and wavy black hair (8:17; 12:6).

described as "almond-shaped."[7] Added by her all-black outfits, Amy is a walking mass of darkness.

With such a multi-color, but non-black, ideal of beauty and with no other Asian around, Amy naturally falls for only Caucasian boys, a very common motif in Eurocentric literature where Asian characters (mostly women) are always falling in love with Caucasian characters. There are a total of four boys in Amy's life: Simmie, the most handsome boy on campus, has golden hair and sea-green eyes; John Adams is a tall redhead; Emmett is also tall and slender with dark green eyes, long black eyelashes and slightly wavy dark hair with red highlights; and Nikos Smith is "gorgeous" with his dark eyes and curly dark hair.[8] Hence, the pattern continues where Asians are typically paired off with Caucasians, further adding to the near non-existence of major Asian couples in Eurocentric American literature. In contrast, Gina Hawkins, the only other non-Caucasian girl in the series, falls for a fellow African American. Instead of developing or dealing with another African American boy-girl relationship or a possible biracial relationship between a European American and an African American when Themba leaves the country, the author drops Gina out of existence from the series. All this perpetuates already popular images of couples in Eurocentric literature where Africans generally stay paired among themselves, Asians do not fall in love with fellow Asians, and the most ideal biracial couple is Asian-Caucasian, preferably Asian woman-Caucasian man.

As a result of the totally Caucasian environment in which Amy Ho is immersed, several other common motifs seen in Eurocentric literature with Chinese characters can also be found in the Pen Pals series—that is, the conservatively negative Chinese parent and the great white savior motifs, both of which go hand-in-hand. In this formulaic treatment, Chinese parents consistently occur as "traditional," old-fashioned, sexist, and tyrannical, who do not respect, understand, or communicate with their children. Consequently, the Chinese protagonist fights against his/her parents who function as obstacles to freedom and love. He/she is eventually shown the "way" with the help of progressive and kind-hearted characters who are inevitably Caucasian. In the end, the Chinese parents repent or learn their lesson, and yield to the child.

---

[7]Amy's black hair is especially singled out at a Halloween party when her suitemates remind her that because she has black hair, she cannot dress as She-Ra, a blond-haired super-heroine (1:97–98).
[8]The only other Chinese American characters with romantic partners are Amy's father and older brother, Alex. No mention is made of their women friends' ethnicity.

In the Pen Pals series, Henry Ho wants Amy to go to an all-girl school so that she would not think about boys, and instead concentrate on her studies to become a scientist. He is strongly against her ambition to become a singer. When living at home in New York City during the holidays, Amy feels like a prisoner because her parents would not let her pierce her ears, dress the way she wants, or let her out of the house without her brother Alex chaperoning her. Finally, the father's favoritism of Alex over Amy completes the formulaic treatment of the sexist Chinese parent.

As a result, the protagonist rebels and finds solace, guidance, or help elsewhere. Since Amy has only Caucasian contacts, it is no wonder that, with the exception of Alex, practically all her supporters are Caucasian men. Those who have been the most supportive of her and who, unlike her father, have told her she has talent or should strive for a singing career are Professor Graham Bernard, her voice teacher, and three older teen-aged musicians named Michael Oliver, Rain Blackburn, and Emmett. This formulaic setting pits and contrasts Chinese parents, representing tyranny and conservatism, against white saviors representing individual freedom and love. Naturally, the latter helps the Chinese American protagonist win. In the Pen Pals series, Amy's father succumbs to Amy's desire to sing by first allowing her to take voice lessons, and then by telling her how he likes her singing and promises to communicate with her in the future (SS1:158). As with most of these plots, Henry Ho learns his lesson and ends up apologizing to his daughter.

One must look deeper into this superficial treatment of Chinese parents and realize that Amy's father is not behaving particularly Chinese, but is behaving like most parents. There is no sacred universal law that says only Chinese parents are sexist, strict, unreasonable, conservative, and tyrannical. Such traits are found among all parents, especially when seen from the eyes of teenagers during their formative years of seeking independence. Nevertheless, many pre-adult literature with Chinese American characters attribute these traits only to Chinese parents. The parents of the other Pen Pals characters do not display these negative traits—some are actually portrayed as being open-minded and kind. Unlike Henry Ho, Palmer's father expresses sympathy for Amy's desire to become a rock-n-roll singer (10:31). The underlying effect is clear: the Chinese American parent is once again depicted negatively as unreasonable while the white parent is depicted as understanding. As such, the repertoire of positive Caucasian role models continues to increase with the addition of yet another negative Chinese role model.

Finally, because the Chinese family is almost always depicted as sexist while the European American family is viewed as more progressive, Amy's family setting becomes an ideal battleground for the issue of sexism, which surprisingly does not appear as a problem with her other suitemates who also have brothers. This issue of the son being more important than the daughter is not resolved in the Pen Pal series. Amy's victory in finally earning some respect from her father superficially appears like a resolution, but it is not because the parent fails to deal with Alex. Henry Ho sees this as an issue of growing up, not sexism. Once again, sexism among Chinese families is perpetuated in Eurocentric literature, whereas sexism is non-existent in the idealized European American family.

Amy is already seen early in the series as being sensitive and aware of gender bias. She speaks in defense of womanhood during a classroom discussion of Romeo and Juliet, stating lots of girls are more mature than boys and they are able to state their own opinions (6:21). She is also upset when John Adams tells her that "men and women don't have the same sort of intelligence" (4:43), implying that women are inferior. In response to a boy cousin who says a woman can never be President, she calls this a "caveman mentality" and argues that there are women leaders in other countries doing a great job (8:90–91). Within the same conversation, some of her suitemates express the opinion that a woman should go wherever her husband's job is, and they laugh at the Mr. Moms at home. Amy disagrees with them: "...nobody's going to tell me where to live, even if he is my husband.... I wouldn't even mind if I did all the work outside of the house and my husband stayed home and did the housework" (8:90–91). Thus, it is not surprising to find Amy feeling that it was not a "smart move" for Nikos' mother to give up a ballet career to "do laundry and dishes" (SS2:33).

Just how feminist is Amy Ho? Several major volumes in the series focus directly on Amy and the gender issue. In every situation, she defends womanhood and puts down all the male chauvinists. However, Wyeth has failed to create a truly modern female teenager. For every step forward that Amy claims in the name of womanhood, she regresses several steps because she gives in to the boys. Despite apologies, none of the boys with whom she has confrontations change their sexist attitude or behavior.

For example, when Amy changes the sex in John's song and names it "Willameena," which later proves to be a better version than John's "The Ballad of Young Willie the Poet," she still ends up apologizing to John:

> ...I really love "Willameena" and I cannot give up my words just because you don't want the song to be about a woman. It would be murdering someone. I hope we can still be friends. And, like I said, I apologize. But I will not change the words to my song because I think

they are better. And making the song the best way you know how is what is most important. (6:15)

Although John admits that Amy's version is good, he does not accept her apology, so Amy has to apologize a second time because she needs a date for a dance: "To think *she'd* almost ruined everything—and all because of a silly song [emphasis added]" (6:32). John eventually accepts the second apology even though Amy's talent is proven to be superior to his. In other words, no matter how good a woman is, her abilities are trivialized and she must yield to a man's ego. It is no wonder that by the end of the series, John becomes more sexist.

In another episode when Amy auditions to become the lead singer of a rock band called Emmett and the Heartbreak, it first appears that Amy is struggling to achieve individual freedom and choice. Nothing is more important to her than this opportunity to attain her ambition to be a professional singer. In the process, her personality changes when she violates school regulations, argues with her suitemates, and breaks up with John, whom she accuses of being chauvinistic. Amy is blinded equally by her ambition and attraction to Emmett, the band leader. She refuses to believe that he is a liar and has stolen her song for himself, insisting vehemently that this is an issue of choice and nobody makes decisions for her (15:90). Yet, for a strong girl, Amy is willing to let Emmett dictate to her what she should wear in terms of dress and makeup (15:59), and she even quits her singing lessons when he tells her that they are damaging her voice (15:58). Amy's talent and individual goals are once again compromised for a chauvinistic man who later dumps her after using her.

The last major incident that is supposed to illustrate Amy's feminism occurs during a softball game at Camp Emerald, where her new pen pal, Nikos, ends up being another male chauvinist. He persuades her to pitch for his softball team. Although Amy pitches a no-hitter game, Nikos slowly removes her and the other girls in the co-ed team, eventually making it an all-male team. He claims the girls cannot get any runs, yet he ignores the fact that the boys also have not scored. The ensuing argument resulted in other comments like "girls aren't as good at sports as boys" and "girls are a bunch of quitters" and "whiners" whenever they do not get what they want (SS2:73). This triggers a major war of the sexes, where Amy and Nikos become leaders representing their respective gender. Amy believes she is "fighting for the pride and dignity of women" and that if the girls challenge and beat the boys in the next game, they "would become a symbol of hope for girls all over the country" (SS2:77). She writes a new anti-boy song:

Love is major trouble and romance is just a myth.
I'm fed up to my teeth with boys, especially Nikos Smith!
He's a fourteen-karat oinker, a muscle-headed goon.
The next time he comes near me, I'll send him to the moon.
(chorus) Sisters of the world unite—
Let's do away with guys!
They're loud-mouth, bragging, macho geeks
Who all belong in sties! (SS2:67)

Unfortunately, the girls in camp slowly lose interest in this battle of the sexes and want to be with the boys again. Even Amy begins to feel lonely and admits that "pride and anger at Nikos" are the only reasons why she is still fighting (SS2:110). She has forgotten and has forsaken the principles upon which the battle is based. In the end, Nikos rescues Amy from an attack of hornets and apologizes for pulling her out of the game, but without admitting to any wrong. As with all the other incidents, Amy's sense of feminism takes second place to her need for boys. Again, the message is clear, a woman's individuality, abilities, and ambition can never be equal to that of a man's.

In conclusion, what does Amy Ho symbolize for the teenage audience reading the Pen Pals series? As a Chinese American character, she is a "fortune cookie," so aptly described by Shanon because she finds Amy to be "crispy-sweet and full of good advice" (11:118). Amy is the stereotypical Chinese American woman found usually in Eurocentric literature: she has only Caucasian boyfriends; she does not have any Asian friends; she does not speak Chinese except for the few angry words she learned from her grandmother (6:3); she does not write Chinese but she does "draw" Chinese (11:117); she celebrates Chinese New Year; the only Chinese food she can cook are fortune cookies from her Australian friend's cookbook recipe (10:72); and she is the only character in the series wearing clothes described as "exotic"—even Shanon's boring outfit is transformed into something "exotic and unusual" when she puts on Amy's patchwork cotton vest from China (7:70).

Wyeth does deviate from the stereotypical image of the quiet, smart, and submissive Chinese girl when she makes Amy an outrageous punk teenager who is athletic, always wearing black, and strumming the guitar. However, in this effort to individualize the character, the punky Amy sticks out more as an oddity on campus, especially when she is the only Asian in an all-white environment. Amy's weird appearance and behavior are not unnoticed when even her friends tell her to dress more conservatively during Parents Weekend (10:32).

As a symbol for female teenagers, Amy is the only character fighting for women's rights and dignity, but she compromises her beliefs and gives in too easily to her need for boys. Actually, the entire premise of the Pen Pals series is male-based. Suitemate Palmer Durand states clearly why the girls began their pen pal adventure: "Besides giving you something to look forward to at mail call, having a pen pal means automatic dates" (14:6). After boys and dating, the girls' next major concern is clothes and makeup, which is ultimately done to attract and please boys. At first, Amy differs from this concern because she says her way of dressing is a "personal statement" (7:109). However, when Amy meets Nikos, she would change her clothes four times within three minutes (SS2:13) or spend over 20 minutes to go through "a major overhaul" for him (SS2:31–32), all of which contradicts her earlier stand about clothes and individuality. When women do things in their lives to attract and please men only, then they lose their individuality and become too dependent on what men want.

Finally, whenever Amy fights for her right as an individual and as a woman, she has to apologize or make sacrifices and compromises—without the boys having to make any substantial concessions. The boys in the Pen Pals series show that they can survive without girls, but not so the girls, who always seem to need boys. All this only perpetuates the image that women are of secondary importance and should be subservient to men. Amy's character growth is stunted as she does not realize this in the end, as the true meaning of being a free woman constantly eludes her. Amy does not have a self, and she has a long way to go in order to be "the fearless crusader for female equality."

With 20 books written about the same recurring character, Wyeth could have influenced a large audience into seeing Chinese American women as human beings. But she seems to lack a feminist and an ethnic consciousness. As a result, Amy Ho is no improvement over the many stereotypical Chinese American women portrayed in Eurocentric American literature. Therefore, it is fortunate that the Pen Pals series has ceased publication as of 1991. We do not need any more fortune cookies.

Undoing and Redoing the Hegemony of Western Culture in Diasporic Writings by Chinese American Women

SHIRLEY GEOK-LIN LIM

English Department, University of California, Santa Barbara

American literary tradition has been, until recently, constructed on a canon produced by "white, middle-class, male(s), of Anglo-Saxon derivation" (Baym 69); the master narrative identified an Adamic romance, "a confrontation of the American individual ... with the promise offered by the idea of America" (Baym 71). Recent feminist and ethnic interventions insist further on the national identity of the texts they seek to privilege. The multicultural project now being undertaken in the U.S. can be read as a trajectory of an imperializing culture that appropriates all manners of differences. At the heart of critical consciousness, as Said argues, is the cooperation between filiation, which is chiefly natal, and affiliation, the pressure to produce new and different ways of conceiving human relationships provided "by institutions, associations, and communities" (614).

Using these categories, we can examine how a reading of Chinese American writing as unambiguously American-national totalizes the diasporic writer as a free agent writing the great American epic. The narrative of the immigrant's "assimilation" elides the history and present of illegals, refugees, poor, and working class, and it represses knowledge of how the hegemonic epic of the U.S., as the nation of limitless opportunity, freedom, and triumphant individualism, recasts these people as "others," and reproduces through the few who do succeed its controlling narrative of individual autonomy, economic competition, and race-consciousness.

Re-theorizing the relationship between the filiative and the affiliative as contestory rather than cooperative, this paper analyzes works by two Chinese American women writers as either negotiating or surrendering in these contestory relations. I theorize two other categories: of *ex-filiation,* which I define as the condition of exilic experience, and of *a-filiation,* an imagined condition not temporally situated on its way toward another totality, but fragmented, complete in its incompleteness, demonstrating provisionality and exigency, what Deleuze and Guattari have defined as a literature of the transnational demonstrating a deterritorialization of language, and of imagination attending "the decomposition and fall of the Empire" (25). I argue that Lin Tai-Yi's little-known novel, *The Eavesdropper* (1958), attempts an act of deterritorialization, by locating itself in a position of a-filiation, while Jen's popularly received *Typical American* (1991) is concerned with affiliative cooperation, to re-knit American sociopolitical hegemony.

The disparate receptions to these works produced within United States borders underline the care with which we should distinguish between what is American national fantasy and what is Chinese different. The reception of Kingston's and Tan's novels, for example, as representations having something to say about China, must itself be contextualized critically, as a mode of appropriating the name of China for what is, after all, an American myth. Benedict Anderson, in his study of nationalism, points to the entry of print-capitalism (46) or print-language as laying the bases for national consciousness. One can read in the privileging of recent Chinese American novels the convergence of capitalism and print technology to create the possibility of a new form of imagined community, a community/nation that is America rather than China.

The Eavesdropper comes from another tradition of writing by Asian diasporic women, in which the West is but one agent in a diplomatic axis of China and the West, with China as the other agent. This tradition sets out problematics of affiliation that suggest a different history of the individual imagination as modulated by at least two cultural systems, each undermining and reconfiguring the other in a dynamic of *inter/trans/nationalism* that is the contested ground of diplomatic history. The absence of recognition of this tradition, postulating a difference from the controlling frame of *national* affiliation, explains how *The Eavesdropper* remained, in Said's terms, "simply left out" of United States literary consciousness.

To understand what accounts for the different receptions of Lin's and Jen's novels, we have to turn to the different histories of diplomatic relations between the U.S. and China in the '50s and in the late 1980s. For *The Eavesdropper*, the signifying date is 1949, marking the fall of Shanghai to the Communist Army, the defeat of Chiang Kai Shek's Nationalist Army forces, and the creation of two Chinas, the P.R.C. (People's Republic of China), diplomatically unrecognized by the United States until January 1, 1979, and the R.O.C. (Republic of China) set up in Taiwan. For *Typical American*, the significant date is Nixon's 1972 visit to China and the issuance of the Shanghai communiqué which marked the re-visualization of China in U.S. popular imagination.

George R. Packard points out that the dramatic shift in U.S. attitude toward China between 1949 and 1972 was anticipated in the history of U.S. relations with China: "Relations between the American and Chinese peoples have, from the beginning, been marked by turbulence and surprises on both sides of a deep cultural, historical, and political chasm" (1).

Similarly, Michael Hunt notes that the myth of a "special relationship" between the U.S. and China in the 19th century "underscored the role of American benevolence, Chinese gratitude, and mutual good will;" but it also masked a "cultural, economic, and diplomatic interaction [between] two countries widely separated by culture and geography in a relationship notable for its breadth, complexity, and instability." This instability helps explain "the mid-20th century collision and estrangement between a U.S. ascendant in Asia and an intensely nationalist China." The dangers of American paternalism remain, as seen in the popular response to Nixon's 1972 visit, which "reawakened in a public long hostile to Communist China as ignorant, 'warlike,' 'sly,' and 'treacherous' a nostalgic vision of Chinese as a 'hard-working,' 'intelligent,' 'artistic,' 'progressive,' and 'practical' people" (312). "The history of U.S. dealings with China," Hunt cautions, "illustrates how likely Americans ... are to ignore diversity in the world and instead reduce cultures radically different ... to familiar, easily manageable terms" (313).

The Eavesdropper begins in New Haven and in New York, tracing the course of a Chinese émigré graduate student and his absorption through marriage into a Chinese American family (13–112). It concludes with Shutung's binational consciousness: "My mind kept spanning the breadth of the ocean, flying back to Shanghai, and then snapping back again like an elastic band, abruptly to New York" (232). Although half of the novel treats his experiences in the U.S., *The Eavesdropper* was not viewed by the publishers, author, or reviewers as an immigrant story. It was received as a story of China, an un-American story at a time in U.S. history when the McCarthy hearings were fresh in popular memory, and Chinese were stereotyped as a Communist threat.

Yet, while the narrator oscillates between the two national cities, the novel constructs other mentalities that suggest a different grounding. The patriarch, Henry Yee, is first seen as a "resident alien": he "stepped from an old China right into a modern America, and he did not know it" (57). Living in a Tudor-style house at Great Neck, he reconstructed "the inside ... of an old-fashioned Chinese home," in which an archaic China "uniquely saved from his times" was preserved (58). The nostalgia of the "resident alien," however, cannot withstand the pervasive force of what Said calls the hegemonic culture:

> ... a continual process of reinforcement, by which a hegemonic culture will add to itself the prerogatives given it by its sense of national identity, ... by its vindicated power as a victor over everything not itself." (612)

By the novel's end, the "oasis of China which Henry Yee had built on the breast of America must have merged with the land itself.... This land of barbarians had become for him the land where his son and grandchildren were born, and he must have realized ... that he could not hold out forever" (233).

Unlike the father who is economically assimilated but culturally separatist, the son Fulton, named after a street and subway stop in Brooklyn, operates as a monocultural nomad in the majoritan world of American colloquial speech and capital. Driving a Studebaker, Fulton "was saying that he was in tiptop shape every morning and rarin' to go, and he thanked his lucky stars for it, too, because by golly, if he didn't feel so good, he sure couldn't stand up to the strain of his crowded schedule" (13). The passage's parodistic surface mocks Fulton's crass Americanness, represented as a combination of optimism, eagerness, boastfulness, and busy-ness in the service of money-making. Fulton is also interested in language:

...it's gotta be original. Now I been fooling around with a lot of names, like Lotus Garden or Bamboo Inn ... but I have always to turn them down in the end ... 'Cause words like that are redundant ... Redundant means something stale and got no life." (14)

Aware of what is dead about an original Chinese culture in modern Manhattan, his response to cultural redundancy is to surrender to American hegemony. Parodying the assimilated American, he wishes to name his new restaurant, "Fulton Yee's Melting Pot" (15).

Shutung embraces instead a phenomenological significance. Attempting "to achieve a complete objectiveness" (16) over his impoverished émigré situation, he finds security in the metaphysical "continuity of remembrance of things past" (22). His opening dream replays the historical drama of China's paralysis, collapse, and loss in his unconscious, a thematic phantasmagoria seized by critics such as Amy Ling as defining and/or preceding the experience of dual cultures. The paradigm of "between worlds" assumes that Chinese diasporic writing is located in cultural longing, the desire for and surrender to the Anglo Other. Shutung's point-of-view, however, is one of resistance to U.S. civilization, which is presented as seductively easy to penetrate. Arriving alone, "gathering my sudden Asian self about me like an island," he is corralled by Lilien, whose family exemplifies the successful assimilation of Chinese into American capitalist society (53). His opening ex-filiative mode is distilled through his disillusioning return to his native China to an a-filiative position. Through history's fatal mark, he loses not simply a home, but a patriotic sentimentality. When the novel concludes with the famous novelist transformed to a small-time Chinatown travel agent, the transformation is both an ironic reduction on the dispersal of affiliation/home to visit/China and a valorizing metaphor for Shutung's attainment of "detachment":

> There are mornings when I go to Chinatown feeling as if I were merely a shell of myself ... as if the last thread in this piece of fabrication had been brought into place ... the expertness with which this had happened suffused me with the joy of release." (250–51)

A-filiation encodes both aesthetic virtue, the satisfactions of closure, and spiritual grace. The self-reflecting subject is both empty and complete: a subject position outside the material of history that is China and outside the history of the material that is U.S. culture.

Shutung voices an uncommon resistance to U.S. culture. The novel's conclusion constructs a home-less subject, ideologically related to the Buddhist valuation of detachment or non-affiliation. Such Sino-Anglian writing of the Chinese diaspora that resists the master narratives of American culture—narratives of affiliation, of attachment to the New World—continues to remain invisible today.

In contrast, Chinese diaspora literature that re-thematizes American cultural hegemony is a highly marketable product. *Typical American* also begins with a boyhood in China and a protagonist who leaves Shanghai, in the throes of the Nationalist defeat, for the U.S. Unlike the idealist Shutung, Yifeng Cheng is a materialist. The novel collapses Yifeng's (now Ralph's) assimilation into the American socioeconomic world in the space of two pages: "By August he'd moved nine times, in a spiral away from his Chinese friends. They and the university still formed some center to his universe, but only as a point of origin" (32).

This spiraling away from origin is described as "Natural Process," "the slow shift of a pendulum's swing into a different plane" (32). The operation of hegemonic forces in dislocating the individual from a natal community is naturalized and simultaneously assumes the inexorable mechanic force of a giant clock. Killing "hours upon hours of chickens" in a store basement, Ralph enters the American working class: "The first week he vomited daily from the stench of the feces and offal and rotting meat. But the second week he only blanched, and by the third he worked as though indigenous to this world" (34).

He metamorphoses from home-less subject to an indigene/indigenous in the underworld channel-house. In the progression from China origin to U.S. indigenous, China/home is constructed as always already absent: "He might gild it [home], but in truth it was lacking. Lacking what? Something, everything" (33). The void of origin prepares the reader for the construction of the U.S. as material vitality.

Much of *Typical American* narrates the Changs' near vertiginous climb through successful professional certification and accelerated material appetites. For Helen, America is a house in the suburbs. Even as Ralph, Theresa, and Helen distinguish themselves from typical 'no-good,' 'don't-know-how-to-get-along' (67) Americans, they are inexorably drawn into the culture. Their assimilation is constructed as innocent and natural; these Chinese immigrants "slipped from tongue to tongue like turtles taking to land, taking to sea" (124); "they were all innocence ... 'going up,' every day" (124).

The novel's counter-movement is situated in the instabilities inherent in the master narrative of capitalism. Like *The Fall and Rise of Silas Lapham*, the overt didactic frame—related to the Puritan attempt to control the excesses and pleasures of capital formation—reframes the novel's representation of material success. Ralph's discontentment with mere academic tenure leads him into a partnership with the shady Grover Ding, a self-proclaimed millionaire. The discourse of capital explicitly penetrates the book; Ralph papers an entire wall of his office with inspirational quotes, "ALL RICHES BEGIN IN IDEAS," "DON'T WAIT FOR YOUR SHIP TO COME IN, SWIM OUT TO IT" (198). His desire for money, success, and power brings pain and near-disaster to the family.

The novel's last section critiques its earlier capitalist drive: "a man was as doomed here as he was in China .... He was not what he had made up his mind to be" (296). The America of endless invention, the possibility of containing everything and satisfying every desire, is glimpsed here as a cultural fantasy. The promise of capital, progressive improvement, change, and accumulation is set against the limits of human ability: "A man was the sum of his limits; freedom only made him see how much so. America was no America" (296). This "bleak understanding" of universal limits undermines the signature of American culture and interrogates the naturalizing of an ideology composed of contradictory themes: progressive social mobility and community cohesiveness, increasing wealth and intensifying consumer patterns, hyper-individualism and strong family bonds. Ralph's meditation explodes the contradictions in this myth of America.

But if "America is no America," there is no China either to function for that other swing of the pendulum. In its conclusion, the novel shifts to an image of Theresa and Old Chao "floating on twin inflatable rafts, in twin blue wading pools of water" (296). Evading that winter's "understanding" for an image from the "heat wave of the summer," the novel enacts a rhetorical violence of extremities that re-represents the totalizing pressure of American culture. The infantile play, the lightness of being that resonates in the image of adults in a suburban idyll, closes the novel, reinforcing the seduction of the capitalist text with its promise of future pleasure.

Works Cited

Anderson, Benedict. *Imagined Communities: Reflections on the Origin and Spread of Nationalism*. London: Verso, 1983.

Baym, Nina. "Melodramas of Beset Manhood." In *The New Feminist Criticism*. Ed. Elaine Showalter. New York: Pantheon, 1985. 63–80.

Deleuze, G., and F. Guattari. "What is a Minor Literature?" *Mississippi Review* 22 (3): 13–33.

Hunt, Michael. *The Making of a Special Relationship: The US and China to 1914*. New York: Columbia, 1983.

Jen, Gish. *Typical American*. Boston: Houghton Mifflin, 1991.

Kingston, Maxine Hong. *Tripmaster Monkey*. New York: Knopf, 1989.

Lin, Tai-yi. *The Evesdropper*. Cleveland and NY: The World Publishing Co., 1958.

Ling, Amy. *Between Worlds*. New York: Pergamon, 1990.

Packard, George. "The Policy Paper: China Policy for the Next Decade." In *China Policy for the Next Decade*. Eds. U. Alexis Johnson, George R. Packard, and Alfred D. Wilhelm, Jr. Boston: Oelgeschlager, Gunn & Hain, 1984. 1–46.

Said, Edward. "Secular Criticism." In *Critical Theory Since 1965*. Eds. Hazard Adams and Leroy Searle. Tallahassee: U. Presses of Florida. 605–622.

Tan, Amy. *The Kitchen God's Wife*. New York: Putnam's Sons, 1991.

The No-Good Kuei:
A Look at Two Modern-Day Chinese Ghost Stories

WILLIAM BOWEN
Department of Anthropology, University of California, Riverside

We all love a good story or tale. But besides pleasing us, stories and tales have deeper, more informative, more educative, and more enculturating functions. Their primary purpose is to help shape our attitudes, perceptions, and orientations toward the material and cultural context (Wilke 1986). They do this in a roundabout fashion, through the transmission of underlying symbolic, meaning-laden, or metaphoric messages.

While stories and tales often contain factual or objective information, they also contain culturally-determined explanations for the unknown or unknowable; warnings about what to fear and models for appropriate problem-solving behaviors. Stories and tales are, thus, layered, functioning on several levels simultaneously. We listen for fun, we bond in our mutual enjoyment, but we also learn something about how we should see, understand, and behave in the worlds we inhabit.

The telling of stories and tales must be considered a deep function innate to human communication. Storytelling dates to primitive man, who told stories about the hunt and about creation. For early or preliterate societies, the educative function of stories was perhaps greater than today's. Stories were one of few ways for individuals to learn the culture and lifeways of their people (Biesele 159; Gordon 6). Through stories, social facts were preserved, and the history, wisdom, and world view of the people passed down for posterity (Edeson 1975; Vasina 1965; Minc 1986).

In storytelling, an underlying "subtext" (symbolic message or metaphor) is concealed under the overt and entertaining narrative story line. The underlying contents make an impression on deeper, perhaps unconscious, levels of the mind where they are then retained, awaiting activation through association in appropriate social and material settings and contexts.

This paper focuses on two Chinese stories. The point is to demonstrate that a reading of both the surface and the underlying metaphoric, symbolic, or message-laden aspects of these stories can help us better understand their multi-leveled function. The goal is to see how they enculturate or perpetuate a vision, an understanding, and a set of relevant behaviors through the transmission of traditional cultural values and beliefs, deemed important for "survival" in the world.

Chinese Ghost Stories. In January 1991, in his home in San Diego, California, Chinese Taoist Master Share K. Lew told this author two modern-day Chinese Taoist folk tales (or ghost stories). Master Lew, the story-teller, is a temple-trained Taoist monk who immigrated to the United States in 1949.

Master Lew, currently employed as a healer and a Chinese massage and herbology teacher, was trained in Tao Ahn Pia (Inner Elixir Style) kung fu at Wong Lim Kwan (Yellow Dragon Monastery), which is located on Mount Lou Fa Shan, west of Canton between Xinzuotang and Boluo.

The folk tales he told, which are transcribed below, are about female "kuei." Kuei is the Chinese word for a hungry ghost, demon, or disembodied spirit. The two ghost stories entitled "The Two Brides" and "Jo Mo Gay Exorcises the Clam Spirit," while entertaining, contain embedded traditional Chinese male beliefs and values about primary relationships and their dangers. They concern primary relationships because, while on the surface they are about relationships with the living dead, in a deeper symbolic sense they are about relationships with members of the opposite sex (females). The beliefs associated with these stories are not idiosyncratic to Master Lew or Taoism, but resonate with a larger enduring cultural pattern that can be found in other forms of narrative in Chinese culture (Wile 1992).

Kuei in Traditional Chinese Culture. To understand what kuei means to a Chinese person, one first needs to know that the traditional Chinese belief is that people, like natural objects and places of the world, have their own unique and characteristic energy or "qi."

When a human dies, his or her spirit, or "shen qi," an aspect of their overall "qi," goes to the next world. However, if a person dies prematurely, or dies in an untimely manner, such as in an accident, battle, or catastrophe, and the body is not found, or there is no relative to care for and show respect for the departed spirit, he or she may become a kuei—a ghost or demon who wanders the earthly realm, deprived of final rest in heaven (Chace 1992).

Kuei are not seen as inherently evil or bad. As our storyteller, Master Share Lew, says, "Some are good and some are bad, just like people." Nevertheless, a kuei is inherently unhappy and incomplete, and hence the potential exists for expression of that unhappiness or incompleteness.

Kuei have the ability to change their form. They are shapeshifters or changelings. They may become an animal, like a fox (vixen) or a clam, or they may even take on human attributes. They may stay in one place, wander about at sunset, or travel from China to the United States in a teak wood dresser drawer, if so inclined.

The chief thing to fear about kuei is that they can enter a living person's body and possess them. Possession can cause sickness, and will drain the life energy of a human to the point where he or she may die. In ancient China, kuei were blamed for many illnesses—and they knew no limits. They would even stoop to harming a fetus in the womb (Hume 1975)! No wonder some modern-day Chinese will avoid an accident victim on the road or pay a handsome reward for the recovery of a drowned body, out of fear that a kuei may be on the loose and perhaps is looking for someone to possess (Chace, ibid.).

Kuei and Ancestor Spirits. The worship of dead ancestor spirits is a pillar of Chinese civilization. Ancestor spirits are seen to take an active interest in their human offspring. In fact, they are in many ways responsible for the guidance of their descendants. Since death is merely a change in outward substance, it does not affect the duties of blood relatives, nor does it change the relationships between generations or change the interdependence of the living and the dead.

Piety and devotion to the ancestors and promotion of their happiness in the other world are a sacred duty and right of a living Chinese person (Anderson 1991). One must show respect or filial piety for departed relatives, who in turn act as guides for life in this world (Hume 1975).

If respect is not shown to an ancestor spirit, he or she will cause problems for the living. The types of problems the spirit can cause are remarkably similar to those that can be caused by bad kuei. Both kuei and ancestor spirits have the ability to reach out from the land of the dead and cause harm to the living, and both can only be appeased with proper respect or the appropriate ritual.

The scientific explanation for such beliefs about unhappy ancestor spirits and malevolent kuei is that they are primarily used to help explain random or chance events, such as accidents, catastrophes, or untimely illnesses. In other words, kuei are blamed for these occurrences.

Beliefs about kuei and ancestor spirits also serve as a culturally-constituted mechanism of social control, in that both are internalized as a class of images responsible for self control in the individual. Both kuei and ancestor spirits are like policemen in the psyche. If one does not follow expected normative cultural behavior, the individual may risk the wrath of a kuei or ancestor spirit, which are really internalized spirit images functioning somewhat like a conscience or punitive Freudian "super ego." Further, though the image of the angry spirit actually comes from within and exists only in an internal representational world, an individual may project this image out on to the world, seeing it as real. He may then make himself sick through psychosomatic mechanisms or sabotage his life through ill-advised "subconscious" choices, all the while blaming spirits.

Female Kuei. The relationship of kuei, ancestor spirits, and some cultural functions has been expressed above, but what of the cultural connections between kuei and women in Chinese culture? What cultural beliefs does a kuei that is female point to?

It is important to note that both kuei and women are viewed as potentially unstable and dangerous in traditional Chinese society. Both need to be strictly controlled because, as they say in popular belief, "Both brides and demons are kwai," or queer: yin unbalanced by yang (Topley 1974 in Feldman 64).

Ancestor spirits and kuei are dangerous because if they are offended or are restless, they can cause sickness or bad fortune for a man. But women are similar in that they, too, possess the ability to injure a man's interests (Furth 1987:29).

Since traditional Chinese society was extremely patriarchal and oppressive to women, Chinese men must have had a very strong fear of women, as they did kuei.

There are many understandable reasons for a Chinese man to be fearful of his relations with a Chinese woman. First, a Chinese male experiences unease at his dependence on women as childbearers; they have the ability to give him a male heir or not. This makes a man anxious because he wants a male child.

Second, women do not have the ability to control their emotions, which is why Chinese doctors say they are more prone to illness than men and are harder to cure (Furth 1986:49, 59). But the real problem is that women can spread their emotional disharmony to men. Since excess emotion is a major cause of illness in Chinese medical theory, men can easily become ill if they are contaminated by the excess emotions of women.

Third, women suffer menstruation, and menses are dangerous and polluting to a man (Furth 1986:48). As it is stated in traditional medical theory, "Women's menses are rank and dirty and so the gentleman avoids them, considering them unclean and liable to injure his yang" (Li Shih-chen in ibid.). Even modern medical texts reiterate this traditional belief: "dirty menstrual blood [that] carries disease," states the Xinfunu duben (Studybook for the New Woman in Barlow 719).

Fourth, women possess negative sexual power and have the ability to wear out a man through sexual dissipation of vital energies (Furth 1986:63; 1987:9). There is a rich Chinese folklore of male illness caused by sexual exhaustion (Furth 1986:63). Master Lew often told his Anglo students the story about how, in China, fox spirits would turn into beautiful young women and seek out young Taoist monks in order to steal their "ching" (vital/sexual) energy through sexual activity, to the point where the young monks became so depleted they died. The monks were often warned by their elders in the temple to watch out for these beautiful fox spirits.

All told, the combination of a kuei and a female, as in a fox spirit or a female ghost, must be considered as a highly dangerous entity: a symbol for deep cultural fears of primary concern to a Chinese male.

Sifu Lew's Taoist Folktales: The Two Brides. There was once a Chinese boy who was taken by his immigrant parents back to their home village in Mainland China. Their wish was that the boy would find a Chinese bride to marry and bring back to the United States.

One evening at sunset, the boy was walking through the streets of his family's village. He passed a very pretty young girl. He smiled at her and she smiled back. The boy was struck by her beauty and immediately fell in love with her, even though not a word passed between them. The boy went home thinking about the young girl. He began to think more and more about her. It grew to the point of obsession. Everyday he would walk the village streets hoping to see her again. But he didn't. Consequently, he became increasingly withdrawn and consumed with fantasizing about the girl, and he deteriorated to the point of avoiding interaction with all of his relatives.

Finally, the boy's Uncle asked the father what was wrong with his son. Why was he acting so strange? The father was surprised. He really wasn't aware that there was any problem. But he promised the Uncle that he would talk to the boy.

One day the father took the boy aside and asked him, "What's the matter? You not happy? You wanna go back to the United States? We can go back if you want. Maybe you don't like any of the girls here?"

"No, no. I am happy," said the boy. "I don't wanna go back yet. There is a girl I like but I don't know her name."

"Oh. I see," replied the father. "Well, we can get the village picture book (of eligible brides) and see if we can find her in there," said the father. "Okay? I'll bring the picture book and you can select a bride."

"Okay," said the boy.

So the father got the village picture book and brought it home for the boy to look through. The boy looked and looked, but he could not find the girl he liked so much. He did not want to tell his father this. He did not want to disappoint him. So to please his father, he chose another girl to marry. A wedding date was set.

It was day of the wedding. The potential bride was brought in on a carriage carried by several strong men. But when the carriage door was opened, out stepped two identical brides! They looked exactly

315

alike down to the last detail. Everyone was shocked. The family and the wedding guests looked at each other in shock and whispered. Finally someone stepped forward and exclaimed, "What is this? Why are there two brides? Who is the real bride?"

The first girl stepped forward and said, "I am the true bride. I want to marry the boy."

But then the other girl, who was identical in every way, stepped forward and said, "No, I am the true bride. I want to marry the boy."

Everyone was flustered. Who was the true bride?

Finally, someone suggested that the bride's mother be called over to decide who the true bride was. But she became confused, unable to tell them apart, and said, "I don't know which one is my daughter. They both seem like my daughter!" And then she burst into tears.

The chief carrier was then consulted.

"Only one girl entered my carriage," he stated firmly. "I don't understand why there are two brides. We did not stop anywhere and no one else entered the carriage."

By now everyone was totally confused and frustrated. Finally the boy's father stepped forward with an idea.

"We will take the two brides to court to see the judge. He will know what to do."

So both girls were brought before the judge. The problem was whispered to the august judge by an assistant. The judge's eyebrows raised up as he heard the issue. He then looked down at one girl and then at the other.

"Who is the true bride. You tell me true!"

The first bride stepped forward and said, "I am the true bride. I wish to marry the boy."

But just as quickly, the other bride stepped forward and said, "No, I am the true bride. I wish to marry the boy."

The judge eyed them both carefully, looking first to one and then the other. He knew something was fishy. He had been trained in Taoism, though not in a monastery. The judge suspected that one of the girls was a kuei who was imitating the true bride. But he was unable to tell which was which. So he decided to put them through a test.

"Okay," he said, pulling out a "fu" (magical talisman) and holding it up high. "You say you are the true bride and you say you are the true bride. We will find out. We will have a test."

The judge pointed the fu at each girl threateningly and said, "If you don't participate I will use this fu against you."

Both girls agreed to the test, which was to take place at noon the next day.

At exactly 12 o'clock sharp, both of the brides were taken out of the court where they were held during the night. It was a very hot, sunny day. The judge made the brides stand out in the hot sun with no protection. The rays of the raging sun beat down mercilessly upon the girls. The judge watched them carefully. He was looking to see which of the girls would sweat. The judge knew that kuei did not sweat because they were not human.

Finally the judge saw a bead of sweat run down the brow of one of the brides. Quickly he pulled the girl aside and gave her to the boy.

"This is the true bride!" he exclaimed.

He then turned and confronted the other would-be bride.

"I know who you are. You are a kuei!" he said, pointing menacingly at her. "Why are you doing this?"

"It wasn't my fault," pleaded the kuei, her head hanging low. "That boy, he liked me and I liked him. He wanted to marry me, so I doubled as the bride so we could marry."

"But you know that you could never marry this boy. He is human. If you married him, he would die!"

"I know," said the kuei, "but he liked me."

"Alright, alright," said the judge, feeling compassion for the kuei. "Look, you have got to leave. I will not hurt you and no one will prevent you from getting to rest in heaven, but you must go back to where you came from. If you go willingly, then I will give you anything that you want."

"I want my name in the record book and I want respect."

The judge looked at her and said, "Okay, I can arrange that."

So the judge told the kuei that he would make a marriage for her with a member (now deceased) of the boy's family and that her name would be placed in the family's lineage group where she would be accorded proper respect. The kuei was delighted.

The arrangement so struck, a brisk wind suddenly rose up and in a puff of smoke, the kuei was gone and the wedding of the boy and his human bride was underway.

Jo Mo Gay Exorcises the Clam Spirit. In China, after the second World War, there was a very famous and highly regarded Taoist priest, whose name was Jo Mo Gay. Jo Mo Gay was a very powerful high man who knew kung fu and many different kinds of Taoist magic. Jo Mo Gay was what is known as a "wandering Taoist," in that he spent his time traveling all around China, helping people, exorcising demons, and healing the sick.

Whenever Jo Mo Gay traveled to Kwangtung City in South China, which was every two to three years or so, he would stop into Ho Ming restaurant to visit the owner, Tu Ming Ju Dong, who had been his good friend for many years. Ho Ming was a very popular restaurant with excellent food. The head cook was known far and wide for his many delectable dishes. Ho Ming was always crowded and very successful.

On one particular visit to Kwangtung City and Ho Ming restaurant, Jo Mo Gay was introduced by Tu Ming Ju Dong to his head cook, of whom he was justly proud.

Later, after their brief visit, Tu Ming Ju Dong and Jo Mo Gay were sitting alone talking in the boss' office. Tu Ming Ju Dong asked, with a big broad smile, what Jo Mo Gay thought of his head cook. Jo Mo Gay looked at him straight in the eye and dryly said, "He's very sick, he only five days of life left."

"Sick! Five days of life left!" exclaimed Tu Ming Ju Dong. "What... What... He's never been sick a day in his life!"

Jo Mo Gay crossed his arms over his chest and repeated, "Only five days of life left."

"I can't believe this!" shouted Tu Ming Ju Dong, visibly shaken. He began to pace the floor, fretting and wringing his hands. If his cook was really sick, how would he replace him on such short notice, what would happen to his successful restaurant?

Suddenly Tu Ming Ju Dong stopped in his tracks and turned to face Jo Mo Gay. "I don't believe you," he exclaimed.

"You don't believe me, huh?" said Jo Mo Gay. "Haven't I been your good friend for many years? I've never lied to you. I've always helped you. Isn't that true?"

"Well... Yes, that is true, you have been my good friend," Tu Ming Ju Dong replied in a low voice, backing down somewhat. He respected Jo Mo Gay's judgment. "If you say so, I guess he must be sick. Can you help him?"

"Have him come and see me tonight," instructed Jo Mo Gay.

That evening after work, the cook came around to the room where Jo Mo Gay was staying.

"The boss told me I should come and see you. He said it was very important. Is something the matter?"

Jo Mo Gay looked at him intently. Softly but firmly he stated, "You only got five days of life left."

"Five days of life left!" shouted the cook. "How can you say that?" He was visibly ruffled.

"Okay, you listen. Isn't it true that every day at 12 noon you go outside on your break and sit under the tree and take a nap?"

"Yeah, that's so," replied the cook.

"And you see a pretty girl in your dreams?"

"Yeah."

"And you 'have a good time' with her?"

The head cook cocked his head to the side and eyed Jo Mo Gay. He hesitated a moment before answering.

"How do you know that?"

"I know," said Jo Mo Gay. "That girl is not human. She is a kuei."

"A kuei? You... You... mean a fox spirit?" asked the cook.

"No, no. A clam spirit."

"Clam spirit! Oh no!" exclaimed the cook. Now he was really worried. "How can you know such things?"

"I see it. I see the true," replied Jo Mo Gay. Indeed, the truth was that Jo Mo Gay had very many psychic abilities, including the ability to read the future and the past on a person's face.

"That girl is not human," Jo Mo Gay repeated. "She is a kuei."

There was a long pause and silence between them.

"You want long life, don't you?" asked Jo Mo Gay.

"Of course I want long life," replied the cook. "I don't want to die!"

"OK, maybe you say that to me, but in your heart you still not believe me, so I will give you proof."

Jo Mo Gay then picked up a pen and a piece of paper and drew a magical character on it. He handed it to the cook and said, "Okay, tomorrow when you go out at noon to take your nap under the trees, carry this with you. When the girl comes to you in your dreams, don't show it to her, and by no means give it to her. Just keep it in your pocket. See what happens. If you carry this and she is a kuei, she will not be able to come close to your body."

The next day at noon the cook went out under the trees, put up his feet up and fell into a deep sleep. In a flash, a beautiful young woman was sitting next to him. Sensing her presence, the cook opened his eyes and said, "Come sit close to me."

The girl started to move closer but suddenly fell back, a painful look on her face.

"No... No, I can't," she said. "I am afraid."

"You're afraid? How come? Everyday you go with me and have a good time. How come not today?

"How come not today?" asked the cook again, louder.

"No! No! No! I can't," cried out the kuei, covering her pretty face, and in a whisk she disappeared.

Ten minutes later the cook was still sitting there, confused and feeling a little sick. His heart was pounding.

That evening the cook went back to see Jo Mo Gay again.

"What happened?" asked Jo Mo Gay, an expression of deep concern on his face.

"The girl would not come close to me," said the cook, his head hanging down.

"She *could not* come close to your body because I gave you some 'fu.' That special magical character I wrote down for you has big power," stated Jo Mo Gay confidently.

Jo Mo Gay then turned and looked out the window into the moonlight and said, "The problem is that this fu will protect you, but after she leaves you, she will go after other people and do the same thing. We must kill her."

"Kill the girl?" asked the cook. "We have to kill the girl?"

"Absolutely—that girl is not human. She is a no-good kuei!"

The next day, Jo Mo Gay told the restaurant boss to build him a temporary makeshift temple and to stock it with food. In addition, he was to hire five strong, young men and five strong, young women and give each a shovel.

The following day, all the preparations were ready. A large crowd had assembled because Jo Mo Gay's power was well known to the people and the word of his undertaking had quickly spread through Kwangtung City.

It was a clear, sunny day. Jo Mo Gay stood outside the makeshift temple surrounded by a large crowd. He was straddled by the five young men and five young women, all of whom held their shovels tight. The boss and the head cook were standing close by, each looking quite nervous and fidgety.

Jo Mo Gay began the ceremony. His hair was tied up in Taoist ritualistic fashion and he held a magical sword made of "liu ji" wood, which he used for fighting kuei. For about one hour, Jo Mo Gay worked breathing exercises and did magical ritual.

Suddenly a wind came up and dark clouds rolled in overhead. The air was charged with electricity and a sense of malevolence. The crowd became frightened and some ran off. The wind began to blow so hard that it blew down Jo Mo Gay's hair, which he had tied up, and it now hung down in front of his face and on his shoulders. At the height of the atmospheric disturbance, Jo Mo Gay swung the sword around mightily and threw it high into the air. The sword went up and up into the clouds. Suddenly the wind stopped and the clouds rolled back and the sky was silent and clear. For a moment there was dead silence. Nothing stirred. Not a bird or breeze. Then with the deafening sound like an airplane falling out of the sky, Jo Mo Gay's magical sword roared back down from the heavens and stabbed straight into the earth.

"Dig there!" exclaimed Jo Mo Gay, pointing to the embedded upright sword.

The five young men and five young women rushed over to the sword and began to dig. They dug and they dug and they dug and dug. Finally, a shovel hit something hard and made a "thud."

They continued to dig, uncovering what was a giant clam. The clam filled the air with a terrible smell. Little children held their noses and women covered their faces because they could not bear the stench. The ten young people finally were able to lift the giant clam out of the hole where it had rested and they put it on a pyre. They set it, the temple, and all the ritual accouterments on fire and let them burn. The fire burned for hours.

As the flames crackled, Jo Mo Gay turned to the crowd and explained that the clam was actually a kuei that had taken on human form. Using the disguise of a pretty young girl, the clam kuei stole vital energy from unsuspecting men and eventually killed them. For the good of all, the kuei had to be destroyed. The crowd felt relieved and left with a sense of security. Tu Ming Ju Dong was elated to have his cook back and in good health. He thanked Jo Mo Gay profusely before the monk wandered off to help other people in need, and he made doubly sure that the cook took the medicine that had been specially prepared for him to restore his lost vital energy.

Conclusion. In conclusion, it is evident that these two ghost or kuei stories share elements in common with similar stories which were collected by Jon Lee in the 1930s (Lee & Radin 1940). The common elements include a beautiful young woman who is not what she seems, a priest or person trained in traditional religion who recognizes possession, the shapeshifting of the kuei into human form, a marriage or union between the dead and living, the use of a magic sword or other such talismans ("fu"), and disguised warnings about young women.

Specifically, the second tale about Jo Mo Gay fits Eberhard's (25) classification as a B-5 type of ghost story: a ghost establishes a sexual relationship with a human. Eberhard found that in this type of story, the ghost was always a female.

Although the first story contains cultural beliefs about the need for the dead to have a lineage and respect, both of these stories carry a strong cultural message about the dangers and deceptiveness of women. In this first story, the judge reminds the kuei that she could not marry the boy because he would die if they married (and had sex). To have sex with a female kuei is to dissipate the vital fluids, even if it is the result of a "wet dream," as in the second story about Jo Mo Gay (Chace 1992).

In the literature of Chinese martial arts, medicine, and Taoism, there are other such references to this cultural theme of the danger of dissipating sex with women. For example, in early classic Taoist sex manual "The Hand Book of the Plain Girl (Su Nu Ching)," it is stated: "Semen is man's most precious possession and every emission will diminish his life force" (in Qigong Bimonthly 12) and "Every time he reaches orgasm he is harming his system" (ibid. 14). Saving semen, as in Taoist sexual yogic hygiene, will "make the semen return and strengthen the brain, preserve one's vital powers, cause hair to turn black again, new teeth to replace the lost, and lead to the development of higher spiritual energies" (ibid. 10, 11).

Master Lew also often spoke of the need to conserve sexual powers for good health and long life. Once he explained a way of figuring out how often one could safely have sex depending upon their age. The older, the less frequent the sex.

Master Lew's concepts were restated by a well-known, modern-day Tai Chi Chuan martial arts master named George Zu, a one-time gold medal winner in Shanghai Tai Chi competition before he immigrated to the United States. Zu told a story about a 21-year-old African American male student of his. The student claimed he engaged in daily sex. Master Zu warned that the passionate young man would get a horrible disease or would die young because of his excessive sexual activity.

The cultural theme in the ghost stories, ancient sex manuals, and statements of the martial arts masters is the same. Sex with women, thus female sexuality, i.e. the lure, is deceptive and dangerous. Dangerous things must be recognized and then appeased, controlled, or destroyed. This is the message concealed within the symbolic tryst of the human male and the female ghost. Just as the buried, smelly clam destroyed by Jo Mo Gay was a symbol for a woman's vagina, so too the kuei that sprang from it was a metaphor for the dangers of women in general.

The transmission and perpetuation of these traditional male beliefs, even to Anglo students in America, is the underlying enculturating function of the above ghost stories told by Taoist Master Lew. The message about the dangers of women and their sexuality for men are conveyed covertly and unconsciously by way of entertaining story metaphors, hereby upholding traditional Chinese cultural values, if only in the subscribed world of Chinese martial arts practice in America.

A Brief Biography of the Story Teller. The story-teller, Taoist Master Share K. Lew, is an ordained Taoist priest of the Pole Star sect. The sect was founded by the Taoist Immortal Lui Dan Bin during the T'ang Dynasty, about A.D. 618.

Master Lew, called "Sifu" (Cantonese for teacher-father), speaks Toishan Cantonese, but he has learned a rough English from his students since coming to the United States.

Sifu Lew was born in a village a few miles northeast of Taishan in South China. When he was a teenager, his parents were killed by the Japanese. Sifu and two other orphaned teen-aged boys were taken by a wandering Taoist monk to live with him at his monastery on Lou Fa Shan.

In the monastery, Sifu had to do chores, such as sweeping the grounds for several years before the monks would teach him martial arts. The other two boys he came with lost their patience and left after a couple of years, but Sifu remained in the monastery for 13 years.

Sifu's personal teacher at the Taoist temple was a very powerful monk whose name was Chin Po. Chin Po was supposedly able to stop anyone at his door with just the energy or "qi" he could project from his hand. Sifu says that his master also knew how to leave his body during meditation. Sifu once saw him walking in the courtyard, only to observe the elder monk a few minutes later meditating in his cell. Chin Po refused to teach Sifu that technique of out-of-body traveling because one had to start learning it as a young boy, before he ever had any kind of orgasm.

In 1949, Sifu's uncle, who had been working in America, returned to China for a visit. The uncle came to the monastery and asked Sifu to return to America with him. Both the uncle and Sifu's grandfather had immigrated to San Francisco and had been working as houseboys. One was working for a congressman and the other was working for a lawyer. Sifu did not want to leave the monastery, but his uncle pleaded with him to go. Finally, Chin Po assured Sifu that if he did not like America, he could return to the temple. Bowing to filial duty, Sifu decided to leave. Before actually coming to America, however, he wandered around China for several months before finally working his way over to the United States on a steamship.

Sifu landed in Seattle, Washington and was soon asked by acquaintances to move up to Vancouver, British Columbia. In Vancouver he would go to the park and sit on a bench in the snow. Then he would take off his shirt and do Taoist breathing exercises to break a sweat and keep warm.

From Vancouver, Sifu went to San Francisco where he studied with Choy Li Fut kung fu master Lau Bun, who was the first kung fu teacher in America. Lau Bun only taught Chinese students because he thought that if he taught Anglos, they would use it against the smaller Chinese.

Lau Bun was very powerful and could do many classical martial arts feats of strength. His school was located in a basement of a two-story warehouse-like building in the narrow streets of San Francisco Chinatown. In later years, after Lau Bun's death, the studio, which was run by his senior student, Jew Leong, became a featured stop on Chinatown tours.

While studying with Lau Bun, whom he called "Uncle" (probably a fictive kin term), Sifu was employed as an enforcer for the Hop Sing Tong. He was known as one of their best fighter/enforcers.

Some time later Sifu moved from San Francisco to Los Angeles Chinatown. Around 1970, after Lau Bun died, he began to teach martial arts, Taoist yoga, Tui-Na massage, and herbology to Anglo students. He was one of the first traditional masters to do so.

While Sifu was living in Los Angeles, some students from San Diego began to drive up to Los Angeles on Sundays to study kung fu with him. About 20 of these students were later ordained as Taoist servants under Sifu and Alex Ki Dee, the I Ching scholar, who starred as the evil Wo Fat in "Hawaii Five-O." These ordained students were the first to practice Chinese martial arts and medicine in San Diego.

In 1978 Sifu moved to San Diego. There he married a young Anglo woman who was a part of the spiritual community Sifu's other students were associated with. They had a child together. Sifu has remained in San Diego because he likes the weather. He has been very influential on the first generation of Chinese martial arts and medicine practitioners in San Diego. Many of his students have gone on to teach martial arts or to practice acupuncture. Sifu has given up teaching kung fu, and now he teaches only Taoist yoga, herbology, and massage. He claims this is because he had not found one good martial arts student in his 30 years of teaching in America.

On special occasions such as holidays or the opening of businesses, Sifu will perform traditional Taoist ceremonies which call the gods and/or insure good luck. He once even banished a ghost that haunted the Taoist Sanctuary. The ceremonies are similar to those which were performed in his monastery. Sifu also works on patients with energy healing, Tui-Na Chinese massage, and herbs, and he travels extensively to give workshops in Mexico, Japan, and the Esalen Institute in Big Sur, California. He has gone back to China many times in recent years. He was happy to see that his temple, which was torn down by the Red Army during the Cultural Revolution, is currently being rebuilt as a tourist attraction.

Works Cited

"Taoist Sexual Hygiene." In *Qigong Bimonthly* 1-4 (1987): 10–15.

Anderson, E.N., Jr. Personal communication. 1991.

Barlow, Tani E. "New Constructions of Gender in 20th-Century China." Paper read at UCLA Center for Chinese Studies and Center for the Study of Women, 24 February 1990.

Biesele, Megan. "How Hunter-Gather Stories Make Sense: Semantics and Adaption." *Cultural Anthropology* 1-2 (1986): 157–170.

Chace, Paul. Personal communication. 1992.

Eberhard, Werner. "A Study of Ghost Stories from Taiwan and San Francisco." *Asian Folklore Studies* XXX-2 (1971): 25.

Edeson, Lee. *How We Learn*. New York: Time Life Books, 1975.

Feldman, Jamie. "Gender Definition in American and Chinese Medical Discourse." *Crosscurrents* 2 (1988) 56–72.

Finnegan, Ruth. "A Note on Oral Tradition and Historical Evidence. History and Theory." 9-2 (1970): 195–201.

Furth, Charlotte. "Blood, Body and Gender: Medical Images of the Female Condition in China 1600–1850." *Chinese Science* 7 (1986): 4–66.

Furth, Charlotte. "Concepts of Pregnancy, Childbirth, and Infancy in Ch'ing Dynasty." *China Journal of Asian Studies* 46 (1987): 7–33.

Gordon, David. *Therapeutic Metaphors*. Cupertino, Ca.: Meta Publications, 1978.

Hume, Edward H. *The Chinese Way in Medicine*. Westport, Connecticut: Hyperion Press, 1975.

Lee, Jon (collector), and Paul Radin (ed.). *The Golden Mountain: Chinese Tales Told in California*. Taipei: Cave Books, 1940.

Minc, Leah D. "Scarcity and Survival: The Role of Oral Tradition in Mediating Subsistence Crisis." *Journal of Anthropological Archaeology* 5 (1986):39–113.

Vasina, Jan. *Oral Traditions*. Chicago: Aldine Publishing Company, 1965.

Wile, Douglas. *Art of the Bedchamber: The Chinese Sexual Yoga Classics*. Albany, NY: State University of New York Press, 1992.

Wilke, P.J. Personal communication, 1986.

Redefine Our History/Culture:
Discursive Strategies in
Chinese Canadian Literature

LIEN CHAO
English Department, York University, Toronto, Ontario, Canada

West Indian Canadian writer Claire Harris observes that in contemporary Canadian society, there is an attached understatement to the term "immigrant" that is related to a social double-standard for people with non-European racial backgrounds. She points out: "In Canada, normally so open to immigrants, a blatant ethnocentricity condemns *people of color* to the sidelines: *eternal immigrants* forever poised on the verge of not belonging" [emphasis mine] (115). In a society where racial and cultural backgrounds make a considerable difference in terms of how long an immigrant remains an immigrant, Chinese Canadians are one racial minority group among the "eternal immigrants" in this country. This experience is collectively shared by Chinese Canadians in the last 150 years; it is directly related to their 100-year silence in mainstream Canadian discursive fields from politics to literature. With an interdisciplinary approach, this paper provides a quick survey of the historical conditions of Chinese immigration; it examines anti-Chinese racism in Canadian history produced by politicians and government documents. It explores Chinese Canadian writers' choice of linguistic medium and narrative strategies in order to construct a dialogue with history. The discursive strategies are read as signs of redefining the community history, Chinese Canadian culture, and the individuals in contemporary Canadian society. Silence and voice are read as regularities of a discursive dichotomy embodied in the two literary works chosen for the study: Yuen Chung Yip's novel, *The Tears of Chinese Immigrants* and Sky Lee's novel, *Disappearing Moon Cafe*, winner of the 1990 City of Vancouver Book Prize.

The historical event of Chinese immigration to North America was part of the global migration following the discovery of America. It was recorded as early as in 1788 that 50 Chinese artisans disembarked at Nootka Sound, Vancouver Island, with Captain Meares to help develop a fur trading post between Canton and the natives of Nootka Sound. Later, the Spanish drove out Captain Meares as a threat of future competition; many Chinese crew members settled down on the island; they raised families with the native women, grew old, and eventually died in the New World. Various archaeological artifacts remain today, marking this earlier Chinese immigration a model of successful settlement, based on the settlers' respects for the native people and voluntary assimilation into the native culture, as well as the native people's generosity for the settlers.[1]

To retrieve the historical settlement of the 50 Chinese artisans in the 18th century, I am not applying, but rather challenging, a Canadian sociological theory of power-distribution scheme based on the arrival time of immigrants' racial groups. John Porter, exploring this theory in the 1960s, summarized it as "who-got-here-first-has-the-most-say" in "The Vertical Mosaic" (60). This well-accepted, but quite problematic Canadian social law became "who-got-here-*second*-has-the-most-say" (emphasis mine), as Manoly R. Lupul notes on Canadian multiculturalism (3). As both versions are derived from Anglo-French colonialism and nativism, without legislative settlement of the native people's rights to their land, without letting in members of native people and visible minority groups into the power structure, the superficial acknowledgment of the aboriginal people and the rhetorical difference between "who-got-here-first" or "who-got-here-second" do not change the fact that the two dominant charter groups still control the power distribution in contemporary Canadian society. In the case of Chinese immigrants in Canada, their undeniable contributions to this nation and to British Columbia in particular are largely untold in Canadian history; thus, unrecognized in Canadian society.

Chinese immigrants are pioneers and nation-builders of Canada. The majority of Chinese immigrants who came to Canada in the 19th century were either lured by the prosperity of the second "Gold Mountain" discovered in the Fraser River Valley in 1858 or driven by famines at home to become indentured laborers upon the shortage of manpower in Canada.[2]

In one mass migration, approximately 17,000 young Chinese men were directly recruited from Hong Kong and southern China for contractor Andrew Onderdonk to build the British Columbia section of the Canadian Pacific Railway (the CPR). At the CPR, Chinese laborers were underpaid to work in the most dangerous areas without safety devices, medical attendance, or fresh food; their deaths, caused by accidents and diseases, were numerous. According to a conservative estimate of Onderdonk's testimony to the 1885 Royal Commission on Chinese Immigration, 600 Chinese died in the construction, making a ratio of more than four Chinese deaths for

---

[1]References with little variation about the Nootka settlement can be found in the following books: Donghai 60; Steiner 154; Chan 3, and Lee Wai-man 17. For pictures of historical artifacts, see Lee Wai-man 22–23.
[2]The term "Gold Mountain" (gum shan) was first used to refer to the gold rush in California in the 1840s; later the discovery of the Fraser River Valley gold mines was referred to as the second Gold Mountain.

every mile of this section (Wickberg 24). According to an estimate made by the Chinese community, 4,000 Chinese died, making a ratio of more than 26 Chinese deaths for every mile of this section of the CPR (Chung-To Lo 60). In 1891, the Chinese Consolidated Benevolent Association of Victoria alone arranged for a collection of more than 300 unidentified corpses from the Fraser and Thompson canyons to be returned to China for a proper burial (Wickberg 24). On July 29, 1885, towards the last spike, no Chinese workers were invited to the ceremony. Little has ever been mentioned about them in the history of the CPR (Li 59), nor have they been remembered in E. J. Pratt's epic poem, "Towards the Last Spike." It was F. R. Scott, who wrote "All Spikes But the Last," who questions Canadian history and Canadian literature, especially canonical writers such as Pratt for wiping out Chinese immigrants from the historical context (190):

> Where are the coolie in your poem, Ned?...
> Did they fare so well in the land they help to unite?
> Did they get one of the 25,000,000 CPR acres?
> Is all Canada has to say to them written in the Chinese Immigration Act?"

Chinese immigrants and Chinese Canadians suffered unprecedented discrimination in Canadian history. From the 1880s to the 1920s, racist hostility towards Chinese immigrants and their descendants increased from almost all social sectors in British Columbia and Ottawa. Chinese immigrants became the indispensable social scapegoats. Anti-Chinese racists seized upon the visible biological differences as targets. When the first Royal Commission on Chinese Immigration was ordered, Prime Minister Sir John A. MacDonald had "the object of the Commission ... to obtain proof that the principle of restricting Chinese immigration is proper and is in the interests of the Province and the Dominion" (Report of the Royal Commission on Chinese Immigration ix). Chinese immigration was also sacrificed for regional interest by politicians. Historian Kenneth Munro examines Commissioner Chapleau as the most important politician from Montreal with a special regional interest of Quebec, who "saw the exclusion of the Chinese as an obstacle to the construction of Canadian Pacific Railway, and consequently, to George Cartier's dream of making Montreal the metropolitan centre of Canada" (91–95). Ensuring that French Canada's interests were protected, with the finished CPR in sight, on May 4, 1885 at the House of the Commons, Chapleau stated that "as European people now could reach the west coast by railway, the people of British Columbia were right to ask that Chinese immigration be restricted" [House of Commons. Debates (Chapleau) 4 May 1885: 1590].

Chinese immigration was targeted for election campaigns. At the 1921 federal election, in order to win the vote of the unionized labor with a national membership of 225,000, William L. Mackenzie King made a promise of "more effective restriction of Chinese immigration." He spoke agitatedly of white racial and cultural hegemony, "that Canada should remain a white man's country is believed to be not only desirable for economic and social reasons, but necessary on political and national grounds" (Lee Wai-man 131–32). In 1947, when thousands of European immigrants landed in Canada on their own choice, Prime Minister Mackenzie King announced the national immigration strategy of excluding Oriental immigrants:

> The people of Canada do not wish, as a result of mass immigration, to make a fundamental alteration in the character of our population. Large scale immigration from the Orient would change that fundamental composition of the Canadian population. (House of Commons, Debates, 1947, vol. III, 2644–46)

Chinese were treated as the unwanted race in Canadian immigration history. Chinese immigrants were the only racial group that was imposed with head taxes and excluded from Canadian immigration because of their race. Native-born Chinese Canadians were treated as immigrants; they were forced by law to register with the Immigration Department. Chinese Canadians were disenfranchised for a century; as late as spring 1949, they were given, for the first time, the right to vote in British Columbia. Only after 1967, when the universal point system was established for Canadian immigration, could wives and children of the aged Chinese laborers—if they were still alive-come to Canada to be reunited with their husbands and fathers after almost a lifetime separation.

Re-reading Chinese Canadian history, it is evident that institutional racism has created a racially stratified Canadian society, in which the skin colors of non-white groups and their cultural traits are depicted as a signifier of non-assimilability; their accents are considered residues of foreignness. Their differences became attributes of "eternal immigrants" to call back Claire Harris' observation. Had the Chinese any access to the mainstream discursive fields of politics, media, religion, literature, etc. in the 19th century, their contributions to British Columbia and to Canada, their cultural virtues, legends, and mythologies would have been incorporated into Canadian history and culture. They would have been honored as a group of pioneer Canadians and nation-builders. Nevertheless, as a result of over 100 years of racial discrimination and segregation, Chinese Canadians have been deprived of their voice in Canadian context. The cultural and racial experience of the Chinese Canadians has been kept by and large in the ethnic ghettos. Most of the writings in the last 100 years have been published in the heritage language other than the official medium languages of English or French. Because of the institutionally imposed solitude, in the mainstream discursive fields, Chinese Canadians have historically been reduced to voicelessness.

The historical silence of Chinese Canadians in English discourse is neither an original muteness or a sign of non-discursive passivity of the Chinese race. I argue that this silence is a reluctant retreat which can be seen as a collective resistance against institutional injustices. Derrida's exploration of the relationship of silence/*logos*/madness serves an enlightening theoretical construct. According to him, silence cannot be said in "logos," but is indirectly and metaphorically made present by its "pathos." Nevertheless, this silence (of madness) is not a non-discourse, but a subsequent silence, a discourse arrested by command. Thus, it is the dialogue being broken off and divided, signifying an absence, a separation, and an institutional solitude (Derrida 37, 38, 72). As silence is a regularity in a discursive system, it is produced by a power machine in its control over the means of communication with the Other. In the case of Chinese Canadians' historical isolation and segregation, they were deprived of the necessity to communicate in English. Chinese language had been for a long time the only discursive possibility and regularity for the Chinese Canadians confined in ethnic ghettos; their silence in English discourse is thus an imposed solitude, rather than a discursive choice.

Yuen Chung Yip's novel, *The Tears of Chinese Immigrants*, is one sample out of numerous texts published in newspapers or in book form in Chinese by the community and its writers before the 1970s (Lacroix 87–111). The English translation of the novel only became available in 1990, thanks to the current Canadian social discourse of multiculturalism and the financial sponsorship of Multiculturalism Canada (8). As a product of the 1950s and set in a mixed neighborhood in Western Canada, *The Tears of Chinese Immigrants* is embedded with historical elements in its textuality. Chinese were still referred to as "Chinamen" (93), a hereditary subhuman term developed for Chinese bachelor laborers in the 19th century. Racist street rhyme "Chinky, chiny Chinamen" could still be heard from innocent kids who learned it from their grandparents (80). Chinese were marginalized as socially unfit as "not different from the Eskimos or the Indians" (94). Chinese did not think themselves as Canadians either, because being Canadian meant being racially white, culturally superior, and discursively domineering in Canadian society (99).

Written in the first-person narrative of Charlie Zhang, the protagonist, the novel is a dialogue between a younger generation of Chinese immigrants and the traditions of the Gold Mountain. Character Uncle Liang's life is constructed as a historical context of

Gold Mountain for all Chinese in Canada. Uncle Liang is one of the thousands of Chinese bachelor laborers abandoned by Andrew Onderdonk after the CPR was completed; they spread eastbound all over Canada in order to open cafes and laundries for a living. They sent money home to help raise their families. They saved all their lives, hoping one day they could afford the return fares or costs to bring their families to Canada. Illiterate both in Chinese and English, the dilemma of Uncle Liang's generation in the Gold Mountain is undefinable. The historicities of their isolation in Canadian society are embedded in both the original Chinese text and the subsequent English translation; in both cases the materiality of the printed words can only recall with "pathos" the silence of the "eternal immigrants," whose reality can be displaced, but never transcended in the materiality of words.

If Yuen Chung Yip and his generation had to choose silence in English by writing in Chinese as a discursive resistance, the choice of English as the linguistic medium by Sky Lee, Paul Yee, and many other younger contemporary Chinese Canadian writers have demonstrated a post-colonial appropriation of the imperial discourse. For the third and fourth generations of the Canadian-born Chinese, English is as their first language as their heritage language learned from home. Their bilingual capability and their emergence into Canadian social and cultural life in recent decades initiate an ethnic psychological regeneration which calls for a re-definition of Chinese Canadian history, culture, and identity in contemporary Canadian context. In *Disappearing Moon Cafe*, Sky Lee brings out the discursive transition from tears and silence of the older generations to the preference of voice by younger Chinese Canadians. The character/narrator Kae Ying Woo, fourth-generation of Chinese Canadians, realizes that silence and voice are both discursive regularities in discourse. Nevertheless, a discursive transition signifies political impact:

> I have a misgiving that the telling of our history is forbidden. I have violated a secret code. There is power in silence, as this is the way we have always maintained strict control against the more disturbing aspects in our human nature. But what about speaking out for a change, despite its unpredictable impact! The power of language is that it can be manipulated beyond our control, towards misunderstanding. But then again, the power of language is also in its simple honesty. (Lee 180)

Similar to *The Tears of Chinese Immigrants, Disappearing Moon Cafe* depicts the bachelor laborers as a historical perspective and contemporary Chinese Canadians as the speaking subjects. Sky Lee employs two narrative frameworks: one is a traditional Prologue/Epilogue structure, which is set in the great-grandfather Wong Gwei Chang's mind, before his death in 1939, to review the experience of the generation of Chinese bachelor laborers. The other narrative structure is centered around the character/narrator Kae Ying Woo, fourth-generation of Canadian-born Chinese, great-granddaughter of Wong Gwei Chang. The relationship between the two narrative structures form a discursive dichotomy of silence and voice.

The Prologue/Epilogue which frames Wong Gwei Chang's memories can be read metonymically as a status of silence, similar to that of Uncle Liang's double illiteracy in *The Tears of Chinese Immigrants*. The Prologue/Epilogue contains the accumulated anger of this generation, which was never given a chance to be transformed timely into words, into "logos," or into English. As their silence can only be sensed as a discursive totality of resistance, and not be said in "logos," the experience of Wong Gwei Chang, Uncle Liang, and the generations of Chinese laborers can probably best be constructed in a third-person narrative and be voiced by a younger generation in their dialogue with the Gold Mountain history. This third-person narrative, which presents a re-constructed historical perspective on Chinese immigrants in the 19th century, displaces their silence with narrative. By giving voice to their silence, the narrative arouses "pathos" in the reader while appropriating the historical silence of the Chinese laborers.

Character Wong Gwei Chang's personal life is constructed in a third-person narrative as a fictional embodiment of the community history. Covering a historical period from 1892–1939, his memories recall the historical Chinese settlement at Nootka Sound with the native peoples in the 1800s (3, 7); they testify to the bone-hunting journey of the diseased Chinese railway laborers along the completed CPR in the 1890s and the arrangement to have them send back to China for a proper burial (2). His memories also witness Chinese immigrants being targeted by societal-wide racism (97) and being imposed with head taxes and the Exclusion Act by Canadian governments (30). As a community leader of the time, Wong Gwei Chang's memories speak with collectivity. He also recalls the successful historical events organized by the Chinese community in response to anti-Chinese racism (76, 226, 227). The body of the novel, written in the first-person narrative of Kae Ying Woo forms a dialogue between younger generations and the Gold Mountain history. The pattern is obvious in the writer's choice of Kae Ying Woo as the speaking subject in her first-person narrative, while her great-grandfather Wong Gwei Chang's experience is recounted in the third-person narrative of memories. The relationship between the two narrative frameworks embodies a political and discursive dichotomy of silence vs. voice, similar to the narrator/narrated relationship between Charlie Zhang and Uncle Liang in *The Tears of Chinese Immigrants.*

I have started this paper by re-reading Canadian achieves on Chinese immigration. I relate institutionalized anti-Chinese racism directly to the 100-year silence of Chinese Canadians in mainstream Canadian discourses. The fact that earlier Chinese Canadian writers chose Chinese as their linguistic medium is read as a sign of discursive silence and resistance against racial and cultural discrimination; while the choice of English language by younger writers today engages the Chinese Canadian writers in a dialogue with Canadian history in order to redefine community history, the collective Chinese Canadian culture, and the individuals in contemporary Canadian society. Therefore I posit silence vs. voice in a discursive dichotomy as equal regularities to construct a post-colonial experience—discursive resistance and appropriation. This political dichotomy is interrelated and interchangeable, controlled by the power machine in society. Thus, the breakthrough from silence to voice indicates further social changes, rather than a shift within the great modes of narrative.

Critics and theorists have pointed out that the conditions of post-colonial literature are based on linguistic, cultural, and conceptual conflicts and subsequent inevitable appropriations. While "much European thinking, history, ancestry, and the past form a powerful reference point for epistemology," post-colonial writers "deliberately set out to disrupt European notions of 'history' and the ordering of time" (Ashcroft 34). By re-writing Chinese Canadian history, the emergence of contemporary Chinese Canadian literature not only produces a non-European literary branch in the family tree of Canadian literature, but also serves to re-define contemporary Canadian culture. As a model of post-colonial possibility, Chinese Canadian literature sets up a parallel cultural reference system next to the existing dominant Anglo-French system in Canada. The result of discursive appropriation will "dislocate" European cultural history, as Derrida foresees, from "considering itself as the culture of reference" for all (Derrida 282).

Works Cited

Ashcroft, Bill, Gareth Griffiths and Helen Tiffin. *The Empire Writes Back: Theory and Practice in Post-Colonial Literatures.* London/New York: Routledge, 1989.

Canada. "Report of the Royal Commission on Chinese Immigration." Ottawa: Printed by Order of the Commission, 1885.

Canada. House of Commons. Debates (Chapleau) 4 May 1885: 1590.

Canada. House of Commons. Debates. vol. III (1947): 2644–46.

Chan, Anthony B. *Gold Mountain: The Chinese in the New World*. Vancouver: New Star Books, 1983.

Derrida, Jacques. *Writing and Difference*. Chicago: University of Chicago Press, 1978.

Harris, Claire. "Poets in Limbo." In *A Mazing Space: Writing Canadian Women Writing*. Eds. Shirley Neuman and Smaro Kamboureli. Edmonton: Longspoon/NeWest Presses, 1986. 115–25.

Lacroix, Jean-Michel. *Anatomie de la Presse Ethnique au Canada*. Cedex, France: Presses Universitaires de Bordeau, 1988.

Lee, Sky. *Disappearing Moon Cafe*. Vancouver/Toronto: Douglas & McIntyre, 1990.

Lee, Wai-man. *Portraits of a Challenge: An Illustrated History of the Chinese Canadians*. Toronto: Council of Chinese Canadians in Ontario, 1984.

Li, Donghai. *Jianada Huaqiao Shi, or History of the Overseas Chinese in Canada*. Taibei: Haidian, 1967.

Li, Peter S. *The Chinese in Canada*. Toronto: Oxford UP, 1988.

Lo, Chung-To. *Canada [Jia Na Da Die Fang Zhi]*. Toronto: Relief Map Service, 1987.

Lupul, Manoly R. "Networking, Discrimination and Multiculturalism as a Social Philosophy." *Canadian Ethnic Studies* 2 (1989): 1–12.

Munro, Kenneth. "The Chinese Immigration Act, 1885: Adolphe Chapleau and the French Canadian Attitude." *Canadian Ethnic Studies* 3 (1987): 91–95.

Porter, John. *The Vertical Mosaic: An Analysis of Social Class and Power in Canada*. Toronto/Buffalo/London: University of Toronto Press, 1965.

Pratt, E. J. *Towards the Last Spike: A Verse-Panorama of the Struggle to Build the First Canadian Transcontinental from the Time of the Proposed Terms of Union with British Columbia, 1870, to the Hammering of the Last Spike in the Eagle Pass, 1885*. Toronto: Macmillan, 1952.

Scott, F.R. "All the Spikes But the Last." In *The Collected Poems of F.R. Scott*. Toronto: McClelland and Stewart, 1981. 194.

Steiner, Stan. *Fushan: The Chinese Who Built America*. New York: Harper and Row, 1979.

Wickberg, Edgar. Ed. Harry Con, Ronald J. Con, Graham Johnson, Edgar Wickberg and William E. Willmott. *From China to Canada: A History of the Chinese Communities in Canada*. Toronto: McClelland and Stewart in association with the Multiculturalism Directorate, and Department of State, 1982.

Yip, Yuen Chung. *The Tears of Chinese Immigrants*. Transl. Sheng-Tai Chang. Dunvegan, Ont.: Cormorant Books, 1990.

The Voice of a "Cultivated" Asian:
Yan Phou Lee and his Autobiography
When I Was a Boy in China

XIAO-HUANG YIN
American Studies, Occidental College, Los Angeles, California

Throughout the late 19th and early 20th centuries, there were quite a few Chinese students sent by the Manchu court, or brought by missionaries to America for advanced education. Although their migration to the United States during this period represented only a tiny fraction of Chinese immigrants, they constituted a disproportionately large part of the literary voice of the early Chinese American community. The reason is not hard to understand. While most early Chinese immigrants possessed neither time nor means to voice their views and beliefs, these students, sponsored by the Chinese government or by missionary organizations, lived a fairly comfortable life. Moreover, as most of them received a good education in the United States and had sophisticated literary tastes, they knew how to write and what audience to address. Therefore, despite the fact that they cannot be viewed as representative of the general population of Chinese in this country, their writing comprises the bulk of early Chinese American literature.

Unlike most of their countrymen, who lived in the segregated urban ghettos and remained outsiders in American society, most of the Chinese students succeeded in assimilating into the mainstream of American cultural and intellectual life. To be sure, they felt frustrated by the racial prejudice against Chinese and shared the resentment over their countrymen's mistreatment at Gold Mountain. But as members of the exempt classes, they never had the same bitter experiences the Chinese laborers encountered every day, and they held a social status that could never be dreamed of by their "undistinguished" countrymen.

In general, their works are characterized by intentions to bridge the racial and cultural gap between China and America. Apparently, their perception of the roots of racism differed from that of other Chinese immigrants—they saw racism largely as a result of total ignorance and common misconceptions about Chinese civilization on the part of Americans, rather than as a product of the social environment and economic conditions. Thus, they believed that with knowledge, there would come improved treatment of the Chinese in this country. In order to accomplish this purpose, they strongly felt that they, first of all, needed to challenge and rectify the negative views and stereotypes about China which then prevailed in American society. They held that, through the dissemination of correct information on various aspects of Chinese culture and society, they could improve the image of their homeland and win sympathy and acceptance for Chinese immigrants.

Based on the life experience of the gentry class from which most of the students came, their explanation of China to Americans is mainly focused on the "high culture" of Chinese society. And they often deliberately sought to present an attractive picture of Chinese civilization, particularly the charming features of the philosophy, religion, literature, and cultural tradition. They hoped that by writing in this way, they could arouse the benign curiosity of average American readers longing for the "exotic Oriental taste," hence raising the position of China in the eyes of the American public. Although the picture they painted was often artificial and offered limited views of Chinese society, their writing represented serious efforts to introduce Chinese civilization to an American audience and defend it, despite racial prejudice. Indeed, it was their writing that first offered many an American reader a broad-eyed glimpse into Chinese culture. Such evidence of the world beyond had obvious value in teaching Americans about the true nature of China and its people. Lee Yan Phou's autobiographical account of his childhood in the old country, *When I Was a Boy in China*, is an outstanding example of such writing. Published by Lothrop Company in Boston in 1887, it was also the first literary work written in English by a Chinese or an Asian in this country.

Born in a gentry-scholar family at a town about 75 miles south of Canton City, Lee was brought to the United States to study by the Chinese Educational Mission in 1873 at the age of 12. Having lived in the United States for more than a decade, he became profoundly aware of the stereotypes average Americans had formed of China and felt frustrated about it:

> I still continually find false ideas in America concerning Chinese customs, manners, and institutions. Small blame to the people at large, who have no means of learning the truth except through newspapers or accounts of travelers who do not understand what they see in passing through our country…. Accordingly, what I tell in this series of articles about Chinese customs, manners and institutions may often contradict general belief. (Lee 41)

Obviously, this is the major motivation that caused him to undertake the work when he was solicited by Lothrop Company to write a book on China.

Covering such subjects as philosophy, education, literature, religion, ceremonies, family, food, and pastimes, *When I Was a Boy in*

China is an almost encyclopedic account of Chinese civilization. It provides readers with a panoramic view of Chinese society and it elaborated on many aspects of Chinese culture. Lee's discussion of table manners in China, for example, is so detailed and amusing that one could almost visually see the scene:

> The younger ones do not presume to sit till their elders are seated; then after making a show of asking permission to eat, when the elders gravely nod assent, the breakfast begins. Soup is taken first; then each person, holding the chopsticks in the right hand and the bowl of rice in the left, lifts his food to his mouth, pushes the lumps in with the sticks, alternating this motion with picking meat, fish or vegetables from the dishes which are common to all. One must take only from the side of the plate which is nearest to him, however. It is a breach of etiquette to reach over the opposite side. When one finishes, he bids the rest to "eat leisurely," which is our mode of saying "Excuse me!" The Chinese invariably wash their hands and faces after every meal. (30)

While contemporary readers may feel bored by detailed elaboration of such trivial matters, there was certainly a need for Lee to write so. Many Americans at that time, especially the middle class Americans who would be the potential audience of the book, were more disturbed by the strange culture and actions of the Chinese than by the issue of cheap labor. The Chinese custom of shooting firecrackers to celebrate their New Year and other holidays, for instance, was deemed a nuisance and a direct fire hazard, and Chinese funerals with their elaborate ceremonies often elicited only the laughter and contempt of the American spectators. The sacrifices to the dead—usually consisting of roast pig, chickens, rice, liquor, and Chinese sweetmeats—were considered by Americans nothing but meals for Indians. A newspaper reporter in the Midwest observes: "Many Indians made a delicious dinner from the provisions customarily put by the grave of the dead Chinaman." (BeDunnah 16). What the reporter forgot or was too embarrassed to mention, however, is that not only Indians, but "white Americans" also frequently appropriated the food left by Chinese after the ceremonies (Chu 164–195).

The attempt to elucidate the American public's misunderstandings about China can also be seen in Lee's argument on why certain cultural activities, which were common in America, did not exist in China. Using dancing as a typical example, Lee explains that there is no such thing in China because Chinese are more practical than Americans with their time:

> A Chinese gentleman would consider it foolishness and an insensate waste of time to hop about and twirl around for a whole night. Amusements requiring so much exertion are not his taste; and as for throwing his arm around a girl's waist in the whirl of the waltz, a Chinese gentleman would not permit himself such an indecorum. (39)

Again, for the same reason of being practical with one's life, according to Lee, "Fishing means work with the Chinese. A man, or boy, goes a-fishing simply for the fish, and not for the fun." Lee then emphasizes, "and I am of the opinion that my countrymen are right."

For the most part, however, Lee's intention is to demonstrate to the American public that despite the seeming difference between the "Middle Kingdom" and the United States, elements from the two civilizations could be combined, and there could be points of compatibility between peoples of the two cultures. Using illustrations and pictures, Lee explains in detail how a Chinese institution functions and frequently compares it with that of other nations. In his opinion, Chinese society is essentially democratic, just as that of America, because, as far as social mobility is concerned, "there is no such thing as caste in China, in the sense that caste exists in India. In China, wealth and literary and official honors ennoble a family and can lift it from a lower to a higher plane." Even in daily life, Lee points out, Chinese and Americans share many things in common. The cover of the book is a good example. With a colorful picture of a Chinese boy running with a flying kite, he indicates that Chinese kids play the same games that their American peers do and perhaps enjoy it more because Chinese kites are made better than American ones. Hence, he suggests: "Kite-flying in America can be much improved. Kites should be constructed of the Chinese shape."

In order to provide legitimacy for his book's acceptance by the American public, Lee also tries to offer something exotic, foreign, and attractive. It is for this reason that he brings a typical Chinese classroom scene into discussion:

> It is six o'clock a.m. All the boys are shouting at the top of their voices, at the fullest stretch of their lungs. Occasionally, one stops and talks to some one sitting near him. Two of the most careless ones are guessing pennies; and anon a dispute arises as to which of the two disputants writes a better hand... All at once the talking, the playing, the shouting ceases. A bent form slowly comes up through the open court. The pupils rise to their feet. A simultaneous salutation issues from a dozen pairs of lips. All cry out, "Lao Se" (venerable teacher)! As he sits down, all follow his example... Then one takes his book up to the teacher's desk, turns his back to him and recites. But see, he soon hesitates; the teacher prompts him... He forgets three times; the teacher is out of

patience with the third stumble, and down comes the ruler, whack! whack! upon the head. With one hand feeling the aching spot and the other carrying back his book, the discomfited youngster returns to his desk to re-con his lesson. (58–59)

The strong sense of humor in the depiction certainly provides readers with an exotic picture.

Here arises an interesting point. The narrative tone of the book is supposed to be Chinese, but we find that it is surprisingly Western. In other words, the Western cultural influence on the author is so overwhelming that one might think the book is written by an American author. Lee's familiarity with English literature is authentic and impressive. Talking about the *erhu*, a traditional Chinese musical instrument, he mentions it can make melody in the hand of a skillful player but would produce the sound "distinguished in the din like the witches' voices above the storm in Macbeth" when it is played by a stranger. Moreover, readers can easily identify the traits of English literature in both the style and organization of the book. Despite the "Oriental taste" Lee adds to the opening part, it looks surprisingly similar to that of an English classic of his time—David Copperfield.[1] Lee must have had in mind Chapter One of the masterpiece "I Am Born" when he was putting down these lines:

On a certain day in the year 1861, I was born. I cannot give you the exact date, because the Chinese year is different from the English year, and our month being lunar, that is reckoned by the revolution of the moon around the earth... and we say, instead of "January, February," etc., "Regular Moon, Second Moon," etc. (7)

The close resemblance between Lee's writing here and the beginning chapter of Charles Dickens' pseudo-autobiography betrays subtly how Westernized the author's mind was, though he could still speak fluent Chinese. The chapter also reveals that Chinese American authors learned to write English mostly from textbooks and great masterpieces, hence their English is usually formal and polished.

Since Lee's main concern is to "present an accurate image of China" in the book, he would naturally focus on things which he thought had been deliberately distorted and would try to correct them. Actually, we can hear an angry tone in his normally calm narration when he comes to the wild stories American journalists spread on the fate of Chinese girls:

---

[1]Whether Lee actually read David Copperfield, we do not know. But given the fact he was so familiar with English literature, it is very possible that he had read the book.

> I am indignant that there should be a popular belief in America that Chinese girls at their birth are generally put to death because they are not wanted by their parents. Nothing can be further from the truth... I venture to say that in proportion to population and distribution of wealth that infanticide is as rare in China as it is in this country. (43)

In order to rectify the distorted picture, Lee time and again argues that Chinese civilization is not only similar, but also superior, to that of America in many respects:

> A "poor relation" there (in China) is treated with much more consideration and affection than in this country. Generosity towards that class of unfortunates is so common, and its practice is so strenuously insisted upon, in the moral code of the Chinese, that it almost ceases to be an individual virtue—it is a national virtue. (44)

Of course, by explaining Chinese culture in such an idealized way, Lee actually presents a picture of the superficialities of Chinese society. Comparisons between the two cultures in this way would, of course, make one feel that Chinese civilization is better and more humane. Nevertheless, we should not be too critical of the author. One has to put the writing into its socio-historical context. To understand why Lee wrote in this way, we should recall that this was the time when many Americans "truly believed" that "the Chinese (are) uncivilized, unclean, and filthy beyond all conception... lustful and sensual in their dispositions" (Chinese Historical Society 4). It was an immense blow to the self-esteem of Chinese immigrants when they heard in testimony at a Congressional hearing in 1877 that their civilization was even more inferior to that of Negroes, and they were incapable of attaining the state of civilization that the Caucasian is capable of (Sandmeyerm 62–63). With so much against Chinese immigrants, it is small wonder that Lee would argue in this way. This is an obstinate voice, meaning to assure Americans of the excellence of Chinese culture, and expressing a "defensive arrogance" to counter the racial bias.

Similarly, Lee's spontaneous expression of nostalgia serves the same purpose. One of the most common accusations laid upon the Chinese at this time was that they lacked feelings and were emotionless. Even a progressive writer such as Jack London would state arrogantly that the Chinese "were a race different from mine," who "were absolutely indifferent and were least sensitive."[2] Against

---

[2]Despite his progressive views on social problems, Jack London is known for his racial prejudice against non-whites. When criticized by his friends that his racial bias was inconsistent with the socialist doctrine, London is said to have

this background, Lee's emotional account of his sad departure from home shows that the Chinese had the same feelings of other races. He tells us vividly how he felt heart-broken when he left his mother:

> I bowed my head four times to the ground upon my knees. She tried to appear cheerful, but I could see that her eyes were moistened with tears... She gave me some pocket-money and bade me be a good boy and write often. (96)

Since Chinese then were labeled as lacking human feelings and holding life less dear than Caucasians, the sentimental description itself can be viewed as the author's subtle protest against racial bias.

Ironically, despite Lee's intentions and efforts to introduce Chinese culture to Americans, the most interesting passages we read today are his comments on life in America. Of course, as a member of the privileged Chinese Educational Mission, his experience at the Gold Mountain was very different from that of most of his countrymen. Being totally unaware of the miserable fate of Chinese laborers in that very city, Lee claims that "San Francisco in 1873 was the paradise of the self-exiled Chinese." This might be true for a person like him "who came to study under the auspices of the Chinese government and under the protection of the American Eagle." But it was surely not the case for those who were subjects of anti-Chinese violence that occurred rampantly under the same Eagle at this time. Only two years before, an anti-Chinese riot in Los Angeles ended with the murder of 19 Chinese "coolies." However, despite the drastic difference in their personal backgrounds, Lee appears to have experienced the same cultural shock as his unprivileged countrymen:

> It was a long time before I got used to those red-headed and tight-jacketed foreigners. "How can they walk or run?" I asked myself curiously contemplating their close and confining garments. The dress of American ladies was still another mystery to me. They shocked my sense of propriety also, by walking arm-in-arm with the men. "How peculiar their voices are! How screechy! How sharp!" Such were some of the thoughts I had about those peculiar people.[3] (98)

If the dress of American ladies alone had already stunned him, then one cannot help wondering how he felt when he actually met with American women. The real embarrassment took place when Lee

---

met the criticism by pounding on the table and exclaiming, "What the devil! I am first of all a white man and only then a Socialist!" (Gossett 206).

[3]Interestingly, Henry James and William Dean Howells sometimes said more or less the same thing (Berthoff 50–125).

was introduced to his American hostess: "She came after us in a hack. As I was pointed out to her, she put her arms around me and kissed me. This made the rest of the boys laugh, and perhaps I got rather red in the face... It was the first kiss I ever had since my infancy."

The most dramatic part, however, is Lee's first impression of American civilization. The chapter entitled "First Experience in America" provides readers with a unique perspective on how 19th century American civilization was perceived by a young boy from a "strange shore." Ironically, Lee claims that a train robbery taught him what "American civilization really means." This statement produces a subtle satire when we compare it to how proud American writers and artists felt about the train, and that the locomotive had become virtually the symbol of progress and modernization in popular American culture at the time (Kulik 495–510). The terrible event occurred on Lee's very first journey eastward across the American continent in a train with his fellow students and teachers of the Chinese Educational Mission:

> We were quietly looking out of the windows when the train suddenly bounded backward... Our party, teachers and pupils, jumped from our seats in dismay and looked out through the windows for more light on the subject. What we saw was enough to make our hair stand on end. Two ruffianly men held a revolver in each hand and seemed to be taking aim at us... Our teachers told us to crouch down for our lives. We obeyed with trembling and fear. Doubtless, many prayers were most fervently offered to the gods of China at the time. Our teachers certainly prayed as they had never done before. One of them was overheard calling upon all the gods of the Chinese Pantheon to come and save him... a brakeman rushed through with a lamp in his hand. He told us that the train had been robbed of its gold bricks by five men, three of whom, dressed like Indians, rifled the baggage car while the others held the passengers at bay; that the engine was hopelessly wrecked, the engineer killed; that the robbers had escaped on horseback with their booty. (107–8)

That the event left a strong and lasting impact on him is obvious, for, after the agony and suspense were over, Lee declares in a sarcastic tone that "one phase of American civilization was thus indelibly fixed upon our minds." Undoubtedly, his comment on the dramatic event here also aims at scoring a neat point against those who truly believed the Chinese were lawless barbarians and would harm the innocent Americans.

Although Lee's depiction of China is limited and artificial, the book is nevertheless of great significance. Being the first book written in English by an "Oriental," *When I Was a Boy in China* provides readers with a picture of the Chinese as exotic, quaint, and delicate in contrast to the popular belief that Chinese and Asians were mysterious, evil, and threatening. The humorous narration and informative discussion must have been quite appealing to Americans, since American commercial publishers soon decided to publish a series of books written by people from Asia. Works such as *A Daughter of the Samurai* and *When I was a Boy in Korea* were modeled after Lee's book (Kim 25–27). In this sense, Lee had set an example by creating a new tradition which today still has its influence on Asian American writers. Although the book is by no means representative of early Chinese American experience, it thus began a tradition that has been carried on throughout history.[4]

Works Cited

Berthoff, Warner. *The Ferment of Realism: American Literature, 1884–1919*. New York: Cambridge University Press, 1981 (reprinted edition).

Chu, Limin. "The Images of China and the Chinese in the Overland Monthly: 1868–1875, 1883–1935." Ph.D. dissertation, Duke University, 1965.

Gold Hill Daily News (Gold Hill, Nevada) 3 July 1880. Quoted in Gary BeDunnah. "A History of the Chinese in Nevada, 1855–1904." Thesis, University of Nevada at Reno, 1966. 16.

Gossett, Thomas F. *Race: The History of an Idea in America*. Dallas: Southern Methodist University Press, 1963.

Kim, Elaine H. *Asian American Literature: An Introduction to the Writings and Their Social Context*. Philadelphia: Temple University Press, 1982.

Kulik, Gary. "Representing the Railroad." *Gettysburg Review* 2:3 (Summer 1989): 495–510.

Lee, Yan Phou. "The Chinese Must Stay." *North American Review* (April 1889).

Lee, Yan Phou. *When I Was a Boy in China*. Boston: Lothrop, 1887.

Sandmeyerm, Elmer C. *The Anti-Chinese Movement in California*. Chicago: University of Illinois Press, 1973 (reprinted edition).

The Chinese Experience in Arizona and Northern Mexico: 1870–1940. Tucson: Chinese Historical Society, 1980.

---

[4]In addition to *When I Was a Boy in China*, Lee also wrote quite a few articles such as "The Chinese Must Stay" (*North American Review* 4/89).

The Course of Exclusion, 1882–1924:
San Francisco Newspaper Coverage of the Chinese in the United States

JULES BECKER
Dominican College, San Rafael, California

The first American legislation to put restrictions on the immigration of foreign nationals was passed in 1882. This concluded an effort which began about the time that California Governor John Bugler suggested a ban on the landing of Chinese laborers in a special message to the legislature in 1852, when substantial numbers of Chinese first arrived in California. Two decades after the initial Chinese Restriction Act became law, Japanese were the targets. In 1924, Japanese joined Chinese on the exclusion list.

I plan to refer to Japanese exclusion and Japanese as an aside occasionally during this paper to provide a comparison with Chinese and Chinese exclusion.

Chinese immigrants, among the most accommodating and hard-working people ever to enter the United States, were murdered, beaten, and preyed upon by Caucasian Americans, especially in Northern California and the West. But from the 1880s to the first World War, the United States accepted the most dramatic surge of immigration the world had ever seen. Millions of men, women, and children left their homes and their homelands and traveled to the United States to seek better living conditions and a more favorable future. Under these circumstances, why were two particular immigrant groups singled out for exclusion? I sought answers in two major newspapers in San Francisco, the West Coast's most important city at the time, because the *San Francisco Chronicle* and *San Francisco Examiner* played singularly important roles in the campaigns to exclude both Asian groups.

That Chinese and Japanese were targets is not to say that other immigrants were treated well. The story of American immigration is a tale of hardships overcome, of mistreatment ignored, of hard work and long hours, of a society which made room for foreigners grudgingly. Yet foreigners provided the labor and the variety that have made the United States a pluralist nation. There were efforts near the end of the 19th century to establish regulations to restrict the flow of immigrants, and certain identifiable types—paupers, criminals, the insane, illiterates— were barred between 1882 and 1917. Still, no ethnic group, no nationality except Chinese and Japanese, was flatly excluded.

Chinese were the first; while they were under attack, Japanese were the "good" Asians, of whom the *Chronicle* stated, "Of all the foreigners who come to this country it has often been remarked that none assimilates more readily than the Japanese...." But as the campaign against Chinese achieved success, and the Japanese population in the United States increased, Japanese became targets, and the *Chronicle* referred to Chinese as "by far the best of all Oriental coolies...."

After Chinese were barred, it may have been easier to exclude Japanese. Beyond question, Japanese would have been excluded earlier than 1924 had not the government of Japan taken an active role as protector of its nationals in this country. While China took little notice of what was happening to Chinese in the United States during the lengthy period of restriction and, finally, exclusion, the Japanese government reacted quickly and energetically, viewing mistreatment of, or derogatory comments about, its nationals or its emigrants as affronts unacceptable to a sovereign state. At a time when anti-Japanese activity increased because of expanded Japanese immigration, the Japanese government became even more involved, using diplomatic means to forestall United States exclusion legislation. In 1907, it signed a "Gentleman's Agreement" with President Theodore Roosevelt in which Japan committed itself to stop the emigration of Japanese laborers to the United States.

In seeking to learn more about Chinese and Japanese exclusion, one of the reasons I selected the *Chronicle* and the *Examiner* as the source of data on the events of the period was because the papers remained under the same familial ownership throughout the period between the legislation of 1882 and 1924; thus, they provided a continuity of coverage on the issue of Chinese and Japanese immigration. During the entire span of my study, M.H. de Young published the *Chronicle* and exercised direct control of its operation. The Hearst family, first father George, then son William Randolph, published the *Examiner* during these years, although W. R. Hearst guided his West Coast paper from the East Coast after he purchased the New York Journal in 1895.

A caveat: The terms "Restriction Act" and "Exclusion Act" are used interchangeably to describe the same situation—legislation to choke off Chinese and Japanese immigration. The first statute was referred to as a "Restriction Act" because it suspended immigration of Chinese laborers into the United States for a 10-year period. Some 20 years later, after passage of a series of laws, this action became permanent, that is, exclusion. The 1924 legislation never mentioned Japanese, but it prevented all aliens ineligible for citizenship from entering the country; thus, it excluded Japanese as clearly as if they had been specifically identified.

Between 1882 and 1924, a tremendous change occurred in the United States and in the world. In 1881, Vice President Chester A. Arthur, the New York politician whose background typified the Gilded Age, became President. The Civil War had ended less than 20 years before, and the Reconstruction Era had been over almost as long. The telephone had just been invented, but electricity was not yet a factor in American life. Southern blacks were enjoying a respite from the pressures of white opposition to Reconstruction, not the least of which were the activities of the original Ku Klux Klan; they had yet to face the full force of Jim Crow and disenfranchisement. The United States was a turbulent society— politically, economically, socially. Still to come were the Spanish-American War; American expansion into Hawaii, Puerto Rico, and the Philippines; Progressivism; World War I, and the aftermath of that war: political isolationism and economic globalism. The four decades under consideration, from Arthur to Coolidge, encompass as momentous a change in American society as any 40-year period in the nation's history. But at least one common thread ran through this time. The determination to prevent Chinese and, later, Japanese immigrants from entering the country showed itself at the beginning and at the end of this period, and in most of the years in between.

Attitudes toward the two Asian groups showed differences. Chinese were seen as criminals; my review of articles dealing with Chinese and Japanese shows that stories about Chinese and crime provided a substantial part of the coverage in both papers. Japanese, on the other hand, even during the period when they were under attack, were not considered criminals as were Chinese. As the stories about Japanese increased, articles dealing with crime dropped in percentages.

By the time Chinese were excluded, Japanese had become targets, but under different conditions. Exclusion forces objected, but acquiesced, as Japanese agreed to limit their numbers in the United States. Both papers treated Japanese more evenly than they treated Chinese during the periods when exclusion legislation was being considered in Washington. One reason for this more equitable treatment was in the economic benefits which accrued from ongoing friendly trade involving both countries. At one point the *Chronicle* noted that "The significance of the attitude of the Japanese [regarding the passage of exclusion legislation] is that the Exclusion Act is having no effect on our business relations with Japan." A second reason for the different treatment of Japanese was the stature Japan had attained in international affairs, and a third reason was Japan's refusal to permit mistreatment of Japanese immigrants in the United States. China, on the other hand, made little effort which would cause the papers to temper their attacks on Chinese.

Both the *Chronicle* and the *Examiner* were actively involved in the exclusion drama over 42 years between 1882 and 1924. They reported events involving Chinese and Japanese in this country at length, and they furnished editorial support for the anti-Asian efforts. They provided a common thread throughout the period. Questions arise: Did they lead the battle, or did they reflect the attitudes of their readers, the prejudices of their community? Having spent eight years as a reporter, writer, and editor on four major metropolitan dailies in this country, including two Hearst Corporation newspapers, I acquired the background to undertake both a qualitative and quantitative analysis of the news and comment presented in the two San Francisco newspapers.

The combined circulation of the *Chronicle* and *Examiner* during my study reached a substantial portion of the residents of San Francisco. It rose from approximately 20% in 1882, when the *Examiner* showed minimal sales and when there were more than 20 daily newspapers in the city, to more than 40% from 1892 on, when the William Randolph Hearst-brand of journalism expanded his paper's audience. The *Chronicle* was first in circulation, then second to the *Examiner*, during the entire period. Although the papers were read beyond the city, their circulation and influence as the dominant news medium were strongest in San Francisco. The news and comment the two papers offered could, therefore, play a sizable role in shaping public opinion in the city throughout the period. This possibility provides the opportunity to discover whether the two papers led campaigns to eliminate Chinese and Japanese immigration or whether they merely mirrored the views of the community.

I included blacks in my survey of the *Chronicle* and the *Examiner* to determine how the papers covered other non-whites, and to provide a comparison of the coverage of non-Caucasian segments of the American society. During a period when blacks were losing their civil rights and were the victims of deadly violence in other sections of the country, none of this surfaced in San Francisco, although, to be sure, the black population was minimal. The papers show that the enmity toward the Asians, and, in particular, the mistreatment of Chinese, did not extend to San Francisco and West Coast blacks.

Racism can be described as hostility of one race toward another because of different appearance, customs, and beliefs; it presupposes that race determines human traits and capacities. Under this definition, the *Chronicle* and the *Examiner* provide evidence that racism dominated the campaign to exclude Chinese and Japanese. Pejorative descriptions of Chinese continued well past the time that exclusion was law—and had accomplished its purpose. Chinese were "wily heathens" in 1882 and 1887, "wily Chinese" in 1902, "wily sons of Manchu" in 1907, "wily

Orientals" in 1912, "wily Chinese" another time in 1917, and "wily Celestials" in 1922 and 1924. The *Chronicle* and *Examiner* showed more care in language which referred to Japanese, but the use of the term "Little Brown Men" as a derogatory description occurred a number of times in both papers.

A key to the attitude toward both Chinese and Japanese involved the question of the assimilability of both groups, the question of whether they could fit into the American society and culture. When the effort to restrict Chinese immigration reached its peak, a major reason advanced was their inability to assimilate into American society. In 1887, however, the *Chronicle* found that Japanese could assimilate, and "took a special pride in adapting" to America. Five years later, the *Examiner*, while pressing hard for extension of the original Restriction Act against Chinese, commented about the "peculiar American quality of the Japanese nation." But there were only a few Japanese in this country in 1887 and 1892, and the papers viewed Chinese as the major threat. By 1907, when Chinese exclusion had fallen into place and Japanese immigration had increased rapidly, Chinese were the "best Orientals." By 1922, as both papers continued to urge exclusion of Japanese, they made it a point to state that, although they like Japanese as a people and a nation, the Asians were "not assimilable;" they were "virile and competent," but opposition to them was "a matter of assimilation."

San Francisco newspapers did not stand alone in their attitudes toward Chinese and Japanese. In Southern California, the Los Angeles Times accepted the idea of Chinese exclusion almost as a given, commenting as the permanent barrier was being arranged in 1902: "What is needed, and badly needed, is not merely a Chinese exclusion act, but an act which will prevent the entry into this country of all people who would not make good citizens of the United States...." As for Japanese exclusion, when the bill had finally become law, the Times editorialized: "For good or ill Japanese exclusion is now an accomplished fact. The menace of a peaceful penetration by oriental [sic] labor has been conjured away. It might have been done more diplomatically, but the important point is that it has been accomplished. The means have not been permitted to interfere with the ends."

Two major reasons historians give for the effort to exclude Chinese, the opposition of organized labor and political maneuvering, were important in passage of the first Chinese Restriction Act. The evidence is clear in the *Chronicle* and the *Examiner*, however, that over the years, these forces became less significant. John P. Young, editor of the *Chronicle*, reported in published comments outside the paper that labor had to be drawn into the conflict against both Chinese and Japanese. Young wrote that "A brief reference to the agitation which finally resulted in the passage of what is known as the Chinese Exclusion Act will help the reader to divest himself of the opinion ... that the objection to Oriental immigration is due to the machinations of the labor unions on the Pacific Coast...." Referring to Japanese, several years before any anti-alien land laws passed in California and 15 years before exclusion became law, Young warned "Eastern critics of the anti-Japanese immigration movement on this coast that they may be in error in assuming that the attitude of the Pacific Coast on the subject has been inspired by labor agitators...."

The effect of national politics, which one eminent historian of the anti-Chinese movement called "the most effective ally of the anti-Chinese forces," above race and labor, also proved a factor, both for the acts restricting Chinese in 1882 and thereafter, and for the action which barred Japanese in 1924. Especially with Chinese, both papers sought to use the issue of exclusion to help the party they supported. It is also evident that for the *Chronicle* and *Examiner*, two politically involved newspapers, in no year was politics an overriding issue. The amount of their political coverage dealing with Chinese and Japanese exclusion was minimal. Politics played a role in the effort to exclude Chinese, especially through 1902, but in the *Chronicle* and the *Examiner* it was a minor role.

If one compares the amount of both labor and political news in the two papers, plus editorials, with articles on crime and Chinese, one can identify the issue most important for the papers. Reports of Chinese crime, including incidents where Chinese were victims ... because in many cases the perpetrators were Chinese ... demonstrate racial bias in my study; crime stories made up a major part of the coverage of Chinese. The crime articles reported that Chinese were criminals, drug addicts, different and unassimilable, and provided the reasons why they should be, and were, excluded. Despite the activities of labor leaders and politicians on behalf of exclusion, according to the papers, Chinese crime provided the major justification for the campaign against Chinese immigration.

Although the historiography of Chinese exclusion offers a number of reasons for the treatment of Chinese, there is general agreement that the effort to achieve Japanese exclusion developed for one reason: racial prejudice. My study confirms these views, but it goes further. It connects Chinese and Japanese exclusion with a common thread running through the 42-year period, and the newspapers provided that common thread. Racism was the foundation for both exclusion campaigns. The *Chronicle* and the *Examiner* endorsed it and nourished it.

One other point. The exclusion of the Japanese by the United States in 1924 created an international humiliation for the Japanese government. A biographer of President Coolidge noted that it "not only damaged Japanese-American relations in the mid-1920s, but contributed to Japan's feelings of vexation that made easier the overthrow of her moderates by militarists and the coming of war in 1941." The junior Japanese diplomats and junior Japanese military officers in 1924 had become senior diplomats and military officers in 1941. A future study of the papers of these men, their letters, notes, and diaries, with a review of key Japanese newspapers, could perhaps identify more clearly the role that exclusion in 1924 played in the Japanese decisions which led to Pearl Harbor in 1941.

Articles and editorials about blacks in my study indicate the kind of coverage provided another non-Caucasian race residing among the white majority when exclusion was not a factor, that is, news of their activities reflected their minimal numbers in the community. Comparatively few blacks lived in San Francisco; their population growth never kept up with the expansion of the city. There were never as many blacks in San Francisco as Chinese during the 42 years of my study, and there were few stories published about them by the two newspapers. From 1907 on, it was the same with Japanese and blacks. There were a number of articles about lynchings and race riots involving blacks, but not as many as perhaps there should have been. The papers didn't find blacks newsworthy between 1882 and 1924, at least as demonstrated in the years I investigated them.

In the period I reviewed, the publisher was an autocrat; he never considered himself obliged to present both sides of an issue. The amount of coverage both papers gave to exclusion, the headlines used, the pejorative terms which identified both Asian groups, but especially Chinese, the mocking use of pidgin English, the supporting editorials especially when the issues faced crises in Washington, the continual agitation in times where there was no apparent reason for this kind of coverage illustrate the newspapers' leadership in the 42-year effort. They show conclusively that the two papers were at the forefront of the successful campaigns for Chinese and Japanese exclusion.

False Papers, Lost Lives

CHARLES CHOY WONG
Faculty of Humanities, Yamaguchi University, Japan
KENNETH KLEIN
Asian Collection, University of Southern California
Los Angeles, California

After Father's burial and banquet wake, I returned home and began cleaning out his bedroom. Rummaging through Father's belongings in the desk, I found two Seagram whiskey bottles, quart size, containing some dark and smelly concoction. It was not whiskey; I did not know what it was. So, I emptied them out into the kitchen sink—discarding unbeknownst to me a valuable concoction of Di Ta Jue, which is used in healing bruises and muscles. Returning to the bedroom, I pulled out from the small closet two old brown suitcases. I opened one suitcase, and in an envelope I found photographs of a family portrait that included a boy (me), Mother, and a young man... and I immediately surmised him to be my older brother who, until that very moment, had been totally erased from my memory. Rushes of emotion, of recognition, filled my mind and body. My life has not been the same since.

Among other things I discovered in that suitcase was my father's biography—in the form of the things he kept. Among those heartfelt things of sentiment were written accounts of his memorized false paper-son identity and interrogation process: the so-called "coaching papers." These particular documents included three maps and three books neatly stored inside an egg noodles box. The following reconstruction of these accounts provide an archival gold mine of one family's false papers/lost lives. It is worthwhile to note that if my father were alive today, these revelations would not be forthcoming because he would not wish our family tragedy to be a subject of public discourse. In that twisted sense of fate, we dedicate this paper to him, Wong Gun Chown, for providing us the means to tell the Leong/Wong family story of Chinese exclusion and paper-son immigration, double identity, and their consequences.

Source Material. The material on which we base our presentation consists of the collected records of Wong Gun Chown, a man educated and trained in China as an herbalist and physician. Gun Chown took notes and kept documents from key events in his life and filed them carefully away in boxes. We have his tax returns from the 1940s through the 1960s; the ship and airplane tickets for his various journeys between Hong Kong and America; the several loose notes on letter paper, each in its own marked envelope, setting down key relations or events in his life. Gun Chown was meticulous.

The most important of his records, though, are contained in a series of notebooks. The first two we will call Gun Chown's coaching papers. These consist of a series of questions posed to him during his emigration to the United States, and his responses. In the course of reading and translating these papers, it became apparent that, rather than being a set of anticipated questions and prescribed answers, they were, in fact, recorded after the questioning. His ability to recall in detail these lengthy interrogation sessions from memory alone is amazing. We presume they were conducted on Angel Island during his four-month detention and processing. The second volume also contains questions and answers from later years, as Gun Chown was returning to China for a visit and then applying to have his wife and son admitted to the United States. A third notebook records a similar set of questions posed to his wife during her application interviews with the U.S. Consulate in Hong Kong. This notebook is supplemented by some loose notes in an envelope, recording a slightly earlier interview. Finally, a fourth notebook, written in 1967 after Gun Chown's false identity had been discovered by the INS authorities, records the true details and relations of his life. This last source is the essential document which allows us to gauge the degree of distance between Gun Chown's dual identities.

Why Gun Chown wrote down these records, since no one ever read them prior to Charles' discovery of them in 1985 is a question unanswered. Perhaps it was because, in the wavering sea of multiple identities, he felt a need to maintain a clarity of story and dates for future restatements to INS and others; and/or it was his penchant, as a literate person, to document his life.

The Emigration of Gun Chown and Family. Wong Gun Chown was born on September 22, 1907, in Hoi-seun village, in the northern part of Guangdong's Poon-yu county. The fourth of five brothers born to Wong Fook-Quen and his wife, whose surname was Chow, Gun Chown was born into an area, an era, and a family which had set its sights on emigration to America.

It is not clear when Gun Chown's father went to America, or by what means, but he went three times and returned home to China three times, all prior to Gun Chown's emigration. In this sense, Wong Fook-Quen was a very successful sojourner, having finally retired sometime between 1931–1935 to his native village to live out his life; he died in 1968, aged 90. Gun Chown's oldest brother, Wong Jiu Kau, 10 years older than he was, managed to emigrate to America on August 4, 1923. Seven years later, he returned with their father, and on November 6, 1931, the fifth brother, 15-year-old Wong Gun Wai, successfully followed him two weeks later. We can only speculate on how Gun Chown's father, oldest and youngest brothers all passed the U.S. immigration authorities. Whatever paper-son devices that worked for them, though, clearly did not apply to Gun Chown.

In order to emigrate to America, Wong Gun Chown had to secure a "slot" as a son of a bona fide American citizen. The citizen he found was Leong Chung, who was born in 1878, the same year as Gun Chown's father, but in San Francisco rather than in Hoi-seun village. It is not recorded in the coaching papers or Gun Chown's other records exactly how contact was made with this "paper father," but there is strong circumstantial evidence which allows us to piece together a likely scenario.

Gun Chown was married on September 26, 1930 to Sue Jook, a woman born in San-tan village, about one li (one-third mile) away from his village. The Wongs and the Sues were frequent marriage partners, judging from what little we know. Of the nine Hoi-seun Wong marriages we know of, over four generations, three were with Sue women. And when Gun Chown went to school at another neighboring village, he became acquainted with a classmate named Sue Hou-jeung. It is never mentioned in Gun Chown's records how this classmate is related to his eventual Sue in-laws, if at all. Clearly, though, Sue Hou-jeung acted as a go-between connecting the future paper son with his San Francisco paper-father.

Sue How-jeung was a classmate of Gun Chown for about a year, 1921–1922, after which he traveled to America. In San Francisco, in the San-tung-wo store on (Zhen) Street, Hou-jeung met an American-born man whose family came from his own county of Poon-yu and, in fact, from the closely nearby village of Tin-jin. According to what Gun Chown told the immigration officer, he began to correspond with his San Francisco-born father, Leong Chung, at just about that time, when he was 14 or 15.

According to the testimony both Sue Hou-jeung and Leong Chung gave to the immigration authorities when Gun Chown emigrated, they both remember the exact time and place—September 5, 1928 at the Yee Shan Post Office at number 60 Wentworth Street in San Francisco—when Leong Chung asked Hou-jeung to take some money back to his wife and paper son in Poon-yu county. With this delivery made, Sue Hou-jeung then returned to San Francisco in May 1929, this time bringing a letter to Leong Chung from his wife, Gun Chown's paper mother.

All of this falls short of a proof of how the slot Leong Chung had available was filled by Wong Gun Chown. It is very possible that Gun Chown's own father had some part in making the arrangements; at least, in consultation and financial support for his son. We do know, though, that in 1935, when Gun Chown was emigrating to Gum San,

Sue Hou-jeung was the one witness on hand, aside from Leong Chung, to verify the paper facts.

These are the paper facts, the parallel identity, to which Wong Gun Chown had to accustom himself for the rest of his life. First of all, he became Leong Gun Chown, born on September 22, 1907 still, but at number 23 Wing Lok Street, 3rd floor, in Hong Kong. His mother was a Chan, of the Tin-jin village Chans in Poon-yu. His father's family also came from Tin-jin village, but his father, Leong Chung, was born in San Francisco and had lived there his entire life, except for the nine-and-a-half months when his grandmother took him to Hong Kong to get married. This was between July 20, 1906 and May 4, 1907. When he boarded the ship back to America, he left behind his new wife, five months pregnant with an eventual potentially-American citizen.

The learning of his new family relations was simplified by the fact that, as Leong Gun Chown, he, as an only child, and his father, whom he had never met, had only one sister, who had also died young. Leong Chung's father and three uncles had all died long before Gun Chown would have had a chance to know them. The father of his paper mother had died when Gun Chown was three. The only relatives Leong Gun Chown had ever come into contact prior to emigrating were his mother and maternal grandmother.

After a few years in Hong Kong, Leong Gun Chown and his mother moved back to Tin-jin village. Fortuitously, Tin-jin village is only one-half li (one-sixth mile) away from Wong Gun Chown's own Hoi-seun village, in the opposite direction from his real mother's San-tan village. Since the general surroundings of Leong Gun Chown's village were virtually identical to those of Wong Gun Chown's, there would be no need to re-learn completely that aspect of his life. Tin-jin village is made up of two surnames: the Chan and the Leong. Gun Chown did have to learn the details of the house in which he was to have grown up, but for the layout of the countryside and nearby villages, towns, and physical features, he could rely on genuine personal memory.

The economy of paper details which he had to learn and the relatively close fit of his new identity with his real past had to have made Gun Chown's interrogation ordeal easier. On November 30, 1935, leaving behind his pregnant wife, he boarded the ocean liner President Coolidge, and disembarked less than three weeks later on notorious Angel Island in San Francisco Bay. It was then to be over four months, until April 27, 1936, before he was allowed to leave the Island and to enter the country proper.

Over the course of those four months, Gun Chown was questioned in great detail about his family and regional background. In order to try to trip up the immigrants who had memorized, rather than lived, their past, as was the case with Gun Chown, the same question might be asked from two directions: First:

Q: Where did you marry and what is your wife's name?
A: I was married in Poon-yu county, Tin-jin village. My wife's surname is Sue, her given name is Jook.

Then, six questions later:

Q: Did your parents-in-law have children?
A: They had no son and one daughter.
Q: What is the name of your parents-in-law's daughter and how old is she this year?
A: Their daughter is named Sue Jook, and she is 22 this year.

There was also minute questioning about trivial matters for which there would be little way of preparing. The INS interviewers were well aware of the paper-son scheme brought about by exclusion and felt it was their mission to ferret out every possible one. In some cases, actual U.S. Chinese American citizens failed to satisfy the INS interviewers and were deported. This traumatic ordeal experienced by every Chinese entrant to the United States between 1910 and 1940 occurred at Angel Island and is dramatically presented in the excellent play, "Paper Angels," which features representative men and women characters seeking entry into Gum San. Gun Chown's interviewer at one point focused, for instance, on the school he attended:

Q: Does the ancestral temple have a toilet?
Q: How many seats are there in the toilet?
Q: How deep, wide and high is the toilet?
Q: Is the toilet on the east or the west side?
Q: What direction does the ancestral temple face?
Q: Does the door to the teacher's bedroom face the south or the west?
Q: When you study, in which row is your table?
Q: What is the name of the person with whom you sit?
Q: Where is the school's drinking well?

Leong Chung and Sue Hou-jeung were both interviewed as well, to check for inconsistencies and contradictions; Leong being questioned about family relationships, Sue about the region and the school. And they were both questioned about the circumstances of the interactions between the two of them. Gun Chown passed his immigration interrogation and entered Gum San on April 27, 1936. When he went the next year to receive his residency papers, he told the immigration authorities that he was working at Fook Wo Tong &

Co. herbs, at 940 Grant Avenue, San Francisco. This was not the end of the coaching papers, though. Just a week after he left Angel Island, Gun Chown's wife, back in Poon-yu, gave birth. Leong Gun Chown's immigration problem would not be over until his wife and family were also admitted. The War intervened, of course, and the Chinese immigration to the United States was closed off even further between 1936 and 1945. When Gun Chown picked up his record of interviews again, it was November 1946, and he was applying to return to China. From this interview, we learn that his paper father had died in 1941 in San Francisco. Gun Chown by now had relocated to Los Angeles, a small Chinese community of about 4,000 Chinese, where his two real brothers, Wong Jiu Kau and Wong Gun Wai, were situated. He lived at Chung Jen Low, 915 West Temple Street, and was working at Tong King Low, in Little Tokyo, 227 East First Street. His shift from working at his trained profession as an herbalist and physician to restaurant cook was probably due to the fact that the Chinese community throughout Los Angeles county in the 1940s numbered less than 5,000 and could not support many medical practitioners. Also, job referrals within the immigrant Chinese community was by way of clan affiliations and his brothers worked there too, by virtue of their father who was perhaps a part-owner of the Tong King Low restaurant.

It is also in the record of this interview that we find the first mention that Gun Chown's wife had given birth to twins, Leong Leong and Leong Jim, back on May 5, 1936. Gun Chown reported his intention to bring back his now ten-year-old sons to America to study. He did return to Poon-yu county early in 1947 and stayed two years. When he returned to the United States in May 1949, he traveled by airplane. The effort to bring one son, Leong Leong, was denied by the U.S. Consulate in Hong Kong. Also, he left behind one more son, Leong Choy, born in May 1948. And his wife, he reported, was pregnant again.

Sue Jook and her sons moved from Hoi-seun village to Hong Kong on August 21, 1951. In Hong Kong, the effort to have Leong Leong emigrate to America was renewed. Due to some mistaken testimony of his, however, the details of which are not recorded, his application was again denied. This was a serious setback which forced the family to change its strategy. First of all, it was necessary to shed part of the paper fiction of the Leong family, specifically the claim that Leong Leong had a twin brother.

We are able to know that there was never a twin because of the record book Gun Chown wrote in 1967 as Wong Gun Chown, rather than as Leong Gun Chown, setting the record straight after more than 30 years of having to assume a false identity. It is from this 1967 notebook that we learn the full details of Gun Chown's parents and four brothers and their children. Here also, he pens the details of his own life, where and when he was born and where he was married. And he reports having two sons, Wong Leong (who died in 1958) and Wong Cha-li Choy. He is very exacting and, with no reason to leave out any details, he makes no mention of Wong (or Leong) Jim.

In 1952 in Hong Kong, though, Sue Jook still had to account for the fact that she no longer had another son, twin to her eldest, a year before, to the Consulate interviewer. The story she told was that about half a year after coming to Hong Kong, Leong Jim decided to go back to Hoi-seun village to look after the family house. He was accused there of being an anti-communist element, was arrested and then executed.

When asked how she had heard of her son's death, Sue Jook said that she had received two letters telling her of the incident, one from her next-door neighbor, Wong Ngau-si in Hoi-seun, and another from her maternal grandmother. This would be the only possible documented evidence of her son's death, since 1952 was not a good year for getting vital statistics records from China. Sue Jook then said, however, that she was so angry and upset that she told Leong Leong to burn the letters. She thus could produce no documented evidence of Leong Jim's death—or of his life, for that matter.

Sue Jook had shown the U.S. Consulate official a photograph of their family of five taken in 1948—she and Gun Chown, the twins, and Leong Choy. When it was pointed out that one of the 12-year-old boys was two inches taller than the other, Sue Jook explained that when he was a baby, Leong Leong drank all of her milk, leaving less for Leong Jim.

It seems clear that Gun Chown, through the device of claiming an extra twin son (and also his wife's third pregnancy in 1949, later completely dropped in all records), was trying to create new slots of his own to sell. The fact that a 12-year-old boy had been photographed along with the family in 1948 indicates that the slot had been filled. We have no way of knowing exactly why it was decided to drop the effort to bring in that boy as Leong Jim. One possibility is that the new requirement of matching blood types of parents and children, instituted by the U.S. Consulate in Hong Kong in 1951, threatened to expose the family's false paper artifice. Or, just as likely, the failed application of Leong Leong had somehow compromised the chances of the boy posing as Leong Jim, and of the family as a whole.

Whatever was the reason which led to the retraction, it required a non-traceable demise to Leong Jim. Thus, the story of the execution.

The family now decided to begin to apply to have Sue Jook and Leong Choy emigrate, and in 1952, a new series of interviews began, of Sue Jook in Hong Kong and Leong Gun Chown in Los Angeles.

One place in which Sue Jook's account risks exposing itself is when she recounts where she lived after Gun Chown's emigration to America, late in 1935. For a couple of years, she stayed in Tin-jin, a village composed of the Leong and Chan surnames. In 1938, though, Japanese troops came and burned down her house and most of the rest of Tin-jin, wiping the village from the map. She and her sons (including Leong Jim in the story, of course) relocated first to her mother's house in San-tan village, only two li (two-thirds mile) away from Tin-jin. Two months later, she moved to Hoi-seun village, half a li away, where she bought a house. Hoi-seun village was made up entirely of the Wong surname. The official at the U.S. Consulate asked her, "Why are all the people in Hoi-seun village named Wong, while you are named Leong?" Her only answer was, "Because I moved to Hoi-seun village." No other explanation was offered for moving to a village where she had no relatives (on paper), and staying there 13 years. The fact is, of course, that she had moved to her husband's village to be with the rest of the Wongs.

Finally, on February 16, 1954, Sue Jook and her youngest son, Leong Choy, boarded a Pan Am airplane which took them from Hong Kong to Los Angeles. Her oldest son, Leong Leong, was left behind, to die tragically four years later. For the husband and wife and their second son, though, the slot system had won them admission to America.

The Effects of Exclusion on the Wong Family. Because the effects of exclusion are myriad, a short-hand scheme to encode it is desirable. Thus, I shall discuss the effects of exclusion upon our family members in terms of separated family, stranded brother, and secrecy and silence. The central event is the death of number one son, Wong Han Leung, and how it tragically affected the lives of the other family members, especially myself.

Separated Family. Sojourning, as a Chinese emigration directive, ended in 1949. Its principal effect was the separation of families for an uncertain length, perhaps forever, in the case of unsuccessful sojourners. The motif of family separation meant that wife and husband, children and father, kinsmen and kinsmen sacrificed split lives in its most noble sense of sacred duty. However, as former sojourners now tried to bring over their whole families, the prior half-century of paper-son falsehoods produced a maze of relationships that was often difficult to reconfigurate with actual family relations to the INS' satisfaction. In our case, Father had left China in 1935 as a paper-son Leong, leaving wife and child. Upon returning to the United States in 1949, after his two-year village pilgrimage, he recorded to the INS that he had two teen-age sons and had sired another son in 1948;

and in addition, that his wife was again pregnant. Were it not for this audacious effort to obtain two additional slots, perhaps son number one, Han Leung, might have successfully come to America with Mother and myself.

This reconstructed mix of truth and falsehood is revealed in Mother's 1951 Hong Kong interview as she tries to satisfy her gatekeeper interviewer.

Q: What is your name and how old are you?
A: My name is Sue Jook and I am 38 years old.
Q: When and where were you born?
A: I was born on August 14, 1914 in San-tan village.
Q: When were you married?
A: I was married on September 26, 1930.
Q: How old was your husband the year you were married?
A: My husband was 24 when we were married.
Q: Where does your husband come from and what is his name?
A: My husband is from Tin-jin village, Poon-yu county; his name is Leong Gun Chown.
Q: When was your husband born and how old is he now?
A: My husband was born on September 22, 1907, and is 45 this year.
Q: What is your husband's name?
A: My husband's name is Leong Gun Chown, his courtesy name is Jiu-fan.
Q: How many children do you have?
A: I now have three sons and no daughters.
Q: How old are your three sons and what are their name?
A: My sons Leong Jim and Leong Leong are twins and are 16 years old this year. Leong Choy is four years old.
Q: Which of your twin sons, Leong Jim and Leong Leong, was born first?
A: Of my twin sons, Leong Jim and Leong Leong, Leong Leong was born first.
Q: Have you had any children die?
A: No.
Q: How old is your third son and what is his name?
A: My third son is Leong Choy; he is four years old.
Q: When and where were your three sons born?
A: My twin sons, Leong Jim and Leong Leong, were born on May 5, 1936 in Tin-jin village. Leong Choy was born May 28, 1948 in the ? hospital in Pang-wu town.
Q: Do you have any brothers and sisters?
A: I have no brothers or sisters.
Q: Why are your twin sons, Leong Jim and Leong Leong, not going together to America?

A: I could not bear to part with both Leong Jim and Leong Leong and have both go to America, so I will wait a while before letting Leong Jim go to America.

Q: What kind of immigration papers does your husband have?

A: My husband told me he has ?.

Q: Do you know when your husband first went to America?

A: My husband first went to America on a ship on November 5, 1935.

Q: How may times has your husband come back home?

A: My husband has come back to China once.

Q: How did your husband come back home?

A: My husband came back home on March 7, 1947.

Q: What time of the day was it when your husband came back home?

A: It was after breakfast when my husband came back home.

Q: When your husband came home, how many pieces of luggage did he have and who did he bring with him?

A: My husband had a leather suitcase and a trunk; he had someone help him bring it.

Q: When your husband returned home, where were the members of your family?

A: Leong Leong, Leong Jim, and I were in the main room.

Q: When your husband returned home, did you pour a bowl of tea for him to drink?

A: When my husband returned home, I poured a bowl of tea for him to drink.

Q: When your husband returned home, what did he have to give you?

A: When my husband returned home, he brought me a blue dress and a little bodhi tree.

Q: When your husband returned home, what did he do?

A: When my husband returned home, he did not have any work to do.

Q: On the day that your husband went back to America, did you and your sons go out to eat with him?

A: On the day that my husband went back to America, my sons and I and several other people all went out for a three o'clock meal.

Q: On the day your husband went back to America, what was he wearing?

A: On the day my husband went back to America, he was wearing western clothing.

Q: How old were your sons, Leong Leong and Leong Jim, the first time your husband went to America?

A: My sons, Leong Leong and Leong Jim, were born five or six months after my husband left for America.

Q: When did your husband go back to America?

A: My husband took an airplane back to America on May 21, 1949.

Q: How old is your husband this year?

A: My husband is 45 this year.

Q: Does your husband send money back to the family every year from America?

A: My husband sends money to the family every year.

Q: How many times a year does your husband send money and how much does he send each time?

A: My husband sends $100 twice a year.

Q: Why did your son, Leong Leong, not go to America together with your husband?

A: My son, Leong Leong, went many times to the U.S. Consulate to request to be allowed to go to America, but the Consulate said that it was not his turn. So, when my husband returned to America, they could not go together.

Q: When it came time for your husband to return to America, what did he (instruct) you to do?

A: When my husband returned to America, he told me to educate our sons and to look after the family.

Altogether, Mother went through three further interviews at the U.S. consulate office in Hong Kong between 1951 and 1954. Whereas the first interview dealt in detail with family members, in-law relations, Father's return and departure from the village, Father's remittances from Gum San, Mother's different village movements, and why the eldest son did not accompany father back to America, the second interview extending three days, from October 6–8, 1952, began with and focused upon the twin sons, Leung Chien and Leung Liang. By now, the plan was unraveling: Leung Liang had been denied entry to join his father in America. Efforts shifted to securing entry for mother and youngest son, Choy. The twin son, Leung Chien, was explained away through death. The third interview on May 12, 1953 again focused on the twin brothers and Leung Chien's alleged death. By now, Leung Liang's application to join his father in Los Angeles had been rejected. The fourth interview occurred on January 25, 1954 and covers the same ground of identity, former residences, family relations. The short interview is perfunctory, since Mother and I had already been approved to leave.

Q: What is your husband's name and were does he live?

A: My husband is Leung Gun Chown and he lives at 27 North Garfield Street, Alhambra, America.

Q: How many sons do you have?

A: I had three sons, but the second son died, so now I have two sons.

Q: What is your eldest son's name and where does he live?

A: My eldest son, Leung Liang, lives at 54 Chia-lin-pien Avenue, Tower A-2, Hong Kong.

Q: Do you know why the Consulate has not approved your son's going to America?

A: I know it is because his testimony was not correct.

Q: When do you plan to go to America? Do you plan to take a ship or a plane, and to which city are you going?

A: I plan to take a Pan Am Co. plane in the first month of the new year to go to Los Angeles.

On February 16, 1954, Mother and I left Hong Kong to be reunited with husband and father, this time on American soil; but we also left Leung Liang forever. We were met at the Los Angeles International Airport by cousin Ah-Nam, who drove us home to Boyle Heights in his green Chevrolet. Looking out the car window, seeing the wide, clean streets, big buildings, and tall palm streets, I must have said, "What a wonderful place." But, what kind of reunited family would emerge from this previously separated and now mutilated family?

Stranded Brother. It was indeed common for Chinese men to report births, actual or fictitious, upon returning to American shores in order to establish future slots of paper-son eligibility. In this vein, it was not uncommon for Chinese men to report male twins as well, to double the gain. Father tried this maneuver. It failed. The tragic consequence was that the legitimate son, Han Leung, was denied entry. Did Father foresee this very risky possibility? We do not know the answer to this question. We do know that the risk was thought to be worth the gamble, as evidenced by the commonplace occurrence of twin paper-sons schemes. The consequence of denial for Han Leung meant being stranded as a refugee in Hong Kong or returning to the Communist-controlled village in China; neither prospect was remotely desirable.

We do not know about the life of Han Leung in Hong Kong from 1954 to 1958, a young man of 18 to 22 years, except to suggest that he was supported by his parents in Los Angeles, by regular remittances and correspondence. His mother desperately wanted to rejoin her first child and let her husband take care of the second child, but Father, fearful of future re-entry denial, forbade such a plan. We do not know the circumstances of his refugee life in Hong Kong society or the specific circumstances of his death, except to suggest that a failed female relationship may have been the precipitating cause of his suicide by jumping off a tall building.

After the discovery of our family photos, I finally buried Father, symbolically. Writing his eulogy was wrenching, as I released a visceral cry of pain from deep within my chest and shed near-continuous tears: a cathartic process. Afterward, I buried two family photos, one with elder brother, Mother, and me in Hong Kong; the other, Father, Mother, and me in Los Angeles, at Father's Rose Hill gravesite, as I read the eulogy. On a subsequent trip to the village in 1986, I again buried the same two photos at the family cemetery under Grandfather's gravesite.

Eulogy to Elder Brother:

Dear Brother, Han Leung:

Today, I shall finally bury you, my beloved brother—28 years after the fact. A long time, indeed. I bury you for my mother—your mother, my father—your father, and me. Your death, apart from us in Hong Kong, shattered the survivors. In a very real sense, we—each of us— died too, but we did not jointly and publicly mourn the untimely passing of our blood and flesh. Each in his own way coped as he could, unfortunately to the detriment of the family unit and to ourselves. Our mother, heart-stricken to mental distress, our father, perhaps with utmost tragedy, bore in visceral silence the agony, and I—I coped by erasing you from memory as if you never existed. What else could I do? My parents never acknowledged to me your death, your suicide. And no one else, my relatives ever mentioned you, or perhaps I would block, deny, or not hear their sounds. Both Mother and Father carried the burden of unexhausted grief to their own deaths. Your burial plot was but a dead letter. With parental love, they mourned privately. This is not enough.

So today, A-gao, I bury you for all of us—and especially for me. I loved you, cherished you.

What life experiences we shared, as a separated sojourning family trying to survive as many, many other Zhong-guo yen, testify to the anguish of exclusion. Perhaps, in time, I shall be able to recall and fruitfully assimilate the bond of our short time together in China and Hong Kong. I know deep inside it was as Chinese brothers should be: you carrying me on your shoulders, acting as a surrogate father and protector of family. Perhaps, in time, your death will become a positive and nurturing event, transforming death into the gift of life. It is too late for Mother and Father, but not for me. I still have time.

In succession, Providence sent me Joy to help manage Mother's death, Judy to help manage Father's death, and now Cindy to help manage your death. Those here today are my brothers and family. They come to witness your burial on behalf of Mother, Father, and myself. So, until our souls touch again, good-bye.

Your little brother, Ah-Choy

If there is any specific event that symbolizes for me the effect of exclusion, it is the Hong Kong airport departure and family separation scene on February 16, 1954. In preparation for my pilgrimage to China and my village in 1982, I underwent regression hypnosis. The practitioner-counselor led me back to several recalls. Airport departure in those days required walking from the terminal to the propeller airplane on the ground and boarding up the airplane stairway ramp. The scene I recall was Mother and Brother standing a foot apart, crying and sobbing unmercifully as I stood a few feet away. This would be our tortured farewell; that scene etched forever in my subconscious haunts me for it is the first act in our family tragedy.

The subsequent impact of that painful separation has had a lasting effect upon my psyche. It is, I now conclude, the source of a survivor guilt complex. Why was I able to leave and my brother, who certainly was more worthy, not? And even more traumatic: Why did I live and my brother die? It should have been the reverse. Eventually, I must come to the position of acceptance: accepting fate, accepting absurdity, accepting bitter pain. In this sense, the profound indirect psychological effects of exclusion continues, perhaps, until the day I die.

Secrecy and Silence. It is common that the children's knowledge of paper families is very limited and truncated. Understandably, false paper-parents did not trust the children to keep the secrets, the double identities, the double names with relatives, and so forth. As a result, children were told very little and knew even less, due typically to disinterest. It created confusion, for example, when filling out those school health cards. There was always a line for "In Case of Emergency, call: (fill in the blank). After parents, a preferred relative was required. I often wondered why, in translating these instructions to Father, I was never permitted to write in the name, address, and telephone number of Uncle Jack, who lived nearby. But no matter, I soon lost interest in my ethnicity and kinship relations and became a super-acculturationalist by my early teens.

It was not until after our family's 1967–68 disclosure in the confession program brought about by the Immigration and Naturalization Service that I was actually given some facts. This took the form of translating my father's documentation into English, since it was now safe to do so. He kept a copy in the bank's safe deposit box, denoting its importance. Since this was my sole glue to the family tree, I kept a personal copy as well and treasured it as a paper piece of my factual identity and continuity. The one sheet read:

Grandfather born in China on 12-8-1878; Wong Fook Quen died in China on 1-6-1968. Grandmother born in China on 7-4-1880; Chow Shee died in China on 1-8-1969. Father born at Hoy Soon village, Poon

Yee Wong Gun Chown district, Kwantung, China on 9-22-1907. Mother born at Ti Mix They village, Poon Yee Sue Jook district, Kwantung, China on 8-27-1914. Brother born in China on 5-5-1936; Wong Han Leung died in Hong Kong on 1-9-1954. 2nd child born at Pon Wu Huey, Poon Yee district, Charles Choy, Kwantung, China on 5-24-1948. Father entered US: First time arrived in U.S. on Nov. 30, 1935 on SS Pres. Coolidge. Returned to China on Jan. 31, 1947 on SS General Gordon. Second time arrive in U.S. on May 21, 1949 by Philippine Airline. Mother and Charles Choy entered US: Arrived in U.S. on Feb. 16, 1954 on PAA airline, Los Angeles.

In actuality, this paper family possessed very little meaning to me. Grandfather and Grandmother were, by now, non-existent to me. I had no memory, no photograph, no sketch, no memento, nothing. They were only two names and dates on a piece of paper; bare essentials, like on a tombstone at the cemetery. They were indeed buried. Also, since I left the village so young, perhaps, three years old, I could easily accept the dictum that I was too young to remember. Why my father never showed the photographs he had of them, nor told me stories about them, I do not know. Somehow, silence was the modus operandi: Father never said, and I never asked. Similarly, I do not recall Mother bringing up village life and Brother as well. Mother never said, and I never asked.

I do remember Father periodically writing to and receiving letters from China on aerograms, the kind you fold and glue. He did not share the letters with me and I never inquired about them. I assumed they were merely faceless peasants, living peasant lives in the countryside (I did not care to know much about China either). I had little concern for them, having never met them, I thought. In reality, being born in their village, I was taken care of by them, of course! It was not until I discovered Father's papers that I also discovered their photos as well. Simply put, prior to May 1985, Grandfather and Grandmother were only names and dates to me, not real people. This mutual void of silence eventually separated my grandparents from conscious memory.

The same fate fell upon older brother, Wong Han Leung. By my teens, he had been erased from conscious memory: his name, his face, his body, his voice, his biography, his habits, everything. Like my grandparents, he no longer existed. But, of course, there is a huge difference between being separated from a significant other at age three versus age six. The following is difficult to fathom, but true: When I was frequently queried, "Do you have any brothers or sisters?", I would answer, "No," thinking sincerely that I was an only child. I must pose the question: How could such a denial or amnesia be so totally effective? The pain must have been so immense. As I think back upon that early period, I recall Mother wailing privately in the bedroom day and night. So I knew why, but the conspiratorial wall of silence about my brother eventually killed him from my conscious memory. By my mid-teens, I had drawn the curtain shut, a defense mechanism coping with functional survival as Choy, as Charles, as Leong, and later, as Wong.

Strangely, Father was nearly equally non-existent. I knew that he came to America in 1935 and made one return voyage in 1947, from which I was conceived, and returned to America in 1949. "In America for over 30 years and still cannot speak English," I chastised him. Mainly, he labored as a cook. I use the word labored because I rarely saw him. My chief memories are of watching him sleeping in the mornings, since he usually left at 10 a.m. and returned after midnight, perhaps 1–2 a.m., while I was asleep. He took the bus, which I imagine added to his travel time. Excerpts from my personal writing in 1968, age 20, describing our three-member household:

My father has worked feverously through the years to get us to America. He was a Chinese cook, he now receives disability benefits, due to the long hours he worked. He now owns the three units we live in now. He's quiet, around me at least, unexpressive with his emotion to the extent of repression. However, he occasionally blows up! I never knew or know him now for two big reasons: First, he always worked when I was small. I rarely ever saw him and my only recollection was when he was eating or asleep. Of course, we were together sometimes. I associate him as a "bread winner," that's all. The second reason: Although we see each other very often now at home, we have a language barrier. I don't speak Chinese well enough at all and he doesn't speak English well, but we get things across when we have to. I guess the underlining reason we don't communicate is because we have nothing to say. For whatever reason, our relationship is a void. His interest in me is my school work and my future.

My mother and I are much closer. She has worked since we arrived, as a produce worker. I sorta grew up alone. She wouldn't get home until 7 p.m. First, she took me with her to work after school, then later, I played around after school. Although growing up alone, I am spoiled. I expect things done for me even now. She is highly prejudiced, especially of Negroes and Mexicans, and ignorant because of her isolation from new and happy experiences. English is entirely Greek to her still. She cries easily and talks to the wind. She talks out a lot of her hostilities by blaming other people (Father).

Unfortunately, the atmosphere of the house is dry like a bus stop. There exists no romantic ties between them. Perhaps insight into Chinese culture would provide a better answer than mine's... The third dry desert wind is me. I don't make an effort to help make the conditions better. I just go along concerned with myself. Another sad thing is we have few associating friends and relatives.

The climactic impact of secrecy and silence fell upon me in 1968, with the confession program. Suddenly afterward, I was no longer a U.S. citizen, but a green card-holding non-citizen. I was no longer Charles Choy Leong, but Charles Choy Wong, a tainted person with an illegal family history and fractured identity. I was not who I thought I was; the fragile wholeness of my desired "all-American" identity was now cracked into pieces, like Humpty Dumpty. The process of rectifying my official transcript records at college was embarrassing: explaining to friends why I was no longer Leong, as they had known me, as my math teacher had always called me, was stigmatizing; and to strangers, degrading. The subject of my parental and social background was now avoided, as I sought out social distance from my parents, from myself.

Mother died two years later, and there are only a few bits and pieces of shared experiences with Father, pleasant and otherwise, that I can draw upon and hang onto. One noteworthy incident in 1976 was the immediate source of a poem which summarizes my adult relationship with Father. We just had another argument about him wanting me to do something for him that conflicted with my plans. I stormed out of his half of the duplex into mine and, enraged with anger, found release in a burst of words:

Filial piety, an anachronism to be sure; For generations you have reigned; Tying everyone first breath to last; Making eloquent sense of ancestors and generations yet to be; But, filial piety, what functions do you play for me? Except an endless list of what I ought to be. Freedom is the name of life's new game; And spontaneity is the time frame; Do as I please, and do not as I please; Freedom, that is what you mean to me; But, freedom's choice is a lonely dare; For yesterday, today, and tomorrow are all separate affairs; Freedom, what functions do you play for me; Except an endless list of maybes.

Unresolved (1976)

Later that day, in a more contemplative mood, I sought higher ground in a different articulation of words to quell my conflict:

If process is the thread of life, illusions are its fabric; And while stability is the desired camouflage for us all; The ever nakedness of conflict and change; Are constant reminders of life's uncertainties; Yet, amidst the sometime painful disorder of affairs; One can transcend the conflict by finding oneself.

Existence (1976)

The silence, secrecy, and conflict Father and I fronted each other during our life together were sometimes painful, sometimes thankful, sources of growth. As his life came to an end due to cancer at age 78, I sought common ground, the proverbial making peace with unfinished business. In those last few months, we did finally communicate and we cried briefly together in full acknowledgment of his life of hardship and sacrifice, in its sacred duty sense. A few days before his cancer surgery in 1985, I pondered upon our sojourner father-refugee son relationship and wrote to myself words I could not say to Father:

Looking out upon a warm, clear, sunny morning, as often happens after a rainy evening, I note the passing of the seasons, cycles, and contemplate your passing. Today, as you wait for tests and eventual surgery, one friend is taking his wife and two daughters up to San Francisco to visit his mother, a joyous occasion; another friend is tending his brew of kids and manicured lawn and stucco home; and yet another friend is worrying about school deadlines and work pressures; and I, I am sitting here... wondering.

These observations, like the cycles of nature, inform me that we all, each one of us, has his or her own personal cycle. Life has infinite processes going on at once; life and death, sadness and joy, tragedy and opportunity all occur simultaneously—even among our small circle of associates along the way; testimony to the truth that life goes on and that we are but players in the recurring drama of human existence.

Our relationship—sojourner father, refugee son—is, perhaps, not so unusual for all of 130 years of Chinese American history binds us. Yet, our unique expression cannot be denied. Trying to draw meaning from a heretofore disagreeable union, I now realize how fortunate I am; for all the difficulties are but truly opportunities for appreciation. Not knowing each other as a father and son normally would, I now stretch to learn the substance and meaning of love: that it is caring and compassion derived not from personal bond and attachments, but from transcending acceptance and appreciation... and... I now stretch to learn tolerance and patience... and... I now cannot help but still feel a loss. Inseparably, your room with your few well-worn belongings remind me that "we are here for each other." The learning is tough; and I wish I had learned even more from our trying relationship, but am thankful for that measure of spiritual knowledge you have facilitated in me.

As our time draws to a close, I shall draw from the well of spiritual union with you—as indeed, we have on occasions during the last few months—and perhaps we might even bridge the gulf. It seems as we might tie the thread of understanding before the light of life is extinguished, and like a tragedy, "too little, too late." Yet, it is said, that which we leave with, we come back to; that which we close with, we begin with. And so, like recess at school, we shall resume the learning lesson. But while the ending time is still alive, perhaps days, with a sense of urgency, I shall try to learn as much as I can from you.

Thank you, Father. It has taken, for whatever reasons, seven years for Gun Chown Wong's papers to be translated. I am thankful for Ken, friend and collaborator, in making these documents finally possible in English. As I have been writing these effects of exclusion upon the Leong/Wong family, of separated family, stranded brother, and the weight of secrecy and silence, the tragic burden of my family past has been lifted somewhat. Though all my family members are now dead, I am pleased to be able to bring new meaning to our past.

The process of making whole again, of putting Humpty Dumpty together again, is the combination of historical, sociological, and psychological elements; or more simply, call it maturity. Important elements in my case have been the civil rights and ethnic insurgence movements, knowledge of Chinese American history, knowledge in reincarnation, Thoreau, and the Taoist search for balance between being and becoming. And most importantly, the crucial factor in my equation was returning to China, the land of my birth, between 1982 and 1987. From these tours and pilgrimages, I have come back with renewed pride and appreciation in my ethnic cultural heritage, in my village bamboo grove, in my grandfather, in my parents, in myself. Stepping into the house of my birth, seeing the family portraits, including myself, on the wall, eating the welcome home meal, feeling the wood columns, caressing the ceremonial bowls, and hearing old women remembering Ah-Choy, conversing, "Ah-Choy, he has come back," took my breath away.

Conclusion. Breaking the silence and secrecy of the Leong/Wong family is the required process of making the Wong family whole again, of reclaiming the pride and dignity of our past. For Sue Jook Wong, who lived a life of unfulfilled dreams in America, exclusion created a mutilated Chinese American family. No less for Gun Chown Wong, who lived a life of sacrifice and unrecognized skills as physician and cook, exclusion necessitated a false identity for more than 30 years. For Wong Han Leung, exclusion from Gum San resulted in an anguished and foreshortened life that ended in suicide.

And for Charles Choy Wong, exclusion fractured a fragile personality. The secrecy of denial, the silence of avoidance, and the split personality of fractured identity is now openly acknowledged. Simply put, the Wong in me now accepts the Leong: we are assimilated. The Choy in me is resurfacing again. It will not be suppressed as occurred during my American teens and young adult years. The Charles in me is an enigma. In the supermarket culture of American life, identity is what you construct and contour it to be, but social identity is not enough. Charles yearns for the unchanging reality and "substance" behind the changing forms.

We are determined that the Leong/Wong family lives; Han Leung, Sue Jook, Gun Chown, Charles Choy shall not have been lived in vain. As a case study of an archetypal pattern of mutilated families, exclusion resulted in immense community and family dislocation and suffering. Its effects continue today among many Chinese Americans who have not successfully come to terms with their personal legacy of false papers/lost lives. It is our ultimate mission to present the Leong/Wong family story within the historical context of the 1930s to the 1980s in China and America. Finally, we look forward to the day when Gun Chown Wong's papers and artifacts will become part of the permanent collection of the Museum of Chinese American History in Los Angeles.

Paper Partners—Paper Sons:
Evidence of Exclusion

WAVERLY B. LOWELL
National Archives, Pacific Sierra Region, San Bruno, California

The National Archives and Records Administration (NARA) was founded 1934 to preserve and make accessible the permanent, historically significant records of the United States Government. NARA is responsible for the main building in Washington D.C., the Presidential Library system, a nationwide program of regional archives, and federal records centers and the new Archives II facility in College Park, Maryland.

The Regional Archives System, founded 1969, consists of 12 regional archives in metropolitan areas throughout the country. Each regional archive carries out a full range of archival activities (appraisal, accessioning, preservation, description, reference) and educational programs (classes, presentations, workshops, exhibits, publications, curriculum development, volunteer involvement).

Within the National Archives, records are organized by agency into record groups (RG), as a method of maintaining organizational context. Most records related to Chinese travel and immigration can be found in the records of the Immigration and Naturalization Service (RG 85), the U.S. District and Circuit Courts (RG 21, RG 276) and the Bureau of Customs (RG 36).

The largest body of records documenting Chinese immigration and travel are those generated by the Chinese exclusion laws (1882–1943) and contained within the records of the Immigration and Naturalization Service. While most of the regional archives hold some of these records, the highest number of case files are among the holdings of the National Archives, Pacific Sierra Region in San Bruno, CA.

Simply stated, opposition to Chinese immigration arose in California as a result of racism and the depression of the 1870s, the belief that Chinese laborers were a threat to the workers of America. The completion of the railroad and the Panic of 1873 combined to begin the long history of agitation against Chinese immigration. Before the first exclusion law in 1882, there are few federal records specifically documenting the Chinese in California. These include Census records and specific court cases, such as Levi Strauss v. Kan Lun, a patent infringement case over tailor Lun's use of metal rivets in men's work pants (Civil Case #1468).

Ironically, the federal government doesn't generate systematic documentation until it does something to you. Therefore, the bulk of the records documenting Chinese in America begin in 1882 with the

Chinese Exclusion Policy, commonly referred to as the Chinese Exclusion Act. This policy was actually implemented through a series of acts beginning with an 1880 treaty allowing the U.S. to legislate against Chinese laborers, and it ended with the repeal of the Chinese Exclusion Acts by the 78th Congress on December 17, 1943.

The U.S. Bureau of Customs was responsible for enforcement of the Exclusion Laws until the establishment of the Immigration and Naturalization Service in 1891. This is why pre-1900 records are arranged by vessel name and the date the passenger carrier entered port in the U.S. at San Francisco. These limited case files contain material that provides the subject's name, place, and date of birth, names and ages of family members, occupation, street address, status of residency (most claimed U.S. birth), date, and vessel of departure from the U.S., and usually a brief autobiographical narrative (through an interpreter). Photographs of the subject may also be included in the case files.

These and the other Chinese immigration and travel records were generated as a result of a series of laws passed as part of the 60-year U.S. policy of Chinese exclusion. Different laws required different kinds of forms and documents. As a result of this ongoing legislative process, the records came to the archives grouped roughly into series by the particular statute. It helps to identify the terms of some of the laws so that one can begin to see the kinds of documents that they generated.

The Chinese exclusion laws began with the treaty of 1880 that allowed the U.S. to "regulate, limit or suspend, but not absolutely prohibit, the coming and residency of Chinese."

The Act Of May 1882 implemented this treaty. This act, often referred to as the Chinese Exclusion Law, suspended immigration of Chinese laborers for 10 years; permitted reentry of certain Chinese laborers who left the U.S. temporarily and created the Section 6 status for teachers, students, merchants, and travelers to be admitted upon presentation of a certificate from the Chinese government; however, naturalization of Chinese was prohibited.

Exclusionary Acts included the suspension of immigration for Chinese laborers by the 47th Congress on May 6, 1882. The Scott Act of October 1888 voided certificates which had already been issued and immediately denied entrance to returning laborers; The Geary Act of May 1892 allowed Chinese laborers to travel to China and reenter the United States, but its provisions were generally more restrictive than anything preceding it. It was this Act that required Chinese to register and secure a certificate to use as proof of their right to be in the United States, essentially shifting the burden of proof to the defendant. Imprisonment and deportation were the penalty for those who failed to have the required papers. It was this act that generated the majority of the records.

Between 1882 and 1910, essentially prior to the establishment of the Immigration Station on Angel Island, thousands of Chinese, held onboard ship by Customs, filed Habeas Corpus cases for release (Salyer 91–117, Fritz 347–372).

These can be found in the court cases in Admiralty in the records of the U.S. District Court for the Northern District of Northern California. Types of records found in the Habeas Corpus case files include Chinese passports, documentation as to the legitimate reasons this individual may come into the U.S., a photograph of the individual, application for return certificate, return certificate, and letters or testimony that explain how someone had lost their return certificate, or how they might need to stay in China longer than the one year permitted by the law.

Records Of Exclusion. The Angel Island Immigration Station (1910–1941) was the place that thousands of Chinese-born subjects, Chinese wives and children of legally domiciled merchants, and Chinese American citizens entered the United States. Cases generated at Angel Island document the subjects' place of birth, occupation, destination in the U.S., and plans for the future (college, labor, etc.). Transcripts of interviews or interrogations are included in nearly every file, and are the richest source of information. In addition to the interviews, applicants and immigrants would provide supporting material, either voluntarily or by INS request, to validate their responses. Following the San Francisco earthquake and fire of 1906, additional documentation was requested as a way for immigration officials to corroborate responses by alleged parents or siblings; or, in the vernacular, to identify paper sons. In addition to transcripts of extensive questioning, files might include photographs, correspondence from family members, drawings of villages, and marriage records.

Deportations took place, although there were fewer than generally thought. Some of these occurred when native Chinese couldn't prove a relationship to legal Chinese citizens, legally domiciled Chinese, or Hawaiian Chinese; if individuals didn't qualify for merchant status; for Chinese laborers without certificates of residence as required by the Act of 1882, and for proxy marriages, drug addiction, and women on moral grounds. At the death of a husband, a woman might be deported as a concubine if she could not prove marriage; and it might become a public charge.

The legislation passed in September 1888 prohibited the entry of all Chinese persons except "teachers, students, merchants or travelers for pleasure or curiosity;" people whose professions were not going to affect the national labor pool, and, ironically, who could promote the goals of the concurrent Open Door Policy, which encouraged trade with China.

"Laborer" was: "construed to mean both skilled and unskilled manual laborers, including Chinese employed in mining, fishing, peddling, laundrymen or those engaged in taking, drying or otherwise preserving shell of other fish for home consumption."

"Merchant" was defined as: "a person engaged in buying and selling merchandise, at a fixed place of business, which business is conducted in his name, and who during the time he claims to be engaged as a merchant, does not engage in the performance of any labor, except as is necessary in the conduct of his business as such merchant.

Merchants were an excepted group, and one who could prove he qualified for merchant status could apply for a merchant's certificate, with which he could travel to China or emigrate to the U.S. This status allowed him to travel and to bring in later his wife and family if he could provide proof of relation. The kinds of records generated by this process included: the merchant's testimony, merchant's passport, testimony by business colleagues or customers, records of the business, partnership lists and photographs.

Merchants attempting to bring in their family had to first prove merchant status and then the family relationship. Often, Caucasian witnesses were used to testify as to the applicant's merchant status, and Chinese witnesses were used to testify as to family relationships. There is one case of a tailor who had a tailor shop in Honolulu for 30 years and attempted to bring in his wife and child. First, he went through a rigorous process of proving the woman was his wife and the child their own. However, during the process, immigration officials determined that a tailor was not a merchant, as he did not sell goods but provided a service. This made him a laborer, and therefore his family was excluded from joining him in Hawaii. These types of files contain: marriage certificates, birth certificates, photographs, wedding certificates, transcripts of interrogations, witness statements, and letters.

One group of records document Chinese business partnerships throughout California. San Francisco's Chinatown is the largest section within the series, but numerous other communities are also represented. These consist of individual business case-files compiled twice yearly at the request of the Department of Labor in Washington D.C. Each file contains a description of the business, its location and net worth, a list of all partners and their investment, and occasionally a photograph of the owner. This series also contains street maps of Chinese business locations, by city, throughout California, as well as business listings from 1900 through 1930. A careful review of these records reveals changing status among partners and may indicate a pattern of paper partners. This situation would exist to allow Chinese to immigrate as merchants and to bring in their families and then become "silent partners" and begin other types of lives.

Other Asian groups were also affected by these laws. For a brief period ca. 1907–1910, as part of a gentleman's agreement, some Japanese, particularly picture brides, were also subject to the exclusion laws. A small number of "Japanese picture bride" files are among the records of Angel Island.

An Act of July 7, 1898 extended the exclusion policy to Hawaii, and in August of the following year, steps were taken to extend the policy to the Philippines. The economic story was quite different in Hawaii at this time. Agriculture was booming and the need for laborers was extremely high. There were other differences between San Francisco and Hawaii too: such as the attitude toward bound feet, as revealed in records documenting the attitude of immigration officials charged with enforcing the exclusion laws.

The 1900 law required all Chinese in Hawaii to register and obtain a certificate of residence. To obtain these certificates, the applicant had to submit to an investigation at the INS office. If the applicant failed to satisfy the inspector, the certificate would be denied and the applicant would be subject to deportation. Proof of naturalization by Hawaii and certificates of Hawaiian birth prior to the Islands coming under U.S. territorial status, as well as special birth certificates for Chinese born in Hawaii were used to acquire certificates of residency and citizenship. Records for Hawaii include a series of bound volumes containing "landing statements," which consist of information on Hawaiian-born subjects who visited China and sought reentry into the Territory of Hawaii. These records contain interrogations by the "Chinese Inspector" and record his "decision" as to allowing reentry based on evidence presented by the subject.

The Chinese immigration records for Hawaii held by the Pacific Sierra Region consist of 16,842 individual files; indexed by case number and name and organized by individual law. Some of the documents contained in the files include: Hawaiian birth certificates, photographs, biographical information, petitions for certificates of Hawaiian birth, merchant certificates, and transcripts of interviews with immigrants and travelers and/or family members related to facts and status of Hawaiian birth, marital relationship, merchant status and other details.

Although the laws were repealed in 1943, the amnesty created by the 1952 Walter-McCarran Act, which permitted "paper children" to register properly, kept many files active. Once the laws were repealed, many Chinese became naturalized citizens through the federal court. Naturalization records are available and are another source of information on Chinese in the United States.

Using The Records. The Immigration and Naturalization Service records are personal case files. Federal laws on privacy do not allow public access to any file less than 75 years old. Therefore, files started more than 75 years ago, or in 1919, are open to the general public, while access to files started less than 75 years ago may be limited. The right to privacy dies with an individual, so if an individual is deceased, that file can be opened to researchers able to provide an obituary or death certificate. Files less than 75 years old with the individual still alive can be made available if permission to view a file from the individual is presented to the archives.

The files are arranged in the archives by series and case number. Fortunately, the Hawaii INS prepared a series of cards by case number and by name, sorted alphabetically. San Francisco records between 1882 and 1906 were kept by date of arrival and ship name. However, many individual cases can be found through the docket index from the habeas corpus admiralty cases in the federal court. After 1906, there is no comprehensive index to Chinese case files. Fortunately, a series of certificate of identity books have been entered on a database by volunteers, so that the names and case file numbers are indexed. However, these only cover the years between 1909 and 1932, and are only for Chinese Americans who wanted to travel and were granted a certificate of identity. Other methods of access to case files are by using passenger-arrival indexes on microfilm, which give case numbers; by using Chinese partnership microfilm indexes, and by requesting case numbers from the Immigration and Naturalization Service. Remember, if someone never left the U.S., chances are they were not affected by the laws and there may be no file.

The researcher must know the name of the immigrant or traveler used on the papers. This may be different than his or her real or commonly used name. It helps if you have the name in Chinese to verify the name on the file.

INS officials often did not understand the arrangement of Chinese names and put family names in the place of personal names and vice versa. In addition, forms of address, marital status, or respect, such as Ah or Shee were taken to be actual names and were listed on the index as names. In other cases, they misheard, misunderstood, or misspelled the actual name. In some cases, Chinese names were converted to Hawaiian names for phonetic reasons, such as Chung to Akuna or Hung to Ahana. It is helpful to know this when tracking family names back to the original Chinese names.

In 1943, all existing Chinese exclusionary acts were repealed by President Franklin Roosevelt. However, the quota of immigrants permitted into the United States from China was limited to 105 individuals. Following this date, there were a number of laws enacted which affected Chinese coming to and living in the U.S. Although not a part of this discussion, these laws, and the records they generated, are deserving of study to continue the story of Chinese immigration.

The Laws. These records were generated as a result of a series of laws passed as part of the 60-year U.S. policy of Chinese exclusion. Different laws required different kinds of forms and documents. As a result of this ongoing legislative process, the records came to the archives grouped roughly into series by the particular statute. I will describe the terms of some of the laws so that you can begin to see the kinds of documents that they generated.

The Chinese exclusion laws began with the Treaty of 1880, which allowed the U.S. to "regulate, limit or suspend, but not absolutely prohibit, the coming and residency of Chinese." The Act Of May 1882 implemented this treaty. This act, considered the Chinese Exclusion Law, suspended immigration of Chinese laborers for 10 years; permitted reentry of certain Chinese laborers who left the U.S. temporarily, and created the section 6 status for teachers, students, merchants, and travelers to be admitted upon presentation of a certificate from the Chinese government. However, naturalization of Chinese was prohibited.

The Act of July 1884 was passed to strengthen the previous law. It allowed for the issuance of a section 6 certificate by other countries having Chinese subjects and for Chinese in transit through the U.S., but it permitted U.S. refusal of this certificate.

Act of September 1888: (1) prohibited the coming of Chinese laborers into the U.S. and (2) in anticipation that the Treaty of 1888 would be ratified by China (open-door concurrent with exclusion), established that a Chinese laborer who left the U.S. was not permitted to return unless he had a lawful wife, child, or parent in the U.S., or property valued at $1000, or debts of like amount due him. A Chinese laborer with these exemptions who needed to depart temporarily was required to secure a return certificate, valid for one year.

Act of October 1888, known as the Scott Act, enacted a month later when China refused to ratify the Treaty of 1888; prohibited the return of any Chinese laborers who had departed from the U.S.; forbade the issuance of return certificates to Chinese laborers and nullified all certificates of identity issued to Chinese laborers who left U.S. for temporary visits abroad under the Act of 1882. As a result, at least

20,000 Chinese laborers who had left with such certificates and about 600 who were on their way back had their re-entry permits revoked.

Act of May 1892. On the 10th anniversary of the original act and known as the Geary Act, (1) prohibited Chinese persons from coming to the U.S. and provided for the registration of resident laborers; (2) extended all Chinese exclusion laws for 10 years; (3) required registration of all Chinese laborers within one year and the issuance of Certificates of residence to those who were legally admitted, and (4) in deportation proceedings, Chinese had the burden of establishing right to remain in the U.S.

This act was amended a year later in the McCreary Amendment and (1) extended the time of registration from one year to 18 months and (2) defined laborer and merchant.

With the annexation of Hawaii, there was the Joint Resolution of July 7, 1898, which was entitled: "Prohibiting the Immigration of Chinese into Hawaii or Their Entry into the United States from Hawaii." This Act prohibited further immigration of Chinese into the Hawaiian Islands except for those who were declared admissible to the U.S.

Act of April 1900, entitled "Fixing Status of Chinese Within Hawaii and Providing for Their Registration," stated that Chinese in Hawaii were also required to register and obtain Certificates of Residence in the same manner as specified under the 1892 Geary Act.

Act of April 1902: (1) extended all Chinese exclusion laws indefinitely and (2) registration and obtaining Certificate of Residence also required of Chinese persons in insular possessions of the U.S.

Act of April 1904: (1) made exclusion laws applicable to the island territories of the U.S. and (2) prohibited immigration of Chinese laborers from such island territory to mainland U.S.

Act of 1921 decreed that alien wives of American citizens, irrespective of race, no longer acquired U.S. citizenship by fact of marriage (this obviously affected Chinese women marrying Chinese-American men).

Act of 1924: (1) established national origins quota system for European countries and (2) aliens ineligible for citizenship not admissible to U.S. (aimed primarily against Japanese aliens), contained relevant subclauses that (a) excluded Chinese alien wives of American citizens—had been about 150 per year between 1906–1924 (b) revoked the right of U.S. citizens of Chinese ancestry to bring their foreign-born Chinese wives and children in the U.S. Ironically, the U.S. Supreme Court, as part of a larger immigration decision, decided that alien wives and minor children of domiciled alien Chinese merchants could enter the U.S. for permanent residence as non-quota immigrants.

Act of June 1930: (1) provided for admission to Chinese wives who were married to U.S. citizens of Chinese ancestry prior to the Act of 1924—about 60 per year 1921–1924 and 1931–1941.

Other Laws Affecting U.S. Citizens Of Chinese Ancestry: Japanese laborers were excluded under the gentlemen's agreement of 1907; Korean and Japanese laborers under the President's proclamation of March 14, 1907; other Asians under the "barred zone" provision of the Immigration Act of 1917; loss of U.S. citizenship by marriage to alien ineligible to citizenship: American-born woman loses her U.S. citizenship upon marriage to persons ineligible for citizenship (i.e., Chinese, Japanese, and other Asian).

Works Cited

Fritz, Christian. "A Nineteenth Century 'Habeas Corpus Mill': The Chinese Before the Federal Courts in California." *The American Journal of Legal History.* 32:4 (October 1988): 347–372.

Levi Strauss v. Kan Lun, 1878. Civil Case #1468 records of the U.S. Circuit Court for the Northern District of California (RG 21).

Salyer, Lucy. "Captives of Law: Judicial Enforcement of the Chinese Exclusion Laws, 1891–1905. *The Journal of American History.* 76:1 (June 1989): 91–117.

Chinese-Language and Foreign-Language Instruction in California Schools

CAROLINE HUANG

Los Angeles Unified School District, Los Angeles, California

A restoration in foreign-language instruction is taking place in California's public schools. This is evident, for example, from the provision for foreign-language instruction in the Hughes-Hart Educational Reform Act of 1983. Both federal and state governments have been establishing funding and grants to promote foreign-language instruction in order to rectify the current trend of increasingly mono-lingual Americans. The Chinese language is emerging as one of the "uncommonly" taught languages attempting to find its place in K–12 schools.

"Looking to California's Pacific Neighborhood," a report to the Governor and the Legislature by the California Postsecondary Education commission, stresses the critical shortage of students studying Chinese, Japanese, and other languages and cultures. One of the remedies for this situation may very well be the early instruction of a foreign language in the K–12 grade.

The Chinese language has been considered one of the most laborious languages to master. It is not uncommon to labor for years of study and still lack a noticeable achievement. Thus, we have the great burden of searching for a modern pedagogy in teaching the Chinese language. Studies and research in this field is sketchy and often outdated. This report provides an overview of the current situations in the "Chinese schools" and the Los Angeles Unified School District, their overall enrollment and enrollment trends, Chinese language instructors, and instructional materials.

In Southern California, there are 94 Chinese-language schools. They are mostly Saturday or "after-school" programs. In 1976, the Southern California Council of Chinese Schools was founded to provide services, i.e., supplying textbooks from Taiwan, organizing teacher workshops, developing supplementary curriculum, and planning summer camps. Since its establishment, the council has grown considerably. More than 80 Chinese schools, which have over 1,000 teachers and 20,000 students, are affiliated with the council. Area-wise, it encompasses a very large region, ranging from north of Santa Barbara, to south of San Diego, to east of Phoenix, Arizona.

A few interesting observations are:

1. Students enrolled in the Chinese schools are all from K–12 grade, with elementary school-age students as the majority. This situation could be attributed to the fact that elementary-age students are much more impressionable than their teen-age siblings. However, many Chinese-language schools are applying for foreign language instructional credit, which is expected to entice more 9–12 grade students to attend Chinese school.

2. Chinese schools rely on volunteers and parents to staff their schools. Unavoidably, teachers are not familiar with the modern pedagogy of communication-based instruction. The Southern California Council of Chinese Schools has organized many workshops to remedy this deficency. Teachers are overwhelmingly receptive to these trainings.

3. Most Chinese schools use the modified elementary K–6 grade textbooks from Taiwan. It is extremely economical because it is financially subsidized by the Taiwan government. It is readily available through the overseas Chinese Cultural Service. The only problem with these inexpensive books, though, was that they fell short on interest level. Efforts are being made to rewrite the text book (12 V.) to meet the Chinese American children's needs and interests.

4. Almost none of the Chinese-language schools have their own classroom facilities. They usually rent the local schools or churches during the "after-hours." The lack of space and the dispute between building owners and Chinese schools are among the major problems for most Chinese schools.

At L.A.U.S.D., Chinese language is being offered at Gardena, Franklin, Belmont, and Venice high schools. I am currently a Chinese language teacher at Venice Foreign Language and International Studies Magnet High School. At L.A.U.S.D., a plan to introduce Chinese bilingual education in elementary school is in use.

Some observations are:

1. In the elementary school, approximately 6,000 students speak Chinese language of various dialects. These students are eligible to be in the bilingual program. However, many parents have limited

knowledge about the benefits of bilingual education. Therefore, they are often not receptive to enroll their children in bilingual programs. "Parents education" is vital to the success of such programs. At the high school level, only a very limited number of students (about 200 district-wide) enroll in the Chinese language classes. Most of the students are of ethnic Chinese origin. Expanding the recruitment in the future to reach the non-Chinese student population is vital to the continuing success of the Chinese-language program in the secondary level.

2. There is a definite shortage of qualified Chinese-language instructors. Training teachers to meet the anticipated increasing demand should be of high priority. Without qualified teachers to staff the program, students' interest in learning will not be stimulated, and they may not be able to pass the Chinese achievement test that is being planned for the year 1994. In the elementary level, a similar shortage of qualified teachers is also quite evident. This further hinders the development of Chinese bilingual education in California.

3. In the secondary level, textbooks are grossly inadequate. The major sources come from postsecondary-level textbooks, which do not meet the secondary students' interest level. The use of simplified characters in some textbooks also complicates the issue. To serve the needs of secondary level students best, it seems that a textbook written locally, adhering to the "Foreign Language Framework" dictated by the California State Department of Education and adopting the "communication based" text, is urgently needed. In the elementary level, the "whole language" approach is widely enacted. Many core literature have already been translated into Chinese.

Chinese-language instruction in K–12 grades is still at its infantile stage. There is a monumental task ahead of us. For example, Chinese-language courses need to be mainstreamed into K–12 curriculum, so the image of "uncommonly taught language" can be changed. There are some concrete tasks that I think we can do to help. Examples include forming advisory committees to conduct workshops to strengthen the instruction and to inspire teachers to learn and to teach Chinese culture; developing a communication-based curriculum for K–12 grades; educating parents of the benefits of having their children take Chinese language courses, and collaborating with the Southern California Council of Chinese Schools to expand community support. A concerted effort by people at various fronts is expected to facilitate the process and to help the flourishing of the Chinese language instruction in K–12 grades.

Chinese-Language Choices and Adaptations in New York City's Chinatown

MEEI-YAU WEI

Indiana University, Bloomington, Indiana

This is a paper about ethnic grouping, as it is expressed in language choices. I argue for a "dialogic" model, as proposed by Bakhtin (Bakhtin 1981), utilizing the rich resources—linguistic, cultural, economic, or political—as provided by the new immigrants. I examine the "model minority," namely those young, wealthy, well-educated, and aspiring Chinese Americans, and their strategies to get on with the local community and to get ahead with the dominant society. I contrast their strategies with those of the first-generation Chinese and how these two distinct cultural types can teach us the possible strategies the new immigrants are going to adopt.

Following Bakhtin, I treat language as a social discourse. It is stratified not only into linguistic varieties, but into languages that are socio-ideological: language of social groups, "professional" and "genetic" languages, languages of generations, and so forth. The making of a language choice is embedded in our understanding of the history. The "dialogic" aspect of this discourse can be best conceptualized as a duel of social forces, economic or political, competing among and within institutions and individuals.

I use the redistricting issue of the 1991 New York City Council election to illustrate the various rhetoric and rationale for ethnic grouping in Chinatown for a political representation. I conclude that there arises a myriad of contesting voices in testifying to the myth of a well-defined ethnic group.

In May 1991, the New York City Redistricting Commission released its plan for 51 new city council districts. From changing the previous 35 seats to 51, this plan aimed to accommodate greater minority representation. The additional seats also required redrawing the previous districting line to increase the number of council districts. There is no single area in the city where Asians are a majority yet; therefore no official representative was ever elected to represent the ethnic population of Asians.

Two different major plans split the Chinatown votes. Plan A would link the core Chinatown area around Mott and Canal Streets west into SoHo and Battery Park city: a predominantly white liberal area.

Plan B suggested grouping Chinatown with the Latino community, stretching north to 14th Street, east to Grand Street, west to Broadway at Canal, and south to Catherine and Madison Streets.

Both plans have strong advocates who are concerned with the welfare of the residents. Informant A, once a hard-line community leader who still has tight controls over conservative social organizations in Chinatown, strongly favors Plan A. He reasons: "Allying with the uptown white liberals will help better the image of Chinatown and stop the negative stereotypes of Chinese as laborers or working class."

He is also opposed to allying the Chinatown voters with the Latinos around the downtown area, as he says: "I know what being poor means, and we don't want to identify ourselves with the poor any more."

Along with his allies, informant A's rationale seems to aim at advancing Chinatown from an ethnic ghetto to a better community. However, this rationale cannot justify the consequences that most of the voters in Chinatown would have to put up with during the transformation of Chinatown from a ghetto to a tourist center. In a labor-intense market with thousands of new immigrants coming from Southeast Asia every week, the most urgent issues are affordable housing, health insurance, and bilingual services, rather than tourism or condominium plans.

Informant B, a well-educated, well-experienced administrator, strongly supports plan B. Through his experience in working with different ethnic groups, he could easily identify the issues concerning various interest groups. As much as the opponents protested this plan, objecting to the incompatibility of grouping Chinese with Latino or black ethnics, Informant B, along with the advocates, praised the sensible alliance with a group whose concern for public assistance is also shared by the Chinese working class.

Informant B reasoned:

> The uptown whites never like us. Grouping the Chinatown voters with them is just a way for them to use us as a rubber stamp to endorse whatever they think is the most important.
>
> Besides, who is better in manipulating the American political schemes? Chinatown workers have a long history in cooperating with the various black and Hispanic coalitions. We share the common concerns and the means to get into the mainstream politics.

The two opposing views are not generated from an ideological vacuum. Informant A and Informant B represent distinct cultural types which many residents can identify with. Informant A's conservative and idealistic socio-political view reflects the traditional perspective supported by most of the older generation. Paying homage to the local family or clan associations, speaking the local tongues, emphasizing harmony, tradition, and performing cultural rituals at important occasions to assure or assert certain forms of cultural reproduction are the social activities practiced and propagated by traditional leaders like Informant A.

Several instances dramatically changed the ethnic make-up of Chinatown, which had a bearing on the evolution of the two cultural types. The 1960s civil rights movement helped awaken the ethnic consciousness of the Chinese. The younger generation, in contrast to the older ones, were American-born and mostly well-educated. They spoke English and they knew the American system. The experience of the American black helped them find a way to break through the ethnic boundaries between themselves and mainstream American society.

Aware of the competitive edge of the neighboring ethnic groups—such as the Hispanic and the black, with whom they had to compete for federal or government funding, as well as a balanced racial representation—the "new Chinese" of the 1960s forged alliances with other ethnic groups, diversifying their strategies as a means of survival. Homogeneity, harmony, and the self-contained ethnic ideology no longer rang true to their aspirations for breaking out and getting ahead. Confrontations, litigations, and protests were all seen as a necessary means to voice one's point of view. Just as Informant A locates his ideology in an ancient civilization which centers "Chinese" while calibrating others, Informant B locates his pragmatism in a dynamic polyphonic context where his position constantly shifts as occasion demands. In contrast to Informant A, who wants to preserve Chinatown as a homogeneous community, Informant B is keenly aware that changes and adaptations are the two essential forces for the evolution of a polyphonic community over time. As much as the traditional leaders hold on to the Chinese cultural capital to articulate their socio-political views, the younger Chinese are optimizing as assorted capital—Chinese, American, and other ethnic groups—to protect or propagate their interests.

Tradition and culture can no longer be grasped within narrow ethnic boundaries by the younger generation. They were born into a different era and into a different culture: America in the 1960s. The civil rights movement, the 1965 Immigration Act, and the increasing wealth or political turmoil in Southeast Asia provided ample inspiration and adoptable social, economical, or political capital for the younger generation to get on with the local community and get ahead in the dominant society. They allied themselves with the many ethnic groups who shared the same concerns, such as minority rights, and felt the need to innovate an objectifiable racial label, "Asian

American," like that of "African American" or "Latino American," for them to compete for the limited resources with other interest groups and to accommodate the many waves of immigrants from China, Hong Kong, Taiwan, and different parts of Asia.

The unique socio-cultural forces from both the first generation like Informant A's and the 1960s American political polyphony also had a bearing on the younger generation's language choice. Speaking Chinese, being Chinese, or interpreting Chinese took on new meaning for the American-Born Chinese like Informant B. His language choice, like many of his generation, is closely revolved around the competing socio-ideologies in a polyphonic context. Speaking English not only empowers Asian Americans to ally themselves with the dominant society, but can avoid the long-term linguistic tensions between Cantonese and Mandarin, or for that matter, any other Chinese varieties used in Chinatown. Various funding from the federal government or business groups become available for the many vocational English programs, which further legitimize the institutional dominance of English language in Chinatown. Those who master the practical aspect of making a language choice will certainly become the legitimate spokesman in dealing with inter-ethnic or inter-racial affairs.

Likewise, adopting another objectifiable racial label, "Asian American," can be regarded as a creative strategy to dismiss the historical entanglement among the different ethnic groups of Chinese. Above all, the Asian Americans are Americans when they speak administrative English to their Chinese fellows in Chinatown, Cantonese when they use idiomatic Cantonese slang at events such as the Chinese New Year or the fund raising, Chinese when they carried signs protesting outside the U.N. building denouncing the conduct of the Beijing authorities during the 1989 massacre, Asians when they side with the Japanese Americans or the Korean Americans to break the glass ceiling obstructing their climb up the American corporate ladder, and they are the minorities when siding with the blacks or the Hispanics in demanding rights or protesting ethnic injustice. The ambiguities and fluidity in the "Asian American" construct are responsive to the larger society's demands, and are reflected in their ever-changing social identities. Making a choice of a language or ethnicity in this contested social context simply means to adopt another point of view. As Bourdieu points out:

> This objective element of uncertainty—which is often reinforced by the effect of categorization, since the same word can cover different practices—provides a basis for the plurality of world-views, which itself is linked to the plurality of points of views; and, at the same time,

provides a basis for symbolic struggles for the power to produce and to impose a vision on the legitimate world. (Bourdieu 1990:133)

Thus, the distinction between "self" and "other" is a constant flux of ideological conflicts and contradictions. The fluidity of the unbounded consciousness and self-awareness flows across the bleached ethnic and linguistic lines.

The boundaries between ethnic groupings are always situational, contingent, and ambiguous. To the extent that they are articulated by interest groups and tailored to walks of residents, their effects have to be indeterminate. To the extent that they have to accommodate various ideologies in a dynamic context, they have to be ambiguous. The different ideologies not only conflict between different generations of Chinese Americans, but they also have their effects on the new immigrants numbering thousands a week, mostly from Southeast Asia, in the lower-east side Chinatown, which is still the most densely-populated Chinese community in the Western Hemisphere—a desirable turf for any interest group at a time of racial divisions and limited resources. As Royce in "Ethnic Identity: Strategies of Diversity" points out:

The conflicts have varied from open warfare to silent resistance, but the one constant is from opposition to the idea of incorporation. Without this kind of antagonism, persistent identity systems would fail to develop. It is important to assess the larger society's resources in the struggle to incorporate smaller groups as well as those available to the smaller groups for resisting. (Royce 1982:46)

Thus, I conclude that the best way to study this dialogue of ethnic grouping and language choice is through a detailed ethnographic study and a reflexive narration in order to disclose the contingent forces in play.

A Review of Children's Books on Chinese American History

ANN LAU

Chinese Historical Society of Southern California, Los Angeles, California

SAVIO CHAU

University of California, Los Angeles

What do Chinese American children find when they start to search for their historic and cultural roots through books written about Chinese history and culture?

Do they find a wealth of information presented in a similar way as European history? Will they find the study of Chinese history and culture as a matter of course, no more and no less in importance than in the study of European history? Will they find a well balanced view of Chinese history allowing them to understand the various aspects of Chinese history and culture? Will they find in that information an identity of their cultural and historic roots and thus forge a pride in that part of themselves?

Since books on Chinese history and culture written in the English language are necessarily written for Western consumption, will Chinese American children find in those books a preponderance of Western perspectives on Chinese history and culture as only a matter of curiosity and intrigue with little or no redeeming value? Will they find a reinforcement of stereotypes both in Chinese culture and history—and thus in Chinese as a whole? Will they find inaccuracies and misinformation that reflect a Western bias as well as a political bias? Will they obtain only a shallow impression of Chinese culture and history and thus treat such information with disdain? Will they, as a result of such information, become ashamed of that part of their heritage and thus reject that part of themselves?

This paper was prompted by two experiences of our authors. The high school text of one of our authors mentioned the Opium Wars but never explained that it was the British who shipped opium into China that bought on the wars. As a result, many students automatically assumed that it was the Chinese who shipped opium to England. While searching for books on China for children several years ago, one of our authors came upon a full-page photograph of a Chinese man with fingernails over a foot long. Such a photograph should have more appropriately belonged in a book of *Ripley's Believe It or Not.*

Since those times, have books on Chinese history and culture changed? We wanted to find out. In looking for books to review, we have gone to three major sources. We went to public libraries and randomly borrowed children's books about Chinese history and culture. We went to our local school book depositories and asked for history text books, social studies text books that have topics on Chinese history and culture. We went to Chinatown and Monterey Park Chinese bookstores and browsed through many of the bilingual children's books. What we have found was rather surprising. We shall now detail some of the many things we found.

China, a History to 1949. Published by Children Press Chicago 1983, for grade school and middle school. This book has a revised edition which reduced the size of its original full-page photograph of the Chinese man with foot-long fingernails to a quarter of the page. Yet, the photograph still appears in its section of the Sui Dynasty (A.D. 589) about Mandarins, although the photograph itself was dated to 1914. We cannot understand why the editor could not let go of such a photograph.

Asian Civilizations, the Human Story. Published by Silver Burdett Press 1986, for grade school. Translated from the French with professor Moeller of Temple University as its English consultant. From the book:

> Chinese Wisdom—The Chinese had three major religions, Buddhism, Confucianism and Taoism... Confucius was the founder of a religion and for two thousand years the patron saint of a social stratum known as mandarins.

It is, of course, a major error to say that Confucianism is a religion. Although the Chinese called Confucius the "Big Saint," such a status is quite different from that of sainthood as understood by Catholicism. Within the Chinese Confucian context, Confucius had attained the status of a superior man. Within the study of Taoism, there are actually two separate studies; there is Taoism (Tao Chiao) as a religion and there is also Taoism (Tao Chia) as a philosophy. It is misleading to summarily state that Taoism is a religion.

Early China, the Civilization Library. Published by Gloucester Press 1986, for grade school. From the book:

> The four classes: shi—state officials, nobles and scholars whose ability counted far more than birth. Next came the nong, the peasant farmers ... The gaong, the artisans ... Still lower were the shang, the merchants, perhaps because their great wealth constituted a threat to the princes who wanted to control the economy.

This book did quite well in explaining the first three classes, but why did it insist on misrepresenting the reason why the merchant class was considered the least important at the time? The author of this book must have known that the merchants were considered the least important class because they were deemed to have contributed nothing to the society.

From the book: "Rich families ... They ate snails in vinegar, dog meat and tangerines and drank wine, coconut milk and fermented palm juice."

There is a Chinese saying, "Hang a sheep's head, sell dog meat" to mean a merchant trying to fool his clients who want to buy mutton. So is dog meat really a steady diet of the rich? One can only conclude that the author merely wanted to sensationalize the Chinese's range of diet.

From the book: "Confucius taught a practical way of life, based on loyalty to the family, ancestor worship and obedience to the laws of society. His philosophy put emphasis on ceremonies and order."

Perhaps it is difficult in a children's book to really present Confucius' ideals, but the way presented here and in many other books as well, Confucianism was presented as a rigid ceremonious practice. Since the book mentioned that Confucius taught a practical way of life, it would help the young readers if the author mentioned some of the practical ways of life that Confucius advocated. From the book:

> Let the past serve the present—with these words, Mao Zedong, leader of the People's Republic, admitted the importance of early China to the modern day. He encouraged archaeological investigations, which will continue to add to our knowledge of one of the most fascinating civilization on Earth.

The above paragraph appeared in the last page of the book. It is certainly a very curious part of the book since the book covered only the early history of China. Perhaps when the book was published in 1986, it was necessary for the author to write in what is generally considered a "visa" paragraph to guarantee a visa back to China.

World History: A Basic Approach. Published by Coronado Publishers 1984, a middle school text book. From the book:

> This period (A.D. 220–590) was called China's "Dark Age." However, China's Dark Age was not completely "dark." The Mongol invaders soon learned the Chinese ways of living. Chinese schools continued to teach students the ideas of Confucius.

The concept of Dark Age does not exist in Chinese history. Chinese people consider their civilization as always continuous and never interrupted, even under the control of invaders. In fact, the invasion of the northern tribes (the term "Mongol invaders" is an over-simplification since there were five major tribes in that period) only caused a shift of the cultural center to the Yangtze region, but the influence of Chinese civilization prevailed throughout the land. The Toba tribe that unified the northern China was systematically assimilated in A.D. 494. The Equal Field system, which was the cornerstone of the land distribution system in Sui and Tang Dynasties, was also developed in this period. The authors apparently tried to model Chinese history in this period after the fall of the Roman Empire. Unfortunately, such a model is inaccurate and inconsistent.

From the book: "The Tang Dynasty did not allow freedom of religion."

Although it did mention that "During most of Chinese history, every Chinese was allowed to worship as he or she wished," the statement made about Tang Dynasty is grossly misleading. The fact was the Tang Dynasty was most famous for its religious tolerance. Many foreign religions, including Islam and a sect of Christianity, were introduced to China at that time. The purging of Buddhism by Mu Tsung (A.D. 845) was only an exception within the 289 years of Tang Dynasty. The authors apparently compared the purge of Buddhism in China to the persecution of Christianity in the Roman Empire or the Spanish Inquisition by the Catholic Church. In reality, although Buddhism was purged three times in Chinese history (A.D. 446, A.D. 574, A.D. 845), none of them was long-lasting. Moreover, there has never been any large scale religious war in Chinese history. (Note: There were rebellions under the guise of religions. However, they fought against corrupt government rather than other religions.) Any fighting between the Taoists and Buddhists were limited to monks. Common people seldom involved themselves in religious bickering, since religion usually was relegated to the uneducated and considered more a superstition by most Confucian scholars. When asked about religion, Confucius said, "I do not even know about this world, how can I tell you about the after world?" Religious tolerance throughout Chinese history helped China avoid the religious wars that plagued Europe.

Exploring World History: A Global Approach. Published by Global Book Company 1969, a middle school text. From the book: "The people (Chinese) did not think very much about the world outside China. They were very happy with their life and thought that they lived the best way possible."

This is an over-generalized statement. While the Chinese people used to think they were more advanced than the people in neighboring countries, they did not always ignore the outside world. Expeditions were encouraged by the Han, Tang, and early Ming dynasties. Famous explorers included Zhang Qian (Han Dynasty, 139 B.C.), Yuan Juan (Tang Dynasty, A.D. 631), and Chang Ho (Ming Dynasty, A.D. 1405). The Chinese were outward-looking when the country was strong and withdrew from the outside world when the country was weak. The authors' view that the Chinese were not interested in the outside world was probably originated from the Europeans' contact with China in the 19th century. Indeed, China became a closed country after the middle of the Ming Dynasty. However, up until then, there were more than a thousand years of exploration, military and political expeditions with the outside world. Western scholars tend to stereotype China with the impression they got from the Ching Dynasty. However, Chinese culture and civilization, just as any other civilization, have always been changing and will continue to change. Casting Chinese culture in stereotype is the major reason for misunderstanding.

Exploring Our World: Eastern Hemisphere. Published by Follett Publishing Company 1977, a middle school text book. This text omits all the history of China before Marco Polo (Yuan Dynasty), except for a discussion of Confucianism and Taoism. Ching Dynasty was only briefly mentioned. This oversight can only result in superficial understanding that may subsequently distort one's understanding of the long history of the Chinese people.

Exploring World History, a Global Approach. Published by Globe Book Company 1969, revised 1977, a high school text. From the book:

> Confucius ... His lessons can be summed up in the golden rule; Do unto others as you would have them do unto you. Another religious leader, named Lao-Tze also tried to find a way to end the wars among the people.

Here again, it is implied that Confucius was a religious leader.

Exploring Our World, Eastern Hemisphere. Published by Follett Publishing Company 1977, a high school text book. From the book: "Confucius also said that only educated people were fit to run the government."

This is an erroneous assumption, even though Confucius considered the goal of education is to be a virtuous man and only virtuous men should govern; it did not necessarily mean that Confucius considered only educated people were fit to rule.

China, from Emperors to Communes.

Published by Dillon Press 1983, for middle school age. From the book: "Indeed, people sometimes think that Chinese speakers are shouting at each other ... But how the Chinese say a word can completely change its meaning. And so they speak loudly to make the pitch clear."

We don't really know how to comment on this sentence. Certainly, as Chinese speakers, we do not believe we shout at one another. Perhaps the only way to gauge this is to have a scientific study made on the decibels reached by different spoken languages and determine if we Chinese speakers really speak loudly as the author contends.

From the book: "In 1911 a popular revolt overthrew China's last emperor."

It is understandable that the author provided only one sentence on the revolution of 1911 if the book wanted only to concentrate on emperors and communes. But to all Chinese, Dr. Sun Yat Sen was considered the father of modern China and the event that happened in 1911 was considered a Revolution since it was the overthrow of a dynasty and the first establishment of a republic in China. This may be due to the writings of Professor John Fairbanks, whose writings had probably dominated the study of modern Chinese history in the United States prior to 1970s. From the book:

> Most landlords thought only of growing rich and doing as little as possible ... Mao started a communist society. Instead of landlords, the government owned the land. It distributed food and clothes according to people's needs. Mao built schools and hospitals that were open to everyone. In old China, officials never did hand labor. Mao made everyone till the land or work in a factory. In the days of the emperors, only the scholars could read and write. Now all girls and boys went to school.

While this book gave a glowing account of Communism in China, it failed to mention the human sufferings under Communist rules. Because the author failed to mention about the social changes after the revolution of 1911, he also failed to mention that boys and girls were already attending school prior to the Communist revolution.

From the book: "Today many Chinese immigrants come from Taiwan and Hong Kong, and they often start their life in America in a Chinatown."

Although the book did explain how the Nationalists ended in Taiwan, it did not explain why so many Chinese chose to leave China for Hong Kong. Furthermore, since Chinese immigrations to the U.S. from 1949 onward have been very much influenced by political turmoil in China, why didn't the author mention why the Chinese felt they must leave their homeland?

Enchantment of the World People's Republic of China.
Published by Children's Press Chicago 1984, for grade school age. From the book:

> Pu Yi (the last emperor of China) ... was to learn to ... appreciate the value of hard work.... Pu Yi began to study communism. He read works by Karl Marx, V.I. Lenin, Mao Tse-tung and other communists. They wrote of a way of life exactly the opposite of the life Pu Yi had ... Communists want to get rid of ruling classes. They believe that everyone in a country should share the wealth. Communists think that workers, through their government, should own their country's resources and manage them for the benefit of all people.

Although this book covered the history of the Peoples' Republic through the 1970s, it gave a very sanitized version of that history. It did not mention any of the human tolls as the Communist government attempted to consolidate power and to build a classless society. Even as it mentioned the failure of the Great Leap Forward, it failed to mention the famine and the human toll. For a book aimed at grade school age children, it certainly seemed to give approval to the idea of Communism.

The Land and People of China.
Published by J. B. Lippincott 1989, for middle and high school. From the book: "For Confucius, the perfect gentleman was characterized by the five virtues; ren, or benevolence, yi or righteousness, li or proper order, zhi or understanding and xin or trustworthiness."

Besides this book that mentioned ren, there is a text book, *A Message of Ancient Days*, published by Houghton Mifflin Company, 1991, which also mentioned "ren." On two different occasions, Confucius was asked to define "ren." Once, he defined it as the golden run and another time he said that "ren" is to love people. It is interesting that although Chinese Confucian scholars never failed to mention "ren," "li," "yi," thrift and knowing shame, we cannot find any books that mentioned thrift and knowing shame as virtues. One can understand why the teaching of Calvinism and conspicuous consumption would be frowned upon by those following the teachings of Confucius.

From the book: "The republican revolutionary movement that finally took the lead in overthrowing the Qing Dynasty is nearly synonymous with one of modern China's greatest figures, Sun Yat-Sen."

This sentence reflected the view of most Chinese scholars about Sun Yat-Sen, as opposed to the views held by John Fairbanks and many other western scholars. Surprisingly, the author was a student of Fairbanks but did not follow Fairbanks' view. From the book:

> It was a time for settling old score; millions of people were executed for real or imagined crimes against the people. In the cities, intellectuals, businessmen and other people of even modes, wealth and privilege were shown, sometimes forcibly, that in the new China everyone was supposed to be equal, even if that meant being equally poor. Many more people fled to Hong Kong or Taiwan.

This is probably the only library book for children that we have found that did not glorify the Communist Revolution in China. This book truly indicted Chinese Communism and explained why the Chinese left China. Instead of the glowing reviews of Chinese Communism presented by other books and by respected authors like John Fairbanks, this book reflected a wide perspective on Chinese Communism as it affected the lives of millions of Chinese during its tumultuous years.

China. Published by Crestwood House Macmillan Publishing Company 1990, for grade school and middle school. From the book:

> Mao said that he had asked for one hundred flowers but had gotten weeds instead. He was bitter about the way intellectuals were criticizing him. Many of those intellectuals were rounded up by the government and sent away to labor camps—some for as long as 20 years.

This book started with the 1989 Tiananmen Massacre and went back to cover 1949 until the Cultural Revolution and the return to power of Deng Xiaoping. It gave a quite fair account of the history and explained to the young readers what was wrong without giving a glorify account.

Various Texts on the Opium Wars. We wanted to find out if there were changes in text books regarding the Opium Wars since our high school days, so we browsed through a few text books.

We found two general treatments on the Opium Wars. For American history text books, usually only the Open Door policy was discussed and the Opium Wars were not mentioned. For world history text books, however, the reasons for the Opium Wars were usually mentioned and the more recent text books are more candid about the British opium trade. Only one text book we found failed to mention the reason for the Opium Wars; but it also left out the word opium. It wrote:

> The British did not like the way the Chinese treated British merchants in Canton. The Chinese said that the British living in Canton did not obey Chinese laws. War finally broke out between China and Great Britain in 1939. The British won the war.

None of the text books reviewed really faulted the British for starting the war.

The Overseas Chinese Library of the Republic of China, Foreign Language Press of the Peoples' Republic of China, Wonder Kids Publishers of Taiwan, and Sun Ya Publisher of Hong Kong.

There are many translations of Chinese classics for high school- and college-age students. But except for an occasional folk tale, we could not find any books on Chinese literature or stories for children in our local public libraries. The best sources we have found are in the bilingual section of the Chinatown Branch Pubic Library and in Chinese book stores.

The Overseas Chinese Library of the Republic of China is a publishing company associated with the Republic of China. It has published some very outstanding bilingual books on Chinese literature and stories about historical events and people. Many of these books may be obtained through Chinese schools and from the Chinese Culture Center in Los Angeles Chinatown. These books are often provided free of charge to the registered Chinese schools. We highly recommend the series of books on Chinese sayings; not only do they have the sayings printed in Chinese characters, they have the history and stories behind these sayings. Although the series is aimed for middle and high school levels, we recommend it for anyone who has not been exposed to Chinese literature and literary sayings.

The Foreign Language Press of the Peoples' Republic of China has published many English-language story books for children. However, one must be prudent in selecting children's book from this publisher, as it is a propagandist arm of the Peoples' Republic of China. A children's book we browsed at in the Chinatown library with the title *Walo Hamlet* had this to say at the end of the story:

> Team leader Chen said, "We've waged a lot of fierce struggles for emancipation through the generations but none succeeded. Only

when we are led by the Communist Party have we been able to throw off the oppression and exploitation by the reactionary ruling class."

Many of the books promote class hatred that is not appropriate for children here.

We highly recommend The Wonder Kids Publishers, which has a series of books on Chinese history, classics, and folk tales that surely will delight lower grade school age children. These books are not as well researched in the historical aspects as the Overseas Chinese Library of the Republic of China.

Sun-Ya Publisher is also another private publisher that has published many bilingual books appropriate for children. The books are for grade school and middle school children.

Island, Poetry and History of Chinese Immigrants on Angel Island. Published by Him Mark Lai and others. Although this is not a children's book and its poetry is not considered to be of much literary value, this book should be used as a model for future books and poetry written for our children. This book has the original Chinese poetry in Chinese with annotations and references on its translations. It has such a wealth of historical references that it truly bridged Chinese immigrants with their historical and cultural past. It is also an example of how important our knowledge of Chinese history and literature is in understanding Chinese American history.

Conclusion. Before we started our project, we were ready to uncover some horrific errors and bias; yet by the end of this project, we were relieved that many of our original concerns failed to materialize.

We have found that many of the textbooks published before the early 1980s are quite simplistic about Chinese history and have more Western bias. On the other hand, the text books after mid-1980s are quite accurate, and there is less Western bias.

What is most interesting are non-textbooks published about China. We have come to accept some of the inaccuracies as inevitable, but we are truly surprised by some of the glaring errors and misinformation.

Non-textbooks about China can generally be separated into three periods. Books published prior to late 1970s (before Nixon went to China) are more interested in presenting the intriguing aspects of Chinese history and culture. Because research prior to 1970s was limited, these books were quite heavily influenced by John Fairbanks and Edgar Snow, and thus reflect mostly their thinking. Books published in early and mid-1980s seemed to bend over backward in its praise of Chinese culture and Communism in China. This may be due to the need to ensure a "visa" back to China for the authors. Books published in 1989 and later have more of a comprehensive look at both the good and bad about Chinese history and culture especially about Communism in China.

We hope that future books will continue the trend of presenting Chinese history and culture in a well-rounded way. In text books in particular, we would like a more detailed coverage of Chinese history and culture. For example, as far as influence is concerned, Confucius had a far greater and longer lasting influence than someone like Marie Theresa of Austria. Yet in the text book *Exploring World History, a Global Approach*, published by Globe Book Co., there was more information about Marie Theresa than Confucius.

We hope, too, that more scholars will write about world history in a truly global approach. For example, it would be helpful to point out how the inventions of paper and printing in China affect European history. It would also be interesting to point out how the Chinese invention of gunpowder, crossbows, and cannons affect the way the knights conducted their wars and, ultimately, the effect on European history. One should also realize the importance of the American idea of democracy and how the writings and speeches of Abraham Lincoln affected Dr. Sun Yat Sen and subsequently changed the history of China.

We hope that the values, as taught by Confucius, are taught to our children not as simply Chinese culture, but as values we should live by. Confucius defined "ren" as "love people" and as "what you do not wish for yourself, do not do to others." These should be taught to our children from kindergarten onward. Perhaps through such teachings, Chinese culture can help to redefine the future of what is considered as American. If pizza can be considered as American food, then Confucian values can also become American food for thought.

Chinese American Name Styles and their Significance

EMMA WOO LOUIE

Chinese Historical Society of Southern California, Los Angeles, California

"Names are full of historical, cultural, and sociological information," concluded the author of *What's In a Name?*, a book about American names and name practices (Ashley 31). Studies have shown that names reveal such information as language, national origin, religious affiliation, and social class (Loesell 224). Names, therefore, disclose our social values, family traditions, and individual whim—overall reflecting the society we reside in.

Societal changes also affect the selection of given names. For instance, following the social turmoil and the rejection of long-held customs and mores during the 1950s and 1960s, American parents no longer named their children Mary or John with the same high frequency as in the previous two centuries. Onomasticians—people who study names—noticed that by the 1970s, many traditional given names were dropped in favor of newly coined ones, respelled old ones, or names that were not in popular use for some time. The pendulum, though, seems to be swinging back again to traditional names (Ashley 121, 126).

The latest in American name fashions can be detected in the "Red Eggs and Ginger Party" announcements often reported in *AsianWeek*. And like the names for the majority of Americans, the names of the infant honorees at these parties almost always consist of two Western given names: *Christopher Michael Woo, Ashleigh Noelle Lung, Kendrick George Dea*, and *Marissa Rebecca Wong* (Gan 24). In comparison, their parents and grandparents have names such as the *Howard Woos, Mr. and Mrs. Hom Gok, Dr. and Mrs. K. C. Wong*; names likely to be found for an older generation.

Other records show Chinese Americans having name patterns closer to their Chinese cultural heritage. For example, the listing for the 1987 graduating class of South Pasadena High School includes such names as:

Asli C. F. Chui, Myvan Hua, Yaping Joyce Liao, Wen-Tao Tien, and *Leilani Chia Chi Wong.*

Limited as these samplings of Chinese American personal names are, we can observe the influence of both American and Chinese cultures. The purpose of this paper is to discuss what "historical, cultural, and sociological information" can be gleaned from the popular name styles used by Chinese Americans. Name styles are particularly useful because, regardless of the choice of given names, we all write or state our names in specific ways.

According to Elsdon C. Smith, author of several books on name customs in America, there are seven distinct American name styles (118, 135). If Stephen Louie, for example, has only one given name, he may write his name as 1) *Stephen Louie* or as 2) *S. Louie.* Or he may call himself 3) *Steve Louie.* If Steve has a middle name, such as John, he has the option of three more name styles: 4) *Stephen John Louie,* 5) *Stephen J. Louie,* or 6) *S. J. Louie.* If he prefers to be known by his middle name, he writes his name as 7) *S. John Louie.* The name style involving an initial between the given name and the surname, Smith pointed out, is an especially American custom.

These name styles are used by Chinese Americans irrespective of having a Western or a Chinese given name. But there are 10 more name styles for Chinese Americans due to their observance of Chinese name customs and to the different ways of structuring the transcribed Chinese given name. These 10 name styles are listed below with typical examples (Louie 225–237):

1. Chinese personal name with the surname first: *Lou Sheng;*
2. Chinese personal name composed of three or more separate words: *Ieoh Ming Pei, Chow Kwan Kam Oi;*
3. hyphenated Chinese disyllabic name, with the second word in lower case: *Chi-yuan Lin,*
4. hyphenated Chinese disyllabic name, with a capitalized initial in the second word: *Han-Sheng Lin;*
5. Chinese disyllabic name written as one word: *Renqiu Yu;*
6. Western given name plus a Chinese middle name: *Jean Yun-Hua King;*
7. Chinese given name plus a Western middle name: *Sao-Ke Alfred Sze;*
8. three initials for the Western and Chinese given names: *V. L. C. Chuan* (*V.* stands for *Victor* and *L. C.* for *Lu-Chi*);
9. two initials for the Chinese given name: *Tracy S. Y. Wong;*
10. one initial for the Chinese disyllabic given name: *Robert T. Poe* (*T* is for *Ta-Pang*).

Before proceeding further, I should explain that the term *personal name* refers to one's given name and surname. Americans, however, often call the given name the *first name* since it customarily precedes the surname or family name. Not surprisingly, we call the latter the *last name*. These terms *first name* and *last name* can be confusing when discussing Chinese personal names since the surname always comes first whenever these are written or stated in Chinese. I prefer the term *given name* because it is an exact description; most people are *given* a name, usually by a parent. And when individuals name themselves—as new immigrants may do in conforming to the customs of their adopted country—they become their own namegiver.

To facilitate discussing Chinese American name styles, I have grouped personal names into three main categories, the second having four subcategories:

1. names consisting of Western given names only;
2. names consisting of Chinese given names only:
   a. written as separate words,
   b. written as initials,
   c. written as hyphenated names,
   d. written as one word;
3. names incorporating Western and Chinese given names.

In the first and third categories, the surname always follows the given name(s), as in European American name tradition. In the second category, the surname could be either at the beginning or at the end of the name.

Names Consisting of Western Given Names Only. George R. Stewart wrote in his book on American given names that most Americans, since the middle of the 19th century, possess two given names. This was so commonplace that it was presumed by the time of World War I (1914–1918) to be true for every American (20–21, 30).[1] I don't believe this can be presumed for Chinese Americans at that time or even today. According to the 1980 federal census, the majority of this population is foreign-born, which is no doubt true to this day (Gardner, Robey and Smith 3–12, 36–41).[2]

---

[1] Our American custom of having two given names—a first and a middle name—began with the Germans, who settled in Pennsylvania toward the end of the 17th century.

[2] Since the 1965 Immigrant Act, the percentage of foreign-born in the Chinese American population greatly increased. The statistics in this booklet place it at over 60%. Unfortunately, the data for the 1990 census did not include the percentage of foreign-born vs. native-born. But no doubt this figure continues to

My impression while growing up in San Francisco's Chinatown, before the end of World War II (1939–1945), was that my generation, the second generation whose parents were born in China, had only one Western given name that was bestowed at birth. However some Chinese Americans have been known to give themselves a second Western name in the belief that an American should have two given names.

The late Louise Leung Larsen, whose autobiography was published posthumously by the Chinese Historical Society of Southern California, gave a charming account of how she came by her name "Louise." She was named *Mamie Leung* at birth. During the 1920s, her best friend in college was Eleanor Chan, whom the author thought was "more Americanized." As she wrote: "Eleanor's full name was Eleanor Ransom Chan, which I thought sounded most elegant. She said I must also have a middle name; we finally, after much argument, settled on 'Louise.'" This later became the name that was used professionally (125, 213).

Another impression of name customs for my generation was that most of our parents had Chinese names. My parents each happened to adopt a Western name because, as they later explained, this made it easier for the non-Chinese they met at work to remember. But these names were not used by Chinese-speaking relatives and friends. For that matter, my parents did not call me by my Chinese name—if they did, I knew I was in trouble! A final impression was that everybody in Chinatown had Chinese given names to go with our family names of Chinese origin.

However, prior to World War II, the full Chinese given name was rarely written in English. Sometimes it hid behind a middle initial, as in *John C. Wong*. Or else only half the name was transcribed, as in *Bessie Ying Lee*. In all probability, there were two syllables to those Chinese given names.

Names Consisting of a Chinese Given Name, Written as Separate Words. Most Chinese given names are disyllabic, consisting of two characters. In comparison, family names are overwhelmingly monosyllabic. The monosyllabic given name, consisting of one character, has had a longer history of usage, but the disyllabic given name prevailed since the Song Dynasty (960–1279). Today, the trend among parents in mainland China is to bestow a child with a one-character given name (Ning Wen 1989, Lu 275, 277).

When Chinese emigration to America began during the mid-19th century, it was common to write the disyllabic given name as separate words: *Ng Poon Chew, Moy Jin Mun*. The disyllabic family name was also

---

hold true because of the steady flow of immigrants from the People's Republic of China, Taiwan, and Hong Kong, each with its own annual quota. Hong Kong's quota will be increasing to 25,000 by 1995. See Ng 6.

rendered the same: *Soo Hoo Nam Art.* This name style is still used today; it fits in well with the way Chinese words are written—with a space between each character.

Yet of all the name styles for Chinese Americans, this one has generated the most confusion over the surname. We cannot be certain, just from looking at the spelling for a Chinese personal name, whether the surname lies at the beginning or at the end. This ambiguity arises from the fact that many given names have the same spelling as family names bearing the same or nearly the same sound, as in *Chen Lin Yuan* and *Chung Wong Leo.* The early immigrants, such as those mentioned above, tended to keep the family name first. Today the family name is more likely placed last, according to European American custom. But one can never be sure. For example, several years ago, in a photographic exhibit about Locke, a Chinese American town, there were several photographs identifying a *Mr. Wong Buck* and his wife, *Mrs. Buck.* Sometimes the caption called the husband *Mr. Buck.* Fortunately, Chinese characters were included that revealed his surname to be *Wong.*

Spelling cannot reveal the precise Chinese word it represents because the Chinese language is extremely rich in homophones. For example, there are over 29 words spelled *Wu* in my computer desk accessory, out of which seven are surnames. As the late Dr. Yuen Ren Chao (1892–1982), the internationally known Chinese linguist, once pointed out, most systems of transliteration "work only one way and are not reversible" (47). Incidentally, Dr. Chao used this name style and he always placed his surname last. At other times he initialed his given name, as in *Y. R. Chao.*

Names Consisting of a Chinese Given Name Written as Initials. Now, in most cases, there is no question about the position of the surname when the Chinese given name is initialed. Evidently, initialing the given name was quite a fad among the early students and scholars who came from China for their education. In the 1905 issue of *The Dragon Student,* almost all the names of the foreign-born students were rendered in this fashion: *Y. C. Chang, S. T. Kong,* and *T. Shen.* In a Chinese Students' Monthly publication for the end of 1920, most of the names of the staff were in initials; presumably for Chinese names.[3]

Perhaps the Chinese given name was initialed to avoid having it continually misspelled or mauled in pronunciation. Perhaps initialing was in emulation of prominent Americans in certain business and social circles. For example, *J. D. Rockefeller* (Smith 88). This name style, though,

---

[3]Out of 56 names listed as staff, managers, and representatives, given names were initialed for 38 persons.

seldom appeared among the names listed in a 1943 Chinese student directory.[4]

Perhaps the students who came from China were paying heed to an edict issued by the Ministry of Education in 1933. According to a Chinese writer, it was enacted to stop students—especially in Christian missionary-sponsored schools—from initialing their names or adopting "foreign" names. Instead, students were to spell their names in full and according to Mandarin. "Certainly," this writer scolded, "the use of initials in place of the given name is a most un-Chinese custom, while the adoption of a foreign given name may be regarded as an evidence of denationalization, a despoliation of the country's spiritual heritage (T'ang 117).

While this edict may have discouraged this name style, certainly by the 1940s, a new style in the form of a hyphenated name—as in *Sun Yat-sen*—was making its appearance in the names of foreign-born Chinese college students.

Names Consisting of Chinese Given Names Written as Hyphenated Names. Hyphenating the disyllabic Chinese name has been attributed to Herbert A. Giles, co-author of the widely used Wade-Giles romanization system for Mandarin. He used this name style in his *Chinese Biographical Dictionary*, published in 1898, which served as a guide for transcribing Chinese personal names (Bostwick 868, Hummel 1006–7).

The hyphenated name shows up with great regularity in the aforementioned 1943 Chinese student directory, but it could be a bias; the editor may have had a preference for this name style. It is especially a name style favored by immigrants from Taiwan since the Wade-Giles transcription is favored in that country.[5] The hyphen is very useful because it distinguishes between given name and family name.

An important feature of the Giles method is to write the second word that follows the hyphen in lower case, as in *Sun Yat-sen*. Chinese Americans today, however, like to place the initial of the second word in upper case, as in *Sun Yat-Sen*. The Chinese writer whom I just quoted thought that this was "more logical and in accordance with the nature of the Chinese characters (T'ang 119).

Names Consisting of Chinese Given Names Written as One Word. What then exactly is the nature of a Chinese disyllabic given name? In his presentation at a conference on Asian genealogy held in 1969,

---

[4]*Directory of Chinese University Graduates and Students in America*, New York: Committee on Wartime Planning for Chinese Students in the United States, 1943.
[5]Ling-hu 5/12/89. The Office represents the government of the Republic of China in Taiwan. However, according to Mr. Ling-hu, there is no law in Taiwan requiring the use of the Wade-Giles system.

Thomas Chinn equated the first of the two characters to an American middle name and the second character, to the "first name" (224). Accordingly, the *yat* in Dr. Sun Yat-sen's name would be a middle name and *sen*, his first name. In other words, Chinn regarded the disyllabic name as two separate given names.

Mary Seeman, who has studied and written on names in Canada, believes that the disyllabic given name is a "dithemic" name; meaning it is one name composed of two elements (129–137). The Anglo-Saxon names *Alfred* and *Edith* are good examples. The first element in Alfred originally stood for "elf" and the second element was "raed", meaning "counsel." The first element in Edith was "aed", meaning "rich" and the second was for "war" (Stewart 3). According to this explanation then, the *yat* in Dr. Sun's name is the first element, meaning "quiet" and *sen*, its second element means "immortal." "*Quiet immortal* "—a fitting name indeed for the founding father of the Republic of China in 1911.

To Lin Yutang (1895–1976), the famous writer, the two characters of a name constitute two syllables of one name. Therefore, as he wrote in 1935, the disyllabic name should be written as one word. As an analogy, we would not write *David* as *Da Vid* or *Johanna* as *Jo Han Na*. "The mystification over Chinese names," Dr. Lin remarked, "is entirely due to our own making"—the "our" referring to the Chinese themselves (366).

As with the hyphenated name, writing the disyllabic name as one word helps to differentiate between given name and surname. Dr. Lin thought this could also be accomplished if the family name was always kept first, a Chinese custom, as seen in his name. Dong Kingman, the famous artist (born 1911), is a notable example of a Chinese American who did so. Otherwise this name style was rarely used by Chinese Americans.

Although writing the disyllabic name as one word predates communism in China, it is often seen today with names transliterated into Pinyin, the system of spelling promulgated by the People's Republic of China during the late 1950s. But it is not until the late 1970s, when students or scholars from mainland China came once again to study in American colleges, that we began seeing more of this name style. Even though it is not an officially sanctioned name style in the People's Republic of China (Ning Wen 1989), its usage will undoubtedly increase as a Chinese American name style as immigration from that country continues to take place.

Names incorporating both Western and Chinese given names. The last category of popular name styles among Chinese Americans is the juxtaposition of a Western name and a Chinese disyllabic given name; a practice born out of the desire to maintain the Chinese identity while conforming to American name customs. For example, note the names *Victor Lu-Chi Chuan* and *Cecilia Siaw-ling Zung*. Although Chinese

Americans on the U.S. mainland did not use this name style prior to World War II, I have been told that the Chinese in Hawaii have long had this practice. The 1943 student directory indicates that foreign-born college students who had Western names preferred having two initials for the Chinese name instead of writing it in full, as in Leslie T.C. Kuo.

Sometimes the Chinese given name comes first, as in *Vi-Kyuin Wellington Koo*. Dr. Koo (1887–1985), who was the first diplomat to sign the United Nations charter in 1945, also styled his name *V. K. Wellington Koo* and *V. K. W. Koo*. It is far more common, however, for the Chinese given name to serve as a middle name: *Walter Yuen Ng, John Kuo Wei Tchen, Janet Jen-ai Chong, Kristal Elun Lui, Theodore H. C. Chen, Ginger Y. Chiu,* and *William S-Y. Wang*. (There is no period after initial *S* in his name, Dr. Wang once informed me.) All the usual methods for structuring the Chinese disyllabic given name, as discussed above, can appear in this name style.

Since the 1950s, when the Chinese American population began to transform from a small homogenous group of predominantly Cantonese-speaking people into a more diversified group of various speech and geographical background, we have been seeing more of this name style. Interestingly, some Chinese Americans use this name style for their children even though they themselves do not own such names. My niece, who is a sixth-generation native-born married to an African American, named her son *Marcus Wing Yen Murray*. A friend's daughter, a third-generation American of Chinese ancestry who is married to a Filipino American, named her child *Araceli W. Tamayo-Lee*—the W stands for *WaiYun*. These are truly American names.

This brings me to one last observation: Nothing can be assumed about the single middle initial that is found in many Chinese American personal names. I have discovered in my research that it can stand for different things—a Western middle name, a monosyllabic Chinese name, a disyllabic Chinese name or part of it, or a family name.

For example, many Chinese American married women use their maiden name as a middle name, as I have, whether initialing it or spelling it in full. The feminist movement notwithstanding, retaining the maiden name is an ancient Chinese custom. A middle initial in a man's name could also represent the actual family name because many Chinese Americans have a "paper" surname or a "new patronymic." The description "paper surname" refers to a surname acquired through an illegal entry while a "patronymic" is a surname based on the given name of a grandfather or father (Louie 101–108). For instance, if Eugene Wong Moy wrote his name as *Eugene W. Moy*, his real family name would be hidden.

To Ginger Y. Chiu, it is more logical to have two initials for her Chinese name *Yiu-Kum*, but she felt that American legal forms allow room for just one. On the other hand, simplifying a double-barreled name to one initial may be due to just the dynamics of living in America. Victor Lu-chi Chuan said that when he first came to America as a student during the 1940s, he was advised to spell both his Western and Chinese names in full. As time went by, he reduced his Chinese name to two initials. Sometimes he wrote his name as *V. L. C. Chuan*. Then as more time went by, he dropped the second initial to the Chinese name, finally legalizing his name to Victor L. Chuan.

In summary, Chinese American personal names are a synthesis of American and Chinese cultures that reflect the social values held in both societies. And as social values inevitably change with the times and as name fashions fluctuate by generation, name patterns, too, are affected. The significance of the 10 Chinese American name styles is that these dovetail also with the chronology of Chinese American history.

The immigrants who came during the last half of the 19th century and prior to World War II customarily wrote the Chinese disyllabic given name as separate words. Their descendants would be observing mainstream American name customs and yet continue to bestow Chinese given names to the next generation. Students from China who were admitted as one of the exempt classes during the Chinese Exclusion laws (1882–1943) liked to initial the Chinese given name; preferring the hyphenated name style for their Chinese names at a later time. The settlement of several thousand foreign-born students and scholars after the People's Republic of China was established in 1949 added to the variety of name styles used by Chinese Americans. Structuring the disyllabic Chinese name as one word has increased in usage with immigration from mainland China during the 1980s.

Personal names have always been important clues to the development of a society, to the different stages of its history. Historically, it was rare for early Chinese pioneers to write their disyllabic names other than as separate words. Therefore, to arbitrarily rewrite a documented Chinese American personal name would result in distorting historical facts. And names have to do with facts.

By and large, the personal names of Chinese Americans reveal a strong desire, despite conformity to mainstream American name customs, to retain the Chinese identity. This occurs in newcomer families, as well as in those with several generations of native-born who cannot speak the Chinese language. But names do speak of a common cultural heritage.

Works Cited

Ashley, Leonard R.N. *What's in a Name? Everything You Wanted to Know.*
    Baltimore: Genealogical Publishing, 1989.
Bostwick, Arthur E. "Modern Chinese Personal Names." *Library Journal* 57:18
    (1932): 868.

Chao, Yuen Ren. *Language and Symbolic Systems.* New York: Cambridge University Press, 1968.

Chinn, Thomas W. "Genealogical Sources of Chinese Immigrants to the United States." In *Studies in Asian Genealogy.* Ed. Spencer J. Palmer. Provo, UT: Brigham Young University Press, 1972: 224.

Consul Ning Wen of the People's Republic of China. Telephone interview. 12 May 1989.

Directory of Chinese University Graduates and Students in America. New York: Committee on Wartime Planning for Chinese Students in the United States, 1943.

Dunkling, Leslie Alan. *First Names First.* New York: Universe Books, 1977.

Gan, Carolyn. "Bay Area Merry Go Round." *Asian Week* 2 February 1990: 24.

Gardner, Robert W., Bryant Robey, and Peter C. Smith. "Asian Americans: Growth, Change, and Diversity." *Population Bulletin* 40:4 (1985): 3–12, 36–41.

Hummel, Arthur W. "Transcription of Chinese Names." *Library Journal* 57:21 (1932): 1006–1007.

Larson, Louise Leung. *Sweet Bamboo: A Saga of a Chinese-American Family* Los Angeles: Chinese Historical Society of Southern California, 1989.

Lin Yutang, *My Country and My People.* New York: Halcyon House, 1935.

Ling-hu, Bruce, Executive Secretary for the Coordination Council for North American Affairs Office in Los Angeles. Personal interview, 12 May 1989.

Loesell, Eunice Devere. "A Comparative Study of Names and Naming Patterns in Selected Cultures." M.A. thesis, University of Southern California, 1952. 15–17.

Louie, Emma Woo. "Name Styles and Structure of Chinese American Personal Names." *NAMES* 39:3 (1991): 225–237.

Louie, Emma Woo. "Surnames as Clues to Family History." In *Chinese America: History and Perspectives* (1991): 101–108.

Lu Zhongti, "Chinese Given Names Since the Cultural Revolution." *NAMES* 37:3 (1989): 275, 277.

Ng, Johnny. "Bush Signs Immigration Act." *Asian Week* 7 December 1990: 6.

Seeman, Mary V. "Name and Identity." *Canadian Journal of Psychiatry* 25:2 (1980): 129–137.

Smith, Elsdon C. *Treasury of Name Lore.* New York: Harper, 1967.

Stewart, George R. *American Given Names: Their Origin and History in the Context of the English Language.* New York: Oxford University Press, 1979.

T'ang Leang-li, ed. *China Facts and Fancies. China Today series 7.* Shanghai: China United Press, 1936. 117.

The Chinese Students' Alliance in the United States of America. *The Chinese Students' Monthly* 16:1 (1920).

The Dragon Student. San Francisco: Chinese Students' Alliance of America, 1905.

Chow Mein Sandwiches:
Chinese American Entrepreneurship in Rhode Island

IMOGENE L. LIM and
JOHN ENG-WONG
Department of Anthropology, Brown University, Providence,
Rhode Island

...Carol led them in a dancing procession to the dining-room, to blue bowls of chow mein, with Lichee nuts and ginger preserved in syrup.

None of them save that city-rounder Harry Haydock had heard of any Chinese dish except chop sooey [sic]. With agreeable doubt they ventured through the bamboo shoots into the golden fried noodles of the chow mein...

-Sinclair Lewis, *Main Street*

"Chop suey" and "chow mein" have been in the American English vocabulary since the late 19th century. The inclusion of these food item terms in Sinclair Lewis' award-winning novel, *Main Street*, marked their early mainstream status in middle America (79). Both the Oxford English Dictionary (1989) and *A Dictionary of Americanisms* (Mathews 1951) note the American appropriation of these Cantonese words, citing examples of their usage as early as 1898 and 1903, respectively, for chop suey and chow mein. This is an indication of the foothold established at the beginning of this century of Chinese-style foods in the American dietary landscape.

Chinese eateries evolved as natural service accompaniments to the emerging settlements of migrant Chinese seeking futures and fortunes in North America. After mining and railway building vanished as industries, Chinese food service establishments became one of the two major economic opportunities open to Chinese immigrants. These restaurants, as well as hand laundries, were often the first sites of contact for most Americans with Chinese. This simple observation is the foundation for our positing that Chinese (or ethnic) restaurants are "cultural outposts"—places where the transactions of daily life take on

417

representational meanings that tend to fix American notions of ethnicity; in this case, Chinese-ness. Restaurants, like laundries, were spread across the landscape. Establishments in American towns were usually the enterprises of single men or a single family. These places especially deserve the label of "outpost" because the proprietors were either the sole member or members of ethnic communities numbering no more than a few hundred. And the proprietors, distinguished by color and appearance, almost always were perceived as acting for all of China. By extension, the Chinese restaurant also represented all that was/is China. Laundries were outposts as well, but we argue that restaurants assumed a larger significance in this role of cultural outpost.

Beyond the abstraction of the restaurant being a cultural outpost, the restaurant was, and continues to be, a meaningful source of income for many Chinese, providing for families in China and in North America. Food service became one of the primary fields of entrepreneurial activity for Chinese Americans. This paper is a first step toward documenting this activity and creating a framework for analysing its impact.

Chinese words and persons provided restaurants with instant credibility in the marketplace. The decision to open a restaurant created surplus value in a Chinese identity by profiting from being an outsider; thus, transforming a social negative into an economic positive. Beyond image, there were substantial barriers to success as a restaurateur. The first barrier was financial (start-up capital), then skill in cooking and managing, and, finally, labor (staff). Also, even though Chinese cuisine acquired a popular following in America, neither the regulatory climate nor the society at large was always friendly. Since restaurants were family businesses for many Chinese, the study of Chinese restaurants also presents an opportunity to examine the social adaptations of the Chinese American family.

In this case study of Chinese American restaurants in Rhode Island, we explore the development of entrepreneurship and this idea of Chinese restaurant as cultural outpost.[1] Through the social history of Chinese restaurants, we learn how these immigrants survived by adapting to local clientele and foodways. This adaptive strategy is exemplified in the serving of a food item known as a chow mein sandwich.

---

[1]From initial interviews and enquiries in Providence and vicinity, the research has expanded into the southeastern portions of Massachusetts. For this paper, we specifically focus on Rhode Island businesses. This attention to Rhode Island does not exclude supporting data from Massachusetts.

Chinese in America: Image and Reality. Rhode Island was an early participant in the China trade, so there were many merchants in Providence who had direct experience with China. Such experience was not the case for the general public, whose perception of China and Chinese was of exotica and curiosities.

Before any census record of Chinese in Rhode Island, the people of Providence were introduced to "The Chinese Lady—Afong Moy" in 1835. She was presented as a curiosity at the Providence Museum. Since direct contact was limited for the majority of the populace, the early image of the Chinese and their culture was more often formed through familiarity with the China trade and the portrayal of the Chinese in magazines and newspapers, such as the following description of Afong Moy:

> Afong Moy will be richly dressed in her Chinese Costume and seated in a "Splendid Saloon" tastefully composed of beautiful Canton Satin Damask, figured in crimson and gold, decorated with Paintings of their deities, Beauties and Chinese Characters, Brilliantly illuminated in the evening with Chinese Lanterns. The whole presenting a correct and imposing scene of Eastern magnificence. Various curiosities will be shown and explained to the visitors. Afong Moy, is about 16 years of age, mild and engaging in her manners. She will occasionally walk before the company, in order to show her astonishing *little feet*, being little more than four inches in length. [original emphasis] (*Providence Daily Journal* 8/31/1835)

Afong Moy's display in a museum was typical of the time, that is, revelling in the differences of people as curiosity or exotica. Also, since admission was based on the payment of 25 cents, viewing Afong Moy was limited to a more select audience than the distribution and/or readership of the *Providence Daily Journal*.[2] This display of an individual to represent a culture to an audience (of primarily European background) has occurred even more recently as illustrated in the frontispiece of Sally Price's Primitive Art in Civilized Places (1989). The photograph shows a Maori warrior bare-chested with spear in hand on display at the Metropolitan Museum of Art on the occasion of the Te Maori 1984 exhibition.

America's Chinese restaurants had inherited an "exotic" pedigree from early perceptions of Chinese promulgated by magazine and newspaper descriptions. From this exoticism, they were able to exploit and create a cuisine distinct and different in sight, smell, and taste. Part

---

[2]In 1835, twenty-five cents was half the fare for travelling on the steamer "King Philip" from Providence to Fall River. Subscription to the newspaper was $8.00 per annum.

of the marketing of this kind of food was an image that promoted this pedigree. Therefore, this difference, a difference that was simultaneously self-conscious and imposed by the dominant culture, helped to develop and perpetuate the restaurant's role as a cultural outpost.

The Chinese in Rhode Island. The first official documentation of Chinese was in 1865 when the RI Census began listing nativity; previous censuses had not. By 1905, the Chinese numbered 301 and now included four women (see Table 1 below). This latter figure is deceptive in its interpretation if viewed alone. On reading the description, one learns that of these native women of China, "[t]hree of them are whites born in the Flowery Kingdom, while only one— the wife of a Chinese merchant—is a genuine Chinese female" (RI Census 1907: 37). The majority of these people located in Providence County and initially began laundry businesses, since minimal language skills and start-up costs were required. In Footnote 2 of the 1885 RI Census (1887: 413), Rev. J.P. Root noted: "About a dozen years ago two Chinamen opened a laundry in Providence. The number of this people has gradually increased in this city, till 47 of them are now industriously pursuing their humble avocations." Prior to 1940, the number of Chinese in Rhode Island (366) peaked in the same year of 1900 as did the number of Chinese laundries (109) (see Table 2 next page). Both Chinese populations and laundries decreased after 1900, with only the Chinese population seeing a resurgence. In 1992, there were only two Chinese laundries left in Providence.

Table 1. **Rhode Island Census: Number of Chinese**

1865–1905   **1900–1940**

Year	Men	Women	Year	Men	Women
1865	1	0	1900	361	5
1875	9	0	1910	262	10
1885	31	0	1920	201	24
1895	135	0	1930	170	27
1905	297	4	1940	227	30
			1950	299	104

Note: For 1885 and 1895, 2 and 9 Japanese, respectively, were included.

The profits of the laundry business appear to be one important source of capital for the building and founding of restaurant dynasties. Such was the case for the Tow family, founded by Ting Tow (a.k.a. Chang You Tow), who reputedly operated a hand laundry during the late 19th century in Pawtucket (home of the first textile mill in

America), a town immediately north of Providence. In one account, Ting's son, Fong, was Rhode Island's first Chinese restaurateur. He operated in succession the King Fong and Young China restaurants (*Providence Journal* 1935 and *Evening Bulletin* 1974). The latter of these was probably one of the two Chinese restaurants in Providence documented in an 1896 article on Chinatown in the *Providence Sunday Journal*. In 1906, this number had grown to six, and by 1910 to 13. Of these 13, the Port Arthur, founded by Fong Tow and his son, He Gong "Charlie" Tow, in the heart of the downtown (191 Weybosset Street, later moved to 123 Weybosset Street), was the longest-lived, surviving into the 1960s. The Port Arthur in 1918 was the first Chinese American dine and dance establishment in New England (*Providence Journal* 9/7/35).

The names of the other establishments competing with the Port Arthur would be familiar in any town today: Pacific Cafe, Hong Kong, The American-Chinese. At the same time, there were places with Chinese names like Hong Fong Low, the Mann Far Lo, the Bun Fong Low, and Hing Mee Wah Eatinghouse; others in Sampson & Murdock's Providence Address Directory (1910) were identified only by the address and/or notation, such as "Chinese restaurant and Weybosset Bowling Parlor."

Table 2. Chinese laundries in Providence, Rhode Island

Year	Total
1876	3
1880	10
1890	41
1900	109
1910	87
1920	56
1930	44
1940	48
1950	33

Note: The year 1876 marks the first documented presence of Chinese laundries.
Compiled from the annual Sampson & Murdock, Providence Business Directory.

Beginning in the 1890s, the Chinese began to congregate on Burrill and Chapel Streets, where a number of Chinese businesses were established. The Chinese here were basically a labor community which worked in laundries and restaurants, with no real merchant or well-to-do class. As such, there were few who could support the cultural activities (temple, opera, and theater, to name a few) found in larger Chinese communities as in Boston and New York City. At this time, the area was not considered a Chinatown:

> "CHINATOWN" here in Providence is not confined to a given portion of the city, as it is in Boston, on Harrison Avenue, or in New York on Mott Street. There is no district here which is populated abnormally by representatives of the land of the pig tail, the sacred yellow jacket and the pagoda. The little Chinamen are scattered all over town, locating wherever they see a chance to earn a living...
> (*Providence Sunday Journal* 11/15/1896)

Prior to that, and for nearly 20 years, Chinese had been operating laundries in various parts of the city, but there had been no attempt at colonization until a descent was made on the old rookeries of Burrill and Chapel streets. This was in 1902. Here was established the first Chinese grocery store, flanked on either side by laundries. Eventually a Chinese restaurant was added, then the colony was extended down both sides of Burrill street, from Weybosset to Westminster and along Chapel street to the Music Hall building. There came an overflow which was accommodated by taking in two of the buildings on Westminster street, next west of Burrill street. It was on Burrill street that the first Chinese Masonic Temple was established (*Providence Sunday Journal* 2/16/1913).

The U.S. Census of 1910 shows that Chinese were concentrated in the 4th and 5th Wards of Providence. The embryonic Chinatown had also shifted a few blocks north to include much of Empire Street at the western edge of the downtown district. On Empire Street, at numbers 47, 55, 56, 57, 61, and 63, were boardinghouses filled with Chinese; at numbers 62 and 64 were Chinese fancy-goods shops, and at 51 and 53 a Chinese grocer occupied the storefronts.

These Empire Street establishments were demolished and/or dispersed with the widening of the street in 1914 (*Providence Sunday Journal* 12/13/1914). The scattering of the Chinese population was encouraged as they were viewed as unlawful in the extreme. According to Police Superintendent Murray:

> If the Empire street Chinese are well scattered we will know that the appearance in any location of any considerable number of them means that gambling is going on. The Chinese are inveterate gamblers; the vice is inherent in the race. Only by scattering them can we ever hope to minimize the unlawful practice.
>
> ...I don't mind having you say that I will do everything in my power to check the licensing of not only the chop suey houses, but all other eating places maintained on the second story of a building because of the menace they are to young girls who foolishly frequent

them and are there made the recipients of attentions which bode them no good. (*Providence Sunday Journal* 2/16/1913)

Chinese establishments were regularly under surveillance and were not desired by other merchants in the area. The above comments of the Police Superintendent and the 1909 order by the Police Commission that all draperies be removed from every booth, stall, and room of Chinese restaurants for full viewing at all times was, in part, a response to the murder of a young woman by a Chinese suspect in New York City (*Providence Daily Journal* 6/25/1909, *Providence Sunday Journal* 6/20/1909). Besides the negative stereotype of unlawfulness (gambling and opium smoking), Chinese were believed to prey on the sympathies of young women who were in charge of Chinese at the Sunday schools. With complete, open viewing, the police believed that they could prevent non-food related activities from occurring in restaurants and prevent suspicion and innuendo of such.

The authorities exploited these negative stereotypes toward hindering and blocking the settlement of this particular immigrant group. This was during a period of increasing anti-Chinese sentiment throughout the continent that culminated in the 1917 Asiatic Barred Zone policy that virtually banned immigration from all Asia.

The actions of the authorities were supported by other downtown businesses. Letters written by merchants to the *Providence Sunday Journal* (2/4/1917) voiced opposition to Chinese restaurants due to "damage, both to property and to retail trade, that these establishments [Chinese restaurants] would cause right in the centre of the store district on our main shopping district." City ordinances in restricting Chinese restaurants were successful. The number of establishments was constant for the years 1910 and 1920, it declined thereafter (as Table 3 shows).

Table 3. **Chinese restaurants in Providence, Rhode Island**

Year	Total
1895*	2
1906	6
1910	13
1920	13
1930	7
1940	17

*1895 information from *Providence Sunday Journal* (November 15, 1896).
 Compiled from the annual Sampson & Murdock, Providence Business Directory.

The record shows that the opposition of downtown businesses spoiled the ambitions of several would-be Chinese restaurateurs. The negative images were compounded when the murder of a Chinese brought the Chinese community into the public view in the headlines of the 1920s. This act of violence may have contributed to the decline of the restaurant trade in Providence. However, by 1930, at the beginning of the Great Depression, the general economic climate probably contributed to its decline. The Chinese restaurant count in Providence for that year was seven.

The period of the Depression proved to be a time of renaissance for Chinese restaurant businesses in Rhode Island. The most likely factors which led to this entrepreneurial revival were: the price of meals, improved Sino-American relations, and the unmistakable resurgence of Chinese immigration. By 1940, there were 17 Chinese eateries operating in Providence, the majority of which were in the downtown business district. Since then, there has been a steady decline of businesses in the downtown area, as well as the number of Chinese restaurants. Of the many Chinese restaurants that were located in the downtown area, there are now only two reminders of this past. There is, as well, one lone remnant of downtown Providence's Chinese settlement—the On Leong Merchants Association building on Snow Street.

Restaurants and the American Dream. As alluded to earlier, laundries and restaurants provided early Chinese immigrants with basically their only means of economic opportunity. Even for Chinese Americans with formal educations, opportunities were limited, and many returned to operating restaurants or related businesses (noodles, bean sprouts, groceries).

Only in the last three decades have Chinese Americans increasingly moved into the larger labor force and out of traditionally associated jobs (Amott and Matthaei 1991). And of these traditionally associated jobs, only the restaurants have managed to survive in any number. Chinese laundries decreased in number with the development of steam laundries, the increasing presence of washer/dryers in the home, and, of course, permanent-press fabrics.

The story of one immigrant arriving in a town and eventually being joined by another family member is a common tale among the diaspora of Chinese. As already mentioned, some of the early restaurants were the "schools" for later restaurant operators, so one is able to find families of restaurateurs in Providence. Typically, the relative arrived and was put immediately to work as a dishwasher. Gradually, he (not she, since the majority of immigrants who came during the first half of this century were men) learned all the other kitchen skills from butchering the meat, to prepping other ingredients, to finally cooking. One informant (JL), who arrived in Providence in 1937, followed in the footsteps of his grandfather's and brother's passages to the United States. He came at age 14 and immediately began working in a restaurant, and he continued to do so with his brother prior to World War II. After serving in the war as an electronics technician, he returned to restaurant work in order to save enough money to open his own restaurant. That early restaurant schooling helped in his successful operation of two restaurants.

In this particular case, JL managed to open his first restaurant on his own (with bank assistance), but in the 1930s, restaurant spin-offs were frequently the result of several workers pooling their resources as partners. These workers were often related, as well. For example, according to JL, the Hon Hong was opened with seven shares in total, held by several partners. Some of the partners had only half a share (like his brother) and only two or three partners had full shares. Each share was worth $1500. Besides the Hon Hong, other workers later opened the Hon Fong, and the Mei Hong (JL 1992).[3] This cycle of spin-off restaurants has continued. From the 1970 period, 90% of those who had worked at the Cathay Den opened the following: Tai-Dee Garden, The Islander, China Bright, Ho Ho, Imperial Villa, and Golden Pacific (AL/DL 1992). Spin-offs were not always a case of wanting to be more than just an employee in order to reap the benefits of one's own business, but sometimes from discontent with the manner of the operation of the "parent" restaurant.

The number of spin-offs may be a reflection of the various waves of Chinese immigration. After the San Francisco earthquake of 1906, many Chinese were afforded the opportunity to come to the United States as "paper sons" in the following years as the children of merchants or native-born American Chinese. With birth records destroyed, the Chinese were able to take advantage of this loophole in the Exclusion Act.

The Immigration Act of 1965 also opened the door for many other Chinese immigrants. It abolished the national-origins quotas and exempted from the quota of numbered immigrants the immediate family members, namely spouses, minor children, and parents of U.S. citizens. Through this new immigration act, the number of Chinese immigrants increased dramatically from 1960 to 1985, that is, 236,084 to 1,079,400, to make them the largest Asian group in the United States (Kwong 22).

Changes to the immigration act increased the number of immigrants from all parts of the world and saw changes in the settlement pattern from urban to suburban areas as former immigrants and their children moved away from the city proper. The Chinese,

---

[3]Initials and date indicate an informant source.

likewise, moved to outlying areas of Providence, seeking opportunity in the movement of Rhode Islanders. According to one restaurateur, JL, he was the first to open Chinese restaurants in Warwick and in North Kingstown. Although JL's moves occurred in the 1950s and 1960s, there had been other Chinese who predated him in establishing restaurants outside of Providence. There is one in Woonsocket that has been in continuous operation since 1908, despite changes in ownership and restaurant names. In each of these families, the son took over from the father (JC 1992; CR 1992). Other multi-generational operations are notable in several of the older Chinese restaurants. One such restaurant is the Young China Restaurant of East Providence. It has been in operation since 1935 and is under the aegis of the second- and third-generation, serving fourth-generation clients (EY 1992).

The niche in which this family has found acceptance is evident by the continuity established between the restaurant and its clients. This is particularly striking, given the rather negative reception of early Chinese businesses and settlement in Providence (as noted earlier). The Young China Restaurant family was the first Chinese in East Providence. When the family had to move from the original location of the Young China Restaurant (due to a dramatic increase in rent), the community rallied around the recent widow and her six children and found the present location for them. One of the town councilmen was in real estate, and he checked the zoning so that the mother could continue operating the business and still look after her young family. This was only possible if the family could live over the business establishment. From a beginning of four booths in 1940, there was a total of twelve by the end of the war (EY 1992).

To survive in a fluctuating economy, restaurateurs must know their business and clientele. And the existence of these multi-generational operations is testament to their acumen. What strategies have they adopted to survive?

Survival Tactics of the Restaurateur. For many of the early restaurants, the menu consisted of variations on chop suey, chow mein, and fried rice, plus the standards that might be found in an American restaurant, that is, veal cutlet, pork chops, etc. These restaurants were of a hyphenated variety, Chinese-American: not truly one or the other. This combining of food types was a way in which the restaurant could accommodate the tastes of its dining clientele who might be less familiar or adventuresome in experimenting with foods different from the home. In fact, one restaurateur commented that veal cutlet and roast beef were on the menu because of, respectively, Italian and English customers (JL 1992).

Anglo Americans found most acceptable those foods that resembled the cooking of England. Root and de Rochemont note that there was a tendency toward the Americanization of a dish rather than risk introducing a genuine foreign dish. This might even mean creating "an American dish with a foreign name and a vague resemblance to a foreign creation, but which is actually, and reassuringly a native-born citizen of the American kitchen" (276–277).

Chop suey is an example of this Americanization phenomenon in Chinese cookery. Prior to the 1890s, chop suey had not been invented. Different stories have circulated as to its origin (see Root and de Rochemont 277; Hooker 286; Anderson 212–213), from railroad gang cooks to Chinese cooks. The Americanization or transformation of chop suey into the item served in today's restaurants was not likely an immediate conversion. Boiling or stewing was counter to traditional Chinese cooking of stir-frying or quick sauteeing of vegetables. In the 1896 *Providence Sunday Journal* article on Chinatown, the reporter noted "the unusually short period of time" in which the waiter-cook reappeared with "smoking hot dishes." One of the dishes sampled was chop suey, which he translated as "stewed mixture of meat." The readers were provided with a list of ingredients so that they might try the dish themselves. The only cooking instructions were to "mix well and fry." One can only speculate that these instructions became translated into a more American dish than that served the reporter. And through this transformation, chop suey was re-invented for the Chinese restaurateur. It became popular because it now fit in with the Anglo American conviction of vegetable preparation, that is, it should be boiled for a long time. In the 1932 *Pictorial Review Standard Cook Book*, the recipe for chop suey called for an hour and a half cooking time (Hooker 287).

Through the creation of chop suey, Chinese were able to gain the patronage of the dominant culture. It permitted the Chinese to acquire a clientele that, almost a century later, still requests this item. Its acceptance in the American food repertory is noted by its inclusion in *Larousse Gastronomique* (261–262).

The one other food perception that Chinese restaurateurs had to overcome (or adjust for) was the idea promulgated by professionals of the New Nutrition during the early decades of this century that the food habits of immigrants were uneconomical (in terms of energy expenditure to digest). Nutritional science took exception to mixtures of food and the spiciness commonly found in immigrant diets: "Strong seasonings that made bland but cheap foods tasty were denounced for overworking the digestive process and stimulating cravings for alcohol" (Levenstein 103). Blandness was considered healthy, and prior to World War II, blandness was also viewed as more patriotic than exotic seasonings (Stern 12).

Both restaurateurs and clients have commented on the increasing acceptance of spicier foods. One client commented that her impression of Chinese food was that it was "very spicy" and "more exotic than before;" another stated, "back then [in the 1950s], it wasn't spicy, almost bland compared to the taste of today" (DM 1992; CR 1992). Restaurants that considered their cuisine to be basically Cantonese began adding the spicier dishes of Szechuan cooking to their menus in the 1970s (BC 1992; JC 1992). Of course, the addition of such dishes is based on clientele tastes and in some cases, this is modified to the specific area of business. For example, EY commented, "our customers [are] more on the conservative end and don't go for hot-hot but mild-hot [food]" (1992).

With traditional Chinese cooking, there are also regional variations. This also shows up in Chinese American restaurants, not so much in terms of Chinese regional cooking styles but in the manner of chow mein styles. In this area, the restaurants distinguish between Boston-, Fall River-, New York-, and Chicago-style chow mein. Sometimes the difference is only in the sauce:

If we hire a person from Massachusetts, we always explain that they must make the sauce darker; in Rhode Island, people are used to a darker sauce—New York and Massachusetts have a lighter [colored] sauce. (EY 1992)

Fall River chow mein is strained chow mein, that is, noodles and sauce, no vegetables; Chicago chow mein has green peppers, onion, bok choy (bigger large pieces), dark brown sauce, and regular fried noodles; Boston chow mein is mostly shredded celery, bok choy, onion in light [colored] sauce and deep-fried straight noodles; Cantonese chow mein is grilled noodles [with] ingredients sauteed in light sauce garnish[ed] with meat on top. (BC 1992)

Since these perceptions of chow mein are almost institutionalized, a new restaurant entering an area learns quickly if it is to survive. For example, one well-established restaurant in Providence opened a branch in Fall River. Though it originally did not serve chow mein, but only lo mein, soon thereafter, a sign appeared outside stating that it sold chow mein (RS 1992). To the people of Fall River, "real" Chinese restaurants serve chow mein. Fall River chow mein is unlike others because of the sauce's watery consistency. The sauce's thinness is, in all likelihood, an adaptation to the people of Fall River's needs. As a predominantly Catholic area, customers would request that the gravy be strained so that they could abide by their religious stricture of meatlessness on Fridays. With a thick gravy, you could not strain it (AW 1992). This adjustment to religious needs is also seen in the chow mein served at the Young China Restaurant. No meat is included in the regular chow mein or chop suey on Fridays unless requested (EY 1992).

One accommodation made by Chinese restaurateurs that appears unique to the area is the serving of the chow mein sandwich (also chop suey sandwich or chow mein/chop suey mix sandwich). The senior author has sampled several of these sandwiches (all variations of the regular). It is served between a hamburger bun or between sliced white bread; if the latter, brown gravy is served over it in the manner of a hot turkey sandwich. At one restaurant, it was even served between thick slices of Italian bread. To an information request, over 60 respondents, up to 70+ in age, recall eating this sandwich in the New England area. Two restaurateurs in Providence continue to maintain this item in their repertoire even though it is no longer on the menu. This is strictly for customers of an older generation (basically individuals who are in their late 50s or older) (SC 1992). It is less popular than during its heyday in the 1930s and 1940s, but for some restaurants, its popularity has not changed. Young China Restaurant sells between nine and 10 dozen a day (EY 1992) and one restaurant in Fall River has reputedly sold over two million during its 40-year existence (WC 1992).

Although this food item is typically found on the menus of older establishments, it was discovered in a restaurant that is no more than 10 years old, serving Chinese and Vietnamese cuisine. The owner, when asked about the sandwich's menu inclusion, stated that since the restaurant was located in an economically depressed area, he had wanted to have something on the menu that locals could afford. The idea for the sandwich came from looking at old menus.

The rationale for serving the chow mein sandwich today and in the past was most likely the same—an item that many people could afford. As noted by the maker of the chow mein noodles, "for low cost, you could get a meal that would fill" (AW 1992). And those who ate these sandwiches reveal the same sentiment:

The Chow Mein sandwich was a real treat in the early 1930s. The Chinese restaurants were a real God Send [sic], to us who were on the poor level. We were able to be served a whole Chinese dinner (Chow Mein or Chop Suey) for 25 cents. (CD 1991)

We went quite often for chop suey sandwiches and, as I recall, were made on what was much like a hamburger bun. Well, it was so loaded with filling that when we took them home, my mother made two sandwiches from one. I recall the price at the time [late 1930s and early 1940s] was 25 cents each. I might add here that they were delicious and it was considered quite a treat. I also recall going there about once a week for an old aged couple who operated a small variety store in the neighborhood. This would have been their dinner that night. (RC 1992)

My mother gave me 15 cents per day for my cafeteria lunch. I would fudge my lunch money, go without the bottle of milk, and after school, on my way to the library, joined the clique at a restaurant run by a Chinese family... I can't tell you when or how they originated but I have a strong suspicion that they may have been concocted by restaurateurs because most people simply could not afford the 30 or 40 cents for full orders [during the 1930s]. (LH 1992)

The chow mein, as well as the chow mein sandwich, served in Rhode Island is particular to this area. And as noted by Root and de Rochemont (277), such food inventions "are often restricted to the areas which created them." The maker of the chow mein noodles (AW 1992) commented that his business is "of limited appeal, a radius of 50–100 miles, in southeastern New England in particular." AW also noted that Boston did not like this noodle (compare with BC's description of Boston-style chow mein). Not surprisingly, the chow mein sandwich does not appear to have existed in Boston. A fan of the sandwich wrote to say that in 1944, when she and her husband attempted to get one in a Boston restaurant, they had to describe the sandwich. They ended up with two sandwiches, each consisting of a whole order of chow mein between two pieces of bread (BF 1992).

Restaurateurs managed to discover the specific tastes of their clientele, as well as discover general Chinese restaurant trends, by listening to their clientele, talking with friends who were restaurant people, testing out new items on their menus, trying out other restaurant's food, as well as studying others' menus (BC 1992; JC 1992; JL 1992; EY 1992). One informant (JL) was explicit in describing the manner of menu selection. He had three criteria for an item's inclusion: popularity (he collected menus for the names and prices of dishes), profitability, and timing, that is, the turn-over time in order to give better service. Relying on another's menu is a common strategy; for example, the chow mein sandwich at several was a carry-over from a previous restaurant (BC 1992; JC 1992).

By basing a menu on the popular standards and experimenting with the new, restaurateurs satisfy a wider range of tastes without alienating any of their clientele. Chan's Fine Oriental Dining of Woonsocket manages to cater to both local and non-local clientele with its menu. Chan's owner (JC) notes that two different groups patronize the restaurant. Those who come for the live entertainment (jazz) are typically not from the area and are more experimental in their tastes, whereas the locals prefer the older menu of chow mein, chop suey, and fried rice.

Part of the attraction of the older menu is the quantity of food obtained for the cost, as well as the familiarity of the items. As one informant said, "This is New England, nothing changes" (RR 1992). Some restaurant goers are completely consistent in their orders, never varying from their standard, whether it be combination plate #3 or fried rice and chicken wings (SG 1992; JR 1992).

Restaurateurs managed to survive by adapting traditional Cantonese cuisine to the tastes of Anglo Americans and the general perceptions of the time of good and healthy foods. Flexibility in adaptation may be the hallmark of Cantonese cuisine since the manner of cooking is as critical to the product as are the ingredients. As noted by Anderson (209): "No other cooks can be so eclectic while maintaining the spirit of the tradition."

Chinese restaurants in Rhode Island are dispersed throughout the state. In many cases, those first restaurants represented the only contact between Chinese and the local population of the outlying areas. As noted in the brief history of the Chinese in Rhode Island, what was considered Chinatown disappeared relatively quickly after its formation. Thus, direct first-hand knowledge of Chinese and their culture was somewhat limited to the contacts obtained at restaurants where there were intra- and inter-personal transactions.

Cultural Outposts. The Chinatown that had existed in Providence was unlike the other east coast Chinatowns of Boston and New York City. It was more of an enclave for the population rather than a tourist locale for the dominant culture to experience the "sounds, the sights, and the smells of Canton" or "wander in the midst of the Orient while still in the Occident" (advertisements quoted by Takaki 247). Takaki (1989) has implied that Chinatown was a cultural island or ethnic island, but in Providence it was one closed to the outsider. Notions of Chinese-ness thus were limited to representations in the media and, more directly, to those perceptions of ethnicity accessible through Chinese restaurants.

For the ethnic European populations of Rhode Island, the Chinese restaurant was a "cultural outpost." The use of the term "cultural outpost" for an ethnic restaurant is helpful in thinking about the introduction of one culture to another's, that is, an outpost in a cultural frontier. Of the three definitions of "outpost," we have appropriated two for this discussion. From the *Oxford English Dictionary* (1989), an outpost implies a settlement "near a frontier or at a remote place in order to facilitate the commercial contacts of a larger and more centrally situated town or settlement," which in this case is either Boston or New York City. The other meaning for outpost, as used here, is "the furthest territory of an empire," that is, a representative of a main group. In this case, the group is the Chinese or, if in keeping with the notion of empire, as noted in early newspaper articles, "the Celestial Empire."

As a cultural outpost, one can also find the sounds, sights, and smells of another culture in an ethnic restaurant. Besides the difference in the cuisine itself (sight and smell), there are other markers of a culture to be found in a restaurant—eating utensils and decor (sight) and perhaps language and/or music (sound). For Chinese, there are chopsticks and perhaps lanterns, figurines, embroidered or shell pictures, to name a few items; or for Mexican, there are sombreros, textiles and ceramics, murals, pictures; or for Indian, there are replicas of monuments and deities, carved screens, traditional dishware. Each item is in some way representative of the culture, and collectively (the total context of sight, smell, and taste) they evoke ideas or memories associated with an ethnicity. Various informants (restaurant clientele) have commented on the sensory impact of their early recollections of Chinese dining: "impressed by vivid smells—ginger, Oriental tea" (AL 1992); "looking Oriental-fans, dragons, chrysanthemums, ... range of motifs" (JG 1992); "that type of restaurant in '50s [1950s] outside had an architectural element, [such as, a] roof line which I saw right away as an identifier of a Chinese restaurant" (DR 1992); "exotic-different tastes, mixtures" (DM 1992); Chinese restaurant "obviously with the Chinese people working there, the food was different, a whole different environment from what you were accustomed to going to" (RR 1992).

This notion of introducing a culture through foodways is notable in this example of children visiting a Chinese restaurant for a meal after their study of China:

> [The] children from the schools would come to the restaurant for a Chinese meal after finishing their study on China. I would take them down into the cellar to see the sprouting beans. It was a big thing—the children would be fascinated by the process. Their eyes would open up wide to see the lids of the crocks being pushed up by the growing sprouts. (EY 1992)

Restaurateurs are very much aware of their representing what is Chinese culture at that surface level. As noted by one restaurateur (JC 1992), "people who come to a Chinese restaurant like to see Chinese objects. If I liked Chinese music, I would play it [in the restaurant]." Another restaurateur (JL 1992) emphasized the "use of Chinese symbols" in his Chinese restaurants in order to present a "Chinese cultural image." Also discussed by JL were the three factors that contributed to his choice of names for his restaurants. Two of these applied specifically to the Chinese-ness of the restaurant, that is, a famous name that would be easy to remember (Canton) and something strongly associated with China (Pagoda). His other factor in considering names was ease in pronunciation.

Chinese culture was sometimes introduced to non-Chinese indirectly by the restaurants through food service contracts (another survival tactic of early restaurants, prior to this service being known as catering). Through that initial contact, some would then go to the restaurant itself.

> Old Colony Bank was a customer for 30–35 years, every third week was "Chinese meal day" in the cafeteria ... Some of the employees who ate the food service contract stuff knew which restaurant made it so [they] would come into the restaurant. (EY 1992)

As an outpost, the restaurant served as an agent of change in diet, as well as fixing notions of ethnicity. This dialogue between restaurateur and client affected both in their perception of one another and their responses to these views. One result was the Americanization of the cuisine into Chinese American; another was the appropriation and exploitation of certain stereotypes. For example, the catering service of Chan's Fine Oriental Dining is known as "House of No. 2 Son Catering." Indeed, the owner is the second son and he felt that the play on words was humorous, as well as familiar to a populace that had grown up with Charlie Chan films (JC 1992). Also, Chinese men were often called Charlie or John by non-Chinese, rather than their given names (even when they had a Christian name). These names were based on media presentations of "John Chinaman" and "Charlie Chan." Such responses between restaurateur and clientele were active. This dynamic has distinguished in one significant way the impact of restaurants, versus laundries, as cultural outposts.

The laundries were cultural outposts, but with a difference. As outposts, they, too, were often isolated in ethnically European neighborhoods. Chinese were associated with laundries, but the service they provided was not Chinese per se. Laundries were typically family-run and did not require outside local workers, so that in some senses, the people were less known than those who owned restaurants. Also, the time spent interacting with launderers was minimal—exchanging dirty clothes for clean.

For the observant, there were material artifacts to identify the Chinese-ness of the business beyond the individual. Paul Siu's landmark study (1987) on the Chinese laundrymen documented markers of ethnicity, including physical ones such as the abacus, the laundry ticket, and the "ironing" bed. Even today, ethnicity is marked in the hand laundry's successor, the laundromat. During a rare visit to the corner laundromat, the senior author noted that a Chinese couple appeared to be operating the business. They could have been either new employees or the owners, but minor changes to the decor indicated that the latter was the case. A Chinese painting now hangs where paintings reminiscent of an African folk art tradition once hung, and a silk flower arrangement in a Chinese vase now sits where the counter had been bare. Although Chinese laundries were also cultural outposts, their impact on the larger society was less than a restaurant with its full range of sights, sounds, and smells.

The interactions of restaurant workers (non-Chinese) and the public with the owners also increased the understanding of what is Chinese at a level beyond the material culture among these people. One informant who had worked at two different Chinese restaurants in Woonsocket commented on the big New Year's parties hosted by one of the restaurateurs that included everyone from employees and friends to lawyers and councilmen. At these parties, "special dishes, things you don't normally get in restaurants (although perhaps not special in some restaurants today)" (CR 1992) were served. This individual also became aware of Chinese medicinal food practices, such as foods given to a mother after the birth of a child. Perhaps this knowledge of Chinese culture was a result of the relationship held between employee and owner. Working for Chinese owners was "not like [an] employee-boss relationship," it was "more like family, at least for me" (CR 1992).

The Chinese restaurant as a cultural outpost is a useful construct in thinking about how perceptions of Chinese are generated and perceived between Chinese and non-Chinese. The authors also believe that this construct has utility in examining other ethnicities, as alluded to earlier, and suggest further study of European and non-European cultures to test this out. Cultural representation is ascribed by the self-definition of an ethnic restaurant; thus, an ethnic restaurant is an outpost in a cultural frontier.

Works Cited

Amott, Teresa L., and Julie A. Matthaei. *1991 Race, Gender, and Work: A Multicultural Economic History of Women in the United States*. Boston, MA: South End Press, 1991.

Anderson, E.N. *The Food of China*. New Haven, CT: Yale University Press, 1988.

Census—Rhode Island: 1867 Report upon the Census of Rhode Island, 1865; 1877 Report upon the Census of Rhode Island, 1875; 1887 Rhode Island State Census, 1885; 1898 Census of Rhode Island, 1895; 1907 Rhode Island State Census, 1905.

City Directories: 1887–1939 The Providence Directory and Rhode Island Business Directory. No. 47 (1887/88)–No. 99 (1939/40). Providence, RI: Sampson, Murdock & Co.

Hooker, Richard J. *Food and Drink in America: A History.* New York: The Bobbs-Merrill Company, Inc., 1981.

Interviews with consumers of Chinese food: JG 29 June 1992; SG 16 June 1992; AL 26 June 1992; DM 3 July 1992; CR 18 July 1992; DR 2 July 1992; JR 13 July 1992; RR 13 July 1992; RS 26 April 1992

Interviews with restaurant owners: BC 21 July 1992; JC 30 July 1992; SC 14 July 1992; WC 26 April 1992; AL/DL 8 February 1992; JL 6 July 1992; AW 20 July 1992; EY 15 July 1992

Kwong, Peter. *The New Chinatown.* New York: The Noonday Press, 1987.

Larousse. *1984 Gastronomique.* London: Paul Hamlyn, 1988.

Letters: LH 3 January 1992; RC 1 January 1992; CD 24 December 1991; BF no date, postmarked 10 January 1992

Levenstein, Harvey A. *Revolution at the Table: The Transformation of the American Diet.* New York: Oxford University Press, 1988.

Lewis, Sinclair. *Main Street: The Story of Carol Kennicott.* New York: Harcourt, Brace and Howe, 1920.

Mathews, Mitford M. *A Dictionary of Americanisms: On Historical Principles.* Chicago: University of Chicago Press, 1951.

Oxford English Dictionary. Oxford: Clarendon Press, 1989.

Price, Sally. *Primitive Art in Civilized Places.* Chicago: University of Chicago Press, 1989.

Providence Daily Journal. "Order to Chinese Restaurants—Proprietors Are Ordered to Remove Draperies at Rooms." LXXXI(151): 25 June 1909: 1.

Providence Daily Journal: "Great Attraction for the Commencement Week Only at the Providence Museum—The Chinese Lady: Afong Moy." VII(35): 31 August 1835: 2.

Providence Journal Evening Bulletin. "Charlie Tow Keeps Tasting." 21 February 1974: A-1.

Providence Journal Evening Bulletin. "Yat K. Tow; Civic Leader Owned Chinese-American Restaurants." 18 July 1990: G-4.

Providence Journal: "Mourners Throng Chapel for Funeral of Fong Tow." CVII(215): 7 September 1935: 3

Providence Sunday Journal: "A "New China" Here Too." XXVIII(33): 16 February 1913: V-5, 10.

Providence Sunday Journal: "Chinatown on the Move." XXX(24): 13 December 1914: V-7.

Providence Sunday Journal: "Chinatown." XII(20): 15 November 1896: 18.

Providence Sunday Journal: "Letters—Merchants Opposition to Chinese Restaurants." XXXII(32): 4 February 1917: III-3.

Providence Sunday Journal: "Murdered Sigel Girl Enamored of Chinese." XXIV (51): 20 June 1909: I-1

Root, Waverley, and Richard de Rochemont. *Eating in America: A History.* New York: The Ecco Press, 1976.

Siu, Paul C.P. *The Chinese Laundryman: A Study of Social Isolation.* New York: New York University Press, 1987.

Stern, Jane, and Michael Stern. *American Gourmet.* New York: HarperCollins Publishers, 1991.

Takaki, Ronald. *Strangers from a Different Shore: A History of Asian Americans.* New York: Penguin Books, 1989.

Chinese Vegetable Farming:
A Case Study of the Mok Farm in Woodland, California

PETER C.Y. LEUNG and
TONY WATERS
Asian American Studies, University of California, Davis

Vegetable farming by California's Asian American population has played an important role in the state's economy since the 1850s. In the 1870s, Chinese farmers produced two-thirds of the vegetable crops in the state, and they introduced new crops such as sugar beets, celery, strawberries, and asparagus (Eu 1985). They have, of course, both produced for the general markets and specialized in consumption within their own ethnic communities. Yamaguchi (1973) has perhaps written most specifically about this market, though Dahlen, Phillipps (1983) and Harrington (1978) have written more generally about cultural requirements. Older references to oriental vegetable production in the United States include Porterfield (1951) and Chung and Ripperton (1929). Recently, several production/informational manuals on Oriental vegetable crops, such as "Bitter Melon," "Edible Pod Pea Production in California," "Glossary of Oriental Vegetable," and "Pesticide Safety with Laotians" have been written and published by Small Farm Center, Cooperative Extension, University of California. These manuals are not only important for identifying the problems of growing ethnic vegetable crops for specific minority groups, but can be used to test or promote the possibility of such crops becoming another future California commodity.

During the last 140 years, the role of farming, both for California's Asian Americans and the state as a whole has shifted significantly. How and why these shifts have occurred reflect social and economic changes that Asian Americans have experienced in California. The influx of Asian immigrants into California since 1966 has resulted in a demand for Chinese vegetables. This paper discusses how the combination of economics, taste preferences, and social conditions have shaped the Chinese vegetable markets, and in particular, how one Chinese immigrant family, over a period of 20 years, developed a Chinese vegetable farm as a means to support three families (see Table 2 on page zzz).

The family farm is disappearing in California. Since 1900, there has been a substantial decrease in the number of family-owned and operated farms. Replacing these farms are the large corporate entities—farms which are capitalized with millions of dollars worth of equipment, hundreds or thousands of acres of land, and a highly specialized permanent staff with an unskilled itinerant workforce.

These corporate entities use capital-intensive and land-extensive techniques which have largely replaced the small, diversified truck farm in California agriculture. For those traditional family farms which continue to exist, their futures are generally considered to be bleak. If they are not forced out of business due to economic hardship, they most likely will lack family members willing to carry on the family farming tradition.

Little research has been done to understand farms that specialize in ethnic crops and the farming experiences of immigrants in California today. In other words, given the problems common to immigrants, such as poor English language skills and lack of capital, how can a small family farm be established or operated? For this paper, oral interviews were used to document one farm family's experience and the economic and social conditions from the 1970s to the 1990s which made their specialization in Chinese vegetables possible.

There may still be small agricultural niches into which an aspiring immigrant farmer can fit, if abundant family labor is available. However, such niches are increasingly narrow and specialized, and they require a substantial amount of hard work and "luck" to develop. They also require some years to capitalize and make profitable. The competitive advantages increase as the farms become better capitalized, and the economic niche into which they have slipped simultaneously becomes better developed. In the case study described here, this means that the farm has shifted from land leased to land purchased on credit, and finally to land burden-free of any debt. In terms of machinery, the shift has been from a roto-tiller operation to a tractor one. Finally, an opening in the market which has the potential for expansion needs to be identified.

This is the story of the Moks, who arrived in the United States from Hong Kong in 1966. They began growing Chinese vegetables on leased land in 1969 with little more than family labor. By 1990, they had developed a labor-intensive, but fully-capitalized, 27-acre farm to a point where the farm provided its founder and two second-generation families with major incomes. They did it by filling a specialized niche—Chinese vegetables—which in the 1970s was suitable for labor-intensive specialization of farming techniques, and was a part of a specialized and expanding market which had roots in a growing ethnic community. But because the farm is located on the fringe of a developing suburban area, how long this farm can continue depends on the rate of housing development near it.

Certainly, survival of the Mok farm is, to a large extent, attributable to hard work, persistence, and luck. But it is also due to a certain amount of business acumen—Mok Chinese Vegetable Farm has always been a full-service operation. Everything from tilling to marketing is done by the family members, with the help of a few hired laborers during peak harvest times. This has been as true since it was started in 1969, using a single-row roto-tiller for plowing, as it is today, when plowing is done by conventional discing with a 90-horsepower tractor. Only crops suitable for such a generalized labor pool are grown—meaning that they do not compete with crops such as corn and tomatoes grown by "agribusiness" growers in the region. The initial strategy was to ask for a premium price in a market so limited that larger farms would not be tempted to enter. Likewise, the crops grown and harvested would have minimal seasonal peaks in labor demands. Regular cash income (see Table 1 on page zzz) from direct sale of produce could offset the family expenses and avoid high interest loans from commercial banks, so that capital-intensive investment in non-family labor would be avoided.

Methods and Sources. This study focuses on two levels: (1) the role that farming has played in the lives of the farm families—in particular, how labor has been divided and how intergenerational skills and attitudes have affected the development of the family's life—and (2) the constraints that such a strategy places on production and marketing practices. This is discussed in the context of the broader ethnic and agricultural communities which have influenced the operation of the Mok Chinese Vegetable Farm.

Interviews with all family members were conducted in Cantonese and English as appropriate, between 1985 and 1990. One of the sons, Check Mok, also provided valuable background information to the author. Because he graduated from UC Davis in 1984–85 with a degree in Agricultural Economics, he was willing to share a great deal of information that would have been difficult to obtain from his immigrant parents. Other Chinese vegetable farms in the Davis/Woodland area and Fresno were visited between 1985 and 1990, and the emerging literature about small-scale vegetable production for ethnic markets were reviewed.

The Mok Family. The Mok family was among the earlier of the "new wave" Chinese immigrants who arrived in the United States since the immigration reforms of 1966 (see Table 3 on page zzz). Mrs. Mok's father had arrived in the United States in 1929. When he returned to China in 1959, he encouraged his wife and daughter's family to emigrate to the United States. After leaving for Hong Kong in 1962, passage was finally arranged for Mrs. Mok's mother in 1965, and for the daughter's family (then numbering five) in 1966.

Shack Mok was 41 years old when he arrived in California with his family, and he immediately began work as a general restaurant helper in Colusa, California, where his father-in-law lived. He was paid $200 per month, but he quit a few months later when too much responsibility for general management was assigned to him. He then moved himself to work as a kitchen helper with wages of $300 per month in Chinatown, San Francisco. During summers, his wife, two sons and one daughter assisted by picking prunes in nearby farms in Colusa. Dissatisfied with the inadequate income of $300 per month, not to mention the principle of "working for someone else," he decided to pursue a dream of becoming a vegetable farmer. However, it took three years of working and saving in San Francisco in order to identify the markets for Chinese vegetables which he could serve in San Francisco, and to save enough money from the earnings by himself, his wife, and children to capitalize his first venture on leased land.

Farming is, of course, an unorthodox dream for an immigrant whose previous job was a street vendor in crowded Hong Kong and a delivery person in rural China. Indeed, Shack Mok had no specific experience with agricultural production before arriving in the United States, except for a casual exposure during a childhood spent in a rural area of China. Of course, the labor-intensive rice culture typical of his home village area was a far cry from farming in California's Central Valley. However, Shack Mok's start in agricultural production in 1969 did not occur in a complete vacuum—it followed discouraging attempts at Chinese vegetable farming in California by both Mok's father-in-law and uncle in the early 1960s, attempts which were abandoned because they was unable to find adequate markets for their produce.

Shack Mok's late entry into vegetable farming fortunately coincided with a surge in immigration from Hong Kong. This caused an expansion in the market demand which was adequate for the Moks' effort. This fortuitous occurrence—what second son Check today calls "luck"—meant that with hard work and perseverance, the Mok family would earn enough money from the farm to support themselves.

In 1969, with money saved from the mother and children's summer earnings, the Mok family leased five acres in Colusa, 120 miles northeast of San Francisco, and planted yard-long beans and hairy melons. Son Check today recalls that "the decision to start the farm was made out of necessity." His father, with no education or knowledge of English, and already 41 years old, had difficulty supporting the family on $300 per month from the job in San Francisco. Although he had only limited experience in growing vegetables, he knew from the two years of living and working in San Francisco's Chinatown that Chinese vegetables were in short supply while the demand was high. The small markets were full of shoppers, and the vegetables in the markets were usually sold out in a short time.

Cultivation on this first farm was done using a hand-held roto-tiller, which plowed "one row at a time." The soil was poor for row crops, and only the yard-long beans and choy sum (tender greens) could be grown. Marketing was also done by Shack Mok himself, as it is today. Trips to San Francisco Chinatown were made twice per week in order to sell produce through contacts with the small Chinese specialty markets. The first year, though, was a disaster. Sales of vegetables did not cover their investment, and the family had to rely on support from Mrs. Mok's father for several months.

A switch to a new plot with better soil and a diversification of vegetable production (10 crops on 10 acres!) improved production, and in the second year, results were better. The long days and the two marketing trips per week to San Francisco began to pay off. In the second year (1970–71) the Moks realized a gross income of about $10,000.

Production continued in Colusa from 1969–72 on leased land. This was an important period in the evolution of the family's farm as farming techniques for the unusual crops were developed. This was typically done by the first son, Chuck, then aged 16–19, who had responsibility for contacting county extension agents. He, in consultation with his father, was fast developing a wealth of practical experiences. Such advice, in combination with trial and error, was a basis for the developing commercial production techniques of Chinese vegetables in the Mok farm. In 1972, with savings of several thousand dollars, the family was able to purchase 12 acres near Woodland, California, with a small down-payment and a bank loan.

This decision to relocate the farm was based on two factors: (1) a need to reduce transport costs (Woodland is 40 miles closer to the main Chinese vegetable markets in San Francisco than Colusa) and (2) the purchase of land also meant that land would always be available for future production. This purchase was made possible through a $21,000 bank loan and a $4,000 down-payment. The purchase meant that, until 1977, most of the farm income went to debt service rather than what son Check calls "the luxuries that most American families cannot do without." On the positive side, it also meant that the Moks had a relatively high equity share in their farm, which made continued production possible, even after Chinese vegetable prices began to stagnate in 1978.

Paying off the land, though, was not the end of the Moks' struggle. After the land had been paid off in 1977, prices in Chinese vegetables began to level off. Larger companies using mechanized production began to enter the market. An influx of Southeast Asians who initiated kitchen garden production had led to competitive forces, which increased the supply. The Moks responded with the purchase of one tractor and the construction of a storage shed for winter melons.

Much of the improvement has coincided with a gradual change in generations of management. The eldest son, who, from the earliest days, served as a translator, purchasing agent, and advisor to the father, left the farm to work in a civil service position, and to dabble in small business ventures such as a video rental store. The second son, Check, graduated with a degree in Agricultural Economics from UC Davis, and has since taken over management of the farm in steps. In 1986, he assumed responsibilities for bookkeeping, and in 1988, he assumed complete management duties. Much of the expansion into more heavily capitalized ventures has taken place under his direction. This is a difference that both father and son attribute to "style," a difference that is still a source of good-natured disagreement.

Production and Labor. Described below are the competing demands for crop selection, mechanization, and scheduling which have shaped the Moks' lives in the United States.

The crops grown on the Mok farm today typically include five major crops: bok choy, choy sum (tender greens), and Chinese broccoli, which are all grown year-round, and winter melon and yard-long beans, which are seasonal. Other crops such as hairy melons, snow peas, turnips, and Chinese Napa cabbage have also been grown, though were dropped because of the labor intensity and declining prices. Of these crops, only bok choy is typically found since the late 1970s in many American mainstream markets. Consistently, the Mok's market has continued to be Chinese immigrants in urban areas, who are unable to have kitchen gardens and are willing to pay for the vegetables which are otherwise unavailable.

A close look at the crops grown on the Mok farm—winter melon, yard-long beans, Chinese broccoli and bok choy/choy sum—illustrates how the Mok farm operates with different facets of the Chinese vegetable to support their families in the United States.

Winter Melons. These are planted in February in greenhouses, and are transplanted to the field when frost danger has passed, i.e., early spring. Young seedlings are started in April and are planted in six feet interrow in 10- to 12-foot wide plots. There are 70 to 80 plants in a row. Like other melons, they grow quickly in the hot Woodland summers. They prefer sandy loam soil. The quick growth requires about four applications of nitrogen fertilizer before flowering in August, and it also requires spraying for mites at two-week intervals between June and August. The matured melons are harvested in late summer and fall. The melons can be stored for use from winter through spring. They can weigh from 10 to 100 pounds each. Portions of melon are cut and sold in Chinese grocery stores.

Harvest is done in October, when the 10- to 100-pound melons are collected carefully for storage in the 100-ton capacity facility. The excess is sold immediately on the fresh market at lower prices. With a bulky yield of up to 25 tons per acre, care must be taken in storage.

The price of winter melon is volatile, with wholesale prices at eight cents per pound at the harvest in October, and rising to 30–40 cents per pound in May. Despite the fall harvest, "winter" melon is relished by Chinese for use in soups year-round.

Some winter melon farmers sell their entire crop after harvest in October. Although storage costs are saved, the wholesale prices are too low. Much higher prices can be obtained around February to July, when supplies are limited. Retail prices can reach $1.00 per pound from late May to August, until the next harvest is available.

Bok Choy and Choy Sum. Although bok choy and choy sum are sold to the same ethnic market as winter melon, they require a different production schedule. They are grown year-round. They mature in six to seven weeks if planted in the summer, while a winter crop planted in November does not mature until February. Six producing plots are arranged in rotation. Care and harvesting move from plot to plot every two weeks. Summer crops mature much more quickly as a result of the warm weather, but winter crops fetch a higher price. Wholesale prices range from 25 to 40 cents per pound, depending on the season.

Summer harvests occur daily over a two-week period, with the leafy fresh cuttings made on a daily basis. It is necessary to store the bok choy and choy sum for two to three days in order to accommodate the twice per week delivery schedule. Refrigeration facilities (960 cubic feet) are purchased for this purpose. Bok choy and choy sum plants can be cut up to four times before being plowed back. There has been some inter-generational disagreement about the most profitable way to conduct the bok choy/choy sum harvest, which accounts for at least 50% of the labor required, since later harvests are more difficult and time-consuming than the earlier harvests. Son Check believes that the most cost-effective way to handle the harvest is to hire supplemental laborers and complete the harvest in one week before plowing under the field. Such a method eliminates the secondary shoots cutting which Check believes does not provide an adequate return on the extra labor required to sort and cut. Shack Mok on the other hand, would rather use family labor and complete the harvest in two weeks, claiming that the laborers "don't understand the distinction between 'fresh,' like Chinese. They just do the work and don't care about the result." Check adds that this is perhaps true, "but what can you expect for $5 per hour?"

Chinese Broccoli (gai laan, Cantonese): *Brassica oleracea* L. Chinese broccoli has only a slight similarity in taste to the common Italian broccoli. The stalks and young leaves are the major edible parts. Year-round crop can be grown in California. They are only available in special Chinese restaurants catering to Chinese customers and banquets.

Chinese broccoli has a similar production pattern to bok choy. Summer crops sell for 35 cents per pound, while slower growing winter crops fetch 70 cents per pound. Unlike bok choy, though, the succulent stems are harvested and marketed. For Italian broccoli, the immature flower is harvested. Like bok choy, the Chinese broccoli involves a short labor-intensive harvest period which represents some 60% of the total production costs.

Yard-long Bean or Chinese Long Bean (dau gok): *Vigna sinensis*. Two common cutivars, one is pale color and the other is darker green. Immature pods including seed. Pods vary from 18 to 24 inches in length. Harvest period lasts about 10 weeks during summer and early fall.

Yard-long beans are a fifth crop typically grown on the Mok farm. Like winter melon, yard-long beans are a seasonal crop which is planted in the spring and harvested in the summer. On the Mok Farm, two varieties are grown: green and white. They have slightly different harvest schedules: white long beans are harvested from July to October, while green long beans are harvested from July to August. They usually plant about one-and-a-half acres, which can yield 400 to 500 pounds per day in three weeks' peak harvest. A whole crop yields about 10,000 pounds per year at about $1.25 per pound. Although the profit on the yard-long beans is low, the beans are planted every year due to the exigencies of the family-based labor supply. The beans are grown on wooden trellises, which means that Mrs. Mok can participate in the harvest, despite the back troubles which make stoop work on the farm very difficult for her. Like most of the crops on the Mok farm, the yard-long bean harvest requires a large investment in time and labor. Picking the beans requires a certain feel. Mrs. Mok points out that it is necessary to twist the beans off at the node, rather than break them off, as done by the vegetable farms in the Fresno area. To do this quickly requires practice.

What the Moks' claim to be their key marketing advantage is insuring fresh quality in a manner which they claim their competitors (e.g., the farms in Fresno) do not. They claim that there is a clientele in San

Francisco which specifically asks for Mok farm produce and are willing to pay higher prices to get it. Shack Mok points out that they deliver boxes of harvested greens to the refrigerator quicker because his laborers deliver finished boxes to the refrigerator immediately after harvest, rather than wait for a truck to pick up an entire load. Care during the yard-long bean harvest insures that the bunches of beans have and retain the right moisture content. And, of course, selection of only the unspoiled greens insures that their quality is maintained, albeit at a cost.

Besides family labor, hired labor comes from Woodland's Mexican immigrant community, since Cantonese-speaking Chinese are unavailable. When laborers are hired, they are managed by Shack Mok's nephew, Stanley, who has been a working partner since 1983. The nephew works with the laborers trying to set the pace of the harvest. He has also developed a passable competency in Spanish. Communication is facilitated somewhat with the Mexican laborers' familiarity with the Chinese vegetables, since such vegetables are also grown in Mexico (see also Yamaguchi 362). As a result of a long-term relationship established by the Moks with specific laborers during the last two years, a language mixture of Cantonese, English, Spanish, and hand signals has been developed. The laborers are often invited to the family's midday meal.

Marketing and Operation. The Mok family has made plots as small as 17 acres to support the family. This requires a careful match between the small markets (typically specialty markets and open-air markets within a 90-mile radius of Woodland) and the allocation of land and resources. Because many of the sales are done on a personal basis as the result of contacts developed during the last twenty years, this "match" is typically developed on a personal level. While the Cantonese language is a prerequisite for the specialized trade, actual prices are set by individual bargaining between grower and seller, rather than by an institutionalized marketing board.

This was particularly true during the first 10 years of the operation, though, as Shack Mok notes, his familiarity with the markets and buyers now means that there is little of the haggling that once occurred. Son Check notes that "the prices are determined by the subjective judgments of supply and demand by the store owner and farmer during bargaining." During a one-month period when Shack Mok visited China, Check did the marketing and price setting. He remembers this period with amusement: "The buyers told me, 'When your father did this, he always gave us more.' But when every buyer said this, I became suspicious..." In this respect, bargaining traditions probably reflect cultural practices, rather than those to which American farmers are accustomed. This means that Shack Mok must be well aware of what is happening on other Chinese vegetable farms which sell their produce in the area and what their planting, production schedules and quality might be. Prices in such a small specialty market are enormously sensitive to the planting schedule of other growers in the state (see Yamaguchi 362)—or the installation of a post-harvest storage facility such as the one the Moks built in 1979.

Marketing also typically requires bypassing large buyers and having a well-coordinated harvest which does not stress storage facilities, refrigerator facilities, or the capital investment represented by the delivery truck. Sometimes, as many as 10 crops are grown on an area of 17 acres, meaning that pesticide applications, watering schedules, and harvest schedules must be carefully coordinated with the family labor supply and the specialized storage needs of each crop. For vegetables, fertilizer is applied one more time, a week before flowering. Weed control is a particularly heavy consumer of family labor, and this chore dominates scheduling, particularly in spring and early summer. If labor is not available, some selective herbicide may have to be used. Storage and marketing of the bulky (but low-priced) winter melon are also concerns if premium off-season prices are to be achieved. Because of the specialized nature of such crops, techniques generally had not been well-developed before the entry of the Moks into the market.

The farming techniques employed include a combination of traditional and modern ones which have been adapted to local conditions. Notably, none of the Moks brought extensive agricultural experience to their endeavor. Shack Mok had lived in rural areas of China as a child, though not in a farming family. After that he worked as a street vendor, in Hong Kong factories, and as a busboy and kitchen help in San Francisco.

As a result, the initial knowledge required by the Moks was developed both in a trial and error manner, and in consultation with county extension agents in Colusa and Yolo Counties. Communication with the county extension agents was done through a teenage son. In practice, this meant that labor-intensive methods of harvest and post-harvest storage were combined with the application of modern fertilizers. Informal seed selection techniques of the father were applied, as well as the advice provided the sons by agricultural extension agents. At times, misapplications resulted in the loss of certain crops, but notably, both approaches have had learning impact for improving the farm.

The issues of pesticide use have, particularly in recent years, become more and more serious. State regulation and supervision have been tightened since 1986. Crackdowns have resulted in citations to other Chinese vegetable farms during the last several years, affecting their ability to market produce. Check notes that this is particularly so on the small farms which often have had a "nuke 'em" philosophy towards pesticides and insects. Use of gloves and masks can also sometimes be problematic. Check attributes this to a lack of education in some of the immigrant farmers—the difficult warning labels on the pesticides, which are in English, are sometimes too difficult to read.

Check feels that even the pesticide companies are responding to the new regulations, and this has an influence on how the farm is managed. Today, the companies are less pushy or likely to recommend to him excessive applications, as they once did. There is much more today what Check calls a "work with Mother Nature" philosophy to farm operations in general, and to his farm in particular.

Management responsibilities have been delegated among the family members on the basis of position within the family and skills. In this respect, at least, the operation has been based on a Chinese-style system of "family corporation" rather than American business models emphasizing delegation. Even though day-to-day management is now with Check, he notes that "I still regard my father as head of the farm." Likewise, each day usually starts with a short conference between Check and his cousin Stanley, where neither is really the "boss." Still, the father has always had both titular authority and "final word," though for practical reasons, he has always delegated substantial authority to his son. The father also still conducts the twice a week marketing trips to San Francisco, since it is through his personal contacts and knowledge of the market that prices are set.

Mrs. Shack Mok has been responsible for lighter farm chores, such as the yard-long bean and snow peas harvest, hand weeding, and meals preparation. She also keeps a careful eye on marketing and advises about pricing and marketing practices. This is true for the older son who helped establish the farm in Colusa and later in Woodland, and who enjoyed authority because of his English-language abilities, as well as for the second son, because of his English abilities and agricultural economics training. Indeed, since son Check graduated, the father has gone into semi-retirement, with day-to-day farm management done by Check, and the bookkeeping done by a daughter-in-law. Shack Mok, though, in traditional fashion, retains titular control, while expressing his opinion only on limited occasions.

Earnings and Finance. So, what does this example tell us about the future of the family farm for immigrants? There is, of course, a big difference between what the Mok farm was in 1969–70, or better yet, its first profitable years in 1973–78, and what it is in 1990. On the other hand, a look at how the farm is capitalized demonstrates the immigrants' ability to defer gratification. To a large extent, this is attributable to the parents' social life, which Check describes as a "social life limited to the visits to San Francisco during produce delivery." But this has meant a low debt, which means that a lower rate of return has been needed on the Mok's farm in order to turn a reasonable income or small profit. In large part, this is because the labor-intensive operation requires less capital investment in machinery, which in turn means that depreciation and interest are low when fuel, chemicals, repairs, and wage costs can rise.

A look at the Mok farm's income and operating expenses for 1984–85 in Table 1, and 1988–89 in Table 2, provide a clearer view of how exactly the Chinese vegetable market continues to be viable for the Moks. Its gross income is four times higher than the average farm gross of $40,000 reported by Christensen of Bilingual Small Farmers in California.

Most notable is the steady year-round sales of crops. While there are seasonal peaks, e.g., sale of fresh summer crops in September and a sell-off of stored winter melons in February and May, the emphasis is on year-round delivery of produce. Again, this is a reflection of the narrow market niche which the Moks have identified, and the need to provide full-services, i.e., from farm to market, and to take year-round advantage of the major investment that the delivery truck represents.

Conclusion. Income from the Mok Chinese vegetable farm supports three families today. It is the type of rags-to-riches story that we Americans enjoy. On the other hand, much of the heartbreak which goes into making such stories should not be forgotten. The past farming failures of the grandfather and uncle, the hours the children spent working on the farm, and the 80-hour weeks that the father and mother devoted to the farm should not be forgotten. Indeed, the long days of stooping in fields have caused the backaches for both Mr. and Mrs. Mok, as well as for the children.

In the immediate Woodland area, there are three other Chinese vegetable farms, ranging in size from 15 acres to 100 acres. Like the Mok farm, such farms typically rely on a heavy input of immigrant labor, but unlike the Mok farm, they do not have a capital investment in land. Whether this dependence will expose these farms to unmanageable pressures to move frequently, as suburbanization puts pressures on such farms, remains to be seen.

California's Southeast Asian refugees have also played an important role in Chinese vegetable production. Entry into the market by Sacramento's Southeast Asian kitchen gardens has effectively blocked Sacramento's markets for commercial-scale farmers such as the Moks. Indeed, Check has pointed out that "the proliferation of backyard, small kitchen plots has effectively blocked the Moks from sales to the large Chinese immigrant market in nearby Sacramento."

Illustrating how this works are Leonelli's (1986) and Vasquez's (1989) studies of Hmong gardeners in Sacramento and San Joaquin Counties. Leonelli's (1986) description indicates that such farming ventures are important to the Hmong sense of self-identity, even if they do not provide a commercial profit from which the family can subsist. Government transfer payments often provide the refugee families with the bulk of the subsistence income. Holmes (1985) identifies a similar problem with some Vietnamese gardeners in Sacramento in 1983.

Just how difficult such marginal ventures can be is indicated by Vasquez (167), who collected income information about the two largest Hmong farmers in the substantial San Joaquin County community. These farmers had a net profit of $12,600 and $7,700, respectively, on farms of 21 acres and 11 acres. Both farms provided only 60% of the families' incomes, even though three adults and three children, and three adults and four children, respectively, worked on each farm. Vasquez (1989) estimates that the Hmong farms had a turnover of 90%. In other words, for every 10 farms begun, nine do not survive after the first year.

Most recently, Edna Bonacich has described the role that such immigrant enterprises can play in exploiting immigrant labor (119–128). Unprotected by workman's compensation laws, 40-hour work weeks, or minimum wage laws, such small enterprises are potentially self-exploitative. While the Mok farm can continue to be operated, they have been self-exploited in this manner. This would seem especially true for the many unnamed and undescribed Chinese vegetable farmers who must have farmed for one, two, three, or more years, only to stop because their labor was rewarded only by a debt. In other words, extreme caution is the watchword for farmers contemplating a move into the ethnic specialty vegetable market.

Acknowledgments. We are grateful to Mr. and Mrs. Mok and their family for their cooperation to provide all information for this article. Special appreciation is also expressed to Check Mok, who was so helpful to provide valuable personal data for the completion of this article. The project was partially funded by the Agricultural Experiment Station, Department of Applied Behavioral Sciences, University of California, Davis.

Table 1. **Gross Income Receipts, 1984–85**

Month	Gross Income
July	$4,600
August	4,400
September	8,400
October	5,800
November	7,000
December	7,000
January	4,900
February	8,700
March	6,600
April	7,300
May	8,000
June	$3,000
Total	**$75,700**
Monthly Averages	$6,308

Operating Expenses, 1984–85

Jul.–Sep. 1984	rent	$1,250
	tractor	$3,700
	repairs	$3,500
	chemicals	$1,000
Oct.–Dec. 1984	insurance	$1,000
	other	$1,000
	gas	$1,000
Jan.–Mar. 1985	rent	$1,250
	insurance	$1,700
	gas	$1,000
	other	$300
	1984 taxes	$6,850
Apr.–Jun. 1985		not available

Table 2. **Gross Income Receipts, 1989**

Month	Gross Income
January	$14,235
February	8,355
March	6,985
April	9,479
May	12,601
June	9,880
July	10,746
August	17,632
September	21,572
October	21,377
November	14,137
December	$11,737
Total	**$158,736**
Monthly Average	$13,228

Operating Expenses, 1988 and 1989

	1989	1988
Chemicals	$5,321	$3,853
Depreciation	$10,733	$5,639
Freight	$1,120	$950
Fuel	$4,711	$4,250
Insurance	$6,451	$5,528
Interest	$1,462	$1,253
Interest/Other	$1,409	—
Wages, Check & cousin	$49,486	$38,680
Wages, hired laborers	$9,000	—
Wages, Mr. & Mrs. Mok	$25,000	$25,000
Machinery	$6,075	—
Repairs	$12,008	$7,925
Taxes	$7,390	$7,255
Utilities	$6,269	$4,012
Other	$4,983	$2,832
Total	**$151,421**	**$107,177**
Sales	$158,736	$115,683
Profits	$7,315	$8,506

Table 3. **Chinese in the United States, 1950–90**

Census Year	Chinese in U.S.
1950	150,005
1960	237,292
1970	436,062
1980	812,178
1990	1,645,472

Source: U.S. Census Bureau

Works Cited

Bonacich, Edna. "The Social Costs of Immigrant Entrepreneurship." *Amerasia Journal* 14(1) (1988): 119–128.

Christensen, L. Clair. "Glossary of Oriental Vegetables." Cooperative Extension University of California, Small Farm Center, UC Davis, 1983.

Christensen, L. Clair. *Pesticide Safety* (Laotian translation). Cooperative Extension University of Cailifornia, Small Farm Center, UC Davis, 1984.

Chung, H.L., and J.C. Ripperton. "Utilization and Composition of Oriental Vegetables in Hawaii." *Hawaii Agricultural Experimental sttion Bulletin* 60, 1929.

Dahlen, Martha, and Karen Phillipps. *A Popular Guide to Chinese Vegetables*. New York: Crown Publishers, 1983.

Eu, March Fong. "Proclamation Relative to Honoring California's Chinese Pioneers." Secretary of State's Office, Sacramento, 1 November 1985.

Harrington, Geri. *Grow Your Own Chinese Vegetables*. New York: Macmillan Publishing Co., 1978.

Holmes, Paul. *"The Northgate Small Farm Project, a Case Study."* M.A. thesis in International Agricultural Development, University of California, Davis, 1985.

Johnson, Hunter, Jr. "Bitter Melon." Leaflet 21399, Cooperative Extension University of California, 1985.

Leonelli, Laura. ""We Are What We Eat: Food Use Patterns of Hmong and Mien in Sacramento." M.A. thesis, Department of Anthropology, CSU Sacramento, 1987.

Porterfield, W.M. Jr. "The Principal Chinese Foods and Food Plants of Chinese Markets." *Economic Botany* 5 (1951):3–37.

Valenzuela, Louie H. "Edible Pod Pea Production in California." Leaflet 21328, Cooperative Extension University of California, 1983.

Vasquez, Michael. "The Expansion of Simple Commodity Production at the Core: The Case of Agriculture in CA." Ph.D. dissertation, University of California, Davis, Department of Anthropology, 1989.

Yamaguchi, M. "Production of Oriental Vegetables in the United States." *Hortscience* 8(5) (1973): 362–70.

Families Make Good Business:
The Case of Finance Factors, Ltd.

MICHAELYN P. CHOU
University of Hawaii at Manoa, Honolulu, Hawaii

In 1952, several ethnic Chinese and Caucasian investors in the Territory of Hawaii formed a small corporation to make industrial loans. They called the new business Finance Factors, Ltd., and elected a broad-based, experienced, and creative Board of Directors headed by President Hiram L. Fong, an attorney, politician, and businessman. Other early Directors included Mun On Chun, a skilled realtor; Lawrence B. C. Lau, an organizer and consumer loan expert; Daniel B. T. Lau (no relation to Lawrence), a key insurance executive; and Clifford H. N. Yee, a veteran accountant and administrator.

The founders could not have foreseen that in 40 years their $300,000 capitalization would expand into a diverse, highly successful, self-proclaimed "Family of Companies" featuring industrial and consumer loans, real estate development, home building, investments, life insurance, and other components spread out over more than 26 separately incorporated subsidiaries that shared interlocking directorships. In 1976, a corporation called Finance Enterprises, Ltd. was formed as the new parent, with Finance Factors, Ltd. as a major subsidiary. Finance Enterprises' worth is currently set at over $80 million in equity and assets of half a billion dollars.

Except for minor holdings by others in its investment and general insurance subsidiaries, Finance Enterprises is still privately owned by the surviving founding families, all of whom are ethnically Chinese. Finance Factors is Hawaii's independently-owned consumer finance company, and it is believed to be the largest American Chinese-owned industrial and consumer finance corporation in Hawaii. From the beginning, Finance Factors was operated like a "family," both in terms of subsidiary incorporation and in how the owners/managers perceived and treated the employees.

This paper is based on oral histories, interviews, and printed sources in private collections and in the Hawaiian Collection at Hamilton Library, University of Hawaii, Honolulu, Hawaii. The significance of the founders' Chinese heritage upon management, decision-making, personnel, and other business practices was determined by reviewing three corporations established during the first decade: Finance Factors, Ltd.; Finance Realty, Ltd., and Grand Pacific Life Insurance Company, Ltd.

From a Casual Question to Incorporation. Finance Factors, Ltd. began one day in 1952 with a casual question, "Can you raise $75,000?" It was asked of Hiram Fong by Mun On Chun, an old friend who had already brought Fong one major real estate deal. When Fong said yes, Chun displayed figures showing that $1,000 to $2,000 a month could be earned. "What kind of business is this?" Fong asked. "You mean to tell me you could make this kind of money?"

What Chun proposed was the formation of a corporation to make industrial and consumer loans. At the time, Chun handled real estate for Honolulu Trust Company (HTC), a small trust firm owned and operated by Chinese families with backgrounds in banking. HTC was a mortgage loan correspondent for Occidental Life Insurance Company, and it handled general insurance, a real estate brokerage, and property management. Other HTC staff members involved in the proposal were Lawrence B. C. Lau, head of the consumer loan department; Daniel B. T. Lau, an insurance expert, and Clifford H. N. Yee, chief accounting officer.

It was an opportune time. World War II was over. For many years, the Territory of Hawaii had earnestly pursued its goal of Statehood, and now success seemed imminent. Political, economic, and social changes were reshaping the Islands' future by lessening the hold of the Big Five, the Caucasian-owned companies that had controlled Hawaii for over 50 years. And modern technology and communication were ending the Islands' geographical isolation.

In 1952 another Hawaii Statehood bill died in Congress... President-Elect Dwight Eisenhower visited Honolulu after his November election... Parking meters and television sets made their debut... Waikiki had a new hotel, the Surfrider... Woolworth announced plans for a million-dollar downtown store... And there was a shortage of home loan funds.

Until the late 1940s, Hawaii's major banks controlled the consumer loan industry. Reluctant to support ethnic minority businesses, the banks effectively slowed down progress for minority groups. On April 18, 1952, Finance Factors, Ltd. was incorporated with the following officers elected from the Board of Directors:

President: Hiram L. Fong
First Vice-President: Mun On Chun
Second Vice-President: Lawrence B. C. Lau
Third Vice-President: George Thornally
Secretary: William Mau
Treasurer: Clifford H. N. Yee

Other early stockholders included Ah Get Chang, Fong Choy (Hiram's distant cousin), Benedict Lau (Lawrence's brother), Daniel B.

T. Lau, Dr. Lup Quon Pang (medical doctor), and Joseph Pao (real estate developer). While the team had the requisite components for success, the best-known owner/director was Fong. The son of poor, illiterate Chinese immigrants, Fong had capped his struggle for an education with a Harvard Law School degree. A life-long Republican, Fong entered territorial politics and immediately gained a reputation for independence from GOP party bosses and an ability for forming bipartisan coalitions to pass legislation that benefited Hawaii's diverse populations. From 1949–1953, he was Speaker of the House of Representatives, the first of his ancestry to hold that key position. "His word was good," the powerful International Longshoremen's and Warehousemen's Union said of Fong.

As President, Fong's reputation for hard work, intelligence, and honesty—important qualities in any endeavor—coupled with his Harvard degree and flourishing legal office—were definite advantages in Factors' quick growth. Of course other Directors contributed significantly. George Thornally operated a successful car dealership, and through his wife's connections, he was able to obtain a line of credit from the Bank of America.

Lawrence Lau and Clifford Yee were the dynamos who sparked the new venture. With an MBA from New York University, New York banking experience, and several years of local consumer loan expertise, Lawrence Lau also brought contacts and creativity to Finance Factors. Clifford Yee graduated from the University of Hawaii and, having had broad experience at Honolulu Trust Company, returned there as Chief Accounting Officer after his wartime service. At Factors, Yee kept abreast of developments in modern accounting and data processing while also becoming an able administrator. Yee became Secretary-Treasurer when William Mau left the corporation, and he could always be counted on to quickly assume additional responsibilities as directorships and top management staff changed over the years.

Finance Factors. Ltd. opened for business on July 1, 1952 at 58 North King Street in Honolulu with a skeleton staff. Before the end of the first three months of business, the requested $300,000 capitalization was in sight, prompting Fong to approach his distant cousin, Fong Choy, about purchasing the latter's Canton Jewelry Company site at King and Smith streets for Factors' new home. What transpired was indicative of how some investors joined in. When Fong Choy learned that some $80,000 had been deposited in Factors, and that his cousin had invested about $25,000, Fong Choy said: "I go in with you." Hiram Fong demurred, saying: "But you don't know what we're doing. You don't know this and that." But Fong Choy insisted: "As long as you're in it, I go in with you." Finance Factors moved into its new headquarters on September 1, 1952.

On his way home from attending the 1952 GOP Convention in Chicago, Fong stopped in San Francisco to confer with Bank of America officials about Factors' line of credit. Back in Honolulu, he described Factors' lending and borrowing relationship with the giant bank as "large-scale." While it was unlikely that the Bank would locate in Hawaii per se, Fong noted that Mainland money was already in the Islands for automobile and appliance financing, that such funds had no direct relation to Hawaii's tight money mortgage situation, and that Finance Factors represented only a new enterprise in a fertile financial field.

When Factors had a million dollars in assets, a big newspaper ad proudly announced it. "It was a great thing then. Larry Lau was the man that really knew the business. He ... and Clifford Yee worked hard. I was just on the fringe of it because I was a practicing attorney," said Fong. After six months of business, Finance Factors' resources stood at $2,179,000, increasing to $2,776,000 a year later. Assets reached $3,609,000 by the end of 1954.

Business Philosophy. From the beginning, the philosophy guiding Finance Factors was basically conservative. Fong explained that "money came in so easily" that if one were "not disciplined ... not honest ... not conservative," one could get into "a lot of trouble." For example, loan companies that advertised for money and paid high interest rates attracted many deposits—which then had to be put to work in order to pay the high interest. Questionable, even marginal, loans might be made, leading to serious problems like those involving the nation's failed savings and loans companies of recent years.

Fong continued, "We have run our business in a very conservative way. If you go down there to the counter and look at the people that come in and put their money in here, you realize the responsibility that you have. Old people, who have their life savings—people on Social Security ... people who need this money to send their children to school ... to buy a home. Now these are hard-earned monies ... deposited with you because they have confidence in you. And if you break that trust, you are doing a lot of damage to that individual. And that's why I always remind my people here: Look at the [person] at the counter... How could you not guard his money? We give a lower rate of interest and [loan] it out more conservatively. Our primary objective is to safeguard the principal. Never mind the profit."

The directors meet weekly, hearing reports as needed from management and staff before making decisions by consensus. This method enables them to move quickly in times of crisis or to take advantage of opportunities. The first decade brought much growth, and a crisis.

The "Family of Companies" Begins with Finance Realty, Ltd.
Within a year of its founding, the directors "decided that [they] should have a second prop to the business, and since Mun On Chun knew something about real estate, we said let's go... We started Finance Realty with $2,000 apiece, $18,000 from nine of us," recalled Fong. The practice of raising capital internally for new projects and subsidiaries effectively reduced the need for outside monies, enabling the owners to tightly and privately control their companies. Finance Realty, Ltd. was incorporated on July 15, 1953. Led by Executive Vice-President Mun On Chun, a University of Hawaii graduate and a respected church deacon, Realty moved quickly from its first project, the 12-acre Anoai subdivision in cool Manoa Valley, to the 435-home Waipio Acres project on 120 acres in 1955. In 1958 Finance Realty bought 9,000 acres on the Big Island of Hawaii and then developed and completely sold out 8,000 acres as its Fern Forest Vacation Estates. Fern Forest was one of a few Hawaii Island real estate successes. Other real estate deals, including rentals, followed. By 1977, Realty had assets of around $17 million dollars.

The success of Finance Realty illustrates how the Family of Companies grew. It was a logical step from land development to construction support services. Finance Home Builders, Ltd. was incorporated on October 4, 1957, as a subsidiary of Finance Realty. Today, in addition to building residences for Finance Realty, Home Builders takes on commercial and renovation projects for outside clients.

In 1959, Hawaii achieved Statehood. Investment money and new residents poured into the 50th State. There is no doubt that Finance Factors benefited through the political achievements of its President, Hiram Fong. Following an intensive campaign for Hawaii's first Congressional delegation, Fong won a seat in the United States Senate. He was the first American-Asian in the Senate, the first American-Chinese in the Congress, and the only Republican to serve Hawaii in the Senate. Throughout his historic career, which ended when he retired in January 1977, Fong remained as president of Finance Factors and each of the subsidiaries. On January 1, 1987, Fong became Chairman Emeritus of Finance Factors but continued as Chairman of Finance Enterprises, the holding company incorporated on September 22, 1976 as the parent of Finance Factors, Finance Realty, Grand Pacific Life Insurance, and about 18 other corporations. Clifford Yee succeeded Fong as Chairman of Finance Factors, which at the time had some 157 million dollars in assets.

Finance Realty Develops Oahu's First Planned City—Makakilo. A year after Statehood, Finance Realty contracted with the Estate of James Campbell to develop a residential community on a

1,300-acre West Oahu hillside. Located 1,000 feet above the Ewa Plain, the site is said to have been used by ancient Hawaiians as a lookout, and it retains its Hawaiian name—Makakilo—which means "watchful eye." The climate is pleasantly cool, and there are sweeping vistas across the ocean and down to Hawaii's trademark Diamond Head.

In ground-breaking ceremonies on a rocky hillside on December 11, 1961, Senator Fong, as President of Finance Realty, invoked a vision of Oahu's first completely planned city—a community of 5,000 homes to be built at a projected cost of $116 million. Vice President Chun detailed a master plan involving schools, shopping facilities, recreation areas, and many open spaces. When Makakilo was introduced, the only access roads were through sugar cane fields because the Hawaii defense highway, better known as the H-1 freeway, did not extend past Kunia. With the H-1 now completed, Makakilo is only 21 minutes of non-stop driving from Honolulu.

The people of Hawaii were invited to come out to see Makakilo's first 60 completed homes with a full-page newspaper ad on July 4, 1962, and if they brought shovels, they could dig for a "bag of gold" worth $1,000—an effective advertising gimmick to ensure that people would make the then-lengthy trek to Makakilo. In those days, a $450 down-payment bought a three-bedroom home with an all-electric kitchen. Home prices ranged from $14,900 to $17,500. Lease rent from the Campbell Estate was $60 per year for 75 years—the best deal in Hawaii. Since 1976, every home and homesite has been offered in fee simple and the majority of leasehold residences has been converted.

Thirty years later, many of Makakilo's charter families still live there. The community consists of 3,500 families and a population of approximately 12,000. The original homes are now valued at more than $240,000. Current Makakilo for-sale listings range from $249,000 to $1,150,000. Garden apartments, townhomes, single-family homes, and homesites offer a choice of living styles. An additional 2,500 homes are planned through the year 2000, bringing Makakilo's population to about 20,000. Makakilo Ridge, the hillside's first gated community, has a portfolio of custom homes designed by three architectural firms to simplify the building process.

At Makakilo, the emphasis is on families and community life. As part of its 30th anniversary celebration, Finance Realty published a colorful 12-page section of the Sunday paper that focused on the community's youthful residents and their future. There are two elementary schools and numerous safe playgrounds. The active Makakilo Community Association sponsors community events in addition to representing the residents. The Makakilo Recreation Center is popular for various activities, and there are basketball courts, a baseball field, and a City and County swimming pool. Makakilo's 18-hole golf course will be completed in 1993. Makakilo enjoys proximity to several major employment centers, including Campbell Industrial Park, Barbers Point Naval Air Station, Ko Olina Resort, and St. Francis Medical Center-West. As a result, many residents escape heavy commuter traffic that plagues other communities. And the growing "Second City" of Kapolei brings many new opportunities. The vision that Finance Realty and Finance Factors had three decades ago has been actualized.

Grand Pacific Life Insurance Companies, Ltd. With Finance Realty launched successfully, the directors decided on another prop to their business in the form of life insurance. Reaching into their own pockets for funding, they incorporated Grand Pacific Life Insurance Company, Ltd. (GPLIC) on August 12, 1957. Care was taken to provide good management, to build products, and to select agents. Wadsworth Yee, an attorney and the nephew of Hiram Fong's wife Ellyn, headed operations. By 1965, GPLIC made a modest operating profit for a third time. Best's "Recommended Life Insurance Companies" cited Grand Pacific Life as one of 347 firms for "soundness, stability, permanence of operation, and safety from the viewpoint of the policy-holder." The firms—one-fifth of all United States and Canadian life insurance companies—held 96% of the assets and 98 per cent of the life insurance in force. Grand Pacific Life was among the youngest companies cited, ranking particularly high in its ratio of net yield to assets.

Within 10 years, GPLIC was the only Hawaii life company licensed to do business in California. It had more than $100 million of life insurance in force and insured over 25,000 lives in Hawaii and California. By 1970, Grand Pacific Life was also operating in Idaho, Washington, Alaska, Montana, Nevada, Utah, Wyoming, Oregon, Colorado, Guam, and the Trust Territories. In 1967, insurance in force totaled $128,704,000. There were over 30,000 policy holders serviced by 57 full-time agents and 24 home office staff members. In the first decade of operations, more than $1,480,000 was paid out in claims, but assets amounted to over $3,000,000.

Sales mounted steadily. A net investment return of 6.09% was reported. There was a modest profit for 1971 in contrast to losses of $292,000 and $86,000 for the years 1968 and 1969, respectively. Wadsworth Yee was the guiding force behind GPLIC's outstanding record. He was promoted to President in 1971. At the time, he was also a State Senator. Daniel B. T. Lau, one of Finance Factors' founders, became Executive Vice-President of GPLIC.

Daniel B. T. Lau graduated from the University of Hawaii with a degree in Business and Economics and completed Harvard University's Advanced Management Program. The offices he held reflect the structure of the interlocking directorships of the Family of

Companies. In 1992, Lau was Chairman of the Board and Director of Grand Pacific Life Insurance Company; Vice-Chairman, Secretary, and Director of Finance Enterprises; Vice President, Secretary, and Director of Finance Realty Co.; Secretary and Director of Finance Factors, Finance Insurance and Finance Investments; and officer of numerous other Companies. Like other Directors, Lau had also been a Director of the First Interstate Bank of Hawaii. He had taken active roles in church and community affairs. His past offices included President and Director of the Hawaiian Humane Society and Chairman of United Church of Christ. A veteran of World II, Lau was awarded the Purple Heart with Oak Leaf Cluster. Other honors include awards from the insurance industry, as well as from baseball and softball leagues.

A massive jump in life insurance in force was accomplished between 1972 and 1973, from $290 million to over $800 million, an increase of 177.6%. Much of the increase was due to Grand Pacific Life's new contract with the Hawaii State Public Health Fund which amounted to $480 million. Assets jumped 23%, while total income rose 32% during 1972–1973. A milestone—the billion dollar mark in life insurance in force—was reached in 1974. Profits from operations were $158,000, despite "a year when gloom and doom pervaded most of the business community," reported Wadsworth Yee.

The corporation continued to identify and service the needs of the people. In 1980, Grand Pacific Life issued the first "for women only" policy of a Hawaii-owned life company. The policies are based on the actuarial fact that women live longer than men and on the changing needs of increasing numbers of independent women. The growing business required more space. When the firm moved a second time, to expanded quarters in the historic McCandless Building in Downtown Honolulu in 1990, it also unveiled its new marketing logo, "Family for Life," at the annual family picnic that July. Wadsworth Yee said that the bulk of the business would remain in Hawaii and the South Pacific and the Pacific Rim countries, although it was hoped to expand to New Zealand, Australia, and Taiwan. A cross-selling program with Finance Insurance, Ltd., a separate entity, was begun in 1991 for the customers' convenience, as well as to strengthen their business relationships with the Family of Companies.

In 1992, Grand Pacific Life Insurance Company, Ltd. was ranked 158th of the top 250 companies in Hawaii. With Daniel Lau as Chairman of the Board and Wadsworth Yee as President, Chief Executive Officer, and Chief Operations Officer, the firm had 60 employees and sales of $35.1 million in 1991, up from $30.6 million the year before.

Finance Factors' Growth: Headquarters and Branch Offices.
Finance Factors weathered volatile economic and industrial changes
to become one of Hawaii's largest finance companies. Current
financial products include mortgage loans on residential and
investment properties, home equity credit lines, and personal loans.
Its savings accounts and investment time certificates offer the security
of insurance by the Federal Deposit Insurance Corporation (FDIC).
Finance Factors is also a member/stockholder of the Federal Home
Loan Bank of Seattle, which provides expanded service opportunities
to local customers.

The growth of the Family of Companies can also be seen in office
space requirements, as well as in the establishment of Finance Factors'
branches on the Neighbor Islands. Land was purchased in Downtown
Honolulu at the corner of King and Alakea streets. In 1958, the Family
of Companies had a new address—the seven-story Finance Factors
Building at 195 South King Street.

The first branch office was opened in Hilo, Hawaii in August
1954; the second followed just one month later in Wailuku, Maui.
More branches were established to serve growing communities
throughout the Honolulu area (which is synonymous with the Island
of Oahu). By 1961 Finance Factors was also doing business on Kauai,
completing the sweep of the major Islands in the Hawaiian chain.

One reason for Finance Factors' success was that the company
took a different approach. Instead of small offices in many locations,
Factors' opened regional branches, much like banks, that were
generally larger and more impressive than the competition.

In 1966, net profits after taxes were up a healthy 14% over the
previous year, although money was hard to come by. Finance Factors
had reserves for a rainy day, and ties with West Coast and local banks
held up during that time of lean money supply. By the end of 1966,
Finance Factors' 15 branch offices and the seven-story main office had
a total of 42,157 square feet of office space—a dramatic increase for the
first office's 1,000 square feet.

At least once or twice a year, managers of all the branches are
flown to a central meeting location, usually at a major hotel in
Honolulu or a Neighbor Island, for a weekend of workshops, expert
speakers, and the opportunity to relax in pleasant surroundings and to
get better acquainted with each other. Since the wives are usually
included, the weekends encourage Family togetherness and a feeling
that the employees' families are also important to Finance Factors. The
trips also served to reduce the sense of geographic isolation usually
associated with Neighbor Island living.

Each branch manager is qualified to perform far more than loan
and collection activities; each is a licensed insurance agent, and each
undergoes constant training in order to be knowledgeable in all types

of lending, in thrift investments, and in the overall economic picture of Hawaii, the nation, and the world. Each branch office represents every service offered by the Family of Companies. Each community served by a Factors' branch is thus fully accommodated, in the shortest time possible. All staff members are encouraged to take active roles in the community where they work and live.

During the 1971 shipping strike, Finance Factors made news—and gained friends by jumping ahead of all other financial institutions to offer customers an across-the-board deferment of all loan and mortgage payments for the duration of the strike. Payments made at the strike's end would not incur additional interest, and existing loans could be refinanced. New loans made during the strike required no repayment for 90 days.

In 40 years of operation, some branches were combined or relocated as new ones were opened. By 1991, there were seven branches on the Neighbor Islands and 13 on Oahu (excluding the main facility in the Finance Factors Building) for a total of 20. With the recent purchase by Finance Investment of a 16-story building at 1164 Bishop Street for approximately $43 million, Finance Enterprises' inventory of prime office and commercial space in the central business district comes to approximately 300,000 square feet. Before the year's end, all the Companies, now located in six different buildings in Downtown Honolulu, will have the same home address—1164 Bishop Street. From this new home, Finance Enterprises expects to continue growing with Hawaii.

Personnel and Service: Members of the Family. The Companies can be seen as a Family not only because they have a common parent, or holding company, but also because the founders have an almost paternalistic attitude toward their employees, reminiscent of the traditional Chinese family. They exhorted, and expected, all employees to be loyal, hard-working, ambitious, and team players. In turn, the Companies treated their workers well. Almost all promotions come from within, although in later years, outsiders who had special expertise were brought in, usually with the assistance of hired management consultants like Harry Coder. The consultants also evaluate existing personnel as the need arises.

Young, alert, friendly workers were selected at most of the beginning job levels. In-service training was provided annually at company expense, and taking the Dale Carnegie course or its equivalent was encouraged. Tuition was paid for employees enrolled in real estate, insurance, or related classes, and certification was encouraged. At Finance Insurance, all supervisors were Certified Life Underwriters; at Finance Investment, the property manager was certified, and two key executives were graduates of the National

Installment Banking School. The senior management team were also graduates of the Harvard Advanced Management Program.

By 1967, Finance Factors' minimum staff in 1952 had grown to 277 employees of various ethnic backgrounds and were deployed on all the major islands. The Company's payroll rose from an initial $38,000 to over $800,000 in 15 years. Vacation and sick leave benefits were expanded into one of the Hawaii's finest benefit programs. Health, group life, and salary protection insurance and recreational programs were added so that by 1967, each Factors' employee received $2,085 in benefits per year in addition to his/her salary.

In 1955, Finance Factors was among the first companies in Hawaii to offer profit sharing to the fullest extent of the law.

From an initial $16,000, the fund grew to a market value of $1,467,963 at the end of 1969. Each company has its own profit-sharing plan which is individually administered, but with funds pooled into a common Contract Fund handled by Hawaiian Trust Company. No employee contributions are required, but there is a 10-year vesting period. Loans can be made against individual accounts. Long-time employees have been known to retire with over $100,000 accumulated through profit-sharing.

Monthly newsletters were published regularly, except for a few years in the 1980s, both to inform employees of significant events and to build a sense of close family ties among the owners, managers, and employees. Informal snapshots of the entire group at company-sponsored annual picnics and other events evoked warm memories. Results of bowling contests, baseball leagues, and other sports appeared regularly, and they helped to build staff morale. While company emphasis was on profits and guarding the principal, community service was not neglected. In 1958, Finance Factors Foundation was established as the eleemosynary arm. Funded by annual donations from the parent company based on a percentage of corporate profits, the contributions have been used to support educational and charitable causes decided by the Board of Directors. In honor of its 40th anniversary, the Foundation allocated a sum of $40,000 *above* the current level of support to be given to organizations which assist Hawaii through programs aimed at social problems, education, and the environment. Organizations can submit applications for funding. In October, all 355 employees will have the opportunity to evaluate the organizations—*and to vote their choices.* "In this way, we feel we will make a genuine Family decision to help meet *our* community's needs."

The Family of Companies credits its "very special, dedicated employees" for its success. The nine-employee-force has grown to 355 employees whose average length of service is 8.49 years. Over 13% of them had given more than 25 years of service. A color picture of the old-timers, identified by full name under the heading, "We are Family," appeared in a special newspage. This statement also appears: "The Family of Companies supports activities which promote employee participation. Whether benefiting the community through projects such as the Aloha United Way, Food Bank Drive, Walk America, the Bobby Benson Relays or recreational activities such as golf, volleyball, softball, or company events, all employees are encouraged to do things together."

Following a Crisis, the Sky's the Limit. The four-decade development of Finance Factors and the Family of Companies did not happen without internal stress and strain. During the first 10 years, it was perhaps inevitable that the Directors' different business philosophies would surface around the large oval table in the Board Room. While decisions did not have to be unanimous, consensus was expected before action could be taken. As the corporation grew, individual career choices brought about changes in ownership. One instance occurred when Joseph Pao thought more emphasis should be placed on real estate projects. When the others failed to go along, Pao left to pursue his own interests. Ah Get Chang left at about the same time. Rather than seek other capital, the remaining owners bought the shares of those who left.

A major upheaval took place early in 1962. It centered on Lawrence Lau. An action-oriented man with a strong personality, Larry Lau had specific goals and timetables in mind for the company he helped put together. He felt strongly about turning Finance Factors into a public corporation, but was voted down by the conservative majority. When he was offered the presidency of American Security Bank, he decided to leave Finance Factors. Benedict Lau followed his brother out the door. Again the remaining owners had to dig deep into their own pockets to pick up the Laus' shares.

The ownership shakeup could have destroyed confidence in Finance Factors, for it was no secret that Larry Lau had been a key player in the companies' successes. While Hawaii's business community wondered how deeply Factors was hurt in a potentially explosive situation, the remaining founders used the crisis as an opportunity to display how versatile a management team they had developed. Management depth, it was soon apparent, was two, three, and even four men deep as promotions within the corporation were quickly announced.

Clifford Yee stepped immediately into the post of Executive Vice-President and also assumed the title "Coordinating Officer." He took charge of a diverse staff of 200 employees, while Edward Matsumoto took over Yee's operating Vice-President's duties. Yee commented:

"We believe in providing job opportunities for our people. Our assistant vice presidents average under age 35."

Hiram Fong remained as President. Before returning to Washington, he told employees: "There's no question but that the sky's the limit in our operation. The future promises as much dynamic growth as we are prepared for. Our directors are ready, are you? We will move as far and as fast as you are ready to go! I hope all of you find this as exciting a challenge as I do.

"We will always work hard at Finance Factors," Fong continued. "We are proud of our spirit and our zest." But much like a father, he also emphasized: "We also understand that the purpose of work is to enrich living. It is not an ends but a means. We want you to enjoy your family, your friends, your home. We want you to enjoy a balanced life." He said that with hard work should come "a pride, a satisfaction" that makes for "great business organizations and great employees." He encouraged all employees to discuss opportunities with management, which was ready to give them fair chances to prove themselves. Much like a father dispensing wisdom to his children, he asked employees to examine the concepts of the business and to pledge or refuse their loyalty to Finance Factors: "You give much of your life and substance to your work—respect it, believe in it, be loyal to it. Personalities come and go but the impact of your work goes on forever." He asked them to think of him not just as a Senator, but as "one of your co-workers."

Clifford Yee added that "we must never lose sight of our goal of service: service to the community in general and to individuals in particular. Sound ideals and practical profit go hand in hand. If we serve genuinely, honestly, and with personal interest, there is no question but that our earnings will automatically fall into place. I promise you a future that will be exciting and rewarding. And I send this same message to the wives and families of every employee as well—for you too are a vital part of our future and our strength."

It was soon apparent that the Companies continued their progress without Larry Lau. In 1962 ownership rested in six founders: Hiram Fong, Mun On Chun, Fong Choy, Daniel Lau, Dr. Lup Quon Pang, and Clifford Yee. There were no changes in the top team for the next 30 years, until the recent passings of Fong Choy and Dr. L. Q. Pang. As was their practice, the surviving owners did not invite in new stockholders, but continued to fund expansion programs with re-invested profits.

All in the Family: The Second Generation Comes on Board.
The six founders remaining after the 1962 shakeup took a look at the future. All were married with children, and insofar as was possible,

each family began to place one to two of their children into appropriate companies. The current lineup follows:

> HIRAM L. FONG:
>> Marvin Fong—Finance Factors, Ltd.; Finance Realty, Ltd.
>> Merie-Ellen Fong Gushi—Grand Pacific Life Insurance Company, Ltd.

> FONG CHOY:
>> Patrick Fong—Finance Insurance, Ltd.

> MUN ON CHUN:
>> Patrick Chun—Finance Home Builders, Ltd.

> DANIEL B. T. LAU:
>> Russell Lau—Finance Factors, Ltd.
>> Jeffrey D. Lau—Finance Factors, Ltd.; Finance Realty, Ltd.; Grand Pacific Life Insurance Company, Ltd.

> LUP QUON PANG:
>> Wendell Pang—Finance Factors, Ltd.

> CLIFFORD H. N. YEE:
>> Valerie Yee—Finance Factors, Ltd.

Conclusion. Did the founders of Finance Factors, Ltd. succeed mainly because of their Chinese heritage? The evidence does not bear this out. As the Companies developed along their several but related lines, the Directors found it more and more to their advantage to keep control within their families. Thus, a well-qualified individual like a son of Dr. Pang's, Wendell Pang, was brought in for specific training before moving into the presidency of Finance Factors, Ltd. Their personnel policies and practices supported the hiring, retention, and advancement of all employees without regard to ethnicity or religious persuasion. While a high premium was placed on employees' loyalty, hard work and dedication, these qualities were also demanded of the Directors and management. This is not unique to Finance Enterprises. The same qualities are valued by successful companies owned and operated by other nationalities all over the world. Finance Enterprises' newsletters and press releases never publicize the Chinese ancestry of the surviving founders, although it's apparent from their pictures and their names. Even their charitable donations show no distinctively ethnic bias.

The phrase "Family of Companies" is (1) an effective play on words to describe and to show appreciation for the parent company/child subsidiary relationship and (2) while specific to

Finance Enterprises, Ltd., it is not unique in concept to Chinese corporations because many other companies foster similarly strong bonds among owners/management/employees.

In establishing the Family of Companies, the founders and directors of Finance Factors were following good Western business practices. While they were perhaps more comfortable doing business with others who share their Chineseness, nonetheless they engaged in endeavors to capitalize on the profit/benefit/service mode rather than on ancestral grounds. The 40-year-old success story of Finance Enterprises, Ltd.—the Family of Companies—is for all intents and purposes a good ole Yankee success story that proves "Families make good business."

Works Cited

"A Day in Makakilo." Finance Realty insert in the *Sunday Star-Bulletin & Advertiser*, 19 July 1992.

"The Finance Factors Story." Advertisement in the *Sunday Star-Bulletin & Advertiser* 5 July 1992: F12.

Chou, Michaelyn P. "The Education of a Senator: Hiram L. Fong from 1906 to 1954." Unpublished Ph.D. dissertation, University of Hawaii, 1980. 655, 662.

Finance Factors, Ltd. News releases, 6 July 1967, 1 April 1970, 20 April 1971, 21 April 1971, n.d. probably 1975.

Finance Factors, Ltd. Newsletters, August 1990, January 1991.

Finance Factors, Ltd. *The First Fifteen*. Honolulu: Finance Factors, Ltd., 1967. 5.

Finance Family 3(1) (January 1962): 1.

Finance Family 3(1) (January 1962): 4.

Fong, Hiram L., Honolulu, Hawaii. Oral history interview. 6 April 1977.

Fong, Hiram L., Honolulu, Hawaii. Telephone interview. 6 June 1992.

Fong, Hiram L., Honolulu, Hawaii. Telephone interview. 29 July 1992.

Fong, Hiram. "The First Fifteen Years of Finance Factors." *Hawaii Business and Industry* 12(10) (April 1967): 29–32.

Grand Pacific Life Insurance Company, Ltd. Press releases, 23 September 1965, 15 April 1968, 17 September 1980.

Hawaii (Ter.) Treasury Dept. [Application] No. 4735D1, 12 April 1952.

Honolulu Advertiser 19 August 1971.

Honolulu Star-Bulletin 8 December 1986: A13, 15 August 1952: A1, 15 August 1952: A1.

Honolulu Star-Bulletin, vol. 38, no. 2 (August 1992): 115.

Lau, Daniel B. T. President William McKinley High School Hall of Honor nomination form, 1992.

Lau, Daniel B. T., Honolulu, Hawaii. Personal interview. January 1992.

Zalburg, Sanford. *The Spark Is Struck!* Honolulu: University Press of Hawaii, 1979. 453.

Trailing the Feng Shui Master:
Some Basics and Case Studies

ANGI MA WONG

Chinese Historical Society of Southern California, Los Angeles, California

Two men were taking a walk through an exclusive Southern California development. As they stopped in front of one particularly attractive house, the younger of the men turned to the other, "Master, here is my new house, what do you think?" His companion took a long look at the house, then turned around, looking around to scrutinize the neighboring buildings.

"Your home is acceptable," he told the first man.

"But will I prosper here?"

"You will do fine," came the reply, "but your house is across the street."

The younger man stared unbelievingly, for he had dismissed the house in question as being smaller and far less desirable than his new home.

"You will achieve a great wealth should you buy that house," insisted the master.

The next day, the young man bought the house across the street.

Throughout communities with large Asian populations, non-Asian businesses are learning about *feng shui*. One cannot be involved in real estate or building in the West without having heard about deals that were made and canceled, appointments and escrow closings that were rescheduled, or contracts that were never signed due to mysterious reasons. *Feng shui* is responsible for a good many of those reasons.

What is *feng shui*? In the introduction of her book *Feng Shui: A Layman's Guide to Chinese Geomancy*, Evelyn Lip explains:

> Geomancy is defined as the art of divining the future for good or ill fortune, from the figure suggested by dots or lines placed at random on the earth's surface. It is said that the fortunes of men depend on how well their ancestors were buried with respect to geomancy and also how correctly their own dwellings were built with respect to orientation, planning, construction, etc. according to *feng shui* or geomancy. The words *feng shui* in Chinese mean the wind and the water. It stands for the power of the natural environment—the wind and the air of the mountains and hills; the streams and the rain; and the composite influences of the natural processes.

Derek Walters' *The Feng Shui Handbook* states:

> The principles of Feng Shui are based on precepts laid down thousands of years ago in the Chinese classics, particularly the *Li Shu*, or *Book of Rites*, a sacred book that enshrines the basic tenets of Chinese religious belief. It is concerned with order, the harmony of heaven and earth, and with the ways in which humanity can best keep the balance of nature intact.

Comingled with geography and astronomy is the influence of Taoism. Everything in the world is changing, inter-related, complementary, and interdependent. Yin and yang, dark and light, hard and soft, male and female—the universe is an entity composed of two equal but opposite parts. Nothing moves or happens without affecting something else ... the basic law of physics and the wisdom of Chinese ancients.

When trying to explain the most basic concept of *feng shui*, one example particularly comes to mind. A person might think about the home in which he lives now and remember the period prior during which he went apartment-hunting or house-shopping. He may have walked through five, ten or even twenty places, but how did the person ultimately decide which he wanted to be his home? In addition to the obvious reasons of locations and price, what was the final determining factor?

The answer is that he *felt* as if he belonged there, and to borrow an expression from the 1960s ... the *vibes* were right. Those same "vibes" or karma are affected by the terrain, the flora and fauna, the spiritual, events, and the shape of property.

Feng shui is based on the belief that balance and harmony can be achieved on one's physical self and environment through proper manipulation. It melds an intimate knowledge of geography and astronomy with philosophy, religion, folk wisdom, and common sense. Its main component is *ch'i*, the cosmic energy that connects all living things with the land and which can be manipulated to harmonize with nature. The character *ch'i* in the Chinese language can be translated into English as "air" or "energy." It is believed that this universal energy exists in the contours and terrain of the land and in all living things.

In nature, *ch'i* is the flowing energy that flows through the land which can be altered for better or worse by man-made modifications such as roads, tunnels, and buildings. Other interior and exterior structural features that are taken into consideration of good or bad *feng shui* are pillars, chimneys, posts, roofs, flagpoles, doors, windows, beams, walls—all elements of any building. In homes and offices, it can be interpreted as air circulation. In some buildings, the air is stagnant; in others, there are drafts. Too much or too little *ch'i* is undesirable and unhealthy. By applying the principles of *feng shui*, any construction can enhance the prosperity and growth of an area; if ignored, calamities and disaster will befall.

The opposite of *ch'i* is *sha*, a negative, noxious force which is represented by straight lines, roads, or corners of buildings directed toward other buildings, in which case it is called an *arrow*. A structure which is sited at the base of two roads forming the letter T is subject to such negative energy, e.g., the White House! "Band-Aids" to offset *sha* or improve or redirect *ch'i* are mirrors, plants, wind chimes, aquariums, screens, ponds, fountains, and in extreme cases, walls.

Many examples of *feng shui* principles abound in Chinese communities throughout the country. From 1788 when the Chinese first settled in Hawaii, Chinatown streets and structures throughout the United States were constructed under the influence of this ancient practice. In the 1990s, *feng shui* is evidenced in the Buddhist temple located in Hacienda Heights, the Hong Kong Fragrant Garden Restaurant in Millbrae, and Ming's Restaurant in Palo Alto, to name a few. A walk down the street in any major Chinatown, U.S.A., and one might count many eight-sided mirrors to repel evil placed over the main entrances of various businesses.

Did the architect and the landscaper for the Torrance offices of the *Daily Breeze* know about the "killing arrow"? The building is situated at the point where two streets meet in a "T". Palos Verdes Boulevard points to the building and ends, directing *sha* right at the two-story structure. However, at least three outstanding features deflect the negative energy thought to be rushing toward the building. First, there is a monument-like small structure constructed of Palos Verdes stone, on which are anchored the numbers of the publication's street address.

Secondly, a pond with rushing water, a waterfall, and a ring of water spouts is sited directly in front of the main doors. Last, but not least, are three tall flagpoles which could direct any adverse currents up and away from the building.

Traditionally, a spot which features a mountain behind, two smaller hills to the sides, with a wide view in front is considered having auspicious *feng shui*, similar to the seat of an armchair. Preferably the front view includes water in some form—a river, ocean, or lake—for water equates to wealth. In Southern California, the most sought-after property is located in Palos Verdes, Beverly Hills, the hills of Glendale-La Canada-Flintridge area, Malibu, Spyglass Hill overlooking Fashion Island in Newport Beach, and more recently, Rowland Heights, Hacienda Heights, and Walnut. All of these areas boast higher elevations with an expansive view in the front. A drive around your own city or just examining a road or topographical map can reveal the most auspicious areas.

There have been no surveys taken as to what percentage of the Asian population believe or practice geomancy, but a Chinese architect based in Monterey Park estimated that over 80% of his clients believe in *feng shui*. His office building was designed under the supervision of a geomancer and his staff jockeyed for the best office location in the new building expansion. Danny Chang, a realtor in the San Gabriel area of Southern California, thinks that 70% of the people he shows homes to embrace this doctrine. Others believe it's only superstition.

Although *feng shui* originated in China thousands of years ago, its followers can be found not only in Chinese-speaking communities worldwide, but also in Japan, Vietnam, Singapore, Malaysia, and Korea. In the United States, advertisements in Chinese-language newspapers and magazines publicizing the services of one master or another are common. But not every homebuyer of Asian descent believes in *feng shui*. Much depends on whether a person is a new immigrant, what his religious background is, how much and the kind of education he has, how traditionally he was brought up, and a myriad of other factors.

"Wind-water doctors," as they are also called, may charge by the square footage of a house or the property to be assessed, by a flat fee, or not at all. In the last case, the owner of the property may pass along gift money in the form of cash inside a lucky red envelope. By using a special compass called a *luopan*, the geomancer can determine the most favorable orientation for a person's home and/or business. Many geomancers in the United States are ordinary folks who are already in another profession—for example, teaching or Chinese medicine. Some are born with psychic abilities; others study for many years to learn their craft from "master teachers."

Basically, there are two "levels" of belief. For example, most people want the feeling of harmony and balance in one's life and trust their "gut feel" or "sixth sense" which tells them the furniture looks and feels better positioned a certain way in a room or if something doesn't *feel* right. On the other hand, a person who believes fervently in *feng shui* will hire a "wind-water doctor" to make calculations based on his birth date, hour, year, and place. This person most likely will not make a personal or financial move without a consultation. While there are many general guidelines, *feng shui* can also be highly individualized and personalized.

A businessman from Taiwan who was building a 30,000 square foot home in Palos Verdes costing $15 million took no chances. Not content with just a second opinion, he consulted *six* geomancers and paid for their transportation from Hong Kong and Taiwan to inspect his property before one handful of soil moved. The six advisors came to one major consensus which became a nightmare for the man's architect: west was unlucky and all water had to drain in that direction. Moreover, no windows were permitted to face west in the new home.

Mr. Wu, an engineer who grew up in Hong Kong and has lived in the Los Angeles area for over 25 years, is not a believer, but his mother is. Wu was involved in a terrible automobile accident several years ago in which he almost died. His mother engaged a *feng shui* master to assess her son's home. The master proclaimed the Wu's residence was good for the mistress of the house but not the master. Furthermore, the geomancer calculated that the most auspicious direction for his client would be 15 degrees east.

When Wu decided on a parcel of land on which to build his new home, the geomancer was consulted again. Because a tree in the neighbor's back yard and a streetlight in front formed an invisible line that dissected the proposed footprint in two, calamity was predicted. But Wu liked the neighborhood and the community, so proceeded to spend over $6,000 in architectural fees and permits to re-situate the house on site. The master bedroom was designed so that at sunrise, the rays coming through a window would be directed exactly at Wu's bed. The right side of the house, being the *male* side, had to be larger than the left side, considered *female*. The original plans for a nine-foot ceiling in the living room were changed so that the new vaulted ceiling would increase the volume, and therefore "his" influence over "hers." Finally, a fishpond was constructed outside one wall of the house.

A second professional, Mr. Lin, was a manufacturer in Hong Kong before he recently immigrated to California. As a former classmate of Wu, Lin bought a home in the same development so he and his family could be close to their friends. After putting a deposit on his new home, Lin returned to Hong Kong to settle his affairs, one of which was to consult his favorite *feng shui* master. The master informed Lin that he would have many obstacles in the course of purchasing his home, but it was a financially advantageous move for him. In this house, Lin's personal wealth would be such that "he would be picking up gold nuggets from the ground."

Using a rough floorplan sketched by Mrs. Lin as a guide, the geomancer then indicated which rooms would be assigned to which members of Lin's family to ensure the good fortune and health. Every major piece of furniture was designated to a specific location within a room—nothing was overlooked or left to chance. Lin was then instructed as to the exact date that he should move the master bed into his new home and also when the landscaping on the front yard had to be completed.

True to the geomancer's prediction, Lin did experience a great deal of trouble obtaining a loan during the spring of 1991. His wife and daughter became ill during the first several weeks after their move into their new house. More recently, Mrs. Lin has consulted the master again for advice on how to improve marital harmony in the home. She claims that she and her husband have fought daily since they moved in!

Feng shui masters are often consulted when businesses and stores are established. Such was the case when a Gardena manufacturing firm relocated from its old offices three blocks away to a building it had purchased. An advisor was engaged by a friend of the company's partners to make recommendations to ensure prosperity for the business.

The evaluation took two hours in the empty shell of the building as well as the outside property. From the accounting department to the president's office, from the factory floor to the atrium garden—every room was assessed and assigned according to *feng shui*. It was determined that because the company was the fourth tenant since the construction of the building and the three previous businesses had not done well at this particular location, unique solutions were required.

The advisor found that there were too many references to death or the number four which in Chinese is a homonym for "to die." Four benches were on the front patio, this company was the fourth to occupy the building, four steps led from the offices to the fishpond, and the two recessed space hiding the light fixtures resembled open gravesites. To offset the bad luck, numbers six and nine were employed throughout. Six large potted plants were placed along the window in the triangular-shaped foyer, three on each side of the main door. Six pieces of outdoor furniture were situated on the front patio and six indoor plants decorated the interior's main corridor.

In the room that was designated to become the accounting office, all desks were advised to face toward the two doors, and the president's was positioned so that it was perpendicular to the window and forty-five degrees from the angled door leading into the room. Advice was given on the placement of furniture in every office, from sales to engineering.

Generally the overall comments were positive or neutral as the advisor made his way through the building until he reached the end of the wide corridor to a glass door which led out to a Japanese garden with a fish pond. Immediately, he became quite agitated and in a space of one moment, the positive comments were canceled.

"The pond is a bad influence," he stated. "First of all, it requires four steps from the door to the edge of the pond. Secondly, the shape is that of a Chinese cleaver, but the cutting edge is facing the back wall of the garden instead of toward the door.

"Furthermore, the handle part of this pond should be blocked off and filled up so that the shape becomes a harmless rectangle. In addition, the water is stagnant (dead), representing a stalling of business. The garden is overgrown and neglected as is the pond. Both need to be cleaned up and a pump installed so that the water is moving. If business continues to be poor, the pond should be completely filled and an aquarium with fish should be placed next to the window facing the garden.

"Finally," he concluded, "on either December 18 at 9:45 p.m. or January 9 at 6:09 p.m., six or nine large black fish should be placed in the pond. These fish will portend the business success of the company so if they become ill or die, the handle part of the pond should be blocked off and filled as soon as possible. If business still does not improve or gets worse, the entire pond should be filled. This location has potential, but it could be manifested either in explosive growth and prosperity or total failure. It is a tricky spot so even the moving date should be carefully chosen."

While the owners of the business did not put the fish in the pond on the required time and date, they nevertheless filled the handle of the pond as well as change the water and relandscaped the garden. From all recent accounts, the business is thriving.

Reprinted with permission from author from *Chinese American Forum*; also excerpted chapter from author's book *TARGET: The U.S. Asian Market, A Practical Guide to Doing Business* ©, published by Pacific Heritage Books, 1993; second printing 1994.

News from the Underground:
History and Archaeology
Meet at the Station

ROBERTA S. GREENWOOD
Greenwood & Associates, Pacific Palisades, California

It is a pleasure to preview with you the highlights of recent discoveries in Los Angeles' first Chinatown. It is particularly appropriate to bring the news to a conference like this, since it is only due to the historians, Chinese Historical Society of Southern California, many other experts and scholars, and so many other interested parties that this work took place. It is in conjunction with this kind of interdisciplinary approach that the results are being interpreted.

The story begins with history, both of Chinatown and of the railroad station. The Union Station that you may have entered on this trip is not the first one built in Los Angeles; there had been three before this, in different locations. By 1915, the city was concerned about the dangers of many grade crossings and was eager to consolidate service by the three railroads which came into L.A. Fierce battles ensued between many different interests about where to locate the new station, and the question was only finally settled by the U.S. Supreme Court in 1931. The land was acquired and the property was cleared by 1934. The location was old Chinatown.

When planning for Metro Rail began in the early 1980s, the law required certain procedures to identify, preserve, or recover any significant archaeological (or paleontological) resources affected by construction. Before such regulations and guidelines, many other Chinatown sites all over California and the West were simply destroyed. In Downtown Los Angeles, some of the very earliest Chinese deposits in and around the Pueblo were already lost. Some remains of Old Chinatown were exposed during the construction of the San Bernardino Freeway in 1951, but no law then required any attention, and the remains were disregarded as "just trash." Many of the reports generated from the earlier digs illustrated only the whole, or more glamorous items, and didn't consider what the items meant within the total way of life.

Our work for Metro Rail began in 1987, monitoring during construction. The real archaeology began when construction reached the Union Station property. Preliminary historical research had demonstrated that the railroad tracks were actually built on top of 14 feet of fill, so Chinatown was probably still there, although deeply buried. Historical maps provided the location and names of the old streets, buildings, and even house numbers. By computer magic, the old plot plans were overlaid on current streets, Union Station, and the Metro Rail right-of-way so that we could know exactly where we were—110 years ago.

But this was hardly a leisurely excavation. The construction contractor had his own tight schedule and priorities; he even had to move the railroad tracks from day to day to keep the trains running while building the Metro Rail tunnels and station right under the passengers' feet. We were limited to brief periods of time and had limited access. In one area, for example, our work space was so small that a backhoe had to be lowered into the 14-foot hole by a crane. In another, a bridge was built right over our heads, reducing the stand-up space below it to only four feet. The general hubbub of massive equipment being used all around us, the roar and rumble of trains passing over our heads, and the amusement of construction workers running their huge machines while we dug out fragile porcelains with a dental pick—memorable sidelights.

But beneath the 14 feet of fill, Chinatown was still there. A layer of brick rubble, with some walls and foundations intact, marked the demolition, and below that were streets and sidewalks, 57 separate features, and an incredible volume of artifacts from only a very small space. Just to suggest some idea of the quantities, over 2000 stoneware jars used to ship foods, oils, wine, grains, and even cosmetics were found. Of these, 800 contained wine, 350 soy sauce, 350 pickled vegetables or dried fish, 80 were very large (over two feet) for bulk products, and 400 were lids to these jars. We have tallied about 800 rice bowls (sorted by pattern), 450 large serving bowls, 400 tea bowls, 400 soup spoons, 90 teapots, 140 toothbrushes, 160 dominoes, 600 medicinal vials which held herbal remedies or pills, and 370 Asian coins. Less dramatic in quantity, but of great interpretive value, were the children's toys, women's jewelry and shoes, Chinese ink stone and many American glass ink bottles, works of sculpture in stone and clay, and ceremonial candlesticks and incense burners. Last, but not least, were the abundant food remains, from bone to eggshells to fish scales, and the cleavers and clay stoves used to prepare them.

Analyzing a collection of this size and diversity is truly an interdisciplinary endeavor, enlisting the expertise of specialists in glass beads, coins, and seeds, and specialists in mammal, bird, fish, and reptile bones. For insight into some of the artifacts and for translations, we are deeply grateful to professors from UCLA and Sheng Du University (Szechuan Province), and to special friends of the Chinese Historical Society of Southern California.

From the beginning of Chinese sites archaeology, certain truisms had been accepted: that the national origin of things Chinese could be readily recognized even when the function was not apparent; that settlements were spatially limited and populations unmixed; that the quantity of cultural material was usually very high; that dating artifacts which were very conservative in form, pattern, and technology was difficult, and that women were few or absent. The primary assumption was that the people maintained the traditional way of life, manifest most obviously in the preparation and consumption of food, various forms of recreation, and the healing arts. For the early sites of the Gold Rush, this was explained as largely a matter of choice, since the argonauts did not expect, nor wish, to remain permanently, and thus lacked incentives to adapt. But for later communities, it has been explained, in part, as a response to the prejudice and persecution amply documented in the historical resources.

Let's look at a few of these assumptions. The statement that women were few in number is true—but it must be considered in the context of the state, or nation, as a whole. Certainly, the immigrants of the Gold Rush were predominantly men who left wives and children at home while they sought their fortune in the mines. But then the labor force in the mines, railroad camps, or agricultural fields would be male, no matter what the national origin of the workers. In 1850, prior to the greatest immigration of Chinese, there were 12 men to every woman in California, and a more accurate census in the remote mining regions would probably have been even more unbalanced. The scarcity of European American women was, in fact, the reason why Chinese men were at first welcomed so heartily to work in laundries, restaurants, and domestic service. In 1870, the overall sex ratio was 20–1 for the whole state; in this broader context, the ratio of Chinese men was much less remarkable.

Women and children were most certainly present, increasing in numbers through time. Archaeologically, we find the marbles, dolls, and other toys of boys and girls, and also women's cosmetics, jewelry, and clothing parts. Kindergartens and schools were established by the 1880s for Chinese children by church missions and women's service clubs, in Los Angeles as well as San Francisco and Ventura. As families were formed, of course, more and more of the young people were born in America. In 1890, of the 1871 Chinese in Los Angeles, only 2% were native born. In 1900, 10% of the 2111 Chinese were born here, and by 1910, 24% were born here.

Another stereotype is that all the Chinese were unskilled laborers and that the culture was rigid and unchanging. Actually, there were distinctions between the more and less prosperous, rural and urban areas, large and small settlements, and most particularly, there were distinctions through time. At first, those who came to the city after the railroads were completed monopolized truck gardening, raising and peddling most of the vegetables and fruit consumed in Los Angeles. This changed for several reasons. As large-scale corporate agriculture emerged in the San Joaquin Valley, many of the Chinese growers turned to wholesale brokering. Furthermore, the Chinese who arrived later in the century was a different kind of immigrant—in place of origin, economic status, and intention to remain. Especially after the turn of the century, many came from the newly emerging capitalist middle class in China, many from Shanghai or the industrial and commercial districts. Many were speakers of Mandarin, rather than Cantonese, and together with the second- or third-generation residents who had achieved some measure of advancement, they formed a new elite and added to the stratification of Chinese Americans. Chinese archaeological sites can no longer be treated as all the same, or as lacking in distinctions which can be traced through historical and archaeological sources.

In the 1880s, there were 60 licensed Chinese vegetable peddlers, the principal occupation. But in 1900, census records for the block of Apablaza Street where we worked revealed the following occupations: 12 professionals (doctors, teachers, druggists, and interpreters), 59 business owners (14 types of enterprise), 119 persons engaged in sales (store clerks and peddlers), and 184 wage earners in places such as laundries, barber shops, and cigar factories. There were also two fortune tellers. There were 184 shops in Chinatown, most with living quarters behind or above.

The crowded conditions and general appearance of the community were typical of most Chinatowns. They usually developed on property considered undesirable by others: near the ports and docks (San Diego and San Francisco), near the railroad station (Boston, Pittsburgh, or St. Louis), and on lands subject to flooding or of low value (Ventura and Los Angeles). The Los Angeles Chinatown was near the smoky, smelly gas plant, adjacent to the noisy, sooty, and dangerous railroad tracks, with only two of the existing 13 streets and 22 alleys paved. Those who prospered moved out and dispersed throughout the city, their places filled by new arrivals.

There were certain regularities in the architecture. The structures most often had high, steeply pitched gable roofs, and they maximized the use of space by subdividing the blocks. The buildings were long from front to back, but narrow, so that as many shops as possible would face the street. Balconies on two-story buildings were another device to increase the usable space, as it is still done in China. In Los Angeles, where lumber was scarce, brick dwellings replaced the early adobes. Typically, houses were flush with the street, with no front yards, and they were contiguous so that property lines were not visible.

Inside, the rooms had no other light or ventilation beyond what penetrated from the front. There was no provision for heating, and only a few had either gas or electricity—none of the property was owned by Chinese. This was in 1922. The crowded conditions are suggested by the fact that in San Francisco Chinatown, as late as World War II, an average of 21 persons shared each bathroom and 13 shared each kitchen. In Los Angeles, a typical boardinghouse had 32 tiny, dark rooms on one side of a narrow center hall, and 34 on the other. One community kitchen, often outdoors between two buildings, would be shared by the tenants. Finally, the local school principal described that "hundreds of men" slept in the corrals at night, sharing space with the horses and the produce to be peddled the next day.

The census and other kinds of historical data can be used to compile far more than only population numbers, addresses, and occupations. For example, the transition to giving the children European American first names is another symbol of acculturation, if not a result of pressure from the schools. Well into the 1930s, burial records still show the use of Chinese names. But the kinds of behaviors, traditions, or customs continued are not apt to be found in formal written histories, which is how archaeology contributes to a more accurate total picture.

The Union Station site is particularly important for research because the settlement was not a reoccupation of older buildings, and it was not used later by any other group. It was built on previously vacant land, and it existed intact and unmixed until it was destroyed in the 1930s. Obviously, the deep fill, railroad station, and tracks have preserved the remains from looting or other disturbances ever since. Some of the research questions are whether the ratios of Chinese to American ceramics, medicines, and foodstuffs increased or decreased over the years; whether the use of imports from the homeland reflected availability of alternate goods, or was a deliberate choice as a means of maintaining group identity; whether the goods shipped into Los Angeles were different in type or place of origin from those which came through the ports of Mexico or the northwest, and the extent to which assimilation can be measured through some combination of history, archaeology, and other disciplines.

Our consultants have said that their interest is in the Chinese experience in America. Those who have more recently arrived, and from countries other than China, know little of this. The American-born are as much as a century removed from the experience; the elders who might recall are mostly gone. Most are eager to teach the children about the past, reclaim their place in local history, and see in the archaeological record both the proof of their presence and illustration of their way of life. There is some irony in the thought that while the archaeologist may be looking for some measures of acculturation, the Chinese community is searching for what made them separate and distinctive. The goals are not incompatible, however, and it is a distinct pleasure to think that we are giving back the lost generations to the population being studied.

There are still more intact deposits at Union Station, should future construction pose an impact. Even inside the station itself, work on an elevator shaft, indoors, encountered one trash pit substantially below the present floor. Some of the artifacts are already on exhibit in Downtown, and we are preparing a full and lengthy descriptive report on both the history and archaeology. It is through such unmixed deposits and interdisciplinary studies that research can advance in recognizing the dates, types, and places of origin of both the artifacts and their owners—and in applying the material culture to illustrate the non-material aspects of life.

The Archaeology of Chinese Sites in Arizona

JAMES E. AYRES
Tucson, Arizona

Interest in the archaeology and history of Chinese Americans in Arizona has been manifest for a relatively long time. It really began with the advent of a serious interest in historic sites archaeology across the country and its formal development as a separate field of inquiry in the late 1960s. This interest was energized to a great extent by Arizona studies, especially the classic 1959–1960 Johnny Ward's Ranch project (Fontana and Greenleaf 1962). In its later life, the ranch was a Chinese occupied site, but only two Chinese porcelain cup fragments were found there. These supported historical documents that suggested the presence of at least six Chinese males on the site between 1886 and 1903.

The passing of the Historic Preservation Act of 1966 also spurred an interest in historic sites archaeology, but it was not until 1974, several years after it was passed, that regulations were finally implemented and the act became effective. It and subsequent legislation led to a burgeoning, contract-oriented archaeology that today accounts for nearly all of the historic sites archaeology performed in the United States. Most of the archaeology of Chinese sites in the United States is a direct result of federal historic preservation legislation.

In Arizona, only the Johnny Ward's Ranch study and the urban renewal project in Tucson, which was begun in 1967, were not affected by this legislation because they predated its implementation. All subsequent historic sites projects are a direct result of it.

Most of Chinese site archaeology in Arizona has been carried out in urban areas (Tucson: Ayres 1968; Tempe: Stone and Ayres 1985, and Phoenix: Rogge, Keane, Luckingham, Ayres, Patterson and Bostwick 1992), although some have been performed in rural settings. The Stone and Fedick study of the Mobile railroad construction camp (1990) and the San Bernardino Ranch survey by Stone and Ayres (1982) are the major examples of Chinese rural sites. The Mobile camp, located in west central Arizona, is a Chinese railroad work camp dating to the 1890s, and the San Bernardino site, located in the southeastern part of the state within a few feet of the Mexican border, includes the ruins of a Chinese-occupied house that was in use from at least 1905 to 1915. Both sites were recorded, mapped and dated; limited excavation was performed at the Mobile site.

All five of these projects have provided some insight into the Chinese in Arizona, their lifestyles, occupations, artifacts, level of acculturation and assimilation, and so on; but they obviously do not fully reflect the distribution of Chinese in Arizona, nor do they necessarily reflect the diversity present.

Other rural and urban Chinese sites are known throughout the state, but no archaeological or historical studies have been made of them.

Chinese individuals are known in Arizona from the 1860s. There are no records of their presence before 1863; by 1868, 20 individuals are known to have been at work at the Vulture Mine near Wickenburg (Fong 6). There were 21 men and no women listed in the 1870 federal census for Arizona, and by 1880 the census recorded 1630 Chinese, the majority of whom were employed in the construction of the Southern Pacific Railroad (Keane et al. 15).

Chinese could be found in every Arizona community of any consequence after about 1880; in every major, and many minor, mining camps; on large ranches; in construction camps, and many other places throughout the state. Their distribution across the state was much wider in the late 19th and early 20th century than it is today. Today, the vast majority of Arizona's Chinese residents live in an urban location. The reasons for this rural to urban migration would make an interesting research project.

Next, I want to review, in more detail, two of the largest Arizona projects, that in Tucson and the one recently completed in Phoenix.

Tucson. The site of Tucson was first settled by Europeans in 1775 when the Spanish erected a presidio, or fort, on the east side of the Santa Cruz River in what today is the downtown area.

The first record of Chinese in Tucson occurs about 100 years later in the mid-1870s; by 1879, 30 Chinese were reported in the city (Lister and Lister 1). No Chinese were listed on the 1870 federal census, but while this document may be correct, one should not always accept the census as being totally accurate during this period. The 1880 census lists 160 Chinese, the 1900 census lists 222, and the 1910 census lists 257. The coming of the railroad in 1880 is credited with the influx of Chinese in that year.

The center of the Chinese population in Tucson from about 1880 to about 1910 was on the north edge of the business district around the intersection of Main Avenue and Alameda Street. After 1910, when the Chinese moved from this area, the population became more dispersed, but with part of it concentrated on one block located south of Broadway Street between Main and Meyer avenues on the south edge of the downtown business district. Despite the tendency to cluster, at no time was there a stereotypical "Chinatown" in Tucson. A greater or lesser percentage of the Chinese population was always scattered throughout the business district and elsewhere within the community.

The Tucson archaeological project began in 1967 as a result of a Federal Department of Housing and Urban Development-sponsored urban renewal project in the downtown area, which destroyed hundreds of historic buildings and their associated subsurface archaeological remains. The archaeology project was initiated by the late Dr. William Wasley of the Arizona State Museum, University of Arizona, who turned it over to me shortly after he organized it. I expanded the project, defined its scope and goals, and directed it until 1973, when it was brought to a close.

The project was undertaken at a time when there was virtually no interest in historic site archaeological resources at the professional level at the University where I worked, and literally none at the city level, except for the City of Tucson's Director of the Tucson Urban Renewal Administration. So the project was conducted with minimal cooperation for six years, but we managed to study early Tucson architecture before it was destroyed and collected about one million artifacts dating from the Spanish period to about 1920. During the project, over 200 wells, privies, and trash dumps were excavated within a 39-city-block area by nearly 300 student and other volunteers.

Approximately 25 of the excavation units were from formerly occupied Chinese properties. One of the very first excavations was a Chinese trash dump dating to the 1890s. This large deposit generated an interest in Tucson's Chinese and led us to search intensively for others during the course of the project.

The Chinese proveniences were of two types. One was privies, wells, and small trash dumps containing buried deposits that were excavated, and the other was a recently abandoned residential and former business complex owned by the Ying On Merchants and Labor Benevolent Association, where numerous artifacts were collected from a number of rooms and from excavations. The privies, wells, and dumps are common urban archaeological features that produced Chinese ceramics, opium smoking paraphernalia, glass gaming pieces, brass buttons, and occasionally other Chinese-made glass and metal artifacts of all types. For the most part, the Chinese artifacts were the common types widely seen and reported throughout California and the other western states.

Of particular interest are the artifacts that were collected from the Ying On property, which covered approximately three-quarters of a city block south of Broadway Street, between Main and Meyer avenues. The complex consisted of a series of contiguous adobe buildings around a large central courtyard. Those on Main Avenue were originally used for business purposes, and the others were used as residences.

Included within the complex of 51 rooms, some of which had been abandoned for decades, were large quantities of ordinary trash, furniture, cooking utensils and other household goods, and personal effects. Many of these abandoned items were of Chinese manufacture or were made especially for the Chinese market. More specifically, these items in the collection were traditional Chinese clothing, ceramics, household goods, musical instruments, banners and flags, objects relating to gambling, medicine, writing implements, pillows, large lacquered trunks with brass fittings, business records, photographs, immigration records, and many, many others. Also found were hundreds of artifacts related to opium smoking from China, Hong Kong, Macao and Mexico, and several that were homemade. All the Chinese-related material was systematically collected. The artifacts from the Ying On property dated from about World War I to the early 1960s. While the excavated Chinese artifacts are identical in most cases to those found elsewhere in the West, the artifacts recovered from the Ying On property remain an unique collection (Lister and Lister 1989).

Phoenix. The City of Phoenix was first settled in the late 1860s, and the original town site was platted in 1870. The first Chinese in Phoenix arrived there in the early 1870s, about the same time as they came to Tucson; they appear to have settled near the north end of the present central business district at First and Adams streets. This area was ultimately designated "Chinese Quarters" on the 1893 Sanborn map for Phoenix. As in Tucson, this group moved after several years to a new location. This was accomplished in 1895 when the center of the population moved a few blocks south to the First and Madison streets area, which, at least by 1915, was known as "China Alley" (Rogge et al. Table 2-1). The move was forced by non-Chinese Phoenix businessmen (Keane et al. 45). What prompted the similar move in Tucson is uncertain, but most likely it had to do with changing ownership of property. The Phoenix Chinese were not all located in the "China Alley" area, but were thinly scattered throughout the rest of the community as well.

By 1872, there were two Chinese men in Phoenix who ran a laundry, and by 1880 the population had risen to 109. Many of these individuals, mostly men, undoubtedly came to Phoenix as a result of the construction of the Southern Pacific Railroad in that year. In 1880, the Chinese accounted for 4% of the total population of the relatively new community of Phoenix. At the same time, Tucson's Chinese residents represented only 2% of its population. Phoenix' Chinese population increased to 200 by 1890, but by 1910 it had decreased to only 110, after which it began a steady rise, never again to decline (Rogge et al. Table 2-1; Keane et al. 35). The reasons behind the temporary decline after 1890 are uncertain, but anti-Chinese activities in the community during the 1890s probably are at least partially responsible.

The Phoenix archaeological project, conducted by archaeologists from Dames and Moore, Inc., was the latest effort in Arizona to excavate an area of former Chinese businesses and habitations; in this case, "China Alley," the second "Chinatown." This project originated as a result of plans to construct the America West Sports Arena on the site, which encompassed all or parts of four city-blocks. These blocks, characterized as an area of declining commercial activities, once contained numerous commercial and residential buildings, most of which had been demolished some years before the project began. Only one building, the Chinese-owned Sun Mercantile building, was saved.

The project was carried out in several phases. The first, performed in 1989, evaluated all or parts of six city-blocks for possible subsurface remains, using historical records such as the Sanborn fire insurance maps. Because remains were expected to be present, a second phase was performed in early 1990, that of carrying out archaeological test excavations within four city-blocks and preparing a report that would provide recommendations for mitigation of the impacts to the important subsurface remains. In July and August 1990, there was excavation of selected features to recover artifacts and information about the remains of historic architecture. Excavated were 34 privies, wells, and trash dumps.

The Phoenix Department of Community and Economic Development funded the first three phases. Unfortunately, no funding from that agency was made available for analyzing the artifacts and for the preparation of a final report. Ultimately, limited funding was found by matching City Historic Preservation funds with a State Historic Preservation Office (SHPO)/Certified Local Government (CLG) grant and with donations from the Phoenix Chinese community. Limited funding at this level allowed intensive analysis of only 13 of the 34 excavated features (Rogge et al. i, iii). Additionally, the remaining features were quickly "canned" for some information. The three-volume final report is currently in draft form.

In the 13 features were over 17,000 whole and fragmentary artifacts representing an estimated minimum of nearly 7,000 objects. The faunal assemblage from all 34 features included nearly 9,000 pieces of bone. Only about 120 Chinese-made artifacts, more than 40 Japanese-made ceramic items, 20 Mexican-made ceramic vessels, and over 120 Pima Indian ceramic vessels, including water storage ollas and bowls used for cooking purposes were recovered (Rogge et al. iii). Chinese artifacts included a wide variety of ceramic forms, game pieces, opium smoking paraphernalia, and homemade lamp chimneys from beer bottles. Of course, most of the artifacts were European American.

Final Thoughts. The archaeology of Chinese American sites in Arizona has a relatively long history. Indeed, the Tucson Urban Renewal Project was the first in the United States to excavate large and important Chinese sites. The Phoenix project is the latest in Arizona and undoubtedly will not be the last; however, we are rapidly losing this unique and valuable resource, especially in our urban areas.

Both of these projects were conducted under the worst possible circumstances. Both were forced by pending construction to proceed with inadequate funding, hurried construction schedules, time constraints, and other less than desirable factors. Both were plagued with indifferent city departments and officials. In general, these factors apply to much of contract archaeology today throughout the country. The end result is the loss of valuable information about the Chinese and other minorities which is available from no source other than archaeology, because we all know that such groups are under-represented in the historical record.

Works Cited

Ayres, James E. "Urban Renewal Salvage Archaeology in Tucson, Arizona." Paper presented at the Annual Meeting of the Society for Historical Archaeology, 1968.

Fong, Lawrence M. "Sojourners and Settlers: The Chinese Experience in Arizona." In *The Chinese Experience in Arizona and Northern Mexico*, (1980):1–30 (reprinted from Journal of Arizona History, Vol. 21). Arizona Historical Society, Tucson.

Fontana, Bernard L., and J. Cameron Greenleaf. "Johnny Ward's Ranch: A Study in Historic Archaeology." *Kiva* 28(1-2) (1962): 1–115.

Keane, Melissa, A. E. Rogge and Bradford Luckingham. "The Chinese in Arizona 1870–1950." Intermountain Cultural Resource Services Research Paper No. 3. Dames and Moore, Phoenix, 1992.

Lister, Florence C., and Robert H. Lister. "The Chinese of Early Tucson: Historic Archaeology from the Tucson Urban Renewal Project." In *Anthropological Papers of the University of Arizona No. 52*. Tucson: University of Arizona Press, 1989.

Rogge, A. E., Melissa Keane, Bradford Luckingham, James E. Ayres, Pam Patterson, and Todd Bostwick. *First Street and Madison: Historical Archaeology of the Second Phoenix Chinatown*. Phoenix: Dames and Moore, 1992.

Stone, Lyle M., and James E. Ayres. "A Description and Evaluation of Archaeological Resources, San Bernardino Ranch National Historic

Landmark, Cochise County, Arizona." Archaeological Research Services, Inc., Tempe, Arizona, 1982.

Stone, Lyle M., and James E. Ayres. "An Archaeological and Historical Evaluation of Proposed Redevelopment Parcels on Blocks 50, 53, and 59, Tempe, Arizona." Archaeological Research Services, Tempe, Arizona, 1985.

Stone, Lyle M., and Scott L. Fedick. "The Archaeology of Two Historic Homestead and Railroad-Related Sites on the Southern Pacific Main Line near Mobile, Maricopa County, Arizona." Archaeological Research Services, Tempe, Arizona, 1990.

Hidden Heritage:
Chinese Historical Archaeology and the Asian American Comparative Collection

PRISCILLA WEGARS
Laboratory of Anthropology, University of Idaho, Moscow, Idaho

The Chinese presence at numerous sites in the United States and elsewhere is confirmed by the kind and variety of artifacts they left behind. Although in the beginning, the first arrivals may have had to make do with western substitutes for their usual items of consumption, the increasing numbers of Chinese arriving in this country since the 1850s made it profitable for merchants to exploit their preferences for familiar foods, beverages, smoking materials, and other items imported from the homeland.

Ships regularly docked at San Francisco and other Pacific Coast ports with cargoes of Chinese merchandise—products that also made their way by boat, wagon, and pack train to the smaller communities and isolated camps many hundreds of miles inland.

Within the past few years, an increasing number of these 19th- and 20th-century Chinese sites have been investigated. In most cases, the artifacts comprising the Chinese components of the excavated assemblages bear a remarkable similarity to one another. Excavators are almost certain to find utilitarian food and beverage containers, ceramic tablewares, medicine bottles, opium smoking paraphernalia, gambling-related items, and miscellaneous hardware and implements.

In the early 1980s, the Alfred W. Bowers Laboratory of Anthropology at the University of Idaho in Moscow, under the direction of Dr. Roderick Sprague, began a program of archaeological excavations and historical archaeological field schools at Chinese American sites, including one in Downtown Moscow, Idaho. In 1982, I established a Chinese Comparative Collection of artifacts and bibliographical materials at the Laboratory of Anthropology in order to assist with the identification of Chinese sites and the analysis of artifacts from them. Since then, Laboratory of Anthropology personnel have directed or participated in archaeological investigations of Chinese sites in Idaho, Oregon, Washington, and New Zealand, and they have conducted or assisted with the analysis of Chinese artifacts from sites there as well as ones in Nevada, California, Montana, Utah, Wyoming, and Colorado.

At first, the artifacts acquired for the Comparative Collection were of Chinese origin. Later, however, objects of Japanese manufacture also began to be included. Japanese Americans, Filipino Americans, and other groups began to be represented in the bibliographical and slide holdings as well.

The repository's present name is the Asian American Comparative Collection (AACC), thereby reflecting our involvement with archaeological sites and artifacts reflecting the broad spectrum of people with Asian antecedents.

The AACC is likely to be found in an archaeological context in the United States, Canada, and elsewhere. A related objective is the obtaining of relevant documentary materials. These are concerned not only with the artifacts and their associated archaeological sites, but also with the history of the Asians who used those artifacts and occupied those sites during the 19th and early 20th centuries. The objects in the Collection have been acquired from excavation, purchase, or through donations from interested individuals. Bibliographical materials such as books and articles have been purchased, donated, or photocopied to form the nucleus of a reference library emphasizing site reports and artifact identification. Well over 1000 slides, mostly of sites and artifacts, are also available for study.

Using whole examples or illustrations in the AACC for comparison, researchers can readily identify their excavated artifacts and can also obtain supporting documentation for artifact analysis and report writing.

The AACC now functions as a clearinghouse for persons needing assistance with research on, and identification of, most classes of Asian artifacts. Presently, it has not only a national, but also an international, reputation and relevance.

Publications, which include a bibliography on opium-smoking paraphernalia and a quarterly newsletter, reach an enthusiastic audience. The forthcoming book that I have edited, entitled *Hidden Heritage: Historical Archaeology of the Overseas Chinese* (Baywood, 1992), discusses Chinese archaeological sites in more detail. Since the AACC receives no state funding, newsletter subscriptions and book sales are vital to the survival of the AACC.

Typical Chinese Artifacts. Many archaeological sites throughout the American West and elsewhere were occupied by members of different ethnic and national groups during the 19th and early 20th centuries. Usually, however, the artifacts recovered from such sites do not reflect the ethnicity or nationality of the persons who once lived there. Sites once occupied by Chinese immigrants, however, produce artifact assemblages with readily identifiable ethnic origins. Because Asian artifacts are quite different when compared with their European American counterparts, it is useful for archaeologists to be able to recognize the types that occur most frequently on sites once occupied by people from China.

We will first briefly look at some of the typical kinds of Chinese artifacts that occur on most 19th- and early 20th-century Chinese archaeological sites, not only in the United States, but also in Canada, Australia, New Zealand, and elsewhere. In general, those items are ones that were imported by, or to be sold to, Chinese immigrants. Also interesting, but not included in this discussion because of time and space constraints, are Chinese export wares—artifacts made in China and exported to non-Chinese markets in places such as Southeast Asia, the United States, and Mexico.

Utilitarian Food and Beverage Containers. Some of the most common artifacts found on overseas Chinese sites are brown-glazed stoneware shards from beverage and food containers. Alcoholic beverage bottles, in several sizes and shapes, are often represented. The same highly-alcoholic Chinese "tonic" that came in a flared-rim ceramic vessel was also available in glass bottles. The latter have so far appeared only in 20th-century contexts.

Fragments of spouted soy sauce pots are frequently found on Chinese sites. Although these vessels are usually round, square ones are also known, so far from just British Columbia and Idaho. Other food containers include wide-mouthed shouldered ones for various kinds of preserved or pickled foodstuffs; several sizes of straight-sided vessels; squat, bulbous food jars; large globular jars, and large barrel-shaped jars. Ceramic lids for the various jars came in an equally varied assortment of shapes and sizes. Several sizes of brown-glazed stoneware shallow dishes have been most often interpreted as pans for cooking and storage.

Foodstuffs were also packaged in green-glazed stonewares, although this color is much less common than the brown. A green-glazed jar having the same form as the barrel-shaped brown-glazed jar is sometimes seen.

Other green-glazed utilitarian wares include small straight-sided jars in several sizes and ginger jars in several forms. Other ginger jars had blue-on-white and blue-on-beige designs. These would have had straight-sided ceramic lids with flat tops. Glass Chinese "fruit jars" are occasionally reported. Typically, these were manufactured in San Francisco in the 1920s.

Table Ceramics. Dishes for serving and eating were usually of porcelain or porcellaneous stoneware. The pattern most often found archaeologically, but only as a rice bowl, is a blue-on-white one that is now most commonly known as "Bamboo." Numerous vessel forms decorated with the polychrome enamel "Four Flowers" pattern are reasonably common, as are pale-green celadon tablewares. However, we must be careful here in ascribing celadons to a "Chinese" suite of ceramics, as recent research is providing evidence that at least some of them appear to possess glaze characteristics having more in common with Japanese than Chinese wares.

Other less common designs on Chinese table ceramics include the blue-on-white "Double Happiness" pattern, generally seen only on rice bowls, and only on early sites; the 20th-century "Attributes of the Eight Immortals" pattern, in orange; other blue-on-white designs, and a variety of enameled and handpainted miscellaneous motifs.

Medicine Bottles. Nineteenth- and early twentieth-century Chinese medicine bottles came in a variety of shapes and sizes—most are less than 2.5 inches high. They would have held a single dose of medicine, in pill, powder, or liquid form. A very common rectangular version is often erroneously called an "opium bottle." Apart from the fact that opium is too gummy to get in or out of the small aperture, numerous bottles have been found in museums or private collections still bearing intact paper labels. The Chinese characters on these, when translated, invariably indicate that medicinal products were contained in the bottles.

Opium-Smoking Paraphernalia. Chinese archaeological sites are often recognized by the presence of opium-smoking paraphernalia. Highly sensationalized by the dominant white culture, opium smoking by the Chinese is still imperfectly understood. Evidence now indicates that, of the Chinese who used the drug, most did so in moderation, much as many of us today enjoy a "happy hour" beverage after work. After all, opium could be legally imported into the United States until 1909. Some non-Chinese persons also smoked opium, a fact which is now largely ignored.

Opium came in rectangular brass cans, most of which have what is probably a brand name stamped into the lid and sometimes another stamp, perhaps the name of the manufacturer or shipper, on the bottom of the can. Although importation was legal, opium for smoking was heavily taxed. As a result, a brisk smuggling trade grew, centered on the two British Columbia cities of Vancouver and Victoria, where opium for smoking was manufactured for the Canadian and American markets. Since tax stamps and other paper labels are subject to decay, they do not usually survive for archaeologists to find in the ground, but sometimes they remain on opium cans housed in museums. Other opium-related items usually found on sites include ceramic opium pipe bowls, in dark gray stoneware or reddish orange earthenware; metal fittings for opium pipes; metal tools and accessories, and opium lamps, or parts of them. The opium pipe stem itself is often bamboo, so it would not usually survive archaeologically.

Gambling Paraphernalia. Various objects from Chinese gambling games are known from archaeological sites and museums. Small, hemispherical, white and black glass gaming pieces are seen quite frequently. Because the black ones had a higher value, much like different colors of poker chips, they are found less often than the white ones. Under special conditions of preservation, wooden dominoes have been found, as have portions of paper lottery tickets. Another item associated with gambling is a brass object shaped like an inverted bowl with a handle. Called a "spreading-out cover," it was used, while bets were being placed, in the game of *fan tan* to cover a portion of the coins used as counters.

Miscellaneous Chinese Objects. Writing implements, or portions of them, such as ink grinding blocks, dishes, and ink bottles, are occasionally found on archaeological sites. Chinese combs and jewelry have been recovered, as have metal cooking utensils, cleavers, and other tools. Other small objects which are sometimes found are brass Chinese buttons, locks and keys, and portions of scales and their ivory rules.

Chinese Sites and Associated Artifacts. Over the years, a large number of Chinese archaeological sites have been investigated. Most of them are in the United States, particularly in the West, while others are in places such as Canada, Australia, and New Zealand. Of the sites in this country, the majority have simply had their location recorded by a government agency such as the Forest Service or the Bureau of Land Management. Some of these and others have been the subject of historical background research. Only a few have been excavated, mostly by federal agencies, university-sponsored groups, or private firms under contract. Sites that have yielded Chinese artifacts, or have the potential to do so, are therefore numerous, and include both rural and urban locations. They represent a variety of industries such as mining, laundries, restaurants, railroads, and fishing camps.

During the mid-19th century, thousands of Chinese headed to remote locations in many countries to participate in gold mining opportunities. Excavations at mining sites such as at Pierce, in northern Idaho, often produce both Chinese and European American artifacts, including ones on display at the Laboratory of Anthropology, University of Idaho. Another mining site, in Butte County, California, yielded an unusual find of paper fragments from a label that was once affixed to the front of an opium can—paper, of course, does not usually survive in archaeological contexts. Of the many Chinese mining sites to be found in Australia, only a few have been recorded, and fewer still have been excavated. The Palmer River gold field in Queensland, northeastern Australia, was one area that was intensively worked by Chinese miners. A stone-walled dam and a stone wall with a water race are two features there that are believed to have been built by Chinese miners.

In New Zealand, a new dam and consequent reservoir construction necessitated a large program of archaeological excavation on numerous Chinese mining sites before they were inundated with water. Cromwell's Chinatown was one of these; the entire site, together with a reconstructed Chinese miner's dwelling, is now flooded. Following archaeological excavation, however, it had become such a popular tourist attraction that the Arrowtown Chinese settlement, not threatened with flooding, was excavated as a replacement Chinese mining site to interpret to the public, together with the nearby Ah Lum's store.

The University of Idaho has also been involved with archaeological investigations in northeastern Oregon since 1985. An extensive area of hand-stacked rock tailings, known as the Ah Hee diggings, was built by Chinese miners who were in the area from at least 1867 to the 1890s. A nearby terrace had fragments of large woks on the surface of the ground, together with cans having embossed Chinese characters for the word "oil."

This and other evidence indicate that the terrace served as sort of a "mess hall" for the Chinese placer miners in the vicinity. Remote locations, such as the Mon-Tung Chinese mining site on the Idaho's Snake River, often show Chinese ingenuity in modifying or recycling artifacts for new purposes. There, a soy sauce pot or shouldered food jar was found cut down to make a bowl. In New Zealand, archaeologists frequently find small metal trays used to hold servings of opium; these were manufactured from metal recycled from opium cans. Oregon's Union Creek Chinese mining site yielded a cut-down opium can that was divided into two parts to make a stamp pad and name stamp container. One half contained string soaked in red ink and the other half contained a carved wooden signature stamp that once belonged to a man named Yang Fu Yi.

Railroad-related Chinese sites have been investigated in a number of places. One, Cabinet Landing in northern Idaho, was the scene of a large Northern Pacific railroad construction camp which housed both white and Chinese workers for several months in 1882.

Chinese fishermen worked in Alaska and at canneries along the Columbia River. The former fishing village of China Camp in Northern California is now a state park. The interpretive sign there states that "China Camp was in operation by 1870" and that it was "one of the earliest, largest, and most productive Chinese fishing villages in California."

The variety and abundance of the artifacts found during excavations there illustrate both the activities and the quality of life available to the site's occupants. The artifacts, many of which are stored at the California Department of Parks and Recreation in Sacramento, included brown-glazed stoneware utilitarian vessels, porcelain tablewares, and assorted stoneware and porcelain ceramics, as well as opium paraphernalia and miscellaneous objects.

Few buildings that can be confidently attributed to former Chinese owners remain. Of those that do, such as Gin Yet Wah's at North Bloomfield, in California's Malakoff Diggins State Historic Park; the Chew Kee Store in Fiddletown, California; the Chinese temple at Weaverville, California, and the Kam Wah Chung building in John Day, Oregon, have the potential to yield even more invaluable information about their former owners.

In general, urban sites tend to yield a wider variety of Chinese artifacts than rural sites do. The Riverside Chinatown excavations produced numerous intriguing artifacts, such as opium pipe bowls and other objects. The same was true for excavations on the San Francisco waterfront, in San Jose's Chinatown, and at Tucson, Arizona. Chinese artifacts still litter the ground near Chinese buildings in Oroville, California.

Dating. While some Chinese artifacts are very easy to date, they are not necessarily useful for dating sites. Coins, for example, which were minted during the reigns of certain emperors, still circulated more than 200 years later. Those which are most commonly found on sites in the western United States, in fact, are those of Emperor Qianlong (Ch'ien Lung), who ruled from 1736 to 1796.

Some Chinese ceramics have reign marks on their bases, and these can be useful for dating purposes, to a certain extent. Unfortunately, such examples are not commonly found on archaeological sites, and when they are, they are often so faded that they are illegible. Marks which are much more common, and almost always legible, such as the "Eternal Knot," often seen on "Four Flowers" vessels, and the blue base marks on celadons, have not yet yielded any meaningful dates.

Artifacts marked "China" occur on later American sites. Generally, such pieces date to 1891 or after, when the McKinley Tariff Act decreed that imported goods must bear the name of the country of origin written in English.

Some preliminary work has been done on the dates of the introduction of the various ceramic patterns that were brought here for use by Chinese immigrants. These are distinguished from Chinese export wares that were imported for sale to European Americans. For example, Paul Chace has determined that the "Double Happiness" pattern is the earliest, since it occurs on pre-1870 mining and railroad sites in the absence of any of the other ceramic patterns. The more common "Bamboo" pattern is not found on sites that were unoccupied beginning in 1870 and in Idaho and Montana—at least, it apparently does not occur on sites only occupied after 1890.

Significance. Chinese Americans are often surprised to learn that everyday, household objects from their culture have value in interpreting the past experiences of Chinese American pioneers. In fact, their importance in this regard cannot be overstated. Historical archaeologists work with two main bodies of source materials: namely documentary records and artifacts excavated from archaeological sites. In the case of overseas Chinese archaeology, the great majority of the relevant documentary materials for particular sites such as census records, newspaper accounts, and personal reminiscences, were compiled by persons who were not Chinese. In contrast, any Chinese artifacts found were almost certainly used only by persons of Chinese ancestry; thus, they have the potential to provide the least biased indicator of the presence and activities of the Chinese inhabitants of a site.

Chinese artifacts can help in investigating larger questions of trade patterns, production centers, and dating of sites. For example, archaeologists are attempting to learn which items were usually brought by new and returning Chinese laborers as part of their personal gear; which ones were exported from China, as a standard practice, for purchase by overseas Chinese; and which ones might have been smuggled illegally into the country or even manufactured here. More work needs to be done in China on identifying production and distribution centers for the everyday objects that are found in large quantities overseas. Careful study of archaeologically-collected artifacts may enable other types or patterns to emerge—ones which can be associated with definite time periods or with particular geographic areas.

Using the Asian American Comparative Collection. Most items in the Collection, including books, slides, and artifacts, can be borrowed by interested researchers. I often take AACC artifacts to my classes and public appearances, and have shared them with a wide variety of audiences who appreciate the "hands-on" approach offered by such a presentation. Loans of interpretive exhibits to government agencies, local historical societies, and public and university libraries provide some people with their first realization of early Chinese contributions to the economic development of their region.

Conclusion. Archaeological sites occupied in the 19th and early 20th centuries by people of Chinese ancestry are easily identified, once archaeologists know how to recognize objects both brought over and imported by Chinese immigrants. The wide variety of such artifacts points to the people's persistence of preferences for familiar foods, beverages, smoking materials, and other items. Unfortunately, the resulting artifacts, even if marked, are often of little value for absolute dating. Researchers with problems of identification and documentation of Asian sites and artifacts can obtain assistance from the Asian American Comparative Collection at the University of Idaho's Alfred W. Bowers Laboratory of Anthropology, at Moscow, Idaho.

Selected Abstracts

A Distinct Chinese Institution: The Chinese United Methodist Church in the 1920s (Ch. 4). Shirley Sui Ling Tam, Case Western Reserve University, Cleveland, Ohio. Most institutional studies on Chinese Americans are about the traditional associations. Chinese churches, composed of Chinese members, but founded for the worship of a Caucasian religion, were seldom studied systematically. The purpose of this study is to explore more deeply the role of this distinct Chinese institution and its relation with the Caucasian society. The Chinese United Methodist Church is chosen for detailed analysis since it is one of the oldest Chinese Christian churches in the Los Angeles area. The period of the 1920s was essential for the study of Chinese American history because many scholars of this period shift their attention to the study of the Japanese and ignore the Chinese as a whole.

A thorough analysis of the correspondence and conference reports between the Chinese United Methodist Church and the Mission Board demonstrates that the latter was not ethnocentric and discriminatory as previous studies indicate. The parent board was actually solidly supportive of the Chinese against restrictive immigration laws and showed much respect to the Chinese Church. On the other hand, the Chinese United Methodist Church also assumed a different role among the local Chinese. It became an agent for assimilating fellow Chinese into American society through different classes and activities. Their programs fully challenged the charges that Chinese institutions only engaged in perpetuating Chinese customs and traditions. The Chinese United Methodist Church was a distinct institution in bringing the Chinese into the melting pot.

Artifact and Meaning: Funeral Practices of the Chinese in Gold Mountain (Ch. 4). Vivien T.Y. Chen, Center for Folklife Programs and Cultural Studies, Smithsonian Institution, Washington, D.C. A funeral suit in the collection of the National Museum of American History at the Smithsonian Institution in Washington, D.C. is the catalyst for this study of Chinese funeral practices in 19th- and early 20th-century American life. Chinese American funeral processions attracted substantial public interest, but were often misunderstood and labelled "heathenish" and "weird." In fact, they were powerful expressions of a strong belief system maintained by Chinese

American communities in towns and cities throughout the west. To other Americans, these funeral processions—with their banners, music bands and public mourners dressed in white—provided a colorful and exotic experience. To the Chinese, the procession was a religious necessity, a public show of unity, and a cultural statement.

Despite difficult adjustments to life in America, immigration restrictions, and racial hostility, Chinese Americans developed inventive adaptations of traditional burial customs to their new environment and resources. Family and masonic associations arranged for the proper performance of rites for the deceased, held processions down main streets, observed mourning periods, made food and paper offerings at the cemetery, and believed in a vision of the afterlife and continuity of the soul. The observance of "feng-shui" (wind and water) meant a continual search for suitable cemetery sites that would be protected by hills and would be close to running water. After seven years, the remains of the deceased were often exhumed and transported to China for permanent reburial in native villages. There, one could be assured of relatives caring for graves during the Ch'ing Ming Festival and throughout the year.

Painted with colorful symbols of life, happiness, and fortune, the funeral suit is a presentation of the Chinese world view and auspicious symbols for fertility and well-being. It is a gift to the future generation. After the 1920s, funeral practices among Chinese Americans varied from traditional to westernized to bi-cultural services.

The Crossover (Ch. 4). Cy Wong, Chinese Historical Society of Southern California. *The Crossover* is an unpublished semi-fictional human interest story that talks about the first 15 pioneer Chinese immigrants that came to the South from Cuba, to New Orleans and northwest Louisiana under voluntary conditions in 1867 with a Frenchman, Jules Honorat Normand. The story serves as the base for the life of one Chinese named Philippi Wong and the four generations that follow. It reflects the unknown American history that has yet to be fully explored or developed. I write about how these people wre frugal and hard workers. Also, how they managed to control the plantation system for which they worked for a period of time. After the expiration of their three to five year contract, they moved into the communities, became farmers, and married women of color--including Creoles, blacks, and Indians. Thus, the wheels were set in motion for the mixed generations. There have been stories and accounts written by sociologists and anthropologists about the Southern "pure Chinese," but never before has there been anything written by an offspring who happens to be a fourth generation of mixed black and Chinese.

In Search of Gold Mountain: A Photographic History of the Chinese in San Diego, California (Ch. 4). Tom Hom and Murray Lee, Chinese Historical Society of Greater San Diego and Upper Baja California, San Diego, California. This is primarily a highly mobile photographic exhibit consisting of 11 double-sided 4'x6' lightweight panels prepared by the Chinese Historical Society of San

Diego. The purpose of this exhibit is to provide a comprehensive visual history of the Chinese settlement in San Diego from the mid-19th century until the present. The exhibit begins with the early origins of the San Diego Chinese in Guangdong Province, the factors precipitating their emigration, and the ways in which they came. Five panels treat the early activities of the Chinese in mining, fishing, railroad, and other construction, agriculture, and merchandising. Unique San Diego activities such as the first San Diego Bay fishing industry, building the California Southern Railroad, the Flume, and the Del Coronado Hotel are emphasized. Special attention is given to two of the prominent early families, Ah Quin and Quon Mane. Early organizations and social activities from the late 1880s to World War II are covered in three panels. The Anti-Chinese Movement, which had such a negative impact on Chinese everywhere in the U.S. is treated. The decline and present-day remnants of San Diego's Chinatown are explained. The marked demographic changes in San Diego's Chinese are illustrated with two panels showing areas of origin of recent arrivals from China and Southeast Asia with photos and biographic sketches of representative immigrants. The current activities of the Chinese in San Diego are covered through their organizations in three panels. Individual accomplishments of a representative cross-section of San Diego's prominent Chinese Americans are shown. Finally, the results of the acculturation process is demonstrated with examples of Chinese who represent those factors, which indicate an acceptance into the mainstream of American society, or as the successful conclusion of the exhibit's title suggests: "The Discovery of Gold Mountain."

Chinese American Women Organizations in Los Angeles: A Photo Exhibit (Ch. 4). Organization of Chinese American Women-L.A. Chapter, Los Angeles, California. Julie Lee, president. Chinese American women's organizations played a major role in the development of the Chinese community and the Los Angeles community into what it is today. Brought together by various reasons—war relief, philanthropy, social, and others— these Chinese women shaped their own goals and accomplishments for themselves and their community. The 1930s saw the growth of a number of activities bringing women and girls together. The beginnings, activities, and legacies of these groups are chronicled in a photo exhibit organized by the Organization of Chinese American Women-L.A. Chapter. Through personal photos and oral histories, the stories and accomplishments of such groups as the Women's New Life Movement Association, Los Angeles Chinese Women's Club and Jr.'s, Women's Auxiliary of the Chinese American Citizens Alliance, the Mei Wah Club, and others will be shared.

Museum of Chinese Historical Society of America (Ch. 4). Philip P. Choy, Chinese Historical Society of America, San Francisco, California. The Chinese Historical Society of America (CHSA), founded in 1963, can be credited as the first society to be established. Since then, a number of regional historical societies have emerged, increasing the consciousness of Chinese American history. Ultimately, artifacts are collected and displayed to demonstrate the Chinese American experience. While the number of such institutions will increase, it does not follow that each society shares with the other a common goal or purpose. CHSA was founded by members who grew up in an era of exclusion, discrimination, and privation. Its purpose was to research and document the history of the Chinese in America to fill a void left in most American history books; in general pointing out the contributions of the Chinese in the development of the western frontier.

In the span of 140 years of Chinese American history, the Chinese population has not been homogenous. It is characterized by the early immigrants and their descendants and the recent newcomers and their offspring. Each holds a perspective in response to his or her experience within the socio-political climate of their time. On the other hand, the newcomers of the 1980s arrived under a liberal open immigration policy. Not having experienced the anti-Chinese policies of the previous decades, few have an affinity with the historical past of the earlier Chinese. Instead, their emphasis is on cultural contributions.

Therefore, what is Chinese and what is Chinese American needs to be more clearly understood. A re-evaluation of what our problems are; what our purpose is; who our audience is, and how information should be desseminated is necessary to determine what belongs in a Chinese American museum. The museum is a place for visual experience. If the contents are mis-interpreted, it will perpetuate myths and stereotypes of an ethnic population.

The Museum of Chinese American History in Los Angeles: A Community Challenge (Ch. 4). Suellen Cheng, El Pueblo de Los Angeles Historic Monument, Los Angeles, California. Creating the Museum of Chinese American History in the City of Los Angeles has been a dream for many in the Los Angeles Chinese community. Today, the appropriate historic site for the museum has been allocated in the city's El Pueblo de Los Angeles Historic Monument, where the original Chinatown was located. Substantial support from the community, as well as from city officials, does exist, yet the project is far from being completed after seven years of effort. This presentation will describe the history and the development of the project, its accomplishments, and a summary of the project plan. Accomplishments include services as a resource center, community reach-out programs, and a widespread academic and public movement in the pre-planning. The challenges ahead for both the community and its government partners will be delineated.

The Reconstruction of Ng Shing Gung: A Case Study of a Partnership Project (Ch. 4). Sarah Heigho Nunes and Nancy Valby, San Jose Historical Museum, San Jose, California. The Chinese have played a significant role in San Jose's history since 1852. From 1888 until 1949, the Ng Shing Gung Building served the Chinese population as a temple and community center. Although the building was demolished by the City in 1949, the altars and other temple furnishings were preserved and placed in storage. When the City of San Jose Historical Museum was established in the 1970s, the temple artifacts were transferred to the Museum. A replica of the Ng Shing Gung was included in the Museum Master Plan, which calls for a combination of restored and reconstructed structures to represent San Jose around the turn of the century. The Museum made several attempts to raise money for the project over the years. A series of discussions with interested members of the Chinese community led to the formation of the Chinese Historical and Cultural Project (CHCP), a coalition of Chinese community organizations and individuals, in 1987. CHCP's purpose was to reconstruct Ng Shing Gung as an exhibit building to interpret the history and contributions of the Chinese of San Jose and the Santa Clara Valley. CHCP raised over $500,000 and entered into a contract with the City of San Jose for construction of the building on the Museum grounds. The building and its exhibits opened to the public on September 29, 1991.

Flora Bell Jan, Writer and Flapper: An Atypical Second-Generation Chinese American Woman (Ch. 3). Judy Yung, San Francisco, California. I first met Flora Belle Jan in the Survey of Race Relations papers at the Hoover Institute, Stanford University. She had been interviewed in the 1920s in a study on race relations under the direction of sociologist Robert Park. What struck me then was her unconventional answers about generational and cultural conflicts, as experienced by herself and her peers as second-generation Chinese Americans coming of age in the 1920s. Since my initial discovery, I have been able to learn more about Flora Belle's life history and deterred aspirations to become a famous writer through a collection of letters she wrote to her best friend Ludie from 1918 to 1949, her published writings of poems, short stories, and newspaper articles, and interviews with her family. (Flora Belle Jan died in 1950 upon return from living in China with her husband and children through the war years.)

Like her peers during the pre-World War II years, she was subjected to cultural circumscription by her Chinese parents and community, as well as discrimination in the larger American society. But unlike her peers, she chose to reject the "old-fashion" ways of her parents and insisted on "keep[ing] pace with Dame Fashion" and sought "fame and fortune" through writing. Flora Belle's life story offers us another view of the second-generation Chinese American woman's agency to define gender roles for herself in the face of cultural and racial oppression.

Three Generations of Chinese American Women: A Feminist Reading (Ch. 8). Iping Liang, University of Massachusetts at Amherst. This paper connects three Chinese American fictions, Louis Chu's *Eat a Bowl of Tea* (1961), Maxine Hong Kingston's *The Woman Warrior* (1975), and Amy Tan's *The Joy Luck Club* (1989), and it analyzes the transformation of Chinese American women from a feminist point of view. The three texts crossing three decades yield a conducive time frame for my investigation, and I argue that the women characters presented in these books delineate a transformation from the old traditional Chinese women to the new Chinese American "women warriors." The whole process exemplifies Chinese American women's awakening to the feminist search of self-identity. The first woman, Mei Oi (in *Eat a Bowl of Tea*), represents the old-world Chinese women who are docile and malleable. She is brought to America on an arranged marriage to fulfill the role of a traditional housewife. Mei Oi therefore signifies the first generation of Chinese American women who adhere to the old way of life and remain untouched by the American horizons. In Maxine Hong Kingston's landmark memoirs of the second-generation immigrant daughter, Chinese American women turn to be the "women warriors." The story, told from the daughter's point of view, reveals her resentment of being a "girl" and the adamant self-determination to become a Fa Mu Lan. Depicting the typical second-generation revolution, *The Woman Warrior* powerfully declares Chinese American women's feminist manifesto—the aspiration for an independent "American" identity. The portrayal of "women warriors" continues in Amy Tan's *The Joy Luck Club*. Different from Chu and Kingston, Tan is able to weave the two generations in a joyous harmony and contour a genealogy of Chinese American women in a group portraiture. In the paralleling of Chinese mothers and American daughters emerge the third-generation Chinese American women, who are able to assert the American *and* to understand the Chinese.

Reconstructing the Frontier: Racism and Identity in Maxine Hong Kingston's *Tripmaster Monkey* (Ch. 8). Nina Y. Morgan, University of California, Riverside. The signification of the frontier, as Richard Slotkin has said, is affected "less by maps than by illusions." in Maxine Hong Kingston's *Tripmaster Monkey*, the illusionist is Wittman Ah Sing, a poet/playwright whose desire to lasso and capture the wild individuality representative of the American Frontier and to venture out into the mythic space of self-definition is too often frustrated, leaving Wittman dingle-dangling on his rope as his visions vanish into thin air. Wittman is trapped in the "tilted City," and as a Chinese American in 1960s San Francisco, he is also, in the words of James Baldwin, "trapped in history and history is trapped in... [him]."

The instant city of San Francisco, a city of the American West, is not only a construct that reflects the sociological nature of the western community, but is constitutive of the cultural strategies and sign systems that literally built the West. For Wittman Ah Sing, the West has yet to be won. His image as purely American has been denied him by the racist constructions of California writers such as Bret Harte and Frank Norris, whose literary depictions of the immigrant American haunt Wittman even today. It is Wittman's poetic dream to challenge the City to see him not as a "Tricky," "twinkling little" "heathen Chinee," but as an American artist with insightful and meaningful observations to make and with a theater to create.

In an analysis based upon *Tripmaster Monkey*, I will discuss the revisionist role of contemporary Chinese American literature in the reconstruction of the image of the Asian American both within the literary landscape and on the frontiers of American society.

Chinatown: Contested Terrain, Conflicting Images (Ch. 11). K. Scott Wong, Williams College, New York. Based on primary sources written in both Chinese and English, this paper will examine textual images of American Chinatowns prevalent during the late 19th and early 20th centuries, as envisioned by visiting Chinese elites and European American politicians and public figures of that period. The differences and similarities between these two sets of images reflect larger trends in racial and class biases held by both Chinese and European Americans during this period in Chinese and American history. Therefore, this paper situates conflicting and complementary images of American Chinatowns in the context of the intersection of Chinese, American, and Chinese American social, political, and intellectual history.

A Tale of Two Cities: A Comparative Discussion of Chinese Societies in San Francisco and Vancouver, B.C., 1946–1980 (Ch. 11). Wing Chung Ng, University of British Columbia, Canada. It has often been assumed that the Chinese American and Chinese Canadian experiences are fairly similar in terms of encounters with racism and discriminatory legislation, immigration patterns, demographic evolution, and so on. Comparable as they certainly are, this paper seeks to highlight a few more subtle, but at the same time substantial, differences behind these commonly held generalized categories of resemblance.

The themes of variation in the local history of the two Chinese societies in San Francisco and Vancouver in the post-World War II period are explored as follows:

1) The nature of renewed Chinese immigration at the end of the "exclusion era" in the U.S. and Canada, and its impact on the existing Chinese minority population in the two cities.
2) The different trajectories of the two native-born Chinese groups (i.e., the ABCs and the CBCs) in terms of their relative size, cultural orientations, and influences within the two Chinese societies.
3) Extralocal home-country influences in the form of Taiwan hegemony in the two Chinatowns and the tug-of-war between the pro-Taiwan and pro-Mainland China forces.
4) Canadianization and Americanization: the different processes of incorporation into the large society, culture, and polity.